PERSONNEL ADMINISTRATION
A Point of View and a Method

PERSONNEL ADMINISTRATION
A Point of View and a Method
Seventh Edition

Paul Pigors
Massachusetts Institute of Technology

Charles A. Myers
Massachusetts Institute of Technology

McGraw-Hill Book Company
New York   St. Louis   San Francisco   Düsseldorf   Johannesburg
Kuala Lumpur   London   Mexico   Montreal   New Delhi
Panama   Rio de Janeiro   Singapore   Sydney   Toronto

Personnel Administration: A Point of View and a Method

567890DODO79876

This book was set in Times Roman by Rocappi, Inc. The
editors were Richard F. Dojny and Joseph F. Murphy; the
designer was Merrill Haber; and the production supervisor was
Ted Agrillo.
The printer and binder was R. R. Donnelley & Sons Company.

Library of Congress Cataloging in Publication Data

Pigors, Paul John William, 1900–
    Personnel administration.

    Includes bibliographies.
    1. Personnel management. I. Myers, Charles
Andrew, 1913–   joint author. II. Title.
HF5549.P468 1973   658.3   72-5550
ISBN 0–07–050010–X

Contents

Preface

In the 26 years since the first edition of this book appeared, the staff function of personnel administration has moved into the front offices of many corporate and nonprofit organizations. Moreover, managers at all organizational levels have become increasingly concerned with effectively utilizing and developing human resources, recognizing that such concern is fundamentally a line responsibility. Yet much remains to be done so that practicing managers and students aiming for careers in management may make the most of available opportunities for reexamining their current conceptions about managing and developing people at work.

The essential point of view and method which distinguished this book at the outset are still retained. We try to present a comprehensive and consistent point of view at the policy level and to offer brief, general descriptions and analyses of techniques and procedures which organization-centered thinking can help to implement. The selected and updated references at the end of each chapter provide the student, teacher, and management reader with suggested reading to guide his thinking about managerial policies.

Many of these are merely touched upon in this compressed text. Understanding of the complex interrelationships between personnel policies, procedures, and practices can be deepened by careful supplementary reading.

Despite much new material, this edition is shorter than the preceding one. The field of personnel administration, as presented in the growing literature and in practical experience, is continually changing and expanding. No single book can hope to expand sufficiently to cover every subject in depth. We have been selective in emphasizing those developments which seem to us most important. We have drawn heavily on new findings in the behavioral sciences but have avoided burdening the reader with details of controversies which have been raging in the professional literature.

Beginning with Section A, in revising Chapter 1, for example, we have brought in some of the doubts raised about the McGregor and Likert approaches. We have also presented briefly the new concept of "human resources accounting" growing out of Likert's earlier work. Chapter 2 has been reorganized and rewritten to indicate some of the blurring of line-staff distinctions that has occurred with the increasing use of project managers. In general, however, we are convinced that these distinctions continue to be useful in analyzing many difficulties in organizational relationships. Chapter 3 has new material on manpower planning and forecasting and on recent developments in recruiting and appraising new managerial talent. In particular, we offer a brief examination of the "assessment center" approach. Chapter 4 has been entirely rewritten to reflect new developments associated with the urban crisis, the counterculture of the "Now" Generation, and the New Feminism. The appearance of a new breed of employees confronts managers with new opportunities and difficulties. More sophisticated developments in automation and computerization also demand careful attention by forward-looking managers.

In Section B, Chapter 5 has been condensed but retains its essential emphasis on the role of listening and mutual understanding as vital elements in effective interpersonal communication. Chapter 6, also somewhat condensed, presents new material on productive interaction, emphasizing a multidimensional concept of inner motivation. Our principal interest centers on asking, and suggesting answers to, the vital question: What might all these hypotheses mean for a practical manager? Chapter 7 has been greatly condensed but now also contains new material on how to enrich the job of a first-level supervisor so that he can function as a genuine member of management. Chapter 8 has been updated, with an expanded treatment of unionization of government employees, including teachers. There is a new section dealing with problems facing public-sector managers in collective bargaining and settling labor disputes.

In Section C, Chapter 9 has been greatly condensed, retaining its essential points about the importance of "situational thinking" and giving case examples. Chapter 10 has also been somewhat revised. The new title for Chapter 11 emphasizes the role of personnel research in helping personnel administrators and managers diagnose the state of organizational health. In this chapter, and also in Chapter 12, there is new material on ways of dealing with difficulties (such as high absenteeism and turnover) suggested by indexes of poor organizational health. This chapter includes a new section on the use and limitations of exit interviews. Chapter 13, on analyzing and handling complaints and grievances, has been streamlined but contains a new section on adjusting grievances in the federal service.

The chapters in Section D have been revised to highlight recent developments. In particular, Chapter 15 has expanded sections on recruiting and hiring the disadvantaged, manpower forecasting, and computer-based personnel data systems. There are minor revisions in Chapters 16 and 17. Chapter 18 includes a new section called "A Special Case: Needs for Discipline on Campus." Chapter 19 contains new sections on the human aspects of plant relocation and the increasingly popular 4-day, 40-hour week.

In Section E, "Providing Pay and Services," Chapter 20 has been revised to take account of recent research and developments. Chapter 21 condenses and integrates Chapters 21 and 22 in the earlier editions; it has a new title, "Pay Incentive Systems; Sharing Productivity Gains." Similarly, the former Chapter 23, "Employee Benefits and Services," has been dropped because some of the material is more logically incorporated in the benefits section of Chapter 21. Chapter 22 (previously Chapter 24), entitled "Programs for Employee Health and Safety: An Ecological Approach," has been completely rewritten. It calls attention to the need for reappraising and possibly reorganizing a company's health and safety function in the light of recent research and developments. In addition to a greater emphasis on the workmen's compensation movement, this chapter includes material on the Occupational Health and Safety Act of 1971 and contributions made by the relatively new science of ergonomics.

Chapter 23, the concluding chapter and formerly Chapter 25, has been revised completely as a result of readers' comments. Instead of presenting a summary of the essential points developed in the book, we have now chosen to look ahead, asking: "What Future for Personnel Administration?" This question is directed as much to students of management and practicing managers as it is to those who aspire to become personnel administrators or are now serving as personnel managers in organizations. This chapter is a revised and expanded version of a paper by one of the authors entitled "The Changing Role of the Personnel Manager," which appeared in the inaugural (August 1971) issue of *Personnel Review,* a new British journal.

In Part 2, three new cases, 5, 11, and 19, have been added to illustrate new problems facing managers today. Four of the old cases have been dropped and one has been rewritten, but many have been retained because students and teachers have found them useful over the years. Even though some of them took place years ago, readers have told us that the situations they illustrate are not out of date. Many of the cases include relationships with organized labor. In the text itself, case illustrations have been used liberally, so that case material is not confined to Part 2, which includes an expanded introductory section entitled "Cases and Case Method: Notes from Experience."

This seventh edition, like all the others, has benefited from comments made by students, teachers, and colleagues overseas as well as by practicing managers. The publishers asked a number of teachers who have used the book to review our outline for this edition. We are particularly indebted to the suggestions made by Professors Morrison Handsaker of Lafayette College, Alton C. Johnson of the University of Wisconsin, Donald W. Magoon of Eastern Michigan University, and Alfred Stoess of the University of Nevada. We were unable to incorporate all the suggestions, but we have used a great many.

As in all the earlier editions, we also acknowledge our great debt to Faith Pigors, wife of the senior author. She has worked very hard to make the text more readable and has also contributed much that is substantive to a number of chapters. Her continuing interest in the ways in which managers can make work more human has been of great value to both of us as we worked on this revision. As in earlier editions, we have had the unselfish help of Mrs. Laura Carchia and Miss Ellen Humez in the Industrial Relations Library. They checked many references and kept us informed of recent publications we might otherwise have missed. We are also grateful for the patience with which Miss Patricia Macpherson of the M.I.T. Industrial Relations Section staff has borne the pressures we have faced in having parts of the manuscript ready to meet our time schedules.

Paul Pigors
Charles A. Myers

PERSONNEL ADMINISTRATION
A Point of View and a Method

Part 1

Section A

Management and Personnel Administration

INTRODUCTION

The central theme of this book is the personnel responsibility of line managers. Chapters 1 to 4 show interaction, in a changing world, between management concepts, the personnel function, general organization planning, and career development for managers.

In Chapter 1 we consider various managerial concepts, managing by centralized direction and control, and managing by shared objectives and self-control. The relevance of behavioral science research to effective managerial thinking today is summarized, and external pressures which affect managerial concepts are noted. Within any organization, top management's ideas and attitudes establish the climate for personnel relationships.

Chapter 2 centers on the organization of the personnel function in management. Staff members in the personnel or industrial relations department have personnel functions which they perform in a service and advisory capacity. Every line manager has such personnel responsibilities as coordinating the activities of individuals who report to him and helping them to develop their full potential for serving the organization. No manager can delegate those responsibilities without abdicating his managerial function. Some common misconceptions are examined, line-staff relationships are analyzed and illustrated, and the relatively new role of the project (or program) manager is touched upon. Special attention is given to different ways in which the "control" function is exercised in personnel administration according to different concepts of managing. Finally, there is an outline of broad functions of the personnel administrator as one who provides advice and services to line managers and who may also act as an enabler in the process of change.

Chapter 3 shows how the lifeblood of the organization can continually be rejuvenated by effective management development. It offers suggestions as to how managers can be helped to develop within an organization by changes in organization structure, advance manpower planning, coaching, joint performance appraisal, and, most of all, self-development within an environment which favors psychological growth. The personnel administrator, in a staff role, has exceptional opportunities to help line managers at all organizational levels understand and meet their responsibilities for leading and teaching subordinates.

Chapter 4 centers on four interactive factors that are influencing managerial attitudes and behavior today: (1) The desperate plight of many major cities presents managers with problems that may seem insoluble. Will new kinds of knowledge and new techniques (such as systems thinking) be used by managers to develop innovative and socially responsible solutions? (2) A "new breed of employee" (many of whom espouse the values that characterize the "Now" Generation) will not accept traditional ways of managing. (3) The New Feminists confront managers with insistent demands that women who work (and women who want to work) should enjoy rights equal to those accorded to men. Neither of these latter phenomena can productively be coped with by authoritarian ways of managing. Only participative management can meet the new demands and satisfy the new motivation while also contributing to organizational productivity. (4) Finally, technological advances, especially in automation and systems integration, have begun to transform the world of work. Will managers be able to create new jobs and set up a new climate in which the new breed of employee and the New Feminists can work productively with one another at all organizational levels? And can this evolving world of working and managing include a symbiotic relationship between men and machines such that social and technological advances can be beneficial for each organization as an integral whole and also for the larger society of which business and industrial organizations are a vital part?

CASES IN PART 2 THAT RELATE TO SECTION A

1 The Old-line Foreman
2 Who Owns the Improved Tool?
3 Dissatisfactions of an Expatriate Engineer
4 The Girl and the Computer
8 A Need for Policy-centered Thinking

Chapter 1

Managers and Their Personnel Concepts

All the activities of any enterprise are initiated and determined by the persons who make up that institution. Plants, offices, computers, automated equipment, and all else that a modern firm uses are unproductive except for human effort and direction. . . . Of all the tasks of management, managing the human component is the central and most important task, because all else depends on how well it is done.

Rensis Likert [1]

What is the nature of the managerial process? There are perhaps as many formulations as there are writers on or practitioners of management. One central theme is that managers perform several essential and unique functions which distinguish them from other people with professional training, such as lawyers, doctors, engineers, or scientists. In various degrees, managers undertake risks and handle uncertainties; plan and innovate; coordinate, administer and control; and supervise. The first undertaking is more pre-

[1] Rensis Likert, *The Human Organization: Its Management and Value,* McGraw-Hill Book Company, New York, 1967, p. 1.

cisely an *entrepreneurial* function, the next two are managerial, and the last is often the main task of lower levels of management, for management is also a hierarchy of persons, ranging from the chairman of the board and chief executive down through middle management and various staff specialists to first-level supervision.

The essence of the managerial process, therefore, is planning, innovation, coordination, administration, and control. If there is a key word to describe management it is probably *coordination.*

Coordination includes some decision-making: establishing broad objectives, initiating and approv-

5

ing changes in key personnel and in management organization, approving decisions of various matters in terms of the approver's interpretation of broad objectives, approving decisions on specific matters to avoid conflicts with other decisions.[2]

Management in this broad sense is not confined to private enterprise. It is also essential for the successful operation of a government department or agency, a public enterprise, a trade union, a nonprofit organization, or a college or university. In other words, managing is organizational leadership, and one of its central tasks is effective coordination and utilization of available human and nonhuman resources to achieve the objectives of the organization. These objectives may be, for example, to maximize profit or increase the firm's share of the market in business enterprises; to improve efficiency or expand the scope of services provided by a governmental bureau or department; to get more members or to bargain more effectively for members in a labor union; or to improve the quality of instruction, expand facilities and enrollment, and undertake new research in a college or university.

While the human resources available to management in an organization are only one part of resources which must be coordinated, it is through the combined efforts of people that monetary and material resources are utilized for organizational objectives. Without *human* efforts, organizations cannot accomplish their objectives. Consequently, the organization and motivation of human effort—*the personnel function of management*—are a central responsibility of managers everywhere. Indeed, the managerial hierarchy itself involves interpersonal relationships, in few or many layers from the top executive downward. The effectiveness with which *managerial* and *professional* human resources—high-talent manpower—are coordinated and developed accounts in important measure for suc-

cess or failure in achieving organizational objectives.

Most organizations are hierarchies of individuals performing different roles; some are at the top level of management, others are at intermediate and lower levels of the managerial group. In one sense they are all colleagues or associates in helping the organization achieve its stated objectives; but in another sense some are in the organizational role of being responsible to others at a higher organizational level. The effectiveness with which the organization functions depends to an important degree on how strongly the members of the organization are committed to organizational objectives. This in turn is importantly determined by the personnel concepts which managers hold. As we shall see, however, the interaction works both ways: manager's personnel concepts are influenced by the behavior of subordinates (or assumptions about their behavior), and subordinates, in turn, often adjust their behavior to what their organizational superiors expect of them.

THE IMPORTANCE OF MANAGERS' PERSONNEL CONCEPTS

Every manager makes assumptions and holds convictions about the way people behave in organizations. Sometimes these are explicit: "You have to keep people hopping and check on them closely or they'll take advantage of your absence." Sometimes managers' personnel concepts are demonstrated by the way they behave toward their subordinates in day-to-day relationships. Actions often speak louder than words. Even the manager who prides himself on being practical and having his feet on the ground, scorning any "theory of management," may reveal himself a philosopher about life and people when he has the opportunity. The personnel concepts which managers believe in and communicate in action therefore become well known to people in the organization. This is one meaning of the term "organizational climate."

[2] Robert A. Gordon, *Business Leadership in the Large Corporation,* The Brookings Institution, Washington, D.C., 1945, p. 53.

Why are these deeply held convictions important for a consideration of personnel administration? They are important because concepts managers hold affect organizational structures and the ways in which human resources are utilized. An authoritarian manager will develop a highly centralized organization, with subordinates expected to carry out his directives. A different type of manager will seek the ideas of his associates on policy formulation and implication before personnel policies and procedures are developed.

The purpose of this chapter is to consider different personnel concepts or theories of management, with special emphasis on the traditional or conventional theory of management by direction and external control in contrast to a newer concept of management by shared objectives and self-control. These are two extremes, which are described for purposes of sharpening the differences in concepts of management. We shall consider the implications of behavioral science research for these concepts and the environmental pressure affecting them. Finally, we shall examine possibilities of developing an effective managerial personnel concept applicable to different situations and the importance of a systems approach.

THE TRADITIONAL CONCEPT OF MANAGEMENT

Management by centralized direction and control is probably the most frequent concept of management anywhere. This authoritarian pattern has deep roots in the long and apparently successful experience of such organizations as the church and military organizations, although even in these organizations there have been considerable changes in recent years. The line of authority or chain of command traditionally goes directly from the top down through the various layers of the organization, with some delegation of authority but full and detailed accountability up the line. At each organizational level, supervisors are linked to the next and lower levels by position descriptions and inflexible directives. These statements establish the degree of authority each management representative has to take action for the company. They usually also specify *how* that action shall be performed. All general directives received from top management are progressively particularized as they flow downward along the chain of command. At the work level they are usually specific and unconditional orders, but at every organizational level they are designed *to tell people how to carry out the ideas, principles, and purposes of top management.*

The assumptions behind this view of management have been well expressed by the late Douglas McGregor, who called it "Theory X":

1 The average human being has an inherent dislike of work and will avoid it if he can.

2 Because of this human characteristic of dislike of work, most people must be coerced, controlled, directed, threatened with punishment to get them to put forth adequate effort toward the achievement of organizational objectives.

3 The average human being prefers to be directed, wishes to avoid responsibility, has relatively little ambition, wants security above all.[3]

Many of the principles of organization which are found in the literature of management are derived from these assumptions. Much of the early scientific-management movement attempted to control worker behavior by breaking down jobs into specialized elements, establishing norms of production, designing equipment so that the worker's pace would be more or less controlled, and devising intricate systems of in-

[3] Douglas McGregor, *The Human Side of Enterprise,* McGraw-Hill Book Company, New York, 1960, pp. 33-34. An earlier paper of the same title is reprinted in Paul Pigors, Charles A. Myers, and F. T. Malm, *Management of Human Resources: Readings in Personnel Administration,* 3d ed., McGraw-Hill Book Company, New York, 1973, selection 1. Later ideas developed by McGregor are found in a posthumous book, Caroline McGregor and Warren G. Bennis (eds.), *The Professional Manager,* McGraw-Hill Book Company, New York, 1967.

centive wage payment to reward the superior workers and penalize the laggards. Accounting and budgetary controls were intended to make sure that subordinate managers did not deviate from established standards. Centralized organizational structures reflected these assumptions about human behavior, and the "one-man" firm was an extreme case. The boss never really trusted his subordinates. Therefore, he carefully limited the amount of responsibility and information he gave them.

Managing by rules and orders establishes a pattern of decisions for meeting most of the ordinary difficulties that confront subordinate managers. When an unusual situation occurs—an exception to the rule—supervisors refer to their immediate superiors any matters for decision which (in their opinion) are not covered by previously established rules. In extreme cases, such problems continue their way up through the chain of command until they are brought to the attention of the top executive. *He decides.*

There is much to be said for this way of managing. It "gets results"—at least in the short run, when people respond to pressures and controls partly out of fear of the consequences of not following orders. Subordinate managers are not likely to make the kind of mistake that comes from assuming too much responsibility. But what about the situation in which a critical decision must be made and no available management representative is willing to make it? The following example shows what can happen.

A Case Example:
The Cable Splicer's Dilemma[4]

In a telephone company, during a business recession, an unconditional order had been issued by higher management forbidding supervisors to authorize overtime under any circumstances. One day, a cable splicer was working in a wet

[4] One of the authors learned of this case in his fieldwork with the company.

manhole on a toll cable running through marshy territory near the sea. About an hour before quitting time, he realized that he could not finish the job within the regular working day. He asked the supervising foreman whether he should stay overtime to finish the work. He estimated that the job could be completed in another 3 hours. The supervising foreman, having no authority to grant overtime, telephoned the supervisor of cable splicing. The latter, unwilling to make an exception to an order whose importance had been so strongly stressed, telephoned the superintendent of construction, who told him to use his discretion. The "decision" was transmitted down the line to the supervising foreman, who, however, still feared the possible consequences (for himself) of giving the order dictated by his own judgment. He therefore told the worker to wrap the splice securely and leave it to be finished in the morning.

During the night, an unusually high tide entered the manhole, penetrated the wrappings, and spoiled the cable. It took several days to repair the damage, and the toll line was tied up during all that time.

Does this example show that management by direction and control cannot always be efficient—even technically? The system of rules and unconditional orders is devised to meet specific requirements. When the rule makers are not there to size up the situation, lower-management representatives fear to make exceptions even when the underlying purpose of the rule (cost saving) might be achieved. The routine action—which they have learned to take—*supports the system* rather than the management objectives which the system was set up to attain. Under these conditions, can there be much *sense of achievement,* which is one of the key factors in job satisfaction for subordinates? Does management by rules stifle the initiative of subordinates and reduce the possibility of innovations which might increase productivity?

A PERSONNEL-MINDED CONCEPT OF MANAGEMENT

Experience like the cable splicer's dilemma under management by centralized controls and rules differs from other work-group experiences reported by skilled managers. Furthermore, recent behavioral science research does not support the traditional view, as we shall see later in this chapter. A contrasting concept of management is based on the belief that the most effective way to get results in any organization is to work *with* people rather than *through* them. The quality of the relationships is what Mary Parker Follett, an early perceptive writer on management, called "co-action," as contrasted with coercion.[5]

This concept of management is not soft or laissez faire in contrast to tough or decisive management. Neither is it "kid-glove" management based on various techniques of getting other people to do what the boss wants them to do without quite realizing that they are being manipulated. All these variations on management by centralized direction and control (except for laissez faire management, which simply leads to chaos) are based on the same assumptions about human behavior and motivation that underlie the traditional concept.

An alternative management concept does not involve abdication of managerial responsibility. Management is still responsible for achieving organizational objectives. But this personnel concept of management makes quite different assumptions about human behavior and motivation. A satisfied need is not a motivator of human behavior. In addition to lower-level physiological needs, most people have other needs (for safety or security, social acceptance by the group, and "egoistic needs" for self-respect, achievement, recognition, and self-actualization. In Chapter 6 we consider motivation theory in more detail). When work does not provide fulfillment of some of these other needs, it becomes a

punishment to be undergone in order to enjoy life off the job. Employees then tend to become "clock watchers."

The implications of all this for alternative concepts of management were well expressed by Douglas McGregor:

> Above all, the assumptions of Theory Y point up the fact that the limits on human collaboration in the organizational setting are not limits of human nature but of management's ingenuity in discovering how to realize the potential represented by its human resources. Theory X offers management an easy rationalization for ineffective organizational performance: It is due to the nature of the human resources with which we must work. Theory Y, on the other hand, places the problems squarely in the lap of management. If employees are lazy, indifferent, unwilling to take responsibility, intransigent, uncreative, uncooperative, Theory Y implies that the causes lie in management's methods of organization and control.[6]

In what McGregor calls "Theory Y," the assumptions about human behavior in organizations are as follows:

1 *The expenditure of physical and mental effort in work is as natural as play or rest.* The average human being does not inherently dislike work. Depending upon controllable conditions, work may be a source of satisfaction (and will be voluntarily performed) or a source of punishment (and will be avoided if possible).

2 *External control and the threat of punishment are not the only means for bringing about effort toward organizational objectives. Man will exercise self-direction and self-control in the service of objectives to which he is committed.*

3 *Commitment to objectives is a function of the rewards associated with their achievement.* The most significant of such rewards, e.g., the satisfaction of their ego and self-actualization needs, can be direct products of efforts directed toward organizational objectives.

4 *The average human being learns under proper conditions, not only to accept but to seek responsibil-*

[5] Mary Parker Follett, *Creative Experience,* Longmans, Green & Co., Inc., New York, 1924, p. XIII.

[6] *The Human Side of Enterprise,* p. 48.

ity. Avoidance of responsibility, lack of ambition, and emphasis on security are generally consequences of experience, not inherent human characteristics.

5 *The capacity to exercise a relatively high degree of imagination, ingenuity, and creativity in the solution of organizational problems is widely, not narrowly, distributed in the population.*

6 *Under conditions of modern industrial life, the intellectual potentialities of the average human being are only partly utilized.*

These assumptions lead to a managerial approach which emphasizes the principle of *mutual responsibility* and *shared objectives.* They recognize the fact of *interdependence* in human organizations. This system is *not* "democratic" in the sense that managing is done by majority vote, but it is "participative" in the sense that superiors seek out their subordinates' ideas about proposed courses of action before a decision is made. However, top management still makes all official decisions for the organization as a whole. At each organizational level the person in authority—after taking account of the experience and ideas expressed by his associates—is accountable for making the final decision.

Concepts Similar to Theory X and Theory Y

McGregor's Theory X–Theory Y concept has had a growing impact on managerial thinking in an increasing number of organizations. So have two similar and more recently developed systems for managing human effort. One is the Blake-Mouton "managerial grid" approach; the other is Likert's System 1–System 4 concept, developed from extensive research studies in a large number of organizations.[7] The Blake-Mouton

---

[7] Robert R. Blake and Jane S. Mouton, *The Managerial Grid: Key Orientations for Achieving Production through People,* Gulf Publishing Company, Houston, 1964; and Rensis Likert, *The Human Organization: Its Management and Value,* McGraw-Hill Book Company, New York, 1967. Some of the work reported in this latter book is an extension of research findings and their implications first presented by Likert in *New Patterns of Management,* McGraw-Hill Book Company, New York, 1961.

grid has two dimensions: high-low concern for people and high-low concern for production. For example, at one point on the grid, managers can be *too* considerate of people's needs for satisfying relationships, with the result that production suffers; or, at another point, it can arrange conditions of work technologically so that the "human element" interferes to a minimum degree, showing that its concern for people is lower and for production higher. But in what Blake and Mouton call "9,9 Management," with high concern both for people and for high production, "work accomplishment is from committed people; interdependence through a 'common stake' in organization purpose leads to relationships of trust and respect."

Likert uses a continuum of four managerial systems, from System 1, which is characterized by "direct hierarchical pressure for results," to System 4, which uses "the principle of supportive relationships and group methods of supervision." System 4 is characterized by high trust, high performance expectations, and participation. Likert also stresses the significance of "linking pin" relationships within this type of system between a manager at any organizational level, his superiors, his subordinates, and his organizational associates in other areas of responsibility.

While McGregor's Theory Y, Blake-Mouton's 9,9 Management, and Likert's System 4 are not identical, there are important similarities between them. These theories and other behavioral science applications (such as those of Chris Argyris, Frederick Herzberg, Abraham H. Maslow, William Foote Whyte, and others) have been widely discussed in management development seminars and have been experimented with in a number of firms.[8]

---

[8] See Harold M. F. Rush, *Behavioral Science: Concepts and Management Application.* Personnel Policy Study No. 216, National Industrial Conference Board, Inc., 1969. Among the firms applying these concepts, case studies have been published for American Airlines, Armstrong Cork Company, Corning Glass Works, Genesco, Hotel Corporation of America, Raymond Corporation, Steinberg's, Syntex, Texas In-

BEHAVIORAL SCIENCE RESEARCH: SUPPORTIVE OR QUESTIONING?

A number of studies of people in organizations have resulted in conclusions which tend to support the concepts just discussed. But there have also been studies which raise some questions about the general applicability of these concepts, and, in particular, about the causal relationship between job satisfaction and performance of productivity. Is a satisfied employee a higher performer? Or is the higher performer a more satisfied employee—or what? Can employees in highly repetitive operations engage in a meaningful "participation"? Or do they want and expect their supervisor to give them clear instructions and hold them to expected standards of performance? These questions oversimplify some of the assumptions examined in recent research, but they indicate that continued behavioral science research in organizations will be needed to test some of our present concepts.

Only a brief summary of the supportive and questioning research findings can be summarized here. We shall make reference to these and other studies throughout the book, particularly as they apply to the individual in the organization, the measures of organizational health, and elements of an integrated personnel policy system.

Research Findings Supporting the Newer Concepts of Management

These have principally emerged out of the extensive field studies by the Institute of Social Research at the University of Michigan, under the direction of Rensis Likert.[9] They are not isolated studies; they have been conducted in a variety of industries such as insurance, automobiles, heavy machinery, public utilities, railroads, chemicals, delivery service, and others. They have covered many thousands of employees from unskilled workers to scientists in research laboratories. Some of the significant findings of this research group include the following.

1 *There are significant differences in the leadership patterns of supervisors of high-producing groups and those of low-producing groups.* The former tend to be employee-centered—concentrating their attention on the human aspects of their subordinates' problems and on building effective work groups with high performance standards. The low-producing supervisors are more production-centered, using pressure to "get out the work" but neglecting important needs of their human organization. While both types of supervisors enforce the rules, arrange work, and make work assignments, the employee-centered supervisors recommend promotions, transfers, and pay increases, inform their subordinates about what is happening in the company, keep them posted on how well they are doing, and hear complaints and grievances more often than the production-centered supervisors. In one company, when high-production managers were switched to low-production divisions, these divisions gained in productivity faster than the formerly high-production divisions lost under the low-production managers, who continued close, job-centered supervision.

2 *Freedom to set one's own work pace is directly related to productivity.* Contrary to the widespread impression that people will "goof off" unless a supervisor is breathing down their necks, these studies showed that departments in

---

struments, and the Systems Group of TRW, Inc. For other case studies of Polaroid, Texas Instruments, H. P. Hood & Sons, American Telephone and Telegraph, and American Velvet, see Fred K. Foulkes, *Creating More Meaningful Work,* American Management Association, New York, 1969. The Texas Instruments experience is fully presented in M. Scott Myers, *Every Employee a Manager,* McGraw-Hill Book Company, New York, 1970.

[9] These are reported in Likert, *New Patterns of Management,* and also in two of his earlier articles reproduced in Pigors, Myers, and Malm, *op. cit.,* selections 2 and 21, under the original titles "Measuring Organizational Performance" and "Motivation: The Core of Management." See also his later book, *The Human Organization,* chap. 2.

which men feel most free to set their own pace have above-average productivity, while those in which men feel least free to set their own pace have below-average productivity. In repetitive operations, the pace of work may be controlled by the machine, but in many other types of jobs it will vary with the employee's ability and will to work.

> Managers who achieve high performance in their units accompanied by a sense of freedom supervise by setting general goals and objectives and providing less specific direction than do the managers of low-producing units. . . . They use more participation and achieve higher involvement, greater interest in the work, and more responsibility for doing it than the low-producing managers. [10]

These findings also apply to supervisors themselves, in relation to their superiors in higher management and to scientists in research laboratories.

3 *An effective interaction-influence system is required for high performance.* A study of 40 sales offices showed that "a complete set of interdependent cooperative relationships exist between the manager and the men and among the men in successful enterprises." [11] Subsequent studies of 38 additional sales units identified four leadership dimensions: managerial support, interaction facilitation, goal emphasis, and work facilitation. The essence of this has been put succinctly by Mason Haire: "The amount of influence a superior has with his subordinates depends on the degree to which they can influence him." [12] This is consistent with other research findings which stress the importance of the manager's role in helping an organization to change. "The more the system which must change participates in decisions about how to manage the

change, the less likely it is to resist the change and the more stable the change is likely to be." [13]

4 *Superiors at all levels in an organization generally underestimate the extent to which their subordinates believe the "boss" understands their problems.* In one study, people at different levels were asked how well they thought their superior understood their problems and, in turn, how well they thought they understood their own subordinates' problems. Of the men in the work group, only 34 percent said their foreman understood their problems, but 95 percent of these same foremen stated that they understood the men's problems well. Again, only 51 percent of these foremen said their own boss (the general foreman) understood the first-level foreman's problems well, but 90 percent of the general foremen asserted they understood the foreman's problems well. Finally, when the general foremen were asked how well their superior in management understood their problems, only 60 percent gave a favorable reply. A similar finding was made in the power plants of a public utility; the higher levels of management always said they sought their subordinates' ideas much more frequently than the subordinates said their superiors asked for their ideas. These studies illustrate the well-known gap between downward communication and upward communication in an organization. Actions speak louder than words.

5 *Pressure through traditional management methods will bring impressive short-run results, but at a disproportionate cost in human assets. Participative methods enhance human resources for longer-run gains.* This was shown in a year's experimental study of 500 clerical employees in four divisions which were similar in organization, technology, work, and employee attitudes. Before and after measurements of productivity, employee attitudes and supervisory behavior were

---

[10] Likert, *New Patterns of Management,* pp. 20–21, and *The Human Organization,* chap. 3.

[11] Likert, *Human Organization,* p. 70.

[12] Mason Haire, *Psychology in Management,* 2d ed., McGraw-Hill Book Company, New York, 1964, p. 212.

[13] Edgar H. Schein, *Organizational Psychology,* Prentice-Hall, Inc., Englewood Cliffs, N.J., 1965, p. 102. Schein also points out (p. 105): "Good leadership and good membership blend into each other in an effective organization. It is just as much the task of a member to help the group reach its goal as it is the task of the formal leader."

carefully tested. In two of the four divisions, supervisors were trained in participative management methods, and in the other two there was an increase in closeness of supervision and centralization of decision making. These were called "hierarchically controlled"; the first two divisions were called "participative." Now for the results.

All four divisions knew that management sought an increase in productivity through a reduction in the number of clerks in each division. Clerks in the participative divisions took part in the decision to reduce the work force, while the managers of the hierarchically controlled divisions were ordered to cut staff by 25 percent through transfers and not replacing persons who left. As might be expected, the flat order did result in a 25 percent payroll reduction. The participative groups achieved only a 20 percent reduction during the experimental year, although the better of the two groups achieved as much as the two hierarchically controlled groups, while staff in the other participative division (which had been the poorest of the four before the experiment began) was reduced by only 15 percent. There were other significant differences, however. "The productivity increases in the hierarchically controlled program were accompanied by shifts in an *adverse* direction in such factors as loyalty, attitudes, interest, and involvement in the work. Just the opposite was true in the participative program." [14] Thus at the end of the experimental year, the people in the hierarchically controlled groups were resentful toward management, their supervisors, and the high producers; some had quit in disgust. In other words, the human resources of these divisions were being dissipated, and productivity would very likely begin to fall (although the experiment was not continued long enough to test

this conclusion). Possibly something like this happens when a manager "gets results" by pressure over a time span of a year or two, then moves on through a promotion or transfer while a new manager takes over his old job and finds he has inherited a sullen and resentful work force.

Human asset accounting. This study led Likert to suggest the need for some form of "human asset" accounting, to show the improvement in or deterioration of human assets, just as existing accounting systems report changes in physical assets. Furthermore, under these systems, recruitment, training, and other "investments" in human resources are treated as current costs. Subsequently, some of Likert's associates with an accounting background developed what they believed to be the first human resource accounting system. This was begun in 1968 with 96 management people in the R. G. Barry Company, a Columbus, Ohio, manufacturing firm with 1,300 employees. "Outlay costs" (some salary and nonsalary costs) represent organizational investments in human resources; "positional replacement costs" of human resources are the outlay costs which would be necessary to secure a replacement for a manager who leaves his position. Even though this new form of accounting is in an early stage, the researchers claim beneficial results for "organizational and manpower plan ning which underlie and sustain corporate growth." [15] Subsequently, in 1969, the system was refined and extended to cover factory and clerical employees in several plants.

6 *In a favorable organizational climate, participative management methods reduce resistance to change and increase productivity.* An earlier experimental study in a garment factory demonstrated more positive results from participative

[14] Likert, *New Patterns of Management,* p. 65. This experimental study is reported in detail in Nancy Morse and E. Reimer, "The Experimental Change of a Major Organizational Variable," *Journal of Abnormal and Social Psychology,* vol. 52, pp. 120-129, 1956. For a discussion of later studies with similar results, see Likert, *The Human Organization,* pp. 80-100.

[15] R. Lee Brummet, William C. Pyle and Eric G. Flamholtz, "Human Resource Accounting in Industry," *Personnel Administration,* vol. 32, no. 4, pp. 34-46, July-August 1969. For later experience, see William C. Pyle, "Monitoring Human Resources—'On Line,'" *Michigan Business Review,* vol. 22, no. 4, pp 19-32, July, 1970. Also reprinted in Pigors, Myers, and Malm, *op. cit.,* selection 3.

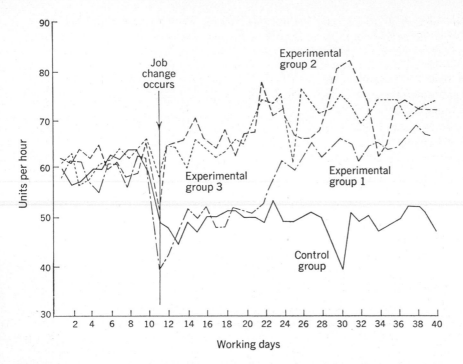

Figure 1-1   The effect of participation on production. Contrasting effects of participation and traditional managerial methods on productivity. Note that the control group, in which there has been no participation in designing the new job, has restricted output to around 50 units per hour. *(Source: Lester Coch and John R. P. French, Jr., "Overcoming Resistance to Change,"* Human Relations, *vol. 1, no. 4, p. 522, 1948.)*

methods in cost reduction, as contrasted with a control group in which traditional management methods were used.[16] A new production standard for the control group was set by management, explained to workers, and put into effect. In experimental group 1, the problem was dramatically brought home to workers when they could not distinguish between two similar garments, although one cost twice as much to make as the other. Their interest was aroused, so they agreed to effect savings and approved management's plans to introduce new methods and rates. Special operators were trained and made many good suggestions. Experimental groups 2

and 3, which were smaller, held similar meetings on the need for cost reduction, and all operators participated directly in designing the new jobs and making suggestions for improvements.

The results before and after the changes are shown in Figure 1-1. Starting from similar levels of production, the control group dropped in productivity, and the others rose. Later, the control group was exposed to the full participative approach and the results were similar to those of the other participative groups.

When this same company acquired a company in another city, the parent company began some management training programs and took other steps to change the approach of the existing managerial approach of the new company toward a more participative one. These changes resulted, according to a study of these experi-

[16] Lester Coch and John R. P. French, Jr., "Overcoming Resistance to Change," *Human Relations,* vol. 1, no. 4, pp. 512–532, 1948.

ences, in a 26 percent increase in productivity over a 2-year period. This increase was accomplished without a single replacement of management or supervisory personnel. [17]

Similar productivity increases have resulted in Scanlon Plan companies characterized by a Theory Y-type management. Since the Scanlon Plan also involves sharing productivity gains, we shall discuss it in more detail in Chapter 21.

The effect of participative management is also given by a case study of an automobile plant where a new manager succeeded one who had managed by centralized directives and pressure. The new manager began by learning about the needs of the organization as seen by his subordinates. He listened. There was increasing participation in problem solving by the higher management group, and this spread throughout the managerial organization. After 2½ years, this plant became the outstanding plant of seven in the division of the company. [18] A more extensive research study of "mental health" of automobile workers indicates the contribution made by personnel-minded management concepts. [19]

Research Findings Which Raise Questions

Much of this research is of recent origin; some goes back to questions raised about the general applicability of the Theory X-Theory Y type of

concepts. Briefly, here are the principal findings: [20]

1 *Instead of high employee job satisfaction leading to high performance, the reverse may be true. High performance is more likely to lead to high job satisfaction, through rewards which the employee receives for high performance and which he perceives as equitable.* If the rewards (pay, promotion, feeling of accomplishment, etc.) are believed by the employee to be unrelated to high performance, dissatisfaction results. The Porter-Lawler model is the clearest expression of this relationship. [21]

2 *Extrinsic rewards (e.g., pay and benefits) may be less important rewards for high performance and hence high job satisfaction than the intrinsic rewards of higher self-esteem and prestige, greater autonomy in one's work, and fulfillment of self-actualization needs such as opportunity for growth and development, feeling of self-fulfillment, and feeling of accomplishment.* One study of 200 middle and lower managers in a Pennsylvania steel mill showed that the highest correlation was between performance and fulfillment of self-actualization needs, but the correlations for the lower-order needs for security and social relationships were not significantly different from those for esteem and autonomy. While supporting the

[17] Likert, *The Human Organization,* pp. 29-40. Likert calls these a "System 4" management approach. For a more detailed research study of these experiences, see Alfred J. Marrow, D. G. Bowers, and S. E. Seashore (eds.), *Strategies of Organization Change,* Harper & Row, Publishers, Incorporated, New York, 1967. For a similar change in a hotel chain, see Richard Beckhard, "An Organizational Improvement Program in a Decentralized Organization," *The Journal of Applied Behavioral Science,* vol. 2, no. 1, pp. 3-25, January-March, 1966.

[18] Robert H. Guest, *Organizational Change: The Effect of Successful Leadership,* The Dorsey Press and Richard D. Irwin, Inc., Homewood, Ill., 1962, chap. 7.

[19] See Arthur Kornhauser, *Mental Health of the Industrial Worker: A Detroit Study,* John Wiley & Sons, Inc., New York, 1965, chap. 12, especially pp. 263, 281, 284.

[20] This section draws heavily on the excellent summary of research and presentation of new findings in the symposium organized by Professor Raymond E. Miles, "A Complementary Collection: Work, Performance, and Satisfaction," (a series of four articles), *Industrial Relations,* vol. 9, no. 4, pp. 405-474, October, 1970.

[21] Lyman W. Porter and Edward E. Lawler III, *Managerial Attitudes and Performance,* Richard D. Irwin, Inc., Homewood, Ill., 1968; and Lawler and Porter, "The Effect of Performance on Job Satisfaction," *Industrial Relations,* vol. 7, no. 1, pp. 20-28, October, 1967. Leaders or managers may also be affected in their leadership styles by the *level* of performance of their subordinates; the leaders of high-performing groups becoming more supportive than those of low-performing groups. For experimental evidence, see George F. Farris and Francis G. Lim, Jr., "Effects of Performance on Leadership, Cohesiveness, Influence, Satisfaction, and Subsequent Performance," *Journal of Applied Psychology,* vol. 53, no. 6, pp. 490-497, December, 1969.

Porter-Lawler model, the question might be asked: Are these findings inconsistent with the basic assumptions of McGregor's Theory Y, or Likert's System 4 management? The same question could be raised about another study which concluded that dissatisfactions among laboratory engineers were greater than among field engineers when the latter had greater responsibilities and autonomy in their work and the former saw themselves as often being underutilized or misutilized.[22]

3 *Managers need to recognize that the nature of the production technology and the consequent organization of the work will affect leadership styles.* For example, in organizations with well-defined, predictable tasks, with highly structured technology (as in assembly-line operations), and with a well-defined and structured product, there tends to be a hierarchy of authority, with centralized management, explicit division of labor, and wide use of rules and procedures. But when organizations have less well-defined tasks, as in a research and development laboratory, for example, highly centralized organizational structures with centralized managerial controls work poorly. The same appears to be true of firms with complex and changing technology, or with rapidly changing markets, or concerned with the development of new products. In these cases, *uncertainty* requires more decentralized organization structures, which draw upon the capacity of people at subordinate levels to contribute toward task solutions and toward the integration of team efforts to achieve organizational objectives.

Some of these conclusions grow out of research in Great Britain in the 1960s by Woodward, by Burns and Stalker, and in this country by Fiedler.[23] A more recent study of two organizations with high performance and two with lower performance indicated the complex relationship between supervision, task, and performance. In the high-performance container manufacturing plant, management and supervision were highly directive, the work was technologically structured, and employees were highly motivated. But so were the employees in a high-performance industrial research laboratory, in which participative management was necessary to motivate professionals to high performance. In contrast, the two lower-performance organizations were (1) a comparable manufacturing plant which had too little structure and a participative type of supervision, and (2) a comparable industrial research laboratory which had too much structure and supervision that was too directive for effective research performance. The researchers concluded that "competence motivation is most likely to be fulfilled when there is a fit between the task and the organization," and that a "contingency theory" is necessary to characterize the "task-organization-people fit."[24]

[22] These two studies, part of the Miles symposium, are as follows: John W. Slocum, Jr., "Performance and Satisfaction: An Analysis," and R. Richard Ritti, "Underemployment of Engineers," both in *Industrial Relations*, vol. 9, no. 4, pp. 431–452, October, 1970. Raymond E. Miles was one of the coauthors of a study which concluded: "We interpret our results here as providing support for three links in the McGregor-Likert, et al., logic—that democratic-participative leadership behavior is related to satisfaction and to performance—and some suggestion of support for the fourth link in the chain, that attitudes of support and confidence in subordinates are related to the other three variables." But they add: "Our best guess is that these relationships, if they exist, are circular...." Karlene Roberts, Raymond E. Miles, and L. Vaughn Blankenship, "Organizational Leadership Satisfaction and Productivity: A Comparative Analysis," *Academy of Management Journal*, vol. 11, no. 4, pp. 401–414, December, 1968.

[23] Joan Woodward's early studies and later research are found in her book *Industrial Organization: Theory and Practice*, Oxford University Press, London, 1965; Thomas Burns and G. M. Stalker, *The Management of Innovation*, Tavistock Publications, London, 1961. For the importance of the task and the situation, see F. E. Fiedler (ed.), *A Theory of Leadership Effectiveness*, McGraw-Hill Book Company, New York, 1967.

[24] John J. Morse and Jay W. Lorsch, "Beyond Theory Y," *Harvard Business Review*, vol. 48, no. 3, pp. 61–68, May–June, 1970. See also Paul R. Lawrence and Jay W. Lorsch, *Organization and Environment: Managing Differentiation and Integration*, Division of Research, Graduate School of Business Administration, Harvard University, Boston, 1967; and Harold J. Leavitt, "Unhuman Organizations," *Harvard Business Review*, vol. 40, no. 4, pp. 90–98, July–August, 1962 (also reprinted in Pigors, Myers, and Malm, *op. cit.*, selection 4).

The question-raising research reviewed above offers little support for traditional concepts. But it does suggest a modification in the general applicability of the personnel-minded concepts of management characterized by Theory Y and System 4. However, is there not still much room for management application of these latter ideas, especially within management ranks and with professionally trained people whose tasks are "knowledge-based"? Are not many more organizations facing changing technology, products or services, and markets? And, finally, aren't external environmental factors bringing pressures on top managements to move in the direction of the newer concepts?

ENVIRONMENTAL PRESSURES FOR CHANGE

The following developments in the external environment affect the nature, values, and expectations of new recruits and replacements drawn by organizations from today's labor force. These developments may be expected to have a greater impact if they persist over a period of years. They are characteristic of the United States labor force but may have validity for other countries as well.

1 *The growing predominance of white-collar employees, particularly in the technical and professional employee group.* Table 1-1 shows this trend

Table 1-1 Employment by Major Occupational Group, 1900–1960 and Projected for 1980

Occupational group	Percent of labor force				
	1900	1920	1940	1960	1980*
White-collar	17.6	24.9	31.1	43.3	50.8
Professional, technical, and kindred workers	4.3	5.4	7.5	11.4	16.3
Managers, officials, and proprietors except farm	5.8	6.6	7.3	10.7	10.0
Clerical and kindred workers	3.0	8.0	9.6	14.8	18.2
Sales workers	4.5	4.9	6.7	6.4	6.3
Blue-collar	35.8	40.2	39.8	36.6	32.7
Craftsmen, foremen, and kindred workers	10.5	13.0	12.0	13.0	12.8
Operatives and kindred workers	12.8	15.6	18.4	18.2	16.2
Laborers except farm and mine	12.5	11.6	9.4	5.4	3.7
Service workers	9.0	7.8	11.7	12.2	13.8
Private household workers	5.4	3.3	4.7	3.1	
Service workers except household	3.6	4.5	7.1	9.1	
Farm workers	37.5	27.0	17.4	7.8	2.7
Farmers and farm managers	19.9	15.3	10.4	4.1	
Farm laborers and foremen	17.7	11.7	7.0	3.7	

* Note the relative importance by 1980 of professional, technical, and kindred workers, and of clerical and kindred workers, as compared to operatives, laborers, and farm workers.

Sources: Occupational Trends in the United States 1900 to 1950, U.S. Bureau of the Census, pp. 6–7; *Manpower Report of the President,* April, 1971, Table E-10, p. 297.

clearly, and it indicates other developments which the reader can determine for himself. Compare the preliminary estimates for 1980 with the actual percentages for two-decade intervals from 1960 back to 1900.

2 *These trends also reflect a better-educated labor force.* More than 95 percent of the fifteen-to-nineteen age group attend secondary schools in the United States, and in recent years an increasingly high proportion (approaching 50 percent) of the graduates have had the advantage of some form of higher education. In 1970 over 7 million students were enrolled in higher educational institutions. With their first job often delayed beyond the age at which their fathers or grandfathers started work, these young people tend to expect more from work than did their forebears, some of whom were immigrants.

3 *Changes in values held by people at work and in the society.* Some managers complain that young people no longer want to do a "fair day's work." Possibly. And perhaps this reflects the view that work and material accumulation aren't the main goals in life. But others, who are "turned off" by their work experience, may be repelled by highly structured work organizations directed by centralized management with a more or less authoritarian outlook. It is the latter group which brings pressure on management to move in the direction of Theory Y–System 4.

4 *Scientists and engineers, especially in research and development groups, have different work values than those in other parts of the organization.* As a number of studies have shown, they tend to think in terms of career development in their profession. And the respect of their peers outside the organization may seem more important than approval by their organizational superiors. As the authors of one study concluded:

> Surely the need for participation increases in the industrial research laboratories with many highly trained specialists at work on complex and rapidly-changing technologies. For industrial research the need for blending the authority of technical competence with hierarchical authority is vitally necessary. . . . The administrator needs the help of tech-

nical experts in ascertaining what is readily knowable and in estimating probabilities in "areas of ignorance."[25]

5 *Pressures from labor unions.* Unions of blue-collar workers and unions of some white-collar workers have challenged the unilateral exercise of managerial authority in plants, stores, and offices. Management decisions on hiring, promotion, transfer, layoff, discipline, wages and salaries, methods of wage payment, fringe benefits, etc., are subject to provisions of collective agreement. While management initiates decisions, the union may question them through the grievance procedure, arbitration, and in some cases through the concerted withholding of labor (the strike). Thus, managers have to consider more carefully than formerly the impact of their actions on employees. Managers in private enterprise are increasingly aware of this fact, but the recent unionization of government employees (especially at the state and local levels) and teachers is forcing government officials and school boards to learn the same lesson again.

6 *Shortages of high-talent manpower.* There have been shortages not only in managerial personnel but also among professional, technical, and skilled employees. The possibility that a dissatisfied employee may leave for another position is a continual pressure on management to pay greater attention to human aspirations. This has been true of the scarce high-talent man-

[25] See Ralph M. Hower and Charles D. Orth III, *Managers and Scientists: Some Human Problems in Industrial Research Organizations,* Harvard Graduate School of Business Administration, Boston, 1963, p. 307. Also William Kornhauser, *Scientists in Industry: Conflict and Accommodation,* University of California Press, Berkeley, Calif., 1962; Simon Marcson, *The Scientist in American Industry,* Princeton University, Industrial Relations Section, Princeton, N.J., 1960; Eugene Raudsepp, *Managing Creative Scientists and Engineers,* The Macmillan Company, New York, 1963; and Herbert Shepard, "Superiors and Subordinates in Research," *The Journal of Business* (The University of Chicago), vol. 29, no. 4, pp. 261-267, October, 1956. Donald C. Pelz and Frank M. Andrews, *Scientists in Organizations: Productive Climates for Research and Development,* John Wiley and Sons, New York, 1967; and Frank M. Andrews and George F. Farris, "Supervisory Practices and Innovation in Scientific Teams," *Personnel Psychology,* vol. 20, no. 4, pp. 497-515, Winter, 1967.

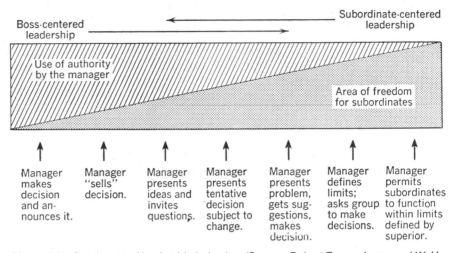

Figure 1-2   Continuum of leadership behavior. *(Source: Robert Tannenbaum and W. H. Schmidt, "How to Choose a Leadership Pattern,"* Harvard Business Review, *vol. 36, no. 2, pp. 95–106, March–April, 1958.)*

power which an advanced industrial society requires. Even if various devices are introduced to reduce labor turnover, such as pensions, vacations, and other benefits tied to continuous service with the organization, employees may still withhold their full efforts and energies by controlling the pace of work, restricting output, and doing only enough to "get by." When a well-informed observer can state that "it is no secret that our creative professionals, especially our scientists and engineers, are the most dissatisfied employees in industry,"[26] traditional management is surely under considerable pressure to change its managerial concepts and practices.

7 *Increasing role of government.* Government regulation of the terms of the employment relationship has increased during the past 40 years. Hours of work and overtime payments are regulated by various federal and state laws; the right to organize and bargain collectively is protected; federal and state mediation agencies are likely to intervene if a serious labor dispute occurs. Perhaps these are only indirect constraints or controls, but they do restrict the exercise of unilateral managerial authority over employees.

[26] Raudsepp, *op. cit.,* p. 113.

8 *Growth of professional management.* Finally, the growth of a professional managerial class in American enterprises and organizations has largely replaced family management. There are still many family-owned firms, but they are mostly small ones. Larger enterprises such as the Ford Motor Company are now professionalized, and their stock is increasingly owned by the public. This separation of ownership from control, which began in the 1920s in this country, has spread further. Professionalization of management has been accelerated by the growth of undergraduate and graduate schools of business administration and management and by the spread of professional management organizations. These are often transmission belts for newer management concepts and techniques.

DEVELOPING AN EFFECTIVE PERSONNEL CONCEPT OF MANAGEMENT

Much of what we have reviewed in the preceding sections suggests the need for a more effective personnel concept of management, which is more consistent with the findings of behavioral science research as well as with the variety of external pressures on management to move away from older, traditional concepts. A number of possible managerial styles or patterns can be represented as points on a scale or continuum. Figure 1-2 shows seven stages ranging from a higher degree of authority by the manager to considerable freedom by subordinates.

The place on this continuum occupied by a particular manager or supervisor depends on a number of factors. First, his own value system, as reflected in his confidence in his subordinates, his leadership inclinations, and what Tannenbaum and Schmidt call his "tolerance for ambiguity" as opposed to the certainty of rules and procedures, will affect where he is. Second, he will be influenced by the behavior of his own subordinates, a factor that reflects their perception of him and of the work situation and which also expresses their own values. (Scientists differ from workers on the assembly line.) Third, factors inherent in the immediate situation may affect the managerial concept used. For example, if the organization is large and geographically dispersed, possibly more centralized controls will be necessary than in a small research organization. Research organizations are also dependent upon considerable sharing of information; this is less true of a routine clerical operation or one which has been computerized. Finally, the pressure of time and the need for rapid decision making may inhibit the degree of participation that can be permitted at a particular moment.

These factors have led to the suggestion that "sensitive flexibility" is needed in executives, who must strike a balance between different styles of management.[27] Certainly flexibility is desirable, but it should be in response to an *awareness* of the factors at work in a particular situation and of how the manager can effectively operate in this situation. As Tannenbaum and Schmidt have observed:

The successful leader is one who is keenly aware of those forces which are most relevant to his behavior at any given time. He accurately understands himself, the individuals and groups in which he operates, and certainly he is able to assess the present readiness of growth of his subordinates . . . the successful leader is one who is able to behave appropriately in the light of these perceptions. If direction is in order, he is able to direct; if considerable participative freedom is called for, he is able to provide such freedom.[28]

In other words, management strategies may change with the needs of the particular situation confronting the manager. *If his assumptions about human behavior grow out of a belief in management by shared objectives, he will have the flexibility to move along the scale—even to using directive methods when the situation requires it, as in an emergency or crisis.* Under these circumstances his subordinates are more likely to accept a firm hand at the helm. The manager whose rigid concept is one of centralized direction and control restricts himself to the left end of the scale in Figure 1-2, either because he lacks confidence in the potentialities of his subordinates or because he is himself an authoritarian personality. He has limited his flexibility.

It is also important to ask: Over the long run, in which direction is the management of an organization likely to move on the scale? This will be in response to the long-run changes which are likely to occur in the internal and external environments, rather than as a result of the factors in the particular situation of the moment. We believe that a preponderance of these changes in an increasing number of organizations is forcing managers to move in the direction of management by shared objectives and self-control. But the road will be long, with intermediate stages on the way. There is a risk in management moving too quickly from one degree of control to the opposite. Abrupt changes in management ap-

[27] Eugene E. Jennings, *The Executive: Autocrat, Bureaucrat, Democrat,* Harper & Row, Publishers, Incorporated, New York, 1962.

[28] *Ibid.,* p. 101.

proaches arouse suspicions, doubts, and even resentments. A short step in the direction of more participation will be more effective than introducing full participative management at once.

Meanwhile, there will continue to be managers with the philosophy of Benjamin Jowett, the famous Master of Balliol College at Oxford during the latter part of the nineteenth century. He explained his methods of administration in the following words: "Never retract, never explain. Get it done, and let them howl." Perhaps this approach was effective then, but it is unlikely to be effective today in running a university, a research laboratory, a government department, or a business enterprise.

THE NEED FOR LOOKING AT MANAGEMENT AS A SYSTEM

Modern management concepts stress the importance of a *systems approach*. From one point of view this means a system which involves complex interrelationships between sales, marketing, production, inventories, finance, personnel, and other functional areas, and between the internal environment of the organization and its external contacts, both in the present and in a foreseeable future. Techniques of operations research, PERT, and computer-based managerial information and control programs are increasingly used to implement this systems approach.

But it is also possible to view different personnel concepts of management as "systems" in the sense that each must have an internally consistent set of personnel policies. One policy cannot be changed without affecting the others. For example, a personnel concept of management characterized by McGregor's Theory Y (or Likert's System 4) will not be effective unless the organization structure supports it and personnel policies are consistent with it. This means that communication methods, selection procedures, promotion policies, performance evaluation through an emphasis on management by objec-

tives or self-control, discipline, wage and salary policies and methods, sharing productivity gains, and employee services, health, and safety programs—all these will have different content and administrative methods than if management adopts a Theory X approach.[29] New managerial techniques, such as computer-based management information systems, will also be determined by the personnel concepts of management. A top manager who believes in management by integration and self-control (Theory Y, or System 4, or 9,9 Management in the Blake-Mouton managerial grid) will utilize the computerized information system to provide each level of management with that information which will help it to monitor its progress toward the achievement of subunit and organizational objectives (self-control), instead of using this information to tell subordinate managers what they should do (centralized direction and control).[30]

Finally, there is another way in which systems thinking applies to the managerial process. Management is part of an economic and social system external to the enterprise or organization but interacting with it. For example, decisions which modern managers make about personnel hiring or reductions are affected by the state of demand in the industry and in the economy generally or by budgets set for nonprofit organizations. Similar decisions are influenced by such developments as the poverty program, urban renewal, and the civil rights movement, particularly the pressure to employ more blacks or other members of minority or disadvantaged groups supported by legislation and government pressures. In Chapter 4 we consider in more detail these implications for management.

[29] For a detailed discussion, see Likert, *The Human Organization,* chap. 7, "The Need for a Systems Approach."

[30] For a more detailed discussion, see Charles A. Myers (ed.), *The Impact of Computers on Management,* The M.I.T. Press, Cambridge, Mass., 1967.

Another example is the spread of national business overseas. Managers in a foreign country relate their activities to the economic and social structure of the host country as well as to the demands of the home office. "International business" is a wider system than that of a one-nation firm. We shall have more to say on this important subject in Chapter 3

SUMMARY

In this chapter we have considered the importance of managerial personnel concepts, contrasting the traditional concept of managing by centralized direction and control (Theory X, or Systems 1 and 2) with the newer concept of managing by participation and self-control (Theory Y or System 4). We have also considered other comparable managerial concepts. These can be thought of as points on a scale or continuum. It is important to ask: In what direction is management moving? It is possible to move in either direction, and there are clearly situations in which management by centralized direction and control is necessary. But a number of environmental pressures, as well as the findings of behavioral science research, tend to call for more management by participation in shared objectives. The appropriate styles of managing at any one time should be based on an awareness of the forces present in the particular situation.

The essence of good management is getting effective results—not only in the short run, but also in the long run through building and maintaining a productive human organization. This simple truth emphasizes the overriding importance of the personnel function in management. The personnel concept of management, which permeates every organization, has a profound effect on how this function is organized and carried out at all levels of management from the top down.

These considerations demonstrate the importance of a systems approach, which recognizes and uses the interrelationships between managerial concepts, organization structure, and personnel policies.

SELECTED REFERENCES

Argyris, Chris: *Integrating the Organization and the Individual,* John Wiley & Sons, Inc., New York, 1964, chap. 13.

Bennis, Warren G.: *Changing Organizations,* McGraw-Hill Book Company, New York, 1966.

Blake, Robert R., and Jane S. Mouton: *The Managerial Grid: Key Orientations for Achieving Production through People,* Gulf Publishing Company, Houston, 1964.

Guest, Robert H.: *Organization Change: The Effect of Successful Leadership,* The Dorsey Press and Richard D. Irwin, Inc., Homewood, Ill., 1962, chap. 7.

Haire, Mason: *Psychology in Management,* 2d ed., McGraw-Hill Book Company, New York, 1964.

———, Edwin E. Ghiselli, and Lyman W. Porter: *Management Thinking: An International Study,* John Wiley & Sons, Inc., New York, 1966, chaps. 1, 2, 6.

Lawrence, Paul R., and Jay W. Lorsch: *Organization and Environment: Managing Differentiation and Integration,* Graduate School of Business Administration, Harvard University, Boston, 1967.

Leavitt, Harold J.: "Unhuman Organizations," *Harvard Business Review,* vol. 40, no. 4, pp. 90-98, July–August, 1962 (reprinted in Paul Pigors, Charles A. Myers, and F. T. Malm, *Management of Human Resources: Readings in Personnel Administration,* 2d ed., McGraw-Hill Book Company, New York, 1969, selection 4).

Likert, Rensis: *The Human Organization: Its Management and Value,* McGraw-Hill Book Company, New York, 1967, chaps. 2, 3, 4, 7.

———: *New Patterns of Management,* McGraw-Hill Book Company, New York, 1960, chaps. 2-4, 8, 14.

McGregor, Douglas: *The Human Side of Enterprise,* McGraw-Hill Book Company, New York, 1960, chaps. 1-4.

———: *The Professional Manager,* McGraw-Hill Book Company, New York, 1967, chaps. 1-5.

Miles, Raymond E.: "Human Relations or Human Resources," *Harvard Business Review,* vol. 43, no. 4, pp. 148-156, July–August, 1965.

Pelz, Donald C., and Frank M. Andrews: *Scientists in Organizations: Productive Climates for Research and Development,* John Wiley & Sons, Inc., New York, 1966.

Porter, Lyman W., and Edward E. Lawler III: *Managerial Attitudes and Performance,* Richard D. Irwin, Inc., Homewood, Ill., 1968.

Raudsepp, Eugene: *Managing Creative Scientists and Engineers,* The Macmillan Company, New York, 1963, chaps. 6 and 7.

Schein, Edgar H.: *Organizational Psychology,* Prentice-Hall, Inc., Englewood Cliffs, N.J., 1965.

Tannenbaum, Robert, and Warren H. Schmidt: "How to Choose a Leadership Pattern," *Harvard Business Review,* vol. 36, no. 2, pp. 95-106, March-April, 1958.

Chapter 2

Personnel Administration and the Line Organization

Operating executives generally reported that they are quite satisfied with the services and performance they receive from their personnel departments. However, they and the chief executives frequently complain that personnel managers do not have enough line experience, knowledge of general management, or understanding of the company's operations.

Dalton E. McFarland[1]

During most of the twentieth century in the United States, and more recently in other advanced industrial countries, the personnel function has evolved from a narrow concern with employment interviewing, testing, and welfare programs to a general management awareness of the importance of the human factor in effective organizational performance.[2] In Chapter 1 we noted some of the behavioral science research and external pressures that have helped to bring about this change in management attitudes. The same influences induced many organizations to establish personnel departments, but there have been considerable confusion and friction about the proper function of a personnel department.

Should the personnel department "handle personnel problems," or should it assist operating managers in handling their *own* personnel problems? How can managers at all levels get help instead of hindrance from the personnel administrator and his staff? These are the central questions which will concern us in this chapter. They are not new questions, but they are persistent ones in many organizations.

[1] Dalton E. McFarland, *Company Officers Assess the Personnel Function,* AMA Research Study 79, American Management Association, Inc., New York, 1967, p. 18.

[2] For a historical review of personnel administration, see Frank B. Miller and Mary Ann Coghill, *The Historical Sources of Personnel Work,* New York State School of Industrial and Labor Relations, Cornell University, Ithaca, N.Y., 1961; Cyril C. Ling, *The Management of Personnel Relations: History and Origins,* Richard D. Irwin, Inc., Homewood, Ill., 1965; and Gerald E. Kohler and Alton C. Johnson, *The Development of Personnel Administration,* Monograph no. 3, Graduate School of Business, University of Wisconsin, Madison, Wis., 1971.

WHAT IS PERSONNEL ADMINISTRATION?

A point of view which has been emphasized in earlier editions of this book, and which is still widely held by practicing personnel administrators as well as by top managers, is the following: *Personnel administration is a line management responsibility but a staff function.* While we shall subsequently show how this distinction has been blurred in practice in many organizations, it is useful to start with as a working principle.

Some years ago, a group of leading personnel administrators, sprinkled with a few academic specialists, developed a statement on "The Function and Scope of Personnel Administration." It concluded with the following words:

The responsibility for carrying out a company's program of personnel administration in any of its organization units must rest with the officer or executive in charge of the unit. In addition to fulfilling the administrative duties which the program prescribes, he should demonstrate its spirit by his example. He should be the official representative of the company in its relations with his subordinates, as members of the organization.

Each manager must concern himself with the interest and ability in personnel administration of each of his subordinate managers. He should stimulate this interest and help each to develop this ability. Though he may receive counsel and aid from personnel specialists in such endeavors, he cannot avoid ultimate responsibility for the personnel function.

All executives should continually concern themselves with the success of their subordinate managers in carrying out the company's personnel program, should note failures in executing any of the program's features, and should assist each subordinate executive in correcting such failures.[3]

[3] "The Function and Scope of Personnel Administration," *Personnel*, vol. 23, no. 1, pp. 5–8, July, 1947. This statement was developed by the members of a group which continues to meet yearly to review current issues in personnel administration.

Since management aims at getting effective results *with* people, personnel administration is a basic management responsibility permeating all levels of management in any organization, beginning with the chief executive. He can be effective only to the extent that he achieves results with the assistance of his vice-presidents and general managers, who in turn depend on the cooperation and skill of the superintendents and supervisors under them. And first-level supervisors have the task of building effective work teams of people whose performance will meet or exceed expected standards.

However, in too many organizations, top management has given middle managers, who in turn have given first-line supervisors, so many technical responsibilities that they have little time for their personnel responsibilities. If top management really believes that other managers should improve the performance of their human organizations, they need to provide time in their job assignments for this and reward them as the people they supervise achieve results.

Personnel administration also permeates all types of functional management, such as production management, financial management, sales management, and research management. It applies in nonindustrial organizations, government, nonprofit institutions, and the armed services. Unless these managers themselves expect to perform all the duties for which they are responsible, they have to secure the cooperation of other people within their part of the total organization. In short, every member of the management group, from the top down, must be an effective "personnel administrator" because he depends on the cooperative efforts of his subordinates.

This view has sometimes been challenged by those who assert that the personnel administrator is the "agent" of the chief executive and should act for him on all matters affecting personnel. But a recent report based on interviews with company presidents expresses a view consistent with our own: "In short, each manager is responsible for getting his men to do—and continue to do—a good job, and this responsibility cannot be shared. Any attempt to share it, even in part, with the personnel department can only stimulate confusion and the inevitable line-and-staff conflict."[4]

What, then, is personnel administration as a *staff* function? In 236 companies surveyed by The Conference Board, the most important role for the corporate personnel department in 148 was to "advise and counsel top management in initiating and recommending changes," and the most important in 78 more was "service to the line and other staff groups."[5] Another analysis of 249 companies showed the following level of reporting by the head of the corporate personnel department, reflecting its high status:

Chairman or president	161
Executive vice-president	74
Finance executive	10
Other	4

In terms of titles of personnel department heads, 138 were vice-presidents (9 of these were senior, or executive, vice-presidents), 92 had "director" in their title, and 19 "manager" or "general manager."[6] The world's largest industrial corporation, General Motors, has a "vice-president, personnel" reporting at corporate headquarters directly to an executive vice-president.

[4] *A Look at Personnel through the President's Eye,* Management Bulletin no. 66, American Management Association, New York, 1965, p. 8.

[5] *Personnel Administration: Changing Scope and Organization,* Studies in Personnel Policy, no. 203, National Industrial Conference Board, Inc. (now The Conference Board), New York, 1965, table 4, p. 16.

[6] *Ibid.,* tables 2 and 3, pp. 14–15. Some of these titles included "personnel manager," "employee relations manager," or director or vice-president of "industrial relations." These terms are often used interchangeably in practice and reflect past history in particular firms. "Labor relations" and sometimes "industrial relations" refer primarily to the relations between management and unionized labor. This is discussed in more detail in chap. 8.

LINE AND STAFF RELATIONSHIPS

Before turning to a further examination of the staff function in personnel administration, we need to consider briefly the formal concepts of "line" and "staff."

Line (or operating) managers are those who have full responsibility for the success or failure of their units in achieving the assigned goals or tasks. They receive orders and instructions from their superiors and are responsible for carrying them out by giving instructions to, and getting cooperation from, their own subordinates. There is delegation of authority from the board of directors to the chief executive. He then delegates some of his authority to the operating vice-president or general manager, who, in turn, delegates some of his authority to superintendents or department heads and, through them, to first-level supervisors. The important point, however, is that line managers have complete responsibility and accountability for the results achieved by the people in their plant, department, or section. Authority can be delegated, but responsibility for action taken by a subordinate still rests with the superior manager.

Staff specialists, on the other hand, are those who provide specialized services to line managers and advise and counsel them in the performance of their responsibilities. An example of this is the in-house attorney, who provides legal assistance and advice to management. The comptroller or chief accounting office has, or should have, a similar relationship with the line. He keeps control records that enable him to advise the chief executive on prices to be charged for products or services, but he does not set the prices himself. Further, he tells department heads and supervisors when their costs exceed "standards," but it is not his responsibility to correct this variance. Sometimes this function is called a "control" function, but ideally the control should be exercised *through* the line and not *on* the line. Staff "control" is "inspection," which involves bringing the results of this inspection (information) to the line's attention *for action by the line.* In other words, staff control involves an information feedback to line managers, so that *they* can take corrective action if they have not properly applied predetermined standards or policies.[7]

APPLICATIONS WITHIN THE ORGANIZATION

The traditional line-staff relationships involving personnel administration can be illustrated by a formal organizational chart. Figure 2-1 shows a company organization with key line and staff officials reporting directly to the president. The relationship of delegated authority from president down to foreman is shown by heavy solid lines. The president also gives orders to his staff specialists. Therefore, a line relationship is also indicated between them, as well as between the personnel administrator and his own subordinates. The staff specialists provide advice and service not only to the chief executive but also to each other and to all lower levels of management. Dotted lines might have been added to indicate these staff functional relationships. The essential staff nature of the personnel administrator's function needs emphasis even though there is a variety of apparently successful experience in support of different organization arrangements.[8] Reality is always more complex

than an organization chart indicates. (We shall expand this point later in the chapter.)

The role of a personnel administrator attached to the product division, branch office, or plant of a decentralized organization is a particularly difficult one. He is responsible to the division or branch manager in a line sense and subordinate in a functional or staff sense to the chief personnel administrator in the home office. The local personnel administrator is expected to help develop in the division or branch the personnel program and policies that have been established for the whole company. Yet, in seeking to gain acceptance of these programs and policies, he will not have the support of the division or branch manager unless the latter is as impressed with the importance of good personnel administration as is the chief executive of the company in the home office. As a staff specialist, the local personnel administrator cannot give orders to the division branch manager. If he cannot convince this man of the wisdom of a particular course of action, he can only report his difficulties to the chief personnel officer, who will then endeavor to get from the president of the company better support down the line for the personnel program.

Centralization of management and the responsibility for personnel administration, however, has been carried to excess in many firms, and the result is a countertrend toward decentralization, geographically and within the company organization. Product division and branch plants, in which each manager has full responsibility for results, develop executive tal-

---

[7] For further discussion of line and staff organization and problems, see William H. Newman, *Administrative Action,* 2d ed., Prentice-Hall, Inc., Englewood Cliffs, N.J., 1963, chap. 12; Herbert A. Simon, *Administrative Behavior,* The Macmillan Company, New York, 1947, chap. 11; Robert Sampson, *The Staff Role in Management,* Harper & Row, Publishers, Incorporated, New York, 1955, chaps. 3, 4. For opposing views see C. A. Efferson, "In Defense of the Line-Staff Concept," *Personnel,* vol. 43, no. 4, pp. 8–15, July–August, 1966; and Gerald G. Fisch, "Line-Staff Is Obsolete," *Harvard Business Review,* vol. 39, no. 4, pp. 67–69, September–October, 1961.

[8] For further discussion of this point, see John T. Dunlop and Charles A. Myers, "The Industrial Relations Function in Management: Some Views on Its Organization Status," *Personnel,* vol. 31, no. 5, pp. 406–413, March, 1955; Dalton E. McFarland, *Cooperation and Conflict in Personnel Adminis-*

tration, American Foundation for Management Research, New York, 1962; Charles A. Myers and John G. Turnbull, "Line and Staff in Industrial Relations," *Harvard Business Review,* vol. 34, no. 4, pp. 63–81, July–August, 1956; Melville Dalton, "Changing Staff-Line Relationships," *Personnel Administration,* pp. 3–5ff., March–April, 1966 (a specific study of a research-based organization); J. K. Bailey and Allan H. Savage, "How 'Pure' Should the Staff Role Be?" *Personnel Administration,* vol. 28, no. 4, pp. 3–5ff., July–August, 1965 (for a survey showing the spread of functional authority for personnel officers).

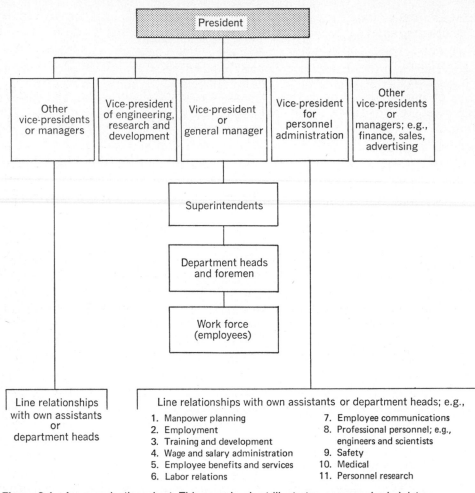

Figure 2-1 An organization chart. This sample chart illustrates personnel administration at the vice-presidential level, reporting to the chief executive along with other vice-presidents, and with line relationships with his own assistants or department heads. For examples of many other types of organizational arrangements reflecting multiplant and multiproduct organizations as well as nonindustrial organizations, see *Personnel Administration: Changing Scope and Organization,* National Industrial Conference Board, Studies in Personnel Policy, no. 203, New York, 1966.

ents better than situations where the chief executive wields all the authority. When managerial jobs are decentralized in this way, responsibility for personnel is an essential part of the manager's job, and the personnel administrator in each division or plant advises, counsels, and services that manager, who is his organizational superior.

This same pattern seems to be evolving in the growing number of companies with international operations. A few have assigned responsibilities for dealing with the special problems of overseas personnel—selection, orientation, and compensation for United States nationals and foreign nationals working for the firm overseas—to the corporate personnel department or an international specialist in it. But most firms with international divisions have a personnel department attached to that division at headquarters, possibly with regional overseas personnel staff people reporting to it. There is also likely to be coordination between domestic and international personnel policies, so that the "international director of personnel relations sees the role of his department as primarily that of helping the foreign operations to shape solutions to their local problems in ways that will be compatible with the corporation's concepts of management and human relations."[9]

Further Roles for the Personnel Administrator

Except within his own department, where he has *line* authority, the personnel administrator is unwise if he issues orders to managers or their subordinates. Instead, he advises the president and other top executives on good personnel policies and on their consistent, uniform application throughout the organization. If he cannot persuade or convince a line manager that his advice is sound, he might suggest that they jointly report the disagreement to their line superior. He may thus perform a control or inspection function, but it must be exercised sparingly if he is to win the confidence and cooperation of line management. His personality should be the kind that makes managers (both line and staff) want to work with him instead of against him. If a personnel administrator has any "authority," it is the authority of established personnel policies and procedures that he has helped to formulate and the authority of his specialized knowledge rather than the authority of his position.[10]

When a personnel administrator initially faces opposition from managers in persuading them of the usefulness of his advice, *he can succeed only if he is seen by managers as a source of help and not as a threat.* Furthermore, the help must be *wanted,* not *imposed.* This assumes, first, that the manager recognizes that he has a problem, and second, that the suggested solution fits his conception of the problem. Exploration of organiza-

tional or departmental difficulties, undertaken together and carefully done, should lead the manager to select a course of action consistent with his departmental needs as well as with organizational policies and objectives.[11] A personnel administrator can thus help the manager to develop the skills to handle future problems more effectively. In this way personnel administration can be developed as a line responsibility.

Since this means developing the skills and understanding of other managers in the organization, the personnel administrator is a "change agent," beginning in some cases with his own top management. His role is to help managers think through the implications of prospective or actual management decisions concerning the human organization, particularly on the capacity of that organization to change constructively with environmental or technological developments. Some basic knowledge of behavioral science applications to management will enable him to become a more effective change agent;[12] but the kind of interpersonal skills he must have go beyond an intellectual knowledge of his field.

Responsibilities within His Own Department

The chief personnel officer is, of course, a *line* manager in relation to his own subordinates. In a large personnel department, found in most medium-sized and large organizations, he is directly

---

[9] "Organizing for 'International' Personnel Work," *The Conference Board Record,* vol. 3, no. 10, p. 31, October, 1966.

[10] For further discussion, see Myers and Turnbull, *op. cit.,* pp. 113–124. For a follow-up study, see Maynard N. Touissaint, "Line-Staff Conflict: Its Causes and Cure," *Personnel,* vol. 39, no. 2, pp. 8–20, May–June, 1962.

[11] For an example of this approach, see Glenn A. Bassett and R. H. Hawk, "Function and Dysfunction in the Organization," *Personnel,* vol. 42, no. 5, pp. 23–31, September-October, 1965.

[12] "Organization development" (OD) is a growing area of application of behavioral science concepts, some of which were summarized in Chapter 1 and which will be developed further in Chapters 5 and 6. For a good summary of the OD approach, see Richard Beckhard, *Organization Development: Strategies and Models,* Addison-Wesley Publishing Company, Inc., Reading, Mass., 1969. TRW Systems Group, part of TRW, Inc., has used the OD approach to develop line management and personnel staff skills in improving interpersonal relationships, problem solving, and communications to make matrix organization with project management groups work more effectively. Thomas H. Patten, Jr., "OD at TRW Systems," *Newsletter,* vol. 9, no. 1, pp. 5–6, Fall Quarter, 1970, School of Labor and Industrial Relations, Michigan State University, East Lansing, Mich.

responsible for supervising the activities of such subordinates as the employment manager, wage and salary administrator, director of training and development, manager of employee benefits and services, the labor relations director, and such other section heads as the size of the company and the scope of its personnel and labor relations activities may require. (Refer again to the organization chart, Figure 2-1, on p. 28.) Here a personnel administrator has an opportunity to demonstrate in practice the validity of concepts about getting results with people which he is trying to help instill in other members of the management group. If he is considered an autocrat by his own subordinates within the personnel department, it will be obvious that he does not practice what he preaches. On the other hand, if he is able to develop one of the best-run departments in the organization—an enthusiastic team of men and women who do their jobs well—then he has shown that the concepts he supports can be applied successfully.

One of these concepts—management by participation and self-control, as discussed in Chapter 1—entails establishing objectives. The personnel administrator, no less than other staff and line managers, should set objectives for his area of responsibility with the help of his organizational superior. His contribution to the overall organizational objectives will then be evaluated on the basis of how well he achieves the objectives he and his boss established earlier. [13]

There may be other, hopefully temporary, occasions when an experienced personnel director assumes line responsibilities for personnel matters which properly belong to operating or line managers. For example, when a new supervisor or superintendent lacks skill or knowledge in dealing with personnel problems, the personnel manager may show how these can be handled by

initially making the decisions himself. The exercise of the control function, which we shall consider in more detail later in this chapter, may also be seen as an exercise of line authority by those whose actions are "controlled." Admittedly, some personnel directors do exercise line authority in more matters than others, but the hidden danger in the former case is that they are likely to be resented by the very managers who ought to be seeking staff help in discharging their own personnel responsibilities.

Qualities Needed

To repeat, a personnel administrator and his departmental associates need to be seen as sources of help by the different levels of the organization, not as usurpers of power, empire builders, or constant needlers whose interference is continually resented. The successful personnel administrator needs to have patience, understanding, empathy (an ability to put himself in the other fellow's shoes), a willingness to listen first and talk afterward, and competent professional knowledge of his field. Since he works constantly with members of the line organization on their problems, it is usually helpful if he has had some prior experience in a line or operating position himself. The personnel man who trains as a specialist and enters an organization as a specialist is more likely to remain out of touch with the real personnel problems faced by managers in doing their jobs. [14] Nevertheless, a well-trained person-

[13] George Odiorne, "Yardsticks for Measuring Personnel Departments," *The Personnel Administrator,* vol. 12, no. 4, pp. 1-6, July-August, 1967. For a specific example, see Douglas McGregor, *The Human Side of Enterprise,* McGraw-Hill Book Company, New York, 1960, chap. 5.

[14] In the United States there is no widely accepted professional training for personnel administrators, some of whom are former line officials. One-third of the personnel directors in 1,000 firms in 1958 came from outside the department; others were promoted from within; 65 percent were college graduates, and of these 6 percent had law degrees, 17 percent M.A. degrees, and 1 percent Ph.D. degrees. Dale Yoder and Roberta Nelson, "Industrial Relations Salaries and Staffing Ratios, 1958," *Personnel,* vol. 35, no. 1, pp. 15-22, July-August, 1958.

The practice in Great Britain is somewhat different. The Institute of Personnel Management has for some years attempted to establish standards of qualification for the personnel specialist and in 1955 introduced an examination which qualifies a person for membership in the institute. This

nel administrator, like an increasing number of line managers, needs a solid grounding in the behavioral sciences and economics.

THE STAFF ROLE IN PRACTICE

We believe that the personnel administrator should remain in a staff role as we have defined it: offering advice, service, and consultation with respect to the managerial functions that directly involve the line manager or supervisor and his work group. *The responsibility for achieving results with members of his work group belongs to the manager, not to the personnel administrator.*

In many firms, however, particularly in large ones facing strong national unions, there has been a tendency to give increasing responsibility for certain personnel functions to the personnel or industrial relations director. Sometimes this involves the control function discussed earlier, but in a manner which leaves the foreman or supervisor with the feeling that the personnel director is really giving him orders. As one personnel officer said about an erring line supervisor: [15] "I bring the fellow in and say, 'These are the rules. Get on the ball or there is no place in the organization for you!'" "Sell, then tell the supervisors" is the way some personnel directors approach the control function and the handling of grievances.

To be sure, when managers have learned that the personnel administrator's advice is usually good, as in avoiding grievances in unionized plants, they are likely to follow his advice more often in the future, and it may appear that the personnel administrator is "calling the shots." This may also be true in questions of the inter-

pretation and application of the collective labor agreement which the personnel administrator has helped to negotiate. There is, however, an important distinction in practice between a manager's *seeking* the advice and assistance of the personnel administrator and having to accept it whether he wants it or not.

The increasing complexity of union-management negotiations has led some firms to place more and more authority for negotiation and interpretation in the hands of a specialist—the labor relations director. We shall consider the problem of dealing with unions in Chapter 8, but here it should be noted that it is perfectly possible for top management to delegate part of its authority in union negotiations to a labor relations specialist who may have the necessary patience, skill, and technical knowledge to deal with experienced union negotiators. There is a hidden danger in giving the specialist too much authority and responsibility. This happened in one large multiplant firm where the labor relations director consulted only the company president before negotiating the union agreement. Other operating managers were left in the dark and felt that "labor peace" was being bought at the expense of their ability to manage their divisions or departments.

In contrast, the executive vice-president in another smaller multiplant company handled the union negotiations himself, with the advice and assistance of the personnel director. Supervisors in this firm said, "There are times when we'd like the personnel department to handle labor problems, but on second thought, we realize that we can't divide our job. We're held responsible for results; and we have to select and motivate and reward or discipline our people. The personnel department can't do this for us."

In an increasing number of companies and organizations, line-staff conflicts in personnel administration are becoming less important because there is a "unity of purpose" among members of the management organization. Here both

---

"includes written and oral tests designed to assess the candidate's personal suitability, his theoretical knowledge, and his ability to apply theory to practice." M. B. Foreman, *The Personnel Function of Management,* Institute of Personnel Management, Occasional Papers, no. 9, London, 1956, appendix, p. 11.

[15] Quoted in Myers and Turnbull, *op. cit.,* p. 118. See also Dalton E. McFarland, "The Scope of the Industrial Relations Function," *Personnel,* vol. 36, no. 1, pp. 42-51, January-February, 1959.

line and staff people appreciate the importance of human resources and of how they should be treated. In these situations, the personnel administrator can make decisions affecting the line without any apparent ill effects on the line; his ideas are more acceptable.[16] In these organizations, there is a blurring of line-staff distinctions, because the managerial team includes people who perform *both* line and staff functions for the achievement of common organizational objectives.

This development is especially important in the "temporary organization" characterized by a "project" or "matrix" type of management, in which a group of managers—line and staff—is assigned to a project or program to work as a team until the task is completed. A related example is the work group performing cross-functional coordination and applying personnel policies to a particular problem. Likert shows this as a part of a larger, multiple, overlapping group structure, with horizontal as well as vertical linkages under a System 4 type of management which emphasizes participative management. Here again line-staff distinctions are blurred.

Another blurring of line-staff distinctions, which represents an occupational role conflict, may occur when personnel administrators do in fact make decisions affecting line managers, even though they believe that their role should involve less decision making and more information and advice for decision making by others. This was one of the findings of a study of characteristics and attitudes of a stratified sample of the 4,500 members of the American Society for Personnel Administration, the largest of several professional personnel organizations in the United States.[17] The respondents reported that they spent 17 percent of their time on "information and advice," 17 percent "supervising subordinates," 13 percent "making decisions on personnel matters for other departments in the company," and the remainder in activities which might broadly be called "staff functions." The authors of the study point to the "paradox" about decision making, and conclude: "An interpretation of this paradox is that the 'should' probably represents a continuing subscription to the occupational myth which their self-reported actions contradict." Whether this is really a "myth" depends on how one regards the personnel function. The authors characterize as a "manipulative decision maker" a personnel manager who is quoted by another study as saying:

> We can't tell the managers or the foremen what to do. Of course we do set the policies and they have to follow them. We could make a big fuss if they don't follow policies, but usually we don't have to. As a matter of fact, they are in on the policy decisions in the first place, and usually we can get them to understand the reasons why they must act as we have planned. . . . When the guys in the line don't want to follow a certain policy or practice, we usually think there is a reason for it. Then we try to find out what that reason is, so we can help them. We know that there is more than one way to skin a cat, so we find out what they want to do; we find a legitimate way to get the cat skinned.[18]

This subtle or manipulative approach may work, but it may also be so transparent to line managers that they know they are being manipulated. Can there be trust and understanding between line and staff if one is manipulating the

[16] See O. Glenn Stahl, "The Network of Authority," *Public Administration Review,* vol. 18, no. 1, 1958 (reprinted in Pigors, Myers, and Malm, *op. cit.,* selection 9); 3d ed., New York, 1973, selection 9; Myers and Turnbull, *op. cit.,* pp. 75–80; and Hall H. Logan, "Line and Staff: An Obsolete Concept?" *Personnel,* vol. 43, no. 1, pp. 26–33, January–February, 1966.

[17] George Ritzer and Harrison M. Trice, *An Occupation in Conflict: A Study of the Personnel Manager,* New York State School of Industrial and Labor Relations, Cornell University, Ithaca, N.Y., 1969. The lengthy questionnaire study was completed during 1967.

[18] Quoted in Dalton McFarland, *Cooperation and Conflict in Personnel Administration,* American Foundation for Management Research, New York, 1962, p. 126.

other? Is manipulative management consistent with the traditional concept of management or with the newer concepts of managing? Is it possible that personnel administrators adapt to the personnel concepts held by their own top managers?

MANAGEMENT'S USE OF THE PERSONNEL DEPARTMENT

How can a staff group such as the personnel department be used most effectively by line managers? In the preceding sections, we have seen some of the consequences of misconceptions about the staff role, and we have noted various ways in which personnel administrators and their assistants might be helpful to managers at different levels. In this section the question is turned around: In what ways can managers get help from the personnel staff?

Under Centralized Management

The answer depends largely on the personnel concepts or patterns of management discussed in Chapter 1. Management by centralized direction and control will tend to delegate considerable authority to staff departments, including the personnel department, for developing and administering a complex of management controls. In the personnel area, this entails checking up on subordinate managers to make sure they are correctly implementing personnel policies, and reporting failures to do so to the higher management levels. Under this concept, then, the personnel administrator becomes a policeman for top management. In this role he is likely to be feared by subordinate managers, who take pains to make sure they are not "caught." Management by centralized direction and control may also ask the personnel department to perform a number of specialized services such as recruiting, testing, interviewing, keeping all kinds of personnel records, job analysis, job evaluation, etc.

These functions are performed by staff specialists *for* the line managers at the request of top management. The personnel administrator accustomed to this way of managing may welcome such assignments as ways of proving his specialized skills and services to otherwise apathetic subordinate line managers. By exercising the control function, he keeps these managers on their toes and respectful of his authority. Or at least, he may see his role in this light, since many staff people hunger for more "authority" and "recognition." Although line managers are often resentful, they are forced to rely increasingly on the personnel staff for favorable reports to top management and for specialized services of various sorts. Thus, staff groups like the personnel department have achieved considerable power in many companies and organizations. More often than not, however, they are seen as threats to most line managers below the top level, rather than as sources of needed help. Managers are subjected to personnel programs and procedures which the personnel department is "selling" to them as something which they *ought* to have. The initiative always comes from the staff group.

Under Management by Shared Objectives

Under a managerial concept tending toward management by shared objectives and self-control, the staff role is different. We have noted earlier that, ideally, staff is a source of help on problems *as seen by the line managers*. As in the relationship of the client to the lawyer, the home builder to the architect, or even the patient to the doctor, the initiative in seeking help starts with the manager, who relies on the staff for advice, counsel, guidance, and service in the staff man's area of competency.

For example, top management may need help in developing adequate personnel policies and in planning ahead to meet manpower needs. Here the personnel staff specialist can be helpful in suggesting alternative policies, sources of new manpower, and other ways of meeting organizational requirements.[19] If the personnel administrator is worth his salt, he will be well informed on personnel policies which might fit the particular organization's needs, and he can help draft policies for top-management approval. But the personnel director who is alert to current organizational needs will not always slavishly provide what the chief executive requests. He may have strong convictions that a proposed policy is not in the best interests of the human organization. If so, he will make his views known to top management in an effort to persuade them of the desirability of a different course of action. In rare cases, he may run the risk of having to submit his resignation. Sometimes, he may find that management's problem as first expressed is not the real problem; further probing and discussions in the best staff-counseling sense will bring out a problem lying much deeper which requires a different approach. Top management may then see the personnel specialist as a source of help on a new policy problem.

Managers at all levels may seek help from the personnel staff in solving more immediate problems. For example, advice may be sought on handling a particular grievance, on administering disciplinary action, on transferring a dissatisfied employee, on reclassifying a changed job in the job-evaluation program, on handling a technical change which will affect a group of employees, or on other specific personnel problems. Here the line manager knows that the personnel administrator is familiar with the ways in which these problems have been handled most effectively elsewhere in the organization, and he seeks professional guidance for situations which may be new to him. The personnel administrator, in turn, will weaken the line-staff relationship if he "tells" the manager what he should do. Instead,

he will suggest several possible courses of action, outlining possible consequences, and leave it to the manager to decide which he will adopt. The decision should be the line manager's, not the personnel administrator's, since this helps build managerial competence in personnel matters.

What about help in providing managerial controls? The control function is the one in which many line-staff conflicts develop. Under the pattern of management by shared objectives and self-control, managers at all levels may expect help from their own personnel staff in being informed when they are "out of line" in administering personnel policies or taking personnel actions. Self-control is best advanced when it is understood that the staff man will not report his knowledge of a line man's deviation to anyone else but that line manager, unless both are willing to go to their common line superior for clarification. As McGregor has emphasized, "The helping role and the role of policeman are absolutely incompatible roles. To place an individual in the latter is to destroy the possibility of his occupying the former one successfully."[20]

Finally, as under the traditional concept of management, the manager operating with an alternative approach also needs certain services from the personnel department. These include assistance in developing job descriptions, recruiting, screening, and testing candidates for employment, assistance in developing specific training programs, guidance in making performance appraisals, staff assistance in developing and administering a job evaluation program for setting relative wages and salaries on different jobs, and administration of employee benefit, service, safety, and health programs. The line manager may also seek advice in diagnosing organizational health if he has confidence in the personnel administrator's skills in situational thinking, case analysis, and developing measures

---

[19] Responsibilities of the top personnel executive as an aid to top management are stressed by Frank E. Fischer, "The Personnel Function in Tomorrow's Company," *Personnel*, vol. 45, no. 1, pp. 64-71, January-February, 1968.

[20] McGregor, *op. cit.*, p. 169.

of employee morale, including labor turnover data.

If the personnel staff becomes too preoccupied with the administration of these services, however, there is a real danger that it will not be available and competent to provide the help in policy making and problem solving which line managers more urgently require. Managers at all levels will fail to make best use of the personnel department if they look on personnel staff people as administrators of services rather than as advisors and colleagues in helping to meet the hu-

man problems involved in the superior-subordinate relationship.

EXAMPLES OF COOPERATIVE LINE-STAFF RELATIONSHIPS

Our discussion of the difficult problems of line and staff in personnel administration may be illustrated in Exhibits 2-1 and 2-2, showing in two areas the personnel responsibilities of department supervision (line), and the staff functions performed by personnel specialists to assist line

Exhibit 2-1 Line Responsibilities and Staff Functions in Employment

Department supervision (line)	Personnel-employment specialist (staff)
1 Prepare *requisition* outlining specific qualifications of employees needed to fill specific positions. Help create reputation that will attract applicants. [First step.]	1 *Develop* source of qualified applicants from local labor market. This requires carefully planned community relations, speeches, advertisements, and active high school, college, and technical school recruiting. [Second step.]
2 *Interview* and *select* from candidates screened by Personnel. Make specific *job assignments* that will utilize new employees' highest skills to promote maximum production. [Fifth step.]	2 Conduct *skilled* interviews, give *scientific* tests, and make thorough reference checks, etc., using requisition and job description as guides. Screening must meet company standards and conform with *employment laws*. [Third step.]
3 *Indoctrinate* employees with specific details regarding the sections and jobs where they are to be assigned—safety rules, pay, hours, "our customs." [Seventh step.]	3 Refer best candidates to supervisors, after physical examinations and qualifications for the positions available have been carefully *evaluated*. [Fourth step.]
4 *Instruct* and *train* on the job according to planned training program already worked out with Personnel. [Eighth step.]	4 Give new employees preliminary *indoctrination* about the company, benefit plans, general safety, first aid, shift hours, etc. [Sixth step.]
5 *Follow up, develop,* and *rate* employee job performance, *decide on* promotion, transfer, layoff, or discharge. [Ninth step.]	5 Keep *complete record* of current performance and future potential of each employee. [Tenth step.]
6 Hold separation *interview* when employees leave—determine causes. Make internal department *adjustments* to minimize turnover. [Eleventh step.]	6 Diagnose information given in separation interviews, determine causes, and take positive steps to correct. [Twelfth step.]

Exhibit 2-2   Line Responsibilities and Staff Functions in Training

Department supervision (line)	Personnel-training specialist (staff)
1 Recognize and *decide* on department training *needs;* advise Personnel on focus needed and specific application.	**1** *Research* to develop over-all plans, objectives, responsibility, and needs; develop outside contacts and information.
2 Sincerely and *actively implement* executive development according to over-all plans. *Share information,* provide challenging assignments, and *coach.*	**2** *Help* president develop over-all *approach* and *plan* for supervisory and executive development to meet organization needs. Administer and coordinate program.
3 *Utilize* Personnel training specialists to help decide on tailor-made programs to meet department needs for jobs, apprentice, and supervisory training.	**3** Give *advice* and *assistance* to spark-plug company units in planning, organizing, conducting employee and supervisory training and educational programs.
4 Give daily *coaching* and individual *training* to subordinates to meet job standards; judge their progress and suggest areas for improvement.	**4** *Prepare* training outlines and visual aids in accordance with latest research in education in order to accelerate learning.
5 *Assume* responsibility, in some areas, for running department training to develop potentials of people.	**5** *Train* department supervisors to develop teaching skills in order to conduct their own training most effectively.
6 *Decide* on future training as result of evaluations of past training activities.	**6** Provide conference leadership in certain types of training; *evaluate* results.

supervision in carrying out these responsibilities.[21]

The reader can check these results against the discussion of line and staff responsibilities for personnel matters under different concepts of management. Under management by centralized direction and control, for example, the employment section of the personnel department would have full authority to hire new employees for line supervisors, who could normally not refuse candidates referred to them. Under management by shared objectives and self-control, the division would function as indicated in Exhibit 2-1. Can the reader draw a similar distinc-

tion with reference to the training responsibility? What would be the responsibilities for other functions such as safety, labor relations, and wage administration?

THE PERSONNEL SYSTEMS APPROACH

We have mentioned (in Chapter 1) the importance of the systems concept in management and its relevance to modern personnel administration. This has been summarized succinctly by the vice-president, personnel, of International Business Machines Corporation:

> I conceive this basic mission [of personnel administration] to be a *huge balancing act*. Personnel is charged with the job of balancing the demand for people with the supply of people, of balancing the corporation's need for certain skills and experience

[21] Taken from Robert Saltonstall, "Who's Who in Personnel Administration," *Harvard Business Review,* vol. 33, no. 4, pp. 75–83, July–August, 1955 (reprinted in Pigors, Myers, and Malm, *op. cit.,* selection 8).

with the manpower market's supply of these skills and experience. Everything personnel does has an effect on one side of the balance or the other.[22]

Computers have been programmed in IBM and other companies to provide a "skills inventory" of present employees, with projections of future needs based on forecasts of production, sales, and future expansion. Computers have been used in other personnel functions, such as salary administration, computation of fringe-benefit costs, etc., although generally the personnel field has lagged behind other areas of management in the application of electronic data processing.[23] This is surely an area of continuing challenge for the personnel administrator. We shall discuss this systems approach again in later chapters.

SUMMARY

Personnel administration is a *line* responsibility and a *staff* function. It is a basic management responsibility, permeating all levels and types of management in all organizations, private or public. Personnel specialists help line managers in providing advice, counsel, services, and various types of controls to help management secure uniform administration of personnel policies which

serve individual needs and further organizational objectives.

The principal staff functions of the personnel administrator and his associates can be summarized as follows:

1 To advise and counsel line managers in the personnel approach; in other words, to be an effective exponent of the personnel point of view in formulating and administering policies and in helping with the problems handled by all managers. Familiarity with behavioral science research will be helpful here.

2 To diagnose organizational health by means of various indexes of teamwork, such as productive efficiency, absenteeism, accidents, labor turnover and internal mobility, and complaints and grievances, and to keep managers informed of actual or potential difficulties that need their attention. This is an important area for personnel research within the organization, drawing on the best of current research outside, as is the next point. The various indexes also serve to evaluate the effectiveness and contribution of the personnel program.

3 To provide personnel procedures and services as an aid to managers in getting more effective results with the people in their work groups. Among these procedures and services are job descriptions, initial recruitment of new candidates for employment, employment interviewing and testing, induction or orientation programs, various types of training programs, wage and salary surveys and administration, the management of change, safety engineering and education, and employee-benefit programs.

4 To secure coordination of these activities and uniform administration of personnel policies (the "control" function) through discussions with managers and inspection reports to the chief executive, who has the final responsibility for seeing that policies and procedures are uniformly and consistently administered.

Functions 1 and 4 summarize much of what has already been discussed in this chapter. Methods of diagnosing organizational health are con-

[22] John J. Bricker, "The Personnel Systems Concept," in *The Systems Approach to Personnel Management,* American Management Association, Management Bulletin 62, New York, 196 , p. 16. See also Edwin B. Geisler, *Manpower Planning: An Emerging Staff Function,* American Management Association, Management Bulletin 101, New York, 1967. For another analysis of the systems approach, see Mason Haire, "Approach to an Integrated Personnel Policy," *Industrial Relations,* vol. 7, no. 2, pp. 107-117, February, 1968; and Haire, "Managing Management Manpower," *Business Horizons,* vol. 10, no. 4, pp. 23-28, Winter, 1967 (also reprinted in Pigors, Myers, and Malm, *op. cit.,* selection 10).
[23] For a critical evaluation, see Richard T. Bueschel, "Real Time Data Processing for Industrial Relations," *Management of Personnel Quarterly,* vol. 5, pp. 24-30, Spring, 1966; and Elizabeth Lanham, "EDP in the Personnel Department," *Personnel,* vol. 44, no. 2, pp. 16-22, March-April, 1967.

sidered in Chapters 9 to 13, against the background of the discussion of the individual and the organization in Chapters 5 to 8. Organization planning, management development, and the problems entailed in managing and working in a changing world are discussed in Chapters 3 and 4. Procedures and services that are essential to an effective integrated personnel administration program are discussed in the remaining chapters of the book. In these chapters, more emphasis is placed on the policies that need to be developed and the kinds of problems that are likely to arise in their formulation and application than on the details of the particular policies or procedures. These details, and the paper forms which accompany them, will vary from firm to firm and organization to organization, depending on particular circumstances and needs.

Since personnel administration is a basic line-management responsibility, the development of effective managers is a central top-management obligation. The organizational structure and climate within which managers are developed and develop themselves are also important. These are the central concerns of the following chapter.

Note on Source Materials for Personnel Administration

Personnel administrators and students hoping eventually to become personnel administrators need to keep abreast of current developments in the field; so do line managers who hope to improve their handling of personnel and labor relations. The following professional journals and other sources are helpful:

Personnel (bimonthly journal of the American Management Association) and the AMA's *Personnel Series* (papers presented at semiannual meeting until 1957, when the series was discontinued).

Harvard Business Review (published bimonthly by the Graduate School of Business Administration, Harvard University).

Other graduate business school journals such as *The Journal of Business* (The University of Chicago), *California Management Review* (University of California), *Columbia Journal of World Business* (Columbia University), *Business Horizons* (Indiana University), *Business Topics* (Michigan State University), *Industrial* (now *Sloan*) *Management Review* (Massachusetts Institute of Technology), *Business Quarterly* (University of Western Ontario), *Michigan Business Review* (University of Michigan).

Industrial and Labor Relations Review (published quarterly by the New York State School of Industrial and Labor Relations, Cornell University).

Industrial Relations (University of California).

Journal of Human Resources (University of Wisconsin).

Management of Personnel Quarterly (University of Michigan).

Monthly Labor Review (U.S. Department of Labor).

International Labour Review (ILO).

Conference Board Record and *Studies in Personnel Policy* (National Industrial Conference Board, Inc., New York—now The Conference Board).

Research studies by university industrial relations sections or centers, and by Industrial Relations Counselors, Inc., New York.

Behavioral science and scholarly journals such as *Academy of Management Journal, Administrative Science Quarterly, American Journal of Sociology, American Political Science Review, American Sociological Review, Annual Review of Psychology, Human Organization, Journal of Applied Behavioral Science, Journal of Applied Psychology, Organizational Behavior and Human Performance.*

Labor Law Journal (mainly for legal aspects).

Personnel Administration (Society for Personnel Administration) and *Public Administration Review* (for discussions of personnel problems in public service).

The Personnel Administrator (American Society for Personnel Administration).

Advanced Management Journal (Society for Advancement of Management).

Personnel Journal.

Personnel Management Abstracts (University of Michigan).

Personnel Psychology.

Training and Development Journal.

Daily or weekly services for current developments, such as *The Daily Labor Report* and *Labor Relations Reporter* (both published by Bureau of National Affairs, Washington), and loose-leaf services published by Commerce Clearing House and by Prentice-Hall, Inc.

Canadian Personnel and Industrial Relations Journal (Federation of Canadian Personnel Associations, Toronto).

Journal of Management Studies (British).

Management International Review (International University Contact for Management Education).

British Journal of Industrial Relations.

Personnel Practice Bulletin (Department of Labour and National Service, Commonwealth of Australia).

Personnel (formerly *Personnel Management;* Institute of Personnel Management, London).

Occupational Psychology (National Institute of Industrial Psychology, London).

SELECTED REFERENCES

American Management Association: *A Look at Personnel through The President's Eye,* New York, 1965.

―――: *The Systems Approach to Personnel Management,* Management Bulletin 62, New York, 1965.

Bailey, J. K., and Allan H. Savage: "How 'Pure' Can the Staff Role Be?" *Personnel Administration,* vol. 28, no. 4, pp. 3–5ff., July–August, 1965.

Blood, Jerome W.: *The Personnel Job in a Changing World,* American Management Association, New York, 1964.

Firsch, Gerald G.: "Line-Staff Is Obsolete," *Harvard Business Review,* vol. 39, no. 4, pp. 67–69, September–October, 1961.

Fischer, Frank E.: "The Personnel Function in Tomorrow's Company," *Personnel,* vol. 45, no. 1, pp. 64–71, January–February, 1968.

Logan, Hall H.: "Line and Staff: An Obsolete Concept?" *Personnel,* vol. 43, no. 1, pp. 26–33, January–February, 1966.

McFarland, Dalton E.: *Company Officers Assess the Personnel Function,* American Management Association, Research Study 79, New York, 1967.

McGregor, Douglas: *The Human Side of Enterprise,* McGraw-Hill Book Company, New York, 1960, chaps. 11 and 12.

McLaughlin, David: "Roadblocks to Personnel Department Effectiveness," *Personnel Journal,* vol. 50, no. 1, pp. 46–50, 79, January, 1971.

Myers, Charles A., and John G. Turnbull: "Line and Staff in Industrial Relations," *Harvard Business Review,* vol. 34, no. 4, pp. 113–124, July–August, 1956.

National Industrial Conference Board: *Personnel Administration: Changing Scope and Organization,* Studies in Personnel Policy, no. 203, New York, 1966.

Ritzer, George, and Harrison M. Trice: *An Occupation in Conflict: A Study of the Personnel Manager,* New York State School of Industrial and Labor Relations, Cornell University, Ithaca, N.Y., 1969.

Saltonstall, Robert: "Who's Who in Personnel Administration," *Harvard Business Review,* vol. 33, no. 4, pp. 75–83, July–August, 1955 (reprinted in Paul Pigors, Charles A. Myers, and F. T. Malm, *Management of Human Resources: Readings in Personnel Administration,* 3d ed., McGraw-Hill Book Company, New York, 1973, selection 8).

Chapter 3

Organization Planning and Management Development

Many companies appear to think of a management development program as something that is done to the individual rather than as a step in a continuous and integrated management process, involving not only the motives and development of the individuals but likewise the philosophy, objectives, and organizational structure of the corporation.

John F. Merriam [1]

The quality and depth of the management of any organization are its greatest asset. Managers develop themselves through their own experiences on and off the job, and they are developed by the way in which their previous and present superiors deal with them. The structure of the organization in which they function also affects the organization's capacity to develop increased managerial competence. Finally, the personnel concepts of management held by the chief execu-

tives are important determinants of management development, as we have seen in Chapter 1.

There is usually a shortage of competent managers in every organization, and in expanding companies, the shortage is often acute. This has led increasingly to a concern with management-development programs for providing a continuing supply of good managers at all levels, and especially at the higher ones. Organization planning is a part of the process of management development because of the intimate relationship between them. If we again view the organization as a system, the shape of the organization structure, the personnel concepts of management, the way in which managers develop, and the ele-

[1] Albert S. Glickman, Clifford P. Hahn, Edwin A. Fleishman, and Brent Baxter, *Top Management Development and Succession: An Exploratory Study,* Supplementary Paper no. 27, Committee for Economic Development, New York, November, 1968, p. viii.

ments of personnel policies are all interrelated. But the subsystem which we here call "organization planning and management development" also has interrelationships which deserve special attention.

In this chapter, we shall review these interrelationships and consider those approaches which give the greatest promise of developing and utilizing managerial talent most effectively. The contribution which the personnel administrator can make to these efforts will also be pointed out.

ORGANIZATION ANALYSIS AND PLANNING

Before top management can determine future executive needs, it must have a clear picture of the present organization structure and desirable future changes based on projected expansion, mergers, or acquisitions, as well as on new products or functions which may develop.[2] An organization chart showing current positions and lines of responsibility is therefore essential. But management thinking might be projected ahead into an "ideal" organization chart, which will serve as a guide when it is possible to make improvements either in operations or in personnel. This ideal chart can take into account not only retirements of present managers but possible realignments of responsibilities.

Such an analysis of present and future organizational structure naturally raises important questions. For example:

● Are some responsibilities assigned to certain positions because of special capacities or defi-

ciencies of individuals now occupying those positions? Should these positions be realigned if these men were transferred, promoted, or retired?

● Are all the present positions necessary, or can responsibilities be regrouped for more effective operations now?

● Is each position so organized that the individual holding it knows what is expected of him or has participated in setting his objectives and knows what his responsibilities are?

● Would a different grouping of responsibilities be more effective if the organization should grow in size during the next 5 or 10 years? For example, some companies have changed from functional divisions such as manufacturing, sales, research, engineering, etc., to product divisions, with each of these functions coordinated by the division manager to achieve maximum profit for the product division. Would this type of organizational structure be more effective in developing all-round executives?

● Do staff people have so much responsibility for procedures and methods that line managers no longer feel responsible for results and tend to "pass the buck" to the staff?

Answers to these questions should be based upon an analysis of present positions and the qualifications of the individuals needed to fill them. In all this, however, it is important to think in terms of the people involved in the present organization structure and to avoid a mechanistic approach to organization analysis and planning. Abstract principles of good organization are no longer accepted without question, for they may not apply to the special situation which confronts a management. The well-known principle of "span of control," for example, in which it is said that a manager cannot effectively supervise more than half a dozen subordinate managers, has been found to conflict with another principle of job enlargement and a "flat" organization structure in which increasing responsibilities are delegated from one manager to a large number

[2] Donald H. Grubb, "Organization and Manpower: A Flexible Approach," *Personnel,* vol. 43, no. 5, pp. 29-31, September-October, 1966; and William F. Glueck, "Where Organization Planning Stands Today," *Personnel,* vol. 44, no. 4, pp. 19-26, July-August, 1967. For a more comprehensive discussion, see Ernest Dale, *Organization,* American Management Association, New York, 1967. The internal organization planning of 500 profitable firms is examined in detail in Joseph J. Famularo, *Organization Planning Manual,* American Management Association, New York, 1971.

of subordinates who are not constantly reporting to, and checking with, him.[3]

Decentralization—or More Centralization?

If there is one principle of organization planning which has gained increasing acceptance over the past 25 years, it is "decentralization," even though an occasional firm has carried the process too far and has had to "recentralize." Alfred P. Sloan, Jr., is properly known for his pioneer work in introducing principles of decentralization in General Motors during the early 1920s, about the time that the Du Pont Company was "evolving from a centralized type of organization common in the early days of American industry." But he has also pointed out that "General Motors was emerging from almost total decentralization" under the creative but rather chaotic management methods of the founder, William C. Durant. "General Motors needed to find a principle of coordination without losing the advantages of decentralization," and it did this by retaining some centralized controls over decentralized operations.[4]

The intimate relationship between decentralization and management development has been succinctly expressed by the chief executive who was responsible for initiating a decentralized organization structure in the General Electric Company about 1950:

The decision to decentralize the Company, which means to decentralize responsibility and authority for operating decisions, was made in part because it is a way to accelerate manpower development. Men become strong and self-reliant managers when they are responsible for profit-or-loss decisions. . . . The net result of decentralization, after thirteen years, has been to build up in General Electric an unusual depth of experienced, confident, and self-reliant managerial talent.[5]

While decentralization is widely used by large firms, there is the possibility that the spread of "information technology" with the electronic computer will permit recentralization of management because accurate data on all operations is now available more quickly.[6] There is also the prospect that middle and lower management will be affected by having routine and structured duties taken over by the computer.[7] This is certainly possible, but recentralization may well be only one result of information technology. Managers who believe in centralized direction and control will certainly utilize the new technology to enforce more centralization; but those who manage by shared objectives and self-control may see the computer as providing more accurate and rapid information on the basis of which managers of decentralized operations can judge their

---

[3] For research on this question, see Lyman W. Porter and Edward E. Lawler III, "The Effects of 'Tall' vs. 'Flat' Organization Structures on Managerial Job Satisfaction," *Personnel Psychology,* vol. 17, no. 2, pp. 135–148, Summer, 1964 (reprinted in Paul Pigors, Charles A. Myers, and F. T. Malm, *Management of Human Resources: Readings in Personnel Administration,* 2d ed., McGraw-Hill Book Company, New York, 1969, selection 14). Mason Haire found that the number of line production workers supervised by first-line foremen averaged 13, and ranged from 11.5 to 21 in four firms he studied intensively. Chap. 10 in Haire (ed.), *Modern Organization Theory,* John Wiley & Sons, Inc., New York, 1959.

[4] Alfred P. Sloan, Jr., *My Years with General Motors,* Doubleday & Company, Inc., Garden City, N.Y., 1964.

[5] Ralph H. Cordiner, "The Nature of the Work of the Chief Executive," address to the International Management Congress, New York, September, 1963, reprinted by the General Electric Company, Schenectady, N.Y. Subsequently, under a new chief executive, GE has recentralized, somewhat, with a new top-level group in the president's office.

[6] For a discussion of this possibility, see Thomas L. Whisler and George P. Shultz, "Information Technology and Management Organization," in Shultz and Whisler (eds.), *Management Organization and the Computer,* The Free Press of Glencoe, New York, 1960, pp. 3–36.

[7] For extended discussion of this impact, see Herbert A. Simon, "The Corporation: Will It Be Managed by Machines?" in Melvin Anshen and George Leland Bach (eds.), *Management and Corporations, 1985,* McGraw-Hill Book Company, New York, 1960, pp. 17–55 (reprinted in Pigors, Myers, and Malm, *op. cit.,* selection 18).

own progress under predetermined objectives.[8] Thus the *use* of information technology may reflect management concepts as well as influencing the future jobs of managers within the organization structure.

Making Organization Changes

Decentralization, recentralization, or any other organizational change resulting from careful planning is achieved best with the participation of key members of the management group. The decision cannot be made and sprung full-blown on the organization; it must grow out of the experience and conviction of those who will be most affected by it. This is why a number of leading American companies have made major organizational changes only after careful study and planning by a representative management committee, sometimes with the advice of specialists and consultants.

In addition to or in place of traditional management consultants on organization planning, some firms have used consultants and personnel specialists in "organization development," which draws heavily on research and experience in the behavioral sciences. OD, as we have noted in Chapter 2, is a change process, helping to change a managerial strategy or personnel concept (as toward Theory Y), or to help an organization move from a family-owned, family-managed firm to a family-controlled, professionally managed firm.

OD has also helped management to change the organization structure and roles in the structure, to improve intergroup collaboration, to open up the communications system, and to cope with organizational and human problems in mergers. The change processes include diagnosis of the problem, strategy planning with top management, educational and problem-oriented programs to improve managerial competence and skills, further consultation and training efforts, and, as a final step, organizational evaluation.[9]

ADVANCE MANPOWER PLANNING AND FORECASTING

An analysis of the present and projected organization structures makes it possible to determine the need for replacements as present managers retire or are transferred or promoted to other positions. An analysis of age groupings of present managers will frequently reveal surprises in terms of the need for replacements within a few years. There is also the possibility that some managers may leave the company or may die or become physically handicapped before retirement.

All this requires advance manpower planning, which is a staff function assisting general management.[10] The manpower audit or replacement table is simply a convenient way of summarizing the kind of information that the chief executive and the manager of each major line and staff unit of the organization need to have for advance manpower planning. The current organization chart is used. The following facts about each incumbent are indicated by code in the chart or listed in a separate table: (1) age, (2) years of service with the organization, (3) current performance, (4) promotability and how soon, and (5) possible replacements, their ages, years of ser-

---

[8] For further discussion of this possibility, see Charles A. Myers (ed.), *The Impact of Computers on Management,* The M.I.T. Press, Cambridge, Mass., 1967.

[9] See Richard Beckhard, *Organization Development: Strategies and Models,* Addison-Wesley Publishing Company, Inc., Reading, Mass., 1969. Beckhard uses four case studies to describe the organizational conditions which called for efforts leading to organization change and improvement.

[10] Manpower planning and forecasting obviously applies to all human resources employed in an organization, but the high-talent resources represented by managers and professionals are the most critical. See Eric W. Vetter, *Manpower Planning for High Talent Personnel,* Bureau of Industrial Relations, University of Michigan, Ann Arbor, Mich., 1967, p. 194. Vetter says, "Locating the activity in the personnel department makes good sense."

vice, current performance, and promotability.[11] This information is also essential in planning for future recruitment for managerial positions, including management trainees. The manpower audit or replacement table, therefore, is a highly confidential document prepared and kept by the top-management group for its own guidance in manpower planning, especially in an expanding organization.

Case Example

Harris-Intertype Corporation, a Cleveland-based printing equipment firm, planned in 1964 to boost sales from $100 million to $250 million in 1969 as a major goal of its fifth 5-year plan, according to the company president.[12] Despite position descriptions, appraisals, and progress reviews, the company's growth (partly through acquisitions) forced the conclusion that "very simply, we hadn't been developing our future management manpower in sufficient depth or detail." The existing junior management development program was enlarged and strengthened "to provide and train an adequate supply of young men," and a senior executive program was instituted "aimed at more rapid development of high-potential experienced managers in the 30- to 40-year-old bracket." There were annual development plans for each participant.

The main feature of the new program, however, was a management manpower-planning program in which the manager of each division appeared annually before corporate top management (including the vice-president, personnel) to discuss his organization structure and re-

view individuals in the top three levels of his management organization, including plans for developing them in relation to his division's current annual operating plan and 5-year guide plan. Each individual's picture (with pertinent data) was mounted on a fabric board in present organization-chart form and color-coded to indicate prior performance ratings (discussed with each in a "progress review"). Pictures could be moved around to indicate possible future changes.

During the first 2 years, the president spent about a quarter of his total time on this effort, and in the second 2 about 15 percent, viewing it as "one of the most important uses of executive time." The 1969 sales goal was reached 1 year ahead of schedule, and the president felt that the company was better prepared to handle the new corporate 5-year plan than it was the previous one.

Alternative Approaches

While many manpower-planning programs probably resemble this example, a few firms have experimented with an alternative approach. One large national company has a job-posting and job-bidding system for managerial and nonmanagerial vacancies, although probably most of them are filled below the top level by this method, which has been described as an "open market" system, or one which emphasizes the choices open to those who want to "throw their hat in the ring" rather than find themselves moved around like checkers on a checkerboard.[13] The danger of the latter is that individuals are not as free to plan their own careers, and capable candidates may be overlooked in large, multiunit organizations by a centralized process which depends on the top managers knowing all qualified people in the subunits.

[11] For examples and fuller discussion, see "Management Inventory," chap. 8 in *Developing Managerial Competence: Changing Concepts, Emerging Practices,* National Industrial Conference Board, Studies in Personnel Policy, no. 189, New York, 1964, pp. 95–100.

[12] Richard B. Tullis, "Manpower Planning Today, Management Power Tomorrow," *The Presidents Forum,* vol. 8, no. 1, Spring, 1969 (published semiannually for members only by the Presidents Association, Inc., an affiliate of the American Management Association, New York).

[13] For a discussion of this approach, see Theodore M. Alfred, "Checkers or Choice in Manpower Management," *Harvard Business Review,* vol. 45, no. 1, pp. 157–167, January–February, 1967 (reprinted in Pigors, Myers, and Malm, *op. cit.,* selection 11).

A variation of the job-posting–bidding method may be provided by the capabilities of the computer. An increasing number of large organizations have developed skill banks or skill inventories of managerial and technical manpower. The data base contains detailed information on each individual in a form that can be readily retrieved in answer to specific queries. For example, IBM has a computer-based Personnel Data System with three basic files for each individual: basic personnel file, personnel skills inventory, and educational objectives and attainment data. The file is used to search out people who might fill vacancies at any one of the company's many locations in the United States, beginning at the local or plant level, then the division, and finally corporation-wide.

The file can also be used to estimate future manpower losses in any year due to retirement and other causes, or to estimate shortfalls in future needs based on higher projections for certain types of managers, engineers, or technicians. A number of other firms have developed similar systems for internal use. The central benefit in each is that the computer search process is eventually organization-wide, turning up candidates who might easily have been overlooked in a manual searching process. [14]

FORECASTING MANAGERIAL REQUIREMENTS

The case example given above included some forecasts based on 5-year sales goals. Many firms do, as a part of the long-range planning process, forecast sales, capital spending, and volume of production or services to be supplied for 1 to 5 years ahead. Until recent years, however, specific forecasts of managerial requirements related to these other forecasts have not been part of the planning process. Increasingly, large firms and organizations are finding it necessary to attempt to forecast their managerial requirements as a part of the management-development process as well as of the general planning process.

A report on the experience of 14 firms which were doing sophisticated manpower forecasting in 1967 showed that all of them made forecasts of *managerial* requirements. [15] As examples of the forecasting methods used, the following were cited:

- The regional telephone company uses relationships among managerial and nonmanagerial employment, the number of telephones, the number of customer accounts, the forecasts of business growth, to predict employment levels for six company divisions by various managerial grades, and for total nonmanagerial employment.
- A rapidly growing manufacturing concern employs a regression of manpower requirements against two separate measures of demand—sales of new equipment and sales of replacement parts. This allows manpower forecasts to reflect the changing composition of product demand.
- An electrical equipment producer employs an unusual equation to forecast the size of its managerial work force. Working from historical data for their firm, the manpower planning staff

---

[14] For a discussion of the IBM experience, see John J. Bricker, *The Systems Approach to Personnel Management,* Bulletin no. 62, American Management Association, New York, 1965. This experience and that of other firms are summarized in Paul S. Greenlaw and Robert D. Smith, *Personnel Management: A Management Science Approach,* International Textbook Company, Scranton, Pa., 1970, pp. 37–43, and chap. 2, "Skills Inventories," pp. 65–86. This book also summarizes other management science applications to the personnel function.

[15] Peter B. Doeringer, Michael J. Piore, and James G. Scoville, "Corporate Manpower Forecasting and Planning," *The Conference Board Record,* vol. 5, no. 8, pp. 37–45, August, 1968. For a later survey of 69 firms in Minnesota, see H. G. Heneman, Jr., and George Seltzer, *Employer Manpower Planning and Forecasting,* Manpower Research Monograph no. 19, Manpower Administration, U.S. Department of Labor, Washington, D.C., 1970. Heneman and Seltzer report (pp. 13-14) that forecasting activities had begun within the last 5 years in three-fifths of the firms, and that managerial and professional requirements were often the most difficult to forecast.

discovered that the annual percentage increase in supervisory employment, either in total or by broad grades, is directly related to the percentage increase in sales 1 year earlier. If sales did not rise in the preceding year, this lagged relationship is replaced by a forecast of zero net change in managerial needs.

Actual managerial manpower requirements at the plant or division level will be a function not only of such forecasts but also of other data reflecting attrition rates among present managers, promotions and transfers between plants or divisions, and prospective promotability of junior managers. Short-range forecasts (up to 2 years) will probably be easier to make than intermediate- (2 to 5 years) or long-range forecasts (beyond 5 years). Some of the factors that enter into each are summarized in Exhibit 3-1.

Recruiting and Assessing New Managerial Talent

If managerial forecasts for 5 years can be made despite the uncertainties involved, then most organizations need to consider recruiting new people at the bottom of the managerial ladder. Some experienced managers may be hired further up the ladder, either through raiding other organizations or employing those who become available for various reasons. Executive-recruitment agencies may be effective middlemen here.

But most organizations promote from within existing managerial ranks. This means that new recruits must be sought for future development and promotion as managerial needs expand and as numbers are reduced by normal attrition due to retirements, resignations, and deaths. Most new managerial recruits come from two sources:

Exhibit 3-1   Three Ranges of Manpower Forecasting

	Short range: 0-2 years	Intermediate range: 2-5 years	Long range: Beyond 5 years
Demand	Authorized employment (including growth, changes, and turnover)	Operating needs from budgets and plans	In some organizations the same as "Intermediate"; in others, an increased awareness of changes in environment and technology—essentially judgmental
Supply	Employee census less expected losses plus expected promotions from subordinate groups	Manpower vacancies expected from individual promotability data derived from development plans	Management expectations of changing characteristics of employees and future available manpower
Net needs	Numbers and kinds of employees needed	Numbers, kinds, dates, and levels of needs	Management expectations of future conditions affecting immediate decisions

Source: James W. Walker, "Forecasting Manpower Needs," *Harvard Business Review,* vol. 47, no. 2, p. 156, March–April, 1969. For an application to one firm (American Oil Company), see Walker, "Manpower Planning: An Integrative Approach," *Management of Personnel Quarterly,* vol. 9, no. 1, pp. 38–42, Spring, 1970.

(1) colleges, universities, and graduate schools of management; and (2) noncollege supervisory or nonmanagerial ranks. Organizations compete with other organizations in hiring the first group; and college recruitment is a major spring effort of many companies and other organizations. Company officials visit a number of campuses for this purpose.

The selection process frequently includes an interview on campus and a visit to the employing organization for further interviews for mutual exploration of possible employment.

After employment, there may be further efforts to assess managerial potential in order to make initial job assignments. One of the best-known programs of this type is the "assessment center" process used (both for college hires and new noncollege managers advanced from nonmanagerial positions) by the American Telephone and Telegraph Company and its affiliated operating companies. The "Management Progress Study" which grew out of the initial establishment of the center reviewed the experience of 422 men employed in six Bell System companies over several years. Each had spent 3½ days in the assessment center in a group of 12. Among the techniques used were a lengthy interview; the in-basket exercise of some 25 written memos, phone calls, and other written communications on which action must be taken; a manufacturing problem; group discussion; projective tests; paper-and-pencil tests; and questionnaires. These were all designed to test for managerial skills desired in candidates.

Subsequent performance as shown by management level and salary achieved correlated significantly with the initial assessments made of the newly hired managers. This study then led to setting up modified assessment centers in two-thirds of the operating companies as an aid in selecting persons for managerial positions, including promotion from nonmanagerial jobs.[16]

THE ESSENCE OF MANAGEMENT DEVELOPMENT

Organization planning, manpower planning, and forecasting are parts of the process of management development but not the essence of it. Management development occurs in every organization in some way, as subordinates learn from and respond to the example of their superiors and try to improve their own performance on the job. The organizational climate established by top management, including the personnel concepts which they hold, is the single most important influence on the development of subordinate managers at all levels.

To overemphasize formal management-development programs is to neglect the important point that "the climate management creates and the way the business is run are the controlling forces in executive development. Companies can't develop executives; executives must develop themselves."[17]

Not all people in management want to get ahead; some are satisfied to remain at a certain status and income level rather than take on added responsibilities. But for those who aspire to higher managerial positions, the way in which top management runs the organization will determine whether they will have opportunities to develop themselves within the organization or must seek better and more challenging opportunities elsewhere. If younger managers have opportunities to "repot" themselves as they outgrow their present positions, they will remain in the organization and grow with it. But if superi-

[16] John P. Campbell, Marvin D. Dunnette, Edward E. Lawler III, and Karl E. Weich, Jr., *Managerial Behavior,*

Performance, and Effectiveness, McGraw-Hill Book Company, New York, 1970, pp. 213-232. See also Douglas W. Bray, "The Assessment Center Method of Appraising Management Potential," in Jerome W. Blood (ed.), *The Personnel Job in a Changing World,* American Management Association, New York, 1964, pp. 225-234.

[17] Robert K. Stoltz, "Getting Back to Fundamentals in Executive Development," *Personnel,* vol. 30, no. 6, p. 456, May, 1964. For a more extensive discussion, see Robert L. Desatnick, *A Concise Guide to Management Development,* American Management Association, New York, 1970.

ors discourage such repotting and fail to communicate their reasons effectively, young managers often leave for greener pastures. This was the conclusion of a study of a sample of young managers remaining within a number of AT&T operating companies as compared with those who left voluntarily over the same period.[18] Job repotting, if initiated by the young manager himself, is a part of his own career planning, as opposed to having his career within the company planned *for* him. Some who left voluntarily were dissatisfied with their career opportunities within their company, but they may also have been more "mobile managers" who thought they could advance their managerial careers by moving from one company to another.[19]

For example, a study of 900 top executives indicated that "only a third of America's leading corporation executives are in the same firm they started with, 26 percent had been with another company, and 40.5 percent had been with two or more." The conclusion was that a company "must understand and recognize the drive for self-development and self-renewal and thus give its ablest members the right to maximum choice and flexibility."[20]

Effective management development programs have three principal components: (1) an organizational climate—including advance organizational and manpower planning—conducive to managerial self-development, (2) appraisal of managerial performance, and (3) various opportunities for further managerial development.

The remainder of this chapter will deal with the latter two. They cannot be effective without the direct involvement of top management from the beginning; its active participation in planning, analysis, and appraisal; and recognition of the example it sets by its own behavior. This has been described as a "commitment approach to management development," and its importance cannot be overemphasized.[21]

APPRAISING MANAGERIAL PERFORMANCE

While some firms and other organizations have hesitated to adopt a formal system of appraising managerial performance, the fact is that this performance is evaluated in some fashion whether or not there is a formal system. In every organization, some managers (including those at the top) do a good job of evaluating the performance of their subordinates and discussing the evaluations with them as a means of helping them to improve their work and chances for promotion. Frequently, however, the lack of uniformity among divisions and departments is obvious, and some systematic way of appraising management performance throughout the company is therefore desirable. The objectives are to help each manager to improve his present performance and to identify the individuals who show the greatest potential for higher managerial positions.

Performance appraisal, of course, is not confined to management positions. It is used by many firms in evaluating the performance of employees below the management level; we shall discuss this experience in Chapter 17. But unless there is some method of appraising the work of managers at all levels, including first-line supervisors, it is unlikely that an employee performance appraisal system will work well. As in

[18] Warren P. Miner, *Job Repotting—A Model to Aid in Retaining an Effective and Experienced Management Team* (unpublished master's thesis, Alfred P. Sloan School of Management, Massachusetts Institute of Technology, Cambridge, Mass., 1970). This study drew on the "repotting" concept first developed by Robert N. Ford, *Motivation through Work Itself,* American Management Association, New York, 1969.

[19] Eugene E. Jennings, *The Mobile Manager,* University of Michigan Press, Ann Arbor, Mich., 1967, p. 19.

[20] Robert C. Albrook, "Why It's Harder to Keep Good Executives," *Fortune,* vol. 78, no. 6, November, 1968, pp. 137 and 180.

[21] Robert J. House, *Management Development: Design, Evaluation, and Implementation,* Bureau of Industrial Relations, The University of Michigan, Ann Arbor, Mich., 1967. See the chart on pp. 46–47.

most aspects of personnel relations, management sets the example.

Performance appraisal systems vary considerably, and there has been a controversy over the most effective approach to stimulating improved managerial performance. This controversy reflects the underlying personnel concepts of management. Under management by centralized direction and control, appraisals are worked out by superior managers, sometimes in consultation with other superiors at the same or higher levels, and communicated to subordinate managers. There is little opportunity for two-way discussion of the manager's performance; he is told *how* he stands and what he must do to progress further. In contrast, under management by shared objectives and self-control (as discussed in Chapter 1) the superior encourages his subordinate manager to evaluate his own past performance with him, to establish new objectives for the coming year or another calendar period, and to evaluate his subsequent performance against those mutually established objectives. However, relatively few organizations have as yet approached this latter type of appraisal, which we shall consider later in this chapter.

Appraisal by the Superior Manager

Perhaps the most frequent method of appraising managerial performance has been to use a standard form listing a number of factors which are thought to be important attributes of effective management. For example, one such form used by a large chemical company included the following major headings (with many subheadings under each): "Accomplishment," "Thinking," "Administration," "Relationships," and "Knowledge." A box after each major factor and subfactor was provided for the rater to check, much as in a student report card, A (outstanding), B, C, D, and E (unsatisfactory)! This appraisal system also provided for a forecast of potential for the next-higher managerial posi-

tion, using the same factors and grading or rating symbols. Other similar "factor" or "trait" systems avoid the grading method by asking the rater to write out his thoughts about the manager being appraised under such headings as "Planning," "Organizing," "Delegating," "Executing," and "Relationships."[22] Some systems provide for combined judgments of two or more raters who presumably know the ratee well.

Most of these approaches include a subsequent discussion, based on a previous rating, between the manager and his subordinate. Presumably the manager being rated has an opportunity to comment on the rating, and indeed some forms provide a section in which such comments can be recorded. The difficulty here is that communication is often largely one-way, with little opportunity for the subordinate manager to evaluate his own progress and plan his own development with his superior's help.[23]

Goal Setting and Self-appraisal: Management by Objectives

An alternative approach is a form of appraisal by results, emphasizing the joint efforts of superiors and subordinates in setting short-term objectives or performance goals and then reviewing these subsequently. This is really management by *shared* objectives and grows out of the personnel concept of management characterized by Theory Y or System 4 (as discussed in Chapter 1).

There is a considerable literature on "management by objectives." One study summed up the approach in a few words: "To accomplish anything, know what it is you are trying to accomplish. To know whether or not you have done so,

[22] For illustrative forms and examples, see *Forms and Records in Personnel Administration,* Studies in Personnel Policy no. 175, National Industrial Conference Board, Inc., New York, 1960.

[23] An early criticism of traditional management performance appraisal systems was that by Douglas McGregor, "An Uneasy Look at Performance Appraisal," *Harvard Business Review,* vol. 35, no. 3, pp. 91–92, May–June, 1957.

compare achievements with objectives." After observing that "to many practitioners, these concepts are less theory than common sense," the author concluded: "Indeed from the evidence in a great many companies, very few managers consistently use these ideas with any real vigor."[24]

The "Objective-centered Performance Appraisal and Review Process" used by the Aluminum Company of America illustrates the steps in this approach to management development:[25]

> **1** An individual writes down his *major* performance objectives for the coming year, and his specific plans (including target dates) for achieving these objectives.
>
> **2** He submits them to his boss for review. Out of the discussion comes an agreed-upon set of objectives.
>
> **3** On a quarterly basis he verbally reviews progress toward these objectives with his boss. Objectives and plans are revised and up-dated as necessary.
>
> **4** At the end of the year, the individual prepares a brief "accomplishment report," which lists all major accomplishments, with comments on the variances between *results actually achieved* and *results expected.*
>
> **5** This "self-appraisal" is discussed with the boss. Reasons for goals not being met are explored.
>
> **6** A new set of objectives is established for the next year.

The emphasis in this approach is on mutual planning and problem solving rather than on the

preparation of a form-based judgment of an individual manager's performance by his organizational superior. Under either system, performance as appraised will also be rewarded eventually in salary increases and promotions. We shall consider incentive aspects of management compensation in a later chapter.

An objective-centered appraisal process leads naturally to the next step in management development: guided self-development.

PLANNING FOR GUIDED SELF-DEVELOPMENT

Planning for an individual manager's development must be related to the present and future needs of the organization and to his own abilities and potentialities as shown by appraisals and by his own objectives. It is necessarily individual, for no plan for improvement is likely to be identical for any two managers. The most important elements in any such plan are on-the-job coaching and the systematic exposure of the individual manager to new assignments, so that he can learn and develop from this experience. This may be done in a variety of ways which supplement what the subordinate has already learned from the delegation of responsibility by his superior on the present job. Many different methods are used; the following are more important because they help to make potential higher managers visible and encourage self-development.[26]

Job Rotation

Managers may be rotated among positions in different functions or geographic locations to test their ability to meet new situations and problems. Sometimes an organizational change or the

---

[24] Walter S. Wikstrom, *Managing By—and With—Objectives,* Personnel Policy Study no. 212, National Industrial Conference Board, Inc., New York, 1968, p. 2. See also Raymond F. Valentine, *Performance Objectives for Managers,* American Management Association, 1966, particularly the examples in Chaps. 7-10; and Charles L. Hughes, "Assessing the Performance of Key Managers," *Personnel,* vol. 45, no. 1, pp. 38-43, January-February, 1968. Howard P. Mold, *The Mechanics of Management by Objectives,* Industrial Relations Center, California Institute of Technology, Bulletin no. 37, Pasadena, Calif., 1972.

[25] Wikstrom, *op. cit.,* exhibit 1, p. 3. Wikstrom also presents detailed reports on the programs used by Honeywell, General Mills, St. Regis Paper, 3M (Minnesota Mining & Manufacturing) Company, and Kimberly-Clark.

[26] "Experience and research generally affirm the proposition that greater mobility of managers increases the range of choice and flexibility in the deployment of human resources and most often results in a more adaptable organization." Glickman et al., *Top Management Development and Succession,* p. 57.

need for temporary replacements provides a special opportunity for rotation. The manager affected should be consulted about a proposed transfer in a job-rotation program, however, if he is to avoid getting the impression that he is just a pawn on management's chessboard. Unfortunately, some companies give subordinate managers little opportunity to consider whether they want to make a particular geographical move or how it might affect their families at the particular time. Others consult the junior manager, who is given the opportunity to refuse a transfer if he believes his own development will be better served for the immediate future in his present job. If managers are rotated too frequently, they may not have time to develop their subordinates effectively, with the result that some mediocrity survives in the rapid turnover of managers.[27]

Task Forces and Interdepartmental Committee Assignments

A number of organizations use special "task forces" or project groups to work on particular problems, drawing members from different departments, functions, and levels within the organization. Management committees are formed to develop and administer such programs as wage and salary administration, performance appraisal, quality standards. All these expose managers to new problems and test their ability to work cooperatively with other managers. These experiences may not only reveal latent leadership ability, but they may develop working relationships which improve interdepartmental communication when committee members on the task force return to their own departments.

Understudies for Key Positions

Individuals may be assigned temporarily as "assistants" to key officials, with the understanding

that they will be shifted again to positions of direct operating responsibility. This is sometimes part of "job rotation" and gives junior managers a wide variety of managerial experience. It also enables senior managers to evaluate subordinates in a number of different jobs.

Problem-solving Conferences with Staff Specialists

Problem-solving conferences are discussions in which the staff specialist starts with the problems as seen by the line executives and tries to help them arrive at satisfactory solutions from a human relations point of view. The competent personnel manager thus plays an important role in day-to-day development of managerial skills.

These approaches may, in turn, be supplemented by various programs or conferences designed to develop and broaden management skills in general. An individual might be invited to attend such a conference with some of his colleagues, as a part of his development.

Management Conference Programs within the Organization

The most effective management conference programs are developed and run by the organization's own line officials with the assistance of staff specialists, rather than by outsiders brought in for the specific purpose. The objective is to acquaint management personnel in the organization with internal policies, the staff services available to line officers, and the skills that are important for an effective manager. Development of these skills may involve case discussions, the Incident Process,[28] role playing, sensitivity

---

[27] This same point and others in this discussion apply equally to the development of good supervisors, considered separately in Chap. 7.

[28] For a discussion of this variant of the case method, see Paul Pigors and Faith Pigors, "Learning by the Incident Process," *The Technology Review,* vol. 65, no. 4, pp. 27-29ff., February, 1963 (reprinted in Pigors, Myers, and Malm, *op. cit.,* selection 16). See also Pigors and Pigors, *Case Method in Human Relations: The Incident Process,* McGraw-Hill Book Company, New York, 1961.

training or T-Groups,[29] and other methods of increasing the understanding of the human problems of management. Some large multiplant firms have established residential "staff colleges" which are attended by successive groups of their management personnel for periods of several weeks or months. Examples are the General Electric Company's center at Crotonville, New York; Western Electric's resident corporate education in New Jersey; the staff colleges run at former English manor houses by Imperial Chemical Industries and by the British-American Tobacco Company; and the Tata Staff College organized for the many Tata enterprises in India.

Conferences or Institutes Sponsored by Management Organizations

Examples of conferences or institutes sponsored by management organizations are the management seminar programs run by the American Management Association in New York City and the periodic or annual conferences sponsored by The Conference Board, the Society for the Advancement of Management, and the Industrial Relations Counselors of New York. An early example in Great Britain was the Administrative Staff College established after the war at Henley-on-Thames, near London. This college attracted top-echelon managers from British private and public enterprises and from government departments for study of management in groups of 10 by the "syndicate method." The same pattern is found in the Administrative Staff College of India. A variety of management-training programs has sprung up in other developing countries, as well as in Western Europe. In addition to the management programs of the British Institute of Management, two graduate schools of management have been established in London and Manchester. There are also management training centers in Sweden, France, and Switzerland, in particular.

University Management-development Programs

The oldest university management-development program in the United States is the 12-month Sloan Program in Executive Development begun in a preliminary form at MIT in 1931. The Advanced Management Program at the Harvard Graduate School of Business Administration grew out of a wartime program for senior managers. This program has been followed by similar ones at Columbia, Carnegie-Mellon, MIT, Stanford, and many other universities.[30]

---

[29] This is also called "laboratory training," for it grows out of the experience of the National Training Laboratory at Bethel, Maine, in which small training groups (T-Groups) were used to increase the perception of each member about his impact on the others in the group—his "interpersonal sensitivity." With the inauguration in 1958 of a series of such "laboratory training programs" in Esso refineries, the method has been employed on a limited basis as a means of changing the behavior of people in particular organizations. For a discussion of this and similar experiences, and a general evaluation of laboratory training, see Edgar H. Schein and Warren G. Bennis, *Personal and Organizational Change through Group Methods: The Laboratory Approach,* John Wiley & Sons, Inc., New York, 1965. There is a shorter evaluation of sensitivity training in *Developing Managerial Competence,* pp. 91-94, and in Frank Friedlander, "The Impact of Organizational Training Laboratories upon the Effectiveness and Interaction of Ongoing Work Groups," *Personnel Psychology,* vol. 20, no. 3, pp. 289-301, Autumn, 1967. A review of research indicates "clear evidence" that personal growth results for most participants, but that the value for subsequent job performance is less convincing. Paul C. Buchanan, "Laboratory Training and Organization Development," *Administrative Science Quarterly,* vol. 14, no. 3, pp. 466-480, September, 1969.

[30] Evaluation of the effect of university management development programs in terms of individual performance back on the job is difficult. However, one study concluded that the main value was to the participants, through "change in their perception, interest, attitudes with respect to themselves as individuals (self) or as businessmen (job)." Kenneth R. Andrews, *The Effectiveness of University Management Development Programs,* Division of Research, Graduate School of Business Administration, Harvard University, Boston, Mass., 1966, p. 162. The study covered 60 percent of 10,000 graduates of 39 university programs. Of *Fortune*'s top 500 companies, 268 had no representative. For an account of recent changes in the content of these programs, see Jude O. West and Don H. Sheriff, *Executive Development Programs in Universities,* Personnel Policy Study no. 215, National Industrial Conference Board, New York, 1969.

These are usually full-time programs designed especially for middle- and top-level executives who leave their jobs for shorter or extended periods and are exposed to new ideas and new people from other companies. Other programs, such as those at the Graduate School of Business of the University of Chicago, are extended evening seminars, which do not take the executive off the job. Finally, many universities have off-campus conferences or extension courses for management at different levels and specialized conferences on various functions of management.

Activities outside the Company

Participation in trade or professional association activities and in community affairs offers opportunities for managers to widen their contacts and get administrative experience serving on committees, community agencies, and as elected or appointed officials in local governments. As an example, William G. Caples, former vice-president of Inland Steel Company, served as president of the Chicago Board of Education for several years, and in many cities businessmen are chairmen of annual community fund drives. During the late sixties and early seventies, many businessmen were actively involved in the efforts to hire disadvantaged people through the National Alliance of Businessmen.

Emphasis on Self-development

In listing all these various possible supplementary programs, it must be emphasized again that not every manager needs all of them. Guided self-development should be tailored to fit the needs of the particular individual as he and his boss see them. More important than any of these more or less formal programs is the way in which each manager's superior deals with him—in delegating responsibility, in coaching him, in providing challenging opportunities to tackle new problems, in letting him learn from his mistakes, in not checking too closely, in holding him accountable for results, and in reviewing his performance periodically. Basically, this is the way in which an environment is provided to help managers develop themselves. If the emphasis is on self-development, as we believe it should be, then top management needs to avoid rigid control systems that require detailed reports on the activities of subgroups run by subordinate managers and are clearly in conflict with "management by shared objectives."

MANAGEMENT TRAINEES —OR A CHALLENGING FIRST JOB?

In addition to management-development programs designed to improve the performance of present managers and to increase their potential contribution to the organization, some companies have established special programs for trainees who may in the future become managers. These trainees are usually selected from each year's crop of college or M.B.A. graduates and are assigned to a training program, sometimes lasting as long as 2 years, in which classroom work and seminars are combined with a variety of job assignments within the company.

Many large American corporations have established trainee programs of this type. One of the most extensive is that conducted for 1,000 college men each year by the General Electric Company. When the GE trainee finishes his intensive program after 18 months, he frequently has a choice between several alternative lines of job progression. During his training program, he has been encouraged to develop specific job skills as well as to adopt a broader managerial view.

The assumption of management trainee programs is that there is greater value in a broad exposure to a variety of jobs and functions in the organization and that some further "postgraduate" study in the classroom should supplement this experience.

Among the companies that have not had special management-trainee programs are Du Pont and the Ford Motor Company. They believed in hiring college men for specific jobs and in giving them only a short general introduction in company operations. This avoided, in their view, the creation of a specially favored group of future managers, which tends to develop tensions in the rest of the organization. The emphasis is on self-development through doing a productive job rather than on developing broad managerial skills in a young, picked group who may get the idea that they are the "crown princes" before they have really proved themselves.

However, there is growing evidence that today's college and business school graduates prefer challenging jobs at the outset of their employment and are "turned off" by the longer periods of further training represented by the "management trainee" concept. The old stereotype of the college graduate as "immature, impractical, and incapable" was reinforced by the kinds of job assignments supervisors and managers gave him. Schein argued in 1964 that "top management should always maximize the responsibility given to the college graduate in the initial assignments."[31] His subsequent studies of a panel of master's graduates of MIT Sloan School of Management tended to confirm his belief that the absence of initial job challenge leads many to move to other organizations where more challenging opportunities continue to exist.

A more recent survey of industry practices concluded that "many companies—notably such companies as Texas Instruments, Honeywell, Inc., and the 3M Company—give a good deal of attention to providing challenging job circumstances as a means of stimulating effective managerial performance."[32]

The relationship between early job challenge and subsequent career success in the same organization was examined in a study of 62 college men hired by two Bell System operating companies in 1956 and 1957. The degree of first-job challenge correlated significantly with two indexes computed 5 years later: a success index based on overall performance and relative salary level achieved and a performance index based on annual appraisals.[33] Since these men were selected as a result of the AT&T assessment center procedure discussed earlier, it is possible that those judged more capable then received more challenging job assignments, and that they demonstrated their effectiveness early and were moved up more rapidly. But the evidence still supports the conclusion that there is a positive relationship between early job challenge and subsequent job success.

DEVELOPING OVERSEAS MANAGERS

The selection and development of managers for overseas subsidiaries of international companies (sometimes called "multinational") show how the situation determines the leadership qualities required. The manager who has been successful in a domestic branch may not possess the qualities necessary to work effectively in a foreign culture, where business practices are somewhat

[31] Edgar H. Schein, "How to Break in the College Graduate," *Harvard Business Review,* vol. 42, no. 6, p. 73, November–December, 1964. These findings were substantially corroborated by a later study of two samples of M.B.A. graduates, one of which remained with the original employer. Both samples of graduates rated highest among the factors in their first job the following: "advancement opportunity, challenging work, and responsibility." "Salary" was fourth and "security" last in a longer list. Alton C. Johnson and Jim Simonson, "The College Graduate and His First Job," *Management of Personnel Quarterly,* vol. 9, no. 3, pp. 18–22, Fall, 1970.

[32] John P. Campbell, Marvin D. Dunnette, Edward E. Lawler III, and Karl E. Weich, Jr., *Managerial Behavior, Performance, and Effectiveness,* McGraw-Hill Book Company, New York, 1970. The book is a comprehensive review of research as well as practice.

[33] Cited in Campbell et al., *ibid.,* pp. 224–229.

different and adaptability may be a virtue.[34] There is the further problem of working in an organization staffed largely by nationals of the country, so that the personnel responsibilities of overseas managers take on new dimensions.

The manager assigned from the United States to an overseas subsidiary of an American company, for example, may have the task of developing effective subordinate managers among the nationals of the country so that they can take increased responsibilities as he is rotated or transferred to other assignments in other countries or back in the United States. A case example of a somewhat similar experience of a Mexican general manager with a Belgian engineer is found in case 3, "The Dissatisfactions of an Expatriate Engineer" in Part 2. Increasingly, senior executives of United States international firms prefer local nationals over Americans for overseas posts.[35]

It is no wonder, then, that the top executives of large multinational companies spend considerable time and thought in selecting managers for their overseas operations, taking into account the managerial potential in their organization anywhere in the world. A standing committee of directors of the Standard Oil Company (New Jersey) met 37 times in one year to review senior executive appointments, taking into account not only an appraisal of past performance but an evaluation of the man's social and political skills and growth potential. In this manner, organiza-

tional planning and management development are broadened, as executives of international companies move from one assignment to another, at home or abroad.[36] As firms in advanced industrial countries increasingly develop overseas operations, either in wholly or partially owned subsidiaries or in joint ventures with firms abroad, these aspects of organization planning and management development will become more important than they have been in the past. Top-management support for this effort, especially for developing multinational managers as well as local managers, is essential.[37]

THE PERSONNEL ADMINISTRATOR'S ROLE

Since a basic purpose of organization planning and management development programs is to develop and release the constructive energies of management at all levels in the organization, the personnel administrator is necessarily concerned with them. A major personnel administration goal is to assist in the effective utilization of human resources in the organization. Therefore, the impact of organization structure and management policies on the development of managers and the need to plan in advance for the consequent manpower requirements are vitally important to him.

---

[34] See Harold Stieglitz, "Effective Overseas Performance," *Management Record* (National Industrial Conference Board), vol. 25, no. 2, pp. 2-8, February, 1963 (reprinted in Pigors, Myers, and Malm, *op. cit.,* selection 15). For an analysis of the organization charts of 42 companies from various nations, showing how foreign operations of these companies are organized and integrated with the parent company, see Harold Stieglitz, *Organization Structures of International Companies,* National Industrial Conference Board, Studies in Personnel Policy, no. 198, New York, 1965.

[35] As reported in a survey of 254 executives, Michael G. Duerr and James Greene, *Foreign Nationals in International Management,* Managing International Business, no. 2, National Industrial Conference Board, New York, 1968.

[36] An example is the 1967 appointment of Jacques G. Maisonrouge as president of IBM World Trade Corporation in New York (the international subsidiary of IBM). Starting in the French IBM affiliate, he next moved to the European operations, then to the New York headquarters office, before he was named president of IBM World Trade Europe in July, 1964. After his most recent appointment, he said in an interview: "IBM practices what it preaches about internationalism in its business. Take my case for example, I can honestly say that I never notice a man's nationality but only whether he has, can or will do a job." *The New York Times,* Dec. 24, 1967. Also, "The Man Who Makes It One World for IBM," *Business Week,* July 18, 1970, pp. 90-92.

[37] For a discussion of the failure of some United States firms to do this effectively in Latin America, see John G. Shearer, "Industrial Relations of American Corporations Abroad," pp. 109-131 in Solomon Barkin et al. (eds.), *International Labor,* Harper & Row, Publishers, Incorporated, New York, 1967.

Unfortunately, many personnel administrators are either bypassed in this area of responsibility or do not realize its importance. A study of the personnel function as seen by corporate executives showed that:

In organization design, manpower planning and development, and electronic data processing, line executives are already by-passing personnel departments. Meanwhile, personnel executives are not actively adopting objectives in these areas, nor are they trying to gain greater acceptance of personnel's role in these areas from members of top management. [38]

When he is successful a personnel administrator's function is to work with the line organization, especially top management, as adviser in developing an overall plan for management development that is consistent with the objectives of the organization and the needs of the managers. Lacking such a coordinated approach, the techniques and methods of management training lose much of their effectiveness and fail to provide maximum opportunities for the development and release of managerial talents.

The importance of top-management interest cannot be overemphasized. The responsibility for building a competent managerial organization clearly rests with the chief executive, and he cannot properly delegate it to a personnel administrator, a controller, or a group of outside consultants. An organization plan or an executive-development program is likely to be on paper and not in men's minds unless a chief executive shows by example the importance that he attaches to developing managerial ability.

The staff role in this activity, however, is particularly difficult. If the personnel administrator becomes identified as the boss's "hatchet man" in pruning "dead wood," he is seen as a threat rather than as a help to line management in its task of developing executive ability. The proper staff role is well described in the following words:

In a very literal sense the staff man's function is that of adjunct to a top-management executive and his subordinates in their efforts to carry out their operating responsibilities. He expands, but does not supplant, the efforts of the head executive to assist his managers in self-development. Not being under the day-to-day operating pressures for immediate results, he can think in larger terms and for more distant results than the executives. He can spend the necessary time for a snail's-pace approach. To him the *way* in which he works is of paramount importance. He has no authority and wants none. As an agent for change, his only power comes from his skill in making full use of the participative process. [39]

Thus, a personnel administrator's role is to help all levels of management with *their* problems of developing *their* subordinates as *they* see them, rather than to impose *his* preconceptions about the organization and *his* solutions. He can explore with them the consequences of present organizational relationships and whether a different organization structure would be helpful. He is apt to be more effective in his role as a counselor to the line officials than if he were a mere keeper of the many records that so often accompany a formal system of organization planning and executive development.

The relationship of line responsibility and staff function is illustrated by the experience of a large automobile manufacturing company which launched a management-development program after careful study of similar programs in other large firms. The company-wide committee to develop and administer the program was headed

[38] Dalton E. McFarland, *Company Officers Assess the Personnel Function,* American Management Association, Research Study 79, New York, 1967, p. 22.

[39] Robert C. Sampson, "Train Executives while They Work," *Harvard Business Review,* vol. 31, no. 6, p. 45, November–December, 1953.

alternately by the president and the executive vice-president. Membership was rotated among central-office vice-presidents and divisional operating vice-presidents. The industrial relations vice-president was a permanent member of the committee and had functional responsibility for coordinating the program among divisions. In explaining his approach, he said: "It has been our very careful plan not to superimpose any programs on our various company components, either staff or operating, but rather have them realize largely on their own initiative the value in such a program and thus become eager to adopt it." This approach worked, for within 2 years eight operating divisions, representing a high percentage of management positions, had adopted the program from the small pilot-line beginning in a few divisions.

SUMMARY

The environment in which managers with the necessary leadership qualities can develop is best provided by an organization in which opportunities are constantly presented to challenge managerial capacities and to broaden managerial experience. The atmosphere established by top management is crucial for management development. Delegation of responsibility through decentralization of authority, coaching of subordinates by superiors, and relating individual to organizational goals are important parts of a management-development program.

An increasing number of companies have adopted formal programs, although there is a tendency to rely too much on the forms and procedures and to neglect the all-important factor of a favorable environment in which managers can develop themselves. Elements of a formal program, which help top executives focus on a systematic approach, are (1) organization analysis and planning, (2) preparation of a manpower audit showing present incumbents and possible replacements in each managerial position, tied in

to advance manpower projections, (3) appraisal of management performance, and (4) special planning to guide the development of individual managers. Some companies have also adopted management-trainee programs. However, there is increasing evidence that a challenging initial assignment is more effective than a trainee program.

Management development cannot be delegated to a staff officer, such as the personnel administrator, because the development of managers is a central responsibility of the line organization. However, the personnel administrator can supplement the efforts of line managers, act as counselor to managers in dealing with their own problems, and provide staff assistance in carrying out a formal program.

Management development is important in any growing organization, but it is even more imperative in a rapidly changing world. Managers have never been able to ignore the social, political, and economic environment outside the organization, but recent rapid changes make it imperative for managers to adapt their personnel concepts to technological and social changes because of the way they affect the nature of work in the modern world. The next chapter will explore these implications in two principal areas: (1) the growing urban crisis, with its effects on the disadvantaged segment of our work force, and (2) the changing nature of work resulting from automation, and particularly from the impact of computers, and the systems approach.

SELECTED REFERENCES

Alfred, Theodore M.: "Checkers or Choice in Manpower Management," *Harvard Business Review,* vol. 45, no. 1, pp. 157–167, January–February, 1967 (reprinted in Paul Pigors, Charles A. Myers, and F. T. Malm, *Management of Human Resources: Readings in Personnel Administration,* 2d ed., McGraw-Hill Book Company, New York, 1969, selection 11).

Beckhard, Richard: *Organization Development: Strategies and Models,* Addison-Wesley Publishing Company, Inc., Reading, Mass., 1969.

Campbell, John P., Marvin D. Dunnette, Edward E. Lawler III, and Karl W. Weich, Jr.: *Managerial Behavior, Performance, and Effectiveness,* McGraw-Hill Book Company, New York, 1970.

Desatnick, Robert L.: *A Concise Guide to Management Development,* American Management Association, Inc., New York, 1970.

Finkle, Robert B., and William S. Jones: *Assessing Corporate Talent: A Key to Managerial Manpower Planning,* Wiley-Interscience, a Division of John Wiley & Sons, Inc., New York, 1970.

Glickman, Albert S., Clifford P. Hahn, Edwin A. Fleishman, and Brent Baxter: *Top Management Development and Succession: An Exporatory Study,* Supplementary Paper no. 27, Committee for Economic Development, New York, November, 1968.

Hughes, Charles L.: *Goal Setting: Key to Industrial and Organizational Effectiveness,* American Management Association, Inc., New York, 1965.

McGregor, Douglas: *The Human Side of Enterprise,* McGraw-Hill Book Company, New York, 1960, especially chap. 6 and part 3.

Schein, Edgar H.: "Forces Which Undermine Management Development," *The California Management Review,* vol. 5, no. 4, pp. 23–24, Summer, 1963 (reprinted in Pigors, Myers, and Malm, *op. cit.,* selection 13).

———, and Warren G. Bennis: *Personal and Organizational Change through Group Methods: The Laboratory Approach,* John Wiley & Sons, Inc., New York, 1965.

Stieglitz, Harold: "Effective Overseas Performance," *Management Record,* vol. 25, no. 2, pp. 2–8, February, 1962 (reprinted in Pigors, Myers, and Malm, *op. cit.,* selection 15).

Thompson, Paul H., and Gene W. Dalton: "Performance Appraisal: Managers Beware," *Harvard Business Review,* vol. 48, no. 1, pp. 149–154, January-February, 1970.

Wikstrom, Walter S.: *Managing by—and with—Objectives,* Personnel Policy Study no. 212, National Industrial Conference Board, Inc., New York, 1968.

Chapter 4

Managing and Working in a Changing World

In every domain, when anything exceeds a certain measurement, it suddenly changes its aspect, condition or nature. . . . The liquid boils, the germ cell divides. . . . Critical points have been reached, rungs on the ladder involving a change of state—jumps of all sorts in the course of development.

Pierre Teilhard de Chardin [1]

The central theme of this chapter is the challenge for managers and other employees posed by the rapid and accelerating pace of social and technological changes. First, we consider the urban crisis and two phenomena (the "Now" Generation and the New Feminism) that confront managers with difficulties and opportunities. Second, we focus on technological change, especially the impact of automation and computerization on work and work relationships. Finally, we glance briefly at possibilities for future developments. They are now in the making.

[1] Pierre Teilhard de Chardin, *The Phenomenon of Man,* Harper Torchbooks, The Cloister Library, Harper & Row, Publishers, Incorporated, New York, 1961, p. 78.

PROBLEMS ASSOCIATED WITH THE URBAN CRISIS

In the late 1960s, the term "crisis" was applied to the condition of many major cities in the United States. Today, most of the elements in that crisis have worsened to the extent that "catastrophe" might seem a more appropriate term. For example, the 1970 census showed that nine major cities have continued to lose relatively prosperous residents (and businesses too), while suburbs have kept on gaining. Meanwhile, the exodus of blacks from the rural South to Northern cities has not slowed as much as expected. Thus, in the early 1970s, the population of some core cities

59

consists of a majority of nonwhites.[2] When New York's Mayor Lindsay hosted mayors from 10 other cities in April, 1971, they all told of disastrous conditions.[3] For example, the Mayor of New Orleans reportedly said that his city "was going down the drain." The Mayor of Boston said his was "a tinderbox . . . an armed camp . . . [with] one out of every five people on welfare." And Mayor Gibson of Newark said his city had just about "hit bottom." The other Mayors "talked in the same apocalyptic tones." Meanwhile, taxpayers in cities and suburbs have watched inflation eat away their gains in income, while tax burdens have become increasingly heavy, especially on property owners.

Discrimination

During the 1960s the plight of nonwhites in the inner cities was greatly aggravated by discrimination in housing, employment, and education. However, a study published in the summer of 1971[4] clearly shows that Negroes have made substantial gains, although they still lag behind whites in the following social and economic categories:

Housing In the nation as a whole, black-occupied housing with little or no plumbing dropped from 41 to 17 percent in 1970. But this was more than three times the figure for whites.

[2] According to the 1970 census, blacks constituted 28 percent in the nation's cities with a population of 2 million or more. But in the suburbs, the black population remained at about 4 percent. For further details, see 1970 census figures and article by Jack Rosenthal, *The New York Times*, Mar. 3, 1971, pp. 1 and 20. New York City added a million blacks and Puerto Ricans in the decade from 1960 to 1970. And the old segregated housing patterns were intensified. More than two-thirds of the city's 2,159 census tracts were either 90 percent white or 90 percent black. *The New York Times*, Mar. 6, 1972, pp. 1 and 22.

[3] The following quotations are taken from *The New York Times*, Apr. 23, 1971, pp. 1 and 48.

[4] *The Social and Economic Status of Negroes in the United States, 1970*, published by the U.S. Census Bureau and the Bureau of Labor Statistics, with figures taken from the 1970 census.

Employment In 1970, for the first time since the early fifties, Negro unemployment was less than double that of whites. (It was 8.2 percent for blacks as compared with 4.5 percent for whites. Undoubtedly a factor in the decreased differential was the sharp rise in unemployment for skilled and professional whites.)

Income The median family income for nonwhites rose 54 percent, from $4,001 in 1960 to $6,191 in 1969 (an increase of $2,190). However, during the same period, the median income for whites rose only 35 percent, from $7,255 to $9,794 (an increase of $2,539). Thus, the absolute gap between the two groups widened, despite the greater percentage of gain by nonwhites.

Education During the sixties, the number of blacks in college doubled (rising to 7 percent in 1970). But only one out of six blacks of college age was enrolled in college, compared with one out of three whites. And a diploma was proved to be worth less, economically, to a Negro than to a white. For example, in 1970, a Negro with a college degree earned less ($8,669) than a white with only a high school diploma ($8,829).

All these gains are owing not only to strenuous efforts by Negroes themselves but also to the planning and administrative work done by private citizens and by representatives of government at all levels. However, when nonwhites have compared what they have gained with what they feel are their rights, many of them have become angry. Some have become violent. In fact, impatience and violence—not only on the part of nonwhites—are characteristic features of our times.

Civil Disorders and Strikes

During the late sixties and early seventies, many businesses and industrial organizations, large and small—as well as numberless individual citizens—have been threatened or financially ruined by civil disorders. The relatively new phenomenon of strikes and work stoppages by professional and municipal employees has sometimes created conditions bordering on chaos—notably in New York City. (See Chapter 8 for the effect on public policy of strikes and work stoppages by municipal employees.)

A New and Worldwide Demand: Freedom Now!

It is not only in the United States that developments in the latter half of the sixties and the early seventies are outward and visible signs of a worldwide and accelerating thrust for autonomy. Students in colleges[5] and high schools, members of religious groups, and former colonial states have demanded their right to independence and self-determination. In many instances, these demands have been backed by sufficient force to bring a conciliatory response from those who formerly exercised authoritarian powers.

A New Breed of Employee

In the realm of business and industry, many managers have recently been confronted by "employees [who] are bright, healthy, well fed and well educated compared to those in the time-and-motion study days. They will not accept jobs unless they are their very own."[6] However, the health of a growing number of employees and job applicants has been undermined, during the early 1970s, by drug addiction. This factor, which is new on a large scale and which may increase as more veterans and teen-agers join the

labor force, poses difficult problems for personnel administrators, for first-level supervisors, and for managers. (See Chapter 22, "Programs For Employee Health and Safety: An Ecological Approach," for particulars.) Similarly, as one commentator has said,[7] "employees entering the world of business [nowadays] are unwilling to accept the system of half answered questions [and] half baked opportunities. . . . More than ever, people are actively pursuing meaningful activities to fill and fulfill their lives. . . . The 'new breed' has representatives at all ages and economic levels and is becoming an ever increasing proportion of our workforce."

One symptom of the independent lifestyle of the new breed has been described by Jennings as "co-worldly living."[8] This term denotes insistence by an increasing number of young executives that their private lives be relatively autonomous. "Company loyalty" is still defined in many firms as willingness to sacrifice personal and family life to organizational demands. But during the 1960s there has been a sharp rise in the number of able young careerists who prefer to leave such a company for the sake of a fully-rounded, co-worldly life. Co-worldliness is the new ethic that could possibly reverse the widespread belief among youth that one has to sell his soul to the company.

Even more radical new demands have come from two groups—not all of whose members are currently employed. These ultramoderns may be classified as the Now Generation and the New Feminists.

THE NOW GENERATION: A COUNTERCULTURE

It is easy for the "over-thirties" to turn away in disgust from the outward manifestations of this

[5] Vivid accounts of campus conditions in 1967 and 1968 are given in *The Cox Commission Report: Crisis at Columbia: Report of the Fact-Finding Commission Appointed to Investigate the Disturbances at Columbia University in April–May 1968,* Vintage Books, Random House, Inc., New York, 1968, and John Hersey's *Letter to the Alumni* (of Yale University), Alfred A. Knopf, Inc., New York, 1970.

[6] Robert N. Ford, *Motivation through the Work Itself,* American Management Association, Inc., New York, 1969, p. 198.

[7] W. N. Penzer, "Managing Motivated Employees," *Personnel Journal,* vol. 50, no. 5, p. 371, May, 1971.

[8] Eugene Emerson Jennings, "The Co-Worldly Executive," *Management of Personnel Quarterly,* vol. 10, no. 2, pp. 4-8, Summer, 1971.

new culture; especially since many of the young seem to reject all the over-thirties—lumping them together as fossilized remains of a bygone era. But do they really reject them as individuals? During the spring of 1971, a slogan that was reportedly popular among teen-agers in Paris was: "We are not against the old, only against all the things that have made them old."[9] Regardless of what it is that the young reject in connection with the over-thirties, "oldsters" need not react with a similar dismissal. In trying to understand this new phenomenon, they might start by asking: Are there any good reasons for trying to bridge the generation gap? In what respects is this modern culture actually new? Why do so many of the over-thirties reject the new young?

Why Try to Understand the New Young?

On the ethical level, are not parents, teachers, school administrators, and managers obligated to demonstrate in their behavior their strong belief in productive interaction and their willingness to work for it?

Practical reasons for attempting to understand the new lifestyle are these: In the early 1970s, the new young represent a significant proportion of our youth.[10] Moreover, their numbers are rapidly increasing and their culture is being adopted by many persons in their mid-twenties and even early thirties. (Among the older representatives of the new young are many liberals and veterans of the Indochina war.) Furthermore, the potentially powerful effects of this counterculture can be seen not only in the readiness of some of the Now Generation to demonstrate in the streets but still more significantly in the fact that some

11 million eighteen- to twenty-one-year-olds now have the vote.

Finally, within a decade, many of the new young will probably enter "The System" (still objecting to many of its features). If members of the older generation can make significant headway now toward understanding the new young, "oldsters" will be in a far better position to interact productively with the younger generation after they have entered regular employment.[11]

In What Respects Is This Lifestyle Actually New?

Taken separately, many elements in the "new" lifestyle are at least as old as the history of man. For example, use of drugs for a variety of purposes goes back to man's earliest beginnings. Long hair for men was traditional until modern times. Love of nature and communal (or tribal) living undoubtedly began before the dawn of history (though many experiments, such as Brook Farm, failed to survive). Belief in nonviolence was an early Christian doctrine and has long been practiced by members of the Society of Friends. Young people throughout history have characteristically objected to what they regard as arbitrary authority. And men of Concord, like Emerson and Thoreau, were by no means the first to proclaim the duty to follow one's own truth. However, the combination of these elements, appearing as it does in the highly industrialized and technologically advanced society of the United States, *is* something new. But the newness of this new lifestyle is by no means the only barrier that blocks understanding by members of earlier generations.

Why Do So Many Over-thirties Reject the New Culture?

An emotional reaction against the new ways is a major obstacle.

---

9 Nesta Roberts, "The Fed-Up Generation," *Manchester Guardian,* vol. 10, no. 17, Apr. 24, 1971.

10 The number of persons potentially involved, in the United States, can readily be inferred from the fact that, according to the 1970 census, more than half our population is under twenty-five years of age.

11 See John S. Fielden, "Today the Campuses, Tomorrow the Corporations: Demand for Participation Can Be Good," *Business Horizons,* vol. 13, no. 3, pp. 13–20, June, 1970.

Ambivalent Feelings Slater[12] suggests that feelings of ambivalence are part of the trouble. Issues such as autonomy, as well as free emotional and sexual expression, strike a responsive chord in the subconscious minds of many older persons who have learned to repress the kinds of behavior that once motivated them—and still would if they gave free rein to their impulses. In fighting their own subconscious, many people have found it easy to overreact when confronted with the uninhibited behavior of the young.

Unwarranted Assumptions Another barrier to understanding consists in the assumption that the "young" are all of a kind. Actually, the Now Generation exemplifies a great variety of values and behaviors. Hersey,[13] in describing the "shimmering diversity" of college students whom he knew, emphasizes how inaccurate and harmful it is to lump together "the various student types" instead of trying to understand and work with each one as an individual.

Other blocks to understanding can be overcome by making two more differentiations. First, one must distinguish between the militant minority (with whom it will be impossible to interact productively until they can modify their destructive behavior) and the great majority of young people, whose beliefs are idealistic and whose behavior is nonviolent. Second, it is unreasonable to assume that those with long hair, tattered blue jeans, bizarre accessories, and even lack of cleanliness necessarily lack the qualities that are needed in the world of work.

Questions That Can Lead toward Understanding

In trying to appreciate what constitutes the heart of the many-faceted counterculture, one may well begin with questions that can be answered by referring to objectively verifiable facts.

[12] Philip E. Slater, *The Pursuit of Loneliness: American Culture at the Breaking Point,* Beacon Press, Boston, 1970.
[13] John Hersey, *op. cit.,* p. 12.

Where Do the Leaders of the New Young Come From? Contrary to what many people assume, most of the leaders (both nonviolent and militant) are not poor, nonwhite, or otherwise underprivileged. On the contrary—as in earlier generations, they come from affluent middle-class or upper-middle-class families. And usually they are among the more sensitive, intelligent, and better-educated members of their peer groups.

What Does the Now Generation Reject? To the new young, a horrible aspect of the culture into which they were born is the Indochina war. The senseless carnage and destructiveness of this undeclared war does violence to all their most cherished values. Moreover, the publication of the "Pentagon Papers" reenforced the conviction of the Now Generation that members of The System (whether in business or in government) are hypocritical. Many of the young would reject a society which can enter into such a war and continue it without the "consent of the governed," even if they saw no other serious flaws in the culture of their elders. Another aspect of society that is unacceptable to the new young is what they perceive as gross injustice and callous indifference to the plight of the disadvantaged and the nonwhite. Environmental pollution is a third feature of our current culture that deeply offends sensitive young nowists. They totally reject the idea that this side effect of a highly industrialized society must be accepted as the price of "progress."

Traditional theories and practices of education are also rejected by many of the new young, not only in college but even in high school. Instead of being a "relevant" and effective preparation for living, they see orthodox education as little more than training to do what one is told. In their view, these "obedience" schools are totally irrelevant to the needs of young people who feel responsible for realizing their own potential, for participating in democratic systems of work and government, for helping those less fortunate than themselves, and for enjoying and preserving the natural world around them. However, a mere listing of what the young reject presents only the negative side of this counterculture. The positive side can be seen by looking at the values that undergird the new lifestyle. [14]

What Are the Values of the Now Generation?

Primacy of Self Each human being is unique. He can best serve others by speaking and living his own truth. (This, of course, is straight Emersonian doctrine.) He should never submit without protest to authority that does violence to his own values (Thoreau). From this it follows that no one should ever stand by, inactive, when wrong or violence is done to others.

The Absolute Worth of Each Individual Belief in supporting the rights of others also springs from the related concept that every human being is of absolute worth.

Nowism: The Imperative of Action The new young feel compelled to act on their convictions—if necessary by burning their draft cards or demonstrating peacefully in the streets.

True Community The kind of community valued by the Now Generation is based on the belief that all people are members of the family of man. All are friends, whether or not they have yet met. In the opinion of the new young, this community of friendship makes it natural that all should share in what is available to the more fortunate.

An example: Communal living illustrates values that are central to the new lifestyle. [15] In a true community, everyone is left free to be himself, so long as "doing his own thing" does not prevent him from helping those with whom he lives. Communes come in many different varieties and "may well serve as a laboratory for the study of the processes involved in the regeneration of our social institutions." [16]

Enhanced Awareness For the Now Generation, a strongly motivating force is the urge for enhanced awareness. This drive for heightened sensitivity has led many young people to experiment with drugs, unfortunately many times with serious consequences.

The Preeminence of Feeling For the new young, experience is of little worth "unless it is warmed by *feeling*. 'Openness' is the praised quality. A student can say of a man who throws a public tantrum, 'At least he cares.'" [17]

Feeling for Nature The world of nature strongly appeals to youth groups now (as well as in earlier times). The new young wish not only to experience the world around them vividly but also to protect nature and the environment for future ages by eliminating pollution.

What about Work? This multiple mind-set, made up of what the young reject and what they value, determines their view of what is desirable—or at least tolerable—as work. The new

---

[14] For a penetrating analysis of what many members of the oncoming generation reject, what they consider unimportant, and what they value most highly, see Kingman Brewster, Jr., "Reflections on our National Purpose," *Foreign Affairs,* vol. 50, no. 3, April, 1972, pp. 399–415. (As President of Yale University, Mr. Brewster had extensive firsthand experience of talking *with* students under circumstances of mutual tension.)

[15] By the same token, the new lifestyle expresses opposition to values that have been cherished by earlier generations of Americans. These values include: voluntary sacrifice by individuals for the sake of society or nation; the family as the basic social unit; monogamy as the ideal relationship between the sexes; private property; and regular employment for pay. For more on this topic, see Martin Walker, "Looking for a New Utopia, the Alternative Society," *Manchester Guardian,* Mar. 27, 1971.

[16] Herbert A. Otto, "Communes: The Alternative Life Style," *Saturday Review,* vol. 54, no. 17, pp. 16–21, Apr. 24, 1971.

[17] Hersey, *op. cit.,* p. 30.

young emphasize the purifying value of physical work and of any work voluntarily done in the service of others. Many college dropouts have rendered magnificent service by teaching in ghettos and as volunteers in projects like the Peace Corps and Vista. But leaders of the Now Generation have not felt drawn to business and industrial establishments which, in their view, are dedicated to materialistic values and run in an authoritarian style which they feel does violence to individuality and personal growth.

HAVE WE REACHED A CULTURAL TURNING POINT?

Are the Young Settling Down?

Hersey suggested that, at least for college students, a turning point may have been reached by the spring of 1970. At Yale, Harvard, MIT, and many other universities and colleges, students began to see that faculty members—and even administrators—behaved less like enemies or strangers than like friends who held some of the same values cherished by the young. These students recognized the value of talking things out (rather than merely "trashing," or shouting nonnegotiable demands). During discussions, some sense of community developed between students who urgently felt that some changes were overdue and those in authority who showed readiness to listen, ability to learn, and willingness to consider changes—not only in the curriculum but also by giving students a place on faculty and administrative committees, and thus a voice in decision making.

Moreover, varied experiences in trying to bring about changes—not only in educational institutions but also in politics and government policy—may have convinced many students that working for change within the system (time-consuming and undramatic as it is) can be more effective than public demonstrations, violent or otherwise. From these signs, many observers have concluded that the student mood has changed drastically. Others think that the mood

of the young remains essentially the same. In their view, leaders of the Now Generation have merely changed their tactics. It seems to us unrealistic to take either of the extreme positions. It would be unwise to assume that the feelings of the young have changed to the extent that there is no longer any danger that a militant minority might join with others in revolutionary action. On the other hand, it would be foolish to overlook the fact—tested in experience—that many of the new young respond favorably to honest expressions of friendliness and trust by their elders.

Furthermore, there are many indications that "the overwhelming majority of recent graduates who had moved to the 'left' during their college years will surely not live in communes, or choose to drop out of society and be downwardly mobile."[18]

Which Way Will Managers Turn?

The immediate future will depend not only on behavior by the new young but also on responses by their elders. Will the Now Generation be regarded as "crazy kids?" Those who take that view will tend to react repressively. However, some managers have already shown that they can respond affirmatively to the idealism of the new young and are willing to work *with* them. Key questions are: Will managers, in ever-increasing numbers, accept and recruit members of the new young—including veterans of the Indochina war and former drug addicts (whether or not they are veterans)? Will managers be in a position to demonstrate that their organizations are actually serving socially useful functions and measuring up to their environmental responsibilities? Having recruited or attracted some employees whose values characterize the Now Generation, will executives be willing to experiment

[18] See Seymour Martin Lipset and Everett Carll Ladd, Jr., "College Generations—from the 1930's to the 1960's," *The Public Interest,* no. 25, pp. 99-113, Fall, 1971. Quotation on p. 113.

with a relatively wide decentralization of authority? Will they give young managers more freedom and responsibility than has been permitted under traditional systems of management? Will they offer to every employee opportunities to exercise a degree of creativity and control in his everyday work that can stimulate inner motivation? (See Chapter 6 for more on motivation and productivity.) Certainly the possibility of assimilating, utilizing, and developing members of the Now Generation as responsible members of business and industry will depend in large measure on the imagination and flexibility shown by managers. Personnel administrators should be able to offer ideas and encouragement to executives and managers who are interested in meeting this challenge.

Just as challenging to managers (and to personnel administrators) as the attitudes and behavior of the new young is the accelerating movement to gain equal rights for women. This manifestation of long-held aspirations and deep-seated emotional needs is often dismissed as "that crazy movement, Women's Lib." However, it confronts managers and personnel administrators with difficulties and opportunities similar to those presented by the attitudes of the new young.

THE NEW FEMINISTS[19]

New Feminists base their case primarily on three general principles:

1 *Equal opportunity for all women who want to work.* The constitutional right to equality of op-

portunity has not been enforced in regard to women. A proposed remedy is that an Equal Rights Amendment be written into the Constitution, to read as follows: "Equality of rights under the law shall not be denied or abridged by the United States or by any state on account of sex."[20] Equality on the basis of *race* has been tested and upheld in many courts. But the Supreme Court "has upheld or refused to review state laws and practices making discriminatory distinctions based on sex."

2 *Consideration of individual capabilities and limitations for both sexes.* Feminists deplore discrimination on the basis of any such stereotype as that women are members of the weaker sex. When individuals are considered, it is obvious that some women are physically stronger than some men.

3 *Mutual responsibility and partnership.* If men and women treated one another as equals at work, would it not be more likely (as well as more suitable) for a husband to treat his wife like a partner at home?[21]

No reasonable feminist thinks that these principles could be implemented easily or quickly. But every manager and every personnel administrator would surely wish to consider them.

Brief Historical Background

By 1923, 18 states had laws governing minimum wages for women. But in that year they were declared unconstitutional in a ruling which included the statement that "women of mature age [cannot justifiably] be subjected to restrictions

---

[19] Gerda Lerner in "Women's Rights and American Feminism," *The American Scholar,* vol. 40, no. 2, pp. 235-248, Spring, 1971, defines the following terms: *American feminism* (includes all aspects of women's emancipation, namely, "freedom from oppressive restrictions [biological and societal] imposed by sex"; the *woman's rights movement,* centered on winning legal rights [such as the vote and the right to hold and dispose of property]. The newest and most radical manifestation of feminism is the *women's liberation movement,* which calls for reappraising traditional male and female roles.

[20] See *A Matter of Simple Justice: The Report of the President's Task Force on Women's Rights and Responsibilities,* U.S. Government Printing Office, 1970. The preceding quotation and the next are taken from page 4.

[21] Warren Farrell is optimistic that the Women's Liberation Movement may result in a realistic sharing of male and female roles, whereby women will help to support the family (thus making men more free to look for a job that will be truly satisfying) and be freed from near-total responsibility in bringing up children (thus also giving children and fathers the opportunity to know one another intimately). "The Human Lib Movement," *The New York Times,* I, June 17, 1971, p. 41-C, and II, June 18, 1971, p. 37-M.

upon their liberty of contract which could not be imposed in the case of men under similar circumstances." [22]

However, in 1937, a one-vote shift in the Supreme Court reversed this 1923 decision in a ruling that women's wages should be protected. In 1936, by the Walsh-Healey Act, and again in 1938, by the Fair Labor Standards Act, the same minimum wages and maximum hours were set for male and female employees working on government contracts. However, these laws were often disregarded, and no government agency had power to enforce them.

In 1963, the Equal Pay Act declared it illegal for employers in the private sector to discriminate on the basis of sex in regard to pay. However, when this act was incorporated into the Fair Labor Standards Act, certain exemptions in the latter automatically applied to the former. (One set of exemptions was for executive, administrative, and professional workers.)

State laws limiting hours for working women were enacted slightly later than the first laws concerning women's wages. However, by 1930, 27 states had laws specifying maximum weekly or daily hours for women doing paid work. By 1967, laws limiting hours for working women existed in 46 states, the District of Columbia, and Puerto Rico.

In 1920, Congress set up the present Women's Bureau in the Department of Labor. This new agency has advocated regulation of working conditions for all employees, rather than special protection for female workers.

Title VII   In 1964, on the day when the House was to vote on the Civil Rights Act (which had been planned primarily to protect Negroes) Howard Smith, of Virginia, proposed adding the word "sex" to Title VII—which as previously drafted prohibited discrimination "on the basis of race, color, religion, or national origin." [23] Smith's intention was to defeat the bill by getting it laughed off the floor. However, with strong support from Martha Griffiths and other congresswomen, it was passed.

A controversial point about Title VII concerns the interpretation of the phrase "*bona fide* occupation qualification." This loophole has provided many employers with an excuse not to accept women for certain jobs which, as individuals, they could undoubtedly have performed. But in 1969, the Equal Employment Opportunity Commission (EEOC), reversing a previous decision, declared that prohibiting women from certain occupations (or limiting their working hours) has "ceased to be relevant to our technology or the expanding role of the female worker in our economy . . . and [state] laws will not be considered a defense to an otherwise unlawful employment practice. . . ." [24] Although the EEOC has no enforcement powers, it can conciliate when it receives complaints and also make its influence felt by filing *amicus curiae* briefs in court.

Major Handicaps to Equal Rights for Women

Lack of Enforcement   Equal rights for women are not yet enforceable on states. Although an Equal Rights Amendment to the United States Constitution had periodically been proposed since 1923, it achieved final passage by the Senate only in March, 1972. The vote was 84 to 8. However, to become effective, the amendment must first be ratified by 38 states. In many states, laws set up to protect women (for instance in

[22] Raymond Munts and David C. Rice, "Women Workers: Protection or Equality?" *Industrial and Labor Relations Review,* vol. 24, no. 1, p. 4, Oct., 1970.

[23] The new amendment made Title VII applicable to 21 million white women who did not receive even as much pay as Negro men. At that time, the median income of a white male, working full time, was $6,497; for Negro males, $4,285; for white females, $3,859, and for Negro females, $2,674. Caroline Bird with Sara Welles Briller, *Born Female: The High Cost of Keeping Women Down,* David McKay Company, Inc., New York, 1968, p. 3.

[24] Fed. Reg., p. 11,367 (1969).

relation to jobs considered hazardous, heavy, or requiring night work) have been used to discriminate against them.

Prejudice and Stereotypes   One of the greatest barriers to full equality for women is set up by deeply entrenched attitudes. This "Invisible Bar" (as Bird calls it) is powerful and generally accepted. It has often blocked women from paid employment and from salaries and titles that go with the work they do. Reasons given for rejecting women applicants have included the following: Women are "really" less productive than men, and less reliable. They are more likely than men to be tardy, or absent without notice, or to quit. [25]

Prejudice also keeps women out of jobs that require work with complex machinery, from union and managerial positions that require bargaining, and from high-level political positions. [26] One stereotype that is hard to eliminate is that women make poor supervisors. The gap between earnings by men and women doing similar work has often been explained by the stereotype that women are less capable. And this gap widens in the higher job brackets. [27] The fact that a few women have made it all the way to the top certainly shows that some females have the necessary capabilities. But, too often, prejudice has prevented women from showing what they can do.

Attitudes on the part of some female employees have helped to build up prejudice. Supervisors have found that a few women (like some Negroes) need special handling; for example, with constant praise and encouragement (to help them overcome feelings of inadequacy). Other women have taken advantage of their sex to be tardy, lazy, or absent without excuse. Another kind of prejudice is created by women who exploit their sexual attractiveness to obtain favors and special privileges that should not be given to any employee.

Finally, a backlash against the movement toward full equality of opportunity for women has been created by the exaggerated demands and strident tones of militant women—and still more by militant splinter groups like "the Proud Eagles Tribe," who have claimed credit for senseless acts of vandalism.

Lack of Union Protection   One factor that has unquestionably militated against equal treatment for women at work is lack of union protection (although there have been exceptions to this general rule; e.g., The Amalgamated Clothing Workers).

The Special Situation of Two-career Families A woman who is interested in a career comes up against difficulties that do not exist for men. For one thing, she must work harder than a man (and usually for more years) before she can win acceptance for a top position. But by that time she is nearer to retirement and therefore less acceptable on that account alone. Moreover, if a young woman wants to prepare herself for a career but thinks she may also wish to marry, what is she to do? Many vocational counselors urge girls to limit themselves to teaching, nursing, and secretarial work. If a husband is transferred from one

[25] Little scientific work has been done on differences in productivity between men and women. And there is evidence that—on the same low-rated, monotonous jobs—tardiness, absence, and turnover are higher for men than for women (Bird, *op. cit.* p. 85). See also Jean A. Wells, "Facts about Women's Absenteeism and Labor Turnover," U.S. Department of Labor, Wage and Labor Standards Administration, U.S. Women's Bureau, August, 1969. This report shows that with reference to such factors as absenteeism, labor turnover, job tenure, and labor mobility, comparative cost differentials are insignificant. The favorable findings for women workers emphasize the importance of judging work performance on individual achievement rather than on sex.

[26] The National Women's Political Caucus, founded in 1971, has been working to place women in high political positions, and it may even present its own presidential candidate in 1976.

[27] See "Fact Sheet on the Earnings Gap," U.S. Department of Labor, Wage and Labor Standards Administration, Women's Bureau, February, 1972.

part of the country to another, or even overseas, such skills are certain to be in demand.

However, many college-educated women are as ambitious as their male contemporaries to have careers in which they can develop and use their full potential. Formerly this aspiration was likely to mean foregoing marriage. But feminists (male and female) are greatly interested in a recent development of our changing times. A personnel manager for Standard Oil (New Jersey) has called it "the package deal."[28] The package consists of a recently married couple, both highly qualified and both aiming for executive positions. The Ford Motor Company has been recruiting such couples since 1969, and a few other organizations have successfully followed this lead. From an organizational viewpoint, advantages of this arrangement include the following: When a firm relocates, there is greater likelihood of retaining both executives; on overseas assignments, it is better economics to employ a husband and wife who are both productive than to send a nonproductive wife along merely for social reasons.

This new development for career women may serve as a link between circumstances listed as obstacles and those that have unquestionably favored the cause of equal rights for women.

Favoring Factors

Tight Labor Markets Scarcity of labor, such as was experienced in both World Wars, has caused many employers actively to recruit women (though not for top jobs). Each such opportunity has enabled women to demonstrate their abilities. "Rosie the riveter" may be cited as a familiar example. When each crisis is over, many women have wanted to remain in their jobs and have been encouraged by management representatives to do so.

[28] For details see "Executive Couples," *The New York Times,* Section 3, Oct. 24, 1971.

College-educated Women An increasing number of young women with college education have managed to establish themselves in top-level positions. And each such success encourages other young women to aim for the same goal.

New Jobs and Improved Working Conditions Technological advances have created jobs that do not carry sex labels. Computer programming is one such occupation. For these jobs, women can apply on an equal basis with men. Often their performance has been outstanding (though few women have been promoted to the level of manager). Also, automation has eliminated from many jobs the physical effort and poor working conditions that were formerly an integral part of them. Consequently, protective laws no longer bar women from access to these jobs.

More Flexible Work Schedules Several factors, including the rising cost of fringe benefits, have prompted managers to recruit women for part-time work, either for part of each day or for part of the year.

Presidential Action President Johnson in 1964 announced his intention to appoint 50 women to top posts, thus making the "Federal government a 'showcase' of opportunity"[29] for women as well as for Negroes. In 1967, he ordered that the Civil Service Commission hear complaints of discrimination with regard to Civil Service employees, and that the U.S. Department of Labor investigate complaints of discrimination by federal contractors. The publicity associated with such developments gave rise to a flood of formal complaints. And publicity about such complaints naturally attracted the attention even of managers and personnel administrators in whose organizations no official complaints had been made.

[29] Bird, *op. cit.,* p. 200.

Policy Statement by the AFL-CIO Policy makers in the AFL-CIO have stated their purpose to require managers to raise labor standards high enough so that no special protection for women will be needed. If—or when—this policy is implemented by managerial action and by changes in state laws, it will answer the question raised by Munts and Rice[30] in their subtitle "Equality or Protection?" When adequate protection is extended to every individual, then equality will include protection.

What Remains to Be Done by Managers?

Many managers and personnel administrators agree that the following specific goals are among the most urgent to work toward:

• Develop aptitude and fitness tests for access job even when applicants lack the traditional high school diploma.
• Establish physical and skill tests for women applying for employment on so-called "hazardous" jobs. Such tests will unquestionably show that many women have the necessary qualifications for jobs from which they have been barred.
• Offer opportunities for split shifts and/or part-time work for women who want or need a special work schedule.
• Actively recruit women with professional training for managerial and administrative positions and assist in planning and guiding their career development.
• Eradicate unscientific and sex-based stereotypes that limit placement of women to such supportive roles as secretary, research associate, librarian, and administrative assistant.
• Meet initial difficulties in a managerial assignment by coaching on-the-job instead of indulging in the self-fulfilling prophecy that inability to achieve instant success shows conclusively that women inherently lack the qualities to function as effective managers.

[30] Munts and Rice, *op. cit.*

• Assist married women during the childbearing stage in their family life by providing paid maternity leave without loss of seniority or benefits and, if possible, a given number of days' leave each year—for both parents—to take care of children who are seriously ill.
• Provide adequate child-care facilities (under the Social Security Act, if necessary supplemented at state and local levels of government, with managerial support) so that mothers of preschool children can work. (This change has also been advocated as a significant means of reducing the number of women on welfare.)

These few specific goals may suffice to indicate the range of activities that are required to implement the general principle of full equality for women in the world of work. Managers and personnel administrators who are seriously interested in seeing to it that social innovations keep pace with technological advances will wish to make up their own minds on these matters, as also on questions raised by members of the Now Generation.

THE SCOPE AND PACE OF MODERN CHANGE

All three of the current phenomena mentioned so far in this chapter (the urban crisis, the Now Generation, and the New Feminists) confront managers, personnel administrators, and other citizens of the United States with crucial and unescapable problems. Moreover, all these problems are peculiarly difficult to analyze and cope with because of a characteristic feature of life today: the scope and pace of change.

In an important sense this world of ours is a new world. . . . What is new is new not because it has never been there before, but because it has changed in quality. One thing that is new is the prevalence of newness, the changing scale and scope of change itself, so that the world alters as we walk in it. . . .

To assail the changes that have unmoored us from the past is futile, and in a deep sense, I think it is wicked. We need to recognize the changes and learn what resources we have. [31]

Let us therefore take a look at some of our current resources.

Freedom of Choice In this country, one of our greatest resources has always been a high degree of freedom. For example, managers and employees, members of the Now Generation, and New Feminists are free to choose how they will respond to current opportunities and difficulties—as they perceive them.

Human Resources Will executives, managers, and personnel administrators perceive the new young and the increasing number of educated, able female employees as individuals with special contributions to make? A number of personnel administrators meeting in May, 1971, concluded "that youth today are asking the questions that we have always been afraid to ask, and that every attempt should be made to tap the abilities of these young people who are increasing in number throughout the total work force." This experimental approach can be troublesome at times. But it is essential to the survival of business and industry in an increasingly competitive world. Similarly, if women can demonstrate the worth of their values—especially in their approach to interpersonal relationships—they will be offering a resource that managers cannot afford to disregard.

Technical Resources Current levels of science and technology are resources that make possible many things that were inconceivable even a generation ago. (For details, see the section in this chapter entitled "The Impact of Automation and Computerization," below.)

Systems Thinking This relatively new way of analyzing problems might be classified as a technical resource. But it seems to us sufficiently important to be mentioned separately. It is indispensable as a way of preparing to cope effectively with the complex and interrelated difficulties that confront our society today. The relatively recent and rapidly spreading interest in ecology has introduced many people to the method and significance of exploring part-whole relationships. An executive who takes a broad-gauged and forward-looking systems view seeks to understand key facts, factors, and relationships within and between all the integrally related components of a worldwide whole. Having gotten this far with his mind, an executive is advantageously placed to get farther—impelled by appropriate feelings.

An Emerging Motivation A growing sense of social responsibility may add a new dimension of power. Many businessmen recognize that the urban crisis and the magnitude of hard-core unemployment are at least partly due to things that their predecessors have done—and not done—over the years.

The Manager's Responsibility

As leaders in the world of work and in their communities, many managers have become aware of their obligation to set up work situations in which rank-and-file employees can benefit by changes. Among the new developments that have drastically affected people at work are those associated with automation and computerization. These technological advances have changed the nature of work and eliminated many jobs, as well as creating new occupations and new kinds of work. Indeed our current stage

[31] J. R. Oppenheimer, *The Open Mind,* Simon and Schuster, Inc., New York, 1955, pp. 140-141.

in automation and computerization, early as it is, might well be characterized by Chardin's phrase "a new rung on the ladder involving a change of state."

THE IMPACT OF AUTOMATION AND COMPUTERIZATION

Opinions differ as to whether automation is "good" or "bad" for employees. Some people emphasize the advantages of automation, in providing new jobs and eliminating much heavy physical labor. (As previously noted, these changes have certainly been advantageous for women.) However, many labor leaders are among those who see the consequences of automation as "bad." Some of them are convinced that if automation is carried as far as it can be, a majority of the population will be out of work.

One reason why it is difficult to assess the ultimate effects of automation is that we are still at a relatively early stage of this development. Even today, in a modern city one can see a curious mixture of old and new work methods and equipment being used simultaneously. The following observation, made a number of years ago, could still be made today:

> Men and machines have been constructing the foundations of a small building. After some preliminary skirmishing of men equipped with surveying instruments and sledges for driving pegs, most of the work has been done by various species of mechanical elephant and their mahouts. Two kinds of elephants dug out the earth (one with its forelegs, the other with its trunk) and loaded it in trucks (pack elephants, I suppose). Then, after an interlude during which another group of men carefully fitted some boards into place as forms, a new kind of elephant appeared, its belly full of concrete which it disgorged into the forms. It was assisted by two men with wheelbarrows—plain old-fashioned wheelbarrows—and two or three other men who fussily tamped the poured concrete with metal rods. Twice during this whole period a shovel ap-

peared—on one occasion it was used by a man to remove dirt that had been dropped on a sidewalk; on another occasion it was used to clean a trough down which the concrete slid. [32]

During the next few years (or decades?) of this evolutionary period we shall probably continue to see a juxtaposition of men and machines working together in various ways. And certainly the advance toward greater automation will be uneven, not only on the international scene but also within the United States and even within each business and industry. Interactive variables which will determine the extent and rate of technological advance in a given enterprise include the following:

• The kind of product or service for which the enterprise was established, e.g., making automobiles, selling life insurance policies, or providing health services.
• External forces such as social pressure to supply unskilled jobs or financial pressure from competitors.
• Costs of conversion.
• Size and financial status of the enterprise.
• Local facilities for time-sharing computer use.
• Availability within the enterprise of technically qualified staff.
• Individual differences in the chief executive or top-management group with regard to age, way of managing, and technical orientation.

The combined effect of these interactive variables will become clearer as we consider the distinctive capabilities of men and machines with specific reference to tasks traditionally assigned to top management, middle management, staff experts, and workers at the production level in factories and offices. However, there is already

[32] Herbert A. Simon, "The Corporation: Will It Be Managed by Machines?" in Melvin Anshen and George Leland Bach (eds.), *Management and Corporations, 1985,* McGraw-Hill Book Company, New York, 1960, p. 86 (reprinted in Pigors, Myers, and Malm, *op. cit.,* selection 18).

some evidence that, at least in the short run, the chief executive's attitude may be more powerful than any of the other variables. As one company president put it:

I am 59 years old; in the remaining years of my presidency I cannot expect to become very well acquainted with these new tools. I'm sure they're the coming thing, but I'm not the man to make the best use of them; I've learned business the other way. Maybe the next president of this company should be a much younger man with very different training. But, for the next few years, I'm president. [33]

The Doctrine of Comparative Advantage

In a profit-making enterprise the top-management group must decide whether or where it will pay to substitute a machine for man and systems management for man management. The answer to these questions, of course, will depend not only on the variables just mentioned but also on the existing state of technological advance at the time when the decision is made. However, until both the hardware and the software of computers have advanced beyond the present point (as of 1973), it would not be economically advantageous to use machines for all the tasks now performed in organizations by human beings. Three examples will suffice to illustrate that general statement:

• Field representatives in insurance companies meet certain vital responsibilities which cannot be delegated to existing computers. Distinctively human skills are exercised in face-to-face informal talk with actual and prospective policy holders. Electronic data processing can greatly assist a field representative, e.g., by rapidly providing information about various kinds of coverage, but it cannot (yet) replace him.

[33] John A. Beckett, "The Total-systems Concept: Its Implication for Management," in Charles A. Myers (ed.), *The Impact of Computers on Management*, The MIT Press, Cambridge, Mass., 1967, p. 233.

• A first-level supervisor also has significant advantages over any mechanical device of the present or near future. One such advantage is his capacity to notice not only the *rational* elements of work that he is supervising but also a variety of *nonrational* manifestations in the behavior of individual workers. If he is skilled in projective listening (see Chapter 5) and has some understanding of human motivation (see Chapter 6), his "monitoring" may result in decision making and preventive (or remedial) action that are beyond the scope of totally computerized management (see Chapter 7).

• The chief executive is a third type of (currently) irreplaceable man. (The reasoning behind that statement is developed below in the subsection on top management.)

In each of these categories, and in others as well, economic justification for retaining human beings will be provided by the extent to which each individual develops his full potential as a distinctively human instrument (or subsystem) and devotes these unique capabilities to the advancement of organization-wide goals.

In general, it is probably safe to say that some human beings will be kept on wherever it seems advantageous to employ an "instrument" with the following characteristics:

• It has general-purpose applicability because it is versatile and flexible.

• It is highly mobile.

• It is eminently teachable, even to the extent that it can rapidly reprogram itself, as it learns from experience, by self-education.

• It can be useful in a variety of different situations and under rapidly changing circumstances.

• It is relatively durable and inexpensive per unit (compared to a sophisticated computer).

• It has essential capabilities which are as yet beyond the reach of computers (such as imagination, foresight, and empathy).

However, before going into details about specific skills needed at different organizational levels, it may be worthwhile briefly to consider the capabilities of present-day computers.

Computer Capabilities

In 1962, Shannon pointed out that "computing machines can do anything which can be described in detail with a finite set of instructions. . . . If the human brain is a machine, a computer with access to sufficient memory can, in principle, exactly imitate the human brain."[34] But can the human brain properly be described as a machine? Rosenblith suggested:

> [When] we talk about The Brain, we are certainly overgeneralizing almost as much as when we talk about The Machine. . . . [Evolution has produced an almost incredible variety of brains. They] are multipurpose devices and the intellectual aspects of their activity are not the whole story by any means. Brains are programmed partly by hereditary factors and partly by learning; they are reprogrammed, almost minute by minute, as they are stimulated by the environment. . . . It would seem that the brain disposes of a certain reserve of uncommitted neurons that can be applied wherever and whenever there is a need for information processing. This unusual and only partially understood combination is far from being readily duplicable by our current machines.[35]

However, even in this relatively early stage of computer development, these mechanical brains have demonstrated extraordinary abilities. Among the earliest and most familiar accomplishments of computers have been processing and retrieving information. Their speed, accuracy, and infallible "memories" enable them to outdo man to such an extent that only lack of money makes it advisable for anyone to employ human beings at these tasks today. Computers can also analyze problems. Some experts have said that routine problem solving is the limit of what can be expected from computers. Other experts have asserted that computers can reflect, learn, and, as Simon puts it, handle relatively "ill-structured problems, using humanoid problem-solving techniques. . . . We now can program a computer to evaluate a formula by writing down little more than the formula itself and the instruction: Do. . . . Computers have exercised judgment and exhibited insight."[36]

Scientists who work with computers have noted that the advance of computerization as simulated thinking has been slowed by limited ingenuity of programmers and limited understanding of what human beings do, at best, when they think. Until it becomes possible to identify and analyze everything that happens in a thinking human brain, computers cannot be taught to imitate all the skills exercised by this multipurpose instrument. However, it is agreed that as human thinkers learn more about human thinking, computers can be taught, by heuristic programming, to "think" in more varied, flexible, and sophisticated ways than they can now.

We have already noted another limitation of computers, namely, their inability to detect and respond appropriately to slight differences, say in human speech. Third-generation computers were greatly in advance of the first generation with respect to reading ability; e.g., the first generation could not cope with handwriting translated from a foreign language, but later generations have been designed to do both. However, when it comes to *social literacy*, human beings still leave computers far behind. By "social liter-

---

[34] Claude E. Shannon, in Martin Greenberger (ed.), *Management and the Computer of the Future,* The M.I.T. Press, Cambridge, Mass., and John Wiley & Sons, Inc., New York, 1962, p. 308.

[35] Walter A. Rosenblith, in *ibid.,* pp 320-321.

[36] Herbert A. Simon, in *ibid.,* p. 97. In a similar vein, John Diebold wrote of the *"cybertron,* a computer which does not have to be programmed, in the usual sense of the word, to do a specific task. Rather, it goes through a learning period quite like that of a child. . . . The cybertron will soon be taught to evaluate data from electrocardiograms." *Beyond Automation,* McGraw-Hill Book Company, New York, 1964, p. 41.

acy" we mean reading the signs which indicate human feelings and motivation and communicating in a manner well designed to reach the "inner circuit," which connects directly with what makes a human being tick. (See Chapter 5 for a discussion of the effect of an inner circuit on interpersonal communication.) Until computers have mastered the fine arts of reading and "monitoring" nuances of manner and tone, as well as of observing and responding empathically to nonverbal communication (body language), there will continue to be urgent need for perceptive human beings to bridge the gap between "meaning-for-me" and "meaning-for-him." (See Chapter 5 for an explanation of these terms.)

Other serious charges against present-day computers include the comment that they "follow our instructions too literally and perhaps learn from their experience too little."[37]

Many users of computers have noted their inflexibility. On this charge computers stand convicted by their own record. Even a general-purpose computer cannot equal a man when it comes to being a jack-of-all-trades. Flexibility, sensitivity to small differences, ability to perform unassigned tasks if necessary and continuously to reprogram himself, to work at problem solving not only consciously but also at a subconscious level—all these distinctively human characteristics have yet to be programmed into any computer. Moreover, man has one more priceless advantage over machines: *confronted with a desperate need, he can demonstrate a level of will power which enables him to accomplish the impossible.*

However, competition between men and machines is less profitable to think about than new opportunities for collaboration. These vary according to the tasks to be performed and these tasks in turn differ according to the organizational level at which they are performed and whether performance is by persons, machines, or man-machine systems. In considering the comparative advantages of men and machines and new possibilities for collaboration, let us begin at the top, where there is always plenty of room for making needed changes.

To What Extent Can Top-management Functions Be Computerized?

It has been suggested that the present rate of change requires a new analysis and evaluation of the top-management role. The old familiar list of managerial duties may be rushing toward obsolescence. Even the definitions of what a manager is and what it means to manage may be due for an overhauling.[38] On the other hand, there seems to be general agreement that the advance of information technology makes certain top-management tasks more crucial than ever, e.g., defining corporate goals, making long-range plans, formulating corporate policies (which are attuned to corporate goals and plans); searching out alternatives for action within the policy framework; selecting between possible and relatively desirable alternatives; determining a suitable managerial style; and helping to educate and develop future managers. Briefly considering a few of these distinct but related activities will indicate why few authorities expect computers to take over any of them in the near future and how information technology, even in its present state, can assist and extend management thinking in these areas.

Some of today's challenges for policy decisions geared to corporate goals and plans

---

[37] Claude E. Shannon and Vannevar Bush, in Greenberger, *op. cit.,* p. 310.

[38] For example, the question has been raised: If a manager is defined as one who gets results through people, what about the man who used to manage subordinates but is now assisted only by a computer console? See Donald C. Carroll, "Implications of On-line, Real-time Systems for Managerial Decisionmaking," in Myers, *op. cit.,* pp. 140–173.

were mentioned at the start of this chapter; they include the following:

• Shall we aim, as an ultimate goal, to set up a manless plant? Or have we a social responsibility to provide some relatively unskilled persons with jobs even after technological advances make it unnecessary?

• Shall we drastically change our organization structure, flattening it to match new possibilities of free communication and partnership?

• When it becomes feasible to set up a consolidated data file, should every management representative have access to it so that he can control his own performance? Or shall we use the new technology to centralize decision making and tighten control procedures?

• What is to be the role of middle managers and first-level supervisors?

• How shall we recruit, orient, educate, and reward the "uncommon man" upon whose skills and will to achieve we must depend if we are to remain competitive?

• Do we want to make whatever changes are needed in our attitudes and ways of managing to ensure that all our employees can meet their high-level human needs?

Policy decisions on such questions mesh with long-range planning, which, in this age of rapidly accelerating change, is widely recognized as essential to business success. Diebold has described this essential need as "planning *for change* and its counterpart, planning *necessitated by change.*"[39] He notes that top management's reaction time must be shorter and that successful adjustment within organizations having ever more complex relationships with other organizations requires a high order of planning skill.

Levels of Decision Making In both policy making and long-range, large-scale planning, unstructured (nonprogrammed) decision making is a common denominator. To what extent can such high-level decision making be computer-

ized? On this question, as on so many others where predictions play a part, authorities differ; but there is general agreement that decision making by managers who have mastered the art of systems analysis can be significantly improved by assistance from computers. To see how men and machines can collaborate in high-level decision making (or "problem solving," as it is often called) let us look briefly at what needs to be done.

Characteristics of High-level Decision Making The following are typical requirements:

• Determining whether or not a problem exists in a degree of seriousness and urgency that requires a top-management decision.[40]

• Finding which parts of the environment should be analyzed in searching for a solution.

• Deciding whether the problem actually has been solved after a decision has been made and implemented.

Such intellectual tasks cannot be performed by the algorithmic methods that present-day computers use. They require heuristic methods, applied by managers who "rely on their experience, intuition, and insight." Moreover, executives can learn to identify a potentially serious problem before it has attained significant proportions and tackle it immediately.

Few executives would claim to have all the skill or all the information they need to reach perfect solutions to all their problems. Therefore, machine assistance by real-time time-sharing information systems has looked attractive.[41] Some general computer systems have been constructed by the military, e.g., SAGE and NORAD. These systems permit cooperative problem solving, in

---

[40] In this section we draw on David Klahr and Harold J. Leavitt, "Tasks, Organization Structures, and Computer Programs," in Myers, *op. cit.,* pp. 119–121.

[41] One of the first such systems was developed at MIT in Project MAC (machine-aided cognition or multiple-access

which a human thinker works in a "conversational relationship" with a computer. Moreover, this kind of symbiosis, in which dissimilar organisms live productively together, offers great hope for the future. Significant capabilities of on-line real-time computer systems make available "a current, global data base [and] computational power at the moment of real-time decision...."[42] Of course, the ability of a present-day computer system to "do its best," so to speak, depends entirely on its having been programmed with adequate information and proper instructions. When an adequately prepared computer system is supplemented by a human thinker (or team) with insight and creative imagination, the result exceeds what could be accomplished by man or machine alone. Using heuristic thinking, man can ask "what-would-happen-if" questions. Computers, using the algorithmic method, can come up with the answers in a matter of seconds.

Those who are most optimistic about heuristic programming predict that generalized computer systems of the future will be able to make unstructured decisions. Moreover, as Forrester[43] points out, the distinctions between structured and unstructured decision making are changing fast. Capital investment policy, for example, is perhaps even now within reach of being structured.

Decision making in structured situations is already within the reach of computers. For this reason if technical feasibility alone were considered, the impact of information technology on middle managers might be catastrophic.

Impact of Information Technology on Middle Management

In contrast to the nonprogrammed (and possibly nonprogrammable) decisions made by top executives, many decisions made by members of middle management could easily be made by

computers, following so-called "decision rules." Operational control by computer systems is a reality today, but its installation has been delayed in many enterprises, not only by the doctrine of comparative advantage but also by human and social considerations (as suggested earlier in this chapter).

Top management can tightly control representatives of middle management if it wishes to do so. This can be done by converting to "total systems" control. Then both the number and the freedom of middle (and lower) management representatives can be sharply decreased. Opinions differ as to whether job dilution for management representatives is a welcome or an unwelcome change. Perhaps the difference in opinion results from individual differences. For example,[44] a purchasing agent, credit manager, or controller may say that he welcomes changes which have drastically reduced the number of his subordinates and his scope for independent decision making. Perhaps he is glad to be relieved of the risk and the blame that he incurred when he had to make decisions without adequate information and with nothing to depend on but his own brain and such assistance as he could obtain from colleagues. Certainly he may take pride in being part of a formalized system which works more efficiently than when it depended directly on his own decision-making powers. Other persons, especially those with executive potential, seem more than willing to run such risks as making errors and getting blamed, for the sake of being free to take responsibility and grow on the job. Nevertheless, any manager who is even of medium managerial stature might be glad to be freed by information technology from routine and repetitive duties that typify the "bucket brigade."

Under an authoritarian system of management (by Theory X, or System 2, for example) handling information is the task which has occupied most of the middle manager's time. Muller-

---

[42] *Op. cit.,* p. 164.

[43] Jay W. Forrester, *Industrial Dynamics,* The M.I.T. Press, Cambridge, Mass., 1961, pp. 133–134.

[44] Beckett, *op. cit.,* pp. 222–223.

Thym has estimated that middle managers now spend

> . . . 80% of their time simply handling information and [doing so] in a very primitive and inadequate manner. . . . [Today, some of this information is handled] piecemeal and selectively [by computers. But information systems are still] supplemented by having some middle-manager try to find out what was wrong at a lower level in order to pass the information to his superior, or by managers in a chain trying to force information through many layers to the point where, hopefully, work could be done. This "bucket brigade" approach is extremely inefficient; there is about 50% loss at each transmission.[45]

If the middle manager's role were nothing more than that of an information handler, then that level of "management" could advantageously be computerized. For a chief executive who sees middle managers in that role, the decision is obvious. However, if top management sees a need for imaginative leadership throughout the organization and for a communication chain which links all subsystems together, then neither middle managers nor first-level supervisors will be entirely eliminated, although their numbers have been decreased in many organizations and this trend may grow.

An Accelerating Shift by Line Managers toward Staff Behavior As noted in previous chapters (especially Chapter 2), the boundary separating line and staff has become increasingly indistinct as the emerging style of management proves its worth. Many managers have already accepted the idea that instructions are more suitable than orders (see Chapter 5) for the new class of professional employees, "the uncommon men." Thus, well-educated young managers of today tend to function far more like staff experts than like old-fashioned line managers. They

teach, advise, counsel, and in general provide organizational support to employees in subordinate positions for whose performance they are officially responsible. On the other hand, technical staff people have moved into positions of great prestige and power. Often their advisory relationship to members of top management creates a halo effect which endows their "suggestions" with the character of orders. (The position and behavior of Mr. March, in Case 4, "The Girl and the Computer," in Part 2, illustrate this point.)

What Personnel Functions for Staff Experts?

Aside from purely technical staff duties, will there be any continuing need to meet other staff responsibilities? In our opinion there will. Troubleshooting for human difficulties, both individual and interpersonal, will be needed in the future at least as acutely as in the past, and there will be new reasons, as well as new opportunities, for exercising this skill of personnel administration. One new reason already mentioned is that line managers still have much to learn about working with scientists and engineers in new roles and relationships as well as with the new young and the increasing number of women in positions where they have a considerable degree of authority and responsibility. Similarly, human understanding in troubleshooting will be needed to help workers and union officials adjust to the technological changes which not only alter work assignments but even eliminate whole job classifications (for details, see Chapter 19). If a computer were asked about featherbedding, it would surely answer: It's unjustifiable; cut it out. But experience shows that this is easier said than done. The reasons for stubborn resistance to change must be understood before employees can be helped to overcome them. This needs a socially imaginative mind, one that can see the unreasonable practice of featherbedding through the eyes of a manual worker who needs a job so desperately that he clings to one for

[45] Bernard J. Muller-Thym, "The Real Meaning of Automation," *Management Review*, vol. 52, no. 6, p. 44, June, 1963.

which there is no longer any rational justification. Still another need for understanding has made itself felt in every organization where recruiting among disadvantaged groups, including hard-core unemployed, has brought in employees by whom, and for whom, many kinds of difficult accommodations must be made.

Finally, considerable need for adjusting to changes brought about by automation has already been felt by many rank-and-file workers both in factories and in offices. The specific short-term effects of automation on employees at the work level vary according to the nature and place of work. Let us look first at the factory environment.

Effects of Automation on Factory Employees

Authorities differ about future effects of automation on factory workers, and in any given organization those effects will of course depend on such interactive factors as those listed on page 72. Louis E. Davis predicted that where automated processes are least profitable, jobs will be most plentiful and that in these industries there will be a continued need for the same skills, in many jobs, that have traditionally been required. Davis also gave reasons for thinking that as automation reaches its final stage, men will still work directly with machines.

There is a diversity of opinion about what skills will be needed for what jobs in the future, but technological advances have already greatly changed job requirements for many factory employees.

Changes in Job Content If behavioral psychologists are right, the changes most welcome to many factory workers are those which make for job enrichment. For employees who welcome greater responsibility (and who are not demoted or laid off when their jobs are eliminated), automation has much to offer. Men who work directly with integrated production systems have far greater responsibility than a manual worker

on an old-type machine. Moreover, a monitor who knows the "language or logic" of the new system is in a strategic position to furnish process information needed by engineers and managers. Thus there are many occasions for an exchange of views between blue-collar workers, professionals, and management representatives. "In general, . . . indications are that effectiveness of performance . . . appears to increase as skills, job knowledge, and responsibilities of the job holder are enlarged. [Under these conditions workers seem to respond] in a positive manner to many problems and issues of concern to management."[46]

However, other observers have found that even job enrichment is not welcomed by every machine operator, especially if his previous experience has preconditioned him to expect his job to make relatively slight mental demands on him. Mixed feelings have been evoked from employees by the shift to an automatic production line, where one worker stationed at a control console monitors a number of machines. In other words, whether a change is "good" or "bad" depends on how people feel about it. A personnel-minded manager knows that each employee's feelings must be understood before they can be coped with intelligently. The following comments, in a seamless-pipe mill which was automated over a period of 4 years, may serve to illustrate a range of feelings.[47] The first three comments were made in interviews during "the breaking-in period."

Reason I'm glad about new job is that there is much less physical work than plugging the hi-mill—my old job.

I'd rather have to work hard for eight hours than do nothing physical but have to be tense for eight hours, the way I do now.

[46] Louis E. Davis, "The Effects of Automation on Job Design," *Industrial Relations,* vol. 2, no. 1, p. 63, October, 1962.
[47] Charles R. Walker, *Toward the Automated Factory: A Case Study of Men and Machines,* Yale University Press, New Haven, Conn., 1957.

For a month I was ready to give up. I came home nervous and couldn't sleep. But I'm glad I stayed. I'll *lick it* yet.

During the third round of interviews (3 years later) when the "mill was rolling," most of the men expressed satisfaction. For example:

All in all we are in the swing of things. We have everything timed better . . . and we don't get scared and jumpy like we did at the beginning.

From a money point of view and from a point of view of gaining a lot of experience making the product, I think I have gained in coming to Number 4.

Effects of Automation on Office Workers

While many machine operators in factories have been coming up in the world, many employees in offices have been going down, especially in status and in job content. Many of the features that traditionally set office workers apart from factory workers have been altered by electronic data processing. Here are a few of the interrelated variables that have changed.

Office workers in factories, being relatively few in number compared to production workers, came to regard themselves, and to be regarded, as an office elite. Proximity to the boss was also an important status symbol. But the changing nature of work has, perhaps only temporarily, brought a greatly increased demand for clerical workers. Nowadays, in many offices the enlarged clerical staff sits at long rows of desks, an arrangement similar to work stations in a factory. And clerical production is often controlled by a factorylike work-flow system. Quotas have frequently been introduced, but in most offices no incentive pay is offered for superior performance. Instead, the "incentive" offered to an efficient clerk who has finished her quota may be another batch of work, taken from the quota of some girl who has been falling behind.[48]

[48] For an illustration of this way of rewarding job excellence, see the case "Meeting a Deadline," in Paul Pigors and Faith Pigors, *Case Studies for Management Development, Series III: White Collar Cases.* The Bureau of National Affairs, Inc., Washington, D.C., 1965.

Job Dilution: A New Relation between Clerk and Machine   Electronic data processing has also changed the relationship between clerks and machines. A typist has always been a machine operator, but a typewriter is an adjunct to a typist. When keypunch machines are used to prepare inputs for a computer, it is the other way around. Keypunch operators serve the computer. That kind of service makes special demands, two of which are the ability to endure highly repetitive work and to perform it accurately. (For a case illustrating these difficulties and others associated with a shift from varied office work to preparing data sheets, see Case 4, "The Girl and the Computer.") In a number of offices, the meaning to job holders of such a change in job content has been communicated to managers when complaints, requests for transfer, and even quits have followed what amounts to downgrading.

For a manager who wants to help employees to adapt to new job requirements, time can be used to advantage. A considerable lag is likely to exist between making plans for technological changes and necessary preparations for changeover. This time can be used to advantage in discussing with everyone concerned what can be done, in transferring or retraining some employees, and in cushioning the shock for those whose retirement will be hastened.

British investigators of computer installations in offices arrive at similar conclusions. As well stated in a summary of two extensive case studies:[49]

Introducing a computer is not merely a simple change from one system of work to another. It is something much more fundamental and far reaching, which can affect the structure of a firm, the organization of departments, the nature of work and the attitudes and behaviour of employees. . . . Office automation has quite different implications for different individuals and groups within a firm and in consequence, people will react to it in differ-

[49] Enid Mumford and Olive Banks, *The Computer and the Clerk,* Rutledge and Kegan Paul, Ltd., London, 1967, pp. 16-17.

ent ways according to their own particular needs, values, and interests. . . . [Consequently] the introduction of any major technical change must involve the formulation of policies and strategies which are based on a careful preliminary analysis of all the variables operating in the change situation . . . [including] organisational and human relations factors.

What Lies Ahead?

At the present stage of information technology we are too low on the ladder to have much perspective on what lies before us. But as long as information technology continues to advance and win corporate acceptance, it will certainly affect organization structure.

A New Corporate Design?   Evidence already at hand clearly shows that organization structure will be changed. "Computer technology contains or implies an organization logic incompatible with [traditional organization structure]."[50] A top-management decision to capitalize fully on computer capabilities requires changes in organization structure and ways of doing managerial work. At first, these changes may seem to be relatively modest, consisting chiefly in the relationship between electronic data processing and other departments. However, with the development of integrated data processing, top executives must adopt a complete systems approach and rethink all of their business procedures. Forrester has pointed out that industries which experience the impact of rapid change in science and technology will need to develop a new corporate design. Among the changes he predicted are:

> Elimination of the superior-subordinate relationship.
> Individual profit centers (with individuals or

small work teams set up as decision points responsible for the activities in which the center chooses to engage).

A radial or star-shaped organization with information files at the center, and "on-line" use of computers for both data processing and internal communication [to] provide an information picture that is up to date and fully processed at all times. . . . With such a restructured system, information will be directly accessible to persons who now must operate with too little information either to permit good management or to establish a feeling of security and confidence.[51]

In predicting that these changes will actually be made in some organizations, Forrester admitted that he might be seeing what he hoped to see. But he pointed out that data processing, instead of being incompatible with greater freedom of the individual, actually facilitates it because "the data base can define the rules of the game," permitting each organizational member to know exactly where he stands and where he can go.

Change Agents and Enablers of Change
During the process of accelerating technological change that lies ahead, considerable help will certainly be needed by many organizational members who have difficulty in adapting to organizational changes. At best, much of this help can be given by top management in policy thinking about the organization as a total social system. Forrester explained why he believes that the broadest type of engineering mind is well suited to a task that requires systems thinking of this kind.

> The engineer could become a change agent to precipitate improvements in our social systems. [To do so he would need to broaden and generalize his underlying engineering approaches to design. He would try to clarify the enduring goals and objectives for his organization and the people within it. He would explore new ways of interrelating the

---

[50] George E. Delehanty, "Computers and the Organization Structure in Life-insurance Firms: The External and Internal Economic Environment," in Myers, *op. cit.,* p. 78. See also the research reported by Thomas L. Whisler, "The Impact of Information Technology on Organizational Control," in *ibid.,* pp. 16-49.

[51] Jay W. Forrester, "A New Corporate Design," *Industrial Management Review,* vol. 7, no. 1, pp. 5-18, Fall, 1965.

people, organizations, and information channels within the system.] He would give more attention to the surrounding social system as a whole rather than as an array of isolated parts. He would come to understand why the system operates as it does, rather than merely lamenting that behavior, and then move on to determine a revised basis for internal control. He would consider the transient and steady-state behavior of his organization from the same system viewpoint that he approaches complex physical systems. He would strive to perfect models of social processes that permit simulation studies leading to a better understanding of organization, information links, and policy. And he would bring to actual human organizations the courage to experiment with promising new approaches based on a foundation of design. [52]

Following through on such policy thinking by a top executive, management representatives (including staff members from the personnel department) could work with individuals as enablers of change. [53] Much of this work would be preventive and educational. Its aim would be to help individuals direct their attention away from the question: What is this change going to do *to me?* and toward the question: What might this change do *for us?* [54] In trying to help a middle manager, for instance, to overcome his resistance to a drastic change like conversion to operations control tested means include consulting him before the decision has been made final, inviting him to cooperate in designing the system, and seeing to it that the control system (1) does not rob him of freedom to make decisions, (2) does enable his suborganization to do a better job than before, partly by improvements in communication and coordination, and (3) helps him to

achieve a systems-minded view of major objectives for the organization as a whole.

Greater Freedom to Participate? As we advance along the new road of automation and computerization, will many managers see and respond to the social implications of the new technology to the point where they could agree that "our task is wisely to use our technology, our knowledge of history, and our compassion to make the age of automation a golden Periclean age in which a society based on the work of the machine—not of human chattels—rises to the full heights of which the human spirit is capable"? [55]

Will innovative practices, to implement new policy decisions, be put to work on a scale and at a pace which can turn the tide before our major cities are overwhelmed by civil disturbances, the Now Generation becomes even more alienated than at present, and the New Feminists—goaded by what they consider to be sexist discrimination—are impelled to resort to extremist behavior?

As we look back to the years we are living through, shall we be able to see—on the international as well as the domestic scene—that technological advances were used by mankind in turning away from conflict and toward cooperation? On the world scene, as in our own country, racism and poverty, bitterness and resentment between haves and have-nots are real and present dangers to peace. Yet, internationally, as well as nationally, technological innovations, systems thinking, mutual understanding, and compassion are among the great resources for dealing creatively with differences and with change. A long-range aim toward which business and industrial leaders can work with scientists and other world citizens has been well stated by a world-famous biophysicist: "The new technological abilities make the old Adam a new man; they call for transformation of his traditional competing societies into a single world-wide

[52] Jay W. Forrester, "Common Foundations Underlying Engineering and Management," *IEEE Spectrum,* vol. 1, no. 9, p. 77, September, 1964.

[53] For more on the role of change agents, see Warren G. Bennis, *Changing Organizations,* McGraw-Hill Book Company, New York, 1966.

[54] Adapted from Glenn Gilman, "The Computer Revisited," *Business Horizons,* vol. 9, no. 4, pp. 77–89, Winter, 1966.

[55] Diebold, *op. cit.,* p. 13.

community as the only alternative to mutual destruction.[56]

SUMMARY

This chapter can be briefly summed up by glancing at the major issues which have been considered.

1 *The urban crisis* (in employment, housing, education, race relations, and finances) can be resolved only by effective systems thinking, and by abandoning racism—both black and white. Will managers make the most of their opportunities to reverse the drift "toward two societies, one white one black—separate and unequal?"[57] Will managers develop innovative and practical procedures that enable them to do their share in providing employment and education even to those previously classified as "the hard-core un-

2 A *"new breed"* of *employee,* some of them presenting various aspects of an alternative society, has presented leaders in business and industry with new challenges. Will executives be willing to experiment with the wide decentralization of authority that alone will satisfy those who aspire to fulfill their lives while also making a living? Will managers and supervisors have the imagination and patience to do more than their share, if necessary, to bridge the gap that has separated so many of the Now Generation from the over-thirties?

3 *An accelerating thrust toward equal rights for women* who work—and also for those who want to work, but have not been able to—can either be dismissed as that "nonsense about women's

lib" or accepted as a new means to move toward full utilization of a hitherto largely untapped resource. Will managers, assisted by their personnel administrators, show interest in letting women demonstrate what they can contribute—not only in technical and administrative work but also in ideas and values that are characteristically feminine?

4 *Automation and computerization* have already brought many changes both for managers and for rank-and-file employees. Will executives take full advantage of technological advances—for example, by adapting the traditional corporate structure, and by using technological information as one means to achieve greater participation from all employees, each of whom can become a center of power and of information? Or will technological advances be used for strictly authoritarian ends?

Answers to such questions will be decisive in determining what lies ahead. It is too early now (as of course it always is) to predict the future with any degree of certainty. But this much can be said: Executives, managers, staff experts (including personnel administrators), and supervisors, as well as rank-and-file employees, can play an important part in making the most of new opportunities—those that now exist and those that are yet to come. Will top executives use their new freedom from structured decision making to devote most of their time to innovative long-range planning and policy making? Will members of middle management, freed from the duties of the "bucket brigade," develop their uniquely human capabilities for unstructured decision making and for perceptive personnel administration? Will employees at low organizational levels welcome and make good use of opportunities for job enrichment and for new relationships with employees at higher organizational levels? Will all employees work together to reduce to a minimum the human difficulties entailed in adjusting to a continuing process of technological change? Will they welcome into the world of work large numbers of

[56] Eugene Rabinowitch, *The Dawn of a New Age: Reflections on Science and Human Affairs,* The University of Chicago Press, Chicago, 1963, p. 114.

[57] *Report of the President's Advisory Committee on Civil Disorders,* p. 1. Commission members have been criticized for taking an overly pessimistic view of current history. However, their report (part III, pp. 283–483) includes detailed recommendations for reversing recent trends; and they proposed (p. 413), as a major goal in our time, creating "a single society and a single American identity."

persons whose lack of education (among other handicaps) has caused them to be labeled and treated as unemployable?

By the year 2000 (or before) many of these questions will have been answered. In the meantime, if the answers are to be as technically efficient and humanly satisfying as they might be, employees in all organizations and individuals in every community and throughout the world will need to learn all they can about communicating with one another. To initiate and maintain a true dialogue is very different from merely talking to—or at—another person. The kind of attentive, "projective" response required when another person talks is a long way from the relatively inattentive and passive state so often referred to as "listening." What interpersonal communication can be, and what it can do, are the central themes of the next chapter.

SELECTED REFERENCES

The Urban Crisis

Bennett, Lerone, Jr.: *Confrontation: Black and White,* Johnson Publishing Company, Chicago, 1968.

Birch, David L.: *The Businessman and the City: An Analysis of the Business and Urban Affairs Conference, Sponsored by the Harvard Business School Association, Washington, D.C., May 1966,* Harvard Business School, Division of Research, Boston, 1967.

Chamberlain, Neil W. (ed.): *Business and the Cities,* Basic Books, Inc., New York, 1970.

Janger, Allen R., and Ruth G. Shaeffer: *Managing Programs to Employ the Disadvantaged,* Studies in Personnel Policy no. 219, National Industrial Conference Board, Inc., New York, 1970.

King, Martin Luther, Jr.: *Where Do We Go from Here: Chaos or Community?* Harper & Row, Publishers, Incorporated, New York, 1967 (also Bantam Books, Inc., 1968).

Ross, Arthur, and Herbert Hill (eds.): *Employment, Race, and Poverty,* Harcourt, Brace & World, Inc., New York, 1967.

The Now Generation

Hersey, John: *Letter to the Alumni,* Alfred J. Knopf, Inc., New York, 1970.

Keniston, Kenneth: *Youth and Dissent: The Rise of a New Opposition,* Harcourt, Brace & Jovanovich, Inc., New York, 1971.

Kerr, Clark, Chairman, The Carnegie Commission on Higher Education: *Dissent and Disruption: Proposals for Consideration by the Campus,* McGraw-Hill Book Company, New York, 1971.

Lipset, Seymour Martin: *American Student Activism in Comparative Perspective,* Seminar on Manpower Policy and Program, U.S. Department of Labor, Manpower Administration, January, 1969.

Slater, Philip E.: *The Pursuit of Loneliness: American Culture at the Breaking Point,* Beacon Press, 1970.

The New Feminists

A Matter of Simple Justice: The Report of the President's Task Force on Women's Rights and Responsibilities, U.S. Government Printing Office, 1970.

Bird, Caroline, with Sara Welles Briller: *Born Female: The High Cost of Keeping Women Down,* David McKay Company, Inc., New York, 1968.

Fogarty, Michael P., Rhona Rapoport, and Robert Rapoport: *Women and Top Jobs: An Interim Report,* A PEP Report, London, 1967.

Orth, Charles D. III, and Frederic Jacobs: "Women in Management," *Harvard Business Review,* vol. 49, no. 4, pp. 139-147, July-August, 1971.

The Impact of Automation and Computerization

Gooding, Judson: "Blue-collar Blues on the Assembly Line," *Fortune,* vol. 82, no. 1, pp. 69-71ff., July, 1970 (reprinted in Pigors, Myers, and Malm, *op. cit.,* selection 19).

Mumford, Enid, and Olive Banks: *The Computer and the Clerk,* Routledge and Kegan Paul, Ltd., London, 1967.

Myers, Charles A. (ed.): *The Impact of Computers on Management,* The M.I.T. Press, 1967.

Technology and the American Economy: Report of the National Commission on Technology, Automation, and Economic Progress, vol. 1, U.S. Government Printing Office, 1966.

The Individual in the Organization

INTRODUCTION

Organizational success depends on having a system which partly predetermines individual behavior. However, no system can ensure that every member in the system *will* do all that he *could do* in working toward organizational objectives. What can be done is to establish a climate such that communication between supervisory and nonsupervisory employees helps to stimulate and guide inner motivation instead of repressing it. The first-level supervisor can be an important communication link if he is selected and helped to develop as a representative of management. When building cooperative relationships is an organizational aim, management representatives can talk reasonably and deal fairly with union representatives.

Chapter 5 is concerned with communicating as a managerial responsibility. Questions considered include the following: key differences between a mechanical communications system and an interpersonal communication system; effects of the "inner circuit" as shown by consequences of individual interpretation; reasons why traditional ways of managing inevitably restrict interpersonal communication; listening as a major responsibility of every manager and supervisor; and advantages of a policy-shaping process to implement aims of participative management.

In Chapter 6, the center of interest is the intermeshing of inner motivation, individual goals, and teamwork. Findings from behavioral science help to explain why so many employees, by withholding what they could give, greatly limit what can be accomplished by the organization as a whole while depriving themselves of enduring human satisfactions. Following leads offered by behavioral scientists or acting on their own intuition, many managers have learned much about helping other employees to meet high-level human needs on the job—e.g., needs for responsibility and the opportunity to grow—while working in team relations toward shared organizational aims.

Chapter 7 raises critical issues that arise at the point where management has direct and daily contact with employees at the production level. The role and function of first-level supervisors have changed rapidly and radically since the days when the old-line foreman was an undisputed boss. In many organizations today first-level supervisors do not know precisely what their status is, what degree of authority they have, to what activities they are supposed to give priority during the working day, and what their relationship is with the many staff experts who not only offer advice but also exercise various kinds and degrees of control over employee performance. In recent years, some top executives have asked themselves: What organizational changes need to be made so that the first-level supervisor can do a better job in helping us to meet organizational goals? This question has led, in a few enterprises, to job enrichment of a nature such that the incumbent becomes a first-level manager.

In Chapter 8 we consider employees and labor organizations. Not all employees are union members, but many of them are, especially in certain industries. Through collective action, these employees challenge the unilateral right of management to act in ways they regard as inimical to their interests. By collective bargaining, unions win provisions in labor agreements which affect conditions of work, working rules, and even procedures which were formerly at the sole discretion of managers. The patterns of union-management relations which evolve, whether of "armed truce" or "working harmony," greatly affect the role of the individual employee within the two organizations, the company and the union. In recent years, direct action by unionized members of certain professional groups and by government employees has raised new questions with regard to union policies and the public interest.

CASES IN PART 2 THAT RELATE TO SECTION B

1 The Old-line Foreman
2 Who Owns the Improved Tool?
3 Dissatisfactions of an Expatriate Engineer
5 Managing Highly Motivated Secretaries
6 Conflict of Interest?
11 Will More Money Be a Motivator?
19 Fear? Or Featherbedding?

Chapter 5

Interpersonal Communication

Without the means, the capacity and the will to communicate, what we know as business, government, and community activities could not be. [But it is not enough for] people to talk to others. . . . They need to know how to talk with *others, too.*

Irving J. Lee[1]

Talking *with* managers in "communication forums" supplies evidence that many managers think of communication merely as *information flow* in which complete understanding by receivers can be taken for granted. Here are some frequently raised questions. The first set reveals preoccupation with techniques of information transmission.

1 It's my impression that most of our [communications] problems are in mass communication; for instance, when a plant manager has to communicate to a thousand employees. What's the best way to do it?

2 What is the best form of communication—the most accurate? Written, or verbal, or by pictures?

3 Suppose you have an explanation to make, a one-shot deal—let's say a new salary program. How do you get the same message to every employee?

The next set of questions reveals an uncomfortable awareness that communication blocks often prevent managers from getting their message across.

1 I think in our organization and in others, the big question is: How do you influence attitudes? There's a contest going on for employee loyalty. How does management win?

---

[1] Adapted from Irving J. Lee, *How to Talk with People,* Harper & Row, Publishers, Incorporated, New York, 1952, pp. ix and xi.

2 How do you know when you've got complete understanding from the lowest worker? Is there a way to check how much of the communication is being absorbed by an insensitive, pigheaded employee?

3 How can we get subordinates to report their problems up the line?

Still a different focus of attention is revealed in another set of questions, of which only the second shows a genuinely responsive concern for others.

1 How can we increase our efficiency as listeners, as *receivers* of communications from other people? What blocks to receiving can be avoided, and what techniques can we use to improve our comprehension?

2 How do you prepare a supervisor for bad news? For instance, that one of his subordinates will become his boss.

Such questions indicate a range of attitudes and assumptions about a manager's responsibilities in the communication process. To point up those differences and to indicate the major sections of this chapter, we here introduce further questions of our own.

1 What can be learned by thinking about the basic differences between electromechanical systems of communication and control and the process of psychological communication?

2 When the appropriate response from a receiver depends on shared meaning, what subjective factors interfere with external control?

3 What are some of the consequences for administrative communication of such different ways of managing as the authoritarian and participative systems?

4 How might a chief executive talk *with* organizational members about policies in a way that fosters mutual understanding and acceptance?

It would be presumptuous to offer definite answers to all these questions. But it may be useful to cite research findings and clinical experience on this general subject. We start by inviting comparison of the two communication systems. In an electromechanical network, *all components are things.* Almost perfect control is attainable. In a psychological system, *human beings function as essential components.* Control is at best imperfect and cannot be exercised mechanically.

THE ENGINEERING APPROACH TO COMMUNICATIONS SYSTEMS

In the world of science and technology, communication engineers properly limit their concern to fidelity of reproduction in transmitting signals that carry information. They need not consider semantics. In exercising control, engineers have two great operational advantages: (1) the signals they transmit consist of factual (usually numerical "bits" of data), and (2) the components of the system—reciprocal senders and receivers "transceivers"—are specially designed by them for the communications task assigned to them.

Development of technological communications systems[2] has transformed the world of today into a global village—in the sense that messages can be transmitted through space in a matter of seconds. The NASA manned space program was made possible because signals could be sent and received with perfect fidelity between men on earth and men on the moon. Furthermore, by means of tracking stations and communication satellites, televised pictures of epoch-making events can be transmitted to every part of the globe.

[2] For detailed information on such systems, the interested reader should consult such original source material as Claude E. Shannon and Warren Weaver, *The Mathematical Theory of Communication,* The University of Illinois Press, Urbana, Ill., 1949; Norbert Wiener, *Cybernetics: Or Control and Communication in the Animal and the Machine,* The M.I.T. Press, Cambridge, Mass., 1948; and Richard A. Johnson, Fremont E. Kast, and James E. Rosenzweig, *The Theory and Management of Systems,* McGraw-Hill Book Company, New York, 1967.

How is it then, that when trying to communicate (talk *with* someone) in the same room, barriers to effective communication have often proved insurmountable?

FEATURES OF A PSYCHOLOGICAL COMMUNICATIONS SYSTEM

Although communications technology has enabled man to eliminate the handicaps imposed by distance and establish communication links throughout space, complications arise when human beings themselves function as essential components of an interpersonal communications system.

Consequences of Individual Differences in Human "Transceivers"

Many difficulties for communication with employees follow from the fact that no two people are alike. An appropriate time and an intelligible way for communicating with one individual may be untimely and unintelligible for someone else. Similarly, experience with persons whose motivation is at a low ebb may seem to indicate that everyone can be manipulated, but attempting to manipulate a highly motivated individual in this way may have unplanned and unpleasant results. Case 4, "The Girl and the Computer," in Part 2, furnishes a good example.

Unpredictability in Person-to-person Communication

In addition to the fact that every human sender-transmitter is unique, there are at least two other reasons why it is impossible to predict precisely how another person will "encode" or "decode" the signals he sends and receives: (1) any human being may at any time take independent and inner-directed action, and (2) some of the forces which affect person-to-person communication are not wholly within the control of either a sender or a receiver.

Preconditioning factors The activity of human transmitters and receivers is influenced by such powerful forces as cultural heritage, social environment, and previous experience. For instance, when a member of middle management receives a directive which is to be "recoded" for transmission to other organizational members, *what he makes of it,* both in decoding and in recoding, depends in part on preconditioning factors in him. When the recoded message enters the minds of his associates and/or subordinates (if it does), preconditioning forces within those human subsystems determine how each one decodes the message and how *each receiver responds to his own perception* of what he receives.

The Nature of Meaning Prevents External Control Unlike communications engineers, human senders and receivers are concerned not only with physical reception of information inputs but even more with the *meaning* of what is *taken in.* Meaning is not the same for everyone, nor is it stable. Instead it is unique in each mind and always changing. Subtle changes in meaning occur whenever a message is received into any person's mind. Furthermore, cumulative experience gradually alters the context within which each person interprets his impressions. Hayakawa has put these ideas succinctly: "The meanings of words are not *in* the words. They are in *us.* . . . [And] no word ever has exactly the same meaning twice."[3]

Anyone who reflects on his own experience as a sender-transmitter and as a receiver is in a position to realize that such statements are not farfetched. The multiplicity and mutability of meaning ("message content") derive from the fact that when working toward meaning, a person works in several interlinking contexts. In addition to the preconditioning factors already

[3] S. I. Hayakawa, *Language in Thought and Action,* Harcourt, Brace & World, Inc., New York, 1949, pp. 60 and 292. This excellent book should be read by everyone interested in communication skills.

mentioned, the unique meaning for anyone who receives a verbal message (or perceives an event) is inevitably influenced by ideas, feelings, and purposes that are currently affecting him.[4]

Elements of Meaning

Meaning as a whole may therefore be analyzed as having three components, a rational element, a feeling element, and an element of volition. The *rational* element of meaning-for-me consists in "my" acceptance of words in their dictionary (or other objectively determined) sense or in my use of reason to interpret the significance of an event. But meaning-as-a-whole is often determined more by the interplay of *current feelings and purposes* as a message is processed within a receiver's unique personality. Meaning-as-sent is thus inevitably altered during the reception phase, which takes place beyond the reach of the sender. At this state of the communication process, intended *input* is inevitably modified by *actual* intake. Another change occurs when intake is converted into *meaning-as-perceived* by means of an internal data processing system.

Sometimes a preconditioning factor—e.g., a difficult personal relationship or previous experiences which have resulted in a strong prejudice—can affect a receiver's interpretation to the point where the sender's message is perceived as having a meaning almost opposite to what was intended.

Every manager, supervisor, and other employee has doubtless experienced some such miscarriage of meaning. For example, a first-level supervisor may "read between the lines" of a written communication from an organizational superior. Human nature being what it is, the supervisor is likely to construe the message in the light of what he expects (hopes or fears) to find there. Similarly, a production worker may unconsciously (or sometimes deliberately) twist the meaning of what his supervisor says. Such a distortion of intended meaning is especially likely to occur if the past experience of *this* worker has taught him to distrust *that* supervisor.

Even rough measurements of differences between "message content" as sent and as received would show conclusively that deviations from predetermined plans are so great that if the system were mechanical, it would be called out of control.

The Inner Circuit: An Individual Data Processing Device

Perhaps the inevitable difference between the meaning-as-sent of any message and its meaning-as-received can be clarified by a diagram like Figure 5-1, which points up operative differences between a mechanical communications system and a person-to-person communications system.

WHAT CONTROLS CAN BE EXERCISED BY HUMAN SENDER-TRANSMITTERS?

Organizational communication cannot always be timed or tuned for maximum receptivity by individual receivers. But often it can be. A considerable degree of control can be exercised by a sender who responds perceptively to subjective forces currently at work in a receiver. Such controls can be used most easily and effectively when "signals" are exchanged between two individuals, or in a small group, during face-to-face "informal" talk. When individuals are trying to talk *with* one another, and not merely *at* one another, something that approximates an efficient control system can be applied. A human sender-transmitter can use his own sensitivity and perceptivity as a combined "sensor" and control unit. Partly by interpreting body lan-

---

[4] For an illuminating development of this basic idea, see Carl R. Rogers, *Client Centered Therapy: Its Current Practice, Implications and Theory,* Houghton Mifflin Company, Boston, 1951, especially chap. 11, "A Theory of Personality and Behavior," pp. 481–533. See also his *On Becoming a Person: A Therapist's View of Psychotherapy,* Houghton Mifflin Company, Boston, 1961.

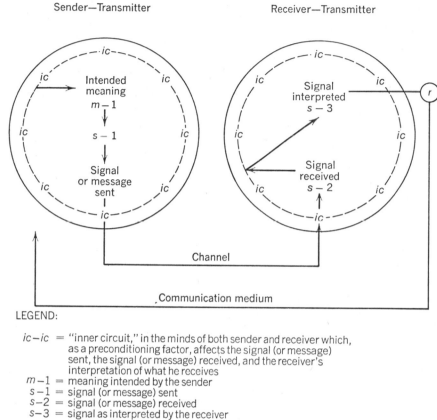

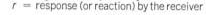

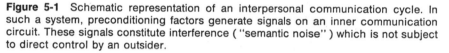

LEGEND:

$ic-ic$ = "inner circuit," in the minds of both sender and receiver which, as a preconditioning factor, affects the signal (or message) sent, the signal (or message) received, and the receiver's interpretation of what he receives

$m-1$ = meaning intended by the sender
$s-1$ = signal (or message) sent
$s-2$ = signal (or message) received
$s-3$ = signal as interpreted by the receiver
r = response (or reaction) by the receiver

Figure 5-1 Schematic representation of an interpersonal communication cycle. In such a system, preconditioning factors generate signals on an inner communication circuit. These signals constitute interference ("semantic noise") which is not subject to direct control by an outsider.

guage, a perceptive sender can rapidly detect and roughly measure a receiver's deviation from the expected response. Good timing and sound judgment tell him when and how to *offer* a corrective input. But the parallel breaks down here. No one can *direct* a corrective input into the behavior of anyone else. Consequently, perfect control cannot be achieved from outside. However, *both senders and receivers can exercise control over their own behavior to a degree that normally keeps the communication process in a state approximating control.*

Listening: A Control Technique

One of the most effective self-controls is listening with understanding. This skill is most easily and effectively applied in face-to-face talk. Even under those favorable conditions, however, there have been many misconceptions about who needs to listen, and at what level, what needs to be listened for, and, at best, what listening can accomplish.

Experienced interviewers have learned that talking is most likely to be productive when senders and receivers *both* listen intensively and continuously.[5]

Such multiple listening requires intense concentration, enhanced by sensitivity, powered by friendly feelings, and guided by social literacy (the ability to read body language). Yet much so-called "listening" amounts to little more than mechanical reception of sound waves which are treated by an indifferent listener as relatively meaningless. Maloney calls this "marginal listening."[6] Steere describes an experience in which his attempts to communicate were foiled by spasmodic and marginal listening when the executive with whom he was trying to talk kept interrupting him to attend to other matters, which evidently interested him more. He "said 'yes' and 'no' now and then, but his mind was elsewhere."[7]

At a somewhat higher level of attention, a person listens to the general tenor of the words that someone speaks, but his interest is primarily in using them as a springboard from which to launch his own (already formulated) opinion. When two speakers "listen" to each other only with the outer ear, there can be no genuine dialogue. Instead there are only "two tangential monologues, neither of which represents any genuine response to the other person."[8]

Attentive listening to spoken words *as clues to another person's meaning* is more demanding. The quality of a listener's silence can "reflect and communicate: (1) friendly feelings, (2) interest not only in what the other person says but also in what he might say if he felt free to speak his whole mind, (3) concern for the meanings [and values] that underlie his words, and (4) a sense of responsibility for what happens in consequence of what is being said, heard, and shared."[9]

Empathic listening has been described by Rogers[10] as a kind of response that can eliminate or greatly reduce two major barriers to effective communication. These are premature evaluation of what someone is saying and an immediate negative reaction to it. Rogers suggests the following experiment as a means to test a high degree of listening with understanding.

In an argument . . . just stop the discussion for a moment and [as] an experiment, institute this rule. "Each person can speak up for himself only *after* he has first restated the ideas and feelings of the previous speaker accurately, and to the speaker's satisfaction." . . . Once you have been able to see the other's point of view, your own comments will have to be drastically revised. You will also find the emotion going out of the discussion, the differences being reduced, and those differences which remain being of a rational and understandable sort.[11]

"Projective listening" is the term applied by Martin Maloney to this kind of attentive response to the total meaning of what a speaker is saying—the emotional and purposive elements as well as the rational components. A person who has developed what amounts to a semantic radar has at his command a valuable control device. Anyone with such a delicate "sensor" can often catch the impression his own words make—or fail to make—on another person's "inner circuit." Such psychological and socially sensitive listening is greatly needed for "quality control" in person-to-person communicating.

---

[5] In this subsection we draw heavily on Douglas V. Steere, *On Listening to Another,* Harper & Row, Publishers, Incorporated, New York, 1955, especially pp. 1–12.

[6] Martin Maloney, "Semantics: The Foundation of All Business Communications," *Advanced Management,* vol. 19, no. 7, pp. 26–29, 1954.

[7] Steere, *op. cit.,* p. 3.

[8] *Ibid.,* p. 4.

[9] Paul Pigors and Faith Pigors, *Case Method in Human Relations: The Incident Process,* McGraw-Hill Book Company, New York, 1961, p. 264.

[10] Carl R. Rogers, *On Becoming a Person: A Therapist's View of Psychotherapy,* Houghton Mifflin Company, Boston, 1961, chap. 17, "Dealing with Breakdowns in Communication—Interpersonal and Intergroup," pp. 329–337, consists of a paper presented at the Northwestern University Centennial Conference on Communications in 1951.

[11] *Op. cit.,* pp. 332–333.

Projective listening can sometimes help another person express ideas and feelings which have been troubling him (or troubling other people through him) but of which he has been unaware. Listening without interrupting may also help someone to talk out a perplexing problem and to find for himself a solution which neither he nor his listener could have envisaged at the start of their talk.

Another use for projective listening is demonstrated when a supervisor functions as an enabler during group decision making. In that role he needs the ability to perceive the different ideas, purposes, and values that speak in various group members. Then he may be able to help them clarify their meanings, a necessary preliminary to working productively from difference toward consensus.

Controls for Written Communications

When a sender tries to communicate in writing, he can have no immediate perception of how his meaning will be interpreted by other minds. But for purposes of quality control certain preventive measures can be applied.

Clarity of Statement   Many receivers of written communications have found it baffling to fight their way toward intended meaning, past obstacles and interferences set up by clumsy wording. Unfortunately, many a sender finds that the motto "always be clear" is easier to say than to live by. For one thing, clear expression requires clear thinking. Furthermore, wording a message so clearly that it cannot be misunderstood by anyone is not always possible. Those who write books will testify to the multitude of misreadings that can distort the intended meaning.

Readability and Style   These also contribute to ease of reception. For readability, Rudolf Flesch[12] has recommended short sentences, few affixes, and many personal references. Other writers and teachers concerned with style have stressed "cleanliness, accuracy, and brevity." E. B. White,[13] recalls his Cornell professor's emphatic and reiterated admonition:

Omit needless words! . . . Vigorous writing is concise. A sentence should contain no unnecessary words, a paragraph no unnecessary sentences, for the same reason that a drawing should have no unnecessary lines and a machine no unnecessary parts. This requires not that the writer make all his sentences short, or that he avoid all detail and treat his subjects only in outline, but that every word tell. [14]

WHAT ABOUT MASS COMMUNICATION TO EMPLOYEES?[15]

The reader should now look back at the first set of three questions quoted at the beginning of this chapter, bearing in mind the general characteristics of person-to-person communication (as contrasted with mechanical communications systems) and the unique nature of each human receiver's built-in data processing circuit. Is it

[12] Rudolf Flesch, *The Art of Plain Talk*, Harper & Row, Publishers, Incorporated, New York, 1946. His later book, *How to Write, Speak, and Think More Effectively*, Harper & Row, Publishers, Incorporated, New York, 1960, is a compendium of his numerous publications on this subject.

[13] E. B. White, *The Elements of Style by William Strunk, Jr., with Revisions, an Introduction, and a New Chapter on Writing*, The Macmillan Company, New York, 1959, p. vii. In a final chapter of his own White notices that "the approach to style is by way of plainness, simplicity, orderliness, sincerity" (p. 55). (New revised edition published 1972).

[14] *Ibid.*, pp. viii–ix.

[15] Mass communication at the level of "rabble rousing" is not considered in this chapter. Administrative communication characteristically takes place at the level where reason can be a controlling factor rather than at the level where personality is submerged and people respond to the contagion of purely emotional appeals. Management communications should always be encoded in reasonable words and ask a reasonable response (even though seasoned managers are well aware that feelings and purposes can play an integral part in every human response).

surprising that communication problems arise when a plant manager tries to communicate simultaneously to a thousand employees? Or would it be feasible, in a one-shot deal to explain a new salary program, getting the same message to each individual employee?

Experience shows that mass communication to employees is likely to be useful only to the extent that the information to be transmitted can be stated briefly, is extremely easy to understand (at the rational level), and has a strong personal appeal for each intended receiver. For instance, use of a public-address system can be an effective way to broadcast such generally welcome news as this: "Because of the severe snow storm, the home office will close at 2 P.M. so that all personnel can get home safely before dark."

But even such a highly communicable message must be followed up by managers and supervisors to ensure that everyone has heard the words and will respond appropriately. Someone may mishear the time or, the following day, may offer that explanation for his failure to return from lunch. Or some highly motivated employee perhaps in R&D or electronic data processing (EDP) may be so absorbed in his project that he fails to hear the announcement and gets locked in.

At the other end of the scale are lengthy written communications intended to transmit large amounts of information to large numbers of employees. Such efforts to communicate may contribute to the stability of a control system when each part is written clearly and briefly and is referred to periodically by those who want to refresh their memories. However, a chief executive cannot afford to assume that he has *communicated with* everyone on the routing slip as soon as his written message has been disseminated.

A Case Example: "Management by Objectives"

In one company, monthly "management memos" regarding long-range corporate objectives were routed to all members (several hundred) of the "management group," including first-level supervisors. After this mass "communication" had been going on for about a year, a consultant was invited to give a course for supervisors and lower-level managers as part of the company's career development program. At one meeting he asked, "How do you help your subordinates harmonize their individual goals with long-term corporate objectives?" A brief silence ensued. Then someone replied, "We can't. We don't even know ourselves what the objectives are."

The consultant was flabbergasted. Waving a sheaf of papers, he said, "I don't understand. What about all these management memos?"

Discussion disclosed that few conferees had read the memos (though many had filed their copies) and even fewer could remember anything of what they had read. This unplanned response was explained when a conferee said, "These management objectives are on such a broad scale that nothing we can do could possibly affect them." Such a sweeping statement is debatable, but it reflected a feeling that had blocked downward communication even within the management group.

One can readily appreciate why written statements about long-range objectives say so little to so many supervisors, but suppose that top management's message concerns a projected reduction in workforce that will affect a large number of employees. How could mass communication followed up by oral explanations from first-level supervisors fail to reach the minds of so many of the employees who later lost their jobs?

A Case Example: The General Manager's Letter

As part of a comprehensive and carefully timed communications program to clarify a projected manpower reduction,[16] the general manager

[16] See L. D. Belzung, John P. Owen, and John F. MacNaughton, *The Anatomy of a Workforce Reduction: A Study of Workers Affected by a 1962 Reduction in Force at the Humble Oil & Refining Company, Baytown, Texas, Refinery,* University of Houston, College of Business Administration, Center for Research in Business and Economics, 1966.

wrote a letter (dated Sept. 1, 1961) addressed to all employees. It included the following explanations of why such drastic action was contemplated: (1) "loss of a large market for products formerly sold to another company for resale through its own service stations," and (2) "construction of a large products pipeline by a group of competitors."

The general manager also issued a directive that first-level supervisors were to distribute his letter and explain to their subordinates the reasons for the projected cutback,[17] which was to begin the following January. A year after the workforce reduction had been completed, interviewers talked with many of the displaced employees.[18] In these interviews 18 percent of the laid-off employees stated (as a fact) that information about the projected cutback had reached them *less than 1 month* before they were laid off.

Such a large-scale contrary-to-fact impression might seem almost incredible to a manager who had gone to so much trouble to ensure that his own explanations would be distributed and followed up *more than 3 months* before the cutback began. However, the failure of that message to get across is easy to understand if one starts from the premise that person-to-person communicating requires individual reception and interpretation of messages that are perceived as having immediate meaning-for-me.[19] Explanations (especially in broad terms) fall on deaf ears if the person has already dismissed the whole topic as something that is not going to happen until next year and probably will not affect him anyway.[20]

The published study does not show to what extent supervisors met their responsibilities as communication links. How many of them effectively translated the general manager's written explanations into words calculated to interest and convince each individual employee?[21] It seems at least possible that at that time they were not expected to practice the fine arts of *interpreting messages* from higher management (to make them as meaningful and acceptable as possible to individuals at the work level) and of *projective listening* (to appraise the extent to which such messages actually had been understood and accepted as relevant). However, such skills are not dismissed as mere frills in enterprises where managers know that long-term productivity depends on widespread participation.

Assumptions about the possibilities of mass communication are closely related to ideas about managing. Some of the assumptions which underlie one way of managing are clearly reflected in the second set of questions which we quoted at the start of this chapter. To paraphrase two of them: How do you know when you have gotten complete understanding from a pigheaded employee? How does management win the contest for employee loyalty? To those questions one might add: If an employee gets the message that a manager regards him as pigheaded, is he likely to make any great effort to understand what that manager wants him to do?

---

[17] The total workforce reduction included 722 employees. Of this number 459 elected voluntary retirement, and only 81 were actually laid off. More than half the displaced employees were maintenance and construction workers, and 59 of the laid-off employees had 14 or more years of service.

[18] "All laid-off workers who could be contacted (two-thirds of them) and a scientific sampling (one-fifth) of the voluntary early retirees."

[19] A vivid example of the relative inefficacy of mass communication, as compared with face-to-face talk, was given in the experience of William E. Zisch, special representative of the Secretary of Commerce for the Negro job program. In the summer of 1967 he sent a form letter to leaders in business and industry, asking for their cooperation with the federal government in providing jobs for hard-core unemployed, chiefly in the ghettos. Results were disappointing, but when he made follow-up visits during the autumn, he obtained proposals which if all had been implemented, would have created some 14,500 *new jobs* (*The New York Times,* Dec. 15, 1967).

[20] Some indication was given during the interviews that many employees who subsequently laid off had believed the projected cutback could be handled entirely by voluntary early retirements.

[21] Some light is thrown on that point by interview data which reveal a preponderantly negative attitude toward the company on the part of many employees who had been laid off. Their statements of management's "real reasons" for reducing the workforce differed radically from those of the general manager; e.g., "contractors could be hired for less" (31.4 percent); "Humble wanted to get rid of some men" (23.5 percent); "Humble wanted to dominate the union" (3.9 percent).

And will he be inclined to respond with feelings of personal loyalty?

Such questions about communication cannot usefully be considered apart from the managerial climate in which administrative communication takes place.

DIFFERENT MANAGERIAL CLIMATES AFFECT ADMINISTRATIVE COMMUNICATION

As we have already stated in earlier chapters, for years progressive managers have acted on the research finding that production-centered supervision yields lower productivity, over the long haul, than employee-centered supervision. It has been less widely understood that similar principles apply to organizational communication. For instance, it is not true that the greater the number of communications sent down the line and the greater the insistence that accurate reports be sent up the line, the more effective administrative communication will be. Behavioral scientists have shown conclusively that without appropriate organizational structure and a permissive managerial climate, productive interaction in communicating is impossible. Organizational structure and managerial climate are more important for effective administrative communication than management's words.

Communication and Control in Centralized Systems[22]

A basic assumption of Theory X (or System 2 management) is that centralized control, emanating from the top of the organizational hierarchy, is the most effective way to get results. In such a managerial system, administrative communication is expected to implement the chain of command by flowing along official communication channels. Relatively inflexible directives go down the line and are translated into increasingly detailed (and restrictive) instructions as they approach the work level. Authoritarian management is sometimes carried to the point where unconditional orders are given even to management representatives and inflexible standing orders prevent supervisors from using their own judgment.[23]

Subassumptions are that top management can (1) keep track of how well an externally imposed system is working by getting accurate and adequate reports up the line, as to quantity and quality of output, costs, scrap, etc., and (2) quickly reestablish control by tightening up the system and perhaps also resorting to punitive measures when reports indicate negative variances from predetermined norms.

Restrictive Management Blocks and Distorts Upward Communication

When the functions of planning and decision making are limited to top management, communication up the line is inevitably and severely restricted. Information that reaches top executives is too little and arrives too late to permit the degree of control required for peak productivity.

Bavelas has vividly described what may be anticipated when a first-level supervisor is confronted by restrictive management:

> [He] may follow one of two courses. He may ask for special guidance and hope that the delay in receiving it will not be so great as to result only in embarrassment—an outcome that might attract undesirable attention to himself. Or he may learn to avoid or simply not see situations that are not "in the book." If, on occasion, he should dare to deal with some local problem on his own discretion, he will probably choose not to report it, whatever the result. Thus any know-how that might accumulate at the periphery would probably remain trapped

[22] See Rensis Likert, *The Human Organization: Its Management and Value,* McGraw-Hill Book Company, New York, 1967, especially chap. 3, "Productivity and Labor Relations under Different Management Systems," pp. 13-46.

[23] The case of "The Cable Splicer's Dilemma," cited in Chap. 1, p. 8, shows how a supervising foreman's literal compliance with a strict standing order involved his company in heavy and unnecessary expense.

there. Performance reports, in such a system, would become largely verifications of the correctness and the wisdom of the decisions being made at the center. The man at the center, on whom everything depends, would find himself in the precarious position of knowing less and less about what was really going on. . . .[24]

Furthermore, employees have it in their power to distort some of the information that does travel up the line and is needed for appraisal and control. The following example shows how easily this can be done.

A Case Example: The Fudge Factor Operates

In one company, random sampling of employee contacts with customers was obtained by automatically recording telephone conversations. Whenever the recording device went into operation, at random intervals, it made a slight but audible click. This signal was soon noticed by employees in one unit. They got the message, and went to work. By effective teamwork, "whoever heard the click promptly alerted the rest of the employees, and the telephone call was immediately taken by one of the most experienced and skilled employees. The performance reports for that unit were outstanding."[25]

From a psychological analysis of what blocks upward communication, Anderson[26] develops the following: too heavy a workload for managers (leaving them with too little attention and perhaps also with too little patience for effective listening); insufficient understanding of subordinates and of their jobs (causing inability of a manager to empathize with individuals and ignorance of key facts to probe for); lack of skill in interviewing techniques (resulting perhaps in failure to select a place for talk that is quiet and where interruptions are unlikely); and inability to summarize and clarify facts and ideas while a subordinate is talking to him (the result being that the manager becomes confused or forgets some of the salient points that he should look into).

Why Don't Managers Know the Score?

If a centralized system of decision making and hierarchical organization structure inevitably restrict and distort information flowing through channels to a single decision-making center, should not both mechanisms be modified? On the other hand, if that reasoning is valid, how can managers have overlooked it for so many years? Likert suggests that if top executives could study reports which show the full cost of System 2 management, they would soon be converted to System 4. Unfortunately, financial reports provided through standard accounting procedures are inadequate because "human asset accounting" is no part of them.[27]

In considering dimensions of the communication process, Leavitt[28] suggests two reasons why many managers prefer the one-way to the two-way direction. The former is faster and more comfortable for a sender. Two-way communication, on the other hand, is more accurate. But this process often entails psychological risks for the sender. Also, establishing, maintaining, and

[24] Alex Bavelas, "Communication and Organization," in George P. Shultz and Thomas L. Whisler (eds.), *Management Organization and the Computer,* The Free Press of Glencoe, New York, 1960, pp. 119-130.

[25] Likert, *op. cit.,* p. 135.

[26] John Anderson, "What Blocks Upward Communication?" *Personnel Administration,* vol. 31, no. 1, pp. 5-7ff., January-February, 1968.

[27] According to Likert's analysis, basic flaws in standard cost accounting procedures are (1) that they fail to incorporate any measurements of gains and losses in human assets (such as morale, teamwork, or even turnover) and (2) that the time span covered by each financial report is too short to show the interrelationships between different ways of managing and human costs. See *ibid.,* chap. 9, "Human Asset Accounting," pp. 146-155.

[28] Harold J. Leavitt, *Managerial Psychology,* University of Chicago, rev. ed., 1964, pp. 138-152.

expanding such a reciprocal system may require changes in organizational structure and administrative procedure that managers do not wish to make.

Participative Management Frees the Flow of Communication

A manager who knows that he can get peak performance only by working *with* employees, not through them, naturally adopts a management system and an organizational structure which, instead of dissipating human assets, will develop them. He decentralizes decision making so that it is carried out within and between interlinking work groups. For such decentralized decision making, an open communications system is essential. Therefore a flow of information in all directions is encouraged so that necessary data will be available wherever and whenever they are needed.[29] Furthermore, in participative management, information about performance is used for prevention—by better planning—rather than for external control. When employees perceive how managers use the information that goes up the line and how they themselves benefit from the results, they feel motivated to supply accurate and adequate information.

However, the favorable climate provided by participative management cannot be expected to bring instant results in improved employee mo-

rale and the development of employees as individuals and teammates. Attitudes cannot be changed overnight. Participative management must be practiced for an interval long enough for employees to come to trust their own experience in the new relationship. The social and human meanings of participative management cannot be communicated once and for all in a "one-shot deal" as a policy statement issued by top executives. The message that participation is genuinely desired and offered as an opportunity for self-realization on the job must be communicated through consistent action, at every organizational level, by every manager and supervisor.

Is Order Giving Obsolete?

In our opinion, belief in participative management does not entail abolishing order giving. But to be consistent with principles of participation, the content and wording of orders and the manner and tone in which they are issued must be demonstrably in keeping with situational requirements. Perhaps words like "instruction" and "request" are more fitting than the term "order" in the context of participative management. A supervisor who wants participation adapts his instructions and requests to such factors as current work requirements, existing relationships (formal and informal) between individuals and groups, and unique characteristics of persons who are expected to exercise initiative and judgment in doing their work. In this way of managing by partnership, a transmitter of directives does not regard himself, or even his position, as *the* source of authority. Instead he tries always to speak for situational requirements.[30]

[29] For statistical data on open communication systems see, A. K. Wickesberg, "Communication Networks in the Business Organization Structure," *Academy of Management Journal,* 1968, vol. 11, no. 3, pp. 253-262. In 35 organizations (ranging from transportation to education), 91 businessmen reported their communication activities during 5 days (Monday through Friday in 5 different weeks). Tabulating the flow of communication showed that managers and nonmanagers alike had directed about a third of their communications to people in other organizational units. Wickesberg's study, supported by findings of other researchers, suggests: (1) that informal communication—most of it task-oriented—plays a much larger part in achieving organizational goals than is recognized by authoritarian managers; and (2) that many employees not classified as managers engage in planning, implementing, and controlling to such a degree that efficiency requires an open communication system.

[30] The content and tone of his instructions and requests range from a "situational hint," a general or a conditional directive or, on occasion, e.g., in talking with new and inexperienced employees, a specific, detailed, and unconditional instruction. See Paul Pigors and Faith Pigors, *Understanding as a Condition of Success in Order-giving,* Industrial Relations Associates, Inc., Cambridge, Mass., 1945. This monograph was revised as "How Can a Boss Obtain Favorable Responses to His Orders?," *Management of Personnel Quarterly,* vol. 1, no. 1, pp. 15-19, Autumn, 1961.

The following example shows how the organizational climate in which order giving occurs may be more significant than the actual words of a specific order (or instruction).

A Case Example:
A Foreman's Leading Question

A factory manager decided to please an important buyer by personally expediting a last-minute order for an essential component. Bypassing the production scheduling department, he went directly to the shop and told the manufacturing foreman to "get this order out right away."

Foreman (cost-minded, and a "yes-but" man by nature): O.K. But would it be all right if I let it wait for about 3 hours?

Manager: Why can't you start on it right away?

Foreman: Because in about 3 hours one of my machines will run out and we won't have to waste time taking a job down and setting it up again.

Despite his impatience to get the order out, the factory manager immediately agreed to this minor modification, explaining that when he had said "right away" he merely meant "some time today."

In this instance, productive interaction during a communication spiral began when the foreman felt free to introduce an operational fact of which the manager was unaware. A second favorable force came into play when the manager felt able to accept an independent but cost-minded suggestion from a subordinate.

HOW CAN MANAGERS GET THROUGH TO EMPLOYEES?

Having considered two ways of communicating associated with different ways of managing, and leading to different results, let us look back at the second set of questions quoted at the beginning of this chapter. A common thread running through them is the search for some manipulative technique by which top management can open the minds of employees with the following desirable results: (1) management "inputs" sent down the line would be taken in—to the point where intended meanings would be completely "absorbed and accepted," and (2) adequate, accurate, and real-time information would continuously flow up the line.

Those who believe in science-based management might suggest that a more profitable line of inquiry would be for Theory X or System 2 managers to ask: Could our way of managing be accountable for our communication problems? What might we do differently so that the meaning of our messages would get through to employees more often and so that they would freely give us the information we need? Productive answers to those questions have been given by managers who recognize that shared understanding and free communication are partly results of mutual endeavor toward shared objectives. These managers offer opportunities for participation in managing instead of merely demanding participation as compliance from order receivers.

To set the tone for productive interaction in genuinely participative management, a chief executive can appropriately start by talking *with* work associates at the level of policy.

POLICY COMMUNICATION FOR PARTICIPATIVE MANAGEMENT

Effective communication between the writers and the readers of these pages must depend in part on shared understanding of the meaning of the word "policy." Unfortunately, that term has been used so indiscriminately that today it has no single, generally accepted meaning. In management literature, "policy" refers to such widely different and mutually incompatible ideas as a vague aspiration (or ethical principle), a long-range plan or organization-wide decision, a practice, a management procedure, even a standing order (or general rule). Here are some examples: "It is our policy to treat every customer fairly. . . ." "We don't give trading stamps any more. There has been a change in company policy." "You can't use any accumulated time off to get an extra day before or after a holiday. That would be contrary to our present policy."

However, "policy" might be given a distinctive meaning by reserving the term for a special kind of decision and directive. A statement of policy—as distinguished from an inflexible rule or unconditional standing order—can invite participation and the use of initiative from responsible organizational members.

To offer guidance, without undue restriction, a policy statement can appropriately and usefully:[31]

1 *Affirm a general principle or long-term corporate aim.* This feature integrates a general decision or directive with a given managerial philosophy.

2 *Commit management representatives to take account of the stated principle.* This feature makes for consistency of behavior among organizational subsystems, without imposing uniformity.

3 *Invite discretion, within appropriate limits, by those who interpret a policy decision.* This feature, which encourages the use of judgment to interpret a policy decision in a specific situation, differentiates action on policy from mere compliance with an inflexible rule.

4 *Be congruent with other corporate policies* (*which together form a comprehensive policy structure*) *as well as with implementing procedures and the necessary minimum of rules.*[32]

[31] See also Geneva Seybold, "Statements of Personnel Policies," National Industrial Conference Board, Inc., Studies in Personnel Policy, no. 169, New York, 1959.

[32] Jay W. Forrester has expressed a similar line of thinking in stating that the efficiency of policies, which he defines as "rules that guide decisions," can be measured along the "four dimensions of freedom, accessibility, source, and consistency." He states that "policy should allow freedom to innovate and should have the fewest restrictions compatible with the coordination needed to insure over-all system strength, stability and growth. Policy should be accessible, clear, and

Many statements of corporate policy meet several of these specifications. The following is one of the relatively few we have seen which incorporates them all.

A Policy on Equal Employment Opportunity[33]

[*Policy.*] The management of the Babcock and Wilcox Company and of its subsidiary companies state that it is *their desire that individuals be provided equal employment opportunity based on merit, competence, and service,* without regard to race, creed, color, national origin, sex, or age.

Applicability. This policy applies to *all aspects* of the employment relationship including hiring, upgrading, transfer, training, and wage and salary administration. It *requires* that *all* employment relationship *decisions be based solely* on an individual's ability and qualifications *except where* retirement policies, service and seniority policies, or labor agreement commitments specify other criteria.

not retroactive. The source of policy should be a process that ensures some consensus by those affected that it is a just compromise for the common good. Policies should be consistent by being designed as parts of a total policy structure that creates the desired dynamic behavior in the resulting system." See "A New Corporate Design," *Industrial Management Review* (Alfred P. Sloan School of Management, Massachusetts Institute of Technology), vol. 7, no. 1, pp. 5–17, Fall, 1965.

Forrester's idea about "the source" of policy is one which we develop, along somewhat different lines, as a participative policy-shaping process (see the next subsection in this chapter).

[33] The statement that follows is quoted from the National Industrial Conference Board Personnel Policy Study no. 201, vol. I, New York, 1966, pp. 71–72. Each of the 12 case studies in vol. I contains a statement of company policy. Our italics added to the company statement emphasize the various policy features. For example, the paragraphs on "applicability" and "responsibility" (1) present a firm commitment for multifaceted implementation, (2) indicate consistency with other policies and with statements in the labor agreement, and (3) spell out needed communication practices. Paragraphs on "limitations" explain why, where, and how much discretion is to be exercised. They also include a three-part statement ruling out action *not* to be taken because it would be carrying the purpose of the policy to the point where it would represent reverse discrimination.

Equal encouragement should be extended to all employees to prepare themselves to assume job responsibilities suitable to their individual abilities, talents, and interests.

Company facilities used by or available to employees or applicants for employment shall be maintained without regard to their race, creed, color, or national origin.

Responsibility. The head of each of the company's divisions and subsidiaries is responsible for the implementation of the above-stated policy. Through responsible subordinates they shall:

1 Effectuate realization of *both the spirit and detailed provisions* of this policy.
2 Deal firmly and promptly with any efforts to impede or prevent compliance with this policy.
3 *Advise each supervisor and management representative* of this policy and direct them to use it effectively in their employee relationships.
4 Maintain *objective data* to support employment relationship decisions.
5 Keep the director of employee relations, staff division, informed of questions and problems concerning the application of this policy.

The director of employee relations, staff division, is responsible for:

1 *Informing* heads of divisions and subsidiaries of Federal laws and regulations believed to be applicable to this policy.
2 *Recommending* new or improved practices which advance the objective of equal employment opportunity.
3 *Obtaining such evidence* of conformity with company policy *as may be desirable.*

Limitations. It is recognized that in some communities, *long-established local customs and practices without the force of law* may make immediate and complete *desegregation of facilities* impractical. *It is expected,* however, that in such localities, *local management* will proceed as rapidly as practicable toward implementation of the [company policy].

This policy is *not intended to foster unsound practices* such as:

1 *Discrimination in favor of any employee or applicant* for employment on racial, religious, or other basis *to the detriment of the employment opportunities* of any other qualified employee or applicant.
2 *Lowering of job requirements or performance standards* for the purpose of favoring any employee or applicant on the basis of his or her race, creed, color, or national origin, age, or sex.
3 *Offering of employment opportunities without regard to individual classifications* of ability, *for the purpose of achieving correlation* between the company's employee population and the population of the community on a racial, religious, or other basis.

In connection with the idea that, as differentiated from a rule, a policy permits discretion, the following statement is of interest.

Unless the company permits the [personnel department] to act broadly under the policy, no really permanent improvement can be effected. The extent of the search to be made for Negro job candidates is one example of the area of discretion; another is the degree of persuasion to be used in convincing a supervisor to accept the most capable job applicant, whether a Negro or not. On the other hand, the personnel director cannot ignore his overall responsibility to represent the best interests of *all* employees in the company as well as to promote the welfare of the company itself.[34]

A Participative Policy Process

Officially issuing a written policy statement is only one step in what can be a participative process of shaping corporate policies. A brief con-

---

[34] Quoted from *ibid.,* p. 92. To that statement one might add that supervisors also need scope for exercising their own discretion under such a policy, e.g., in providing extra training on the job and perhaps extending early stages of the discipline process to allow for more orientation or reeducation than most employees need.

sideration of integrally related phases may show why it can pay off to invite widespread participation in thinking at the level of policy.

Step 1: Initiating Policy Thinking A suggestion that a policy is needed (or that an existing policy needs to be modified) may originate in any subsystem of the organization.

Step 2: Fact-finding and Situational Analysis At this exploratory stage a member at any organizational level may be able to make a useful contribution, derived from his direct and specialized experience. A wide range of experience can be synthesized by a policy committee.[35]

Step 3: Making Recommendations to the Chief Executive Members of the policy committee report to the chief executive considered opinions which integrate their own judgments and findings. Free discussion of these recommendations depends on friendly personal relationships and on mutual confidence between the chief executive and members of the policy committee. If new committee members hesitate to express independent opinions when talking with the chief executive, the personnel administrator should be ready to take the lead. In his regular role as an adviser, he has learned that the "yes-but" approach can be more productive than a mechanical "Yes, Sir" response.

Step 4: Preparing a Written Policy Statement Until a policy decision has been put in writing, it cannot be regarded as a firm and official management commitment. Skill is required to select and adhere to policy language that appropriately states and synthesizes general principles, com-

mitment for action, and scope for discretion. Anyone with a high degree of this skill (preferably from the department chiefly affected by the policy) may prepare the written draft.

Step 5: Discussing a Proposed Policy Statement By this time it is essential to obtain *active participation*[36] from all those who are expected to use the policy as a guide for partly independent decision making. Naturally, this step can be taken most easily and effectively by persons whose participation in policy thinking began at step 1 or step 2.

A chief executive who wants to provide maximum opportunity for participation in managing also makes sure that all who will be affected by new (or revised) policy decisions will get an advance hearing. That opportunity for upward communication should be offered before it is too late for employees to respond constructively to such questions as these: Is this policy clearly stated? Is it demonstrably consistent with other policies in the organization, as well as with established procedures and practices? Is the policy acceptable to all those upon whom management representatives must depend to make it work? If not, what changes need to be made?

Step 6: Issuing a Written Statement of Policy Simultaneous release to all management representatives is in itself a significant communication of purpose. Such timing symbolizes recognition that prompt and complete information in regard to official corporate decisions is one prerequisite for effective performance by all those who are expected to interpret top-management thinking. Simultaneously forwarding copies to union officers can demonstrate top management's purpose to work productively with a union.

---

[35] Membership on this committee should be rotated, but the personnel administrator should be a permanent member. Whether or not a given policy is strictly in the area labeled "human relations," all policy decisions affect what Likert has called "the human organization."

[36] Experience shows that merely circulating a draft "for your comments" is likely to be unproductive. Too often an initialed "no comment" means that the receiver has not even read the document carefully.

Step 7: Interpreting and Living with a Policy Decision Written statements of organization-wide principles and purposes gain depth of meaning as people live with them. In each part of a large organization a given policy decision comes to have a somewhat special meaning. This differentiation takes place as every management representative or other employee interprets its meaning-for-him. Each time a policy directive is processed by the "inner circuit" of an individual mind, there is some variance from the chief executive's initial ideas, feelings, and purposes. However, free and comprehensive discussion at earlier stages of the policy-shaping process can ensure that modifications remain within tolerances appropriate to a flexible policy.

Step 8: Interim Appraisal Management representatives who are guided by a corporate policy and other employees affected by a given policy decision can develop the experience needed to appraise its appropriateness and usefulness. Any serious difficulties with a new or revised policy should be reported up the line, along with constructive suggestions. This upward communication can be counted on if employees have learned that they can command attention and get action from higher management by participating in this way. Thus organizational experience can be recognized as authoritative. It becomes a decisive factor in kinds of decisions which, however, must be finally approved and formally issued by top management before they can become official corporate policy.

Step 9: Officially Reviewing and Evaluating an Existing Policy Members of a policy committee can summarize, for the chief executive, work-group answers to such vital questions as: Does the policy decision realistically reckon with current resources and effectively meet current situational requirements? Or does an existing policy need to be reshaped, or a new policy de-

veloped? Has the central policy principle been flexibly interpreted? Or has it, in any organizational subsystem, been applied as an inflexible rule?[37] Has the policy helped to build mutual understanding and teamwork, enabling organizational members more clearly to understand and more strongly to support some long-term corporate objective?

Step 10: Revising a Policy Statement If during previous stages of policy making a chief executive has *talked with* and *listened to* members of a policy committee, he is in a favorable position to know what revisions, if any, are called for. If he is a newcomer to the organization, he can intelligently discuss needs for policy revision only after devoting time, thought, and effort to familiarizing himself with what a given policy has come to mean for those who have lived with it. However, he need not regard such conferences as unproductive, either for himself or for organizational members who are already familiar with the whole policy system. What better way could there be for him to start creating a climate in which mutual understanding and community of organizational purpose may develop between him and his associates, thus providing opportunities for them to demonstrate and develop executive caliber?

In reviewing an existing policy, as at other stages in a policy-shaping process, a chief executive can demonstrate his willingness to follow situational leads and to learn from other organizational members. What a chief executive says, his response in projective listening, and his willingness to distribute responsibility for leading in decision making demonstrate his genuine belief in participative management.

---

[37] Case 17, "Difficulties Connected with Work Scheduling," in Part 2, illustrates how that natural tendency can deflect the purpose of a policy.

Mutual Responsibility and Responsiveness

Full and sustained productivity can be assured only when employees develop strong feelings of responsibility with regard to organizational goals. However, there is considerable evidence that this participative response from employees can be expected only when employees experience *responsiveness to them,* as whole human beings, from their immediate supervisors. Interest in creating this precondition for productive interaction was expressed in the third set of questions quoted at the beginning of this chapter: How can we improve our efficiency as receivers of communication? How can we help people to accept bad news? A common denominator here is the wish to respond to fellow workers as fellow human beings. Martin Buber[38] described this attitude as "turning towards the other." He saw it as the most important prerequisite for what he called "the life of dialogue." A manager who tries to put this principle into practice needs to know *as an individual* each person with whom he is trying to cooperate and to communicate. For that purpose, he must learn to understand the inner motivation which impels the messages that travel along each individual's "inner circuit." Inner motivation is the subject of the next chapter. But first we sum up this chapter.

SUMMARY

When human beings talk and listen *with* one another, they are doing something much more difficult than what can successfully be accomplished by a mechanical communications system. Engineers exercise almost perfect control over a communications system in which interchangeable "transceivers" send and receive prearranged signals. In person-to-person communication, however, one-to-one congruence between

[38] Martin Buber, *Between Man and Man,* Beacon Press, Boston, 1955, p. 22.

meaning-as-sent and meaning-as-received is impossible. Meaning is a complex and ever-changing whole, compounded of individual ideas, feelings, and purposes. For these reasons, interpersonal communication often operates in ways which engineers would characterize as being "out of control." A sender cannot control what takes place during the reception phase when the meaning he would like to transmit as input is doubly changed: First it becomes actual *intake.* Then, by being processed on an "inner circuit," it is transmuted into an individual interpretation. Finally, the receiver's response to his own interpretation of meaning-as-received is expressed in action (or inaction).

A sender who accepts the idea that he cannot control the inner response of any receiver may feel motivated to develop communication skills which he can exercise as self-controls. One of them is listening. In face-to-face talk, a responsible, socially minded listener who pays attention to unspoken meanings as well as to spoken words may be able to prevent many miscarriages of meaning, or help someone to express troublemaking ideas and feelings, or to resolve perplexing problems.

For written communication, clarity, brevity, and style may be useful as preventive controls because they make reading easier and more pleasant. However, mass communication (especially in writing) has limited usefulness, because no two receivers are identical.

Traditional ways of managing (by inflexible directives and externally imposed controls) inevitably and unnecessarily restrict interpersonal communication, both up and down the line. Participative management, on the other hand, helps to free the flow of communication because it unfreezes individual initiative and stimulates communication between employees as whole persons, regardless of organizational status.

Traditional ways of order giving were based on the assumption that there are inherent differences between those who manage and those who are managed. It was taken for granted that employees can contribute most to productive goals when they stop thinking for themselves and do exactly what they are told. Supervisors who practice the principles of participative management also give instructions with the aim of stimulating employee productivity. However, their instructions are designed (in content, manner, tone, and timing) to facilitate a high degree of employee understanding and acceptance.

The concept of managing by partnership can be further implemented by widespread participation in a policy-shaping process. At best, this process involves every functional group. Thus it can help individual organizational members, as whole persons, to harmonize their personal goals with major objectives that have been established for the organization as a whole.

Basic premises of participative management are that managing and working are interdependent activities and that each requires a strong response from a whole person. A manager who accepts such ideas sees his role as that of stimulating and sometimes also guiding the high-level inner drives of persons in subordinate positions. He tries to learn all he can about how the aspirations of inner-directed individuals can be harmonized with organizational objectives, with benefits all around.

In the next chapter, perhaps the most important question is: What can be done to stimulate the inner motivation of every normal individual who feels that his work is worthwhile in itself and is, at the same time, helping him to develop his full potential?

SELECTED REFERENCES

Argyris, Chris: *Personality and Organization: The Conflict between System and the Individual,* Harper & Row, Publishers, Incorporated, New York, 1957.

Boyd, Bradford: "An Analysis of Communication between Departments: Roadblocks and By-passes," *Personnel Administration,* vol. 28, no. 6, pp. 33-38, November-December, 1965.

Control through Information: A Report on Management Information Systems, American Management Association, Administrative Services Division, Management Bulletin no. 24, New York, 1963.

Feldman, Sandor S., M.D.: *Mannerisms of Speech and Gestures in Everyday Life,* International Universities Press, Inc., New York, 1969.

Fenn, N., and G. Head: "Upward Communication: The Subordinate's Viewpoint," California Management Review, vol. 7, no. 4, pp. 75-80, Summer, 1965.

Gemmill, Gary: "Managing Upward Communication," *Personnel Journal,* vol. 49, no. 2, pp. 107-110, February, 1970.

Hovland, C. I., and M. J. Rosenberg: *Attitude, Organization and Change,* Yale University, Yale Studies in Attitude and Communication, New Haven, Conn., 1960, vol. 3.

Hower, Ralph M., and Charles D. Orth III: *Managers and Scientists,* Harvard Business School, Division of Research, Boston, 1963.

Kellog, Marion S.: *When Man and Manager Talk . . . A Casebook,* Gulf Publishing Company, Houston, 1969.

Koontz, Harold D., and Cyril J. O'Donnell: *Principles of Management,* 3d ed., McGraw-Hill Book Company, New York, 1964, chap. 26, "Communication," pp. 505-516.

Likert, Rensis: *Communication Problems in Superior-Subordinate Relationships,* Foundation for Research in Human Behavior, Ann Arbor, Mich., 1960.

Maier, Norman R. F., Richard Hoffman, John L. Hooven, and William H. Read: *Superior-Subordinate Communication in Management,* American Management Association, Research Study no. 52, New York, 1961.

Pigors, Paul: *Effective Communication in Industry: What Is Its Basis?* National Association of Manufacturers, Lt. Rush Toland Memorial Study no. 1, New York, 1949, especially chap. 5, "What is Meaning and How Can We Share It?" pp. 45-58.

Rogers, Carl R.: *On Becoming a Person: A Therapist's View of Psychotherapy,* Houghton Mifflin Company, Boston, 1961, especially chap. 17, "Dealing with Breakdowns in Communication—Interpersonal and Intergroup," pp. 329-337.

Taylor, J. K. L.: *Attitudes and Methods of Communication and Consultation between Employers and Workers at Individual Firm Level,* Organization for Economic Cooperation and Development, International Joint Seminar, London, Paris, Feb. 26-May 2, 1962.

Van Zandt, Howard F.: "How to Negotiate in Japan," *Harvard Business Review,* vol. 48, no. 6, pp. 45-56, November-December, 1970.

Chapter 6

Inner Motivation, Individual Goals, and Teamwork

Job satisfaction may or may not be tied to happiness. But we will know that we are doing something right if we can change the conditions of the job so that employees will stay on and work productively. For the older workers, the test will be whether they are with us in spirit as well as in body. The way to achieve this end, for new or old employees, is not to confront them with demands, but to confront them with demanding, meaningful work. And the employee will always have the last word as to whether the work is meaningful.

Robert N. Ford [1]

To a given job incumbent, work can be meaningful and satisfying only when it elicits and stimulates his inner motivation. Then his experience on the job can be an integral element in a total life experience during which he moves toward his full potential as a person. This hypothesis is a long way from the assumptions and practices of traditional management by Theory X (or System 1). But there is convincing evidence [2] to support the statement that when a manager helps to release and develop hitherto neglected human talents by offering opportunities for psychological growth on the job, he can increase an em-

---

[1] Robert N. Ford, *Motivation through the Work Itself,* American Management Association, Inc., New York, 1969, p. 199. Reprinted by permission of the publisher from *Motivation through the Work Itself.*

[2] For examples see Frederick Herzberg, "One More Time: How Do You Motivate Employees?" *Harvard Business Review,* vol. 46, no. 1, January–February, 1968; William P. Paul, Jr., Keith B. Robertson, and Frederick Herzberg, "Job Enrichment Pays Off," *Harvard Business Review,* vol. 47, no. 2, March–April, 1969; Frederick K. Foulkes, *Creating More Meaningful Work,* American Management Association, Inc., New York, 1969; Charles Foster, *Building with Men: An Analysis of Group Behavior and Organization in a Building Firm,* Tavistock Publications, London, 1969; Robert N. Ford, *Motivation through the Work Itself,* American Management Association, Inc., New York, 1969; William J. Roche and Neil L. MacKinnon, "Motivating People with Meaningful Work," *Harvard Business Review,* vol. 48, no. 3, May–June, 1970; M. Scott Myers, *Every Employee a Manager: More Meaningful Work through Job Enrichment,* McGraw-Hill Book Company, New York, 1970; and Harold M. F. Rush, *Job Design for Motivation: Experiments in Job Enlargement and Job Enrichment,* Conference Board Report no. 515, The Conference Board, Inc., New York, 1971.

ployee's productivity and thus contribute to organizational effectiveness.

If, then, a manager is interested in trying to stimulate and reinforce the motivation of his employees, what are some of the basic propositions that he should consider? In offering an answer to that question, we begin with Maslow.[3]

Theory of Motivation: Some General Propositions

Motivation Comes from Inside Each Individual Fundamental human needs—such as air, food, and shelter; belonging, "ego" satisfactions (including self-esteem, recognition from others, opportunities for achievement, self-development, and self-actualization)—act as powerful, though often unconscious, motivators of behavior. Inner motivation can be more decisive for behavior than any external influence.

The Whole Individual Is Motivated, Not Just Part of Him A person's basic needs determine to a great extent what he will try to do at any given time. All these needs are interrelated[4] because each "individual is an integrated, organized whole. . . . It is John Smith who wants food, not just John Smith's stomach. [Moreover, because] man is a wanting animal," when John gets what he *has* wanted, he soon feels the need for something more.

While a Need Is Satisfied, It Is Relatively Quiescent During the time when a basic need is adequately met (for a given individual), it loses power as a motivator. In other words, when a need is no longer a *felt* need (even in a man's subconscious mind), it does not determine his current behavior.

[3] In the next few pages we draw heavily on the work of Abraham H. Maslow, Saul Gellerman, Frederick I. Herzberg, Ray C. Hackman, and Carl R. Rogers.

[4] A. H. Maslow, *Motivation and Personality,* Harper & Row, Publishers, Incorporated, New York, 1954, pp. 63-69. See also *Toward a Psychology of Being,* 2d ed., D. Van Nostrand Company, Inc., New York, 1968; and *Eupsychian Management: A Journal,* Richard D. Irwin, Inc., and the Dorsey Press, Homewood, Ill., 1965.

Frustration of Basic Needs Makes a Man "Sick" When anyone is blocked in trying to meet a need which he feels is essential for him, he becomes to some extent mentally ill. However, one of the difficulties in dealing intelligently, and even in communicating, with other people is that not everyone can say—even if he is asked—what needs are currently important for him. And some "sick" men turn themselves into "half-men" by being unable to live up to their own central interests.[5]

Basic Needs Take Effect as Motivators on Different Levels In every individual, basic needs take effect as though they were arranged in a hierarchy. This hierarchy is not rigid. Lower-level needs do not have to be completely satisfied before higher-level needs can emerge as determinants for behavior. Nevertheless, everyone can recognize that different needs have priority at different times. For example, because man is partly an animal, he cannot exist without minimum satisfaction of physiological needs, such as those for air, water, food, and shelter. But because man is more than an animal, he has social, psychological, and spiritual needs which must also be met. Otherwise, he cannot develop his characteristically human potential. At levels higher than mere physical existence, every human being needs opportunities to belong, to give and receive affection and loyalty, to use and develop his powers, and to spend his energies in the sevice of something he believes in.

Psychologists agree that deep and lasting satisfaction can be achieved only to the extent that high-level needs are met. *The higher the level of the need, the greater its power to give enduring satisfaction.* Moreover, frequent opportunities to satisfy a high-level need do not blunt a person's appetite. As Francis Bacon said of knowledge,[6]

[5] See Chap. 11 for difficulties in identifying, and Chap. 22 for opportunities to help, the "half-man" who is on his way to becoming a full-blown alcoholic.

[6] Francis Bacon, "Of Knowledge," in *Essays.*

it provides a kind of satisfaction "whereof there is no satiety."

Some high-level needs seem to be almost universal. But everyone's motivational pattern is somewhat different from that of anyone else.[7]

Motivational Patterns Are Unique Recognizing that John Smith is motivated as an integral and unique organism, a practical question becomes: How is anyone to know who John is (as an individual), still less what he might become (as an organization resource) if he could truly satisfy his deepest human needs? For this reason alone it is essential that every first-level supervisor try to understand each of his subordinates—as an individual.

The Self-concept as a Unifying Force According to Gellerman, unifying forces run through each individual's motivational history. One of the most powerful is the drive to actualize his own image of himself. "The outlines of a person's self-image are fairly well etched in early childhood; thereafter . . . they do not ordinarily change radically. . . . The individual remains true to his symbolic self."[8] For example, a child who early sees himself as a leader will, if possible, try to behave that way in later life. Therefore, anyone who wishes to interact productively with another person should seriously try to answer the questions: How does he see himself? Who does he think he is? What is he trying to do?

Two things that each individual is always trying to do, consciously or otherwise, are: to act like the person he thinks he is, and to get what he thinks he can (and should) have. In short, everyone "is always following a strategy [which seems to him] sensible for getting along in the world he thinks he lives in."[9]

Effect of the Environment as Perceived However, a person's ideas of what he most needs and how he can get it are the product of his *experience in a given environment*. Here a second unifying force makes itself felt. It should be noted that a person's interpretation of what his environment can do for him, and to him, is not a direct response to objective facts. As emphasized by Carl Rogers, what counts, for psychological development, is that part of the phenomenal field which "is experienced [consciously and unconsciously] by the organism."[10]

Sometimes the experiences of an individual's adult life fail to confirm the lessons he learned as a child about how best to handle the events and persons that make up his perceived environment. When adult experiences differ drastically from those in which a person's self-image was formed, that individual is likely to be in serious trouble. For example, if a person continues to assert himself aggressively, although his assigned role is that of a subordinate in a system of authoritarian management, he will almost certainly get into trouble with his organizational superiors.[11] On the other hand, if, in order to avoid having trouble with other people, an employee changes his behavior on the job so much that it no longer matches his own motivational pattern, he is in deep trouble within himself. For instance, a per-

---

[7] John J. Morse and J. W. Lorsch (in "Beyond Theory Y," *Harvard Business Review,* vol. 48, no. 3, pp. 61–68, May-June, 1970) emphasize that every individual is different, although research convinced the authors that all people have one characteristic in common. *Everyone has a need to feel competent.* However (p. 67), differences "in many other dimensions of personality . . . will determine how a particular person achieves a sense of competence."

[8] Saul W. Gellerman, *Motivation and Productivity,* American Management Association, Inc., New York, 1963, p. 184.

[9] *Ibid.,* pp. 197–198.

[10] Carl R. Rogers, *Client Centered Therapy: Its Current Practice, Implications and Theory,* Houghton Mifflin Company, Boston, 1951, p. 483.

[11] For interesting sketches of "a deviant" and "an isolate," see A. Zaleznik, *Worker Satisfaction and Development: A Case Study of Work and Social Behavior in a Factory Group,* Harvard Business School, Division of Research, Boston, 1956, pp. 81–95.

son who is naturally self-reliant and highly motivated may give in to environmental pressure. In so conforming, his response in words and action becomes that of a yes-man. But now that he no longer responds to his inner motivation, his productivity tends to be reduced to the point where he does just enough to get by. Such giving in and giving up is, in effect, "mental retirement."

At the organizational level of lower and middle management, this environmentally conditioned response has been characterized by Blake and Mouton [12] as "the 1,1 managerial style. . . . [A manager with this orientation] has learned to be 'out of it' [doing just enough to avoid being dismissed]. Little is expected of him and little is given by him. . . . The 1,1 approach is unnatural. It comes to those who have accepted defeat. . . . This kind of accommodation amounts to 'being present, yet absent.' "

All Behavior Is Determined, but Not All of It Is Motivated   To some extent, every intelligent and flexible person responds to environmental pressures. As Maslow has pointed out, "There are many determinants of behavior other than motives." [13] Those which make themselves felt in childhood are normally most important. Some are exerted by national culture, geographical location, and the historical period in which a person happens to live. Still other determinants of behavior originate in the situation itself. Here is where ways of managing make a difference—for people at work. Managers at all organizational

levels exert influences that affect the behavior of other employees. Every manager who sees this fact *as a responsibility for him* will ask himself what kind of influence his way of managing exerts on those with whom he works. He will want to know what he can do to increase organizational effectiveness by helping to reinforce, in employees, the drive toward satisfying high-level needs which is potentially a powerful motivating factor. He will want to find out whether newcomers who are members of minority groups have brought with them a feeling that "everyone is down on me anyway, so I could never get anywhere even if I did try." If so, the manager should ask himself: "How can I demonstrate that in this organization people are recognized as individuals, not stereotypes? Promotion is open to everyone who qualifies for it." [14] In seeking answers to such questions, a manager might wish to consider other theories of motivation developed by behavioral psychologists with specific reference to job satisfaction.

A Controversial Theory: The Duality of Man's Nature

Herzberg [15] started from the premise that man's nature has two entirely separate parts: the *animal* nature and the uniquely *human* nature. From there, Herzberg developed a theory of motivation whose salient points are as follows:

---

[12] Robert R. Blake and Jane S. Mouton, *The Managerial Grid: Key Orientations for Achieving Production through People,* Gulf Publishing Company, Houston, 1964, pp. 85, 89, and 105.

[13] In this chapter, we use the word "motivation" in accordance with Maslow's differentiation between inner-directed behavior that is "motivated" and behavior that is merely "determined." A similar concept has been advanced by Herzberg—see next section of this chapter. An apparent contradiction will appear later in Chap. 21, where the more generally accepted meaning of the term "motivation" is used to denote any factor that brings about a change in behavior, regardless of whether the stimulus comes from inside an individual or from outside, as an external incentive or pressure.

[14] For suggestions as to how blacks can qualify for managerial and professional positions in predominantly white business establishments, see John S. Morgan and Richard L. Van Dyke, *White-Collar Blacks: A Breakthrough?* American Management Association, Inc., New York, 1970. The book gives case histories of 44 careers (men and women) and presents helpful interview material on key phases of the employment process.

[15] Frederick Herzberg, Bernard Mausner, and Barbara Bloch Snyderman, *The Motivation to Work,* 2d ed., John Wiley & Sons, Inc., New York, 1966; Frederick Herzberg, *Work and the Nature of Man,* The World Publishing Company, New York, 1966. The former includes a detailed description of Herzberg's method. The second is largely a restatement of his theory. In the following pages, references to the first book will be given as *Motivation* and to the second as *Work.*

• Everyone has needs that derive from his nature as a human animal (corresponding roughly to Maslow's lower-level human needs).

• Insofar as man responds to his animal nature, he is negatively oriented. He tries to avoid pain and unpleasantness by adjusting to his environment. Maximum success in this effort can lead to the absence of discontent with a job. As a dominant orientation, it is conducive to mental ill health.

• The other part of man's nature is uniquely human. Behavior motivated by this set of (high-level) needs consists in *adjusting to one's self.* In this process, achievement leads to the feeling that one is becoming more of a person by growing in the direction of self-actualization. This type of inner-directed adjustment contributes to strong and lasting satisfaction, to greater productivity, and to mental equilibrium.

• According to Herzberg, both sets of needs are "unidimensional." Each relates to only one side of man's nature. It would therefore follow that environmental factors which affect a man's attitude toward his job must also be divided into mutually exclusive categories. This view is in marked contrast to the traditional one-factor theory of job attitudes in which any job-related factor may be a source of both satisfaction and/or dissatisfaction.

In seeking empirical data to test these postulates, Herzberg and his associates developed an interview method by which they could gain insight into individual motivational patterns. They undertook to study as a *unit* the "factors-attitudes-effects" (FAE) complex.

"Satisfiers" and "Dissatisfiers" Findings of Herzberg's first major study are pictured in Figure 6-1, in which the *length* of each block shows the *frequency* with which each first-level factor [16] appeared in the sequence of events reported as satisfying or dissatisfying. The width of each block shows the reported duration of satisfied or dissatisfied feelings.

[16] A first-level factor is defined as shorthand notations of outward events, as reported by the interviewee.

As hypothesized, the directly job-related factors (at the top and right side of Figure 6-1) were found to have a more lasting effect than those at the bottom and to the left of Figure 6-1, which concern the context or surroundings in which a person does his job.

Herzberg's interview data (and subsequent studies made by other researchers using the same method) [17] also confirmed the hypothesis that factors of job content (the satisfiers) can stimulate high motivation and increased productivity. The factors classified as dissatisfiers were reported more often as part of a negative job attitude. Moreover, according to Herzberg, even when they are adequately provided for and occasion no dissatisfaction, they cannot raise employee morale above a neutral level. Among these "Hygiene" or "Maintenance" factors, Herzberg found that "company policy and administration" was the most important in "determining bad feelings about a job," (*Motivation*, p. 71) [18] and that salary "has more potency as a job dissatisfier than as a job satisfier." (*Motivation*, p. 82.)

Critics [19] of Herzberg's motivator-hygiene duality question the validity of classifying money as a hygiene factor. But the feature that has aroused widespread criticism is the idea that satisfiers and dissatisfiers are unidimensional;

[17] Studies undertaken by nine other researchers on a total of 14 populations ranging from agricultural workers to supervisors in utility companies, and from hospital personnel in the United States to engineers in Hungary, showed *achievement* as the top satisfier for 13 out of 14 of the groups studied. For 12 of these groups, *recognition* was second only to achievement. Among the dissatisfiers, *company policy and administration* was verified as the top factor for 13 of the 14 groups studied. (*Work,* Chap. 7, "Verification of the Theory of Motivation-Hygiene," pp. 92–129.)

[18] As an example of company policy which occasioned dissatisfaction, interviewees most frequently mentioned preference for college-educated personnel regardless of the merit of noncollege personnel. Among administrative practices, bypassing was often reported as dissatisfying.

[19] Orlando Behling, George Labovitz, and Richard Kosmo, "The Herzberg Controversy: A Critical Reappraisal," *Academy of Management Journal,* vol. 11, no. 1, pp. 99–108, March, 1968.

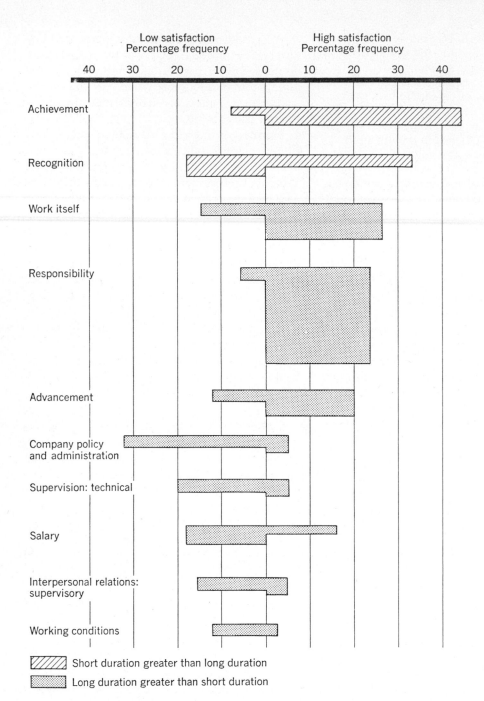

Figure 6-1 Comparison of satisfiers and dissatisfiers. *(Source: Frederick Herzberg, Bernard Mausner, and Barbara Bloch Snyderman,* The Motivation to Work, *2d ed., John Wiley & Sons, Inc., New York, 1959, p. 81.)*

namely that a factor such as achievement, which can be strongly motivating, cannot also be demotivating (demoralizing) when there is no opportunity to satisfy this need.

Interviews which we have held with managers and supervisors during management development seminars have led us to disagree with Herzberg's classification of interpersonal relationships as a dissatisfier and also with his statement that a motivator cannot operate in reverse—as a demoralizing factor. First, there were frequent indications that an interpersonal relationship had been a strong motivator for many people when support—that could have been withheld—was offered by an organizational superior or an associate. Second, our interview material clearly showed that interpersonal relationships can also be a powerfully demotivating factor. Many persons reported that their will to work had been undermined by evidence that an organizational superior lacked integrity and failed to follow through on promised support. This lack of confidence in certain superiors was frequently cited as a primary reason for having requested a transfer or for having quit.

Nevertheless, these interviews have also convinced us that Herzberg's contrast between job content and job context is significant for the understanding of inner motivation. Intrinsic interest of the work itself, opportunity to develop one's potential and growth on the job, were uniformly regarded as more important than the physical surroundings in which such meaningful work was done.

Convincing support for Herzberg's theory of satisfiers (responsibility, achievement, recognition, and career development) has been given by controlled experiments in the Bell Telephone System.[20] The results convinced members of top management that reshaping jobs to provide maximum satisfaction in the work itself is worth far more than it costs—not only because there is

a dramatic reduction in employee turnover, and therefore also greatly reduced training costs, but also in higher productivity and in career development for employees. The large proportion of employees who were able to meet gradually increasing opportunities for responsibility demonstrated their promotional caliber.

Consequently, we find ourselves in complete agreement with Ford[21] that Herzberg has (1) made a great contribution in emphasizing the significance of "work itself" (job content) as potentially motivational; (2) provided a simple and stimulating framework for further research; but (3) overstated the case for disregarding "hygiene or maintenance factors." Unless pay and benefits are high, even a satisfied employee may quit.

Hackman's Multidimensional Concept of the Motivation to Work[22]

Hackman (working independently) agrees with Maslow and Herzberg that there is a hierarchy of basic needs. However, he strongly emphasizes the significance of differences between individuals and notes that there probably are no pure types of motivational patterns. Using a structured questionnaire as part of an attitude survey, Hackman found that the words a person uses to describe his motivational feelings (for example, feelings of recognition, confidence, and accomplishment) indicate his degree of independence. Hackman agrees with Herzberg in differentiating between work itself and the conditions surrounding work. He finds that some people are primarily "task-oriented," while others are "situation-oriented." Both types of responses are classified as "work-activity-oriented." His motivational theory is based on responses to the *total work situation,* including interpersonal relations—especially supervision—as a potentially positive factor in the work situation that can

[20] See Robert N. Ford, "Results of the Controlled Experiments," in *op. cit.,* pp. 45-79.

[21] *Op. cit.,* pp. 130-131.
[22] Ray C. Hackman, *The Motivated Working Adult,* American Management Association, Inc., New York, 1969.

reinforce motivation. Moreover, he is convinced that his system of describing work motivation applies to men and women, salaried or hourly rated, and regardless of length of employment.

According to Hackman, a work-motivated adult can be described by considering seven basic dimensions: (1) His characteristic level of physical energy, and (2) the extent to which his energy—high or low—is work directed. Highly motivated people "are identified with work in a social context that yields closure experiences," e.g, opportunities to complete a given task.[23] Such an adult regards work (3) as a medium through which to exercise skills, or (4) as a means to attain and exercise responsibility over other people and their activities, or (5) as a means to some end extrinsic to work itself (such as wealth, security, or prestige). To some individuals, ordinary pressures of work and of the "conditions which surround it" (6) feel threatening and arouse anxiety, or (7) seem irritating and arouse aggressive reactions.

In summary, Hackman sets up the following classification of motivational patterns: (*a*) "closure seekers," (*b*) "responsibility seekers," (*c*) "instrumentalists"—means-to-end seekers, and (*d*) "emotional types," who feel threatened or irritated by normal work pressures.

Other Motivational Studies

Patchen's research,[24] which was conducted in selected units of the Tennessee Valley Authority,

took account of the following indicators of motivation: "General job interest, interest in innovation, and attendance, as well as pride in work and symptoms of stress." "Aroused motivation" was found to be a function of three variables (one in the employee himself and two in the work situation): (1) an employee's inner need for achievement; (2) the degree of achievement possible in his job; and (3) the probability that increased effort on his part will lead to greater achievement. However, research showed that one cannot expect an employee to be strongly motivated unless all three conditions exist simultaneously. For example, if an employee sees his job as one in which genuine achievement is impossible or thinks that greater effort on his part would not result in greater achievement, what incentive is there for him to exert himself—even if he has an inner drive to achieve?

According to the above findings, the level of performance by an employee who has inner motivation for achievement can be raised by the following features in the work situation: (1) a degree of difficulty in his job that is great enough to constitute a challenge to him but not so great as to induce stress; (2) a considerable degree of control over his own work methods; (3) the existence of appropriate standards for measuring performance; and (4) feedback—that he regards as relevant and reliable—as to his degree of success.[25]

Patchen also emphasizes the importance of individual differences in regard to rewards that people value. For example, some employees value an extrinsic reward, such as money, more than an intrinsic reward, such as opportunity for psychological growth on the job. He also notes that when these four situational variables (a match of individual differences and situational factors) appear in combination, their effect on

[23] A similar drive has been singled out by McClelland as the "achievement motive." See D. C. McClelland et al., *The Achievement Motive,* Appleton-Century-Crofts, Inc., New York, 1953; *The Achieving Society,* D. Van Nostrand Co., Inc., New York, 1961; "Business Drive and National Achievement," *Harvard Business Review,* vol. 40, no. 4, July-August, 1962, pp. 99-112. The article characterizes the achiever as one who (1) likes situations in which he takes personal responsibility for finding solutions to problems; (2) has a tendency to set moderate achievement goals and to take "calculated risks"; (3) wants concrete feedback as to how well he is doing.

[24] Martin Patchen, *Participation, Achievement, and Involvement on the Job,* Prentice-Hall, Inc., Englewood Cliffs, N.J., 1970.

[25] The importance of such a match between employee expectation and experience on the job is also emphasized by other researchers, notably Roche and MacKinnon, Morse and Lorsch, and M. Scott Myers.

motivation is multiplicative rather than merely additive.

Porter and Lawler[26] start by recognizing that behavioral research has long since exposed as a myth the notion that a happy employee is *necessarily* more productive than if he were dissatisfied. However, they make three significant qualifying statements: studies have shown that (1) job satisfaction is often associated with high performance,[27] (2) high satisfaction *is* associated with low employee turnover and low absenteeism, and (3) it may be more fruitful to think about job satisfactions as a result rather than as a cause of high job performance.

In addition to the significant motivational differences noted by Patchen—those between extrinsic and intrinsic rewards and individual differences in value attitudes by employees to a given reward—Porter and Lawler speak of an employee's "expectation"[28] that greater effort on his part will enable him to obtain the kind of reward that he values most. For example, if a rank-and-file employee puts a high value on money but works in an organization where pay raises are given only according to length of service, why should he be expected to exert himself beyond the point where he meets minimum requirements? Conversely, if another employee has strong drives toward achievement and for control over his own work methods (intrinsic rewards), then satisfying these high-level needs tends to result in high performance by him.

M. Scott Myers[29] agrees with major findings summarized in the previous paragraphs. In addition, he draws on experience at Texas Instruments in Dallas, Texas, with reference to the following hypotheses:

• A job becomes meaningful when the incumbent (1) can see that his task relates to a "meaningful chunk" of his personal goals and (2) can plan and measure his achievement according to an effective "do-and-control system."[30]
• To have maximum effect on inner motivation, a goal must be (1) influenced by the employee as a goal setter; (2) visible—that is, by direct feedback; (3) desirable; (4) challenging; and (5) attainable. Such a goal satisfies needs for growth, achievement, responsibility, recognition, affiliation—the need to belong—and security.
• Management systems must satisfy human needs that are both high-level and maintenance-oriented. Participation by lower-level employees in planning and implementing such systems is a form of job enrichment that can give meaning to work experience of an employee whose daily task would not, in itself, appeal to an achievement-motivated individual.

What Might All These Hypotheses Mean for a Manager?

After considering such research findings on motivation, a manager might select those which seem to him most significant, and most practicable, for his organization:

1 Motivation needs to be thought of both in relation to *individual differences*[31] and *in the context of the total work situation.*
2 Inner motivation to satisfy high-level needs can result in high performance on the job if these currently felt needs are satisfied.

---

[26] Lyman W. Porter and Edward E. Lawler III, "What Job Attitudes Tell about Motivation," *Harvard Business Review,* vol. 46, no. 1, pp. 118-126, January-February, 1968.

[27] Victor H. Vroom, in *Work and Motivation,* John Wiley & Sons, Inc., New York, 1964, Chap. 6, reviewed some 20 studies and found that in most cases where data on satisfaction and performance were gathered there was a positive correlation between these two factors.

[28] Note the difference between "expectation" and "probability," suggesting that what a person perceives is decisive for him.

[29] M. Scott Myers, *Every Employee a Manager: More Meaningful Work through Job Enrichment,* McGraw-Hill Book Company, New York, 1970.

[30] At Texas Instruments, "control" includes measurement, evaluation, and correction. "Planning" includes problem solving, goal setting and use of manpower, materiel, and systems. The "do" phase, of course, implements the planning.

[31] Individual differences in personality and value orientation as well as differences in job and position classification, e.g., nonmanagers, managers, and executives.

3 Intrinsic rewards, such as recognition from within and outside the group for attainment of goals, derived from job content, can greatly stimulate inner motivation and therefore high performance. But extrinsic rewards, such as increased pay or promotion, may be seen as appeasers and annoyers if they seem unrelated to high performance.

4 "Hygiene seekers" should not be appointed to managerial positions, chiefly because (*a*) they are to some extent mentally ill; (*b*) they do not naturally plan and organize work for their subordinates so that intrinsic rewards can be attained, and (*c*) their juniors are likely to imitate them.

5 For purposes of placement and selection, (*a*) "closure seekers" should not be given top-management positions because work requirements at that organizational level do not characteristically permit this kind of experience; (*b*) "responsibility seekers" should be placed in managerial and supervisory positions because human relationships are extremely important to them; (*c*) "instrumentalists"—who regard work as means to their own ends—can be useful in hourly rated positions; but (*d*) those who become anxious and irritable, even under normal work pressures, are poor employment risks.

6 Supervisors can stimulate and reinforce inner motivation when they give every employee (their subordinates) the highest practicable degree of responsibility and control in regard to the methods by which they work.

7 Goal setting for each employee should be both career-oriented and task-oriented. Progress toward each goal should be challenging for him, as well as visible and attainable. Even for rank-and-file workers, task-oriented goals can thus satisfy high-level as well as low-level needs.

Any manager interested in testing possible connections between job attitudes, interpersonal relationships, and high performance needs to clarify the meanings of key terms such as "teamwork," "team spirit," "partnership," and "cooperative relationships." These terms have a core of generally accepted meanings, but they also have special connotations for every individual. Here is what the following terms connote to us.

TEAM RELATIONSHIPS

By *teamwork* we mean well-coordinated and effectively synchronized interaction to achieve a shared objective.

Prerequisites for effective teamwork include (1) commitment of all members to shared objectives; (2) a relatively small number of persons—to permit mutual understanding between all teammates; (3) ability of each member to contribute toward the common goal(s); (4) proximity and frequent opportunities for informal face-to-face communication—so that all members can come to know one another well; and (5) constant practice. Only by intensive and continuing practice in interaction with the same persons can anyone come to feel sure of what those individuals can and will do as teammates. That assurance makes it possible, in a crisis, for team members to think and act in concert—with few words or none—effectively meeting shared objectives in a changing situation.

By *team spirit* we mean (1) readiness to join with others in activity toward a common goal, (2) loyalty to other team members individually and to the team as a social unit, and (3) willingness to pay a high price, in personal effort, to accomplish a team goal.

Pablo Casals, in the orchestra which he founded and conducted in Barcelona, created a situation where *team spirit* and the *prerequisites for effective teamwork* enabled him to work with 88 musicians (most of them without previous orchestral experience) and develop an outstanding group of symphonic players. Two rehearsals a day met several preconditions mentioned above. But the spirit developed by members of the orchestra was probably the most significant factor. Casals inspired them with his own feeling of dedication to music:

> I stressed that each musician must learn to play, on the one hand, as if he were a soloist and, on the other, with the constant awareness of being an in-

dispensable part of a team. . . . Human teamwork [in music is] the sense of being one of a group working together to achieve the ultimate in beauty. . . . We share the great privilege of bringing masterpieces to life. We also share a sacred responsibility. We are entrusted with the duty of interpreting these masterpieces with utter integrity.[32]

Prerequisites for team spirit and for partnership are so similar that we have combined them below.

Partnership, according to Webster, is "the state of being a partner; participation." This state of being may be further clarified by describing the feelings which are characteristic of a partner. They are similar to those of a teammate. But what is distinctive about a partner is his recognition that he can contribute to shared objectives by exercising managerial functions. If he is a *junior or working partner,* he does not expect to participate on equal terms in making all major decisions. But he can count on the following: (1) having a share in planning, organizing, directing, and controlling all activities for which he assumes responsibility; (2) being invited to express his ideas in regard to all decisions whose consequences will seriously affect him; (3) having his constructive suggestions judiciously considered (though not necessarily adopted); (4) receiving reasonable explanations as to why any of his suggestions are modified or rejected; and (5) being treated with courtesy and consideration by his other partner(s).

Prerequisites for team spirit and for a spirit of partnership are provided in a situation where individuals have opportunities to participate (1) with their minds and at the level of ego involvement, as well as with mere physical strength or technical skill, (2) in small action groups, where effort is meshed, and (3) in achieving goals which all members see as important.

It is contrary to human nature to expect team spirit to develop before each individual has

learned by experience what teamwork *can do for him.* Moreover, highly competitive relationships between peers (traditionally referred to as "healthy competition") and emphasis on superior-subordinate relationships are incompatible with what motivates a person who feels and functions like a teammate or a partner.

By *cooperative relationships* we mean those characterized by (1) willingness to engage in teamwork, (2) community of purpose with regard to long-term aims, and (3) commitment to a larger whole. Between members of a large organization who have no regular contact with each other, a cooperative relationship is the nearest thing to a team relationship which can prevail. Using the words "teamwork" and "team" for activities which have any tinge of cooperativeness obscures the highly effective interaction (team play) which can be achieved only in relatively small groups.

Prerequisites for a cooperative relationship among all members of a large organization include (1) A style of managing which fosters cooperation and free communication regardless of organization status or specialized function, (2) An organization structure which permits communication as needed between cross-functional work groups, and (3) Corporate policies and goals which encourage feelings of membership and enlistment in the organization as a whole.

Where cooperative relationships exist, a considerable degree of teamwork can rapidly be developed when members of different work teams temporarily join forces on a common project, e.g., to cope with an emergency. Outstanding instances of such temporary teamwork have been given by employees in public utilities. After a hurricane, out-of-state line crews often pour into a disaster area, working with local teams around the clock to restore power. Cooperative relations may also develop into a team relationship when employees are recruited to work together on some special project. Whether or not this happens depends in large measure on the leadership exercised by the project manager.

---

[32] *Joys and Sorrows: Reflections by Pablo Casals,* as told to Albert E. Kahn, Simon and Schuster, New York, 1970, p. 157.

Implementing These Ideas

Most managers know that they need good team-work and strong team spirit but that both can be disadvantageous unless directed toward organizational goals. Having reached this point, an executive may usefully ask himself: Where does teamwork exist in this organization? Toward what goals is it directed? What might I do to facilitate teamwork which could help to advance our major organizational goals?

Taking a Systems Approach   At this stage he might consider, and even consider *doing something about,* ideas presented in the previous chapters. As a starter, he might think of the entire organization as an integral whole, a total man-machine system, in which relationships between the component parts are as important as the parts themselves. Then, in thinking about "the human organization," he could direct his attention to the smallest social units, work groups. Each of these can be regarded as a fundamental building block for a productive organization. Then, recognizing the relationship between individual behavior and environment, a systems-minded manager would not ask: How can we change the behavior of these individuals, so that instead of loafing on the job and resisting managerial controls, they will go all out for management objectives? Instead, his inquiry will be guided by the insight that *behavior* is a *function* of interaction between a *person* and his *environment.*

Taking the total organizational situation as the environment, the executive might then reexamine the components of organization structure, the communication system, and corporate policies. Questions to be asked here include these:

1   Is our organization structure such that planning, decision making, and controlling are sufficiently decentralized to facilitate teamwork at various organizational levels?

2   Is our communication system such that ideas and information flow freely in all directions?

3   Do our policies provide adequate guidance for decision making by management representatives without imposing undue limitations on their initiative and judgment?

4   Are policy statements accessible to all who need to know about them and to use them?

5   How are our policies shaped up? Is all policy thinking done at the top level? Or do policy suggestions and evaluations come from all segments of the organization?

Practicing Consultative Management   After making some such general review, the next step for a chief executive might be to discuss with his immediate work associates the managerial style which they believe in and try to practice. Does he, and do his associates, think that *his* way of managing is one which evokes a high level of participation from other employees? If so, how about *their* way of managing?

A chief executive who invites group appraisal of managing as practiced in the organization is using the consultative approach. In this way he demonstrates a feeling which is appropriate for problem solving as well as for appraising. By encouraging constructive criticisms and a "yes-but" response to his own statements he is practicing participative management.

Studying a Work Situation   An executive's next step toward fostering better teamwork in his own organization may be intensive study of some work situation in which teamwork has demonstrably increased productivity. Such a situation may be observed wherever a management and a local union cooperate on increasing productivity.

In writing about such an experience, Lesieur[33]

---

[33] Frederick G. Lesieur, *The Scanlon Plan: A Frontier in Labor-Management Cooperation,* The M.I.T. Press, Cambridge, Mass., and John Wiley & Sons, Inc., New York, 1958, chap. 4, "What the Plan Isn't and What It Is," pp. 34–49. Except as noted, the following quotations are taken from this source. For further details and experience under the Plan, see Chap. 21.

has emphasized participation and teamwork as keys to its success. This

> . . . doesn't mean giving people a "sense of participation," workers don't want that. This plan means giving them real participation. . . . [It has enabled] management and labor to get together and mutually solve problems that will help them be more competitive. . . . [For a rank-and-file worker] it means working with your brains instead of [merely] with your back.

Some executives have found it difficult to analyze objectively any way of managing which entails close cooperation with a union. Thus there may be advantages in observing how participation and teamwork have been achieved in a hospital before unions entered the picture.

Teamwork and Individual Goals in Nursing

During and after the Second World War, the nursing shortage became acute. To alleviate it, nursing administrators (taking a leaf from the book of scientific management) introduced the so-called "functional method" of nursing. Strictly professional duties, such as giving medication and making rounds with attending physicians, were reserved for professional nurses. Nonprofessionals took over most of the less-skilled work. For example, licensed practical nurses (LPNs) were assigned such duties as taking blood pressures and temperatures or giving baths and back rubs. Auxiliary workers, nurse's aides, and orderlies were assigned to such tasks as making beds, carrying trays, and escorting patients to other departments.

Professional nurses now had more time for highly skilled services. But because of the effect on nonprofessional personnel, this technically efficient system did not work out as planned. Resentment and bickering developed between persons assigned to perform a number of strictly limited tasks for many patients. Nonprofession-

als found their work dull. Many quit for better-paying jobs. And no one had enough contact with any one patient to permit understanding him as an individual. Thus, in the late 1940s, many nursing administrators became convinced that the current method of nursing care was not good enough—either for the patient or for job satisfaction and individual development by nursing personnel.

At this point, forward-looking nursing administrators saw the need and possibility of developing genuine teamwork and team spirit based on concepts of "leadership, organization, partnership, group response to goals, integrated action, and in-service training of supervision."[34] Nursing administrators in New York and Boston launched independent experiments in team nursing at almost exactly the same time.[35] The following hypotheses were the basis for specific plans to reorganize work and work relationships so that nursing personnel (from professionals to aides) could derive direct rewards in job satisfaction while also becoming more productive:

- Participation in nursing care by nonprofessionals needs to be guided and supplemented by professionals. But supervision by professionals need not restrict development of nonprofessional personnel.
- A high level of participation by employees can be expected only when each can function up to the limit of his ability, contributing his experience and insight as well as his technical skill and physical effort.
- When employees have opportunities to participate in making plans they are expected to implement, a high degree of understanding and

[34] Ruth Sleeper, in Dorothy Perkins Newcomb, *The Team Plan: A Manual for Nursing Service Administrators,* G. P. Putnam's Sons, New York, 1953, p. viii.

[35] The results of both experiments were published in 1953 in two monographs which have become classics in the field of nursing education: Eleanor Lambertsen, *Nursing Team Organization and Functioning,* Division of Nursing Education, Bureau of Publications, Teachers College, Columbia University, New York, 1953; and Newcomb, *op. cit.* In this section we draw freely on both texts.

acceptance tends to motivate them toward superior performance.

• Participation at the level of ego involvement is prerequisite for the full development of each individual and for a kind of evaluation (of planning and performance) which can continuously raise the level of group achievement.

• When participation is a strongly motivated response by "the whole man," there is no need for an authoritarian type of inspection and control. Group supervision, group controls, self-control, and self-evaluation can effectively be supplemented by a leader who also functions as a working partner and is thus in a position to understand the individuals with whom he daily works and communicates.

Plans and Assignments Two kinds of interlinking plans and assignments help to weld members of each nursing team[36] into a well-knit action group. The *medical care plan* (formulated by the attending physician) provides a framework within which a *plan of nursing care* for each patient is developed. This nursing plan is designed to meet the needs (psychological as well as physical) of each patient. Thus every team member can feel committed to a unified project and understand how his part contributes to the whole team effort.

However, before a nursing plan is even formulated, the first kind of assignment is made. The head nurse on each unit (ward) assigns specific patients to each nursing team. Then, each team leader tentatively develops nursing-care plans for all patients assigned to her team. On any given day, some part of her own work assign-

ment may highlight the job-centered approach which characterizes team action and disregards status. For example, a team leader may decide to make a patient's bed or to carry in a tray. Such an apparently unimportant (nonprofessional) task is an appropriate assignment for a leader if by performing it she can create a favorable condition for overcoming a communication block which has prevented other team members from reaching a patient.

Another way in which team nursing differs from traditional nursing practice is that a team leader no longer regards any individuals as "my patients." Instead, she keeps herself free to circulate among her teammates, all of whom are helping to care for "our patients."[37]

Participation and Evaluation Each team's long-range objective is continuously to raise the level of care given to each patient. Part of every team member's assignment is to observe the response of each patient and to jot down suggestions for improving the plan for his care. These suggestions are discussed at the daily team conference.

Communication: In Team Conferences[38] and between Individuals A daily conference, conducted informally by the team leader, has the following multiple purpose: (1) to make sure that each member clearly understands the what, how, and why of her work assignment for the day; (2) to discuss and, if possible, solve problems encountered by team members either earlier in the

---

[36] On each team, the leader is always a graduate nurse, with another graduate as her replacement. Other members are LPNs, orderlies, nurse's aides, and student nurses. The specific role of each is determined by previous education and current skill. In theory, each patient is also a member of the nursing team; he is expected to participate, as much as his physical and mental condition permits, in monitoring and implementing a plan of care which is tailored to his needs. When effective communication can be established between patient, physician, and nursing personnel, the needs currently felt by patients can be taken into account during daily reviews of plans for his care.

[37] In this respect, as in others, there is a strong resemblance between attitudes characteristically developed by team nursing and by the Scanlon Plan. In writing about the latter, Lesieur commented on the need, and consequences, of "getting away from the 'I' concept, and going to the 'we'" (*op. cit.,* p. 37).

[38] For a study indicating that there is a positive relationship between (1) the frequency and amount of supervisory communication that is perceived by nonsupervisory employees as satisfying and (2) supervisory effectiveness, see Harish C. Jain, "Supervisory Communication Effectiveness and Performance in Two Urban Hospitals," *Personnel Journal,* vol. 50, no. 5, pp. 392-395, May, 1971.

tour of duty or the day before; and (3) to consider suggestions for improving some plan for a patient's care.

Supervision and Inspection The team leader's daily work assignment enables her constantly to supervise and inspect what other team members do. However, her supervision is not resented because her work associates can see that her professional knowledge and up-to-date understanding can be helpful to them.

When a team leader finds that something has been done incorrectly or inadequately, she is expected to ask: What is accountable? Is the plan for nursing care faulty in some respect? Was the work assignment unwise (perhaps because the person was insufficiently prepared)? Were the instructions unclear? In correcting the performance of teammates, a leader is expected to do so with objectivity and friendliness. The focus of attention is always on the job to be done.[39]

Control Experience with nursing teams has demonstrated that control for quality and quantity of output can increasingly come from mem-

bers of a work group. Members of nursing teams feel responsible for doing their best, in partnership with others who share responsibility for nursing care plans. And each of these plans meshes with a medical care plan, which fits into the whole plan by which each hospital undertakes to meet its major objectives. Thus, team members naturally feel a responsibility toward performance by the hospital as a whole.

Linkage and Cooperation with Other Hospital Personnel The leader of each nursing team serves as a link to a health team. She works with the physician (the leader of that team) and cooperates, as need arises, with other members of a health team, e.g., a social worker, a dietician, or a clergyman. The head nurse is another link member. She confers with physicians and their associates on health teams. Sometimes, it has been in evaluating action taken in an emergency that the need for this kind of linkage could most clearly be seen as a means for suitable expansion of teamwork.

A Case Example: The CPR Team

In one hospital a plan was developed by the CPR (cardiopulmonary resuscitation) team whereby turning on a patient's light alerted nurses to the fact that there might be an emergency. Whoever saw the light first and found that there actually was an emergency requiring the services of the CPR team immediately picked up the nearest telephone and alerted the switchboard operator, who then paged the CPR team both as a whole and individually: "Attention, please, CPR alert, *x* floor." While expert help was on the way, whoever was on the spot would immediately initiate mouth-to-mouth breathing and external chest massage, keeping these up unremittingly until relieved by a CPR team member. If the anesthetist arrived before the physician, he would direct operations until relieved. (Any physician in the hospital was expected to report for duty immediately on hearing the CPR alert.)

[39] A similar way of supervising, in a situation where all members of an experimental work group felt responsible for quality production, turned out to be a key feature in the unexpectedly high productivity of girls in the relay test room during the Western Electric Research Program conducted by Elton Mayo and his associates. There was more supervision in the test room than there had been in the shop; the operators were under constant supervision. But the different quality of supervision in the test room apparently meant that the girls welcomed it as "supportive" instead of resenting it as "suppressive." An evidence of the friendly attitude felt by the test-room operators toward those who were supervising them was given by the girl who said about one of them, "Say, he's no boss. We don't have any boss." The comprehensive report has become a classic. See F. J. Roethlisberger and W. J. Dickson, *Management and the Worker: An Account of a Research Program Conducted by the Western Electric Company, Hawthorne Works, Chicago,* Harvard University Press, Cambridge, Mass., 1939. For an examination of subsequent criticisms made by laboratory psychologists and social scientists of the Hawthorne experiment, see Alan Cubbon, "Hawthorne Talk in Context," *Occupational Psychology,* vol. 43, no. 2, pp. 111-128, 1969.

Hospital personnel not on the CPR team were also able to cooperate. For instance, housekeeping personnel, aides, and orderlies knew that they could be of immediate service by removing all excess furniture to make room for emergency personnel and equipment.[40]

Results In a few hospitals, authoritarian ways were so entrenched that it was impossible to develop the climate essential for the development of team nursing. However, in many hospitals good results of team nursing have included the following:

- At the practical level it has been found that team nursing saves time (and therefore money) and that employee turnover is lower.
- Nursing administrators emphasize as a major gain the continually improving quality of nursing care achieved by full participation from team members working closely with an able leader.
- An associated result is psychological growth on the job. This gain shows up clearly at five levels of the nursing service hierarchy:
  1 The *head nurse* must now learn to delegate. She can still keep in touch with patients and with nursing personnel. But now she has time to concentrate on the core of her job, creating and maintaining a climate conducive to the best possible nursing care.
  2 The *staff nurse,* now functioning as a subleader, can develop her skills not only as a professional person but also in planning, organizing, directing, coordinating, supervising, communicating, controlling, and evaluating work done by her teammates.
  3 *Student nurses,* as early as their second year, are sometimes given opportunities to func-

tion as team leaders. In this role, they can practice the managerial skills which they are thinking and talking about as part of their academic education.
  4 Even a *first-year student* can gain more from her clinical experience when she functions as a part-time teammate. In addition to what she learns by doing with supervision from a clinical instructor, she can also learn by observing and by relating herself realistically to full-time team members.
  5 *Nonprofessional personnel* can learn and develop their full potential for nursing care in what amounts to on-the-job training.

These varied opportunities for self-development can be a major factor in creating job satisfaction and harmonious work relationships for personnel as individuals. Each team member can now be freed from the frustration felt by every highly motivated person who is "capable of doing more than he is permitted to do. The person who is functioning at the highest level of his ability most of the time is the happiest and most effective worker."[41]

SUMMARY

In the first section of this chapter we summarized some of the behavioral research findings that explain why participative management can be beneficial not only to each employee as a person but, by increasing individual productivity and potential, also to the organization as a whole.

We then selected a few working hypotheses that can be tested in any organization.

Finally, after considering the meaning of key terms relating to effective joint effort, we described team nursing illustrating the advantages of applying participative management and a systems-minded approach in a work situation that had formerly been managed in a highly authoritarian style.

In the section on team nursing, supervision was a recurring theme. In the next chapter it is

---

[40] "When employees are oriented to, and psychologically prepared for, emergency measures, a plan can run very smoothly. Everyone experiences a certain joy when he is able to contribute. But he needs preparation [if he is to function effectively, in a clearly defined role] under stress." Sister Mary Lucida Field, "The C.P.R. Team in a Medium-sized Hospital," *American Journal of Nursing,* vol. 66, no. 1, pp. 87–90, January, 1966.

[41] Newcomb, *op. cit.,* p. 30.

the central topic. It has often been said that the first-level supervisor is a key man. But perhaps it is more meaningful to ask: Why is he a key man, and what are his key functions? In seeking answers to such questions, supervisors cannot usefully be considered apart from such interrelated topics as the changing work situation, interpersonal communication, and inner motivation. Therefore, students who take a systems-minded approach to learning will want to carry with them into the next chapter ideas from the preceding chapters.

SELECTED REFERENCES

Argyris, Chris: *Integrating the Invidivual and the Organization,* John Wiley & Sons, Inc., New York, 1964.

Berelson, Bernard, and Gary A. Steiner: *Human Behavior: An Inventory of Scientific Findings,* Harcourt, Brace & Jovanovich, Inc., New York, 1964.

Bockman, Valerie M.: "The Herzberg Controversy," *Personnel Psychology,* no. 24, pp. 155-189, 1971.

Branden, Nathaniel: *The Psychology of Self Esteem,* Nash Publishing Corporation, Los Angeles, 1969.

Gardner, John W.: *No Easy Victories,* Harper & Row, Publishers, Incorporated, New York, 1969.

Kast, Fremont E., and James E. Rosenzweig: *Organization and Management: A Systems Approach,* McGraw-Hill Book Company, New York, 1970, chap. 8, "Individual Behavior and Motivation," pp. 210-240.

Likert, Rensis: *The Human Organization: Its Management and Value,* McGraw-Hill Book Company, New York, 1967.

Maslow, Abraham H.: *Toward a Psychology of Being,* D. Van Nostrand Company, Inc., Princeton, N.J., 1962.

Porter, Lyman W., and Edward E. Lawler III: *Managerial Attitudes and Performance,* Richard D. Irwin, Inc., Homewood, Ill., 1968.

Rogers, Carl R.: *On Becoming a Person: A Therapist's View of Psychotherapy,* Houghton Mifflin Company, Boston, 1961.

Rush, Harold M. F.: *Behavioral Science: Concepts and Management Application,* Personnel Policy Study no. 216, The National Industrial Conference Board, Inc., New York, 1969.

Schwab, Donald P., and Larry L. Cummings: "Theories of Performance and Satisfaction: A Review," *Industrial Relations,* vol. 9, no. 4, pp. 408-430, October, 1970 (reprinted in Paul Pigors, Charles A. Myers, and F. T. Malm, *Management of Human Resources: Readings in Personnel Administration,* 3d ed., McGraw-Hill Book Company, New York, 1973, selection 22).

Stacey, Chalmers L., and Manfred F. de Martino (eds.): *Understanding Human Motivation,* H. Allen, Cleveland, 1963.

Chapter 7

A New Role for the First-level Supervisor

The supervisor of the future knows he is . . . managing . . . a way of life that finds expression [at] all levels . . . of the organization. Through this way of life, people gradually become more knowledgeable and competent, and [move] toward a total commitment which leads to continuing growth, success, and self-renewal for both the organization and its members.

Mark Shepherd, Jr. [1]

In this chapter, the focus is on needs and opportunities to develop a new role for the first-level supervisor, with the aim of enabling him to make a maximum contribution to organization-wide goals. But before offering specific suggestions, it may be helpful briefly to review historical developments starting with the old-time foreman and then looking at the supervisor's job during a long period of transition.

[1] Mark Shepherd, Jr., President of Texas Instruments, Inc., in M. Scott Myers, *Every Employee a Manager: More Meaningful Work through Job Enrichment,* McGraw-Hill Book Company, New York, 1970, p. x.

The Old-time Foreman

In the "good old days," a foreman knew what he could do and where he stood. His job was to get out production and to keep control. As long as he got results, no one asked how he got them. (For a clear-cut illustration of that supervisory style, see Case 1, "The Old-line Foreman.") In the early days the foreman had authority to hire and fire. No union official challenged what he said or did; there was no union. No staff man gave him "advice." He was the expert. He decided how work was to be done. He set standards for job performance. He meted out punishment when he felt it was deserved and praise when he felt like giving it. He was *the boss.* The gang boss of migrant workers is a current survival.[2]

In those days it was not difficult to select a supervisor. An aggressive and competent worker was given a title and a pencil. The title made him responsible for getting out production and gave him the necessary authority. The pencil enabled him to keep track of results. He was given no preparation or training for his supervisory duties.

THE JOB IN TRANSITION

Since those early days things have changed greatly for the first-level supervisor. His role has often been so ill defined and ambiguous that incumbents have been unclear about how much authority they had and even about what they were supposed to do. However, during the years of transition, one primary duty has remained unchanged. The first-level supervisor has always been expected to get out production or service. What has become increasingly unclear to many first-level supervisors is how they can be held accountable for employee performance in a situation where so much planning and organizing are done by other representatives of management and where their authority has been so greatly reduced.[3]

Enter the Shop Steward The foreman's freedom to make independent decisions was greatly circumscribed from the moment a representative

of the union could challenge any decision or order which even seemed to threaten the well-being or job security of a union member. The increasing power of unions brought other changes equally unpleasant to many supervisors.

Enter the Labor Relations Expert One development followed from the circumstance that a standard clause in most labor agreements provides for arbitration as the final step in the grievance procedure.[4] Executives soon learned that arbitrations are costly and their outcome uncertain. Therefore, experts from the newly established industrial relations department were given responsibility to monitor the foreman's handling of employee complaints. (Case 1, "The Old-line Foreman," shows how such changes can affect an old-timer.) In some organizations the labor relations expert was actually made responsible for handling employee complaints. Nor was the labor relations expert the only staff "intruder" upon the foreman's domain.

Enter the Personnel Administrator Specialization of management functions (and in some organizations a desire to keep the union out) had already brought the personnel department into being.[5] The combined impact of these two staff activities deprived foremen of their undisputed authority to hire and fire subordinates.

Enter the Technical Experts In the eyes of many factory foremen no change in the work situation has been so frustrating as the constant "interference" to which they have been subjected by methods men and industrial engineers. Since technological change became a constant feature of the industrial scene, many a foreman has felt (and said) that staff experts are always on

---

[2] For an analysis of typical methods of control see William H. Friedland and Dorothy Nelkin, "Migrant Labor: A Form of Intermittent Social Organization," *ILR Research* (New York State School of Industrial and Labor Relations, Cornell University, Ithaca, N.Y.), vol. 13, no. 2, pp. 3-14, November, 1967.

[3] Major changes identified in the following are not listed chronologically, because they have not occurred in the same sequence everywhere. The points to keep in mind are that all the following changes *have* occurred *and* have interacted to affect the position of the first-level supervisor.

[4] For details see Chaps. 8, Employees and Labor Organizations, and 13, Complaints and Grievances.

[5] Details on functions of the personnel department were given in Chap. 2.

his neck hindering, rather than helping, him in his work.[6]

Effective coordination with staff specialists has required from foremen a range and degree of technical knowledge (lacked by those who came up through the ranks) and a drastic change in attitude, which many foremen have felt unable to make. One foreman, run ragged trying to meet what appeared to him as unrelated and unreasonable demands by operating managers and staff experts, exploded: "I'm damned if I do and damned if I don't. No matter what happens, if we don't get the work out, it's *my* fault. I feel like a fugitive from a chain gang."[7]

Obviously, feelings like these make anything approaching teamwork impossible.

Enter the College-educated Subordinate Foremen who came up through the ranks soon discovered that people with a college education cannot effectively be handled in authoritarian ways. In fact, many of these highly educated newcomers are management trainees. They may start at the work level to learn the ropes, but their heads are full of the latest technical developments and modern ideas about managing. Sometimes they have betrayed impatience to be on their way up the organizational ladder. To first-level supervisors, who are expected to enforce standard operating procedures, such "eager beavers" have been a headache.

Enter the Project Manager The relatively new role of the project (or program) manager has often created tensions for line managers, and not only at the first level of supervision. It has been noted that in an authoritarian system of manage-ment the project manager is an anomaly. Anomalous or not, with increasing emphasis on technological development it seems likely that he has come to stay. The program manager is responsible for some special project which is currently of great interest to the top-management group. This extra prestige empowers him (during an intensive, though limited, period) to cut through established lines of superior-subordinate authority. During such periods, a first-level supervisor may feel that, far from being in the middle of things, where the action is and also the limelight, he is way out in left field and, as usual, more or less in the dark. (Case 4, "The Girl and the Computer," illustrates this point.)

Centralized Decision Making When attitudes and assumptions of executives have been authoritarian, the trend toward centralized decision making has created difficulties for supervisors. In a cold-war climate, the first-level supervisor found that he was supposed to *hold the line against* employees, getting out production in spite of workers who were assumed by managers to be lazy, dumb, and incompetent. The first-level supervisor was in a position to know that such assumptions were wide of the mark. But if he knew what was good for him (under System 2 management), he knew better than to argue with his superiors. In this dilemma, many a supervisor apparently decided that his wisest course was to go back, crossing the line and siding with production workers teamed up in pursuit of their own goals. In doing so, a supervisor may hope to keep on the good side of higher management by getting out production, while also keeping out of trouble with those on whom he must depend for results. (Case 2, "Who Owns the Improved Tool?" pictures this kind of accommodative supervision.)[8]

---

[6] For a classic case history of difficulties experienced by a foreman "in charge of" an assembly line, see A. Zaleznik, *Foreman Training in a Growing Enterprise,* Harvard Business School, Division of Research, Boston, 1951.

[7] David N. Ulrich, Donald R. Booz, and Paul R. Lawrence, *Management Behavior and Foreman Attitudes: A Case Study,* Harvard Business School, Division of Research, Boston, 1950, p. 39.

[8] Such nonsupervision cannot be justified in terms of organizational objectives. But "the man in the middle" has often adopted it as a way to dodge the conflicting demands made on him.

The Man in the Middle

Such changes, often accompanied by few explanations from senior managers, have left many
supervisors with the feeling that the outstanding
fact about their situation is the impossibility of
satisfying all the people who make demands on
them. In a classic statement, published some 30
years ago, Roethlisberger[9] described the foreman as "the man in the middle." Many supervisors, even today, might agree with that description of their plight and would be able to
document it. Caught in a no-man's land between
higher managers and production employees, the
first-level supervisor has been subjected to a
heavy cross-fire of unshared purposes. Perhaps it
is not surprising that, subjected to such pressures, many supervisors have sought support by
retaining membership in whatever craft union[10]
they belonged to before being promoted.

IMPACT ON THE SUPERVISOR'S ROLE

During the 1950s, some higher managers became
concerned about the first-level supervisor. They
asked themselves: Why isn't he doing a better
job at getting out production? What is his actual
role?

Differences in Role Perception

In 1956, under the auspices of the American
Management Association,[11] questionnaires were

sent to 187 first-level supervisors and 53 higher
supervisors in four plants. Many different kinds
of managerial activity were explored, and
degrees of authority retained by supervisors were
studied in relation to each activity. Two significant findings were these: organizational superiors fairly consistently rated the foremen's *responsibilities* higher than the foremen themselves did,
but, in important areas of managerial control,
many foremen thought they had far more *authority* than was conceded by their superiors.

Considerable differences of opinion about the
role of the first-level supervisor have continued
into the 1970s, and it seems likely that they will
persist for some time to come. Consensus must
await two related developments: (1) systems
management will have to become an accepted
way of thinking by those with authority to decide
what the first-level supervisor's position should
be, and (2) there must be a considerable measure
of agreement among all whose expectations and
demands determine what a first-level supervisor
actually does. Research by Kay[12] indicated that
this second advance will be even more difficult to
make than the first.

Kay's concept of "role centrism," points up
the following hypothesis. A person's perception
of another's role is colored by the impact of that
role on *what he sees as his own role* (which is
partly self-prescribed). In other words, if I am a
supervisor's subordinate, *the meaning-for-me* of
his role is largely determined by the *consequences
for me and for my scope of action* of what the
supervisor does—or fails to do. I am predisposed
to appraise his *role performance* as effective or

[9] "The Foreman: Master and Victim of Double Talk,"
Harvard Business Review, vol. 23, no. 3, Spring, 1945. This
article is reprinted in Paul Pigors, Charles A. Myers, and
F. T. Malm, *Management of Human Resources: Readings in
Personnel Administration,* 3d ed., McGraw-Hill Book Com-
pany, New York, 1973, selection 23. Note especially the re-
trospective comment added by Roethlisberger in the *Harvard
Business Review* reissue of this article in 1965.

[10] Elizabeth Faulkner Baker, "The Printing Foreman—
Union Man: A Historical Sketch," *Industrial and Labor Re-
lations Review,* vol. 4, no. 2, pp. 223–385, January, 1951;
"The Printing Pressroom Foreman—Union Man: A Case
Study," *Industrial and Labor Relations Review,* vol. 4, no. 3,
pp. 367–385, April, 1951.

[11] Chester E. Evans, *Supervisory Responsibility and Authority,* American Management Association, Inc., Research Report no. 30, New York, 1957.

[12] Brian R. Kay, "Prescription and Perception of the Supervisory Role: A Rolecentric Interpretation," *Occupational
Psychology,* vol. 37, no. 3, pp. 219–227, July, 1963. Kay's
study was made in seven New Hampshire industries, and
four of the organizations studied were unionized. Using
Flanagan's critical incident approach, Kay interviewed foremen and their immediate superiors. In this phase of the study
he asked for outstanding examples of "effective" and "ineffective" behavior as perceived by interviewees in the following five groups: foremen (153), their immediate superiors
(60), staff personnel (50), subordinates (135), and union stewards (33).

ineffective according to the degree in which it furthers or interferes with what I regard as my legitimate goals and rights.

According to Kay, serious discrepancies between role expectations and perceptions of behavior included the following:

1 *Between foremen and their immediate supervisors:* the degree to which foremen should be, and were, represented in policy-formulating discussions; the adequacy with which foremen communicated organizational policies to their subordinates; and the degree to which foremen met organizational requirements in emphasizing *quality,* as well as quantity, of production.

2 *Between foremen and staff experts:* whether or not foremen knew enough about company rules and regulations, and about state and federal labor laws.

3 *Between foremen and their subordinates:* whether the foreman functioned satisfactorily in his "personal treatment" of subordinates.

4 *Between foremen and shop stewards:* whether the foreman supported his men as he should when he talked with his organizational superiors; and whether he performed effectively in handling complaints and grievances.

Some of his conclusions were:

1 These foremen were aware of contradictory expectations from the various groups with which they interacted.

2 At the time of the study, however, they were not "being torn apart" by their recognition that they could not satisfy all these conflicting demands.

3 At an earlier period, they probably had been deeply disturbed by that recognition, but gradually they had learned to make their own adjustment to this feature of their situation. Some seemed to identify either with their subordinates or with their organizational superiors. Others had retreated into indifference. Many foremen seemed "to recognize that they had obligations toward many groups."

Evidence gathered since this study indicates that, even in the 1970s there are still wide differences of opinion not only as to what the first-level supervisor's role should be but also as to what his organizational status is.

What Is the First-level Supervisor's Place in the Organizational Hierarchy?

In theory there is nothing confusing about the status of a first-level supervisor. Figure 7-1

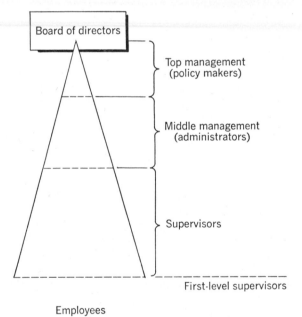

Figure 7-1

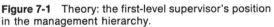

Figure 7-1 Theory: the first-level supervisor's position in the management hierarchy.

shows that his place is at the bottom of the management pyramid, at the line of contact with employees who get out a product or provide a service. In many organizations, however, the place of a first-level supervisor often has been, and continues to be, far from clear. A person's actual status is indicated in a number of ways, one being his official title.

Multiplicity of Titles   In manufacturing organizations, confusion about the foreman's status

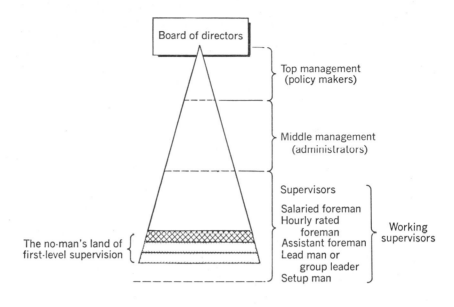

Figure 7-2 Actuality: the "no-man's-land" of first-level supervision.

has been compounded by introducing such varied titles as (1) *salaried foreman,* who spends most of his time planning for and directing the work of others, (2) *hourly rated foreman,* who spends much of his time doing actual production work, (3) several other grades of *working supervisors,*[13] and (4) *assistant foreman,* understudy for the position of foreman and, during the foreman's absence, *acting foreman.*

This range of titles suggests that the position of a first-level supervisor in the management hierarchy could more accurately be pictured as a band or strip than as a single line. Figure 7-2 is, therefore, a more true-to-life picture of an industrial situation in which the foreman's status has confused many people.

The same diagram applies to organizations other than factories. For example, in offices, different kinds of authority are indicated by such

titles as "administrative supervisors," "technical supervisors," "section heads," and "checkers." Likewise, in many hospitals there has been considerable confusion about degrees of authority to be exercised by a "nursing service supervisor," a "head nurse," and a "charge nurse." (Case 17, "Difficulties Connected with Work Scheduling," shows a consequence of such confusion in one hospital.)

Thus, in actual practice there is no clear-cut line between first-level supervisors and their immediate subordinates. In view of this, one may ask: What tells a first-level supervisor that he has finally crossed the great divide and arrived in the management domain? Is it being put on salary? That change has seemed all-important to some foremen in the past, but if the current trend continues, a salaried position will not be a differentiating symbol in the world of tomorrow. Is a supervisor on firmer ground if he gauges his status according to what he actually does, day in and day out?

[13] See George Strauss, "The Changing Role of the Working Supervisor," *The Journal of Business* (The University of Chicago), vol. 30, no. 3, pp. 202-211, 1957.

What Does a First-level Supervisor Actually Do?

Studies of how first-level supervisors have spent their time do not support the view that they function primarily as representatives of management. For example, a British study[14] showed that "tasks and problems dealt with by production supervisors vary greatly from firm to firm, and that even within a single firm the jobs of supervisors in different sections or departments may be greatly different." Observation and research in the United States show that the situation has been much the same here.

For instance, in "a minute-to-minute observation study of production foremen on an automobile assembly line [observers found that] . . . in 480 minutes the foreman performed 876 separate incidents of behavior. In other words, he did something different every half minute."[15]

That general finding is illustrated by the following example taken from the aircraft industry.

A Case Example: "Just In and Out"[16]

A production foreman (recently put on salary) was charged by the union with violating Article X of the labor agreement, which provided that "Supervisors of the rank of Assistant Foreman and higher shall act in a supervisory capacity only . . . except in case of extreme emergency, or for the purpose of instructing employees."

At the hearing, the arbitrator asked a witness (one of the foreman's subordinates, an assembler): "What did you see him do, exactly?"

The witness replied, "Well, he would work a little bit, and then he'd go some place, then he'd come back with something and he'd work a little bit and go some place else. He was just in and out."

Other first-hand reports, as well as clinical studies, suggest that many production foremen spend most of their time in dealing with emergencies of one sort or another. Obviously, such a crisis schedule inevitably varies greatly between different companies and departments and even within one organizational unit from day to day. However, common denominators do exist between these varied activities. Thurley and Hamblin,[17] having studied 16 departments, in five British industrial companies, arrived at the following generalizations:

1 All supervisors studied functioned as part of a control system.
2 All supervisors studied had responsibility for machines and equipment.
3 Every supervisor was responsible for the whole production process within his organizational unit; *he spent most of his time on technical matters.*
4 Direct supervision of operatives, i.e., standing over them and watching them work, took up a significant part of the supervisor's time at only two firms, though even there the time spent on direct supervision never exceeded 8 percent of a supervisor's working hours.[18] In one company, first-level supervisors spent an appreciable amount of time "handling" disputes, by the simple device of arranging for the shop steward to discuss the matter with a member of middle management.

[14] K. E. Thurley and A. C. Hamblin, *The Supervisor and His Job,* Department of Scientific and Industrial Research, H. M. Stationery Office, London, 1963. A condensation of one part of this five-part report is reprinted in Pigors, Myers, and Malm, *op. cit.,* selection 24.

[15] Frank J. Jasinski and Robert H. Guest, "Redesigning the Supervisor's Job," *Factory Management and Maintenance,* vol. 115, no. 12, pp. 105–107, December, 1957.

[16] Paul Pigors and Faith Pigors, "Case of the Hard-working Foreman," in *Case Studies in Management Development: Practical Supervisory Problems,* Bureau of National Affairs, Inc., Washington, D.C., 1955.

[17] *Op. cit.,* pp. 105–107.

[18] This conclusion accords with findings by one of the authors in a large insurance company between 1960 and 1970. In interviews and group discussions, supervisors in that company reported that they had to spend about 90 percent of their time on technical responsibilities, leaving barely 10 percent for administrative duties and responsibilities in personnel relations.

5 In theory, supervisors shared with the personnel department responsibilitiy for training. In practice, however, operatives were either instructed in the training department or learned their job by "sitting next to Nellie."

6 Most supervisors expressed the opinion that the personal problems and general welfare of operatives were "one of their main concerns." But the amount of time spent on those matters indicated that, in practice, such responsibilities had a low priority.

7 The study did not confirm the common assumption that a first-level supervisor is an important communication link. It appeared that supervisors were told little more than operatives about proposed changes or other matters on which they might be expected to be well informed.

However, notable exceptions to that long-accepted practice were indicated by another study, made in the United States.[19] At least a few chief executives recognized that in the difficult task of implementing a new policy for equal employment opportunity, the first-level supervisor was indeed a key man. They therefore took pains to ensure that every supervisor knew precisely what the new policy was, the reasons why it had been adopted, and what was expected of him in helping to make it work. At the Caterpillar Tractor Company, for example, a slide talk for supervisors expressed top management's sense of dependence on first-level supervisors. It included a statement to the effect that the supervisor is the one who must interpret company policy to the work force.

OTHER INDICATORS OF ORGANIZATIONAL STATUS

Other key facts to be considered in regard to a supervisor's status include *the kinds of plans and decisions* he is expected to make and both the *timing and the content of communications* he re-

[19] Stephen Habbe, *Company Experience with Negro Employment*, National Industrial Conference Board, Inc., Personnel Policy Study no. 201, New York, 1966, vol. 1, p. 105.

ceives from management representatives (line and staff) below the top level.

Planning and Decision Making

Technological advances have made many production decisions so complex that no single individual is qualified to make them. Long-range production planning is done a long way from the place where the first-level supervisor has his desk. In many organizations a noteworthy feature of the first-level supervisor's job is that he can do no more than make recommendations on most of the matters which, if he actually were a manager, he would make decisions.

Timing and Content of Communication to the First-level Supervisor

Obviously everyone in a responsible position needs a continuous flow of reliable and up-to-date information on all matters he is held accountable for. Here again, few first-level supervisors have been able to function as managers. For example, if a foreman is to be held accountable for the quality of his production, he needs a daily flow of information from the quality control department. In the past, however, quality control information has usually traveled upward along staff channels, across to operating management at a high level, and then down the line through middle management to the first-level supervisor's boss. The information has thus reached the first-level supervisor when the facts were past history, and all too often its delivery has been more threatening than supportive.

In relation to organization policies, the most that a first-level supervisor could usually expect has been a printed policy statement to put into his Manual. Sometimes this printed material has been accompanied by a meager explanation from his immediate organizational superior.

In organizations where management by objectives has been more than a slogan, first-level supervisors in recent years have been encouraged to participate with their immediate superior in planning for their organizational unit. They have also often received more information on long-range corporate goals and policies than would have been conceivable in the old days. This change does not necessarily tell a supervisor that he has crossed the line separating production workers and management representatives. On the contrary, a major purpose of management by objectives is to erase that line, enlisting all employees in the service of organization-wide goals. This development may augur well for the future, but for the moment, it may leave the first-level supervisor still wondering where he stands.

INTERACTIVE INTERRELATIONSHIPS

Most of the traditional features in the supervisor's position mentioned so far in this chapter

have been perceived by many incumbents as difficulties. This perception of the first-level supervisor's position can be diagramed as in Figure 7-3. A supervisor who thus sees himself as the man in the middle can scarcely be blamed for developing feelings of sharp resentment. Whether achievement, security, or advancement is the strongest motivating force for him, he naturally tends to resent whatever he perceives as a block or even a threat to his progress toward that goal.

However, the organizational design, or plan, of interactive roles (shown in Figure 7-3) can also be regarded as indicating that the foreman occupies *a central position.* Obviously, a person at the center of action might be in a *strategic position,* for purposes of interpersonal communication, from which to generate *power with* others in related roles.

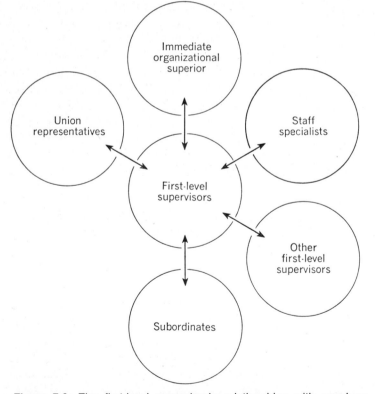

Figure 7-3 The first-level supervisor's relationships with members of interactive groups.

It is now generally accepted that productive interaction in any organization depends in large measure on the harmonization of organizational and personal goals at all organizational levels. Yet the difficulty of achieving such harmony suggests the following questions: Is it reasonable to expect that employees at lower organizational levels will do most of the harmonizing? What if they feel that some long-range, organization-wide objectives, as perceived by them, are incompatible with more important and immediate personal goals? What might be done to restructure the situation that has generated such oppositional attitudes? Our answer to that question is offered in the following interrelated suggestions for making organizational changes.

INTERRELATED SUGGESTIONS

Planning for Changes

A manager who thinks of making any organizational change is well advised to consider the interactive effects of the following variables:

1 Employee feelings about changes of any kind, and their value attitudes toward security, significantly determine their response to change. Such subjective factors exercise a greater influence than either their capacity to reason or the nature of the change itself. Thus managers should anticipate some irrationality of response to change and should recognize that such irrational feelings are likely to be expressed as resistance to change.[20]

2 The general managerial climate, and specific management-employee relations in a unit where a change is proposed, greatly influence the foreseeable consequences of changes planned by managers. (This follows because employee attitudes toward change always play a part in the consequences, sometimes a decisive part.)

3 The manner, timing, and medium of communication about a proposed change may make

a considerable difference in determining how employees perceive and respond to it. (Is there any face-to-face discussion, at a time when employee suggestions could be acted upon? Or is a given change merely announced, as a fact, perhaps only in writing?)

4 Flexible timing in initiating and implementing a change may greatly reduce employee resistance (especially if informal leaders are consulted). Resistance to change varies inversely with the length of time between the announcement of a change and its initiation because it permits time for understanding and accommodation.

To explain this hypothesis one might note that, at best, perception of what is new tends to be delayed, biased, and at least partially blocked by preconceptions derived from previous experiences.

5 The cumulative effect when many changes are made within a short time is likely to be disadvantageous, even though each change in itself is potentially desirable and even acceptable.

Taken together, these variables mean that any change announced and then promptly initiated by someone in authority is likely to elicit a negative reaction from employees. That general idea has been illustrated in countless work situations. The following brief example will suffice to suggest why employee resistance (at any organizational level) is a factor which managers cannot afford to ignore.

A Case Example: Supervisory Resistance Blocks a Technological Change[21]

In a steel foundry, an electronic data processing (EDP) system was introduced. Its primary purpose was to process information for accounting, scheduling, inventory control, and payroll, but its effectiveness depended on accurate inputs

---

[20] This hypothesis is more strongly stated by Arnold S. Judson, in "How I Stopped Worrying and Learned to Live with Irrationality," *Technology Review,* vol. 70, no. 1, pp. 39–43, October–November, 1967.

[21] L. W. Gruenfeld and F. F. Foltman, "Relationship among Supervisor's Integration, Satisfaction, and Acceptance of a Technological Change," *Journal of Applied Psychology,* vol. 51, no. 1, pp. 74–77, 1967; New York School of Industrial and Labor Relations, Cornell University, Ithaca, N.Y., ILR Reprint Series, no. 218.

supplied by first-level supervisors. As it turned out, the EDP system had to be discontinued because the information provided by supervisors proved unreliable. Subsequent interviews disclosed that they had been unwilling to undertake the slight amount of extra responsibility and work required by the new system. During these talks it also became clear to interviewers that the supervisors had been greatly dissatisfied because they felt that they were not treated as members of the management group. The EDP system might have meant greater integration with higher managers. Its use entailed bypassing the superintendent level. However, apparently *what it did mean* to these supervisors was "close and punitive supervision" by higher management.

Suggestions Concerning a New Role for First-level Supervisors

The first-level supervisor's job should be redesigned,[22] his role restructured, and other changes (listed below) should be effected so that the incumbent:

1 Can function as a manager.
2 Can count on consistent support and coaching (as needed) from his immediate senior.[23]
3 Has official relationships with staff experts such that he interacts with them as captain of a cross-functional work team.
4 Has regular contacts with other first-level managers such that mutual understanding and cooperative relationships can develop.

[22] "When technically feasible, the design of a supervisor's job should be in the direction of including authority and responsibility over all the functions required to complete the product or service assigned to his work group, including quality acceptance." Page 189 in Louis E. Davis and Ernst S. Valfer, "Intervening Responses to Changes in Supervisor Job Design," *Occupational Psychology,* vol. 39, no. 3, pp. 171–189, July, 1965.
[23] In applying the principle of supportive relationships, a critical test of success is the subordinate's perception that contact with his organizational senior "maintains and builds his sense of personal worth and importance" (Rensis Likert, *New Patterns of Management,* McGraw-Hill Book Company, New York, 1961, p. 103).

5 Finds that he is expected to establish and maintain cooperative relationships with his counterpart in the union and that when he does so, his achievement is appraised by higher managers as a valuable contribution to an important corporate objective.
6 Is able to allot adequate time to all three major aspects of his job, technical, administrative, and in human relationships.
7 Receives a salary commensurate with his current management status and his managerial potential.
8 Knows that he will be considered, if he so desires, for promotion to higher levels of management.
9 Receives an assistant if the scope of his job is expanded to the point where his so-called span of control exceeds the span of his human understanding (his understanding of subordinate personnel as individuals).

The following examples show that all these changes have already been tested in industrial experience.

A Case Example: Kimberly-Clark Corporation[24]

In 1962, the new plant manager of the Niagara Falls Mills abolished the position of tour foreman. Instead he created that of *shift superintendent.* Tour foremen had done little more than monitor operations, passing along to staff experts and higher managers problems which they felt unable to solve. Shift superintendents were given authority to plan, organize, lead, and control. They were also given a salary about 25 percent higher than that of tour foremen, and they knew that outstanding performance would lead to advancement.

Reducing operating costs and improving quality were primary aims in creating the role of shift

[24] Material for the following two case examples is taken from Walter S. Wikstrom, "Managing at the Foreman's Level," National Industrial Conference Board, Inc., Personnel Policy Study no. 205, New York, 1966.

superintendent. In regard to both these objectives the plant manager appraised results as excellent. [25] Moreover, he expressed satisfaction that "the problems of the mills are now being solved at the mills."

A Case Example: The Pillsbury Company

Here too, the major aim was to reduce costs, the means being the creation of a new role at the base of the management pyramid. The first-level foreman was replaced by a *unit manager.* Under the old system, a serious obstacle to efficiency at the production level had been that no foreman had a complete operation to supervise. With the new system, each unit manager in effect ran his own plant, which both mixed and packaged a product. Other organizational changes concerned interaction with staff experts. Previously, experts from the maintenance and repair department and from quality assurance could shut down the line whenever, in their judgment, this was advisable. Personnel difficulties were passed along to the industrial relations department. Cost information was not routed directly to foremen. Under the new system, unit managers had authority to manage. They were even free to reject advice from staff experts.

Changes in communication procedures enabled each incumbent of the new position to function as a manager. For instance, unit managers made cost projections and then set up operating schedules designed to meet or beat their own goals. To keep them informed, the division controller developed a simplified cost control report. This was sent daily to each unit manager. This on-line information enabled the new managers to keep their costs in line with their plans.

[25] After the reorganization, however, labor relations deteriorated markedly. The Niagara Falls Mills formerly had fewer grievances than any other unit in the corporation. During the mid-1960s, more grievances went to arbitration from this unit than from all the others combined. If cost-accounting procedures had shown the tangible and intangible losses associated with these disputes, the financial picture would not have looked so favorable.

After 3 years' experience in applying the unit manager concept, top management at Pillsbury was convinced that the following results had been obtained: *better management on the scene* (which kept down manufacturing costs), *more efficient labor relations* (most complaints now being settled at the first step of the grievance procedure), and *improved staff-line relationships at the production level* (unit managers learned how to make good use of advice from persons whose specialized knowledge and technical experience were greater than their own). [26]

ONE ORGANIZATIONAL CHANGE CALLS FOR OTHERS

When the first-level supervisor's job is redesigned so that he becomes a *first-level manager,* other changes need to be made in recruiting, selecting, and preparing the "right man" for this new role and in helping his steady development on the job.

Suggestions for Recruiting and Selecting the "Right Man"

A proportion of candidates should be sought among persons with academic education beyond high school; [27] in liberal arts, in some technical field, or both. Having a proportion of graduate

[26] As noted by Wikstrom (*op. cit.,* p. 8), a manager who effectively coordinates specialists can "decide how to do things better than he could by himself."

[27] Kenneth Hopper, "The Growing Use of College Graduates as Foremen," *Management of Personnel Quarterly,* vol. 6, no. 2, pp. 2–12, Summer, 1967. Hopper uses the term "graduate foreman" to denote any educational or technical qualification above the high school level. Hopper notes that census figures for the decade 1950–1960 show an increase of 50 percent in employing graduate foremen in American industry; many companies have encountered difficulties in attempting to recruit college graduates for the old-style position of first-level supervisor, but successes have uniformly been reported in recruiting college graduates for the position of first-level manager. Hopper cites as an outstanding example a young Russian textile engineer who became foreman in a Leningrad factory in the 1930s. His name was Alexei N. Kosygin.

foremen makes it reasonable to expect that some management representatives at the first level will have the following qualifications: They will (1) have the intellectual caliber to make decisions *as managers* instead of merely thinking like workers about managerial responsibilities, (2) be prepared to work *as equals* with staff experts, (3) be promotable, (4) be readily transferable, (5) want to demonstrate that they can handle changes and even initiate them, (6) be able to take a systems-minded view of the organization as a whole or rapidly to acquire such a view, and (7) already have had some of the necessary preparation to function effectively as communication links. A college-educated person is likely to be readier than a noncollege supervisor to report up the line adequately documented difficulties and complaints that are brought to him.

However, some candidates for the position of first-level manager should be recruited from within the organization itself. This second recommendation applies equally to the *activity of selection.* In selecting each candidate, while the position of first-level manager is still in the experimental stage, the final decision should be made in conference between the second-level manager, his immediate superior, and possibly also someone at the executive level. If possible, some persons slated for this new role should be selected (1) from among former supervisors who have demonstrated their ability (before the job was enriched), whether or not these men have had a college education, and (2) from staff experts who are interested in developing their managerial potential. (As an example of the "assessment center" method of selecting new recruits for supervisory positions with college or noncollege background, see Chapter 3.)

Advantages of recruitment and selection procedures which make it possible to have a combination of college and noncollege men at the first level of management include (1) the stabilizing effect within a managerial group of having some incumbents who do not seek further advance-

ment; (2) the leavening effect of having some men who are ambitious for promotion, who welcome change, and whose articulateness facilitates communication; (3) the benefits for personnel relations and employee morale in having some managers who have been promoted from the ranks of hourly rated employees (i.e., men who are in a position to understand and appreciate attitudes, customs, hopes and fears which may seem unreasonable to managers whose orientation is highly technical or primarily intellectual); and (4) a reduction in the number of former first-level supervisors who must be set back even though they have functioned effectively in the position to which they were originally promoted.

Some *criteria for selection* have already been indicated in the subsection on recruiting. In general they add up to managerial ability and potential. Specific characteristics which may be looked for include *high motivation* (a manager needs to be inner-directed and a self-starter), *interest and ability in problem solving* (by group methods, if participative management is company policy), *skill and potential in leadership and communication,* and *capacity to function effectively under pressure.* In a unionized organization, appropriate attitudes and thorough knowledge of the existing labor agreement are also essential (see Chapter 8 for details).

Suggestions for Preparing First-level Managers

Those entrusted with responsibility for preparing and teaching first-level managers should bear in mind that inner motivation and innate capacities are prerequisites for the kind of learning at issue. (Unless there is a strong drive, and considerable capacity, for self-development, no amount of exposure to "supervisory training" or "programs for management development" can produce needed results.) Participation in such opportunities for self-development should come as a result of invitation rather than assignment.

1 Scheduling of a course to help first-level managers prepare for their new job should also take account of inner motivation. As noted by Boyd,[28] the incentive to learn is likely to be greatest just before and just after promotion.

2 Specific preparation for the enriched job should be varied to fit the circumstances and policies of each organization, but certain general practices recommend themselves. For example, whenever feasible, theoretical preparation offered in an organization as part of a formal development program should be given concurrently with preparation gained through practical experience. Many companies have reported good results with traineeship as a final phase of preparation for a managerial position.

3 In helping managers to *develop on the job,* formal courses can be useful. For best results, the following specifications should be met:

a All courses offered should be part of an organization-wide program for manpower development. In this total program, every organizational member from chief executive to file clerk can participate.

b In-plant courses should be supplemented by opportunities to take outside courses. These supplementary opportunities may consist primarily in vocational or technical instruction, in sensitivity training, or in postgraduate courses for executives.

c Members of each course should include staff personnel as well as representatives of line management to ensure cross-pollinization of ideas.

d The content and the learning-teaching method of all in-plant courses should be demonstrably consistent with what is said and done on the job: in planning, target setting, coaching, performance appraisal, and decision making by an incumbent with his immediate organizational senior. Unless the content of formal programs is reinforced by everyday experience on the job, theoretical propositions will soon be forgotten or shelved. However, interaction between these two ways of learning can be positive. What is recognized in firsthand experience as factual and valid can greatly accelerate the process of learning-as-changing which can begin in a well-run formal course.

e The formal program, which should, if possible, be conducted as a cooperative enterprise by members of line and staff, as well as by qualified outsiders, should include a minimum of lectures and considerable use of case method.[29]

Advantages A development program for first-level managers which meets these specifications has the following advantages:

1 A systems approach (to getting results with people) is implemented and illustrated in several ways; for example, because: the program is open to all qualified organizational members, membership in each course covers a range of experience and functional orientation, yet attention can consistently be focused on needs of the organization as a whole.

2 Opportunity for participants to confer, instead of merely listening to lectures, is virtually a necessity if a development program is to match the capabilities, aspirations, and needs of graduate foremen.

---

[28] Bradford B. Boyd, "Worker to Supervisor: Problems of Transition," *Personnel Journal,* vol. 43, no. 8, pp. 421–426, September, 1964.

[29] Zaleznik, *op. cit.,* pp. 226–227, stated his conviction that "case method has real possibilities" as a means to help supervisors develop social skills "which are both the goal of learning and the means whereby supervisors can learn from their [everyday] experience" (p. 220). When he made that statement, no variant of the Harvard case method had been developed which readily lent itself to use by first-level supervisors. Since then, the Incident Process has proved useful in stimulating supervisory development. For detailed information on this and other variants of case method, see Paul Pigors, "Case Method," in Robert L. Craig and Lester R. Bittel (eds.), *Training and Development Handbook,* sponsored by the American Society for Training and Development, McGraw-Hill Book Company, New York, 1967, pp. 174–205.

3 Use of case method has special advantages for supervisory development because it provides favorable conditions:

   a For first-level managers and staff personnel to become acquainted with one another and with a range of problems which may otherwise be regarded by incumbents as none of their business.

   b For practicing skills of situational diagnosis, doing so in a group and with experienced leadership.

   c For testing and developing skills of problem solving in an atmosphere where reasonableness and friendliness tend to prevail.

   d For outstanding participants to demonstrate and test *skills of leadership* by preparing cases from their own experience and leading discussion of them and of *communication,* not only in the role of a discussion leader, but also as a participating observer-reporter. Functions in this role include keeping track of what is said and done during case discussion and then rendering a report to the group on group performance.[30]

Whether or not a given program for supervisory (or managerial) development fits these specifications, any such program is designed to result in kinds of behavior which top management regards as desirable for persons taking the courses. However, a major difficulty which has plagued many perceptive training directors can be indicated by the following questions: Is it possible to train people in making "right decisions" when the same thing never happens twice? Can anyone spell out absolute rules for managing at the first level (or any other level) which guarantee that each incumbent will be able to meet requirements at all times and in regard to all persons with whom he interacts?

---

[30] For detailed role descriptions and other material concerning the what and how of the Incident Process, see Paul Pigors and Faith Pigors, *Case Studies for Management Development, Series III: White Collar Cases,* The Bureau of National Affairs, Inc., Washington D.C., 1965.

IS IT REALISTIC TO FORMULATE RULES FOR SUPERVISORY BEHAVIOR?

In our opinion it is worse than useless to spell out inflexible rules which supervisors are to follow without question. Yet members of top management (and the personnel administrator) are failing to meet their joint responsibilities unless guidelines are offered to help assure consistency (not uniformity) of managerial behavior throughout the whole organization. Rules of conduct, however, have always been popular, and they are still offered in many supervisory training courses. A brief glance at that approach may serve to indicate why they are not more effective.

Traditionally, the first-level supervisor has been held accountable for meeting requirements which can be stated as two (related) imperatives. (1) Get out production. To do that, you must (2) motivate production workers so that they will subordinate their personal goals to organization-wide objectives.

The trouble with the second rule is that it cannot be implemented. As suggested in Chapter 6, a root difficulty for any supervisor is that motivation and the attitudes which reflect strong inner drives cannot be changed by external pressures. A supervisor can influence the behavior of his subordinates, at least for a time. Yet he cannot change the motivational pattern of even one employee (except himself) or the specific attitudes which in the long run determine the extent to which an employee will of his own volition do what he theoretically can and should do.

First-level supervisors have often been told to make employees change their undesirable attitudes; but any perceptive supervisor knows, by intuition, that the only person who can change an attitude is the person who has that attitude. As Haire has pointed out,[31] an attitude is a way

---

[31] Mason Haire, *Psychology in Management,* 2d ed., McGraw-Hill Book Company, New York, 1964, pp. 106–107.

of seeing things. Therefore, a practical way to set in motion a change in attitude is to make some change in the situation which may help participants to see things differently. If it is possible to eliminate some feature which has seemed to employees incompatible with their self-interest (individually or as group members), then a change in attitude may follow naturally. The following example illustrates this point.

A Case Example:
From Resistance to Cooperation

At the Wayside Press, one difficulty had nagged the pressroom foreman for years, and he had nagged the workers about it for years. Since there is a high salvage value for wastepaper from presses when it can be kept flat, the foreman kept urging workers not to crumple it. He told them to fold it neatly on pallets that were conveniently located near each press. The pressmen, however, obstinately continued to find excuses for not doing this. When the "heat was on," there would be sporadic compliance with the foreman's instructions, but before long the pressmen went back to their habit of crumpling up waste paper and throwing it into corners or trash barrels.

This was the state of affairs in the pressroom when management began to experiment with the Scanlon Plan [32] for enlisting participation of employees in production problems. During the first 4½ months after production committees were set up, 197 suggestions for cutting costs or improving production were made. One suggestion came from a pressroom employee. His idea was that wastepaper should be saved in flat form so as to increase its salvage value. The pressroom foreman scoffed at the suggestion. "I've been trying for years to get you fellows to stop crumpling waste paper. There's no point in bringing

that up again." Their committee member explained why they had been unwilling to cooperate before. They suspected that the foreman was trying to check on how much paper each of them wasted. To protect each other, they made it impossible for him to carry out the control system they thought he had devised. Now, however, things were different. "We're all on the same team."

To reach the point where workers feel and function like teammates with management representatives is a goal greatly desired by many managers. But how to reach that goal has often proved to be a puzzling question. The following suggestions as to a general supervisory style, for use at the first level of management, may help to answer that question.

SUGGESTIONS FOR A SUPERVISORY STYLE TO MATCH A NEW MANAGERIAL ROLE

1 Every first-level manager should keep his behavior in tune with the general idea that *managing and working* (at the production level) are interdependent though contrasting activities. They should not be regarded as mutually exclusive opposites. Each requires the other, and each contains an element found in the other. [33]

2 Recognizing that there are three primary aspects to his job, a first-level manager should try to meet his full responsibility not only in regard

---

[32] See Chap. 21 for further description of this plan. Chiefly relevant here is the fact that the plan is worked out in cooperation with union officials and the employees themselves. Thus workers feel that it is their plan and have confidence that it will work to their advantage and not threaten them.

[33] As Wilfred Brown has pointed out in his essay on "What Is Work?," all work done by rank-and-file employees has a "discretionary element" as well as a "prescribed element." If behavior by employees is to contribute fully to organization-wide goals, each must do some planning and organizing of his work. At the top of the organizational pyramid, the work of a chief executive includes a prescribed element. Even he is not free to do whatever he chooses. See Wilfred Brown and Elliott Jaques, *Glacier Project Papers: Some Essays on Organization and Management from the Glacier Project Research,* William Heinemann, Ltd., London, 1965, pp. 54–70. See also Sidney A. Fine, *Guidelines for the Design of New Careers,* The W. E. Upjohn Institute for Employment Research, Kalamazoo, Mich., September, 1967, p. 9.

to administrative and technical matters but also toward all members of the human organization with whom he interacts. His administrative responsibilities for coordination are met chiefly by functioning in team relationships with members of two or more work groups. He can act as *captain* of a team whose other members are staff experts. He can serve as *coach* of a team (or teams) whose members are his work associates at the production level. In trying to stimulate and guide members of this second team, the coach should ask: Am I constantly increasing and developing my human understanding (as well as the level of my administrative ability and technical know-how)? Am I doing all that I could in matching "job development" with "career development" for each of my subordinates? [34]

3 The central position of the first-level manager (in relation to other groups with which he constantly interacts) offers favorable opportunities for him to function as a communication network manager. [35] Communication to and from him needs to be multidirectional.

As suggested in Chapter 5, no human link in an interpersonal communication network can operate an automatic switching system which ensures prompt and efficient transmission of messages. But a manager should attempt to understand his work associates to the point where he can get messages through to their "inner circuits" and receive intelligible messages from these individual control centers.

To be specific, a supervisor-manager who knows his subordinates as individuals knows how to meet his responsibilities for giving recognition and instructions in ways which are meaningful and which stimulate inner motivation. To one person, the most satisfying form of recognition may be freedom to function independently, with considerable opportunity to plan and organize his own work. For another person, however, an unexpected salary increase, or a word of praise (perhaps even in writing) from some higher management representative, may be more satisfying. For a third, the most meaningful kind of recognition may be the news that some idea of his has been put to work.

Practicing the communication skill of projective listening (to sense individual meanings in other persons) enables a supervisor to correct some of his own mistakes, at an early stage, and to clear up many misunderstandings before they do any serious damage. Regardless of specific communication skills, however, every manager should recognize that he communicates first and foremost by resonance. His natural behavior shows what he really believes in and is trying to do. Thus his feelings about what is most important become a factor in the work situation.

4 A first-level manager should take (and try to communicate) a system-minded approach to organizational endeavor. When he does so, he can help his work associates to adopt high performance goals for the organization as a whole.

5 Supervision should also be group-oriented, always being carried out in ways that recognize and foster needs **for** partnership and teamwork. Insofar as possible, a supervisor's planning, organizing, coaching, target-setting, and performance appraisal should be done with participation from the work associates for whose performance he is accountable.

6 Another leadership responsibility for every

[34] In his *Motivation through the Work Itself,* (American Management Association, Inc., New York, 1969), Ford uses the term "job development" rather than "job enrichment" and indicates how a supervisor can use the concept of job design to translate the generalities of corporate objectives into specifics that enable each employee to realize high-level human needs (such as responsibility, achievement, and advancement) while meeting job requirements. For example, among the questions (p. 198) that supervisors should ask and answer are the following: "What can I do for [this employee] that he could not do for himself? What goals could we now set *jointly?* . . . What job could he work toward now? How can I help?"

[35] For detailed comments on specific supervisory responsibilities which require communication skills, see especially Chaps. 10, Interviewing; 13, Complaints and Grievances; 16, Training and Performance Appraisal; 18, Constructive Discipline; 19, Managing Changes in Jobs and Work Schedules, and 22, Employee Health and Safety.

first-level manager is to help his work associates concentrate on *doing the job.* Implicit in this view is the goal of continually improving performance on the job.

7 Planning, organizing, deciding, and other job-related behavior by a supervisor-manager should be based on thorough situational diagnosis (see Chapter 9 for a detailed description of this technique). In thus applying what amounts to a systems-minded approach to personnel relations, a supervisor identifies and explores the relationships between basic variables that are interactive in every situation where human beings play a part. These factors are human nature, space-time dimensions, and technical features. For example, in the situation which developed at the Wayside Press, a supervisor of managerial caliber might have been able to perceive why his subordinates kept crumpling up wastepaper. At the very least, he would not have needed to be told that a formerly negative attitude had been replaced by a feeling that "Now we're all on the same team." And a perceptive manager would know how to take it from there, capitalizing on the newly developed team spirit.

8 It is not enough for a supervisor to practice situational thinking by himself. One of his continuing responsibilities is to interest his work associates in developing their diagnostic skills and helping him to improve his.

9 Every management representative should adopt and communicate an experimental frame of mind. Meeting this managerial responsibility requires, among other things, keeping alert to recognize incipient changes in the situation; being receptive to new ways of doing things; keeping one's mind open to the possibility that one may have made a mistake (as Benjamin Franklin put it, "doubting a little of one's own infallibility"); and being flexible and ingenious in rectifying one's mistakes when possible.

These qualities in a manager are illustrated in the following example.

A Case Example: A Backup Decision

In one company, the chief of a project team feared that team members might come up with a solution which would get him into trouble with his organizational superiors because, although easy for them to implement, it would not meet the organizational objective. He therefore asked each team member to prepare an independent report, planning to combine them and arrive at the final solution himself. In accordance with these instructions, each of his subordinates, working alone, prepared a report which took into account aspects of the problem of special concern to his unit; but none of the four reports gave due consideration to needs of the other three units. Thus the chief found himself with four incompatible sets of recommendations.

At that point he decided to back up and start over again. Using Maier's[36] group decision-making process, he and his four subordinates together worked out a solution which all agreed was better than any of the ones developed independently. As a result of this experience, group decision making became a regular practice on this team. By-products included greater mutual understanding and more candid communication among teammates. For example, they were able to tell their leader (and apparently he was able to accept the statement) that when he instructed them to work independently, he "had made impenetrable" the office wall which, until doors were opened, separated them from one another.

Every manager should always remember that what he says and does (sometimes even what he fails to say and do) has an important influence on organizational juniors who look to him for direction. An important aspect of this managerial responsibility is the obligation to stimulate the interest of subordinates in developing their abilities to coach and teach each other. One way of doing this is shown by the following example, which also summarizes most of the main ideas presented with regard to supervisory style.

[36] Norman R. F. Maier, *Problem-solving Discussions and Conferences: Leadership Methods and Skills,* McGraw-Hill Book Company, New York, 1963.

A Case Example: Coaching for and by Teamwork[37]

In a sales office, a system for group coaching was devised with the purpose of helping new salesmen rapidly acquire needed skills and judgment. The supervisor or manager of each sales unit met periodically with his new salesmen, to hear and analyze reports of what each had recently been doing. The plan was to enable all newcomers to benefit by the supervisor's analysis of each report and recommendations to each individual. After a few months some of the managers who were conducting these meetings noticed that salesmen liked to participate in the process of analyzing and coaching. This interest was encouraged and led to a fundamental restructuring of coaching sessions. Thereafter, these managers no longer dominated the meetings, serving instead as chairmen of discussion groups. Their primary function was to help keep group talk problem-centered, friendly in tone, problem-solving in technique, and directed toward high performance goals which would enable each salesman to grow toward his full potential.

Among the reported advantageous consequences of this system for team coaching were (1) stimulation of inner motivation and improvement of initially planned techniques (brought about by suggestions from teammates offered at and between meetings), (2) development of a strong team spirit (because each salesman knew he could count on coaching and assistance not only from his superior but also from other members of the sales unit), (3) higher sales goals set at group meetings, and (4) greater flexibility and more innovation in implementing predetermined aims and in developing new markets. These interrelated consequences resulted in sales achievements that topped even the high goals set.

[37] Likert, *op. cit.,* pp. 55–57.

ROLE OF THE PERSONNEL ADMINISTRATOR

A personnel administrator who measures up to the responsibilities implicit in his role knows that making organizational changes (like those described in this chapter) often creates new problems and does not automatically cure the old headaches. For example, if the first-level supervisor's job is enriched, a difficulty is created for incumbents not qualified to meet standards for the new role. Moreover, in some organizations it seems that a persistent headache of first-level supervisors has merely been pushed down the line. It now afflicts "nonmanagerial" supervisors (or other persons "in the middle" between managers and production workers) to whom important responsibilities are delegated without the organizational authority to meet them.

When managers are trying to resolve difficulties, new or old, the personnel administrator may be able to help in such ways as the following:

1 As a policy adviser (for details see Chapters 2, 5, and 9).

2 During a preliminary stage, when specific changes are being considered, a personnel administrator who has done his homework (by reading professional literature and keeping in touch with experience in other organizations) can offer and document sound recommendations.

3 At this same stage, a personnel administrator who is skilled in situational diagnosis can predict some of the foreseeable consequences of making whatever organizational or methods changes are being considered. As he does so, he can bring to the attention of line managers current costs and potential gains for the human organization.

4 At all stages in the process of organizational change (from planning, through implementation, and into appraisal) the personnel administrator is obligated to demonstrate and help realize a systems-minded view. What changes must be made by the top-management group for a

proposed change in organizational relationships to become part of an internally consistent whole? (For instance, the new role of first-level *manager* would not fit with policies and assumptions associated with System 2 management.) If the personnel administrator can communicate what he sees, in a way that is persuasive for top management, he will have met a vital responsibility as an enabler of change.[38]

5 When top management has decided to institute a major change, e.g., redesigning the role of first-level supervisor, the personnel administrator should be able to offer useful suggestions about the timing and manner of communicating the proposed change and other possibilities for making the change acceptable to those affected by it.

6 The personnel administrator and members of his department also have specialized contributions to make in relation to any organizational change. As already mentioned, in regard to the new role of first-level manager, changes need to be made in traditional practices of recruitment and selection. It may also be necessary to revise educational programs which seemed good enough for the purpose of "training" old-time supervisors but which are obviously inadequate to meet the needs of promotable managers.

SUMMARY

In the old days, the first-level supervisor was an undisputed boss. He had authority to hire, train, reward, discipline, and even discharge his subordinates. They were regarded as having no right to question his decisions or orders.

During a period of transition, the balance of power gradually shifted away from the first-level supervisor. Other power centers became oper-

ative as workers became unionized; a succession of staff experts (in personnel relations, labor relations, industrial engineering, and other technical specialties) entered the picture; increasingly complex production decisions were taken out of the foreman's hands (many of them being made "upstairs"); and subordinates of a new type expected a considerable degree of autonomy.

At this point, forward-looking managers began to ask questions which might be summed up like this: Why does the first-level supervisor feel like "the man in the middle"? What can be done so that he can function as a man in a central position?

Five interrelated sets of suggestions for achieving this result have been offered in this chapter, all reflecting a systems-minded approach to managing.

The first set concerns planning and initiating changes. These suggestions include taking account of such basic, interactive variables as the human element (represented by subjective responses from individuals and group members in the human organization) and timing (including the possibility of allowing time for accommodation to changes and introducing changes one at a time).

The second set of suggestions adds up to redesigning the first-level supervisor's job and restructuring his role so that he can function as a first-level manager. For this purpose, we suggested (among other things) giving him more scope and authority to plan and organize work and work relationships; the authority and accountability that are commensurate with each other and with his managerial status, and the resources he needs (including on-line information, steady support from his organizational seniors, and staff *assistance*) to function effectively as captain of a management production team and coach of production teams at the work level.

The third set of suggestions relates to educational opportunities for men who are expected to

[38] Edgar H. Schein and Warren G. Bennis, *Personal and Organizational Change through Group Methods: The Laboratory Approach,* John Wiley & Sons, Inc., New York, 1965; chap. 10, "Principles and Strategies in the Use of Laboratory Training for Improving Social Systems," pp. 201-233, especially pp. 208-211.

meet high standards of performance at the critical level where the activities of managing and working are most evidently and constantly interdependent. Specific suggestions included timely preparation for the new job; continuing opportunities for self-development offered in a formal program for manpower development which is organization-wide and internally consistent and in which the case method is used to help managers enhance their intellectual and social skills; and informal coaching on the job by organizational seniors.

The fourth set of suggestions outlines a supervisory style to match the new role. At the level of general principles, this amounts to participative management. Executive pronouncements about managing by participation gain meaning at the work level when words become operational. First-level managers communicate (primarily in action) these attitudes and skills.

1 Recognition that managing and working are interdependent activities.
2 Concern and capacity in all three major aspects of their job.
3 Ability and interest in functioning as effective communication links.
4 An approach that promotes long-term productivity because it is organization-centered, designed to foster teamwork, and job-oriented.
5 Skills of situational diagnosis.
6 An experimental frame of mind.
7 Perceptiveness in helping junior work associates to develop their full potential as productive individuals and teammates.

In such ways a first-level manager can guide and stimulate those for whose performance and development he is organizationally responsible, recognizing each employee as a whole man who can contribute in unique ways to the entire man-machine system.

Relatively detailed reports from two companies and numerous short case examples served to show that many of these ideas have already been put into practice with excellent results.

Such organizational changes cannot resolve all problems once and for all, but the personnel administrator should be able to help with organizational problems, old and new. Can he communicate his recommendations in a way that carries weight with line managers, starting at the top? Over and above the specific services which his department can render, after organizational changes have been decided upon, the personnel administrator is in a position to serve as adviser and enabler in the process of change which every organization is constantly undergoing.

In the next chapter attention centers on a topic which has been touched upon in the preceding pages because of its effect on the first-level supervisor's role. Pressures exerted by strong unions have been experienced by supervisors (and by higher managers, too) as a restriction of their authority. But to organized workers this development has meant power, a power which has enabled them to win material gains and to bargain with managers on equal terms in regard to such important matters as rates of pay, employment security, job rights, and conditions of work.

SELECTED REFERENCES

Bishop, Maxine H.: *Dynamic Supervision: Problems and Opportunities,* American Management Association, Inc., New York, 1969.

Ecker, H. Paul: *Handbook for Supervisors,* 2d ed., Prentice-Hall, Inc., Englewood Cliffs, N.J., 1970.

Gelfand, Louis I.: "Communicate through Your Supervisors," *Harvard Business Review,* vol. 48, no. 6, pp. 101–104, November–December, 1970.

Hepner, H. W.: *Perceptive Management and Supervision,* Prentice-Hall, Inc., Englewood Cliffs, N.J., 1961.

Johnson, A. G. Kahler, and R. Peterson: "The Changing Duties of Today's Foreman," *Management of Personnel Quarterly,* vol. 5, no. 4, pp. 42–45, Winter, 1967.

Lennerloef, Lennart: *Supervision, Situation, Individual, Behavior, Effect,* Swedish Council for Personnel Administration, Report no. 57, 1968.

Meyer, H. H.: "A Comparison of Foreman and General Foreman Conceptions of the Foreman's Job Responsibilities," *Personnel Psychology,* vol. 12, no. 3, pp. 445-452, 1959.

Patten, Jr., Thomas H.: *Manpower Planning and the Development of Human Resources,* Wiley-Interscience, New York, 1971, chap. 8, "Foreman Training and the Predicaments of a Changed Status," pp. 342-396.

Peters, David A.: *The Principles and Practices of Supervision,* Pergamon Press, Oxford, 1967, chap. 2, "The Supervisor's Own Attitude of Mind," pp. 4-8.

Raudsepp, Eugene: *Managing Creative Scientists and Engineers,* The Macmillan Company, New York, 1963.

Roethlisberger, F. J.: "The Foreman: Master and Victim of Double Talk," *Harvard Business Review,* vol. 23, no. 3, Spring, 1945 (reprinted in Paul Pigors, Charles A. Myers, and F. T. Malm, *Management of Human Resources: Readings in Personnel Administration,* 3d ed., McGraw-Hill Book Company, New York, 1973, selection 23).

Van Deraal, William R.: *The Successful Supervisor in Government and Business,* rev. ed., Harper & Row, Publishers, Incorporated, New York, 1968.

Walker, Arthur H., and Jay W. Lorsch: "Organizational Choice: Product vs. Function," *Harvard Business Review,* vol. 46, no. 6, pp. 129-138, especially pp. 135-136, November-December, 1968.

Wikstrom, Walter S.: *Managing at The Foreman's Level,* National Industrial Conference Board, Inc., Personnel Policy Study no. 205, New York, 1967.

Chapter 8

Employees and Labor Organizations

We conceive of labor negotiations as an example of social negotiations, *by which we mean the deliberate interaction of two or more complex social units which are attempting to define or redefine the terms of their interdependence.*

Richard E. Walton and Robert B. McKersie [1]

In the earlier chapters in this section we have considered the individual *within* the organization. But individual employees acting together, through labor organizations or (in some cases) occupational associations, may seek to benefit themselves through collective negotiations with the management of the organization in which they work. Historically, in the United States labor organizations started with blue-collar workers, principally the skilled trades, and later the blue-collar employee of the large mass-production industries. More recently, unionization has

spread to some white-collar groups, particularly retail store clerks, government employees, teachers, nurses, and other hospital employees. Even though the labor force now has proportionately more white-collar than blue-collar workers, the strongest unions are still largely among the latter.

As the headquote to this chapter suggests, the entrance of a union involves complex social interactions between the two organizations, the union and the firm or other employing organization. The union is a challenge for management and to its unilateral decision making. How management reacts and adjusts to this new situation will help to determine the nature of the relationship and its impact on the success of the employ-

[1] Richard E. Walton and Robert B. McKersie, *A Behavioral Theory of Labor Negotiations,* McGraw-Hill Book Company, New York, 1965, p. 3.

ing organization, some of whose members are also union members.

As a member of the *work organization,* the individual is still part of a group which has a supervisor, which has objectives to meet, and which is characterized by the problems of interpersonal communication, motivation, and teamwork reviewed in the preceding chapters in this section. But as a member of a *labor organization* (a union), he may support objectives (higher wages, better working conditions, settlement of grievances) that seem to be in conflict with those which management is prepared to offer. The collective bargaining process—the making of new agreements and their subsequent administration—is the way in which conflicts are resolved in accommodating the objectives of the two types of organizations. Most of the time employees, as loyal union members, are also productive and loyal members of the work organization.[2] This dual loyalty is not unlike the pluralistic attachments most people have to work, to family, to church, to lodge, and to informal groups of all sorts.

FACTUAL BACKGROUND ON UNION GROWTH

Readers already familiar with the growth of union membership in the United States and the reasons for it may skip this section, but an understanding of this background will be helpful to managers and personnel administrators who must deal with unions.

Actually, the growth rate of management's interest in the personnel function has almost paralleled the growth of unions. After the First World War, union membership reached a peak of about 5 million by 1920. Then membership fell off drastically during the twenties, partly because the political and legal environment was

unfavorable and partly because many employers turned to employee-welfare programs as devices to avoid or weaken unions. Employee-representation plans were also started with the assistance of some managements eager to avoid outside unions. With the onset of the Great Depression, union membership dropped further and reached a low point of about 3 million members in 1932.

Rapid Growth of Unionism during the 1930s

The advent of the New Deal under President Franklin D. Roosevelt changed the political and legal environment to one of encouragement of union organization and collective bargaining. A major new law was the National Labor Relations (Wagner) Act of 1935, which gave legal protection to the right of employees to join unions and bargain collectively. Union membership grew rapidly with the organization of the mass-production industries under the leadership of the CIO and through renewed organization efforts by the AFL craft unions, which, in some cases, also organized on an industrial basis.

Post–World War II Developments

With the outbreak of war in Europe in 1939 and America's entry into the Second World War in 1941, labor shortages developed, and union membership continued to grow. Indeed, during the 13 years between 1932 and 1945, American union membership increased fivefold, to a total of nearly 15 million (including some Canadian members). It did not drop off in the postwar years as it had after the First World War, partly because of new union regulations on maintenance of membership and the union shop clauses, which increased during the war. These forms of "compulsory union membership" by which unions sought to prevent the "free rider" from securing benefits achieved through collective bargaining were vigorously opposed by some employers as an infringement of individual rights.

---

[2] For a case study in one large firm, see Theodore V. Purcell, *The Worker Speaks His Mind on Company and Union,* Harvard University Press, Cambridge, Mass., 1954.

Before the merger of the AFL and CIO in 1955, the auto and steel unions were the backbone of the CIO and the craft unions of the AFL. The CIO was established in 1935 in an effort to organize the mass-production industries; the unions engaged in this effort were expelled from the AFL for "dual unionism." AFL unions tended to favor organizations of workers on the basis of crafts, while the new CIO unions argued for organizing all workers—skilled, semiskilled, and unskilled—into an industrial union covering the entire plant. The rival federations prospered, and with the passing of time and the original protagonists, the new heads of the AFL and CIO, George Meany and Walter Reuther, respectively, succeeded in bringing about a merger in 1955. Subsequently, Reuther was critical of the AFL-CIO, and his United Auto Workers Union withdrew in 1968 to form a new Alliance for Labor Action with the Teamsters Union and several others. (The UAW remained in the Alliance after Reuther's death in a plane crash in 1970, but the alliance is close to dissolution).

By 1956 the membership of over 180 United States national and international unions (including over 1 million Canadian members) had reached a peak of 18.5 million, but after that there were no further large increases, and many commentators thought that union membership had reached a plateau. Supporting this view was the fact that union membership in the United States was not keeping pace with the growth of the labor force. Indeed, the percentage of employees in nonagricultural establishments covered by *union* agreements has declined from 1956, when it was 33.4 percent, to 30.5 percent in 1968 and 30.1 percent in 1970.[3]

Along with this percentage drop, actual union membership declined by half a million between 1956 and 1964, when there were 17.9 million members, about 1 million of whom were Canadian members of United States unions. The trend was reversed by 1966 when United States membership increased by a million, or over 6 percent, during the 2-year period. By the end of 1968, United States membership increased another 900,000 to a total of 18.9 million, and by 1970, 465,000 new members had been added. Substantial gains have been reported since 1966 by government employees and teachers' unions, the retail clerks' union, and four of the following six largest unions:

Union	1966	1968	1970
Teamsters (independent)	1,651,240	1,755,025	1,828,500
Auto Workers (independent)	1,402,700	1,472,696	1,485,600
Steelworkers (AFL–CIO)	1,152,000	1,120,000	1,200,000
Electrical Workers–IBEW (AFL–CIO)	875,000	897,114	921,700
Machinists (AFL–CIO)	836,163	903,015	865,500
Carpenters (AFL–CIO)	800,000	793,000	820,000

The reasons for this resurgence of union membership are the continued economic boom during the period through 1968 and the growing interest of government employees and other white-collar groups in union membership. The role of legislation seemed to be less important in the postwar period than it was during the early thirties. While the Taft-Hartley Act (the Labor-Management Relations Act) was passed over a presidential veto in 1947, because of public dissatisfaction with some union abuses and a desire to "balance" the Wagner Act, its impact on union growth, except possibly in the southern textile industry, has been minimal. There are few references any longer to what union leaders then called "the slave labor act." Similarly, the Labor-Management Reporting and Disclosure

[3] For fuller details and other data on union membership, see *Directory of National and International Labor Unions in the United States 1971,* U.S. Bureau of Labor Statistics, Bulletin 1665, Washington, D.C., 1972. Preliminary data in advance of this biennial publication are available in U.S. Department of Labor news releases. Employee association members have now been added to the tabulations, largely in the public sector, but the data in the text above refer only to *union* membership.

(Landrum-Griffin) Act of 1959, passed after congressional hearings on internal union abuses, does not appear to have curtailed union membership, particularly in the teamsters' union, which was the target of the congressional hearings. Nonetheless, there is periodic public impatience with some unions, especially during strikes which affect the public convenience or interest.[4]

Resistance of White-collar Employees to Unions: Will It Continue? These attitudes may explain, in part, why some white-collar employees, particularly the professional and technical group, may have been reluctant to join unions. The different values held by white-collar workers and their tendency to differentiate themselves from unionized blue-collar workers explains much of their aversion to union membership. While white-collar union membership has been growing, so has the percentage of the labor force in the white-collar occupations (see Table 1-1 in Chapter 1). The result is that while white-collar union membership increased by nearly 1 million employees over the decade 1958-1968, it has remained around 11 percent of the nonmanagerial white-collar labor force.[5]

Where is present white-collar union membership concentrated and where has the most rapid growth taken place? About 60 percent of the 3.2 million white-collar union members in 1968 were in transportation and public utilities; wholesale and retail trade; service; and finance, insurance, and real estate (although, apart from industrial agents, few insurance companies are organized

by unions and so are few banks in the United States). Another 28 percent are in government service, and 12 percent in manufacturing (principally in firms where blue-collar unions exist). The most rapid increases have occurred in government service, where about 2.3 million employees were union members in 1970—an increase of about 24 percent since 1966.[6]

Engineers and other professionals have been even more reluctant to join unions, despite organizing efforts. A 1962 study reported that "since 1951, no large group has been added to the unionized area of engineering, but the engineers at Minneapolis-Honeywell, Sperry Gyroscope, and Western Electric have voted their unions out."[7] Despite the feeling of some engineers in industry that management does not appreciate their creativity and that they should not be subject to the usual rules applicable to other employees (such as regular working hours), most of them have not seen union membership as an answer to their discontent. Even those who are represented by independent professional unions for collective bargaining tend to prefer an organization more like a professional society than like a union.[8] By 1967, about 20,000 engineers and 26,000 technicians were members of unions.

The recent growth of unions of government employees, teachers, and nurses may indicate a more rapid increase in white-collar union membership in the next decade. Federal government employee unions grew rapidly after they were

---

[4] For a review of public opinion polls on unions, and views of union leaders, see Derek C. Bok and John T. Dunlop, *Labor and the American Community,* Simon and Schuster, New York, 1970. This book is the best single short review of central issues in collective bargaining.

[5] *White-Collar Unionization,* Studies in Personnel Policy, no. 220, National Industrial Conference Board, New York, 1970, p. 4. For an earlier analysis, see Benjamin Solomon and Robert K. Burns, "Unionization of White-Collar Employees: Extent, Potential, and Implications," *The Journal of Business* (University of Chicago), vol. 36, no. 2, pp. 141-165, April, 1963.

[6] During 1966-1968, membership in the American Federation of Government Employees increased 47 percent; The State, County, and Municipal Employees' Union, 30 percent; and the American Federation of Teachers, 32 percent. All made further gains during 1968-1970.

[7] Herbert R. Northrup, "Engineers, Unions, and Management Organization: A Review Article," *The Journal of Business,* vol. 35, no. 2, p. 195, April, 1962. For a later account of the extent of unionization among engineers, see Archie Kleingartner, "Unionization of Engineers and Technicians," *Monthly Labor Review,* vol. 90, no. 10, pp. 29-35, October, 1967.

[8] However, a significant minority of those interviewed in two California aerospace firms said "both types are needed." Archie Kleingartner, "Professionalism and Engineering Unionism," *Industrial Relations,* vol. 8, no. 3, pp. 224-235, May, 1969.

permitted to bargain collectively by an Executive order signed in 1962 by President Kennedy.[9] The right to strike against the federal government is, of course, not protected. However, employee organizations may establish grievance procedures and negotiate, subject to federal Civil Service regulations, agreements with federal agencies. Unions of municipal employees, such as the transit workers and sanitation men in New York City, have struck despite legal prohibitions.

Public school teachers in some cities—e.g., New York City—belong to affiliates of the American Federation of Teachers (AFL-CIO), while others, in independent teachers' federations (some affiliated with the National Education Association), bargain collectively with school boards. The increase in collective bargaining here reflects the frustration many teachers feel with such matters as comparative salaries, hours, teaching loads, and powerlessness to participate in decision making about education. The fact that teachers have gone on strike, despite prohibitions in many cities and states, is an indication of the degree of their dissatisfaction and possibly the relative inexperience of school administrators and school boards in dealing with professional employment.[10] We shall consider the nature of the bargaining process in the public sector later.

Teachers in junior colleges and in some state colleges and universities have also joined affiliates of the teachers' union, but others seek collective representation through affiliates of the National Education Association and, of course, the branches of the American Association of University Professors. The latter two are usually considered "occupational" or "professional" associations, like the American Medical Association, but there are times when their collective efforts may not be vastly different from those of unions for their membership. Professional and occupational associations are likely to grow as the blue-collar proportion of our labor force continues to shrink.[11]

Union Objectives and Goals

Most American unions are firmly committed to the support of our present economic system and to reliance upon free collective bargaining to attain their short-run, pragmatic goals. Further, these unions are nonideological, in the sense that they have few long-range objectives. It would be difficult if not impossible, however, to generalize beyond these two basic beliefs held by American unions.

Despite the presence of some "big unions," it is a mistake to regard all American unions as either big or similar. On the contrary, there is considerable diversity. Unions vary greatly in membership from under 100 to over 1½ million. Their bargaining aims vary greatly also from narrow, specific objectives to broad, all-encompassing ones. There are unions that are run in a strictly businesslike manner and others that provide an entire way of life for their members. The political orientations of unions vary from conservative to communist-sympathizing. There are the traditional craft unions and new industrial unions. There are blue-collar, white-collar, and professional unions. Many unions have long-proved traditions of democracy and the protection of individual rights, while some others are run autocratically with few safeguards for mem-

[9] Sec. 1 (a), Jan. 17, 1962, Executive Order 10988, *Employee-Management Cooperation in the Federal Service,* provides for "the right, freely and without fear of penalty or reprisal to form, join and assist any employee organization, or to refrain from such activity." For a review of federal and state experience, see Jack Stieber, "Collective Bargaining in the Public Sector," in Lloyd Ulman (ed.), *Challenges to Collective Bargaining,* Prentice-Hall, Inc., Englewood Cliffs, N.J., 1967, chap. 3. President Nixon later issued Executive Order 11491, providing for additional bargaining procedures. By the end of 1971, there were slightly more than a million nonpostal federal employees, representing 53 percent of total eligible employees, according to statistics released in March, 1972, by the U.S. Civil Service Commission.

[10] For a comprehensive review, see Myron Liberman and Michael H. Moskow, *Collective Negotiations for Teachers,* Rand McNally & Company, Chicago, 1966.

[11] George Strauss, "Professionalism and Occupational Associations," *Industrial Relations,* vol. 2, no. 2, pp. 7–22, May, 1963.

bership rights. A few are corrupt. Finally, as we have seen, there are independent unions, which are not affiliated with the AFL-CIO, and the railroad brotherhoods, which also are separate and are not governed by the Taft-Hartley Act.

The emphasis of American unions, unlike many European unions, has primarily been on the attainment of short-run economic objectives through collective bargaining. The increasing role of government in labor relations has been accompanied by greater political action on the part of unions, but collective bargaining remains a very useful instrument for the attainment of pragmatic union goals. Unless there are major changes in union goals and programs, union political action will continue to be a supplementary program to collective bargaining. The objective of nearly all American unions is the signing of a written and detailed collective agreement, and it is estimated that 150,000 such agreements are now in effect.

The process of bargaining generally results in agreements without strikes or lockouts. In 1966, less than 0.2 percent of man-hours worked in the United States were lost through labor disputes; in 1969 the percentage was 0.24 and only 0.34 during the higher strike year of 1970. Wildcat strikes resulting from disputes during the term of a collective agreement are relatively rare, partly because the practice of voluntary arbitration of unsettled grievances has spread to about 95 percent of all agreements. When arbitration is the final step in the grievance procedure, unsettled grievances over management's application of the collective agreement are referred to an impartial arbitrator agreeable to the company and the union. A hearing is held, arguments are presented with supporting data, and the award is final and binding. Arbitrators are sometimes lawyers and often professors of law or industrial relations (including the coauthors of this book).[12]

[12] For discussion of private voluntary arbitration of grievances, see Robben W. Fleming, *The Arbitration Process,* University of Illinois Press, Urbana, Ill., 1965; and Paul Prasow and Edward Peters, *Arbitration and Collective Bargaining,* McGraw-Hill Book Company, New York, 1970.

THE DIFFERENCE MADE BY UNIONISM

When a firm or other organization is first unionized, what are the effects? A basic social change occurs in the structure of employer-employee relationships. A wedge seems to have been driven between management and employees. Many of these employees now profess an allegiance to an outside organization that, if it is affiliated with a national union, has broader interests and problems than those confronting the management. In the initial stages of union relations, therefore, conflict is more probable than cooperation, especially if recognition of the union has followed a bitter period of name-calling, electioneering, or possibly a strike.

The Union Is an Employer-regulating Device

With the entry of a union, furthermore, top management can no longer make unilateral decisions that affect employee relationships. Policies on wages, transfer, layoff, and discharge, to mention only a few, must now be discussed with union representatives and formally incorporated in a written agreement. Decisions on the administration of these policies may still rest with management, but they are frequently subject to question and criticism by union representatives under a formal grievance procedure. As one writer on labor-management relations has observed,[13] "A union is an employer-regulating device. It seeks to regulate the discretion of employers . . . at every point where their action affects the welfare of the men." This relates to the question of management's "prerogatives," which have been the subject of much discussion and conflict in labor-management relations. Faced with an effective challenge to its decision-making authority, top management naturally finds it difficult to accept

[13] E. Wight Bakke, *Mutual Survival: The Goal of Unions and Management,* Harper & Row, Publishers, Incorporated, New York, 1946, p. 7. Professor Bakke, director of the Labor and Management Center of Yale University, wrote this book following extensive interviews with 60 management leaders and 60 union leaders in nine major industrial centers in the East and Middle West. Time has not dulled the validity of his findings.

the new organization wholeheartedly without fear of the future.

The Supervisor's New Role

Difficult as this adjustment is for top management, it is frequently even more difficult for low-er-line officials. Superintendents and supervisors now find their authority challenged as we have seen in Chapter 7. There is another person, the "union steward," who, though subordinate to the supervisor in the company organization, has a new status and position outside the company

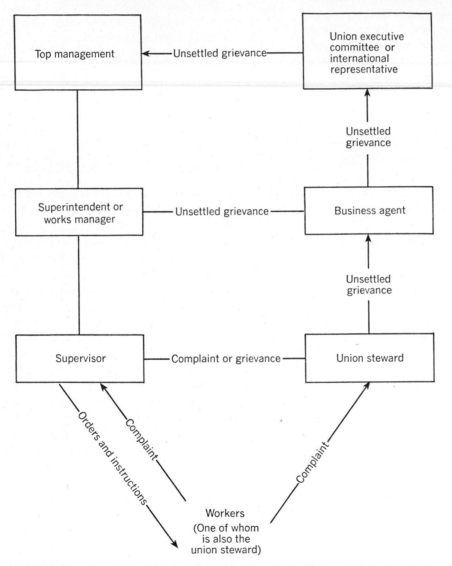

Figure 8-1 Place of the supervisor and union steward in the complaint and grievance procedure. Note the points at which the union can take an unsettled grievance to higher management.

organization structure.[14] This is illustrated in Figure 8-1, which shows a typical complaint and grievance procedure. In Chapter 13 we consider complaints and grievances in more detail. At this point, we are concerned only with the relative organizational positions of the supervisor and union steward in a unionized firm or other organization.

The steward holds his position through appointment by union officers or election by union members in his department. In carrying out his duties, he is responsible to them, not to the supervisor. Employees come to him with complaints and grievances. Acting as the employees' representative, the steward takes these matters up with the supervisor. New stewards, especially in recently unionized firms, are likely to feel that they "are now running the department," and friction with the supervisor often develops. This is a very difficult period of readjustment for the supervisor, who may be especially disturbed unless he clearly understands top management's attitude and policy toward the union. A capable supervisor, working with a shop steward who is usually one of the employees also, can often settle complaints and grievances before they become major problems requiring attention by higher management.

Can Unionism Be Avoided by Nonunion Firms and Organizations?

This question is often asked by managers in firms and such organizations as school systems, local governments, hospitals, banks, insurance firms, and other predominantly white-collar organizations. Failure to provide equitable wages and benefits or to treat employees fairly has hastened union organization. Some managements have

learned that high wages and other economic benefits, which they thought were all their employees wanted, do not prevent unionization. Strong pressures for organized group relationships and for an increasing measure of control over managerial decisions that directly affect them have led blue-collar workers to join unions even in "good" firms. This tendency has been most evident in industries that have already been largely organized by strong national unions, e.g., steel, autos, rubber, and glass.

Managers who have tried to do everything for their employees are often bewildered, hurt, or angered when these employees want to do something for *themselves* through membership in a labor organization. These employers gain little by regarding unionization as an insult or as an evidence of failure on their part. Such an attitude can result only in misunderstanding and bitterness that will delay the necessary readjustments to the new situation. The real challenge is for these managements to deal constructively with this new organization which their employees have chosen to represent them.

The question still remains, however, whether employees would feel the need of unions if management's personnel policies were always sound and all workers considered themselves a real part of the enterprise. Undoubtedly, some personnel men and representatives of line management have based their policies on the assumption that unions could be avoided or weakened by good personnel programs.

There is no doubt that many firms and organizations, including some large ones as well as many smaller ones, have successfully avoided unionization of their employees. Some of these are in manufacturing, and a combination of enlightened (sometimes paternalistic) personnel policies and other special factors has avoided unions. Many more nonunion firms are in such industries as banking, insurance, retail trade, and services, where white-collar employees predominate.

[14] Local union officers may in many cases be employees who find other avenues of promotion within the company structure blocked, so that they get personal satisfaction (as well as some headaches) in being elected to unpaid local union positions by their fellow union members.

Many managers have given greater attention than formerly to the personnel problems of white-collar employees, and especially of professional and technical employees. We have already noted that these employees generally have not yet identified their own goals or interests with union membership. As the numbers of these employees increase, relative to blue-collar workers whom they now exceed in total numbers (see Table 1-1), their attitudes may change more than they already have changed recently. Management policies can help shape these attitudes, for or against union membership. [15]

Management policies geared to the *sole* objective of keeping unions out are essentially negative and may be doomed to disappointment. Employees may still want to do something for themselves. A union may appeal to some of them as a means of preserving what they already enjoy and as an organization that offers them satisfactions as members of a peer group. Local union leadership may also provide avenues of advancement within the union movement to certain ambitious employees who feel somewhat frustrated in their present jobs.

Unionism and Personnel Administration

The entrance of a union does not make good personnel administration any less important. On the contrary, the way in which management deals with its employees as individuals and as members of work groups affects the quality of union-management relations. Employee attitudes are shaped by experiences on the job, and these are bound to be reflected in the attitudes of union members and union officers toward management. Furthermore, personnel administra-

[15] Alfred Vogel, "Your Clerical Workers Are Ripe for Unionism," *Harvard Business Review*, vol. 49, no. 2, pp. 48-54, March–April, 1971. Reviewing opinion surveys, the author concludes (pp. 49-50): "Clerical employees indeed *have* become much less satisfied on most key employee relations issues in recent years (1966 to the present) than in past years (1955 to 1965)."

tion encompasses some matters for which unions do not ordinarily wish to share responsibility with management. Recruitment, selection, training, rating, promotion, discipline, wage administration, and other parts of a well-rounded personnel program are management's initial responsibility, even though wise managements discuss in advance with union officials the proposed action. Most unions prefer to place certain restrictions around these management actions and to raise grievances in behalf of their members. Few desire to share the responsibility for administering these programs that directly affect union members.

POSSIBLE ALTERNATIVES FOR MANAGEMENT

When a union first secures bargaining rights, as well as later, management's position toward the union can be the result of a choice among several attitudes and policies. What are these possible choices?

Fighting the Union

First, management may decide to fight the union. If this decision is put into effect, it must be done in subtle ways, since outright discrimination against union members and refusal to bargain collectively are unlawful. Management may indulge in subtle forms of discrimination and in efforts to discredit the union. Under the Taft-Hartley Act of 1947, it may also speak out against unions and urge workers not to join, so long as there are no threats or promises of benefits. In some cases, management tries to answer what it considers to be untruthful union statements; in others, it may try to discredit a particular union. Retaliation in kind by union spokesmen is part of the pitched battle of words. Constructive labor relations and responsible unions are not developed by this approach. Instead, labor relations are often characterized by bitter accusations on each side and evidences of bad faith.

Armed Truce

Second, management may decide to deal with the union on an "armed-truce" basis.[16] This is done on the assumption that the basic interests of the company and the union are in conflict. Therefore, management's effort is to contain the union and to preserve managerial rights. Management may also attempt, through personnel programs, to strengthen its position with employees.[17] Then a struggle for their "loyalty" ensues. The union, on the other hand, is usually aggressive and under pressure to "get something more" for the members in order to hold their support. In short, the armed truce exists in the context of a power struggle over union security and management rights. In a speech many years ago, a management official who later became head of the Federal Mediation and Conciliation Service said:

> In our company . . . we are going to get about the type of labor leadership that we develop by our actions. If, in dealing with labor organizations, we are ethical, are entitled to the confidence of people, use fair tactics and use friendly attitudes, we will get

that in return; if we are going to be militant, use underhanded tactics, and fight all the time, that is the type of organized labor leader we will get.[18]

Working Harmony

Third, management may structure its dealings with the union so that a relationship of "working harmony" develops. This alternative involves the recognition by management that it has an opportunity to help unions become responsible by taking the initiative in seeking to establish friendly relations based on fair dealing and understanding of each other's problems and goals. Specific and detailed examples of companies and unions which have developed "working harmony" will be found in the series of case studies prepared for the National Planning Association's Committee on the Causes of Industrial Peace under Collective Bargaining. These studies describe labor-management relations in the Crown Zellerbach Corporation, Libbey-Owens-Ford Glass Company, Dewey and Almy Chemical Company, Lockheed Aircraft Corporation, Nashua Gummed and Coated Paper Company (now Nashua Corporation), Marathon Corporation, Colorado Fuel and Iron Corporation, Lapointe Machine Tool Company, American Velvet Company, and the Atlantic Steel Company.[19]

In these cases, management recognized the union's need for security and tried to assure this by actions that strengthened the union and, in many cases, by formal union-shop clauses. The union, on the other hand, appreciated the com-

---

[16] This term, and the two which follow, have been developed more fully by Frederick H. Harbison and John R. Coleman, *Goals and Strategy in Collective Bargaining,* Harper & Row, Publishers, Incorporated, New York, 1951. Their three "models" grew out of an analysis of some 40 case studies involving manufacturing firms varying in size from a few hundred to several thousand employees and located largely in the East and Middle West. For a defense of one variation of this approach, see Herbert R. Northrup, *Boulwarism: The Labor Relations Policies of the General Electric Company,* University of Michigan, Bureau of Industrial Relations, Ann Arbor, Mich., 1966.

[17] For a discussion of the basis for this approach, see George Strauss, "The Shifting Power Balance in the Plant," *Industrial Relations,* vol. 1, no. 3, pp. 65-96, May, 1962 (reprinted in Paul Pigors, Charles A. Myers, and F. T. Malm, *Management of Human Resources: Readings in Personnel Administration,* 3d ed., McGraw-Hill Book Company, New York, 1973, selection 26.

[18] Cyrus Ching, "Problems in Collective Bargaining," *Journal of Business* (The University of Chicago), vol. 11, no. 1, part 2, p. 40, January, 1938. At that time, Mr. Ching was vice-president of the United States Rubber Company.

[19] The final NPA report, *Fundamentals of Labor Peace,* 1953, summarizes the case studies and their implications. A longer summary of the cases, together with the final report, is found in Clinton S. Golden and Virginia D. Parker, *Causes of Industrial Peace under Collective Bargaining,* Harper & Row, Publishers, Incorporated, New York, 1955.

pany's need for lower costs and good earnings in order to provide continued employment. Union-management discussions were centered not on "principles" or "prerogatives" but on problems and how best to solve them. There was sharing of information, and management consulted workers *through their union* about an ever-widening range of company problems.[20]

The importance of communication through the union has been well expressed by Alexander R. Heron, former vice-president of the Crown Zellerbach Corporation (largest paper manufacturer on the Pacific Coast):

> We have seen examples of facts twisted to suit a program of agitation, facts half told in order to create conflict between employer and employee. The more we have barred the sources of information to union representatives, the more dramatic and unfavorable has been their use of the fragments they did obtain; and the more persistent and circuitous have been their methods of obtaining what they could use. Frankness toward the so-called labor politician helps him to become a labor statesman. . . .[21]

> The employer who fails to welcome the union as a channel of information is injuring himself both directly and indirectly. He is inviting a lack of confidence in all the information he shares with his employees through other channels. He creates the suspicion that his facts will not stand up under examination by the union representatives. He provides reason for ill will and resentment on the part of the union officers whom he tries to bypass.[22]

Union-management Cooperation

Finally, management may decide, with the union representatives, that it wishes to develop a program of union-management cooperation on production problems. This type of relationship is much more rare, often it has developed only when the survival of the firm was at stake or its competitive position weakening. Union and management join in trying to reduce costs and increase output, and gains are shared. The implications of this development are so interesting that we shall consider union-management cooperation in greater detail in Chapter 21.

These types of relationships are not so clear-cut as the preceding discussion may suggest. At any one time, there may be elements of both armed truce and working harmony in a particular union-management relationship. Certainly over a period of time the nature of the relationship changes as the parties develop more experience in dealing with each other, or as new management representatives and different union officials enter the picture. This happened, for example, in a subsidiary plant of the Inland Steel Company in Chicago.[23] Relationships may also change or deteriorate as economic conditions and other related factors change.[24]

THE NATURE OF THE BARGAINING PROCESS

These types of relationships reflect, in part, management and union attitudes toward collective bargaining. They involve what two recent authors have called "attitudinal structuring," which is viewed as the third of four interrelated

---

[20] For further discussion of this trend, in relation to personnel administration, see Douglass V. Brown and Charles A. Myers, "The Changing Industrial Relations Philosophy of American Management," in *Proceedings of the Ninth Annual Meeting of the Industrial Relations Research Association,* Cleveland, Ohio, Dec. 28–29, 1956, pp. 84–99 (reprinted in Pigors, Myers, and Malm, *op. cit.,* selection 25).

[21] *Sharing Information with Employees,* Stanford University Press, Stanford, Calif., 1942, p. 177.

[22] *Beyond Collective Bargaining,* Stanford University Press, Stanford, Calif., 1948, p. 145.

[23] For an excellent case study illustrating this change, see William F. Whyte, *Pattern for Industrial Peace,* Harper & Row, Publishers, Incorporated, New York, 1951.

[24] While these points were often made in the original NPA studies, they have been reemphasized by Herbert R. Northrup and Harvey A. Young, "The Causes of Industrial Peace Revisited," *Industrial and Labor Relations Review,* vol. 22, no. 1, pp. 31–47, October, 1968.

subprocesses of labor negotiations.[25] The four are:

1 Distributive bargaining, which determines the distribution of the joint product.
2 Integrative bargaining, which facilitates the resolution of joint problems and integration of the interests of the parties.
3 Attitudinal structuring, which maintains or restructures the attitudes of the parties toward each other.
4 Intraorganizational bargaining, which is designed to achieve consensus within the company (or other bargaining unit) and within the union before the actual union-management bargaining process takes place.

Our view, developed earlier, is that the attitudes of the parties tend to shape the bargaining process and will to some extent affect the strategies and tactics used in the other three subprocesses. Most bargaining does, in fact, include elements of distributive and integrative bargaining, since the "money matters" (wages, salaries, and fringe benefits) are part of the former and the latter concerns itself with such related problems as individual job security and management flexibility, preserving jobs and management efficiency, and institutional security. Usually, changes in the status quo are part of integrative bargaining. Searching for alternative solutions to problems is its central characteristic, and fullest exchange of information is essential.

A Case Example: Restructuring of Relationships in International Harvester

In the postwar period, relationships between the International Harvester Company and the United Auto Workers (UAW) were unfriendly and even hostile. Distributive bargaining primarily characterized the relationship, which each side viewed as a "chance to get even" with

the other. But apparently neither the union nor the company was happy with the results; new contracts were seldom signed until after a strike, and there were wildcat strikes over grievances during the contract period. Management felt it needed to prevent these strikes and improve attitudes which were having a bad effect on employee morale.

About 1955 the parties called in a well-known mediator, David L. Cole, who had earlier served as director of the Federal Mediation and Conciliation Service. Improvements came with time and patience, and the focus was the resolution of a logjam of some 48,000 grievances which had been appealed to the arbitration stage between 1954 and 1959. Starting first in one plant, with top-management support, management and union officials began settling these grievances on the spot, and the approach spread to other plants. In the process, attitudes were restructured, and the 1961 contract was the first signed without a strike. One review of this experience observes:

> The key point about the new look, and one that is perhaps generally applicable to attitudinal structuring, is that it is difficult to change hostile attitudes during contract negotiations alone. The tactical requirements as well as the stakes involved in distributive bargaining place real restraints on the amount of attitudinal structuring that can take place during a single negotiation. Trust can be created more readily in a situation in which the bargaining stakes are not so large.[26]

Distributive bargaining strategies and tactics have received most attention in the growing lit-

---

[25] Richard E. Walton and Robert B. McKersie, *A Behavioral Theory of Labor Negotiations,* McGraw-Hill Book Company, New York, 1965, pp. 4-6, and chaps. 7 and 8.

[26] Walton and McKersie, *op. cit.,* p. 368. The case facts were drawn from pp. 365-367. See also David L. Cole, *The Quest for Industrial Peace,* McGraw-Hill Book Company, New York, 1963, pp. 82-86. For more extensive discussion of successful and less successful collective bargaining experience in various issues, see the classic work, Sumner H. Slichter, James J. Healy, and E. Robert Livernash, *The Impact of Collective Bargaining on Management,* The Brookings Institution, Washington, D.C., 1960.

erature on the theory of bargaining, which is related to game theory.[27] There are many possibilities for agreement or nonagreement (strike or lockout), depending upon each party's real settlement prices,[28] final bargaining positions, degree of commitment to fixed positions, and failure to communicate to the other side the possibility of overlapping final positions which would lead to agreement. The latter possibility is one in which a neutral third party, such as a mediator, may help the parties reach agreement. This, of course, also applies to integrative bargaining, as in the improvement of the operation of a grievance procedure (the International Harvester case).

Management Preparation for Collective Bargaining

The fourth subprocess mentioned above, *intraorganizational bargaining,* entails, on the management side, careful preparation for bargaining.[29] Most agreements are between individual employers and the unions representing some of their employees, but there are also some multiemployer and multiunion agreements. These obviously require more complex negotiations within each group before a unified set of proposals and counterproposals can be presented at the

first bargaining session. In other words, the wider the bargaining unit, the more resolution of intraorganizational differences is required as partial preparation for bargaining.

In multiplant companies, a similar degree of preparation may be necessary, especially if there is centralized bargaining for all company plants or all units of an organization. Some firms and organizations, however, bargain with local unions on a plant-level basis, and here there is perhaps less need for uniformity of position by all plants. Nevertheless, the possibility that unions will "whipsaw" a multiplant firm, by seeking in every plant-level negotiation the most favorable agreements reached in any plant, forces management to coordinate its preparation for bargaining and its bargaining strategy.

Such preparation begins with the collection of data relevant to the issues which will come up: wages and wage levels, fringe benefits, seniority, changes in jobs and job standards, and a host of other subjects covered in collective agreements. The personnel administrator or industrial relations director may take the responsibility for gathering the necessary information, and he may also be responsible for monitoring experience under the expiring agreement so that he can make recommendations for desirable changes in content or contract language. Suggestions may be solicited from plant managers or supervisors.

Members of the management negotiating committee, which may or may not include the personnel or industrial relations manager as an active member, will have been selected by top management before final preparations begin. These preparations include drafting specific proposals for changes in contract language, determining the general size of the economic benefits that can be offered during the negotiations and the final limits acceptable as a last resort, and organizing the supporting statistical data and other documentation. Some advance discussion of bargaining strategy and tactics is also likely.

All this assumes that the union bargaining committees, under the guidance of international

---

[27] In addition to Walton and McKersie, *op. cit.,* chaps. 2 and 3, see Carl M. Stevens, *Strategy and Collective Bargaining Negotiation,* McGraw-Hill Book Company, New York, 1963; and J. Pen, *The Wage Rate under Collective Bargaining,* Harvard University Press, Cambridge, Mass., 1959.

[28] The union's negotiators may have one "real settlement price" but find that their membership refuses to accept a tentative settlement. The membership repudiation of leaders' tentative agreements greatly complicated peaceful collective bargaining beginning in 1967. See Jack Barbash, "The Causes of Rank-and-file Unrest," chap. 3, and William E. Simkin, "Refusals to Ratify Controls," chap. 5, in Joel Seidman (ed.), *Trade Union Government and Collective Bargaining: Some Critical Issues,* Praeger Publishers, New York, 1970.

[29] For a survey of recent experience, see Meyer S. Ryder, Charles M. Rehmus, and Sanford Cohen, *Management Preparation for Collective Bargaining,* Dow Jones and Richard D. Irwin, Inc., Homewood, Ill., 1966.

union representatives, are going through a similar process. Within recent years, however, there has been a new kind of preparation in firms and industries with long bargaining experience, namely, joint study of issues through continuous year-long consultation, either in joint committees to consider specific problems or through periodic meetings of the principal negotiators. The Human Relations Committees in the basic steel industry prior to 1965 were successful in taking some of the misunderstanding and heat out of certain issues, e.g., medical care, seniority, overtime, and extended vacations, but internal changes in the union forced a discontinuance of the formal committee structure. In this industry, however, as in others, it appears that there is consultation of an informal nature prior to formal negotiations.[30]

As the collective bargaining process becomes more factual and less "blue sky" in its character, it will be aided by computerized data banks which contain relevant contract clauses in the locality and/or the industry, as well as data on wages and salaries, fringe benefits, and other costs in the particular organization. The Industrial Union Department of the AFL-CIO has a computerized information system to coordinate the bargaining activities of some 77 corporate or industry-wide bargaining committees.[31] Some firms have been able to use computers to calculate the costs of alternative union demands, but

during the 1960s the possibilities were only tapped.

Coalition Bargaining

An increasingly common type of collective bargaining in private industry involves a number of different unions, which have separate contracts with a large multiplant or multiproduct firm, forming a coalition to bargain jointly with the top management of the firm. One of the early examples in 1966 (tested subsequently in the National Labor Relations Board and through appeal to higher courts) involved the International Union of Electrical Workers (AFL-CIO) and the General Electric Company. The IUE represented at that time over half of GE's unionized employees; the rest were represented by about 80 other unions in nearly 150 bargaining units across the country. Believing that GE had the upper hand in centralized bargaining with separate unions, IUE invited seven other unions to send representatives to its bargaining sessions with GE. GE objected, appealed an NLRB order to meet with the IUE with others present, but finally proceeded under protest when a court issued an injunction on refusal to bargain.

According to one analysis of this and other coalition bargaining experiences with large companies and conglomerates: "Coalition in some form becomes the only way to achieve bargaining effectiveness," from the standpoint of the separate unions. Managements, on the other hand, may have good reasons for remaining under decentralized bargaining, so that plant-by-plant negotiations can be responsive to local conditions and local union objectives. Several firms have taken strikes to preserve this decentralized bargaining, which still characterizes the American system of industrial relations as compared with that of most other countries.[32]

---

[30] One issue on which management-union agreement must be reached if needed action is to be well coordinated is that of equal employment opportunity. Some managements and unions have issued joint policy statements on this issue. But beyond that, continuing consultation is needed to ensure agreement about subpolicies, e.g., active recruiting of so-called "unemployable" persons, as well as about procedures and practices, some of which need to be modified if disadvantaged persons, without any experience as regular employees or as union members, are now to become members of both organizations—a company and a union.

[31] "Computer Sits In on Bargaining," *Business Week,* Sept. 10, 1964, p. 154. For further discussion of this and similar applications in other unions and by management, see Abraham J. Siegel (ed.), *The Impact of Computers on Collective Bargaining,* The M.I.T. Press, Cambridge, Mass., 1969.

[32] For a full discussion of coalition bargaining, see George H. Hildebrand, "Cloudy Future for Coalition Bargaining," *Harvard Business Review,* vol. 46, no. 6, pp. 114-128, November-December, 1968.

COLLECTIVE BARGAINING IN THE PUBLIC SECTOR

We noted earlier the rapid growth of unions at all levels of government, and the militancy of some unions which has led to strikes by teachers and city employees even though these are often illegal. Are there special problems of collective bargaining in the public sector of our economy which are different from the approaches we have reviewed in private industry? One difference has often been pointed out: Union demands and collective bargaining settlements in private industry have to meet the test of the marketplace; public employee bargaining depends on the willingness of government administrators and ultimately the taxpayers to make cost-raising agreements.

Another suggested difference is that unions are permitted to strike in private industry (except where strikes may be postponed by the "national emergency" provisions of the Taft-Hartley Act or in airlines and railroads by the Railway Labor Act). But with few exceptions, most state laws prohibit strikes by public employees; some have "fact finding" with recommendations, and a few (as in Pennsylvania and Michigan, for example) require compulsory arbitration of unresolved disputes involving policemen and firemen. But the issue is far from settled. Some states have no laws whatever, others are considering amending theirs to deal with the problem of continued strikes despite the legal prohibition. The so-called "Taylor Law" in New York State is one example of an approach that has attracted national attention, with court-imposed fines on striking unions and union leaders.[33]

One major difference is in the length of experience with the collective bargaining process. Except for some parts of the federal service, most bargaining relationships between unions and government representatives, such as state agency heads, mayors, city councils, school superintendents, and school boards, are of fairly recent origin. The relationships often have all the characteristics of immaturity: inexperienced negotiators (especially on the management side), belief by management that most noneconomic union demands infringe on managerial prerogatives and must be resisted, long lists of union demands which must be secured in one agreement, and delaying tactics resulting from the fact that agreements sometimes cannot be signed with authority by one side or the other. Despite the longer experience in the federal service, apparently some of these points still apply there, particularly in the military units with civilian employees.[34]

As bargaining relationships in the public sector mature, the scope of bargaining will widen and probably settle down to the more professional approach used in most of private industry collective bargaining.[35] Administration of con-

---

[33] For a concise discussion of these issues, see John F. Burton and Charles Krider, "The Role and Consequences of Strikes by Public Employees," *Yale Law Journal,* vol. 79, no. 3, pp. 418-443, April, 1970. This is part of a larger study of unionism and collective bargaining in the public sector conducted by the Brookings Institution, Washington, D.C.

[34] Philip Shabecoff, "Uncle Sam: Beginner at Baraining," *The New York Times,* Sunday, Mar. 28, 1971, sec. 3, p. 5. A government employees' union national president is quoted as saying that the commander of a large military base, confronted with a union bargaining for his civilian employees, "had no idea of what it was all about. He had no idea about what kind of problems existed among the civilian employees. He had no idea how to talk to union representatives of those employees." As for regular federal government departments, the union president stated: "There are exceptions, but the Federal Government still has too many old-time personnel officers whose word was once law—and who still think it is."

[35] Michael H. Moskow, J. Joseph Loewenberg, and Edward Clifford Koziara, *Collective Bargaining in Public Employment,* Random House, New York, 1970, chap. 9, "The Future of Collective Bargaining in Public Employment." For recommendations at the city level, see *Pickets at City Hall: Report and Recommendations of the Twentieth Century Fund Task Force on Labor Disputes in Public Employment,* The Twentieth Century Fund, New York, 1970. One recommendation (p. 29) was the following: "In government today, especially below the federal level, there is a paucity of experience in dealing with unions and administering labor agreements. Unless the costly and embittering mistakes made in industry at an earlier time are to be repeated in public employment, something must be done to provide those who act for government-as-employer and those who act for government employees with the knowledge and sophistication necessary to negotiate and administer labor agreements capably."

tracts, particularly the handling of grievances, will improve. Public personnel administration, which has had a long history and record of service at the federal level, will be extended to management at the state and local levels, with specialists in labor relations as part of the staff group. In some cases, personnel and labor relations representatives from private industry may help in an advisory role, especially in cities and with school boards. But there is a great need for capable personnel administrators and labor relations specialists in the public service. Many of the personnel concepts and systems developed in this book apply in the public sector as well as in private industry.

STAFF AND LINE RESPONSIBILITIES

Earlier, when distinguishing between "personnel administration" and "labor relations," we said that dealings with unions are not the primary responsibility of the personnel administrator. His field of interest is necessarily broader, for some parts of a well-rounded personnel program do not involve relations with union representatives. But whether or not there is a separate director of labor relations, the personnel administrator must concern himself with union-management relations. Ideally, in his staff role he should avoid being put in the position where he has to make decisions on grievances or contract demands. These decisions are the final responsibility of line management.

Actually, in a number of organizations, the personnel administrator or labor relations specialist may help to negotiate the union contract and may even represent top management at some stage in the grievance procedure. While this organizational arrangement may work well in the absence of a line management competent at all levels to deal with union representatives, we believe that it is better for the personnel administrator to use grievance settlements and contract negotiations as opportunities to help line management, not to relieve them completely of this responsibility.

In his capacity as adviser, the personnel administrator should know something about the experience of other managements in dealing with specific unions, especially in terms of the possible alternatives discussed earlier. If he suggests attempting to achieve either working harmony or union-management cooperation, as we believe he should, he can also assist top management in getting this policy understood and carried out down the line, especially at the supervisory level. New supervisors, and most supervisors in newly unionized firms, need suggestions on building constructive relationships with shop stewards, and here the personnel administrator has an opportunity to bring to their attention the accumulated experience of others in their attempts to meet similar difficulties.

SUMMARY

Unionism springs from the basic aspirations of those employees who become convinced that they can gain more through membership in a union than by "going it alone." Historically, white-collar employees have been less convinced of the need of unions, but some have joined unions. Their numbers may increase, depending upon management policies. If employees do join a union which secures bargaining rights, management is confronted with a new challenge to its authority. Instead of regarding unionization solely as an evidence of ingratitude on the part of employees or a failure by management, wise managers take the initiative in attempting to develop constructive relationships with the new organization representing their employees. An understanding of the nature of the bargaining process, and careful preparation for collective bargaining are essential to the achievement of constructive relations.

The growth of collective bargaining in the public sector presents some new problems, one of which is the lack of experience on the part of the bargainers. In the private sector, new problems have also arisen with the growth of coalition bargaining as separate unions coordinate their bargaining strategy to deal with large multiplant firms and conglomerates.

To the extent that constructive relations are desired, the personnel administrator has a number of tasks and opportunities. He can help to influence and formulate the company's policies in dealing with the union. He can assist top management in communicating these policies to lower levels of management, particularly to first-level supervision. He can advise and assist the different levels of management in handling the labor relations problems that are bound to arise in unionized firms. Beyond this, he may also be called upon to be the company spokesman in contract negotiations, although in this role he is almost certain to appear as a line representative. In the long run, he will be more effective if he assists line management in contract negotiations and grievance settlements, leaving the responsibility for decision making where it belongs.

SELECTED REFERENCES

Bakke, E. Wight: *Mutual Survival: The Goal of Unions and Management,* Yale University Labor and Management Center Series, Harper & Row, Publishers, Incorporated, New York, 1947.

————: "Why Workers Join Unions," *Personnel,* vol. 22, no. 1, pp. 37–56, 1945.

Blum, Albert A., *et al.: White Collar Workers,* Random House, Inc., New York, 1971.

Bok, Derek C., and John T. Dunlop: *Labor in the American Community,* Simon and Schuster, New York, 1970.

Brown, Douglass V., and Charles A. Myers: "The Changing Industrial Relations Philosophy of American Management," *Proceedings of the Ninth Annual Meeting of the Industrial Relations Research Association,* Cleveland, Ohio, Dec. 28–29, 1956, pp. 84–99 (reprinted in Paul Pigors, Charles A. Myers, and F. T. Malm, *Management of Human Resources: Readings in Personnel Administration,* 3d ed., McGraw-Hill Book Company, New York, 1973, selection 25).

Chamberlain, Neil W., and James W. Kuhn: *Collective Bargaining,* 2d ed., McGraw-Hill Book Company, New York, 1965.

Cole, David L.: *The Quest for Industrial Peace,* McGraw-Hill Book Company, New York, 1963.

Golden, Clinton, and Virginia D. Parker (eds.): *Causes of Industrial Peace under Collective Bargaining,* Harper & Row, Publishers, Incorporated, New York, 1955. (A summary of the National Planning Association's case studies.)

Harbison, Frederick H., and John R. Coleman: *Goals and Strategy in Collective Bargaining,* Harper & Row, Publishers, Incorporated, New York, 1951.

Healy, James J. (ed.): *Creative Collective Bargaining,* Prentice-Hall, Inc., Englewood Cliffs, N.J., 1965.

Hildebrand, George H.: "Cloudy Future for Coalition Bargaining," *Harvard Business Review,* vol. 46, no. 6, pp. 114–128, November–December, 1968.

Lester, Richard A.: *As Unions Mature: An Analysis of the Evolution of American Unionism,* Princeton University Press, Princeton, N.J., 1958.

Moskow, Michael H., J. Joseph Loewenberg, and Edward Clifford Koziara: *Collective Bargaining in Public Employment,* Random House, Inc., New York, 1970.

National Industrial Conference Board: *White-Collar Unionization,* Studies in Personnel Policy, no. 220, New York, 1970.

Northrup, Herbert R.: *Boulwarism: The Labor Relations Policies of the General Electric Company,* University of Michigan, Bureau of Industrial Relations, Ann Arbor, Mich., 1966.

Purcell, Theodore V.: *The Worker Speaks His Mind on Company and Union,* Harvard University Press, Cambridge, Mass., 1954.

Ryder, Meyer S., Charles M. Rehmus, and Sanford Cohen: *Management Preparation for Collective Bargaining,* Dow Jones and Richard D. Irwin, Inc., Homewood, Ill., 1966.

Slichter, Sumner H., James J. Healy, and E. Robert Livernash: *The Impact of Collective Bargaining on Management,* The Brookings Institution, Washington, D.C., 1960, especially chaps. 1, 2, 29–31.

Strauss, George: "Professionalism and Occupational Associations," *Industrial Relations,* vol. 2, no. 3, pp. 7–31, May, 1963.

————: "The Shifting Power Balance in the Plant," *Industrial Relations,* vol. 1, no. 3, pp. 65–96, May, 1962 (reprinted in Pigors, Myers, and Malm, *op. cit.,* selection 26).

Ulman, Lloyd (ed.): *Challenges to Collective Bargaining,* Prentice-Hall, Inc., Englewood Cliffs, N.J., 1967.

Walton, Richard C., and Robert B. McKersie: *A Behavioral Theory of Labor Negotiations,* McGraw-Hill Book Company, New York, 1965.

Weber, Arnold R.: "Federal Labor Relations: Problems and Prospects," in *Arbitration and the Public Interest,* Proceedings of the Twenty-fourth Annual Meeting, National Academy of Arbitrators, The Bureau of National Affairs, Washington, D.C., 1971, chap. 6, pp. 148–160.

Diagnosing Organizational Health

INTRODUCTION

To act effectively as an enabler in managing by shared objectives, every manager and supervisor needs to develop the basic skills of personnel administration.

In Chapter 9 we consider situational thinking, a systems view of interactive variables. Some such way of thinking is essential for effective diagnosis of any work situation. Basic variables include technical features, the human element, and space-time coordinates. An organization policy becomes a factor in any situation where it is interpreted and used as a guide. In applying situational diagnosis for purposes of decision making, steps to be taken include *fact-finding* (unfinished until a multiple inside view has been achieved), *weighing facts* (in relation to each other and to organization policies and goals), considering *what is at stake* (not only for a few individuals but chiefly for the organization as a whole), and *evaluating alternatives for action* (not only for the short run and at the level of expediency but also for the long run and at the level of policy). At best, successive cycles of systems-minded decision making become part of a continuing process of learning—with other organizational members, and by experience.

Chapter 10 shows how directed interviewing can be used to obtain and transmit information and how nondirective interviewing is essential for gaining and sharing understanding. A skillful interviewer knows how to create conditions that favor genuine dialogue. Part of what he listens for is what speaks in the other person as inner motivation. Skillful interviewing may be especially needed if new employees have been recruited from among the hard-core unemployed.

In Chapter 11 we shall consider such indicators of organizational health as figures for tardiness and absence and accident records. In working toward a systems view (in which separate inputs will be integrated) a personnel-minded manager or staff expert asks himself: What seems to have motivated the individuals whose behavior produced these results? Ways of looking for this kind of meaning include conducting attitude surveys (a procedure often associated with the Theory X concept of management) and developing an integrative system of measuring significant facts about the human organization (a procedure which implements the central aim of participative management).

In Chapter 12 we see how labor turnover and internal mobility may be advantageous or disadvantageous. For example, turnover may be either a "loss" or a "gain" according to which employees are leaving, and why. When quits are voluntary, neither a systems-minded manager nor his personnel adviser will equate the number of quits with the amount of organizational instability (deriving from employee dissatisfaction). An exit interview, or a follow-up interview some time after the terminated employee has found other employment, may yield valuable insight into what has gone wrong. Similarly, understanding the significance of internal mobility—by transfer—requires consideration of such factors as whether transfers are voluntary (to permit promotion or to provide greater job satisfaction); who is asking for transfers, from and to which organizational units; and whether these moves are occurring at a rate which tends to disrupt work groups.

Complaints and grievances, considered in Chapter 13, may throw light not only on employee attitudes but also on possibilities for improving conditions of work or supervisory techniques. Reviewing formal procedures for handling such evidences of dissatisfied feelings may also prove instructive. Does it seem that more complaints could—or should—have been handled before they became official grievances? Might many others have been settled at an early stage in the grievance procedure, or at least before being submitted to an impartial arbitrator? If complaints indicate that morale is higher in some organizational units than in others, what can be learned—by whom—from that fact? If complaints are widespread, what recommendations for changes might be made?

CASES IN PART 2 THAT RELATE TO SECTION C

2 Who Owns the Improved Tool?
3 Dissatisfactions of an Expatriate Engineer
4 The Girl and the Computer
5 Managing Highly Motivated Secretaries
7 The Good-neighbor Policy
8 A Need for Policy-centered Thinking
9 The "Outside" Inspectors
11 Will More Money Be a Motivator?

Chapter 9

Situational Thinking

To diagnose a situation effectively, a supervisor must first develop an appreciation for the complexity of organization and of human relationships in organization . . . . Secondly, effective diagnosis requires the skill of observing concrete events and relationships. . . . Thirdly, it is necessary to distinguish between the concrete events and relationships, as perceived by an individual, and the words which he uses as symbols to designate these events and relationships. . . . A fourth element . . . is the understanding of the motivations of individuals and groups . . . fifth [is] understanding the distinction between fact and feeling.

A. Zaleznik [1]

Anyone responsible for getting results with people needs to understand each of the elements mentioned in the headquote to this chapter. As noted by Zaleznik, it is also necessary to identify key relationships and relevant distinctions between them. Moreover, to achieve a comprehensive systems-minded view [2] of any organizational situation, insight into other variables is also essential. From our own observation, we would say that the following situational variables are basic and that in any organization the fourth variable needs to be taken into account by everyone who shares responsibility for achieving organizational objectives.

1 *The human element.* In addition to personality and individual differences, we include in this category interpersonal relationships and other social aspects of a situation.

2 *The technical factor.* This category includes such items as equipment and methods used in

---

[1] A. Zaleznik, *Foreman Training in a Growing Enterprise,* Harvard Business School, Division of Research, Boston, 1951, pp. 221-222.

[2] Cf. Sidney A. Fine, "A Systems Approach to Manpower Development in Human Services," pp. 27-37 in *Methods for Manpower Analysis,* no. 3, The W. E. Upjohn Institute for Employment Research, Kalamazoo, Mich., November, 1969, pp. 27-37.

production; management procedures; techniques of job study, wage and salary administration, quality control and the like; and specialized skills in personnel relations.

3 *Space-time dimensions and relationships.* Examples of spatial variables would be the size and location of a plant, office or work station. Interrelated temporal aspects include:

a Timing of a work shift (in comparison with the normal character of individual and community life).

b Continuity of time in human experience, i.e., perseverance of preconditioning feelings and attitudes derived from earlier experiences.

c Stage of development currently reached, e.g., by an individual growing toward maturity, by an employee in his length of service, or in a relationship between individuals or groups.

d Sequence of events and behavior, i.e., what happened before and after some climactic event or behavioral manifestation.

e Pace of events or tempo of activity by individuals and groups.

4 *Organization-wide policies designed to achieve major organizational objectives.* These policies can affect the behavior of individuals within each subsystem. However, policies become operational only to the extent that they are interpreted and used (judiciously or otherwise) by those who manage and those who are managed.

IS SITUATIONAL THINKING PRACTICAL?

Can this concept of basic interactive variables be helpful for purposes of organizational diagnosis and decision making?[3] Each person who consid-

ers applying such a concept must ultimately test it in his own experience. Writers of a textbook can do no more than offer a few case examples to illustrate general ideas and some descriptive material to show how a theoretical concept can be used as a method of asking productive questions about real-life situations.

The following case examples may serve to give substance to the basic variables, as listed, and to indicate some of their interrelationships and interactive effects. In each case example (and in all the cases given in Part 2), a perceptive reader can see that no factor in any of these situations exists in isolation. It is impossible to look closely at any one of these variables without seeing that it is related to, and affected by, other variables.

For instance, our first example may serve to show why it is impractical, and often costly, to treat any feature of a work situation as though it were nothing but a technical matter which could effectively be handled merely by making technical adjustments.

A Case Example: Who Should Do the Touch-up Painting?

An Incident In the works experimental laboratory of a chemical company on the day before shutting down for the annual vacation, Dr. Silvano, laboratory chief, assigned laboratory personnel to do the touch-up painting usually done at that time. The personnel included technicians in both junior and senior classifications. On behalf of the technicians, the union immediately filed a grievance, asserting that this work assignment violated the labor agreement. Union repre-

[3] It may be noted that both the circumstances of the urban crisis (some of which were outlined in Chap. 4) and many of the plans to ameliorate it illustrate the variables listed here. For example, questions to be asked about critical social problems and their solutions include those concerning where, when, for how long, and at what pace (space-time dimensions); how (technically speaking) problems (such as those of the inner city and massive unemployment among members of minority groups) developed and how (by what technical

innovations) they can be solved or their severity reduced; why attitudes (like racism and bitterness) have aggravated practical difficulties, and to what extent other human responses (such as acceptance and nonviolence) might change the climate in which people work on practical problems. In some cities, notably New York, mayors have used the report of the National Advisory Commission on Civil Disorders as a guide to decision making in essentially the same way that policy statements can be used in any organization.

sentatives argued (1) that the work assignment ignored recently formulated job descriptions (of which some pertinent provisions were cited); and (2) that when properly qualified tradesmen (in this instance, maintenance painters) were available, management had no right to assign laboratory technicians to do clean-up or maintenance work.

At this stage of developments, the content of what had been said on both sides of the dispute was purely *technical*. The work assignment was technical. The union arguments were based on technical considerations. However, if anyone had applied a comprehensive system of situational diagnosis at that stage in the grievance process, he would not have overlooked the possibility that subjective factors might be powering the grievance. Moreover, anyone who had looked for evidence on that point might have found it by correlating available information such as the following.

Background Information The company, in which the works experimental laboratory was one subsystem, had recently undergone a 2-week strike, initiated to force recognition of the International Chemical Workers Union as a collective bargaining agent. The strike was terminated by negotiation of the first labor agreement between the parties. Among the dissatisfactions which had led employees to demand union representation was the absence of job descriptions. Employees had frequently complained that they were expected to perform work assignments which were not properly part of their job.

As one consequence of the new labor agreement, management had prepared job descriptions for each classification and incorporated them in the contract. Excerpts pertinent to the dispute between management and the union are as follows:

*[Tradesmen, first class]*shall perform work within the scope of their craft [which, as defined, included painting] . . . and such other miscellaneous work as shall be assigned.

[Laboratory personnel including technicians in all classifications] shall keep equipment, working areas, and storage areas clean, and perform such miscellaneous work as shall be assigned.

One difficulty in this case arose from different interpretations of these descriptive words,[4] but, however efficient the wording of a job description or a contract clause, differences in angles of view and in objectives can make trouble.

Management Action On this occasion Dr. Silvano rejected the union's grievance as being without merit. In his view two facts were decisive. One was past practice. Laboratory technicians had always been required to do touch-up painting. His second argument rested on the job descriptions for laboratory technicians. (He had written them himself.) He pointed out the provision that laboratory personnel, in addition to "work within the scope of their craft," were expected to perform "such other miscellaneous work as shall be assigned."

The laboratory personnel performed the work assignment under protest. Their written grievance was referred to the plant manager. It would be pleasant to report that, at the top level of management, comprehensive investigation and imaginative diagnosis of the situation resulted in mutual understanding with regard to a reasonable work assignment. However, this is not what happened. Actually, the plant manager promptly sustained the laboratory chief. He too brushed aside the arguments presented by the union as being incompatible with management's prerogative to direct the work force. Thus it was

---

[4] The language used in these job descriptions might certainly be criticized on the (technical) ground of being insufficiently precise. This circumstance may perhaps be accounted for by the fact that job descriptions in this company were written in a hurry and for the first time.

only during an arbitration hearing, when the initial disagreement had hardened into an arbitrable dispute, that several significant facts of the case were brought out and weighed.

Facts Brought Out at the Hearing   When the impartial arbitrator was helping the parties to clarify the issue to be arbitrated and to state the remedy that was being sought, a technical feature of the case came into prominence. *The initial complaint had not been made by the tradesmen* (maintenance painters). In other words, this was not a jurisdictional dispute, initiated by employees who claimed that their job rights were being encroached upon by employees in another classification. Instead, the complaint had been made by laboratory technicians and filed by the union, as an official grievance, on their behalf. Furthermore, union officials were interested in a principle; the actual financial considerations were being waived.

When the arbitrator got that far in his preliminary finding, it seemed clear to him that *the issue as perceived by the laboratory technicians* was primarily one of status. Unfortunately, the power of an impartial arbitrator is so limited, and he comes into a dispute so late, that he cannot take the kind of remedial action which is open to management representatives at earlier stages. An arbitrator can only rule which party to the dispute is in the right—under the facts as established at the hearing and under the applicable provisions of the current labor agreement.

Other interactive effects between the human element, the technical factor, and space-time dimensions of this case were also brought out at the hearing when the laboratory chief gave his testimony. In defending his position that the work assignment was appropriate, Dr. Silvano supplied the following information (none of which was contradicted by the union):

Continuity of experience as past practice. For seventeen years, ever since the works experimental lab-oratory was set up, technicians have always been required to do touch-up painting.

Duration. The total work assignment takes only 18-20 hours, and is divided among ten employees.

Interactive effects of techniques and the space-time factor. Touch-up painting can be performed only after each technician has completed his current experiment and cleared his bench and shelf of equipment. Experimental cycles cannot all be completed at the same time.

Spatial and organizational boundaries. The disputed work assignment applies only to the immediate workbench area of each laboratory technician. It never includes any painting of walls or ceiling—the care of which is properly an assignment for plant maintenance painters.

Opinions   After weighing the testimony and studying the labor agreement, the arbitrator sustained the company. But in such a case, can it be held that management won? Should it not rather be said that organizational losses far exceeded gains if one takes account of such intangible costs as lowered employee morale, a wasted opportunity to achieve mutual understanding with employees, and a poor start toward building a sound working relationship with a new union?

In reviewing that case, with the benefit of hindsight and the relative objectivity so easily achieved by outsiders, it looks as though projective listening (a communication technique described in Chapter 5), if applied at an early stage, might have paid handsome dividends. The subjective overtones of the initial complaint should not have been difficult to "hear" even if they were never articulated in spoken words. If the laboratory chief had been an alert and sympathetic listener, he might have responded to the technicians' unspoken question: Who do you think we are, maintenance men?

Even if that earlier opportunity for remedial action had been missed, an experienced labor relations director might have done some useful work in talking—and listening—with parties to the dispute. For example, projective listening might have helped him to answer the question: Why has this union decided to process such an unreasonable complaint? It should not have been necessary to wait until the arbitration hearing to recognize how an unspoken dissatisfaction on the part of the laboratory technicians would sound to officers of a newly established union. What the technicians had almost certainly been feeling, from the moment when their complaint was rejected by the laboratory chief, might be summed up as follows: What is this union doing for us if these job descriptions, now made part of our hard-won collective bargaining agreement, leave us just where we were before? If we can still be required to do work which is unrelated to our technical training and potential, why should we pay dues to a union? That attitude is one to which newly elected union officers feel peculiarly vulnerable. Unless someone can help them to get off the (political) hook, they often support their members by taking to arbitration cases which they know they cannot win.

In case analysis there is always room for differences of opinion. But we hope that the case example has illustrated the idea that the technical aspects of a situation cannot usefully be treated without regard to the human element, which is also a basic component of every work situation.

What Does That Case Example Show?

A single case cannot prove anything. It can only indicate that certain circumstances and consequences are not inconceivable, because they were established facts in one situation. Even citing a hundred case reports could not prove that a concept like situational thinking is valid and universally applicable. Nevertheless, a concept that is illustrated in one case gains substance if it proves applicable to other cases also and useful there, too, for situational diagnosis. For example, every situation where people work together illustrates the idea that employee motivation[5] needs to be considered, along with the technical factor and space-time coordinates. The next example shows what can be accomplished when a manager gives due weight to the human element as a situational factor which inevitably affects production, for better or for worse.

A Case Example: Assemblers Are Given Discretion to Plan, Organize, and Pace Their Work

In a company manufacturing components for television, radio, and control instruments, operators worked on units brought to them on a conveyorized assembly line. Each task, limited to one small segment of the final product, was highly repetitive. Although employees were on incentive, the quantity of output was low. Moreover, quality of the final product was poor. Many dissatisfactions were expressed by assemblers. There was a high rate of turnover.

While employee morale and output were at this low ebb, the plant manager became interested in the concept of job enrichment and decided to apply it. His first step was to abolish the assembly line. In its place, he arranged that individual work stations should be set up in separate cubicles on both sides of the main aisle. Each work station consisted of a semienclosed space, with a U-shaped workbench containing an ample supply of necessary parts. Operators at adjacent work stations could easily talk with one another through the wire mesh. Each operator now assembled a complete component. For his instruction, a finished prototype of the part which he was to assemble was on exhibit at the entrance to his work station. Each operator was left free to determine the method and pace at

[5] See Wretha W. Wiley, "Six Steps to New Careers," *Methods for Manpower Analysis,* no. 3, The W. E. Upjohn Institute for Employment Research, Kalamazoo, Mich., November, 1969, pp. 1–25, especially part I, "Six Tests for Nonprofessional Jobs and New Careers," pp. 3–8.

which he would work. He could assemble an entire component at one time, or, laying out a number of frames on his workbench, he could move from one unit to the next, in effect adopting the progressive assembly-line method. However, even if this choice was made, each assembler could now work at his own pace, instead of having an assigned task move past him at a mechanically preset speed.

There was a minimum of supervision. Each assembler was held responsible for quality control of his own output. The supervisor made himself available as a coach and adviser and walked past each work station at least once on each shift. A pause and a glance sufficed to let him know whether his help was needed.

During an initial period of adjustment, the method of work used by assemblers underwent two changes. At first, most operators preferred to assemble one complete component at a time, but gradually, more and more men went back voluntarily to the progressive assembly-line method. As they compared notes, which they frequently did, it came to be the general opinion that this method was more efficient. Having adopted it by their own choice and being free to pace their own work, they found nothing objectionable in this rationalized work method.

In this company, application of the job-enrichment concept proved highly productive and satisfying. Quality and quantity of output rose markedly. Thus assemblers managed to earn a high rate of incentive pay. Complaints and turnover were sharply reduced.

In this instance, organization goals were achieved by a way of managing which took account not only of technical requirements but also of subjective forces, such as inner motivation and individual preferences within the discretionary element of a work assignment.

In the two preceding examples, policy thinking has not been specifically illustrated. The next two illustrations show how thinking at the level of policy can (or might) help a supervisor to make a decision that integrates requirements which may otherwise seem incompatible.

A Case Example: A Policy Point about Time Off

In one company the policy on sickness and absence was such that an assembler with an infected tooth was excused one afternoon in order to go to the dentist, but no explanation was made to the other girls in her section of the purpose and applicability of the health policy. The next week a female operator in the same section applied for time off to get her hair set. She was indignant when the supervisor refused. "Mary got time off last week—why can't I get off today?" With no understanding of the management purpose underlying the policy, how could this production operator be expected to see that "time off" was not the common denominator between these two requests?

Another brief case example may serve to point up the difference between the discretionary decision making that is needed when a flexible policy statement is to be interpreted and the nondiscretionary faithfulness to the letter which is called for in applying an inflexible rule (or contractual provision).

A Case Example: A Policy Decision on Funeral Leave

When management provides for paid funeral leave, the purpose is to support bereaved employees during the critical period when there has been a death in their "immediate family." Many labor agreements include contractual provisions for granting such leave. To avoid abuse, the term "immediate family" is carefully defined. Usually this term includes wife or husband, children, mother, father, sister, brother, mother-in-law, and father-in-law.

In one case which was taken to arbitration, the following circumstances called for a policy decision. A regular full-time employee was an orphan. Since the age of six he had lived with a neighbor, although he had never been legally adopted. Nevertheless, he looked upon his foster father and mother as his parents. When his "father" died, the "son" applied for funeral leave. On a strictly legalistic interpretation of the relevant clause in the labor agreement, his request was denied, but if the supervisor had been guided by management's policy intention, the employee's request would have been granted.

Having illustrated what we mean by the basic variables, the next question to answer would seem to be: How, and by whom, can situational thinking be applied so that it has practical value for diagnosis and decision making? Naturally, the *how* depends to some extent on *who* is doing the situational thinking, where, when, and with what specific purpose. Nevertheless, both parts of the question can profitably be considered together.

A PHASED APPROACH TO SITUATIONAL ANALYSIS AND DECISION MAKING

Fact-finding

Finding and weighing facts have long been accepted as necessary preliminaries to effective decision making. The importance of these steps was emphasized by the War Manpower Commission in its program Training Within Industry,[6] which won international recognition during the Second World War and is widely used even today.

However, recent attempts to simulate human thinking, by programming computers, have prompted extensive research into the essential nature of the decision-making process. While fact-finding continues to be recognized as a first

[6] *The Training Within Industry Report, 1940-1945: A Record of the Development of Management Techniques for Improvement of Supervision: Their Use and the Results,* War Manpower Commission, Bureau of Training, Training Within Industry Service, September, 1945, pp. 330ff.

step, a systems-minded approach indicates that requirements for comprehensive fact-finding cannot be adequately stated in a few short rules. Furthermore, the relatively simplistic assumptions which underlie fact-finding by many supervisors need to be developed into realistic working hypotheses. For instance, many supervisors have found it natural (and easy) to assume that if a decision maker is a participant in a given situation, his fact-finding need consist in little more than rapidly reviewing what he already knows. Perhaps he may need to verify a few items or at most try to get a little additional information. Also, it is generally taken for granted that fact-finding is a task which needs to be performed only occasionally and at the brink of decision making, except when it proves necessary to justify a decision which has already been made.

Experience suggests, however, that the following hypotheses are more useful:

1 Gathering, verifying, reviewing, and correlating factual information are continuing obligations for everyone with organizational responsibility.

2 Fact-finding gains added urgency, and can be especially efficacious, when the first symptoms of a difficulty are detected. (This timing is efficient because fact-centered diagnosis can then be an effective preparation for preventive action instead of being merely part of a situational postmortem.)

3 A comprehensive system for exploring facts is needed (by insiders and outsiders alike) to reduce the risk of overlooking key aspects of a situation.

4 Sophisticated fact-finding consists in more than merely assembling a mass of unrelated items. Before it is possible to recognize the relevance and significance of factual data as found, it is necessary to explore the "facts" of interrelationship and interaction.

By following through on such general hypotheses, specific procedures can be developed.

Often it makes little or no difference which specific area of a situation is explored first. What matters most is to get adequate coverage. However, subjective factors are usually the most difficult to understand and the most stubborn to cope with (whether in oneself or in other people). Also, management representatives have traditionally been oriented toward technical matters. For these reasons, among others, exploration of facts concerning the human organization has often been less thorough than it should be.

Achieving a Multiple Inside View   Any perceptive case student can clearly see that merely being on the inside of a given situation does not in itself provide a sufficiently all-round view to ensure adequate understanding. Because that point is often overlooked by insiders, many opportunities to clear up misunderstandings are missed. For instance, in the case example "Who Should Do the Touch-up Painting?" the laboratory chief apparently neglected to look at—still less to look into—facts of perception, attitude, and inner motivation on the part of technicians. Yet these intangibles may have been the root difficulty.[7]

In a situation where an individual or group is making difficulty for someone else or has made a complaint, it is useful to ask: What is the source of this difficulty? Is the organizational system or some person in a position of authority making demands on this individual or social subsystem which *are perceived* as unacceptable—or even as impossible to meet? Conversely, is this person or group making demands on the situation that are not being met?

---

[7] Most of the cases in Part 2 of this book illustrate the same general idea. To mention just one, Case 4, "The Girl and the Computer," shows that individual differences in attitude and motivation—ignored by supervisors—made "going across the hall" a totally different experience for one career-oriented employee from what it was to other clerks who were selected from the same work unit for the same temporary reassignment.

Perhaps one reason why insiders so often fail to ask such questions is that they assume they already know the answers. In this respect, an outsider called into a situation to offer advice has a significant advantage. Unless he allows preconceptions or prejudices to stultify his spirit of inquiry, he realizes that he does not know most of what needs to be taken into account for effective diagnosis and decision making in that particular situation. Also, an outsider may find it easier than an insider to appreciate that any situation inevitably looks—and feels—somewhat different to each participant in it. This multiplicity of inside views comes about because not only perceptions but also interpretations and values are determined by individual differences (including those of temperament, previous experience, and currently felt needs).[8]

The following case example is taken from a situation where it was necessary for someone to get the facts (and weigh their significance) concerning the needs and perceptions of an old-timer.

A Case Example: A Self-fulfilling Prophecy

Many years ago a manufacturing company had a serious scrap problem. This technical difficulty gave rise to an organizational problem, a conflict between two department heads. The cost control department had charged the cost of defective work to the machining department, but that department head insisted the cost should be charged to the foundry, where the trouble had begun because of blowholes in the castings. Trying to get at the root of the difficulty, the plant manager decided to supplement the capability of an old-time foundry foreman by providing him with the staff services of a young college-trained metallurgist.

---

[8] For an illuminating discussion of personal factors affecting perceptual behavior see Carl R. Rogers, *Client-centered Therapy: Its Current Practice, Implications, and Theory,* Houghton Mifflin Company, Boston, 1951, especially pp. 483–487.

This was done, but no explanation of the reason for this action was given to the foundry foreman. He therefore made his own interpretation of the unexplained change that so vitally affected him. Naturally, he did so in accordance with his own knowledge, perceptions, and feelings. He knew that higher management valued the technical know-how that he had acquired during years of practical experience, but he was painfully aware that his technical competence at the level of scientific research and theory was open to criticism. Realizing that management now set a high value on scientific background, he feared for his position. To him, therefore, the technical expert appeared as a threat, a college-trained understudy who would replace him as soon as he had learned "the ropes." Therefore, despite his assurance of complete cooperation, he gave the young metallurgist as little cooperation as he dared and resisted many proposed changes. To any inquiry into customary practices, his invariable reply was, "You ought to know. You went to college." Naturally, this antagonistic attitude soon became mutual. The staff expert repeatedly complained that the foreman was not only incompetent but also uncooperative. The foundry foreman's immediate supervisor tried repeatedly to get the foreman to change his attitude. These attempts proved unsuccessful. After a few months, it was decided that the foreman's employment must be terminated. In this way the unhappy result feared from the outset by the old-time foreman was brought about, partly as a consequence of his own negative attitude.

Taking a Person-centered Approach In the foundry situation, hindsight suggests that better results all round might have been achieved if some management representative had found time to talk—and listen—*with* the old-time foreman *before* giving him a young, college-trained staff assistant whose role could so easily be misinterpreted by that particular foreman. But when a management representative does not know what the "facts of feeling" are in some person on whom he depends for results, the manager cannot be sure that he is acting intelligently.

Moreover, merely "getting facts" is not enough. Having factual information in one's possession is of relatively little use unless one takes the trouble to consider its implications. For example, everyone knows—for a fact—that an employee is a human being. Other well-known facts are that human beings have feelings and that feelings affect behavior. But how often have the implications of those familiar facts been overlooked in work situations or brushed aside as irrelevant?

Getting into a Situation by Stages

When someone from outside is called into a situation to make a diagnosis and recommendations, he naturally begins by gathering facts, items related to all situational aspects which he perceives as potentially significant. If some of his fact-finding can be done in advance, he can start to orient himself before he actually goes to the place where he will carry on intensive investigation. By getting a head start, he can save time for those whom he interviews on the spot.

Interviewing Participants Having arrived on the scene, an investigator naturally begins by talking with key people. Even at this point, he may encounter difficulties. Perhaps it now seems that some of the factual information he has brought with him is not so simple, clear-cut, or well established as the written records indicated.

When complaints or disagreements play a part in what the situation has become, the kind of listening needed from an interviewer incorporates (and communicates) close attention, empathy, and objectivity. Attentiveness and projective listening may alert an interviewer to unspoken feelings and attitudes. These represent one kind of fact which needs to be coped with and which can be intelligently handled only when it is understood.

During each such fact-finding interview, whatever the center of attention at the level of spoken words, a personnel-minded interviewer takes an approach which is partly, and temporarily, person-centered. One of his aims is to achieve some understanding of a speaker's *interpretation* of the circumstances being discussed. Even a statement which is unreliable in regard to objectively verifiable facts throws light on the private world from which a speaker is looking at his environment. What he says, therefore, indicates what he sees, especially what he perceives as most important, because it concerns what he feels is currently at stake for him.

Trying to Hear All Sides   An experienced investigator knows better than unquestioningly to accept (as entirely factual) a statement from any complainant. He is aware of the necessity to "get around" by interviewing other insiders. However, before terminating his talk with the first complainant, an interviewer is well advised to mention and explain the procedure that he plans to follow in cross-checking different sources of information. Trying to hear all sides of a disagreement does not imply that he thinks anyone is untruthful. It merely recognizes that different people see different things and assign different values to what they perceive. Even angry complainants rarely resent this practice *if* they receive a timely and adequate explanation. Indeed, each is likely to feel that thorough and impartial investigation will show that *his* report is substantially correct.

As an impartial investigator listens to statements from various participants in a dispute, he may sometimes begin to wonder whether all his informants are even talking about the same situation. (Psychologically, of course, they are not.) Nevertheless, anyone who perseveres in the effort to get a multiple inside view of a situation may count on finding that partially contradictory reports corroborate each other in certain respects. In this way, an investigator can gradu-

ally assemble a nucleus of uncontested verifiable information.

Verifying, Completing, and Correlating Factual Findings

Not all that needs to be done during fact-finding can be accomplished by talking with eyewitnesses. An investigator needs also to make first-hand observations about objectively verifiable facts. What might he be able to see as significant that others have overlooked? Perhaps the heart of a difficulty lies in space-time dimensions. Can a clue to what needs to be done be found by looking into the interactive effects of two or more basic variables?

Interactive Effects of Space-Time Dimensions and Subjective Forces   In the example where assemblers were given discretion to plan their own work method and to set their own pace, a personnel-minded manager spontaneously made the kind of decision that a personnel administrator might recommend. By doing so, the manager converted into organizational assets powerful human forces (of motivation and attitude) which when ignored by managers have often interfered with progress toward organizational goals.

Everyone who practices situational thinking (by intuition or as a set of intellectual skills) knows that space-time dimensions are always worth exploring. The size and location of a plant, a work station, or a manager's office have social (as well as technical) meanings. Sometimes, for certain employees, organizational requirements in regard to space-time assume an importance which to a manager may seem utterly unreasonable.

For example, in one case insubordinate behavior by an employee, who was also president of the local union, led to his discharge. Subsequently, an impartial arbitrator ruled against the company, partly because the restricted parking space from which the employee refused to move his car was not on company property. In weighing available information about that case, it seems clear that if some company representative had talked with the employee in a friendly way, when his attitude toward restricted parking was first expressed in action, an integrative solution to the difficulty might have been found. There was ample parking space on company property. Could not a special place have been set aside for the union president? Apparently what he resented was what he saw as the inequity of reserving special places for officers of the company while ignoring his official status.[9]

In many situations it is easier to change spatial arrangements than to persuade some individual to change his attitude, but a change in an outward circumstance may lead to a desirable modification in employee attitude.

The fact-finding which precedes situational diagnosis and decision making needs to take account not only of interactive effects between basic variables but also of significant differences within individuals. For instance, personnel administrators and personnel-minded managers are aware that organizational requirements involving the space-time factor have different meanings to different employees. To one individual, work on a night shift means hardship. This response is sometimes wholly or partly physiological. Some persons cannot readjust their habits of eating and sleeping to late-shift work assignments, especially when rapid rotation between two or three different schedules calls for frequent readjustment. Often, however, the "hardship" may be primarily social. For example, a young person, permanently assigned to the second shift has only two free evenings a week for taking part in the recreational activities which can seem so important at that time of life. On the other hand, some persons request permanent assignment to a late shift, e.g., a mother of young children who wants to supplement her husband's earnings but cannot leave home until after he returns from work. Or an ambitious student may wish to earn money on the graveyard shift to invest, during daytime hours, in getting a college education. (See Chapter 19 for further consideration of the interactive effects of shift assignments and the human element.)

Case 3, "Dissatisfactions of an Expatriate Engineer" (given in Part 2), pictures a situation in which differences in cultural orientation toward time, combined with a young man's extreme sensitivity about status, precipitated an organizational problem. The young man, a professional engineer who had recently emigrated from Belgium to Mexico, deeply resented having the same work schedule as production employees and having to punch a time clock. Reasonable explanations failed to satisfy him. Until the situation was presented for discussion *as a case* (at a conference led by one of the authors), the Mexican plant manager had apparently not considered the possibility that for a sensitive young Belgian, these organizational requirements might have a meaning which was quite different from that attributed to them by Mexican nationals.

Culturally determined differences in regard to time have often created difficulties between persons, especially when arrogance or lack of relevant information prevents any serious effort at mutual accommodation.[10]

With growing emphasis on overseas operations, appreciation of cultural diferences and

---

[9] For more information on this dispute case, see Paul Pigors and Faith Pigors, *Case Method in Human Relations: The Incident Process,* McGraw-Hill Book Company, New York, 1961, pp. 150-157. A complete discussion plan, designed for use with the Incident Process, is given in Paul Pigors and Faith Pigors, *The Incident Process: Case Studies for Management Development, Series I: Practical Supervisory Problems,* The Bureau of National Affairs, Inc., Washington, D.C., case 12, "The Parking Incident."

[10] For excellent illustrative examples, see Edward T. Hall, *The Silent Language,* Fawcett Publications, Inc., Greenwich, Conn., 1959, especially chap. 9, "Time Talks: American Accents," and chap. 10, "Space Speaks." See also Howard F. Van Zandt, "How to Negotiate in Japan," *Harvard Business Review,* vol. 48, no. 6, November-December, 1970, pp. 45-56.

ways to develop mutual understanding take on increasing importance.

Effects of the Technical Factor Sometimes a personnel administrator is the person who overlooks key facts. Owing to his special orientation and angle of view, he may tend to omit (or scant) investigation of technical features in a work situation. Worse still, his preoccupation with the human element may blind him to opportunities for maximum technical efficiency in his own department. Technical competence in all services rendered by the personnel department is a prerequisite for mutually profitable relationships between the personnel administrator, experts in other staff departments, and line managers. (Chapters 10 to 22 are devoted to specialized techniques by means of which members of the personnel department and the labor relations department, if there is one, can serve their organization.) Only when the work of his own department is efficiently planned, organized, and administered is a personnel administrator (or labor relations director) entitled to expect that line managers will recognize him as someone worth talking to.

Concern for technical proficiency can also help a personnel administrator span the psychological distance between himself and technical experts in other departments. For instance, he can consult experts in electronic data processing about new or better uses for computers. A personnel administrator who communicates his genuine interest in new possibilities for greater efficiency may be able to build a bridge for two-way communication with persons whose specialty has sometimes seemed to put them on the other side of an unbridgeable gap. However, effective coordination by a personnel administrator with other technical experts requires from him more than a readiness to listen. He needs also to acquire a rough working knowledge of the concerns which constitute the heart of the technician's world. In doing so, he will master

key terms in their special language. For instance, a personnel administrator needs to learn the terminology and techniques of cost accounting. He may then be able to render to the organization a greatly needed service by interesting cost accountants in possibilities for extending traditional concepts of their profession. Together, these experts in different fields can develop new concepts and procedures for human asset accounting.[11]

Looking into Technical Features of a Work Situation When a personnel administrator has been called in to some department to diagnose a difficulty, he cannot be expected to be conversant with the whole range of technical features with which qualified insiders are thoroughly familiar. Sometimes he does not even know about a special skill, technique, or technological requirement in which a technical specialist (or a production worker) has achieved outstanding competence. The very fact of such ignorance can be turned to advantage by an outside investigator who is interested and ready to learn. Experience shows that in developing a solution which will be acceptable to those who will have to make it work, an excellent way to begin is by asking them to explain and/or demonstrate techniques and skills with which they have acquired an intuitive familiarity.

Seeing Facts in Relation to Organizational Policies Sometimes what most effectively helps an individual or a group to see familiar facts in a new light is viewing them from the level of policy. Every manager needs the ability to provide this kind of leadership. His subordinates are

[11] The Institute for Social Research at the University of Michigan embarked in 1966 on an extensive research program on this subject. See Rensis Likert, *The Human Organization: Its Management and Value,* McGraw-Hill Book Company, New York, 1967, especially chap. 9, "Human Asset Accounting," See also Robert Wright, "Managing Man as a Capital Asset," *Personnel Journal,* vol. 49, no. 4, pp. 290–295, April, 1970.

entitled to count on his help in the difficult task of seeing relationships between operational realities and the general principles, long-range plans, and overall objectives which are the subject matter of organizational policies. As an exponent of a systems-minded approach to the human organization, a personnel administrator, above all other managers, should be able to play a leading role in policy thinking. (Specific possibilities with respect to shaping and revising organization policies were considered in Chapter 5.) Viewing facts from the perspective of policy can make all the difference in what is seen as most important at the stage where situational diagnosis consists in formulating issues for decision.

Weighing Facts and Formulating Issues

It is impractical to try to draw a hard-and-fast line between finding facts, weighing them, and seeing them in relation to issues. As factual data are correlated, their relative importance emerges. At this point an experienced decision maker also begins to clarify issues, i.e., questions for action. Thus what began as an inquiry into facts can be continued as a search for issues on which decisive action can be useful and timely.

An outsider trying to help other people to resolve a disagreement may find it easy to look with relative objectivity at what is at stake, not only for the individuals or subgroups immediately involved but also for the organization as a whole. Or when a union is a party to the dispute in question, perhaps what is needed is recognition that central requirements of two organizations are at stake. In such a case stating the issue in a way that emphasizes relevant clauses in the labor agreement may be a significant step toward reaching a reasonable decision.

Arbitrators are familiar with difficulties that frequently prevent managers and union officials even from agreeing what the arbitrable issue is, to say nothing of how it can be stated so as to be mutually acceptable. Prolonged discussion at the start of an arbitration hearing often shows that the point of difference as originally stated (by one party or by both) refers only to some relatively insignificant matter. The crux of their disagreement lies deeper.

This same inability to distinguish between root difficulties and surface symptoms often prevents supervisors and managers from working through the basic differences which underlie many personal disputes. (The first, second, and fourth case examples in this chapter illustrate that point, as do several of the cases in Part 2.)

Disagreements as to what is at stake (or at issue) usually have their origin in different angles of view. These, in turn, give rise to differences in value judgments and in opinions about what needs to be done. For instance, suppose an individual's feelings about his personal worth and past services are all that he can see as decisive, while another person (in a position of organizational authority) sees current organizational requirements and ability to measure up to these demands as all that matter. Even an outsider may not be able to help these two people see eye to eye, but he may hope to integrate the partially conflicting views to the extent that each one can see some validity in the other's position. Case 19, "Fear? Or Featherbedding?" highlights the need for understanding conflict situations as a network of interactive variables. Policy-centered evaluation of available evidence might have enabled the contending parties to work out an integrative solution.

Whether the search for an integrative solution to apparently irreconcilable demands is initiated by an outsider, e.g., a personnel administrator or a mediator, or by insiders, the essence of the solution is that it will be advantageous to all parties in the long run, will enable each to maintain his integrity, and will also match requirements in the larger context within which the dispute has arisen.

It is not difficult to recognize, in the abstract, that an integrative solution to a conflict situation is preferable to a solution in which one party wins and the other loses. But it is not always possible to devise a course of action that meets all major requirements of the situation. However, anyone who perseveres in the effort to work with other people toward mutually acceptable and practical solutions can develop the special blend of understanding which is needed for harmonious work relationships.

A Blend of Understanding

Anyone who consistently tries to apply situational thinking as a way of analyzing current situations and making decisions that will stand up is using a kind of understanding which has three components.

Intellectual Capacity   This means the ability to see relationships, to think at relatively high levels of abstraction, e.g., at the level of organization policy, to identify general trends, to think clearly about foreseeable consequences, and to think objectively even about situations in which one's own personal interests are involved.

Perceptivity   This means the ability and the will to appreciate the feelings, attitudes, and inner motivation of other persons. Such subjective factors cannot be wholly "known." In our opinion they cannot be accurately measured, despite recent advances made by behavioral scientists. Nor can their consequences be precisely predicted. However, anyone who develops to the full his innate capacities for observation and intuitive insight can learn to become socially responsive to human needs, even to some which are not expressed in words.

Common Sense   Experienced managers, however, know that intellectual capacity and perceptivity are not enough and that the third essential is *common sense*. In pretesting possible alternatives for any action decision, there is no substitute for a sure sense of what will work and

what will not. This situational response is often assumed to be wholly intuitive, but observation suggests that, like the other components in this blend of understanding, every normal human being starts with some of it and everyone who perseveres can acquire more.

For instance, a sense of timing is an element in common sense. Seasoned administrators act on this kind of extrasensory perception, although they cannot always put into words their reasons for judging that the time is right—or wrong—for a given course of action or that a person can now accomplish something he has never been able to do before. Several cases in this book and countless situations in business and industry illustrate the following points about timing in relation to action decisions:

1 A timely explanation may avert misunderstanding. The same explanation offered after differences have hardened into a dispute may be useless. It may even be perceived as an additional source of irritation. "Now he tells me!"

2 When two-way communication bogs down (or fails to get under way), offering (or repeating) information is so untimely that it may even be worse than useless. Until speaker and listener are on the same wavelength, further one-way talk may aggravate initial misunderstandings or dangerously increase the psychological distance between two persons.

3 The stage and pace of events also offer clues for action decisions. For instance, in negotiating a labor agreement, it is important to consider such circumstances as these. Is the other party a new union? Is a deteriorating situation moving so fast toward a crisis that leisurely discussion of long-term issues is impractical? Is this union president now making unreasonable demands because he feels threatened by a rival union leader or by a militant member of the opposition in his own local?

Supervisors, too, when they make everyday administrative decisions, need intellectual capacity, empathic response, and common sense in regard to the time factor. For example, in trying to help a given employee, is there time for the slow forces of education to take effect? Is education perhaps peculiarly timely because the employee is young, has recently been employed for the first time, and is still on probation? For some employees, should the normal probationary period be extended? For example, perhaps a given individual (hired from the hard-core unemployed) has an unusually great need to reorient himself before he can be expected to meet employment standards which other employees could measure up to before they took their first job. Or, in another case, does a root difficulty appear to be a marked discrepancy between the required pace of work and the natural tempo of a worker? If so, can such an employee be expected to speed up the rate at which he works without pushing himself too far beyond the tempo that comes natural to him? Again, are individual differences in pace, due possibly in part to differences in age, creating friction within a work team? A supervisor needs information and understanding to answer such questions before he can feel reasonably sure that a personnel decision will work out.

Pretesting Alternatives for Decision Often, situational insight is achieved only as hindsight. After a given decision has been put into effect, it may be only too easy to see that it did not match situational requirements and to understand why. Still, anyone who habitually analyzes current situations to search out their meaning for action can develop some skill in foresight. What decisions are called for? To pretest a tentative answer to that question, Maier's "risk technique" is useful. In essence it entails asking: If I were to adopt this particular decision, what risks would I run that I would not incur if I did not act on this decision?

Situational thinking can also be helpful to pretest alternative courses of action, especially when used in group decision making. Discussion-group members can develop basic situational variables into a checklist of questions, for instance:

1 Technically speaking, what looks like the most efficient solution?

2 If we decide upon this alternative for action, might it create difficulties by making demands on other key factors in the situation? For example, does a technically attractive solution call for more resources (equipment, money, time, or manpower) than are currently available?

3 If a course of action passes the pragmatic tests envisioned by foresight, does it also meet systems-minded tests of being in accord with organization policies and demonstrably consistent with major aims and central requirements of other subsystems within the organization as a whole?

Learning from Experience

To develop one's capacity for foresight need not mean neglecting opportunities to learn by hindsight. Every thoughtful person knows that achieving a full measure of situational insight requires reviewing and reflecting on actual developments. Prognosis need not be based solely on current diagnosis. A steadily refined capacity for predicting consequences depends on faithful and objective follow-through by analyzing subsequent developments which still lay in the future when a prognosis was made.

Naturally, busy supervisors do not have time to evaluate and reflect upon every decision they make. But anyone who wishes to improve the caliber of his decisions should make a habit of looking back periodically to compare forecasts and consequences, aims and results. In the field of personnel relations a potentially educational exercise is to review misunderstandings and disagreements, especially those which developed into full-blown disputes or even arbitration cases. By starting evaluative review at the point where such a difficulty first became noticeable, one can profitably ask the following integrative questions:

1 What human shortcomings (or other flaws in the situation) seem to have been accountable for difficulties that showed up in a disturbing incident? (These are unfavorable factors to work *on.*)

2 What factors (people, actions, organizational structure, informal relationships, etc.) can be identified as actual, or potential, forces that tend to favor productive interaction in any such situation? (These are favoring forces to work *with.*)

3 What activities might alleviate current difficulties in such a situation and/or tend to prevent the recurrence of such disturbing incidents? (These planning activities point to long-range goals to work *toward.*)

Situational Diagnosis in Group Discussion
Retrospective analysis offers only limited opportunities as a solo performance, but it becomes increasingly productive when it is carried on in periodical case discussions among organizational members. In this kind of conferring for learning, differences of view can be made into organizational assets. Such differences become apparent as opinions are expressed by insiders and outsiders (in relation to the case being discussed), by line managers and staff specialists, by newcomers and old-timers, and by persons from different departments or at different organizational levels. Achievements and shortcomings demonstrate clearly why persons in certain roles found it easier than others to recognize and meet requirements. One case analysis may reveal that a personnel administrator or higher manager found it easier than a supervisor did to see the need for policy thinking and judiciously to interpret the appropriate policy. In another case it may be apparent that some member of higher management was greatly handicapped because he did not know (or dismissed as insignificant) some fact which any perceptive employee at the work level would have recognized as important.

Looking back is of no value if it means only regret for what cannot now be remedied or criticism of people who it now seems should have known better. Looking back becomes practical insofar as it consists in *looking up* to the level of general ideas and *looking ahead* for opportunities to apply lessons learned from the past. In a study group, *looking around* may also be profitable. Sometimes it has led to a practical insight which may be stated as a working hypothesis. No one person can expect to have an equally perceptive view into all the basic variables to be considered in making administrative decisions. But any well-staffed organization has within its ranks persons whose specialties have helped them to develop keen perceptiveness in each of these areas. Pooling the knowledge, insight, and analytical capacity available in a management group makes it possible to achieve a more comprehensive and objective view than any one member could attain by himself on the basis of firsthand experience.

The practical value of group discussion has been experienced in many organizations, as management representatives have talked together about actual situations, either prepared as written cases or described by someone drawing on his own experience. When the case method was first adopted for purposes of management development, it was taken for granted that first-level supervisors did not have the time or the intellectual caliber to participate productively in case discussions. Some 30 years ago, experiments with the Incident Process[12] in supervisory groups showed that assumption to be unfounded. Since then, this variant of traditional case method has been extensively used to help supervisors (as well

[12] This departure from orthodox practice of case method is briefly described in the introduction to Part 2. See also Robert L. Craig and Lester R. Bittel (eds.), *Training and Development Handbook,* sponsored by the American Society for Training and Development, McGraw-Hill Book Company, New York, 1967, chap. 10, "Case Method," pp. 174–205.

as managers) develop their capacity to learn—together—from experience. Today, a new generation of first-level managers, many of them college-educated, is even more ready and able than their predecessors to use case method as a means to develop skills of situational diagnosis and organization-centered decision making.

SUMMARY

The case examples given in the first half of this chapter illustrated that *technical features,* the *human element,* and *space-time dimensions* may be seen as basic interactive variables at the level of concrete facts. Those same examples also show that *organization policies* may become a factor which affects circumstances, to the extent that someone in the situation interprets and uses them.

The second half of the chapter presented and illustrated an approach for meeting the managerial responsibilities of situational analysis and decision making, as follows: In fact-finding, person-centered interviewing may enable an outside investigator to achieve a multiple, inside view of a given situation. Whether the investigator starts as an insider or as an outsider, he needs to continue his search for information until he has looked into all the basic variables, verified factual data, and organized his findings, looking at them as integral elements in a meaningful whole.

When facts are seen in relationship with one another, with organization policies, and major requirements of the situation as a whole, weights can be assigned to key facts. Within the total system, and viewed from the perspective of organization policies, what do these facts mean for administrative action by decision makers? When a manager with a systems-minded approach is considering issues for action, he naturally asks: What is at stake here, not only for the individuals directly involved but also for the organization as a whole? Answering such a question in a manner that takes account of all basic situational variables calls for a kind of understanding which incorporates intellectual capacity, human perceptivity, and common sense.

Pretesting a range of alternatives for administrative decision can be done by intuition (hunch), by conscious use of situational diagnosis, or by a combination of both. At this stage a systems-minded manager asks: Is this course of action, attractive because it looks expedient, in accordance with organization policies and with long-term objectives of the organization as a whole? Will it be acceptable to those we depend on to make it work?

When opportunities to learn by experience are fully used, decision making can become an integral part of a continuing process in which the power to make valid decisions is developed by reflecting on the consequences of action taken. In retrospect, what seems to have been accountable for results that exceeded expectations or fell short of them?

Situational thinking, for purposes of learning, can usefully be applied during case discussions by members of management who represent a diversity of interests, functions, abilities, and organizational levels. Expressed differences in value judgments, based in part on differences of individual temperament and experiences, illuminate the advantages of obtaining a range of views before making a firm situational diagnosis.

In this chapter, and in earlier chapters, interviewing has been mentioned as a management tool for tapping the experience of others, thus gaining and sharing insight. The next chapter is devoted to a consideration of what needs to be, and can be, done by developing and applying this important skill.

SELECTED REFERENCES

Barker, Roger G.: *Ecological Psychology,* Stanford University Press, Stanford, Calif., 1968.

Barnard, Chester I.: *The Functions of the Executive,* Harvard University Press, Cambridge, Mass., 1938, especially chap. 13, "The Environment of Decision," pp. 185-199.

Barnes, L. B.: *Organizational Systems and Engineering Groups: A Comparative Study of Two Technical Groups in Industry,* Harvard Business School, Division of Research, Boston, 1960.

Fiedler, Fred E.: *A Theory of Leadership Effectiveness,* McGraw-Hill Book Company, New York, 1967.

Hall, Edward T.: *The Silent Language,* Fawcett Publications, Inc., Greenwich, Conn., 1959.

Haney, William V.: *Communication: Patterns and Incidents,* Richard D. Irwin, Inc., Homewood, Ill., 1961.

Johnson, Richard A., Fremont E. Kast, and James E. Rosenzweig: *The Theory and Management of Systems,* 2d ed., McGraw-Hill Book Company, New York, 1967.

Lawrence, Paul R., and Jay W. Lorsch: *Organization and Environment,* Richard D. Irwin, Inc., Homewood, Ill., 1969.

Maier, Norman R. F.: *Principles of Human Relations: Applications to Management,* John Wiley & Sons, Inc., New York, 1952, especially pp. 62-86, "The Risk Technique."

Pigors, Paul and Faith Pigors: *Case Method in Human Relations: The Incident Process,* McGraw-Hill Book Company, New York, 1961, especially chap. 4, pp. 61-94.

Sommer, Robert: *Personal Space,* Prentice Hall, Inc., Englewood Cliffs, N.J., 1969.

Van Zandt, Howard F.: "How to Negotiate in Japan," *Harvard Business Review,* vol. 48, no. 6, pp. 45-56, November-December, 1970.

Whyte, William Foote: *Organizational Behavior: Theory and Application,* Richard D. Irwin, Inc., Homewood, Ill., 1969.

Chapter 10

Interviewing

Real communication occurs, and the evaluative tendency is avoided, when we listen with understanding . . . [seeing] the expressed idea and attitude from the other person's point of view, to sense how it feels to him, to achieve his frame of reference in regard to the thing he is talking about.

Carl R. Rogers[1]

Seeing and accepting an interviewee as a person whose cooperation you value opens the way to a relationship that can be both friendly and productive. Attentive, empathic listening by the interviewer is essential.

An earlier but classic statement of this important idea was made by Fritz Roethlisberger:[2]

When I am confronted with a complex situation involving the interactions of people, what people say is necessarily an important part of the data from which I have to make a diagnosis. Therefore, my first object is to get people to talk freely and frankly about matters which are important to them. . . . In the interview I use a number of simple rules or ideas. I listen. I do not interrupt. I refrain from making moral judgments about the opinions expressed. I do not express my own opinions, beliefs, or sentiments. I avoid argument at all costs. I do this by seeing to it that the speaker's sentiments do not react on my own.

Directive interviewing (where the aim is chiefly to get information about verifiable facts) makes fewer demands on an interviewer—during

[1] Carl R. Rogers, *On Becoming a Person,* Houghton Mifflin Company, Boston, 1961, pp. 331-332.
[2] F. J. Roethlisberger, *Management and Morale,* Harvard University Press, Cambridge, Mass., 1941, pp. 92-93.

talk—than *nondirective interviewing*[3] (where the chief objective is to bring out the interviewee). Both types of interviews are standard tools of social research. Both are needed in personnel administration.

Two Contrasting Interview Techniques

A *directed interview* is planned and led by the interviewer. Before the talk starts, the interviewer knows what the subject matter of the interview will be and centers attention on topics about which he expects to get information by asking specific questions. In planning and conducting a directed interview, it is possible to gauge and control the time needed to achieve the relatively simple and predetermined aim.

In personnel administration, the directed interview is needed when employees are selected and inducted as well as when job descriptions are being prepared. (These specific applications are briefly considered in Chapters 14 to 15.) Any of these interviews may take an unexpected turn. Whenever that happens, techniques of fact-finding may temporarily be discarded to the extent that time and circumstances permit.

The aims of a *nondirective interview* are far more ambitious than acquiring specific information about objectively verifiable facts. Overriding purposes of nondirected interviewing include achieving understanding and building confidence. Often the specific objective is to help a person overcome some difficulty. For any of these purposes, fact-finding questions are not enough. They may even be inappropriate if there is risk that an interviewee may regard them as an

invasion of his private life or as a threat to his job security. An experienced interviewer tries not to lead the talk. Instead, he tries to create an atmosphere that invites candid self-expression, encouraging an interviewee to talk easily about feelings, attitudes, and ideas that are important to him.

Nondirective interviewing requires considerable skill, flexibility, and self-control by the interviewer. In personnel administration, nondirective interviewing often needs to be done by representatives of line management, including first-level supervisors. For example, even an induction interview or a performance-appraisal review is inadequate unless it increases mutual understanding. When a supervisor is confronted with complaints or undisciplined behavior, the need to achieve understanding often calls for open-ended questions—to draw out the interviewee. However, even nondirected interviews should not consist in random talk, nor need they be entirely unplanned. However, it is inappropriate and useless for an interviewer even to attempt to exercise unilateral control when his aim is to achieve mutual understanding. Especially when a nondirected interview is being conducted with a person who is having or making difficulties, a subsidiary objective is to encourage talk that gets somewhere on a topic that is of mutual interest.

Responsive listening by an interviewer helps to increase confidence in him. More important, it can help to increase self-confidence and self-awareness in the interviewee—who must ultimately understand and overcome his own difficulties.

At the level of theory, then, directed and nondirected interviews are clearly distinguishable. In practice, however—for example, in an exit interview—the two approaches may both be needed. An interviewer who is perceptive and flexible will, therefore, change his technique to follow the lead of the situation if time permits. If

---

[3] For a perceptive analysis of these questioning procedures on response, see Stephen A. Richardson, Barbara Snell Dohrenwend, and David Klein, *Interviewing: Its Forms and Functions,* Basic Books, Inc., Publishers, New York, 1965, chap. 6, "Openness versus Closedness, Antecedents and Question-Antecedent Relationships," pp. 138-170. See also Joseph P. Zima, "Counseling Concepts for Supervisors," *Personnel Journal,* vol. 50, no. 6, pp. 482-485, June, 1971.

an interviewer always keeps in mind the overriding aims of achieving understanding and mutual respect, most interviews can be satisfying—or at least acceptable—experiences in human relations.

THE INTERVIEW AS A DEVELOPING SITUATION

No interview need fail in all respects. The interviewer can always achieve more understanding than he started with, even if he does not get all the information he was hoping for. The interviewee should always have the benefit of being recognized as a person sufficiently interesting to be worth listening to. He, too, can get new in-

sight if he wants it; greater understanding about his personal situation, and probably also about technical aspects of the work situation and major objectives for the organization as a whole.

The range of opportunities offered in the course of an interview is shown in Figure 10-1.

A Case Example: Ineffective Interviewing

The following interview was held by a relatively inexperienced personnel consultant. His assignment was to help build a work team and raise morale in the frosting room of a small bakery that lacked a personnel department. By individual interviews, he was trying to pave the way for a group conference. He felt that, by making

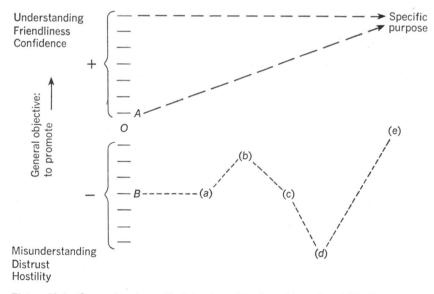

Figure 10-1 General and specific interview objectives. Lines *A* and *B* indicate states of mind of two different employees during interviewing and represent degrees of success achieved during the interview in both general objective and specific purpose. Line *A* starts at the neutral plane where strangers meet and progresses smoothly upward and forward to reach both aims. This is practically an ideal interview, a rare event. Line *B* represents an actual interview (described below) with a person who was hostile to the interviewer at the start. After preliminaries, the interview progressed toward greater understanding (*b*) but then lapsed into increased misunderstanding and distrust—(*c*) and (*d*)—probably because of something the interviewer said. The interview might have ended on this negative note, but by luck or good technique the interviewer in this case was able to reach the neutral plane (*e*).

group decisions and participating with supervisors in remedying unsatisfactory conditions, the girls in the frosting department could learn to think and act as a team.

Mary Ryan had been described by her supervisor as "agressive and a troublemaker." Before the interview, she had branded the consultant, Mr. Anderson, as "just another of those 5-day experts hired by the company to make us all work harder." She had urged her friends not to tell anything to such "scheming outsiders." Starting with this double handicap, Mr. Anderson made matters worse during his talk with Mary by breaking most of the rules for effective interviewing.

The interview was held in a little room above the frosting department. Advance notice to Mary Ryan had been given, without explanation, by the forelady, whom Mary heartily disliked.

Mary (somewhat defiantly): Well, here I am. They told me you wanted to talk with me.   **1**

Mr. A: Thank you for coming, Miss Ryan. Won't you sit down? I should like to talk to you if you can give me a few moments. My name is Anderson. I'm interested in trying to find out how people get along in a small plant like this; whether they like the work and feel they are treated right. Of course, you don't have to talk to me if you'd rather not.   **5**   **10**

Mary: Oh, I'm not afraid. I just don't see any point in it.

Mr. A: Don't you believe in people getting together and talking things over?   **15**

Mary: Sure. Only we don't know you. You come in from the outside and we don't know what you're really after. You say you aren't working for Morgan Brothers Bakery as a . . . a . . . what d'you call it? . . . efficiency expert, but how do we know?   **20**

Mr. A: I'm glad you're frank about it. You're not afraid to talk, but you're suspicious of me. Is that it?   **25**

Mary: Yes.

Mr. A: Well, I don't blame you for that. After all, you don't know me. But that's one reason for my wanting to talk to you. I want to explain who I am, why I'm here, and what I'm trying to do. I had hoped to convince you that I'm here to help you girls, but if you won't take my word for it, of course I can't make you.   **30**

Mary: Why should we believe you? We never met you before. The forelady said you're all right. But we don't know you. Besides I can't understand what you want to do.   **35**

Mr. A: That's why I asked you to come and talk to me. I thought this would be a good chance to explain. I should be glad to tell you anything you would like to know.   **40**

Mary: Well, just what are you trying to do here?   **45**

a *Mr. A:* I should like to talk to you girls and find out what you do, how you like your work, and whether you have any suggestions as to how your department could be improved. I'm interested in anything you have to say about your job.   **50**

Mary: Oh, I see . . . Well, we're all very happy. At least I am.

Mr. A: I'm glad to hear that. What do you do?   **55**

Mary: I'm a froster.

Mr. A: Do you work at that all the time?

Mary: No, as a matter of fact that's one thing that isn't quite right. You see, it takes a long time for a froster to learn her job. For that reason she should get some consideration. But you don't find that here. It doesn't make any difference whether you're just a shipper or a froster or only a beginner; they treat you all alike. I think beginners   **60**   **65** should do some of the dirty jobs. But if the forelady isn't in the right mood, she'll set the green girls to work frosting cakes and make us pick up and clean, or work on stales.

Mr. A: What does "work on stales" 70 mean?

Mary: Oh, stales are the returns from the shops. Most of it is thrown away or sent to the pigs or something. But if the cakes are still in good condition, they're shipped to 75 the stales stores, where they are sold very cheap.

Mr. A: I see.

Mary: Anyway, I don't think good frosters should be called on to do that kind of 80 work.

Mr. A: How many good frosters are there?

Mary: Really good frosters?

Mr. A: Yes, girls who are expert on the 85 job.

Mary: Well, there are two girls who are really good.

b *Mr. A:* That's interesting. I have a good idea who they are. 90

Mary: Who?

Mr. A: The Kearney sisters, isn't that so?

Mary: Yes, all the girls know those two are the best frosters.

Mr. A: How about the others? 95

Mary: Oh, there are three or four who are not so bad. But I suppose there's not much difference, really. Some of the shippers can slap it on pretty good.

Mr. A: Would it be better if some of the 100 good frosters had nothing to do but that?

Mary: Yes, it would. But I'm satisfied anyway. I've no complaints to make.

Mr. A: I'm not looking for complaints. All I'm interested in is to find out how 105 things could be arranged differently so as to make the work more satisfactory. Wouldn't

it be foolish if we could improve working conditions and didn't do it?

Mary: Maybe. But even if I'm not entirely 110 happy, I'm satisfied.

Mr. A: I'm sorry to hear that you're not entirely happy. Has it to do with things at the plant?

Mary: Oh, no. Not at all. Things are all 115 right here.

c *Mr. A:* Has it got to do with things outside?

Mary: Maybe it has. Maybe it hasn't. But I wouldn't tell you. Why do you want to 120 know, anyway? I don't see what it has to do with you.

Mr. A: Oh, I know it isn't any of my business, and I don't want to butt into your private affairs. I just thought it might help 125 you to talk about it.

Mary: No, there's nothing you can do.

Mr. A: I'm sorry.

Mary: Is there any more you want to know? I think Mildred will start looking for 130 me.

Mr. A: Don't worry. She knows you're talking to me and has agreed to let you stay away from work and talk to me as long as you like. 135

Mary: Well, I think I ought to get back to work.

d *Mr. A:* Then don't let me detain you. Thank you for coming and giving me as much help as you did. 140

Mary: I don't see where I've helped you any.

Mr. A: You've helped a lot, and I'm much obliged.

e *Mary* (turning at the door): Well, 145 maybe you're all right. But do you know what? I think you would do better to have a meeting. Why don't you tell the girls we can have a meeting? Then they won't be so afraid to talk. 150

Mr. A: Thanks for the tip. I think that's a good idea, and I'll see whether a meeting can be arranged.

Mary: OK! Well, 'bye now.

Mr. A: Good-bye.   **155**

AN ANALYSIS OF THE INTERVIEW

In briefly analyzing that interview, it is evident that Anderson had two strikes against him before he started and practically put himself out by his unfortunate beginning and by his persistent attempt to elicit from Mary facts that she was unwilling to discuss. At point **a** (interview lines 46–51), when he switched to a line of questioning about the work situation, Mary began to open up and was giving him valuable information and some degree of confidence. But he put her off by his remark at **b** (lines 89–90).

From then on, Mary ceased to cooperate. If he had been more discerning and experienced in interviewing, Mr. Anderson would have realized at point **b** that he should postpone pursuit of his specific purpose until he had reestablished a satisfactory relationship. Once the barometer indicating an interviewee's confidence has dropped below the "fair-weather" level, the longer an interviewer sticks with a predetermined plan, the worse the situation becomes. An agressive worker becomes antagonistic; a timid employee gets more nervous.

In this interview with Mary Ryan, Mr. Anderson showed a distinct lack of perceptiveness and adaptability to Mary's state of mind. At several critical points, he apparently heard no echo of messages that must have been traveling along the "inner circuit" of her mind. It was probably advisable to disregard the clear indications, given at the start of the interview, that Mary regarded him with hostility and suspicion. But Mary's remarks at lines 102–103, 110–111, and 115–116 should have warned him against any such move as his question at **c** (lines 117–118).

His inability (or unwillingness) to read the signs that she gave him almost amounted to social illiteracy. Presumably what blinded him to her state of mind was his preoccupation with his own predetermined objective.[4] Keeping his eye fixed on that, he plunged ahead, making matters worse by attempting to get Mary to discuss her private affairs. At **d** (lines 138–140), he apparently awoke to the impossibility of penetrating Mary's defenses. He then cut his losses and gave up. At that point, luck favored him. Either Mary had a motherly streak in her and felt sorry for him, or she merely responded to his unflagging good nature and courtesy. At any rate, she suddenly repaid him at **e** (lines 145–150) with the very suggestion that he was hoping she would make (that the girls should get together in a meeting). Such breaks are part of the game. For better, as well as for worse, even the most careful planning cannot eliminate the element of chance. When circumstances are sufficiently favorable to allow an interviewer to do his best, what can he do?

PREPARING FOR AN INTERVIEW

Procedures and skills of interviewing vary considerably according to whether the talk is directed or nondirected, and according to the time available before and during the interview. But in interviews (formal or informal) held for purposes of personnel administration, the primary aim should always be achieving and sharing understanding. Therefore, the following steps always need to be taken—if time allows—though the importance of each step varies according to specific aims and circumstances.

---

[4] For an interesting article that describes this common shortcoming in an untrained interviewer, see Norman R. F. Maier and Leonard M. Lansky, "Effect of Attitudes on Selection of Facts," *Personnel Psychology,* vol. 10, no. 3, pp. 293–303, Autumn, 1957. See also Dean B. Peskin, *Human Behavior and Employment Interviewing,* American Management Association, Inc., New York, 1971, chap. 2, "The Perceptual Process and Attitude Formation," pp. 35–61.

Getting or Reviewing Background Information

If the interview is to be conducted by an outsider (a personnel consultant, for example) pertinent information that can be gathered beforehand should be assembled and, if necessary, noted down. This preparation saves time and mental effort during the coming talk and enables the interviewer to sketch in advance at least a general picture of the interviewee and his difficulty. When interviews are to be conducted by representatives of line management (who have time to plan) they should review what they know about the employee and his previous difficulties, if any.

Planning for the Interview

The nature and amount of planning naturally depend on (1) whether the interview is to be directed or nondirected, (2) whether the interviewer initiates it or at least knows about it far enough in advance to permit planning, and (3) whether he is expected to take or to recommend action on what he learns. If official action is to follow, it may be necessary to start with directed interviewing; perhaps asking a number of questions. For this kind of interview, a fairly detailed plan may be useful. In many situations, all that is needed is a simple, flexible plan, something that can be worked out in a few minutes on the way to an interview. Whatever the degree of complexity, such a plan envisages what needs to be learned (or checked) in addition to what is already known. One advantage of advance planning is that the interviewer then has time to think of all the important items on which he lacks information. A second advantage is that, having noted key points on which he needs to get or give information, he is less likely to forget his plan if the interview takes an unexpected turn. Third, having done as much thinking as possible in advance, an interviewer is free during the interview itself to devote most of his attention to listening and observing.

Notifying the Person to Be Interviewed

The prospective interviewee should, when possible, be given advance notice. This should be done in a way that reassures rather than alarms him. The latter point is often overlooked. For example, it seems likely that one reason why Mr. Anderson's interview with Mary Ryan got off to an unnecessarily bad start was that Mary's forelady, whom she disliked, had apparently made no effort to help Mary regard the coming interview as an *opportunity that might help Mary to advance her personal goals.*

An interviewer, especially if his sole purpose is to get information, may easily forget that from the time a person knows he is to be interviewed he, too, is preparing. Is he bracing himself to resist some kind of pressure? Is he preparing himself to be noncommittal, restricting himself to monosyllabic replies, concealing facts that he feels are no one's business but his own? Has experience taught him that when staff experts or supervisors want information, the less said the better? Sometimes, of course, a person holding an interview is unable to get information he needs because communication is blocked by feelings of resentment, guilt or incompatibility of interests. In such a situation, the manner of advance notification would probably make little (short-term) difference. (For instance, in Case 2, "Who Owns the Improved Tool?," tactful advance notice of the talk would probably have been inadequate to persuade members of the work group to tell the methods man what he needed to know.) But often an unnecessarily negative attitude on the part of an employee is evoked, or aggravated, by thoughtless or discourteous notification.

The Setting for the Interview

Success in interviewing depends in part on a suitable setting. Favoring factors include the following:

Privacy and Comfort Important aids to confidential talk are given by surroundings that offer an opportunity to relax, and assurance that talk will not be overheard. When possible, interviews should be held in a private office, with comfortable chairs; but privacy and comfort are states of mind even more than of body. Adequate privacy may be obtained in a corner of the lunchroom, at a deserted workbench, or in any other place where people are not within earshot. Unless the interview seems likely to be of a highly emotional nature, such semiprivacy may be enough. But the relationship between physical and psychological relaxation should not be overlooked. If an interviewee is kept standing, his mental attitude may prove unbending. If he must perch uncomfortably on the corner of a table, it is unreasonable to expect him to lower his guard and reveal what's on his mind.

An Atmosphere of Leisure People cannot be expected to embark on a difficult subject if they feel that they are being hurried through a question-and-answer period that must be terminated in a few minutes. Under ideal conditions, a directed interview can sometimes be conducted in 10 or 15 minutes, but even then a skillful interviewer will convey the impression that he has plenty of time. He knows that leisure is more a state of mind than a matter of minutes. When the subject at hand is complex or difficult and a nondirected interview is needed, talk may have to be prolonged for an hour or more, or even continued in a second session. However long it takes to achieve the aim of the interview, the interviewer should never show impatience or indicate in any way that he would rather be doing something else.

An Informal Opening Even in a directed interview, common sense suggests the advisability of making an indirect start, with a few general remarks which may put the interviewee at his ease and establish the beginning of rapport. In a nondirected interview, it may be left to the interviewee to decide when he is ready to get down to brass tacks. This prelude to the interview is a purely social gesture. As such, it comes naturally to anyone with a flair for human relations.

Sometimes, of course, there is neither time nor occasion for such a gradual start. For example, a dissatisfied or disturbed employee may stop a passing supervisor and launch immediately into a complaint. At other times, a friendly comment from a supervisor who happens to be passing by may turn out to be the prelude to an important and ugrently needed interview.

Establishing and Maintaining Confidentiality It is all-important to help an interviewee achieve the feeling of security which develops in a person's mind when he trusts a listener not to abuse his confidence by repeating what is being said in private. Employees who have experienced, or even heard about, an abuse of confidence tend to be guarded in what they say. The fear of betrayal, even if unfounded in a given relationship, often underlies the negative reaction that balks many an inexperienced interviewer.

If an employee is making a complaint on which he wants action, he naturally wonders how the interviewer can keep confidential what is said in private and also use it as official evidence. But it can easily be explained to an interviewee that these aims are not necessarily incompatible. Usually, the complainant is only one among others who are experiencing similar difficulties. In reporting these difficulties, an interviewer can omit names and other identifying features. Even when a complaint (for instance against a fellow employee or supervisor) is purely individual, respect for the complainant's right to privacy can be shown by *leaving to him* the decision about the next step. He may decide that, in view of the risk, he wants no direct action taken on his complaint. He may prefer some indirect remedy such as transfer out of the group. If, on the other hand, he insists that his case be brought into the open, he should be prepared to substantiate his charge and to serve as chief witness. The interviewer can put the choice clearly before the employee, who thus has an opportunity to make up his mind, knowing that his complaint will not be reported unless he gives the word.

Freedom from Interruptions When an interviewee has thrown caution to the winds and is well launched on a subject that is difficult for him to talk about, a telephone call for the interviewer may spoil everything. During such an interruption, deep-seated attitudes of hostility or suspicion may reassert themselves, and may overpower an employee's sudden impulse to trust an interviewer and talk freely. Even if the interruption does not have any such disruptive effect, it is undesirable. It emphasizes the fact, only too obvious in daily work life, that lower-level employees are considered too unimportant to be put first. Ideally, during the interview, the interviewee does come first. An able interviewer, genuinely interested and concerned, helps interviewees to feel that what they are saying occupies the center of his attention. An interviewer who measures up to his task because he is sincerely interested in what interviewees say need not resort to flattery.

CONDUCTING INTERVIEWS

Of course, an interviewer cannot count on having all these factors in his favor. For instance, perhaps there was no time to plan. (For such a situation, see Case 17, "Difficulties Connected with Work Scheduling." But in that case, as in many other situations, counseling that was greatly needed might have been offered at another time.) Or perhaps no privacy is available when the interview starts because an employee initiates the talk at his work station. If it seems inadvisable to postpone the interview, the supervisor must do the best he can under the circumstances. At such a moment, the abilities and at-

titudes of the interviewer can make the difference between success and failure. Is he flexible enough to think on his feet, playing it by ear and planning as he goes along? Are his powers of concentration great enough so that he can, in effect, create a circle of privacy within which he and the interviewee can communicate as though they were alone? Perhaps most important, has he *the capacity and the wish to cooperate with the other person by listening responsively and with imagination?*

Because the central concern in this book is personnel administration by members of line management, the focus here will be on interviewing needs that could be met by first-level supervisors. Usually, lower-level supervisors lack the specialized education that can be expected from staff experts in the personnel department, but everyone has, in some degree, the essential skills of interviewing. One such skill is the capability to listen with concentration and imagination.

Uses of Listening

Whether the interview is directed or nondirected, attentive listening is essential. Unfortunately this skill is not always practiced in talking with subordinates. Many supervisors take it for granted that their job in an interview is to do the talking, and that the interviewee should do the listening.

Listening to Get Information and to Correct Misunderstandings In a directed interview there may seem to be no need for an interviewer to listen to anything more than what the interviewee says in answering questions. But unless the interviewer also listens for meaning-as-a-whole (including the feelings and purposes of a speaker) how is he to estimate whatever degree of incompleteness and bias there may be in what the interviewee says? Moreover, if the subject matter has emotional overtones, the chances that the interviewee will misunderstand something that the interviewer says amounts to a certainty. For such reasons, "projective listening" to achieve empathic understanding is a skill that needs to be developed by every interviewer. (In Chapter 5 we considered in some detail the difference between merely listening attentively to what is said and listening-with-understanding for clues to deeper meanings.)

Listening for What Other People Hear and Feel An experienced and able interviewer can often prevent or correct serious misunderstandings if he can project his imagination far enough toward an interviewee to get some inkling of how his message is interpreted while being processed on the other person's inner circuit. Many persons do not even try to exercise this skill because they think that knowing what they have said is the same as knowing what the other person heard. An alert interviewer may be able to catch immediately the meaning-for-an-interviewee of something that seems to have shut off communication from that person. For example, in the interview between Mr. Anderson and Mary Ryan, an experienced interviewer might have been able to "hear," at once, the meaning-for-Mary of his interjected remark about the skilled frosters. As it was, he caught the echo of that meaning only after the interview was over. At the time, he was primarily interested in getting new information. Therefore he thought there was no point in letting Mary tell him who the skilled frosters were. He had already obtained that information before his interview with her. But by interrupting her, and giving her the information that she was about to offer him, he committed two tactical errors. When he repeated something he had learned in previous interviews, he may have reminded Mary about the program that she had been trying to disrupt. He also reversed the relationship in which she had been acting as his teacher. Her next remarks say in effect, "If you

think you're so smart, why come to me for information?"

Listening as an Aid to Self-therapy If an employee is under emotional stress, talking freely to a sympathetic listener may be of great therapeutic value. With that purpose in mind, counseling programs have been set up in many organizations.[5]

What can be achieved during such listening was well described by Dr. Richard C. Cabot. As a professional physician (interested in diagnosis as well as in healing), a pioneer in medical social work, and in later life a teacher, Dr. Cabot was a firm believer in listening and a skillful practitioner of that technique. In a book written with a colleague, he said:[6] "It has been our experience again and again to listen while a patient described his problems, to be stumped by them and appalled at our own failure, and prudently to keep silence and make no answer till that very silence drew the patient on to say more than he started to say. Soon he begins answering himself better than we could have answered him."

Effects of Responses from a Listener

In such ways, listening is an active response to a speaker, an effective way of working with him. The listener's responsiveness to what he hears

[5] See F. J. Roethlisberger and W. J. Dickson, *Management and the Worker,* Harvard University Press, Cambridge, Mass., 1939, chap. 26, especially pp. 593–604; W. J. Dickson and F. J. Roethlisberger, *Counseling in an Organization: A Sequel to the Hawthorne Researches,* Harvard Business School, Division of Research, Boston, 1966. See also John MacIver, "The Impact of Psychiatry on American Management: A Psychiatrist's View," *Industrial Medicine and Surgery,* vol. 31, pp. 471–476, November, 1962; and "Practices in Employee Counseling," *Industrial Relations News,* April, 1963.

[6] Richard C. Cabot and Russell L. Dicks, *The Art of Ministering to the Sick,* The Macmillan Company, New York, 1936, p. 193. The excellent chapter on listening should be read in its entirety.

and understands can usefully be expressed by an occasional well-timed and carefully worded comment.

Gardner's "spiral analysis method,"[7] developed as an aid in learning how to listen, could usefully be applied by every supervisor (and by everyone else who has occasion to conduct formal or informal interviews). The method is based on the following observations, all of which can be confirmed by anyone who does much listening: (1) that people tend to talk in circles (especially when they are emotionally involved in what they are talking about), (2) that if they are interrupted (by a listener who injects some thought or feeling of his own), their train of thought may be derailed or they may get stuck in the groove of some feeling, but (3) if a listener can hold up a "mirror" to a speaker, reflecting fairly accurately what is being said and felt, the listener may be able to help a speaker overcome his anxieties, say what he really thinks, and thus break out of the rut which previously prevented him from resolving his own difficulty.

In the opinion of many social scientists, supervisors should be encouraged not to back away from topics about which their subordinates tend to become emotional. Many supervisors seem to be afraid of this part of their job. Therefore, higher managers should make sure that supervisors have adequate time and training to meet their share of responsibility for personnel administration. Many supervisors are so overburdened with technical demands that they could not take time, even if they were willing and able to do so, to interview and counsel an employee who is having difficulties on the job. (See Case 4, "The Girl and the Computer," for a case in point.)

[7] Neely D. Gardner, "The Spiral Analysis Method as a Training Aid in Learning to Listen," *American Society of Training Directors Journal,* vol. 10, no. 6, pp. 13-21, 56-68, November-December, 1956.

Helping an Interviewee to See His Difficulty Clearly

Responsive listening, implemented by a few comments that reflect a speaker's meaning and feelings, can often help a troubled person to see more clearly just what his difficulty is. In human relations it is axiomatic that before a person can be expected to resolve a difficulty realistically, he must be able to see it clearly and with some objectivity. Moreover, if an interviewee wants the interviewer to take official action, on a complaint for instance, it is essential that the interviewer should clearly understand the nature of the difficulty. For this purpose, it is sometimes useful for an interviewer to ask some specific questions—even in an interview that is mostly nondirected

Asking Fact-finding Questions

Sometimes a timely and pertinent question from an interviewer can help to clarify what an interviewee has been saying, especially if the obstacle to clear expression has been either unclear thinking or hesitation to mention something that might easily be misunderstood. The interviewer's question amounts to asking: "Is this what you mean?" For example, suppose a complainant has stated his difficulty this way: "Tom is a stinker. I just can't stand working with him any more." Before seeking a practical solution to that difficulty it is necessary for the interviewee and the interviewer to see clearly just what Tom has said or done that "stinks." After clarifying that key point, it can be decided what needs to be done about it. Is a transfer in order? Or has the interviewee perhaps only run afoul of Tom on an off day? If so, perhaps an apology is all that is needed.

Keeping Alert and Flexible

By listening and asking questions, an interviewer may find his way around in a situation which he is trying to understand with his mind and to appreciate with his feelings. In a nondirected interview, however, the course by which needed understanding is to be reached cannot be laid out in advance. An experienced interviewer presumably has some general plan to guide him, but no one can supply him with a map of the territory he is to explore. Sometimes, as he pursues what looked like a promising avenue of inquiry, he suddenly finds himself blocked by a "No Trespassing" sign. On the other hand, if he is lucky, he sometimes finds that a byway, which he courteously followed because the interviewee indicated a wish to wander there, opens out into a highway that takes him straight to his goal. An interviewer who is able to think on his feet, alert to follow new leads, and willing to embark on ways that he has not traveled before is in a position to take advantage of any lucky break that occurs.

Interpreting Nonverbal Behavior (Body Language)[8]

Often an interviewer can get clues to how he should proceed by observing facial expressions, gestures, tones of voice, and posture. For example, does an interviewee sit on the edge of his chair, tense, with a strained expression on his face, and perhaps also fidgeting with his hands? If so, what do these signs mean—for action by the interviewer? Perhaps he should bend his efforts, for a few minutes, to putting the interviewee at his ease. When such indications of initial nervousness are followed by signs of relaxation, for instance as the interviewee leans back in his chair, crosses his legs, and perhaps

even permits himself to smile, these signs are particularly significant. If direct questions must be asked, for example in trying to get facts about a situation where discipline may be warranted, does the interviewee find it difficult to look the interrogator directly in the eye? If so, what does that mean? Often a person's hands are more expressive of feelings than his face. Many a person whose poker face reveals nothing, gives himself away by nervous motions of his hands. Or perhaps he releases inner stress by tapping with his foot. Tones of voice and inflections of speech also underline or contradict the meaning of spoken words. Some of these signs may tell an interviewer that he needs to take special care to show that he can be relied upon not to repeat what the interviewee might later regret having said.

Taking Notes[9]

An alert interviewer can gather up many more facts and impressions in the course of an interview which lasts an hour or so than he can remember—unless he takes a few notes. But many inexperienced interviewers hesitate to write anything down in a nondirected interview. They fear that to do so would be incompatible with the informal atmosphere which is essential to confidential talk. This difficulty can be prevented by good timing and explanation. Some interviewers also object to taking notes because it is impossible to write and observe at the same time. This difficulty can be overcome by jotting down only the bare minimum of salient facts and characteristic expressions.

Note taking should never begin until after some rapport has been established, but at that point, making a few notes may even have a favorable effect. When an employee trusts an interviewer, he is likely to be pleased that his remarks

[8] Benjamin Balinsky and Ruth Burger, *The Executive Interview: A Bridge to People,* Harper & Row, Publishers, Incorporated, New York, 1959, chap. 6, "The Role of Listening in the Interview," pp. 60–72, especially Sign Language, pp. 62–63. See also Edward T. Hall, *The Silent Language,* Fawcett Publications, Inc., Greenwich, Conn., 1959, chaps. 9 and 10, "Time Talks: American Accents," pp. 128–145 and "Space Speaks," pp. 146–164.

[9] See also Morris Bolsky, *Guide to Gathering Information in Face to Face Interviews,* Ramsey-Wallace Corporation, Ramsey, N.J., 1967, chap. 11, "Note Taking," pp. 46–51.

are considered sufficiently important to be written down. Thus note taking can directly contribute to the interviewer's purpose of showing the employee that someone is concerned to know what he thinks and how he feels about a given situation, and wants to make his report complete and accurate. Sometimes interviewees enter into the spirit of note taking and jog the interviewer's elbow, as it were, by some such remark as, "Now be sure to get this down. It's important." Whether or not this happens, however, the notes are important to the interviewer for follow-through and evaluation—especially if he is conducting a whole series of interviews.

CONCLUDING THE INTERVIEW

The end of an interview is important, if only because it may—retroactively—color all the interviewee's other feelings about the talk.

In a directed interview, following the simple rules of courtesy and common sense is usually all that is required of an interviewer. Even so, in an employment or exit interview for instance, the interviewer may need to exert some self-control. He must not let himself be pushed by his feelings to promise more than he can perform. Nor should he indicate, to an employee who is voluntarily quitting, any feeling that he may have that this departure will be a good thing for the organization.

Toward the end of a nondirected interview, the need for self-control may be even greater. Perhaps the talk has helped an employee to get some perspective on a difficulty but has not enabled him to see for himself how to deal with that difficulty. If so, an interviewer may cancel out most of the benefit derived during the interview if he now tells the employee what he should do. Or if the interview was fruitless, the interviewer may find it difficult not to take out his frustration on the interviewee. Useful self-controlling mechanisms, as the interview draws to a close, are a sense of humor, the habit of courtesy, and

concentration on the overriding purpose of nondirective interviewing: to gain and share understanding by giving the interviewee an opportunity to express whatever ideas and feelings he cares to talk about.

Sometimes, fortunately, concluding a nondirected interview is not necessarily left solely to the interviewer. Often, after an informal talk—even one that has not seemed to the interviewer to be very productive—the employee himself will terminate the interview on a friendly and appreciative note. Perhaps he will say, "Well, thanks a lot. I certainly feel better for getting all this off my chest. I never thought the company was interested in the way we feel about things. I surely appreciate your giving me all this time."

Whether or not this happens, the interviewer should express his appreciation for the opportunity of talking with the employee, and his continuing interest. Perhaps the interviewer does not feel grateful at the moment. But if he is a serious student of human nature and interested in improving his own skills in human relations, he has at least had an opportunity to learn something—even if what he has learned from his experience seems to be chiefly what not to do again.

FOLLOWING THROUGH

No interview is complete unless some effort is made in the direction of a follow-up, even if it involves only showing interest in subsequent developments. Even if the interviewer cannot hope to solve all employees' problems through interviewing, he should always strive to convey to them his continuing interest in their efforts to help themselves and his willingness to assist them.[10]

After a directed interview, following through is likely to be simple, perhaps almost automatic. Records must be completed, but perhaps that is

[10] Leonard E. Himler, "Interviewing: Guides from a Psychiatrist," *Management of Personnel Quarterly*, vol. 4, no. 4, pp. 32–38, Winter, 1966, quotation on p. 38.

all, unless there is other routine action to be taken.

After a nondirected interview, it is not always easy to follow through effectively. For example, if an interview was initiated by an employee who is in difficulties but no definite decisions for action were reached, should the interviewer follow through by initiating a second interview? If so, how soon? Or will it be advisable to wait—and if so, for how long?—to see whether the employee will request another interview? Or suppose the interviewer undertook to make an attempt to get action on a difficulty by appealing to higher management but was unable to get desired results? Is it necessary to tell the employee that nothing has been accomplished? Or is it more sensible to let the employee make that inference for himself when, in due course, nothing happens?

Specific answers to such questions differ according to circumstances and the organizational role of the interviewer. For example, appropriate follow-through by a supervisor is different from the kind of action open to a staff specialist. General rules to keep in mind are these: Proffered help is likely to be most helpful when it is asked for. A solid relationship can be built only on integrity.

REVIEWING AND EVALUATING

When an interview is over, the interviewer's experience is still incomplete. To learn all he can for future interviewing, he should carefully review his notes, going back over the interview step by step to see what went right (and if possible, why), what might have gone better, and where his own skills seem to have been inadequate.

Every interview offers an opportunity to get new ideas about human nature (in oneself and others), about company policies and practices, about current situations and problems, and about what is needed to make talk between two people a worthwhile experience for them both.

Unless ideas on such points are fully clarified while they are still fresh in one's mind (preferably by writing out a summary of each interview), they are apt to disappear.

Writing up his notes so that they form an intelligible statement can do for an interviewer something similar to what talking can do for an interviewee. It helps to clarify ideas and thus to show what is there. To supervisors as well as to members of the personnel department, making a complete (though brief) report of each interview has several kinds of value. For one thing, the completed notes form an important part of a case record. They are also useful for various special purposes; for instance, they can be reviewed before another interview with the same person. Furthermore, the record itself, and even more the cumulative evidence supplied in a number of interview records, reveal significant points about interview method. Everyone can improve his interviewing techniques if he is clear about just what is needed and where he is weak. The record provides clues. Failure in one case may be attributed to bad luck. Failure in many cases indicates faulty techniques.

Study of such interview material often reveals that the interviewer has more food for thought than he realized at the time. As he looks over his notes, comparing them with facts gathered before and with any other information he may later get about a given interviewee, he may find that something jotted down almost at random, or merely because it seemed important to the interviewee, suddenly stands out as significant. Sometimes such new insight does not come until long after an interview, perhaps when another interviewee has a similar difficulty.

SUMMARY

Evaluation brings the process of interviewing full circle as consequences are compared with aims. Does it seem that the interview was a fruitful experience in human relations because both parties gained and shared understanding? If not, why not? What might be done better, next time? Did the interviewer fail in some specific objective because of inadequate preparation, or through overpreparation and inflexibility? Did he permit some goal of his own, perhaps eagerness to get information, to interfere with the overriding aim—to make each interview a satisfying experience for the interviewee? Was the setting less favorable in any respect than he could have made it? In looking back, what evidence can be seen that the interviewee was put off by anything that was said or done during the talk? Does it now seem clear that some comment or sign made by the interviewee had a meaning that was different from what the interviewer understood at the time? Were the interviewer's skills adequate as he listened, tried to hold up a mirror (occasionally) to reflect the interviewee's feeling tone as he asked questions, felt his way along before he had much light on the situation, and observed the nonverbal signs that often reveal more than spoken words? Was he alert to take advantage of unexpected leads? Did he help the interviewee to do all he could for himself? If the interview was an effort to provide counseling, were there any signs that the interviewee gained in self-awareness, in self-confidence, and in ability to see his own problem clearly and find his own way to overcome it?

Interviewing can be a useful means of finding out where other people are, psychologically and emotionally. A skillful interviewer may also help an interviewee to see the need for making some change in his attitude or behavior. Thus interviewing can contribute to the mutual understanding that is necessary for peak efficiency in any organization.

In the next chapter, we consider other ways to gain insight into what needs to be known about an organization. By studying personnel records (for example, of absence and accidents) and by analyzing employee attitudes, management representatives can keep track of employee morale, a significant index of organizational health.

SELECTED REFERENCES

Black, James Menzies: *How to Get Results from Interviewing: A Practical Guide for Operating Management,* McGraw-Hill Book Company, New York, 1970.

Bolsky, Morris: *Guide to Gathering Information in Face to Face Interviews,* Ramsey-Wallace Corporation, Ramsey, N.J., 1967.

Delahanty, David: "Three Aspects of Nonverbal Communication in the Interview," *Personnel Journal,* vol. 49, no. 9, pp. 757–759, September, 1970.

Dickson, William John, and F. J. Roethlisberger: *Counseling in an Organization: A Sequel to the Hawthorne Researches,* Harvard Business School, Division of Research, Boston, 1966.

Fenlason, Anne F., Grace Beals Ferguson, and Arthur C. Abrahamson: *Essentials in Interviewing for the Interviewer Offering Professional Services,* rev. ed., Harper & Row, Publishers, Incorporated, New York, 1962.

Fisher, Waldo E.: *The Interview: A Multi-purpose Leadership Tool,* California Institute of Technology, Industrial Relations Center, Circular no. 34, Pasadena, Calif., 1966.

Lopez, Felix M., Jr.: *Personnel Interviewing,* McGraw-Hill Book Company, New York, 1965.

Peskin, Dean B.: *Human Behavior and Employment Interviewing,* American Management Association, Inc., New York, 1971.

Richardson, Stephen A., Barbara Snell Dohrenwend, and David Klein: *Interviewing: Its Forms and Functions,* Basic Books, Inc., Publishers, New York, 1965.

Sidney, Elizabeth, and Margaret Brown: *The Skills of Interviewing,* Tavistock Publications, London, 1961.

Trull, Samuel G.: "Strategies of Effective Interviewing," *Harvard Business Review,* vol. 42, no. 1, pp. 89–94, January–February, 1964.

Zimpel, Lloyd, and Daniel Panger: *Business and the Hardcore Unemployed: A Management Guide to Hiring, Training and Motivating Minority Workers,* Frederick Fell, Inc., New York, 1970, chap. 3, "The Interview: Vital First Contact," pp. 60–75.

Chapter 11

Indicators
of Organizational Health:
Using Personnel Research

We still make most decisions by the seat of our pants, even though the folklore of management is no substitute for facts. Personnel research is beginning to develop meaningful measurement tools and methods of utilizing data so that the manager's job can be more rational.

Edward A. Robie[1]

In many organizations, personnel records are kept in considerable detail and increasingly in computer-based systems. Managers today recognize that significant indicators of organizational health may be found in individual employment histories and in various behavioral responses by individuals and work groups.

In this chapter and the next two, we consider a number of ways of analyzing some of the personnel information most needed by managers in assessing organizational health. The growing use of personnel research in assisting managers in this effort will be noted in some detail, although personnel research is also helpful in evaluating the effectiveness of personnel policies generally. Its usefulness is certainly not confined to assessing the state of organizational health. However, in this chapter, we shall review the applicability of personnel research to the analysis of tardiness and absenteeism, accidents, and to surveys of employee attitudes or opinions about their work and supervision. We shall also briefly consider problems of alcoholism and drug use not only as they are related to absenteeism but also as a possible cause of accidents.

[1] Quoted in William C. Byham, *The Uses of Personnel Research,* AMA Research Study 91, American Management Association, Inc., New York, 1968. Mr. Robie is vice-president for personnel, Equitable Life Assurance Society of the United States, New York.

Records and surveys contain reports about observed facts. Although facts alone are inadequate to explain what is accountable for whatever is going right or wrong in an organization, they may provide clues to the circumstances or attitudes they reflect. Thus a perceptive manager—possibly assisted by a staff specialist—is concerned not so much with what statistics directly show as with what *shows through* them. He asks himself: Why are these things happening? What is behind them? Are they the long-run effects of some activity that was formerly accepted as "good enough"? Do they point to a need for preventive or remedial action?

When a perceptive manager finds something wrong with a piece of equipment or a component of a product, he does not indulge in moralistic judgments. Similarly, when a level-headed manager examines personnel data which reveal organizational flaws, his attitude is not *Who* is to blame? but rather *What* is accountable? In searching for this kind of insight he is more interested in present observable effects of past failures and tensions, and in possible significance for future action, than in the size of a given figure. For these purposes, analysis by subgroups of employees (according to department, occupation, age, sex, etc.) may be more enlightening than merely looking at overall totals.

Tardiness and Absenteeism

Occasional instances of tardiness are perceptibly disturbing to group efficiency. However, they are not of major concern to supervisors, since they probably reflect external circumstances rather than undesirable attitudes. But a record showing that persistent tardiness is characteristic of some employees (or group of employees in a particular department) suggests the need either for further study or for corrective action by the supervisor.

Some tardiness (and absenteeism) may be expected from new employees who have little prior labor market experience or have pressing personal problems (as in the case of some of the hard-core unemployed). This will require supervisory and managerial patience while efforts are made to help these new employees with their transportation and personal problems. But if a more responsible work attitude fails to develop after a reasonable orientation period, enforcement of expected standards will be necessary. Otherwise, regular employees will feel that double standards are being applied.

Even among some regular employees, lack of integration into the work group and lack of loyalty to the organization are exemplified by the tardy members, who also may form a nucleus among those who rush the time clock at the end of their work day. Anyone may occasionally want to leave work in a hurry, but those who always stand in line or jostle one another to get away at the earliest possible moment are usually giving unmistakable evidence of poor work attitudes.

When chronic tardiness indicates that something is wrong, interviewing may help a supervisor (or personnel assistant) to get at the root of this difficulty. Management may be partly at fault in such ways as not helping employees to recognize that their work is important, in appearing to belittle the individual contribution of an unskilled operator, in not providing supervision of a high quality, or in failing to promote teamwork of a caliber such that group discipline is exercised.

Different Meanings of Absenteeism

The potential value of self-discipline and regulation within each small group is equally clear in regard to absence, which may be a more pronounced symptom of the same attitude that produces tardiness. For example, a statistical study[2] of absences due to "sickness" among women

[2] Norman Plummer and Lawrence Hinkle, "Medical Significance of Illness and Absence in an Industrial Population," *Annals of Internal Medicine,* vol. 39, no. 1, pp. 103–115, July, 1953.

workers showed that "employees with high absence in their first year of employment were in the high absence group year after year."

Various kinds of absence affect group efficiency and stability in different ways and may be significant indicators of individual attitudes toward the work team. Occasional and excused absences, *arranged in advance with the supervisor's permission,* result in a minimum disturbance of group activity and may be justified by unusual demands outside the plant, such as illness at home.

Absence that cannot be prearranged may be caused by an emergency. It therefore becomes an excused absence if the person promptly notifies his supervisor. Such notification indicates a responsible attitude on the part of the person who is absent. The terms "absentee" and "absenteeism" have acquired a moral connotation. For this reason, they should be used with care. Indiscriminate blasts by management against all absences are detrimental to employee morale, because they lump together people whose attitudes and circumstances may be significantly different.

An absence of which the supervisor is not immediately informed interferes with group efficiency, because scheduling is made difficult. Sometimes it is impossible to know at the start of a workday whether a missing person is absent or merely late. However, the fact that no notification has been received does not necessarily indicate a willful disregard of company rules. Sometimes the absence is unavoidable, and for some valid reason notice did not reach the supervisor. Among such reasons are ignorance of company rules, fear of a supervisor, lack of a home telephone, or forgetfulness on the part of someone entrusted with a message.

Chronic unexcused absence is most disturbing to group efficiency and morale. It makes an individual unacceptable on a work team, no matter how much he has to offer when he does come to work. More than any other form of absence, genuine absenteeism indicates low morale and lack of team spirit.

Research on Absenteeism

Analysis of absenteeism is one of the more frequent activities of the personnel research unit within a personnel department.[3] The *number* of absences may be computed weekly or monthly, by plant and department, by hourly and salaried employees, by sex, by duration, and by reason for absence. Comparisons between these variables can then be made and costs of absenteeism computed from lost earnings.

Frequency rates are often computed to provide more valid comparisons when large numbers are involved. The formula recommended by the U.S. Department of Labor for computing the absenteeism rate at the end of each month is the following:[4]

$$\frac{\text{Number of man-days lost through}}{\text{job absence during period}} \times 100$$
$$\frac{}{\text{Average number} \times \text{number of}}{\text{of employees} \quad \text{work days}}$$

$$= \text{Absenteeism rate}$$

Some research on absenteeism, of course, has been done by scholars who study organizational behavior.[5] A comprehensive study of employee

[3] Geneva Seybold, *Personnel Audits and Reports to Top Management,* Studies in Personnel Policy no. 191, National Industrial Conference Board, Inc., 1964, p. 29; "The Role of Research in Industrial Relations/Personnel," *Industrial Relations News,* (no volume or number), p. 2, July, 1962.

[4] *Suggestions for Control of Turnover and Absenteeism,* U.S. Bureau of Employment Security, no. E–61, January, 1962, p. 27.

[5] One study, used in earlier editions of this book, was made during World War II in several comparable firms in the same labor market. See John B. Fox and Jerome F. Scott, *Absenteeism: Management's Problem,* Business Research Studies, no. 29, vol. 30, no. 4, Harvard Business School, Boston, 1943.

Table 11-1   Employee Absence Patterns

Year	Number of problem drinkers	Days lost due to sickness by problem drinkers	Average number of days sickness absence	
			Per problem drinker	Per refinery employee
1953	119	3,559	29.9	10.5
1954	116	2,655	22.8	10.2
1955	109	2,021	18.5	8.6
1956	97	1,718	17.6	8.9

behavior at the Tennessee Valley Authority (TVA) showed that a number of factors accounted for the rate of absenteeism.

By far the strongest predictor of absence is identification with occupation (stronger occupational identification, more frequent absence). Other factors which make a substantial contribution to predicting the level of absence are (in order of their importance ...) chances to use one's best abilities, work difficulty, dependence of co-workers on each other, frequency of time limits (in work), chance to learn, peer rewards for achievement, and concern about work overload. All of the factors predict to less absence with the exception of chance to use one's abilities and concern about work overload, which are associated with greater absence.[6]

Alcoholism: An Important Cause of Absenteeism

Absenteeism among known alcoholics has been estimated, by Dr. Selden D. Bacon, Director of the Yale Center of Alcohol Studies, at 22 days per year. Yet management has frequently failed to heed the tell-tale signs of Monday absences and Tuesday hangovers, the evidence of below-

standard work turned out, the wastage and breakage of good materials and equipment, the disturbance of morale in the plant or office and the incalculable damage that the alcoholic employee may be doing to himself and his family. ... But we do not yet have any dependable way of measuring the losses incurred while friends, fellow workers and even supervisors are covering up for the alcoholic employee, before his problem has been recognized by management. It is impossible to audit the inconvenience and irritation resulting from the disruption of production schedules and the necessity of using inexperienced men for certain operations.[7]

The magnitude of the problem is revealed by a follow-up in Esso Standard Oil Company (New Jersey) by two members of that company's medical department.[8] A review of one plant (28 percent of total population) revealed the effect of employee alcoholism on absenteeism as shown in Table 11-1.

The effect of alcoholism on absence records is difficult to determine when absentees are not full-blown alcoholics. What is shown (and what is concealed) by the continued employment of a person who only occasionally drinks to excess?

[6] Martin Patchen, *Participation, Achievement and Involvement on the Job,* Prentice-Hall, Inc., Englewood Cliffs, N.J., 1970, pp. 148–149, and appendix M, p. 265. On the puzzling finding that chance to use one's abilities is positively correlated with absence, the author points out (footnote, p. 149) that chance to *test* one's best abilities tends to have negative correlation with absence for individuals within each of the major TVA sites.

[7] *A Word for Employers,* Alcoholic Anonymous Publishing, Inc., New York, 1952, pp. 11–12.

[8] J. J. Thorpe and J. T. Perret, "Problem Drinking," in *Archives of Industrial Health* (American Medical Association), vol. 19, January, 1959, cited by James W. Earley, *A Resource for Employee Alcoholism,* a thesis for the degree of Master of Business Administration at Northeastern University, Boston, 1959, pp. 51–52.

What Is Shown, and Hidden, by the "Half Man"?[9]

The continued employment of the "half man" may indicate (1) outstanding competence when he is "all there," (2) team spirit manifested (by fellow employees including his immediate supervisor) in a conspiracy of silence, (3) underlying that conspiracy a lack of confidence by employees in managers, the belief that "they" have little sympathy with *"us"* and *"our"* difficulties and will punish the "half man" unless we can cover up for him, or (4) a top-management policy of "being nice to nice people" (carried to the point of letting sympathy and lack of medical knowledge obscure an organization-centered view.[10])

What is partially hidden by the phenomenon of the half man may include the following:

1 The half person, usually his wife. Often nervous and fearful that her husband's failing will be brought out into the open, her apprehensiveness makes her more subject to accidents than if she were not tied to a half man. She is always distracted and upset when he is on a binge and sometimes unavoidably absent to take care of him, though the "excuses" (both for her absences and for his) must be both fabricated and varied.

2 Reasons for less than capacity performance by a work team. The team is partly crippled when the drinking man is wholly absent or only "half there" because he has a hangover.

3 An incipient case of full-blown alcoholism. This usually takes years to develop and can be most effectively treated in the early stages.

4 Needs for making changes. These include better supervision and communication and a more realistic understanding of drinking (its causes and consequences at various stages).

5 Possibilities for effective cooperation. Cooperation includes that between organizational members and the use of community resources,[11] in health centers, and as help available from Alcoholics Anonymous.

6 The whole man. The man he might be if the half man could be helped to "come out of hiding [and] to become whole."[12]

The alcoholic—who is also likely to be a chronic absentee—needs to be recognized as having a health problem before his rehabilitation through work becomes more difficult. Here the role of the supervisor is important, and training of supervisory personnel within a supportive company policy can speed the recognition and rehabilitation process.[13] The same need exists for a new problem related to absenteeism—the increasing use of drugs by workers in industry, especially by younger workers. A recent survey indicated that the consensus of those interviewed was that the drug problem is serious and growing, particularly in the large urban industrial centers such as Detroit, New York, Miami, and Boston.[14] In San Diego, union sources reported that it began with younger unskilled workers and has spread to skilled crafts. Pushers are even active within some plants. Company medical departments have been able to start rehabilitation programs once addicts realized that their jobs would not be in jeopardy if they sought help. Supervisors are trained to recognize drugs and addicts and then suggest they go to the company medical department for help. An alternative approach is to discharge addicts and report them to the police. However, in the opinion of a large company's medical director, this may simply drive the problem underground.

---

[9] Selden D. Bacon, "Industry, the Public, and Alcoholism," *Manpower Management,* pp. 20–22, April, 1954.

[10] For a case illustration of this fourth possibility, see, "The Life of Reilly," Paul Pigors and Faith Pigors, *Case Method in Human Relations: The Incident Process,* McGraw-Hill Book Company, New York, 1961, pp. 104–106.

[11] See Chap. 22 for suggestions about services which may benefit the half man.

[12] Bacon, *op. cit.,* p. 22.

[13] Harrison M. Trice, "Alcoholism and the Work World," *Sloan Management Review,* vol. 12, no. 1, pp. 67–75, Fall, 1970.

[14] "Workers Use of Drugs Widespread in Nation," *The New York Times,* June 21, 1971, p. 1.

The causes of absenteeism among incipient or actual alcoholics and drug users may seem easier to determine, but behind these immediate causes may be other deeper causes at the level of employee morale and job satisfaction. Causation is often more complex than it first appears to be. The same may be true of accidents, which may also sometimes be the result of alcohol and drugs. Analysis of accident records leads to better understanding of why they occur and why some individuals have more accidents than others.

**What Can Be Learned
from Accident Records?**

In looking at accidents as indicators of the needs and attitudes of people, the two most fruitful methods seem to be comparative analysis and study of the circumstances surrounding special and typical kinds of accidents.

A comparative study of accident records throughout the country, which can be made from the figures published annually by the U.S. Department of Labor, reveals the interesting fact that the lowest percentages of accidents are usually to be found in very small and very large companies. The medium-sized plants have, on an average, a less favorable record. What does this show? It seems to support the belief, also confirmed by experience, that both engineering skill and team spirit can play an important part in keeping accident rates low.

In very large companies, engineering for accident prevention has reached a high level of efficiency (see Chapter 22 for details). In smaller companies, engineering that builds safety into a plant and reduces the hazards that cannot entirely be eliminated is necessarily limited because it is expensive. In very small companies, engineering is even more restricted. In fact, safety engineers are sometimes shocked at the mechanical risks that exist in these plants. Yet, on the whole, people seem to be relatively safe even under such conditions when the total number of employees is small enough so that everybody knows everybody else and when the owner-manager feels personally concerned about employee safety.

Obviously, the human causes of accidents are here sufficiently reduced to outweigh mechanical hazards. Team spirit, manifested in safety-mindedness for others, can be a significant factor in reducing accidents. Moreover, in a very small work force, the skill and intelligence required of all employees mean that each member is likely to have the qualifications that make for personal safety in his particular job. In a medium-sized plant, the caliber of employees is unlikely to be at such a consistently high level, and the sense of belonging to a single company-wide work team is difficult if not impossible to achieve. Thus these companies fall between two stools, as it were. They lack both the expert engineering and the factors of individual skill and team spirit that make for safety.

A Case Example

An illustration of the type of accident that indicates both inadequate engineering inspection by management and unsafe practice by an employee who was not safety-minded for others is given in the following incident.[15] In a shipyard, "a painter had built himself a temporary scaffold and on finishing his work had departed, leaving it in place. Later when several chippers used the scaffold, under the impression that it had been erected by stage builders for their use, it collapsed and dropped the workers and their equipment to the ways." If modern management had developed effective procedures of control, as is usually done in large corporations nowadays, safety inspection would probably have prevented this accident. In a very small concern, the typical safety-mindedness of each worker for all others might be expected to rule out such accidents by eliminating the human cause.

[15] Frank S. McElroy and Arthur L. Svenson, "Basic Accident Factors in Shipyards," *Monthly Labor Review,* vol. 59, pp. 13-23, 1944.

Computing Accident Rates

Comparative analysis is a skill required of every chief executive. Yet it seems that some managers do not even know whether their record for safety is comparatively good or bad. Accidents constitute a major problem both for productive efficiency and for employee morale. Moreover, since accident analysis shows that most accidents are avoidable, it is inexcusable for managers not even to know the facts in regard to the accident record in their own organization. Of course, every executive likes to think that his company record is good, but experience shows that often the wish is father to the thought. It is the duty of the safety director—or if there is none, of the personnel administrator—to find out and report to line managers how well the company's injury-accident record compares with that of other companies in the same industry. This can be done by applying standard formulas to determine the frequency and severity rate. The American Standards Association provides the following formulas:

$$\text{Frequency rate} = \frac{\text{number of injuries} \times 1,000,000}{\text{number of man-hours of exposure}}$$

$$\text{Severity rate} = \frac{\text{total time charges in days} \times 1,000}{\text{number of man-hours of exposure}}$$

The man-hours of exposure are the total of man-hours actually worked by all employees. Time charges for permanent disabilities are based on a standard scale of allowances.[16] The frequency rate includes every accident, however minor; the severity rate is a better indicator of the seriousness of accidents on a comparative basis.

It is also useful to find out about the general liability rate of the industry as a whole, compared with other industries. Managers and other employees are naturally interested to know whether accidents in the company are partly attributable to risks inherent in the type of work. Even when this is known to be a fact, however, it may be regarded as a challenge to build a safety program that will set a record for the industry. Statistics published by the U.S. Department of Labor prove that this can be done. Their figures show that some companies in each of the most hazardous industries have extremely low frequency rates.

The comparison of safety records among different departments in one company may throw light on many features of work life and on the level of teamwork. To be realistic, of course, such comparisons must take into account differences in the rate of accident liability attaching to various kinds of work. When such differences are allowed for, the handicap of a given department is eliminated by using the adjusted frequency rate.

In accident records, the frequency rate is a more significant indicator than the severity rate, because the result of an accident is often a matter of luck.[17] Management's aim should be not merely to reduce the cost of injuries but rather to eliminate all avoidable accidents. Whether or not such a program exists and the extent to which it is implemented by safety procedures may be revealed by analyzing special and typical kinds of accidents.

Special and Typical Accidents

Analysis of the circumstances surrounding individual accidents clearly shows that both me-

---

[16] For greater detail, see *Using Injury Statistics,* U.S. Bureau of Labor Statistics, 1963, Bulletin 255, pp. 8-9. Many companies also compute the number of lost-time accidents, sometimes by department and division. See Geneva Seybold, *op. cit.,* p. 33.

[17] Roland P. Blake (ed.), *Industrial Safety,* 3d ed., Prentice-Hall, Inc., Englewood Cliffs, N.J., 1963, chap. 4, "Appraising Safety Performance," pp. 41-54, especially p. 45.

chanical and human factors (physical, mental, and emotional) play a part in causing accidents. Responsibility for safety is divided between management representatives and nonsupervisory employees. Neither group can do the job alone. Mechanical risks and the quality of supervision are the special responsibilities of management, and even the health and morale of employees are influenced by managerial activity. Inadequacies in either the mechanical or human environment of workers have a depressing effect on employee morale and reduce the possibility of achieving effective teamwork. Therefore, whether or not accidents result in serious injuries, managers should be concerned to learn all they can about their own efficiency in these areas.

A Case Example: Apprehension as an Accident Factor

A case in point was that of an elderly factory worker who had previously been employed in a grocery store. He had this to say at the end of his first week's work: "I was scared; I thought I wouldn't make it. The foreman showed me how to do the job. I guess I spoiled half of the pieces the first week. The foreman bawled me out every day. I was about ready to quit on Friday when I dropped a casting on my foot, and they sent me over to the hospital, and the foreman gave me a bad record for being careless."

No doubt this man made difficulties for his foreman. On the other hand, when the personnel director inquired why he was "scared," why he had not made a better production record on a comparatively simple operation, and whether his instruction had been adequate, the worker replied, [18] "No, I guess he showed me how to do the job all right, but I'd never worked in a shop before. I'd just lost my job that I had been on for 15 years. I wanted to make good, but I was

scared of the noise of the machine shop, I guess. I just couldn't get used to it. And there was a conveyor going over my head carrying some big castings which weighed about 50 pounds apiece. I guess they wouldn't have dropped on me, but I was always looking up at 'em. I guess that's what happened when I dropped the casting on my foot."

Person-centered analysis of this accident suggests that a more careful introduction to his work would probably have helped the employee to make a better adjustment to his new situation. A smoother adjustment on his part would have contributed to the organizational goal of stepping up production. This would have saved both management and the employee the loss occasioned by an avoidable accident. When analysis uncovers such a situation, it indicates the need for improvement in supervisory practices which should constantly interpret for employees top management's concern for their safety and welfare.

Accidents and Supervision

When a company has developed an accident-reporting system in which use of the standard accident-classification code helps to determine causes, the supervisor's report is significant in several respects. To follow up the clues which the report may contain, a series of questions must be asked. For instance, if one supervisor consistently reports that accidents in his section are the fault of employees, what does this show? Does he have an unusually large proportion of incompetent or careless employees? If this is actually a fact, why did he, at the end of the probationary period, accept them as regular employees? Has he done all that he could have done by careful instruction and thorough follow-up to correct their careless habits?

The fallacy is assigning carelessness as a cause of accidents is strongly emphasized by one writer on safety, in the following comment:

[18] T. O. Armstrong, "The New Employee," in Roland P. Blake (ed.), *Industrial Safety,* Prentice-Hall, Inc., Englewood Cliffs, N.J., 1943, chap. 25, p. 281.

Carelessness is not a cause of accidents. Instead it is an alibi for industrial executives, foremen, and others who unthinkingly are placing the blame for accidents on the workers who are injured. It serves as a boomerang, too, for its use condemns the person who uses it; it is an unthinking admission on his part that he is making little or no intelligent effort to control the action of the workers.[19]

Apparent carelessness may be the result of chronic accident-proneness (due, for example, to poor hand-eye coordination) or of temporary ill health of body or mind, possibly due to the after-effects of heavy drinking. If the supervisor is on his toes, he knows what lies behind "carelessness" and does what he can to correct fundamental causes of accidents.

Line and Staff Responsibilities Yet foremen, if unaided by experts, can hardly be expected, among all the urgent demands that are pressed upon them, to think profoundly about accidents as indicators. The safety director or the personnel administrator is responsible for keeping supervisors informed of all that can be learned from accident analysis. In this way, staff and line can work together to supplement each other's understanding and efficiency. When this is done, the result is a gain for both managers and nonsupervisory employees. Accidents can never be altogether eliminated. Human beings will never become entirely stable and perfectly efficient, but when the accidents that do happen are used as educational material for employees at all organizational levels[20] there can be a progressive gain in morale and teamwork. Unless accidents are so used, they not only indicate lapses in morale and teamwork but also tend to

set up a vicious cycle in which employee morale suffers a further depression, which, in turn, further reduces efficiency.

A comprehensive, integrated method of studying accidents is a practical application of situational thinking. In this way, a personnel administrator seeks understanding by correlating information about the human element, technical factors, corporate policies, and space-time dimensions. Safety records can be improved when individual idiosyncrasies, e.g., accident-proneness, are seen in relation to technical features of the work situation, such as job methods and mechanical hazards. Similarly, there is need to consider relationships among current data as to the level of teamwork, the quality of supervision, and the health, strength, and age of individual workers. Moreover, by comparing the company's record with that of the industry as a whole, it is possible to see whether the record is relatively good or bad. Comparison of past and present statistics shows whether the condition is getting better or worse.

EMPLOYEE ATTITUDE SURVEYS

Attitude or opinion surveys have often been used by managers to find out "what is on the worker's mind." This method of determining how an employee feels and thinks about his work was first developed in the 1920s, but not until the late forties were such surveys widely used. Such surveys are now the most frequent activity of personnel research units, although some are conducted by outside consultants.

The word "attitude" has been variously defined. Often it has been used interchangeably with "morale" and "opinion." The following definitions and comment are therefore worth considering.

An attitude is a characteristic of the way in which [a person] sees things. . . . What we mean by morale is the effect of the way the plant force see their working environment. It is the result of certain ways of seeing. To deal with it we need to understand as clearly as possible how [employees] do see

[19] Dean Keefer, "Circumstances Surrounding Accidents," in *ibid.,* chap. 5, p. 51.

[20] For an example with specific reference to overhead-crane operators, see Frank E. Bird, Jr., and George L. Germain, *Damage Control: A New Horizon in Accident Prevention and Cost Improvement,* American Management Association, Inc., New York, 1966, chap. 7, "Anatomy of a Training Program," pp. 121-146.

it, and then to consider what things within them or within the environment lead to this kind of perception." [21]

Written questionnaires, as a means of obtaining information on employee attitudes, may appeal particularly to those managers (especially in nonunion firms) who apparently lack other means of finding out what is on their employees' minds. Assumptions which underlie the use of written questionnaires are that words can be taken at their face value and that answers written by employees (on a form prepared for mass distribution) accurately correspond to what individual writers actually feel and think. An obvious advantage of the written questionnaire method over interviewing is that it is less expensive (in time and therefore in money), it requires fewer trained personnel, and is not subject to such drawbacks as personal bias of the interviewer. [22]

However, many companies have recognized that written questionnaires can usefully be supplemented (at considerable cost and with foreseeable risks) by interviewing, either directed, nondirected, or both. Indeed, unless written data are supplemented by face-to-face communication, attitude surveys may actually be misleading. There is also some evidence that when employees are surveyed on their job locations they tend to respond more favorably about the company than when surveyed off the job. [23]

Criticisms of Attitude Surveys

Use of written questionnaires to collect mass information on anything as personal as an attitude has been severely criticized. For example,

Most of the published analyses of organizations simply present the administrator with written attitudes of masses of individuals usually analyzed in terms of statistical frequencies which are not applicable to the individual case. . . . Moreover, this type of analysis assumes that if a department has "high morale" scores, there is no problem, and if it does not, something is wrong. This is not necessarily so. . . . These results point up another important limitation of the statistical attitude approach to diagnosing human relationships in organizations. It does not provide the administrator with insights into why people have high or low morale, how these attitudes are caused and then maintained, and which of these attitudes are surface manifestations, and which are underlying or basic. . . . Instead of constructing questionnaires, as do the statisticians, to discover attitudes (whose relationship to actual behavior is still very much in question), we construct questions which will help to discover the needs and abilities plus their degree of importance for each individual. The employees are asked about their attitudes, but when this is done, we try to relate them to their needs. Thus two employees may say that they dislike management. Their attitudes are the same. However, one may dislike management because she feels they are frustrating and pressuring her, while the other may need to dislike people in authority. [24]

Likert [25] has compared what shows up in attitude surveys with what is disclosed by a fever chart. All that can be detected is a fluctuation in

[21] Mason Haire, *Psychology in Management,* 2d ed., McGraw-Hill Book Company, New York, 1964, pp. 106–107.

[22] For discussion of the use of questionnaires, see Robert D. Gray, *Manual for Conducting an Employee Opinion Poll,* California Institute of Technology, Industrial Relations Section, Pasadena, Calif., 1966. Experience in Texas Instruments is reported by M. Scott Myers, "How Attitude Surveys Can Help You Manage; A Results-oriented Plan for Texas Instruments," *Training and Development Journal,* vol. 21, no. 10, especially pp. 38–41, October, 1967.

[23] John R. Henrichs and Robert D. Gatewood, "Differences in Opinion-survey Response Patterns as a Function of Different Methods of Survey Administration," *Journal of Applied Psychology,* vol. 51, no. 6, pp. 497–502, December, 1967.

[24] Chris Argyris, *Diagnosing Human Relations in Organizations,* Yale University, Labor and Management Center, Studies in Organizational Behavior, no. 2, New Haven, Conn., 1956, pp. 1–3. For a supporting view based on a British attitude study, see S. Wyatt and R. Mariott, *A Study of Attitudes to Factory Work,* Medical Research Council, Special Report Series, no. 292, H.M. Stationery Office, London, 1956.

[25] Rensis Likert, *The Human Organization: Its Management and Value,* McGraw-Hill Book Company, New York, 1967, pp. 132 and 135.

a symptom. Nothing is revealed as to underlying causes of good or ill health. Therefore, even if management tries to follow through on results indicated by such surveys, action is unlikely either to reach the roots of low morale or to have a positive effect on productivity.

Other Ways to Gauge Employee Attitudes

A different way of trying to measure employee attitudes was developed by General Electric. Their Employee Relations Index is an attempt to measure "the extent to which groups of employees accept, and perform in accordance with, the objectives and policies of the company."[26] The index consists of eight factors: periods of absence, separations (all types), initial visits to the dispensary for occupational reasons, suggestions submitted through the suggestion system, actions incurring disciplinary suspension, grievances submitted through the formal grievance procedure, work stoppages, and participation in the insurance plan.[27] A systems-minded feature of this approach is the fact that it synthesizes eight different behavioral manifestations.

Another approach,[28] geared to the inner motivation of employees, is making "a 'social audit' of a company, which is concerned with the workers as people in their own right rather than as functional parts of the organization. This approach attempts to find out how well—or how poorly—the company is doing in satisfying the basic needs of its employees. . . ."

Likert's Method of Measuring Employee Attitudes

This method implements the central aim of participative management in that "The primary

purpose of measurements, in System 4 organizations, is to provide managers and nonsupervisory personnel with information to help them guide their own decisions and behavior."[29] These measurements "deal directly with the human assets of the organization—for example, measurements of loyalty, motivation, confidence and trust."

For many organizations, however, a serious drawback associated with any such highly sophisticated and complex research method is that it can be administered only under the direction of persons with considerable competence in social psychology, psychometrics, sociometrics, and statistics. As we shall see, few personnel research units possess this competence.

Accurate data are not obtained by merely asking people what they think or how they feel. It takes at least as much sophistication and competence to set up measurements to obtain correct data concerning the causal and intervening variables as is required for accurate accounting. The interpretation of the data and of their use for diagnoses and analyses requires a still greater degree of competence.[30]

Difficulties in Implementing the Results of Attitude Surveys

Although the technical competence of those making attitude surveys has increased in recent years and the data collected are probably more valid, "there is marked uneasiness on the part of both researchers and managers about this ap-

[26] Willard V. Merrihue and Raymond A. Katzell, "ERI: Yardstick of Employee Relations," *Harvard Business Review,* vol. 33, no. 6, p. 91, November-December, 1955.

[27] *Ibid.,* pp. 94-95.

[28] Fred H. Blum, "Social Audit of the Enterprise," *Harvard Business Review,* vol. 36, no. 2, pp. 78-79, March-April, 1958.

[29] Rensis Likert, "Measuring Organizational Performance," *Harvard Business Review,* vol. 36, no. 2, p. 41, March-April, 1958 (reprinted in Paul Pigors, Charles A. Myers, and F. T. Malm, *Management of Human Resources: Readings in Personnel Administration,* 3d ed., McGraw-Hill Book Company, New York, 1973, selection 2).

[30] Likert, *The Human Organization,* pp. 144-145. For further discussion of various attitude measurements, see John P. Robinson, Robert Athanasian, and Kandra B. Head, *Measures of Occupational Attitudes and Occupational Characteristics,* Survey Research Center, Institute for Social Research, University of Michigan, Ann Arbor, Mich., February, 1969; and A. N. Oppenheim, *Questionnaire Design and Attitude Measurement,* Basic Books, Inc., New York, 1966.

proach. This uneasiness stems from the inability or unwillingness to utilize survey research findings."[31] One difficulty arises when survey results are reported only for the entire organization, with the result that individual managers feel little responsibility for doing anything about them. Even when there is subunit analysis of variables and comparisons with other subunits, managers whose results look poor defend themselves with various explanations, such as, "the survey was conducted at a bad time," or "employees always complain—it's their nature." If managers are to take survey results seriously and do something about the faults they reveal, the conclusion is clear: *"Little behavioral change on the basis of survey findings can be expected unless managers feel that such change will be rewarded by higher management and its absence will invoke penalties."*[32]

Of course, survey data must be used by higher management as only one of a number of different inputs used in evaluating performance of managers. It is also important to emphasize the need for future change rather than dwelling on past faults, and to give managers sufficient time to act upon attitude survey results. Recommendations on managerial changes as a result of surveys are best made by the manager's immediate superior in a problem-solving approach, rather than by personnel research people who may lack the managerial experience to make acceptable recommendations.

However, the researchers can serve as sounding boards for managers' ideas in reviewing the data, can relate current results to earlier studies, and can generally perform a staff or helping function. The responsibility for making decisions about implementing changes called for by any study of organizational health, including employee attitude surveys, rests with the various levels of management.

Case Example: Texas Instruments, Inc.

The interaction of personnel research staff and departmental and branch managers in taking action on attitude survey results, presented by a "Vu-graph" method, is illustrated by the accompanying charts (Figures 11-1 and 11-2) prepared by M. Scott Myers.[33]

In this company, which has no union, employee committees are formed (either selected by a manager, selected by an appointed committee chairman, or formed by informal group process) to analyze survey results and make recommendations to their departmental managers for action. This is the "committee" reference in Figure 11-2. These committees are seen as means for involving employees in the analysis and solution of problems, thereby contributing to their personal and professional growth.

THE USEFULNESS OF PERSONNEL RESEARCH

In this chapter, we have indicated various applications of personnel research in the analysis of absenteeism and accidents, and especially in making employee attitude surveys. According to a study of almost 100 executives and behavioral scientist-researchers in more than 75 organizations, most of personnel research "still focuses on selection and opinion research."[34] Other areas of research, reported by 30 percent or fewer of the companies surveyed, were the following: train-

---

[31] David Sirota, "Why Managers Don't Use Attitude Survey Results," *Personnel,* vol. 47, no. 1, pp. 24-35, January-February, 1970. The article is based on the author's experience in a number of organizations, but primarily in one large company (presumably IBM) in which more than 100 attitude surveys had been completed in the preceding 10 years, covering tens of thousands of employees.

[32] Sirota, *op. cit.,* p. 29 (italics are the author's).

[33] *Op. cit.,* pp. 39-40; also in M. Scott Myers, "The Involvement Approach," *Every Employee a Manager,* McGraw-Hill Book Company, 1970, pp. 206-212.

[34] William C. Byham, *The Uses of Personnel Research,* AMA Research Study 91, American Management Association, Inc., New York, 1968, p. 14.

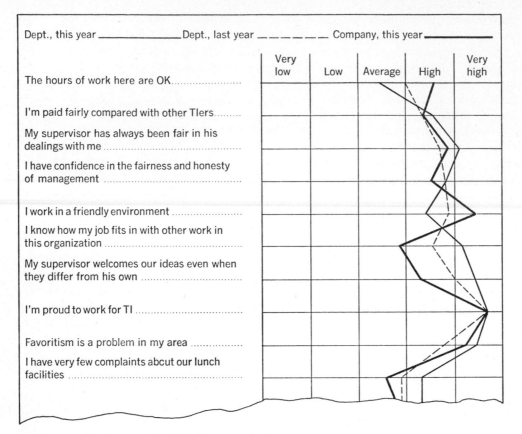

Figure 11-1 Employee Attitude Profile, Texas Instruments.

ing and development, appraisal, motivation and job satisfaction, organizational effectiveness, supervision, accident prevention, and emotional stress. Fewer than one in ten companies did studies of managerial and technical obsolescence, counseling, recruitment, or engaged in so-called "basic research." Respondents indicated that future research activity might be in the selection of minority employees, placing and training the disadvantaged, further analysis of labor turnover, and methods of management appraisal. These topics indicate the widening scope of personnel research and its actual or potential usefulness over a wide spectrum of personnel policies and problems.

Personnel research has come into prominence in many organizations as a result of growing managerial interest in behavioral science research in the universities and in other research institutions. (We have already summarized much of this research in the first eight chapters, and we shall refer to it again in later chapters). But the AMA survey reported in 1968 that only a few companies use behavioral science techniques in their own research, even though the number was said to be steadily increasing. Among those mentioned with a strong behavioral science research orientation were General Electric, Xerox, IBM, Texas Instruments, and Du Pont—companies which also conduct a large

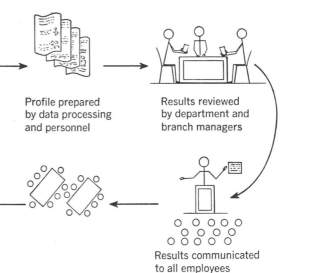

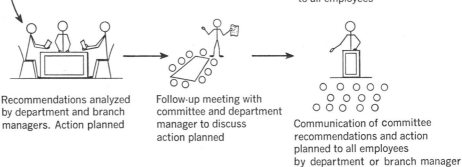

Figure 11-2 Attitude Survey Flow Chart, Texas Instruments.

amount of product research. No listing can be complete, but other firms which have applied behavioral science research techniques to their personnel problems include the Ford Motor Company, Standard Oil of New Jersey, Equitable Life Assurance Society, Bell Telephone Laboratories, and other units of the American Telephone and Telegraph Company.[35] Many of these

firms employ psychologists with Ph.D.'s in their personnel research units, and one survey indicated that nearly 70 percent were industrial psychologists.[36]

Despite the growth of personnel research, there is some ambivalence about its future. Managers and personnel administrators who are concerned with the development and implementation of policies may have lower expectations about the usefulness of personnel research than

[35] Byham, *op. cit.;* Dean F. Berry, *The Politics of Personnel Research,* Bureau of Industrial Relations, University of Michigan, Ann Arbor, Mich., 1967, especially chaps. 9 and 10; and Thomas H. Patten, Jr., "Personnel Research: Status Key," *Management of Personnel Quarterly,* vol. 41, no. 3, pp. 15–23, Fall, 1965.

[36] John R. Henrichs, "Characteristics of the Personnel Research Function," *Personnel Journal,* vol. 48, no. 8, pp. 597–604, August, 1969.

do personnel research managers and their behavioral science consultants. The frustration of researchers when managers fail to act upon research results (of attitude surveys) has already been noted. One study of the role of personnel research in a number of firms concluded that "most personnel research functions are relatively static, not planning their growth and more allied to the professional field than to the organization task."[37]

Personnel research in the years ahead will be greatly aided by the use of the computer for data storage and retrieval of all types of personnel information as well as wage and salary data; for analysis of relationships between independent and dependent variables, using various computer-stored statistical techniques; in simulations of future relationships (as in manpower forecasting); and in developing models of complex behavior.[38]

SUMMARY

Personnel research can contribute to the diagnosis of organizational health in various ways. In this chapter, we have considered in detail the analysis of tardiness and absenteeism, including that occasioned by alcoholism and drug abuse; of accidents; and of employee opinions and attitudes. The role of behavioral science research in analyzing problems indicated by these measures is spreading, and the use of computers in assisting both analysis and simulation of possible future developments will undoubtedly assist personnel research even more in the future.

Research results are of little value to managers if they do not lead to some action when the data suggest that something is wrong. Managers from the top management down to the first-level supervisor have the responsibility for taking such action, with the advice of the personnel department as to the meaning of data and research results. Personnel research staff members can also assist in suggesting ways of bringing research findings to the attention of different levels of management and in helping them to think about getting suggestions from those they supervise on needed next steps.

In addition to indicators of organizational health mentioned in this chapter, two others deserve consideration by line managers and personnel staff. These are labor turnover and internal mobility (considered in the next chapter) and complaints and grievances (in Chapter 13).

SELECTED REFERENCES

Argyris, Chris: *Diagnosing Human Relations in Organizations,* Yale University, Labor and Management Center, Studies in Organizational Behavior, no. 2, New Haven, Conn., 1956.

Berry, Dean F.: *The Politics of Personnel Research,* Bureau of Industrial Relations, The University of Michigan, Ann Arbor, Mich., 1967.

Byham, William C.: *The Uses of Personnel Research,* AMA Research Study 91, American Management Association, Inc., New York, 1968.

Gaudet, Frederick J.: *Solving the Problems of Employee Absence,* AMA Research Study 57, American Management Association, Inc., New York, 1963.

Gray, Robert D.: *Manual for Conducting an Employee Opinion Poll,* California Institute of Technology, Industrial Relations Section, Bulletin 36, Pasadena, Calif., 1966.

Myers, M. Scott: "How Attitude Surveys Can Help You Manage: A Results-oriented Plan for Texas Instruments," *Training and Development Journal,* vol. 21, no. 10, pp. 34–41, October, 1967.

Seybold, Geneva: *Personnel Audits and Reports to Top Management,* Studies in Personnel Policy no. 191, National Industrial Conference Board, Inc., New York, 1964.

Sirota, David, "Why Managers Don't Use Attitude Survey Results," *Personnel,* vol. 47, no. 1, pp. 24–35, January–February, 1970.

[37] Berry, *op. cit.,* p. 244.
[38] John R. Henrichs, "Implications of the Computer for Personnel Research," *Management of Personnel Quarterly,* vol. 7, no. 4, pp. 6–12, Winter, 1968.

Chapter 12

Labor Turnover and Internal Mobility

Just as the high reading on a clinical thermometer is a sign to the physician that something is seriously wrong with the human organism, so is a high index of labor turnover a warning to management that something is wrong with the health of the organization. But, just as the clinical thermometer merely indicates that something is wrong—not what is wrong— so does the turnover rate merely warn, not diagnose. A high temperature may mean pneumonia, measles, or mumps. A high turnover rate may mean poor personnel practices, poor supervisory practices, or poor company policies. Nor should we forget that too low a rate of turnover, like a below-normal reading on the thermometer, can also be a danger signal.

Frederick J. Gaudet[1]

Labor turnover confronts managers with many interrelated personnel problems which are often difficult to diagnose and hard to control. Too little turnover may be as harmful as too much. A certain amount of turnover is unavoidable because of inevitable contingencies such as disability, retirement, and death. Some voluntary turnover is also beneficial if it enables people to utilize their abilities more effectively in other jobs and if it meets the needs of expanding firms and industries in other sectors of a dynamic economy. Thus, turnover which may be a "cost" to one firm may be a "gain" to another firm which is recruiting more people.

What is "normal" turnover for any particular company? What factors should be considered when managers direct their attention to avoid-

[1] Frederick J. Gaudet, *Labor Turnover: Calculation and Cost,* American Management Association, Research Study 39, New York, 1960, p. 12.

able turnover? How can excessive voluntary separations be controlled? These are some of the questions that we shall consider in this chapter.

In dollars and cents, labor turnover is probably management's most expensive personnel problem. "The cost of (avoidable) labor turnover in even a small company is startling. For example, in a company of 200 employees with an adjusted net labor turnover rate of only 2 percent per month, the average cost of labor turnover per year could amount to over $20,000.00." [2]

As we noted in Chapter 1, "human asset accounting" is so new that most organizations don't count the investment in human resources in their balance sheets or the loss of such assets by voluntary resignations. A turnover rate of 10 percent per year in a department may not be as serious to a manager as turnover *loss* of $45,000 of unamortized investments in the people who left. Yet such losses are frequently ignored. How costly it is if a key engineer or scientist leaves an important research and development group in an organization or if a systems designer or key computer programmer leaves before a computerization project is completed! And the loss of a key manager is even more costly.

TWO TYPES OF MOVEMENTS

Many of the tangible and intangible losses connected with controllable labor turnover are also associated with transfers, the shifting of employees within the company itself. From the point of view of change and its consequences, transfer is a similar manifestation on a smaller scale than labor turnover. For this reason, quantitative measurement and qualitative analysis of personnel mobility are important management responsibilities.

A notable field study provided a stimulating comparison of these two kinds of movement. [3] Its author stressed the importance of recognizing the interrelationships of labor turnover and transfers "in the idea of a *system* of worker movement in which control over one segment is necessary and instrumental to control over the other." He added:

The two types of movement are interrelated in fact, and that interrelation may be used to the advantage of all concerned. The type of internal movement which is advantageous may help to prevent the type of external turnover which is disadvantageous. And the type of turnover which is advantageous may serve to prevent the type of internal movement which is disadvantageous (arising from sheer frustration—"*any* job would be better than my present job") and may permit the type of internal movement which is advantageous.

Within due limits, and when skillfully handled, both labor turnover and internal mobility can benefit the entire organization as well as the individuals who make the adjustments. Without the necessary control, or when handled without the necessary skills in policies and procedures, personnel mobility is destructive of individual and organizational stability alike.

EFFECTS OF LABOR TURNOVER
Stabilizing Effects

Labor turnover promotes stability insofar as circulation of employees brings new blood into the organization. The company remains a "going concern" in regard to personnel as long as employees who leave for reasons of age or health are replaced by younger or stronger employees. Moreover, efficiency and morale are raised when necessary replacements can be supplied by pro-

---

[2] Grant W. Canfield, "How to Compute Your Labor Turnover Costs," *Personnel Journal,* vol. 37, no. 11, p. 416, April, 1959. Methods of computing labor turnover costs are discussed in a later section of this chapter.

[3] Neil W. Chamberlain, *Management in Motion: The Corporate Decision-making Process as Applied to the Transfer of Employees,* Yale University, Labor and Management Center, New Haven, Conn., 1950, chap. 1, "Labor Turnover and Internal Movement," pp. 1-15.

motions from within the organization rather than from outside the company.

Similarly, internal mobility may build teamwork when transfers make possible a better adjustment among teammates and when upgrading or promotion meets a worker's needs and thus resolves inner conflicts. An ambitious employee needs to know that promotion will parallel his increased ability and worth to the company. If his job is far below his capacity, he is inevitably wasting ability and is subjected to tensions. Similarly, if he feels that he is in a "blind-alley" job, he is certain to be dissatisfied. The disturbing effect of such strains on his equilibrium may, through him, prove injurious to group morale. Open job bidding permits employees to make themselves available for a wider variety of job opportunities within the organization.[4]

Individual needs can also be met by internal mobility in the form of production transfers to avoid layoffs, remedial transfers to solve personal or technical difficulties arising from improper placement or marked changes in individuals, and sometimes even by transfers for such a purely social reason as an employee's desire to join a more congenial work group or, for some personal reason, to swap assignments with another employee. In such ways, labor turnover and internal mobility may promote individual, group, and company interests by increasing work satisfaction, loyalty, and efficiency, especially when such mobility is encouraged by job bidding in which the employee takes the initiative.

Unstabilizing Effects

Obviously, personnel mobility is not all gain. When a separation occurs for any reason, the organization and the work groups that comprise it must adjust to the loss. Changes in work routine are inevitable, and a group may be shorthanded for a time. If the departing employee is a valued teammate and is laid off or discharged without adequate explanation, his fellow employees become disturbed. Speculation leads to rumors. Gossip and worry reduce work efficiency. A sense of insecurity and resentment may spread among members until it leads to voluntary separations that further upset the group.

When a new member is introduced into a work group, human adjustments must be made by all concerned. Some adjustments are necessary even when a new member is a transferee. If he is a newcomer to the organization, and perhaps also unaccustomed to the kind of work being done there, much has to be done before he is assimilated into the work team.

There are difficult mutual adjustments when the group adapts to a new member or when the probationer makes a place for himself. The strain involved may manifest itself in poor work quality or performance, accidents, or quarrels. Unless the adjustment process can be satisfactorily completed, the whole replacement cycle must be repeated.

Another unstabilizing influence of turnover may be *too little* turnover. Some employees with longer service may simply be "marking time," doing enough to get by while waiting for their retirement benefits. If so, they block promotional opportunities for younger, able people who may leave the organization for better prospects elsewhere. The work group may lose its more vital members while retaining the less vital.

Measuring Costs of Labor Turnover

Since personnel mobility requires adjustments by all concerned, it obviously involves some costs that, unless outweighed by certain gains, constitute a loss to the organization. In most companies avoidable separations and unnecessary or unwise transfers produce unjustifiable

---

[4] For a discussion of this procedure in managerial positions, where it is less frequent, see Theodore M. Alfred, "Checkers or Choice in Manpower Management," *Harvard Business Review,* vol. 45, no. 1, pp. 157–169, January-February, 1967 (also reprinted in Pigors, Myers, and Malm, *op. cit.,* selection 11).

costs not only in human values but also in money. Yet line officials are often unaware of the extent and nature of the damage done even by such an obvious manifestation of poor management as excessively high turnover rates.

In order to reduce the cost of labor turnover to a minimum, it is essential that line officials from the top down be kept supplied with relevant information. At the outset of this chapter, we noted some estimates of the high cost of labor turnover.

In more detail, what are some of these costs? They include:

1 Costs of hiring and training each new employee.[5]
  a Costs incurred by the employment department—time and facilities used to interview the applicant, prepare necessary records, give physical examinations, etc.
  b Training and development costs—time of supervisors and instructors.
  c Wage or salary paid to the new employee in excess of his initial value to the organization. This is as true of newly hired professional and technical employees as it is of pieceworkers paid a "guaranteed minimum" before their productivity exceeds it.
  d Poor performance, breakage, scrap, and wastage of materials in the learning period.
  e Possible costs in accidents to self or others while skill is being acquired.
2 Cost of overtime work required from regular workers in order to maintain the required level of production or service until the new employee can do his share.
3 Loss of production in the interval between separation of the former employee and the time when his replacement is fully broken in.

  a Maximum loss while the group is without a replacement.
  b Loss in group efficiency while regular employees are readjusting to a new member.
4 Expense in equipment or facilities not being fully utilized during the training period.

Several attempts have been made to estimate the amount of these costs. One is shown in Table 12-1. While different organizations may arrive at somewhat different figures, the effort is worthwhile as evidence to management that there are wastes involved in labor turnover. These analyses are unfortunately sometimes necessary in order to enlist the interest of operating officials in a program to reduce excessive labor turnover.

However, these costs can be estimated only when we know how much labor turnover there is at any given time and of what kind. Obviously, from the firm's standpoint the most unjustifiable waste is that involved in "avoidable" separations. In order to determine whether or not this item is concealed among turnover firgures, a personnel administrator must analyze the current rate of labor turnover and distinguish between avoidable and unavoidable separations.

Recognition of high turnover costs may lead to an analysis of the reasons why some employees leave as compared to those who remain. The following example is illustrative of one research approach.

A Case Example: Job Satisfaction and Turnover among Office Employees[6]

During the 3 years preceding 1965, turnover among the female clerical staff in the Montreal home office of a large manufacturing plant averaged around 30 percent. A cost-accounting analysis showed that approximately $1,000 was

---

[5] Costs of hiring (recruitment, testing, etc.) have gone up, as shown by a survey of personnel managers completed in 1969. The average for skilled labor was $149, unskilled $117, secretarial $172, clerical $145, and college graduates from $990 to $1900 each. Personnel Policies Forum, *Recruiting Practices,* Survey no. 86, Bureau of National Affairs, Washington, D.C., March, 1969, pp. 9 and 13.

[6] This information is taken from Charles L. Hulin, "Job Satisfaction and Turnover in a Female Clerical Population," *Journal of Applied Psychology,* vol. 50, no. 4, pp. 280-285, August, 1966.

Table 12-1 Estimate of Labor Turnover Costs for Sample of Firms in Metropolitan Los Angeles

Employment cost, defined as the total of all direct and indirect costs which are specifically chargeable as expenses brought about by the procurement, selection, and placement of employees	$ 43.24
Break-in cost, defined as the expense due to substandard production of new employees while learning their job assignments and becoming adjusted to their work environment	152.97
Breaking-in cost, defined as the dollar value of time spent by supervisors and other employees who assist in breaking in new employees	49.45
Formal training cost, this cost referring only to organized-training-program expenses and not to *on-the-job-training costs,* which are included under break-in and breaking-in costs	29.33
Separation cost, typical expenses would include lost hours of production due to separation processing and exit interview and time lost by personnel department representatives and other persons who are involved in the separation process	3.34
Lost production and extra-burden cost, defined as those costs brought about because of the resultant understaffing of company facilities due to labor turnover, overtime worked to maintain a normal production level, etc.	174.76
Extra Social Security tax cost	17.44
Extra Unemployment Insurance tax cost	10.26
Total average extra cost per separatee	$480.79

Source: Labor Turnover: Causes, Cost and Methods of Control, Merchants and Manufacturers Association, Los Angeles, Calif., 1959. If the first four were considered "hiring costs," the figure should be raised to around $300 for 1965 prices. See "Hiring Costs: Some Survey Findings," *Conference Board Record,* vol. 4, no. 1, pp. 33–42, 1967. This study by the National Industrial Conference Board, in Monroe County (Rochester), N.Y., showed these same costs somewhat lower: $292 for professional, technical, and managerial employees; $130 for clerical workers, $103 for skilled workers, and $94 for semiskilled and unskilled workers; table 4, p. 38.

spent to hire and train one clerical worker, so that total turnover was costing the company $130,000 per year. Comparable turnover rates in other Montreal firms under the same labor market conditions averaged almost 10 percent lower. The company therefore agreed to a research study to determine the reasons for its relatively high turnover among female clerical employees.

The 415 members of the female clerical staff were asked to fill out anonymous questionnaires on job satisfaction, which included an adjective checklist type of scale covering work, pay, promotion, coworkers, supervision, and "atmosphere" (friendliness of the company as a place to work). Over 86 percent (350) participated; most of the nonparticipants were largely on vacation or ill during the survey period. In addition, the questionnaires were mailed to 129 clerical workers who had quit during 1963, and 22 percent were returned. They were also asked how they felt about the company in retrospect. Both groups furnished data on age, education level, job level, mother tongue, and marital status. By December, 1964, 31 more girls had quit, 26 of whom had been in the original 350 control group.

The results may be summarized briefly. When the control group was compared with the quit group, it was found that the latter reported less job satisfaction. But they were also 8 years younger. When each of the 26 who quit was matched in age, education, and mother tongue with two from the control group, there was a statistically significant difference in job satisfaction. Those who remained with the company had higher job satisfaction in each of the six areas.

A follow-up study was done of those who later quit during the 6 months after December 15, 1964: of these 17 had been in the previous control group. Again there was two-for-one matching, but the differences were not statistically significant. However, when the two quit groups were combined and compared to the control group, job satisfaction indexes were significantly higher in the latter group.

The researcher cautioned against generalizing from this study. Female clerical workers

> ... have fewer economic reasons for remaining on any job they are dissatisfied with than would a comparable sample of males. . . . They tend to have readily marketable skills and live in an area in which there is a demand for these skills. . . . On the other hand, workers who are less able to find a new job and who have a number of economic obligations would have pressures on them to remain at their present job even if they were decidedly dissatisfied.[7]

DIFFERENT TYPES OF LABOR TURNOVER

Here, as with other statistical data that are used to further human understanding, the figures are less useful in the form of overall totals than when they are analyzed in more detail. Turnover can be computed for each type of movement in and out of the company. What are these types?

1 Accessions. Hiring new employees or rehiring former employees.
2 Separations. Termination of employment, usually subdivided as follows:
   a Quit. A separation initiated by the worker. Employees who are absent without authorization for 7 consecutive days (or sometimes less) are usually listed among the "quits."
   b Layoff. A termination of employment (expected to last more than 7 days) initiated by the employer because the job is being eliminated or because there is a reduction of employment due to insufficient demand. Such separation is presumably without prejudice to the employee.

c Discharge. A termination initiated by the employer because he is dissatisfied with the employee's performance or conduct. This type of termination is therefore with prejudice to the worker's record, although if the discharge is before the completion of the new employee's probationary period (usually 30 days), it is less severe because no employment rights have been acquired. Some forced "resignations" are really discharges, especially at the upper echelons.
d Retirement or death.

Computation of Rates

Labor turnover is commonly expressed in two rates—one for separations and the other for accessions. The U.S. Bureau of Labor Statistics uses the following method to compute the separation rate:

1 Find the average number of employees by adding together the number on the payroll on the first and last days of the month. Then divide this total by 2.
2 Divide the total number of separations during the month by this average employment figure.
3 Multiply this number by 100 to get the rate per 100 employees for the month.

Expressed as a formula, this method is

$$\text{Separation rate (or percentage)} = \frac{\text{total separations per month}}{\text{average number on payroll for the month}} \times 100$$

Monthly figures may be converted to an annual rate by multiplying the actual monthly rate by a factor equal to 365 divided by the number of days in a given month. Unless this is done, monthly figures are not strictly comparable with annual figures, since months vary in length.

The rate for accessions, quits, layoffs, and discharges can be computed by the same basic formula. When the separation rate is subtracted

[7] *Ibid.,* p. 284. For an illustration of why a low voluntary turnover (quit) rate may not indicate high morale, see Carroll R. McKibbin, "The 'Quit Rate' as a Measure of Morale in the Public Service: The Case of the United States Foreign Service," *Public Personnel Review,* vol. 32, no. 1, pp. 12–15, January, 1971.

from the accession rate, the result is positive or negative according to whether employment is expanding or contracting. If "avoidable turnover" is to be measured, the quit rate is the most useful, and this may be subdivided by "established employees" and "new arrivals" because turnover is usually higher among newer and/or younger employees.

Comparative Measurement of Turnover

Absolute figures for turnover rates are of little significance, however, unless they are compared with a standard and unless they are used as a point of departure for seeking an explanation of employee dissatisfactions. Whether turnover rates are rising, falling, or standing still in the country or in the industry as a whole, it is important to know how the firm's turnover rates compare with others. These comparative figures appear each month in the *Monthly Labor Review,* published by the U.S. Bureau of Labor Statistics.[8] A useful chart can be prepared and kept up to date, showing company turnover rates compared with similar rates for the industry and for all manufacturing.

SOME CRITICAL QUESTIONS ABOUT LABOR TURNOVER

Even if the company figures compare favorably with others, managers and personnel administrators should not be satisfied unless they are sure that the rate of voluntary separations is as low as possible and until they know all that these figures can teach them about how effectively the company is handling its personnel. In following these leads, three sets of questions need to be answered:

Why Are Employees Voluntarily Leaving the Company? Is it because they think they can find a "better job somewhere else"? Are they dissatisfied with working conditions, with supervisors or fellow employees, with shift assignments, or because they feel they are "getting nowhere"? Or are employees leaving the company for "unavoidable" reasons, such as illness, "needed at home," reopening of school, marriage, pregnancy, etc.?

Frequently, of course, management does not know why an employee leaves the company if he goes of his own accord. For example, if an employee quits without notice, even his immediate supervisor may not know what prompted this "irresponsible" action. On the other hand, if an employee gives reasonable notice and leaves in a good mood, he may tell his immediate supervisor why he is leaving; perhaps because another employer has offered him more money or greater opportunity for advancement. But often the alleged reason is not the real one. Many dissatisfied employees tend to follow the counsel of prudence: "Don't burn your bridges behind you." There is always the possibility that at some point in the future they may need a reference from a previous employer.

The Exit Interview as a Source of Information[9] To supplement such rather haphazard communication, many companies have a personnel department representative hold an exit interview when the employee calls for his last paycheck. In theory, such an interview might seem an excellent opportunity to check on administrative and supervisory practices. While covering necessary procedural details, the interviewer may also invite the employee to talk about his feelings concerning the job and work situation that he is leaving. The manner and nature of the employee's response may yield useful insights

---

[8] Data are secured from approximately 7,000 representative firms in different industries. See "Measurement of Labor Turnover," rev. ed., U.S. Bureau of Labor Statistics, 1966, 5 pp.

[9] Refer again to the discussion of the skills in interviewing, Chap. 10. See also John R. Henrichs, "The Exit Interview," *Personnel,* vol. 48, no. 1, pp. 30-35, January-February, 1971.

into his reasons for leaving. It may even prove possible to salvage a desirable employee at this last moment.

However, even to a sympathetic listener, a dissatisfied employee will not be able to talk freely if he suffers from internal conflicts or fears that an argument may ensue. Experience shows that it is extremely difficult to get reliable information by means of exit interviews.

An interview held some time after an employee has left, and presumably feels securely established in his new job, may be a better means of getting reliable information. Widespread discrepancies have been disclosed by comparing reasons that employees gave in an exit interview and reasons that they gave in a postterminal interview—held several months later. The same holds true for subsequent contacts established by sending out questionnaires. For example, exit questionnaires were administered some time after separation to 625 former employees of an aircraft production company. The reasons then given for quitting were compared with the reasons given at the time of separation; 38.2 percent were different. [10]

A more recent study arrived at similar conclusions. [11] A comparison of initial reasons given for leaving and subsequent statements showed a difference of 59 percent in the two sets of information. That employees were reluctant to speak candidly during the exit interview was illustrated by the fact that all of those who said initially they were resigning "for no specific reason" later reported specific reasons.

In view of these findings, we may conclude that while exit interviews may have a certain value as a friendly gesture from management, [12] they seldom yield consistently reliable information as to why employees are leaving. If a manager wants to undertake more promising research into circumstances that prompt employees voluntarily to leave the company, he should rely on objective, statistical methods by looking into a second question.

Where Are Voluntary Separations Occurring?
What segments of industry are characterized by excessive turnover? What departments or sections are workers voluntarily leaving? What kind of work was being performed, in what conditions, and under whose supervision? For example, study of a group of mass-production workers in an automobile assembly plant showed that workers with as much as 12 to 15 years of service gladly left their relatively high-paying jobs for employment which offered freedom from tension and opportunity to exercise some individual initiative. [13]

However, the answers to this set of questions are especially significant if there is a disproportionate turnover in some place where it cannot be readily accounted for by the nature of operations or of working conditions. In such a case the fault may be in the composition and functioning of work teams or in the quality of individual supervisors. For instance, in one company, comparisons of turnover in three departments led to further investigations that definitely pointed to the incompetence of a particular supervisor.

Further insight into reasons for leaving, as well as a more accurate estimate of the expense involved, may be obtained by asking a third question.

[10] Wayne L. McNaughton, "Use of the Post-exit Questionnaire," *Journal of Personnel Administration and Industrial Relations,* vol. 2, no. 3, p. 103, Fall, 1955. For a later study of the same problem, see Julius Yourman, "Following Up on Terminations: An Alternative to the Exit Interview," *Personnel,* vol. 42, no. 4, pp. 51–57, July–August, 1965.
[11] Joel Lefkowitz and Myron Katz, "Validity of Exit Interviews," *Personnel Psychology,* vol. 22, no. 4, pp. 445–455, Winter, 1969.

[12] See James Menzies Black, *How to Get Results from Interviewing: A Practical Guide for Operating Management,* McGraw-Hill Book Company, New York, 1970, chap. 9, "The Exit Interview," pp. 154–168.
[13] Robert H. Guest, "A Neglected Factor in Labour Turnover," *Occupational Psychology* (London), vol. 29, no. 4, pp. 215–231, October, 1955.

What Kind of Employee Is Leaving Voluntarily? The age, sex, marital status, nationality, length of service, and skill of the worker who leaves the company of his own volition are worthy of study. If voluntary separations are chiefly among very young workers of both sexes, or among girls who are getting married, or in the age group above 50, or among unskilled workers with less than 6 months of service, there is less cause of concern than when long-service, professional, clerical, and skilled employees between 30 and 40 years of age are voluntarily leaving the organization. However, management cannot afford to be satisfied when any employee is leaving without regret. Every worker would feel some reluctance to leave the organization if his work and his associations there had been satisfying.

A good deal of unjustifiable smugness is expressed when separations are chiefly among "common labor," for example. It might be more constructive to ask: Could we reduce the number of such separations by improving working conditions or by supplying more and better opportunities for participation and advancement? Similarly, it need not be accepted as true that all young people are flighty or even unreliable today. What specifically is being done in the company to make young people feel that their youth is considered an asset to the organization, that their ideas are potentially valuable, and that the abilities they expect to develop will be suitably rewarded? What educational opportunities are being offered in the company that help to stimulate and to apply their desire for self-development?

METHODS OF REDUCING TURNOVER

Answers to the above three broad lines of inquiry help management and its personnel adviser to ask the final question: Is there any condition in the organization that could be improved, either by management or by the cooperation of management and employees, in or-

der to reduce excessive labor turnover? Since the answer to this question usually is "yes," it is clear that separations furnish the personnel administrator and line executives with a perpetual opportunity for evaluating the effectiveness of their dealings with personnel.

Even when management knows the cost and many of the reasons for high turnover, no single remedy can be used as a cure-all for this symptom of organizational ill health. Participants in the Merchants and Manufacturers Association labor-turnover cost study (mentioned earlier) listed 21 different methods of controlling or reducing labor turnover. The most frequently reported methods, in the order of the number of times cited, were:

Employee orientation, induction, and follow-up	12
Good employee communications (including management communications programs)	11
Sound employee-selection policies and procedures	10
The use of exit interviews	7
Management and/or supervisory training	6
Thorough job evaluation and wage and salary administration program	6
Thorough employee reference investigation	5

Depending on the causes for avoidable turnover, any one or all of these methods can be used in an effort to improve the situation. [14] For example, as a result of its participation in the M & M labor-turnover cost study, a major privately owned public utility inaugurated a program of labor-turnover control. Using the labor-turnover cost figures developed through the formula and tables of representative costs, this company be-

[14] No one list, of course, is inclusive. A more recent survey of a number of personnel administrators all over the United States indicated that the following programs were used successfully to reduce turnover (in order of frequency): improved selection; orientation and related counseling; supervisory training programs; better wage and salary administration; upward communications; exit interviews and other turnover surveys. Personnel Policies Forum, *Turnover and Job Satisfaction,* Survey no. 9, Bureau of National Affairs, Washington, D.C., August, 1970, p. 9.

came aware that undesirable labor turnover was costing between $1,500,000 and $3,000,000 per year. In an attempt to reduce this expense, a full-time staff representative was assigned to the personnel department to analyze where turnover was occurring and how it could be reduced. One of the first studies completed by this staff representative was an evaluation of approximately 50 employees who had separated from the company (failure group) and 50 employees in the same occupation who had good work histories with the company (success group). Analyses were made of a number of factors to determine which would prove the most valid in future recruitment.

Some of the findings developed through this study[15] were as follows:

The employee group that proved most successful had an average age of slightly over 27 years, while the average age of the group that were considered failures was about 24½ years. Of the failure group, however, over 50 per cent were under 20 years of age when hired. The month in which an employee was hired also tended to have some significance. The majority of the failure group were hired during the months April through August, whereas the majority of the successful group were hired in August through November.

Another example from the findings from this company's study indicated that a high percentage of the failure group had resided at their present address less than one month.

Further Case Examples: Restructuring Jobs to Reduce Turnover and Improve Placement

Exit interviews in various parts of the American Telephone and Telegraph system brought out the usual reasons for quitting—inadequate pay, bad transportation, undesirable hours (particularly night work), home problems, poor supervision, unsatisfying or undesirable work. Efforts

were made to deal with some of these problems, although night work, for example, was inevitable. But what about the jobs—could anything be done to make work more interesting and satisfying to the people on them? Could high turnover be reduced by paying more attention to the nature of work itself, and to the conditions under which work motivates people so that turnover is reduced?

The effort begun under the leadership of Robert N. Ford (Personnel Director, Manpower Utilization, AT&T), based on the ideas of Frederick Herzberg (see Chapter 6), showed the relationship between job restructuring or enrichment and the consequent reduction of labor turnover. Studies involving several thousand employees were made in experimental and control groups spread across nine different nonsupervisory jobs in 10 operating companies. In the experimental groups, supervisors in discussion sessions tried to solve this problem:

How can we shape a particular job so that the job incumbent has, not more work, but more responsibility for the work? How can we make him feel that a part of the business is his alone, and that he can make decisions regarding it and personally identify with it? If we can do this, the employee will have a heightened chance for individual achievement. In addition he will have a chance to learn and to grow on his job, perhaps to be promoted. Furthermore, if we can do this, we can make the employee's working life a more meaningful human experience. If we succeed, he will not feel impelled to look elsewhere for good work or to become so unproductive as to be useless to the company.[16]

A number of changes in existing jobs were made by this process, through pushing earlier work stages into the job or pulling later stages

---

[15] *Labor Turnover: Causes, Cost and Methods of Control,* Merchants and Manufacturers Association, Los Angeles, Calif., 1959, pp. 33-35.

[16] Robert N. Ford, *Motivation through the Work Itself,* American Management Association, New York, 1969, p. 186. For a similar approach in Texas Instruments, Dallas, see M. Scott Myers, *Every Man a Manager,* McGraw-Hill Book Company, New York, 1970. Some of this experience was considered in Chap. 6.

back into the job; rearranging parts of the job; and pulling responsibility down from above. After these job changes, it was important to give employees *"direct,* individual feedback on their own performances (not group indexes)."

The results of 19 studies were not all uniform, but there was a 13 percent drop in turnover rates among a large sample of service representatives when the control group (which went along in the old way) had a 9 percent increase. Other measures—productivity, quality of performance, customer reaction—either improved somewhat or held their own in the experimental group.

The second example comes from the studies by the Behavioral Research Service in the General Electric Company. These showed that (1) employees who were dissatisfied with their salaries were twice as likely to have thought of leaving the company as those who were satisfied; (2) engineers who left the company were more aggressive, independent, active, and creative than those who remained with a strong orientation toward engineering work; and (3) certain types of management practices contributed to turnover of "highly regarded" engineers. [17]

Recommendations based on these findings included careful monitoring of salary actions; assignment of young, high growth potential employees to experienced managers who had been successful in developing new talent; and giving these young people more individual responsibility and challenging work, gearing rewards and recognition to performance. Better transfer policies between departments, to reduce quits, were also recommended.

Mention should also be made of a separate study of 395 engineers and scientists in two laboratories not connected with either of the organizations mentioned above. The researcher tested a number of hypotheses on turnover by administering a questionnaire about work satisfactions while they were still employed. Factors most strongly associated with subsequent turnover included the feeling that it would help the person's career, low provisions for rewarding performance, and lower age and technical maturity. Managers seeking to reduce the turnover of high performers in the laboratory, and perhaps encourage some low performers to leave, were advised to select older persons who are strongly oriented toward their lab and weakly toward their profession; and perhaps most important, to reward good performance with higher pay and more opportunities for selection of work goals, advancement, and challenging work. [18]

THE NEED FOR A SYSTEMS APPROACH

These examples indicate the interrelationships between labor turnover and the personnel policy system. There are no simple solutions to the problem of excessive turnover. Careful analysis of the reasons why employees voluntarily leave their jobs, as we have seen in the earlier discussion, will often indicate a variety of factors, including supervisory treatment, feeling of unfair application of promotion or disciplinary policy, poor selection and training, inadequate or inequitable wages or salaries, and many others.

Managers, with the assistance of personnel administrators, need to consider the possible changes in current personnel policies and procedures which would reduce the causes of excessive labor turnover. When one change is made, its impact on other personnel policies should not be overlooked. For example, a change in relative rates of pay may require a reexamination of ladders of promotion. Or an improvement in selection methods may involve more active participation by managers in the selection process. A

[17] Glenn A. Bassett, *A Study of Factors Associated with Turnover of Exempt Personnel,* Personnel and Industrial Relations Services, General Electric Company, Crotonville, N.Y., August, 1967.

[18] George F. Farris, "A Predictive Study of Turnover," *Personnel Psychology,* vol. 24, no. 2, pp. 311–328, Summer, 1971.

sequence of interrelated actions may be necessary for effective reduction of excessive labor turnover.

ANALYZING INTERNAL MOBILITY

When managers show a similar interest in studying data on internal mobility, corresponding improvements in establishing and maintaining effective personnel relations may be expected. Why do people ask to be transferred from certain jobs and departments? Excessive transfer may be a disruptive and costly influence similar to excessive separation. In some ways, the situation is worse, since, whether or not the request for transfer is granted, the employee who was or remains dissatisfied is still a member of the work force and consequently may undermine group morale with his complaints and recriminations. Before concluding that the employee dissatisfactions are unreasonable, management needs to know, for instance, whether there are "blind-alley" or "dead-end" jobs held by employees who are not pensioners. Or are the jobs that employees try to leave simply the lower rungs on established ladders of promotion? If so, do all employees know the established sequence of job progression?

Again, are certain departments serving as training groups for personnel and as feeders of promotional candidates to be used by other departments? If so, why? The reasons for this may be twofold. The work in these departments may be of such a nature that it affords an excellent opportunity for introducing unskilled and semi-skilled workers to the organization. Or these departments may have limited opportunities for advancing employees who show special promise. In any event, management should be fully acquainted with these conditions in order to give supervisors full credit for the extra work involved in constantly breaking in new employees and developing good men. Conversely, the fact that one department head always asks for pro-

motional material from outside his own department may indicate to management that he is not doing a good job in bringing along his own people.

In these ways, analysis of internal mobility can throw light on local conditions and lead to new insight on what needs to be improved if dissatisfaction or even excessive labor turnover is to be prevented.

SUMMARY

Labor turnover can promote organizational health by bringing in new blood as well as providing expanding organizations with the additional human resources which they need. Internal mobility may help individuals and may improve teamwork by raising morale. But both require adjustment in people and among people. In labor turnover, particularly, these adjustments represent a cost, both in money and in human values. In order to determine whether this cost is offset by the gains that result, management needs to know what the cost amounts to, why employees are leaving, where voluntary separations are occurring, and who is quitting the firm. Exit interviews may be helpful, but studies show that employees do not always give the real reasons why they are leaving voluntarily.

Study of labor turnover with available objective data gives the line executive as well as the personnel administrator clues about what needs to be done in order to reduce grounds for dissatisfaction. Other leads may be obtained by analyzing internal mobility in the same way. But neither voluntary separations nor requests for transfer should be taken as a reliable index of the amount of instability that exists in the company in the form of employees dissatisfaction, for when other jobs in the community are scarce, employees are more likely to nurse dissatisfactions on the job than to quit the company. Even when jobs are plentiful, any one of a number of personal reasons may cause an employee to feel that, whatever his dissatisfaction, he must stay where he is.

This suggests that the analysis of complaints and grievances is an essential part of the program to prevent or reduce unnecessary labor turnover as well as excessive internal mobility. We turn in the next chapter to this subject.

SELECTED REFERENCES

Bassett, Glenn A.: *A Study of Factors Associated with Turnover of Exempt Personnel,* Personnel and Industrial Relations Services, General Electric Company, 1967.

Black, James Menzies: *How to Get Results from Interviewing: A Practical Guide for Operating Management,* McGraw-Hill Book Company, New York, 1970, chap. 9, "The Exit Interview," pp. 154-168.

Canfield, Grant W.: "How to Compute Your Turnover Costs," *Personnel Journal,* vol. 37, no. 11, pp. 413-417, 1959.

Chamberlain, Neil W.: *Management in Motion: The Corporate Decision-making Process as Applied to the Transfer of Employees,* Yale University, Labor and Management Center, New Haven, Conn., 1950.

Farris, George F.: "A Predictive Study of Turnover," *Personnel Psychology,* vol. 24, no. 2, pp. 311-328, Summer, 1971.

Gaudet, Frederick J.: *Labor Turnover: Calculation and Cost,* American Management Association, Research Study 39, New York, 1960.

Guest, Robert H.: "A Neglected Factor in Labour Turnover," *Occupational Psychology* (London), vol. 29, no. 4, pp. 215-231, October, 1955.

Henrichs, John R.: "The Exit Interview," *Personnel,* vol. 48, no. 1, pp. 30-35, January-February, 1971.

Hulin, Charles L.: "Job Satisfaction and Turnover in a Female Clerical Population," *Journal of Applied Psychology,* vol. 50, no. 4, pp. 280-285, August, 1966.

Lefkowitz, Joel, and Myron Katz: "Validity of Exit Interviews," *Personnel Psychology,* vol. 22, no. 4, pp. 445-455, Winter, 1969.

Ross, Ian C., and Alvin Zander: "Need Satisfactions and Employee Turnover," *Personnel Psychology,* vol. 10, no. 3, pp. 327-338, 1957.

Saleh, Shoukry D., Robert J. Lee, and Erich P. Prien: "Why Nurses Leave Their Jobs: An Analysis of Female Turnover," *Personnel Administration,* vol. 28, no. 1, pp. 25-28, January-February, 1965.

Shott, Gerald L., Lewis E. Albright, and J. R. Glennon: "Predicting Turnover in an Automated Office Situation," *Personnel Psychology,* vol. 16, no. 3, pp. 213-220, Autumn, 1963.

Suggestions for Control of Turnover and Absenteeism, rev. ed., U.S. Bureau of Employment Security, U.S. Department of Labor, Washington, D.C., 1962.

U.S. Bureau of Labor Statistics, "Measurement of Labor Turnover," rev. ed., Washington, D.C., 1966.

Chapter 13

Complaints and Grievances

The true significance of the grievance emerges only when we recognize the expression of dissatisfaction as a symptom of friction, of malfunctioning somewhere in this living structure of shop relationships.

Benjamin M. Selekman [1]

Dissatisfactions felt by employees, if they were all made known to management, might be the most significant index of organizational health. But unless employees have confidence that the procedure for handling complaints and grievances will bring prompt and fair action, many complaints will be suppressed by resentful employees. It cannot be assumed that what is unknown to management is necessarily unimportant. A suppressed complaint may be more damaging to morale and productivity than one which has been aired through an orderly procedure.

[1] Benjamin M. Selekman, *Labor Relations and Human Relations,* McGraw-Hill Book Company, New York, 1947, p. 110.

Essentially, a complaint and grievance procedure provides an upward channel of communication. A union may perform a useful function by insisting upon such a channel, encouraging employees to use it, and standing ready to protect complainants against reprisals from a minority of supervisors. Or a union may treat a relatively trivial dissatisfaction as though it were a serious grievance. A complaint and grievance procedure, therefore, may provide an opportunity for mutual understanding and solution of genuine complaints, or it may worsen existing relationships. The way in which it is used is often a reflection of the philosophies of management and union representatives. Managements and unions can derive lasting benefit from procedures for handling complaints and grievances only if they wish to learn from their experience. In this book, we are particularly concerned with what management can learn with the assistance of the personnel staff adviser.

DEFINITIONS

In analyzing complaints, it is important to distinguish various forms and stages of employee dissatisfactions. In doing so, we use the three words "dissatisfaction," "complaint," and "grievance," rather than using only the term "grievance," as is often done. It seems to us that it is important to make these distinctions because so many *complaints* are settled by first-level supervisors, and the underlying *dissatisfactions* eliminated, before the expressed dissatisfactions (complaints) become official grievances.

What do these three terms denote?

A *dissatisfaction* may be defined as anything that disturbs an employee, whether or not he expresses his unrest in words. For instance, a worker on incentive may be dissatisfied about the amount of time he must spend in looking for the small tools he needs. An engineer may be dissatisfied because he has to observe regular working hours, is underemployed, or has not received a raise in salary.

A *complaint* is a spoken or written dissatisfaction, brought to the attention of the supervisor and (in unionized firms) the shop steward. The complainant may or may not specifically assign a cause for dissatisfaction. Perhaps a worker complains about the shortage of small tools: "Four times this morning I've had to chase around looking for pliers." His complaint is more specific if he undertakes to fix responsibility, e.g., "I think management ought to give each of us all the tools we need." Or the complaint may be directed against a fellow worker: "We didn't have this kind of trouble before Joe came." Or, in continuous operations, workers on one shift may express their dissatisfaction with workers on the preceding shift: "Look what those butchers have done to our machine!"

In the language of labor relations, and from management's angle, a *grievance* is simply a complaint which has been formally presented, in writing, to a management representative or to a union official. But to most people, the word "grievance" suggests a complaint that has been ignored, overridden, or dismissed without due consideration. It seems unfortunate that the word "grievance" has become the accepted term for all formal complaints and descriptive of the procedure for dealing with them, the implication being that the aggrieved party has been the victim of injustice. Another meaning of "grievance" is a difference between management and the union over the interpretation or application of the terms of the collective bargaining agreement. Furthermore, at times a special kind of disciplinary action arises in connection with the dual function of union stewards and certain elected union officers. As regular employees of a company, these individuals are expected to observe rules of proper conduct that apply to all employees. But in their role as union representatives they are granted specially negotiated privileges to handle employee grievances. Unfortunately, occasions have arisen when managers have felt that certain aggressive union representatives exceeded the agreed-upon freedom to exercise their legitimate union function. "Research of cases published in *Labor Arbitration Reports* reveals that discipline and discharge cases concerning [some alleged impropriety of action during] a representative's grievance work is second only to violations regarding work stoppages as the most frequent area involving arbitration."[2]

---

[2] William H. Leahy, "Arbitration of Disputes over Grievance Processing by Union Representatives," *The Arbitration Journal,* vol. 26, no. 2, 1971, pp. 103–114.

WHAT DO COMPLAINTS SHOW ABOUT EMPLOYEES?

An alert supervisor or manager studies complaints (and grievances) as clues to further investigation. He tries to see them in this light rather than as nuisances to be disposed of. He tries to get beyond the words of complaints to reach the underlying meaning. If management is to act constructively on employee complaints, i.e., to use them as suggestions for improving company practices and procedures, they must be duly verified and evaluated. This process is not always as simple as it sounds, because not all kinds of complaints can be objectively verified. Therefore, it is important to ask: With what kind of complaint are we dealing?

Three Kinds of Complaints

In one of the early classic studies of employee complaints,[3] three types are differentiated according to content. The first type of complaint referred to tangible objects in terms that could be defined by any competent worker or engineer and that could be tested by physical procedures. "The machine is out of order," "This tool is too dull," "The stock we're getting now isn't up to standard," "Our cement is too thin and won't make the rubber stick." Relatively few complaints were of this type.

A second kind of complaint was based partly on sensory experience but depended primarily on the attendant, subjective reactions. "The work is messy," "It's too hot in here," "This job is too hard." Such statements include terms whose meanings are biologically or socially determined. Hence they cannot be understood unless one knows the complainant's background. Except in extreme cases, they are not entirely

verifiable by any objective procedure, scientific or otherwise. Handling wet green hides is a job that would readily be admitted by any reasonable person to be messy. On the other hand, a temperature of 68 degrees Fahrenheit may seem warm to one person and chilly to another.

A third category of complaints involved the hopes and fears of employees. Such complaints cannot be objectively verified unless reworded in such a way that the terms used to state judgments can be agreed upon by all concerned: "The supervisor plays favorites," "The pay rates are too low," "Seniority doesn't count as much as it should," "Ability is not properly recognized here." It was this category of complaint that proved most revealing to investigators, because it showed the importance of determining not only what the employees felt but also why they felt as they did. A necessary step toward remedying the conditions that were occasioning such complaints lay not in verifying the facts (the "manifest content") but in determining the personal reference (the "latent content"). For instance, questioning a worker who complained that his supervisor was a bully elicited the surprising statement, "He doesn't say 'good morning' to the help." Further talk revealed that the worker's dissatisfaction was rooted in his attitude toward *anyone* in authority rather than in the behavior of the supervisor of whom he complained.

This last type of complaint is most difficult to evaluate, as well as to deal with, because of its intermingling of fact and sentiment. Unfortunately, it is also the most frequent. A particularly difficult variant of this last kind of complaint is an employee's feeling that a specific job assignment is unsafe and would jeopardize his safety and health. This preoccupation often leads to direct refusal to obey work orders and exposes the employee to the charge of insubordination. Skill in situational thinking is needed to evaluate available evidence and establish to what extent,

[3] F. J. Roethlisberger and W. J. Dickson, *Management and the Worker,* Harvard University Press, Cambridge, Mass., 1939, pp. 225-269.

if any, the apprehensive employee has reasonable cause for alarm.[4]

COMPLAINTS ALSO SHOW SOMETHING ABOUT MANAGEMENT

By clarifying and studying complaints, it may be possible not only to learn what employees are feeling but also to get a clue to the way in which first-level supervisors are working with personnel. On this second point, more may be learned by studying the source and rate of expressed dissatisfactions.

Where Do Complaints Come From?

Are complaints coming from all over the organization? If so, the fault must lie in some major policy or company-wide procedure. If, however, complaints cluster in one area or a few areas, probably special conditions of work or of supervision need attention. Last, if complaints perpetually stem from a few employees, it may be that these people are misplaced, maladjusted, or suffering from special tension, or they may have other special characteristics. One study showed that grievants tended to have more education than nongrievants, were younger, more active in the union, had more unexplained absences, more tardiness, and lower hourly rates.[5]

The Number and Rate of Complaints

The number of complaints coming from any one part of the company or organization may show

---

[4] For an interesting case example of what an arbitrator upheld, see *Summary of Labor Arbitration Awards,* June 15, 1971, Report no. 147-7 (Arbitrator Charles L. Mullin, Jr., 1/22/71, Hercules Inc., Wilmington, Del., and OCAW, Local 8-667.) The five pages of the full opinion and award are made available by the American Arbitration Association, 140 West 51st Street, New York, N.Y. 10020.

[5] Howard A. Sulkin and Robert W. Pranis, "Comparison of Grievants with Non-grievants in a Heavy Machinery Company," *Personnel Psychology,* vol. 20, no. 2, pp. 111-119, Summer, 1967.

something. The question is: What does it show? If the number is unusually large in any one department, section, or group, it is commonly assumed by members of higher management that this circumstance indicates poor supervision, whereas if there is little or no expressed dissatisfaction in another part of the company, managers often take it for granted that everything is practically perfect there. Such unjustifiable conclusions are frequently used by executives as a basis for comparisons that are unfair to supervisors.

When uninformed judgments lead executives to point out to one supervisor that another foreman is more effective because his subordinates have fewer complaints, supervisors are provided with grounds for dissatisfaction. (Such dissatisfactions are perhaps all the more serious because it is unlikely that they would ever be officially expressed.) It is easy for an executive to offer a snap judgment: "Why aren't you all like Tom McCann? His men are perfectly happy." If it were equally easy for McCann's fellow supervisors to say what they feel, they might retort, "That's what you think!" Actually, the fact may be—and, if so, other supervisors probably know it—that the absence of expressed dissatisfactions is the result of "strong-arm methods" by which a supervisor suppresses complaints. Another supervisor may be receiving and reporting a large number of complaints because he is the kind of person to whom employees can talk freely and who is not afraid to report complaints up the line, if they imply a need for action beyond the scope of his authority.

No one can tell *what* is indicated by the number of complaints unless he takes into account *the rate* at which they are being expressed and understands the situation well enough to know how closely complaints correspond to facts. The rate is significant. A large number of complaints within a short time may be a healthy sign, for example, if it indicates that hitherto suppressed dissatisfactions have suddenly been released. Where there are people, there will be dissatisfactions. This human fact should be the starting point for appraising complaints. If for any reason dissatisfactions have been pent up, they will come out fast when people feel free to speak their minds. When not expressed in words, dissatisfactions will certainly be communicated sooner or later in undesirable actions, perhaps in requests for transfers or even in quits. When top management accepts this fact, it will be easier to help supervisors treat employee complaints not as time-consuming nuisances but rather as opportunities for better mutual understanding.

Thus a small number of complaints is an insufficient index that employee morale is high. The tentative judgment that all is well may be confirmed by taking cross bearings on other indexes of organizational health in the same work group. What is shown by the record for accidents, tardiness, absence, and separations? If all these records are favorable, can the tentative judgment be further confirmed by such positive signs as high productive efficiency and evidences of voluntary participation toward company objectives?

Of course, it may be that a large number of complaints does indicate a low degree of employee morale, especially when the complaints are spread over a long interval of time. In that case, the large number does not indicate a sudden improvement in communication. Therefore, if the complaints stem from one section or department, they may well point to the need for better supervision in that place. Or, if complaints are widely diffused, diagnosis and treatment should be at the level of company policy.

THE COMPLAINT AND GRIEVANCE PROCEDURE[6]

Further understanding of the extent to which company policy is operating to promote organizational health can be obtained by studying the established procedure for handling complaints and grievances. Setting up and maintaining this procedure are responsibilities of top management, whether employees are unionized or not.[7] In organized companies, union officials share this responsibility. There are more than 150,000 labor agreements between companies and unions in the United States, and nearly every one contains a formal grievance procedure. Formal procedures are less frequent in nonunionized firms or for nonunion employees, though no less necessary.

A standard procedure consists of the following steps:

1 The first step is taken when a dissatisfied employee presents a complaint to his immediate supervisor. This interview may be informal. Often the supervisor can say or do whatever is necessary to satisfy the complaint. In unionized companies, a dissatisfied employee usually has the contractual right to demand that his shop steward be present even at this first interview, and a written grievance is often filed, even at this first step.

If the complainant remains dissatisfied, e.g., because his supervisor cannot take action on the complaint or dismisses it out of hand as being without merit, the second step is in order.

2 At this stage, the complaint becomes an official grievance. In organized concerns, the written grievance not only states the original complaint but *also constitutes an appeal to higher management* against the action (or inaction) of a

---

[6] As pointed out on p. 229, it is common labor relations practice to use the term "grievance procedure" for the whole official system of dealing with both complaints and grievances. We think that it is important to distinguish between "complaints" and "grievances." But to avoid constant use of the cumbersome though accurate phrase, "complaint and grievance procedure," we have, where possible, used whichever word applies to the level of action to which we are referring at the time.

[7] For an example, see Reid L. Shaw, "A Grievance Procedure for Nonunionized Employees," *Personnel,* vol. 36, no. 4, pp. 66-70, July-August, 1959; and Neal E. Drought, "Grievances in the Non-union Situation," *Personnel Journal,* vol. 46, no. 6, pp. 331-336, June, 1967.

first-level supervisor. The management representative concerned at this stage is the next higher supervisor, usually the general foreman or the division superintendent. At this second step, the union representative is the chairman of the grievance committee, the business agent, or both.

3 As a final step *within* the organization, an unsettled grievance reaches the top level of local management and, in unionized firms, the international representative of the union or the union executive board.

4 In the great majority of grievance procedures (about 95 percent), the terminal step is voluntary arbitration, i.e., appeal to an impartial arbitrator or umpire whose decision the parties agree in advance to accept as final and binding. Arbitration usually is limited to grievances involving disputes over the interpretation or application of the labor agreement and not to grievances or proposals that might involve a *change* in the agreement. (A diagram showing these steps was presented in Chapter 8, p. 152.)

WHY GO THROUGH CHANNELS?

In saying that a complaint and grievance procedure should start at the level of the first-level supervisor, we are also saying—by implication—that the procedure should be formal, that complaints should go through channels.

However, many people do not share this view. Among those who disagree are many managers of small, nonunionized concerns. In their opinion, a formal complaint procedure is likely to do **more harm** than good. It seems to them that **requiring all** complainants to go through channels is inconsistent with the friendly relationship which a chief executive can and should establish with all his employees.

Many managers who shy away from a formal complaint procedure explain their position more or less as follows: "Of course there will occasionally be differences of opinion, and misunderstandings, between some of our employees and their immediate supervisors. When this happens, we're ready to explore the basis of 'gripes,' in friendly man-to-man discussions. We offer this standing invitation to all our people: 'If something is bothering you, and you don't feel free to take it up with your immediate supervisor, just drop in and let's talk it over.'"

THE "OPEN DOOR"

Managers who issue this invitation are enunciating what is often referred to as the "open-door" policy. At first glance, this policy may appear both suitable and workable, but we are convinced that it is unsound in principle. Experience has shown that, except in very small concerns, it is rarely workable. Of course, in a firm so small that the chief executive (or owner-manager) also functions as first-level supervisor, there is no need for a formal complaint procedure.

In large concerns, however, where there are several levels of management, it is organizationally unsound to invite employees to take complaints directly to a member of top management. Bypassing a lower supervisor in this way has at least two undesirable consequences. First, it prevents the supervisor from getting firsthand information that is stated or implied in the complaint. This is information that he should have, whether it concerns unsatisfactory working conditions or merely the feelings of some employee. Second, when the complaint is not presented to the supervisor by the complainant, members of **higher management** lose a valuable opportunity **to assess** a supervisor's skill. They do not know what action, if any, the supervisor would have taken to correct a ground for dissatisfaction or how effectively he might have helped the employee to accommodate himself to some circumstance that could not be changed.

Another way in which the open-door policy is unsound relates to action taken by top management. If an executive (having decided what is to be done about a complaint) sends an order down the line, he is stepping out of his executive role. He has spent time and thought in doing the work of a lower supervisor.

A further objection is that the open-door policy inevitably weakens line authority of people at organizational levels below and above the supervisor who was initially bypassed. First, such a supervisor loses face with the rank and file when a dissatisfied employee finds that it is possible to get corrective action by ignoring his supervisor and going straight to the top. Second, when the order for corrective action comes down the line, the originally bypassed supervisor is likely to appear in a poor light to his immediate superior. The latter may well ask: "Can't you handle your own subordinates?"

Aside from such purely organizational considerations, *two principles of common justice are violated* by any manager who makes an immediate decision to satisfy an employee who (either explicitly or implicitly) is complaining about his supervisor. These principles are (1) to hear the other side of the story (in any case where two people differ) and (2) to allow the accused to face his accuser (before rendering a verdict). But if the manager is to hear the first-level supervisor's story, then the dissatisfied employee is back where he started, with one important difference. Now the supervisor has, in effect, been called on the carpet, a circumstance that is unlikely to make him feel favorably disposed toward the complainant.

Several practical difficulties are associated with the open-door policy. Here are a few of them. Even if a manager calls in the supervisor and tries to get the whole story, he is likely to be too unfamiliar with the work situation in which the dissatisfaction developed to be able easily to evaluate the information that he gets. If he is to go into the case thoroughly, as though he were an impartial arbitrator, the time required is likely to be out of all proportion to the importance of the complaint.

Two other practical objections are rooted in human nature. One of these is often recognized by some such statement as this: "The open door may be used without prejudice to the employee." Such protection from reprisal would obviously be necessary if the open door were to work. But in making such a commitment, a manager is promising more than he can perform. How can he make good on his assurance of protection? An offended supervisor can bide his time. If he wants to retaliate, he can do so in devious ways. Of course, most supervisors are above such tactics, but there is considerable evidence that employees fear retaliation and are quick to misinterpret subsequent disciplinary action, however justifiable.

It seems that many rank-and-file employees have enough organizational sense to recognize the inherent impropriety and risks of acting on the open-door policy. Even some managers who announce this policy seem not wholly to believe all they say about it. For example, in one company with 21,000 employees, the manager was asked: "How many employees actually used the open door last year?"

He replied, "Eight."

"What did you think of them?"

"To be honest," he replied, "they were screwballs. Every one of them."

The open-door policy may also be improperly used by a personnel administrator. For instance, he may encourage employees to bring their dissatisfactions and difficulties directly to him, without first consulting their immediate supervisor. Such a legalized bypass of first-level supervisors undermines their authority. A personnel administrator has a poor conception of his function if he prides himself on being easily accessible as a person whom employees can trust and confide in. If such informal and direct appeals enable a subordinate to override or modify decisions by his immediate supervisor, the personnel administrator has usurped line authority. This may also happen under a formal union-management grievance procedure. For examples, see Case 8, "A Need for Policy-centered Thinking," Case 1, "The Old-line Foreman," and Case 13, "Factors in Promotion Policy."

Adjustment of Grievances in the Federal Service[8]

During the sixties, considerable progress was made in establishing progressive employee-management relations in the government service. A special task force—appointed by President Kennedy in 1961—held extensive public hearings and consulted various heads of federal departments and agencies. Subsequent recommendations were embodied in two Executive orders: (1) No. 10987, which established agency systems for appeals from adverse personnel actions; and (2) No. 10988, *Employee-Management Cooperation in the Federal Service,* January 17, 1962, providing for exclusive recognition when a union could prove that it represented a majority of workers in the unit and for arbitration of grievances if a union and a government agency made this part of their contract, as some of them had done.

On October 29, 1969, President Richard M. Nixon signed and issued Executive Order No. 11491. This was entitled *Labor-Management Relations* and replaced Executive Order No. 10988. The new Executive order recognized important changes that had taken place and established a Federal Labor Relations Council to coordinate federal policy in labor relations. A vital part of this council is a Federal Service Impasses Panel that handles impass disputes after negotiation and mediation have failed.

With the spread of the collective bargaining process to the public sector, initial differences in the structure and scope of Appeals Procedures for Public Employees are beginning to disappear. "In a recent study of 304 contracts from

state and local agencies, 90 per cent of the contracts contained negotiated grievance procedures similar to the private model; 55 per cent of the grievance procedures in the contracts allowed binding arbitration (an additional 9 per cent provided for advisory arbitration); and the scope of these procedures was quite broad."[9]

In line with these developments, the Air Force voluntarily established an appellate system for use by its civilian employees. This *Appeal and Grievance Procedure, Air Force Regulation (AFR) 40-771,* March 29, 1968, is essentially a three-stage advisory arbitration procedure which is administered by the Directorate of Civilian Personnel, H.Q. USAF.[10] Keystone of this system is the Air Force Appeal and Grievance Examiner. Each of the 18 functionaries was carefully selected in accord with merit principles and (with the assistance of the American Arbitration Association) provided with thorough and detailed training in the concepts and procedures followed by arbitrators. However, he has no authority to render merit decisions and must rely on the quality and persuasiveness of his report. His chief function is to assure due process.

THE LEVEL OF SETTLEMENT AS AN INDEX

When a formal procedure by which complaints can be processed through appropriate channels has been set up, experience with it should be studied for clues to supervisory ability in handling complaints. Of course, the level of settlement affords only a rough test, since many variables in the work situation are beyond the control of lower supervisors. This is most likely to be true if there is a militant union which, for

[8] Harold S. Roberts, *Labor-Management Relations in the Public Service,* University of Hawaii Press, Honolulu, 1970.

[9] James P. Begin, "The Private Grievance Model in the Public Sector," *Industrial Relations,* vol. 10, no. 1, p. 22, February, 1971.

[10] Seymour Alloy, "Grievance Handling without Union Representation—The Air Force Experience," in *Proceedings of New York University Twenty-second Annual Conference on Labor,* Thomas G. S. Christensen and Andrea S. Christensen (eds.), Matthew Bends, New York, 1970, pp. 337-352.

TABLE 13-1   Effectiveness of Grievance Administration Program at the Burbank Plant of the Lockheed Aircraft Corporation: 1960–1968

Year	Grievances filed	Number of employees	Percentage settled at step 1	Grievances filed per 100 employees
1960	3,000	18,000	33	17
1961	2,000	19,000	42	10
1962	2,400	23,000	43	10
1963	2,000	23,000	54	9
1964	2,200	21,000	52	10
1965	1,700	21,000	60	8
1966	2,200	22,000	58	10
1967	3,000	23,000	48	13
1968	1,500	22,000	54	7

Source: J. C. Pettefer, Division Manager of Labor Relations, Lockheed-California Company, "Effective Grievance Administration," *California Management Review,* vol. 13, no. 2, pp. 12–18, Winter, 1970.

internal political reasons, carries grievances as high as possible. However, since the complaint and grievance machinery and the labor agreement (if any) are the same throughout the company, significant differences in supervisory attitudes and skills may be indicated by the number of steps that had to be taken to settle employee complaints (or grievances).

The complaint procedure is functioning effectively if most complaints are being handled informally between the first-level supervisor and employees who feel dissatisfied, or in cooperation with the shop steward. When this is the case, management is to be congratulated both on the caliber of its first-level supervision and on the state of its labor relations.

For example, Table 13-1 shows the results achieved by union-management cooperation at the Burbank plant of the Lockheed Aircraft Corporation in the handling of complaints and grievances.

If, however, most of the complaints are being referred to the shop committee, as grievances for official settlement with the department head or superintendent, considerable delay is inevitable. Thus the ill effects of the initial dissatisfaction have time to grow and spread. Moreover, when a complaint has to be handled by formal negotiation, the opportunities are lost for spontaneous minor adjustments between people who work together and for the growth of mutual understanding that might have taken place during an informal settlement at the first level. In formal discussions, the complaint is usually settled by referring to the union contract—that "formal law of the shop." Necessary and useful as such a contract is, it is not always adequate as a means of settling underlying dissatisfactions. Too often the contract itself is silent on the very point that has led to the dispute.

When grievances cannot be settled before they reach the level of top management and officials of the international union, the situation becomes increasingly undesirable. The initial dissatisfaction has now become an issue that divides management and the union unless, or until, formal agreement can be reached. By that time, the initial complaint is likely to have become obsured by other issues and legalistic protocol.[11] At best,

[11] Grievances that have been reduced to writing gradually take "on the sterile, hygienically-respectable form of any other union-management business communication: crisply recorded, contractually identified by article, clause and paragraph, properly documented, carefully annotated, precisely correct, and precisely unsuited for gaining an understanding of what really occurred out on the shop floor." Earl J. Wyman, "Now Then, about That Grievance," *Personnel Journal,* vol. 50, no. 5, p. 403, May, 1971.

when a complaint is discussed by people who are unfamiliar with the work situation in which it developed, it cannot be understood in the same way as by insiders. [12]

Finally, a maximum expenditure of time and a considerable loss of employee good will are inevitable if the grievance cannot be settled between management and union representatives at any level but must be referred to arbitration. When this is necessary, such a long interval is consumed between the first expression of the dissatisfaction and the time when the arbitrator's decision finally reaches the employee that personnel relations are subjected to a considerable strain. Most complaints should be handled soon after they are expressed, and by the first-level supervisor. However, the opportunity for voluntary arbitration serves as an assurance that the grievance finally will be resolved, and in a way that accords with principles of justice. We do not underestimate the value of voluntary arbitration as a peaceful method of settling labor disputes, but it would be far better if dissatisfactions never reached the point where they required a ruling by an outsider. On the other hand, arbitration is useful not only in settling specific issues but even more because its method may be used as a model. Everyone who uses the complaint and grievance procedure may benefit by learning this method of impersonalizing issues.

An appeal to outside arbitration may result from a genuine incompatibility of the parties' interpretations of a clause in the labor agreement. When this happens, the arbitrator serves as an interpreter of the agreement, substituting his judgment for that of the parties to the dispute. However, if many complaints reach the stage of arbitration and especially if a given management and union are repeatedly unable even to agree on the wording of issues to be arbitrated, this indicates that labor relations are—at least temporarily—at a low level. [13]

The Attitude of Union Officers Makes a Difference

Sometimes resort to arbitration is necessitated by an intransigent attitude on the part of union leaders. For example, in a large machine-tool company, union members revolted against their leaders on the ground that they were becoming too management-minded. A new group was voted into office on the slogan, "We won't compromise with management. We'll take every case to arbitration and win for the union." The result of that shortsighted policy was disastrous. Not only did the grievance machinery become clogged with cases pending arbitration (98 cases on the docket), but with so many disputes to handle, union officers had little time to make an orderly and convincing presentation of the cases. As a result, in every decision the arbitrator had to rule against the union. After 3 months of such unsatisfactory experience, the members lost confidence in their new leaders also.

The action of union officers in unduly pressing complaints or in screening out unwarranted "gripes" is naturally affected by the security of their position. When union officers feel solidly established, they can afford to be reasonable and selective in processing complaints. But when they feel insecure, they may be tempted to press every complaint, regardless of its merit, in order

---

[12] For a case example of the experience in International Harvester, refer back to Chap. 8. The mediator-arbitrator who assisted in developing the system which reduced the backlog of unsettled grievances at the arbitration stage was David L. Cole. See his *Quest for Industrial Peace,* McGraw-Hill Book Company, New York, 1963, chap. 3; and Industrial Relations Counselors, Inc., *Grievance Handling: A Case Study of a New Approach,* Industrial Relations Memo no. 139, New York, 1961.

[13] For the suggestions of one arbitrator on how to improve grievance handling, see Maurice S. Trotta, "Handling Employee Complaints and Grievances," *Management of Personnel Quarterly,* vol. 6, no. 2, pp. 22-24, Summer, 1967. See also Ralph T. Seward, "Grievance Arbitration—The Old Frontier," chap. 6 in *Arbitration and the Expanding Role of Neutrals:* Proceedings of the 23d Annual Meeting, National Academy of Arbitrators, Montreal, Apr. 6-8, 1970, The Bureau of National Affairs, Inc., Washington, D.C., especially pp. 158-159, "Underlying conceptual structure of the grievance arbitration system."

to curry favor with rank-and-file union members whose votes they must have in order to remain in office.

In thinking about the complaint and grievance procedure, a manager (as well as a personnel administrator) naturally asks himself: What features should it have, so that dissatisfied employees may reasonably be expected to use it instead of resorting to direct action, e.g., by creating a work stoppage or going on strike?

DESIRABLE FEATURES OF A COMPLAINT PROCEDURE

It Should Be Demonstrably Fair

The attitude of supervisors is important here. All supervisors should accept the employees' *right of appeal* as long as there is no bypassing. In a unionized concern, supervisors should also accept the employees' right to be represented, if they so desire, by a union official. Such representation assures that a rank-and-file employee has the benefit of counsel from someone in his organization who has training and experience in presenting complaints.

Equally important is the willingness of all management representatives and all union leaders to resort to arbitration if necessary and to abide by the impartial arbitrator's award. Many nonunion companies have been unwilling to go all the way with the employees' right of appeal. They have refused to arbitrate unsettled disputes. In public employment there are many reasons why arbitration is not used as widely as in private industry. However, since 1965, an increasing number of state and local government units are adopting grievance arbitration clauses and placing considerable reliance on arbitration experience in the private sector.[14]

[14] See Joseph Krislov and Robert M. Peters, "Grievance Arbitration in State and Local Government: A Survey," *The Arbitration Journal,* vol. 23, no. 3, pp. 196–205, 1970. See also James P. Begin, "The Private Grievance Model in the Public Sector," *Industrial Relations,* vol. 10, no. 1, pp. 21-35, February, 1971; and Estelle R. Tracy (ed.), *Arbitration Cases in Public Employment,* American Arbitration Association, New York, 1969.

The Provisions Should Be Clear-cut

No grievance procedure can be expected to work satisfactorily unless there are definite provisions, consistently adhered to, determining *what* is to be done, *when,* and *by whom.* For example, every employee should know (1) to whom complaints are to be addressed, (2) in what form (oral or written), (3) what restrictions, if any, there are about when complaints can suitably be presented, and (4) how long a complainant should expect to wait before finding out what action has been taken or planned in connection with his complaint.

Unless these provisions are set up, made known, and consistently adhered to, it is unrealistic to expect that employees will cooperate by expressing their dissatisfactions to the appropriate authority, in the correct form, and at a suitable time.

It Should Be Simple

The complaint and grievance procedure should be sufficiently simple so that it can easily and quickly be explained to each new employee before he begins working for the company, and so that it can be readily understood even by a person who has had relatively little formal education. The success of any procedure for handling dissatisfactions depends on effective communication between employees and management representatives as well as union officials.

It Should Function Promptly

Prompt action is not only desirable from the complainant's point of view; it is also in management's interest. Undue delay can be costly in the growth and spread of employee dissatisfaction. While an employee is waiting to see what, if anything, management will do about his complaint, his dissatisfaction is apt to loom large in his mind. To management, this may seem unreasonable, since, in proportion to the scale of operations in a large enterprise, employee complaints are often so small as to seem practically invisible.

For example, when industrial operations involve millions of dollars, an accidental pay shortage of 21 cents may seem to management so trivial that nobody could possibly get excited about it. But experience shows that this is not the case. Added to other causes of dissatisfaction, even such a trifling matter often contributes to the impression that management does not care how workers feel and that this is simply another instance in which a worker has been "gypped."

It is more realistic to recognize the psychological fact that anything that annoys a person is important to him. He will brood over it and magnify its significance. The longer he broods, the more important it will seem to him, until finally his preoccupation may blot out all his more favorable impressions of the company.

Such a growth of dissatisfaction within one individual is not the only harmful effect of delay in handling complaints. Dissatisfactions are freely communicated among employees during lunch and rest periods, in the washroom, and even during work time. In this way, complaints are spread through work groups. They lose nothing in the telling, finding fertile soil in the latent antagonisms that are so often felt by workers toward higher management. Furthermore, any unnecessary delay (from the worker's viewpoint, any delay that he does not understand) constitutes another grievance. In union parlance, any unexplained delay is "stalling," a frequent and bitter complaint against management.

CRITERIA OF SUCCESS IN HANDLING COMPLAINTS AND GRIEVANCES

If a personnel administrator is interested in evaluating the degree of success achieved in handling a given complaint (or grievance), he may ask such test questions as the following:

1 Was the case handled in such a way that the parties directly involved were able to identify and agree upon what was at stake?

2 Was the incident closed with a sense of satisfactory adjustment by everyone immediately concerned with the original complaint?

3 Was the case handled in a way that strengthened line authority, especially at the level immediately above that at which the dissatisfaction was first expressed?

4 Did the solution result in a better mutual understanding and a better mutual adjustment between a supervisor and his subordinates?

5 Was there any spread of understanding, as a result of this case, to other people (in management and in the union—if there was one—as well as among other employees) who were *not* directly involved in the original complaint? Of course, this objective is not always attainable, but achievement of this aim can be facilitated by circulating decisions or interpretations of cases that were settled at the third or fourth step of the grievance procedure. For example, General Motors Corporation sends out umpire decisions to all members of management. In supervisory and management conferences this material is used as the basis for discussion and for developing policy thinking.

6 Did the solution contribute to operating efficiency?

THE ROLE OF THE PERSONNEL ADMINISTRATOR

Naturally, the personnel administrator should not step out of his role by making decisions, in the name of management, on complaints or grievances. His function is to help people to develop better understanding of causes of dissatisfaction, how complaints should be presented, and how they might be handled. To the extent that he succeeds in meeting these responsibilities, past dissatisfactions can lead to improvements in working conditions and in labor-management relations.

Unfortunately, however, an overly enthusiastic personnel administrator sometimes misconceives his role. He comes to think of himself as a policeman whose function it is to bring foremen into line and *tell* them how to handle complaints. The difficulties that may result from such inappropriate action by a personnel administrator are illustrated by the experience of an electrical-goods manufacturing firm. In this company it had become accepted practice to hold a formal "hearing" in the industrial relations office whenever the foreman and the shop steward could not by themselves settle a complaint.

A foreman who was called into the industrial relations office to give "his side of the story" usually considered himself being "called on the carpet" and was therefore on the defensive. Whereas before, in his own office, he was able to act as a sympathetic listener and "friend," he now found himself in the position of a defendant. The worker and his shop representative were the accusers. The union officials gave their moral support and in a sense acted as "legal aids." The supervisor of industrial relations acted as "trial examiner." The atmosphere of the meeting was legalistic, and both sides were more intent on "proving their case" than on trying to understand the underlying causes of employee dissatisfaction. Under these more formal conditions, foremen sometimes became embarrassed and undecided. They gave reasons and arguments different from what had been used in the shop, thereby blurring the issue. On such occasions, the supervisor of industrial relations was placed in the painful position of having to ask the foreman to clarify his statements or even having to correct him in the presence of workers, a shop steward, or other union official. This tended to place the foreman before the worker as one commanding less confidence than did the shop steward. Foremen naturally resented this, expressing their discouragement as follows: "We are nothing any more. If we don't get licked by the shop steward, we get hauled to the office and get licked there. What's the use? We might just as well sit down and say 'Sure!' to everything they say."

For a detailed example of a foreman's being "hauled to the office" by the personnel director who oversteps his staff position, see Case 1, "The Old-line Foreman."

SUMMARY

The purpose of both a line manager and a personnel administrator in analyzing complaints and grievances is to help raise employee morale and to increase operating efficiency. The method of analysis should include study not only of expressed dissatisfactions but also of the procedures and skills by which complaints (and perhaps also grievances) are handled.

One can profitably start by differentiating among dissatisfactions, complaints, and grievances. It is also important to distinguish different kinds of complaints, e.g., those which revolve chiefly around tangible objects or working conditions and those which seem to be primarily subjective. By using imagination and the skills of interviewing, a supervisor may be able to uncover the latent content of a disguised complaint. If so, perhaps he can bring to light hidden dissatisfactions and thus open the way for (1) improvement of working conditions, (2) more effective supervision, or (3) a better adjustment and a clearer understanding by someone who thought he had grounds for dissatisfaction.

Complaints may show something about the effectiveness of supervision, especially if their number, rate, and spread are studied as interrelated variables.

Top management and the union, if any, are responsible for setting up a formal procedure. In a large concern, the standard grievance process goes through at least *three* steps inside the organization. If necessary, resort to arbitration constitutes a fourth step. Some managers, especially in small, nonunionized concerns, prefer the open-door policy. But there are serious disadvantages to this way of handling complaints, except in companies so small that bypassing does not occur.

When complaints go through channels, the level of settlement is worth studying. If many complaints have to be processed all the way up to top management or even to arbitration, supervisors at lower levels lack skill in dealing with personnel, or the attitude of employees or their representatives is unreasonable, or both. The inevitable delay before settlement at top levels or by arbitration allows time for dissatisfactions to grow and to spread. A large number of arbitration cases usually indicates a low level of labor relations and of personnel relations. Any delay is likely to make matters worse.

Top management is responsible for seeing to it that the complaint and grievance procedure is fair, clear-cut, simple, and prompt in operation. In trying to assess how well such a procedure works, a personnel administrator can look for evidence of the extent to which any given settlement has resulted in (1) a better understanding by and between the people directly and indirectly concerned, (2) better adjustment by, or to, the complainant, (3) a strengthening of line management, and (4) greater operating efficiency.

In a complaint and grievance procedure, the role of a personnel administrator is indirect. His job is neither to settle complaints nor to tell supervisors what they should decide. His concern is primarily as a student and a teacher. What can he learn from complaints and from the way they are handled? If it seems that morale is far higher and supervision is far more effective in some parts of the company than in others, can he do a better job as a teacher? Can he help less effective supervisors to develop more managerial capacity? If complaints are widespread, what recommendations can he make that might remove causes of dissatisfaction which stem from undesirable working conditions?

In addition to learning and teaching all he can in connection with complaints, a personnel administrator naturally turns his attention to other employment activities. In all parts of the company, and at all stages of the employment process, are existing policies, procedures, and practices effectively promoting a high degree of teamwork?

SELECTED REFERENCES

Ash, Philip: "The Parties to the Grievance," *Personnel Psychology,* vol. 23, pp. 13–37, 1970.

Begin, James P.: "The Private Grievance Model in the Public Sector," *Industrial Relations,* vol. 10, no. 1, pp. 21–35, February, 1971.

Cole, David L.: *The Quest for Industrial Peace,* McGraw-Hill Book Company, New York, 1963, chap. 3, "The Grievance Function," pp. 69–94.

Drought, Neal E.: "Grievances in the Non-union Situation," *Personnel Journal,* vol. 46, no. 6, pp. 331–336, June, 1967.

Fairweather, Owen: "A Comparison of British and American Grievance Handlings," pp. 1–18 in *Developments in American and Foreign Arbitration,* Proceedings of the 21st Annual Meeting, National Academy of Arbitrators, Cleveland, Ohio, January-February, 1968, Bureau of National Affairs, Inc., Washington, D.C., 1968, pp. 1–18.

Hart, Wilson R.: "The U.S. Civil Service Learns to Live with Executive Order 10988: An Interim Appraisal," *Industrial and Labor Relations Review,* vol. 17, no. 2, pp. 203–220, January, 1964.

Seward, Ralph T.: "Grievance Arbitration—The Old Frontier," chap. 4 in *Arbitration and the Expanding Role of Neutrals,* Proceedings of the 23d Annual Meeting, National Academy of Arbitrators, Montreal, April 6–8, 1970, The Bureau of National Affairs, Inc., pp. 153–163, especially, Underlying Conceptual Structure of the Grievance Arbitration System, pp. 158–159.

Slichter, Sumner H., James J. Healy, and E. Robert Livernash: *The Impact of Collective Bargaining on Management,* The Brookings Institution, Washington, D.C., 1964.

U.S. Department of Labor: Major Collective Bargaining Agreements: Grievance Procedures, Bureau of Labor Statistics, Bulletin no. 1425-1, Washington, D.C., 1964.

Developing Human Resources: A Personnel Policy System

INTRODUCTION

The six chapters in this section deal with interactive policies, techniques, and procedures which together can help to develop the human assets of an organization. Line managers and staff personnel can cooperate to make sure that all these activities are planned and administered with that aim in mind.

For that purpose all employment procedures and every step in the employment and career-development process need to be consistent with each of the others and also with policies which take account of relevant personnel concepts, e.g., that every employee is a *whole person,* with characteristically human needs, which are also partly unique, and that *inner motivation* can be more powerful than any externally imposed controls in achieving organizational objectives.

Special demands for effective planning and implementation need to be met when new employees have come into an organization from a different culture, perhaps also with relatively little formal education, and possibly with no previous experience of steady employment.

Job description and analysis, presented in Chapter 14, can be important assets in any organization. A complete set of job (and position) descriptions offers a functional view of the whole organization. Job descriptions that (1) clarify current job requirements and work relationships, (2) differentiate between primary and secondary duties, and (3) supply analytical judgments (supported by substantiating data) to show degrees of difficulty associated with job factors can be useful at every stage in the employment process, from recruiting to retirement. Job descriptions can be supplemented by joint target setting during progress reviews. Thus they can offer the incentives for self-development that are supplied at higher organizational levels by position guides.

Recruitment, selection, and placement procedures (Chapter 15) can be designed to attract a suitable number of candidates who are qualified (or can rapidly become qualified) to meet established standards for work and for conduct. By applying tested procedures in these early stages of the employment process, management representatives can do much to ensure that each new employee understands how he can best contribute to organizational goals and is willing and able to do his share as a participating member (and not merely as one who has met minimum requirements for collecting pay). The first placement is both an important decision and a critical experiment in which employees and supervisors test judgments made earlier. A successful placement is one in which a new employee finds that this is a good place to work and proves that he is willing and able to meet high standards for technical performance and to function effectively with other employees in a small work group.

Training and performance appraisal (Chapter 16) are responsibilities which can most effectively be met by cooperation between line managers, staff experts, and the employees who need training and whose performance needs to be appraised. Induction, orientation, and training are ways of preparing employees for productive work. Thus they are at least partly responsibilities of line management. But staff experts can be useful in planning and conducting training programs, as well as revising former programs which fail to meet new needs. The success of training is measured by subsequent performance on the job. That performance can be appraised in any one of a number of ways. Whatever method of appraisal is used, objectivity in making judgments and accuracy in keeping records are essential. Otherwise managers are not in a position to demonstrate that decisions based on performance appraisal are nondiscriminatory.

Promotions, transfers, and separations (Chapter 17) are employment activities in which managers can meet various specific responsibilities within the overall obligation to build the human organization. A company policy for promotion can be accepted by the union when objective evidence is written into the records. Seniority can be accepted by management, as a factor to be considered when a responsible union has agreed that demonstrated ability is a prerequisite for promotion. Implementing procedures can include establishing and communicating clear-cut ladders of promotion, posting job openings, and offering opportunities for employee development. Transfer can be used as a procedure for increasing an individual's job satisfaction, providing opportunities for psychological growth or better teamwork, and avoiding layoff.

If downgrading or layoff becomes necessary, the action taken should always be consistent with affirmative employment policies (such as those implemented in selection, hiring, and promotion). Permanent layoffs should be planned as far in advance as possible, whether the employee's working life is to be ended or merely continued in another environment.

Constructive discipline (Chapter 18) is consistent with personnel policies for managing by shared objectives because its primary purpose is educational and because it can be administered in ways which reinforce self-discipline and group controls. According to this concept of discipline, penalties are applied only after educational efforts have failed. A written statement of company policy, and of implementing procedures, can guide supervisory decisions during a series of steps from a friendly talk, through formal warnings (oral and written), up to disciplinary layoff, or even discharge. A responsible union can accept discharge for "just cause" when that decision has been made after "due process."

Managing changes in jobs and work schedules (Chapter 19) can implement management's purpose to help employees (and union officials) understand the reasons for managerial decisions. By advance planning and consultation, managers can also offer support to employees who must make the adjustments required by technological advances and new work relationships.

CASES IN PART 2 THAT RELATE TO SECTION D

4 The Girl and the Computer
6 Conflict of Interest?
9 The "Outside" Inspectors
10 The Rejected Applicant for Employment (New Engineer)
11 Will More Money Be a Motivator?
12 An Engineer and a Machinist (Need for Orientation and Explanation)
13 Factors in Promotion Policy (Selection of a Head Lift-truck Operator)
14 Discharge for "Proper Cause"?
15 Discharge for "Insubordination"
16 Approaches to Introducing Job Changes
17 Difficulties Connected with Work Scheduling

Chapter 14

Job Description and Analysis

Written job descriptions have been developed by many companies in an attempt to define clearly and without ambiguity the duties and responsibilities of each job. The [job descriptions] can be either an asset or a liability, depending on the way they are used.

Norman R. F. Maier and L. Richard Hoffman[1]

Job description and analysis are topics that evoke a range of opinions—some of them extreme. For example a laboratory manager expressed himself like this: "Job descriptions? No sir, not for me. I'd like to scrap them all. They just limit your freedom to make necessary work assignments. You need somebody in a hurry to take an instrument across the street for calibration. And what do you get? An argument: 'That's not in my job description. I'm a technician, not an errand boy!'"

[1] Norman R. F. Maier and L. Richard Hoffman, "Overcoming Superior-Subordinate Communication Problems in Management," in Norman R. F. Maier et al., *Superior-Subordinate Communication in Management,* American Management Association, Research Study no. 52, New York, 1961, p. 32.

An opposing view, equally extreme, was expressed by the technician who presented the "argument" that his duties precluded running errands: "Without a written job description, I'd be lost. How would I know what my job is? The description gives me a fix on job requirements and shows me how I fit into the organization. Without it I'd be all at sea. Around here, everything is an emergency. But my job description tells me exactly what my job is and what I have to do."

One could go on indefinitely quoting opinions about whether or not job descriptions are useful, but many of these different views have common denominators. They are highly emotional and represent a strictly "I" view (being biased by

247

personal experiences and feelings). Usually they are exaggerated and oversimplified. Anyone who wants to think clearly about the nature and purpose of job descriptions must come closer to verifiable objective facts than he can get by merely listening to what amounts to expressions of individual attitudes. But a good listener, who can analyze and sort out what he hears, can start toward understanding by noting advantages and disadvantages that have been highlighted in such emotional statements.

For example, when a manager rejects the very idea that job descriptions for lower-rated employees should be written down and used, his main argument seems to be that these procedures would deny him the freedom and flexibility which he must have (in his own job and dealing with subordinates) to meet the responsibilities of his position. If that is what he says, he is making a point that needs to be thought about—objectively and in context. Perhaps what has set him against job descriptions is not valid uses of them but frequent abuses.

Often employees have used narrowly defined and inflexible job descriptions as ammunition in the cold-war tactics commonly referred to as "employee resistance to change." When requested to do something a little different from what they have always done, or when instructed to perform a routine task by a somewhat different method, they have balked. Frequently, their union representatives have backed them up, arguing that there should be no deviation from stated job requirements unless there has been a demonstrable and substantial change in the nature of the job. That argument deserves consideration chiefly because it emphasizes the need to think about job descriptions, job requirements, and work assignments as integrally related parts in a total "system" or work situation.

Instead of picking up bits and pieces taken from a range of opinions about job descriptions, we can get to the heart of the matter more quickly by following up a few key questions:

1 What is job description and analysis?
2 How are job descriptions made?
3 What are major criteria for a well-made job description?
4 What are standard uses of job descriptions?
5 How might job description and analysis be most effectively used by managers and subordinates in working toward shared objectives?

WHAT IS JOB DESCRIPTION AND ANALYSIS?

A job description is a word picture (in writing) of the organizational relationships, responsibilities, and specific duties that constitute a given job or position. It defines a scope of responsibility and continuing work assignments that are sufficiently different from those of other jobs to warrant a specific title. For example, the *Dictionary of Occupational Titles*[2] gives standard job definitions, stating in each case *what* gets done, *how* it is done, and, *why* it is done. The job definitions also provide information on (1) functions performed by the worker, and (2) significant aptitudes, interests, and temperament required for adequate performance.

Functions In varying degrees, every job involves the incumbent with *data* (information, ideas, facts, statistics); *people,* and *things* (tangible materials, tools and equipment). In each instance, functions not only form interactive hierarchies, ranging from relatively simple to complex functions, but do so in such a manner that each successive relationship includes those that are simpler and excludes the more complex.[3]

---

[2] 3d ed., Vol. I, *Definition of Titles,* U.S. Department of Labor, Washington, D.C., 1965.
[3] See *Occupational Classification and Industry Index,* 3d ed., vol. II, appendix A, U.S. Department of Labor, 1965, pp. 649-650, for a detailed explanation of relationships within data, people, and things hierarchies. Appendix B (pp. 651-656), provides an explanation of worker trait components.

Exhibit 14-1   A General-purpose Form for Job Description and Analysis

Name of company, department, and section
Date: **Job code:**

I Occupational classification (title of job or position)
II Organizational relationships:
    A Reports to: [Include statement of the kind and degree of supervision received.]
    B Supervises: [Include statement of the kind and degree of supervision given.]
    C Coordinates with:
III Summary: [Condensed statement of primary functions.]
IV Work performed: [Description of specific duties, showing approximate percentage of time spent on each.]
    A Principal duties: [Functional specialties.]
    B Subsidiary activities: [Often subdelegated.]
    C Combination tasks: [May be coordinated with persons in other organizational units.]
V Information on job requirements: [To be used for job evaluation. We omit specific subheadings here because they necessarily vary not only with the level of the job described, but also according to the job-evaluation system currently in use in each organization. Some organizations include in this section qualifications for incumbents, and/or specifications of job standards. For illustrative material, see the factors used by NEMA for hourly rated jobs, cited in Chapter 20, p. 371.] See also *Job Description and Classification Manual—for Hourly Rated Production, Maintenance and Non-Confidential Clerical Jobs,* United Steelworkers of America, AFL-CIO and Coordinating Committee Steel Companies, January 1, 1963.

Exhibit 14-1 presents our concept of a general-purpose form which may be used to list information needed to make systematic job descriptions. This work sheet not only lists static job features to be described and analyzed but also indicates interdependent organizational relationships and opportunities for exercising discretion.[4]

Variations in Nature and Amount of Information

The information that belongs in each subsection of such a form differs according to the nature of the job being described, and so does the length of the document as a whole. For example, the description of a simple, unskilled job can be short. As job content enlarges to include more and greater responsibilities, Sections IV and V need to be expanded. For middle-management positions, lists of duties may cover two or three printed pages and include some 20 different items. Toward the top of the management hierarchy, however, a position description can again be relatively brief. For a chief executive, whose job consists essentially in exercising foresight and judgment, the list of responsibilities emphasizes corporate goals and style of managing.[5]

Different Categories of Job Descriptions

Traditionally, there have been at least three categories:

    1 Hourly rated employees—direct and indirect labor

[4] See Ishwar Dayal, "Role Analysis Technique in Job Descriptions," *California Management Review,* vol. II, no. 4, pp. 47–50, Summer, 1969, for a discussion of these dynamic aspects.

[5] J. C. Wofford, "Behavior Styles and Performance Effectiveness," *Personnel Psychology,* vol. 20, no. 4, pp. 461–495, Winter, 1967.

2 Salaried employees—supervisory, technical, and office occupations

3 Salaried employees—managers, professionals, and executives

Position Descriptions In companies that have written descriptions and analyses of managerial positions, the form used is likely to be somewhat different from that on which hourly rated jobs are described. A survey of 140 companies made under the auspices of the American Management Association showed that the form most commonly used is divided into two or three sections covering the following topics:

> **I** *Function* (sometimes called "basic function," or "objective"). This section provides information similar to that given in the job summary of an hourly rated job. It gives a brief but broad statement of the job as a whole,[6] the mission to be accomplished.
>
> **II** *Duties* (or "duties and/or responsibilites," or "principal activities"). The content of this section corresponds to material given in Section IV of our general-purpose form. Usually it makes up the bulk of a position description, and often it gives a fairly precise account of functional responsibilities.
>
> **III** *Authority* (or "relationships," or sometimes "responsibilities and authority." If the last heading is used, Sections II and III are usually combined into one). Information given under "Authority" corresponds, at managerial levels, to the content of Section II in our general-purpose form.

In many companies, the chief aim (in this section of the position description or guide) is to give a "charter" or "grant of authority." Other

companies stress the other side of the coin, emphasizing the limits of authority. Whatever the emphasis, material given clarifies and amplifies information shown by the organization chart. Many companies describe "authority" and "relationships" in separate sections. Some companies add a final section. This may include specifications for a job holder and standards for job performance.

More important than minor differences in forms used for job and position descriptions, and especially for position "guides," are differences in the purposes for which these documents are written. According to the AMA survey, 74 respondents explained that the difference between position and job descriptions in their companies was that position descriptions emphasize *what* needs to be done rather than *how* assignments are to be met. Referring to "position guides," the National Industrial Conference Board reported that "the position guide does not attempt to describe in detail the specific [current] responsibilities of the job. . . . It does outline the broad responsibilities that must be carried out if the position under study is to carry its weight in an integrated, balanced organization structure."[7] In other words, the position guide points to an ideal toward which the incumbent is expected to strive. According to the AMA survey, the most common explanation for the differences in form and content between job and position descriptions was that the former are written primarily for wage and salary administration, while the latter are designed for use in organization planning. However, that same survey showed that in many organizations, even position descriptions are used entirely for wage and salary administration.

Not all companies have job descriptions for all three of the categories mentioned above. Of the

---

[6] C. L. Bennet, *Defining the Manager's Job: The AMA Manual of Position Descriptions,* American Management Association, Research Study no. 33, New York, 1958, p. 11. For examples of position descriptions, see pp. 192-415.

[7] *Preparing the Organization Manual,* National Industrial Conference Board, Inc., Studies in Personnel Policy, no. 157, New York, 1957; cited in *ibid.,* pp. 12-13.

140 companies covered by the AMA survey, only 30 percent replied that they had descriptions for all positions. But any organization that has job descriptions at all makes them for hourly rated employees, and, historically, describing this kind of job came first. Because job descriptions for hourly rated employees are so generally accepted and widely applied, we shall start by centering attention on them.

MAKING JOB DESCRIPTIONS

What a job description is and how useful it can be—as a practical instrument—are matters that depend in large measure on who made it and how it was made. At worst it is an incomplete list of duties, perhaps also ineptly titled and unclearly worded. Such an inadequate sketch may have been made by a busy supervisor. Perhaps he was in a hurry and possibly also afraid of making the job sound as though it should be more highly paid for than it is. Or the writer may have been an incumbent who was asked to fill out a questionnaire, but perhaps he was so new that he did not yet fully understand what all his duties were, or he may have been on the job for so long that familiarity had blurred the edges of his perception. He knew by long habit what he was supposed to do, but he could not put that knowledge into precise words. Experience shows that although a job holder and his immediate superior can be helpful in providing information and in editing a written statement, neither of them alone nor even both together can be expected to write an accurate, comprehensive, unbiased, and clearly worded description of job duties and report relationships. Nor do they have the specialized knowledge and skills required for job analysis.

An Assignment for a Specialist

For this assignment a specialist is needed. He may be a member of the personnel department, or he may be an outside consultant. Wherever the job analyst comes from, he should bring with him an impartial attitude (he should have no axe to grind) and an ability to understand quickly and to describe clearly job requirements in different work situations. He also needs the specialized training and practical experience which enable him to clarify the difference between primary and secondary duties (to be described in subsection IV, A, and B, in Exhibit 14-1) and to identify and weigh elements of a job that are classified as job factors.

Special Knowledge and Resources The services of a well-informed specialist are most evidently needed in regard to job factors and their relative importance. The job analyst must be thoroughly familiar with the job-evaluation system currently used in the organization (or with a system that he, as a consultant, will recommend). This background tells him what job factors to look for. His task will be to supply the detailed information needed to substantiate his analysis.[8] For example, under the job factor "physical effort," he notes to what extent lifting heavy weights is a job requirement. In making such a determination he is guided by a series of definitions that indicate what degree of physical effort is involved.

Or the question may be whether or not a specific job requires "analytical ability." If so, in what degree? Does the job call for relatively little analysis, merely comparing simple visual forms, such as numbers or letters? Or must the incumbent be able to analyze intangible problems that are difficult to appraise because quantitative measurements cannot be applied?

[8] However, it should be emphasized that *job analysis* is different from *job evaluation.* Information provided by the job analyst is used by another specialist in grading—evaluating—jobs and in establishing a wage and salary structure. See Chap. 20. See also *Job Analysis,* Personnel Policies Forum, Survey no. 79, Bureau of National Affairs, Washington, D.C., 1966.

Practitioners often debate the respective merits of different grading systems. To settle such differences, it may be useful to refer to the *Guide for Analyzing Jobs,* issued by the U.S. Employment Service. In any given organization, an all-important point is this: once a system has been chosen, the *same yardstick should consistently be applied to all jobs in the organization.*

A working knowledge of general semantics is also useful to a job analyst. He may not have taken a college course in that subject, but if he is genuinely interested in thinking out and writing down a description that is as accurate as possible, long practice can sharpen his innate abilities. For example, he can increase his skill in "straight reporting," the ability to describe facts as observed without interjecting opinions. Naturally the job analyst expresses opinions in selecting job titles and in analyzing job factors, but when he undertakes to *describe facts as he saw them,* he should stick to that assignment.

The Process of Describing and Analyzing a Job

Getting and stating facts as accurately as possible are only parts of the job analyst's assignment, which should be carried out as a five- or six-step process, according to whether or not there is a union in the picture.

1 *The first step is to gather factual material.* At best the job analyst (prepared with specialized knowledge and information) does this on the job site. He watches job holders at work and talks with them. If permitted, he may support his findings by taking snapshots. Perhaps he can pick up other illustrative material, such as sample forms for records and reports. He then confirms, corrects, and supplements his initial observations by checking with the immediate supervisor.

At this stage, and later when his first draft is reviewed, the job analyst needs a certain amount of organization sense, and considerable aptitude,

insight, and experience as an interviewer. For example, before talking with a job holder, a job analyst clears with the immediate supervisor. Presumably all incumbents are busy people. If they are interrupted in the middle of a specially urgent assignment they, or their supervisors, or both, may feel annoyed. When a job analyst is making a whole series of descriptions, he can easily adapt the timing of interviews to suit the convenience of supervisors, or perhaps a given job holder is having an "off day." If so, this will be apparent to a perceptive interviewer, who will then find an acceptable excuse for postponing the interview.

When he does talk with the job holder (and others) about a given job, he should have the skills needed to conduct a relatively directed type of interview. He also needs the perceptiveness and self-control which will help him to avoid even appearing to dominate the talk.

Here is an abbreviated statement of some specific suggestions that were derived from broad experience:

> Be sure the worker understands that it is the *job* and not the *person* being described.
>
> [Help the job holder to talk about] "what he is paid for" rather than "what he does."
>
> Control the interview within reason by establishing the "big pieces" pattern [main functions], patiently returning to the subject when digressions occur. But remember that the worker is human and that the analyst must work in a persuasive manner.
>
> Do not tell the worker what he does. Let *him* describe the job.... Help him organize his thinking, but avoid putting words into his mouth.
>
> Give the worker a chance to talk about his job. If he has assembled an outline or exhibits ahead of time, be courteous. Do not brush them aside. Quite often they are helpful. Even more important, avoid giving the impression of rushing the worker or discounting what he considers valuable. [9]

[9] John W. Thompson, "Functional Job Descriptions," *Personnel Journal,* vol. 30, no. 10, pp. 380–388, March, 1952, especially, How to Conduct a Controlled Interview, pp. 387–388.

In preparing a job (or position) description [10] it is essential to work thoroughly, objectively, efficiently, and courteously with the jobholder to accomplish something which together they can do better than either could do by himself. These specifications hold whether interviews are held with hourly rated personnel or with managerial representatives. In a sense, the job analyst is an ambassador. He comes from a realm toward whose "citizens" workers often entertain considerable suspicion and even hostility. The same may be said, with more emphasis, about relationships in many companies between management experts and union officials. Partly for this reason, we recommend that in a unionized concern the job analyst also talk with the shop steward (after interviewing the incumbent and his immediate supervisor), even at this first stage in making a job description. To do so may communicate management's intention to have job descriptions so accurate and job analyses so fair that no reasonable person could dispute them. If the shop steward finds something inaccurate or unacceptable about the job analyst's preliminary observations, it is well to know about the difference of opinion as soon as possible. Perhaps the job analyst has not noticed or been told about something that he needs to know. Or perhaps the shop steward misunderstands the purpose of making, or revising, job descriptions. The sooner such gaps in observation or differences of opinion can be brought to light, the better.

If the job is a new one or has been substantially changed since it was last analyzed, the question of an appropriate title arises. That point may profitably be considered even in the first stage of observing what the job is. Perhaps the job analyst may find it useful to bring up the question of a job title in talking with incumbents, with a supervisor, and even with a shop steward, before he makes his own decision about what title most accurately represents current job requirements.

2 The job analyst now puts his notes together, as a (hopefully) complete draft, using a standard job-description form. Every item of information on it is important, including the date. Precision language (whenever possible in simple, direct verbs) should be used to describe exactly what the jobholder does.

3 The job analyst now takes his draft back to the persons with whom he talked in step 1: the job holder, the supervisor (and perhaps also a shop steward). As they review his draft, what, if anything, will they want to add or to modify?

At this point, suggested corrections or other remarks made may call for self-control by the job analyst. He is frequently tempted to exclaim, "Well, for Pete's sake, why didn't you mention this before?" However, a qualified analyst will swallow whatever annoyance he may feel and patiently listen to what is said now. Perhaps much of the interview material is repetitious or beside the point, but some of it may be new and relevant. Whenever a job analyst is on the job site, he has opportunities to demonstrate to employees and their representatives his thoroughness of method and integrity of purpose. For example, in a second interview, he again asks questions trying to bring out information that is more detailed or more accurate than what he picked up before. Jobholders often forget to mention occasional duties. Information on these can be elicited by asking about record forms or instruments that were not in evidence during the job analyst's first visit. In such ways he can indicate management's purpose to take account of every job requirement, no matter how insignificant it may seem to the jobholder or how infrequently it has to be met.

4 The job analyst now revises his first draft, incorporating any new information that can

---

[10] For a sample interview, conducted at the AMA central office in New York as a demonstration of topics to be covered and skills needed, see Bennet, *op. cit.,* pp. 95-107. In relation to the subject matter of that interview, compare ideas suggested by Hemphill (p. 263 of this text).

make his description and analysis more accurate and more informative.

5 A completed set of drafts can then be correlated by inserting a code number, as the job descriptions are grouped in blocks. Code sequences indicate departments, divisions, or functions so that any manager or staff expert can quickly find whatever job description he needs to use.

Making Position Descriptions At managerial levels, the nature of job duties and the purposes for which position descriptions are to be used have convinced some managers that incumbents (rather than specialists) should draft—or even write—descriptions of their own duties and organizational relationships. Accordingly, the longer process which we have just outlined may be shortened to a two-step process of (1) drafting and (2) reviewing and approving. If higher management thinks that revision is needed, that activity may be interpolated as another intermediate step, and perhaps repeated before final approval is given. An integrative solution between having a manager write his own description and having it done for him by his immediate superior or by a specialist may be to make it a committee project. The incumbent, his immediate supervisor, and a specialist may bring notes to a meeting during which they compare factual information or analytical judgments. Afterwards the specialist (who presumably has more time to devote to this project) can submit a draft which would be reviewed in a second conference among the same three persons.

In relation to job descriptions, what is done next depends on whether or not the firm is unionized, and on management policies and practices for communicating with union officials. If there is a union, and if policy is to review job descriptions with union representatives before issuing the descriptions as official, then:

6 The completed draft may now be reviewed with top officials of the local union. This step cannot be required of any manager, but in our opinion it is good labor relations practice. However, it should be made clear that management is not submitting a draft for union approval. What is being done is extending to the union advance notice of a draft that is ready for final management approval. If union officials have ideas for making changes, management should consider them—as suggestions. Some joint evaluation systems, however, require joint agreement on job descriptions.

Getting Final Approval

We do not include this step as part of the process by which job descriptions and analyses are made, but naturally no such document becomes official until it has been approved by the line manager or staff expert who is responsible for making final decisions on the matter. Sometimes revision—perhaps even more than once—is necessary before a job description is finally approved.

Before a job description *should* be finally approved, what criteria need to be met, in each section of the finished product?

CRITERIA FOR A WELL-MADE JOB DESCRIPTION AND ANALYSIS

This book is not a manual, and therefore detailed instructions about how a job analyst should meet all the requirements of his job are not given,[11] but it will be useful to indicate desirable features of the finished product.

[11] For further information in the context of wage and salary administration, see E. Lanham, *Job Evaluation,* McGraw-Hill Book Company, New York, 1955, especially chap. 8, "Job Analysis," pp. 124-175, and chap. 9, "Job Descriptions," pp. 176-215. See also J. D. Dunn and Frank M. Rachel, *Wage and Salary Administration: Total Compensation Systems,* McGraw-Hill Book Company, New York, 1971, chap. 8, "Job Analysis," pp. 133-149 and chap. 9, "Worker Trait Requirements," pp. 151-164. (Appendixes 3 and 4 also reproduce the "Explanation of Worker Trait Components," and "Explanation of Relationships within Data, People, Things Hierarchies," provided in Vol. II of the *Occupational Classification and Industry Index,* U.S. Department of Labor, 1965.)

The Date

To be useful, a job description must be up to date. The description must correspond accurately to current job requirements. (A job description can be relatively useless or even misleading if it merely gives an accurate picture of what the job used to be.) Provision should be made for periodic review of all jobs, and each description should be revised whenever there is a substantial change in job content or job context, i.e., whenever the requirements or environmental conditions change sufficiently to make the job significantly different.[12] Sometimes a change in the place where some (or all) of the job requirements must be met may substantially change the job. If so, the job description should be brought up to date. On the other hand, a different location of work may not materially affect job content. But in some instances, the relationship between job content and location of work has occasioned differences of opinion between union officials and management representatives. (For one such instance, see Case 9, "The 'Outside' Inspectors.")

A convenient mechanism for keeping job descriptions up to date is to have all supervisors notify the appropriate staff department whenever any change of job requirements is contemplated. That notification alerts the staff department to the need for reviewing that particular job description. A succession of apparently "insignificant" changes may eventually add up to a "substantial" change.

The Title Should Be Apt

The title should clearly indicate the principal demands made by the job on the jobholder. Then it also sets each job apart from every other job.

[12] For example, compare the position description of the tour foreman at the Niagara Falls Mills, Kimberly-Clark Corporation, with the position description of the shift superintendent who replaced the tour foreman. Walter S. Wikstrom, *Managing at the Foreman's Level,* National Industrial Conference Board, Inc., Personnel Policy Study no. 205, New York, 1967, pp. 18-25.

This twofold requirement often calls for prefixes or subtitles.

For example, the job title "truck driver" indicates in a general way what the occupation is. Differences in degrees of skill required should be clarified by prefixes that are derived from the purpose for which the truck is used or the kind of truck driven, e.g., "freight-truck driver," "delivery-truck driver," "milk-truck driver," "trailer-truck driver." Again, operating such special vehicles as tower trucks, fire trucks, or tank trucks may impose special job requirements and call for special skills.

Occasions for considering job titles arise when a new job is created, or when the context of a job is significantly altered—for instance, owing to increased mechanization or advancing automation or to a rearrangement of work assignments so that an employee now has a combination job. Any such change calls for a review of the job title to see whether the original title still matches altered job requirements.

A Case Example: "The Secretary-Assistant"

The importance of an apt job title is related not only to what it *denotes* but also to what it *connotes* for the incumbent. For example, in one company during the Second World War, a secretary's title was changed to "secretary-assistant" (a title which seems to denote a combination job). The purpose of the change was to justify a salary increase which her immediate supervisor felt she deserved. However, that reason was not explained to the secretary, who happened to be an ambitious person. She, therefore, naturally assumed that her new title pointed to a prospective promotion. Acting on that assumption, she kept trying to demonstrate her ability to understudy her boss. She began to use her own judgment in carrying out assignments which she planned for herself. However, each time she attempted to show her caliber as an assistant, her boss made it plain that she was "getting out of line." As it was borne in upon her that the new title did not represent any change in her job she became increasingly frustrated. A few months after her title had been changed she gave notice. Her boss then explained that her altered title was merely a maneuver to get the Wage Stabilization Board to approve the raise in pay which she could otherwise not have received, but the explanation came too late. By that time she had made up her mind to quit, and quit she did.

The Summary Gives a Preview

The summary of primary duties gives an overview of what the job essentially is. It thus serves as a preview of the job description as a whole. It indicates *what* the job is, also *how* and to *what extent* this particular job differs from other jobs.

For Hourly Rated Job Descriptions For example, two descriptions at the Lockheed Aircraft Corporation contained the following statements: [13]

> [*For "inspector: outside production"*] Occupational Summary: This occupation requires the inspection of aircraft parts, assemblies, tooling and material on outside vendors' and subcontractors' premises.
> [*For "inspector: inside precision"*] Occupational Summary: Inspect all types of complex machined parts and precision assemblies received from vendors, for workmanship, dimensional accuracy, interchangeability, and compliance with applicable blueprints and specifications.

Those two statements define and differentiate similar jobs.

For a Specialist's Job Here is another statement, summarizing essential duties of a computer programmer.

> The programmer prepares the program or series of instructions to the computer, directing it to solve a

given problem. He then tests his program on the computer to eliminate any errors he may have made, a process aptly called "debugging."

For Managerial Positions In position descriptions, what amounts to a job summary is given in a section that may have a variety of headings, including: "General Responsibility," "Purpose of Position," "Basic Functions," "Major Function." The text of this paragraph (which almost always comes at the start of the description) plainly reveals the purpose of summarizing essential job requirements. Here are examples:

> [*Boeing Airplane Company, Transport Division: Manufacturing Manager*] Summary: The *Manufacturing Manager* administers and directs all manufacturing activities. In addition, he assists in the development of Division objectives and advises management regarding manufacturing aspects of product proposals. He establishes Transport Division manufacturing philosophy in accordance with overall company policy. [14]

> [*Borg-Warner Corporation, Chairman of the Board and Chief Executive Officer*] Purpose of the Position: To provide leadership to the Board in carrying out its collective responsibility for the management of the property, business, and affairs of the Corporation.
> To focus overall responsibility for the successful administration of the affairs of the Corporation in a single individual. [15]

The Description Should Be Sufficiently Complete but Not Overly Detailed

Meeting the requirement of having a description sufficiently complete but not overly detailed (as given in Section IV of the general-purpose form) calls for clear thinking and good judgment. The essential aim is to come up with a concise description and analysis (with substantiating data) of (1) all normal job requirements (what the in-

---

[13] See Case 9, "The 'Outside' Inspectors" (in Part 2 of this book) for a detailed labor arbitration report with reference to these two jobs.

[14] Bennet, *op. cit.*, p. 221.
[15] *Ibid.*, p. 193.

cumbent does most of the time) and (2) a clear statement of occasional subsidiary activities—such as weekly reports or any other duties that must be performed from time to time.

It is not necessary to list every task that the incumbent could conceivably be asked—with reason—to perform, but if some variation in assignment is part of the job, that fact should be clearly stated. Some indication should be given of the variety and limits of occasional assignments. Some statement, even if only a rough estimate, should be made of the time to be spent by the incumbent on occasional or "incidental" duties. If possible, the amount of time to be allocated to them should be precisely stated.

Case Examples

What needs to be done in describing "incidental" assignments can be clearly seen in the following examples.

The primary duties of a "laboratory assistant" consisted in cleaning utensils. He was also permitted to make occasional routine calibrations. This part of his job was in preparation for upgrading to the next higher classification. Another incidental assignment was driving a small pickup truck. This part of his work consisted in loading and unloading instruments, as well as driving. This assignment had to be performed twice a day. It took about half an hour each time. There was no complete description and analysis of his job, but the primary and subsidiary duties were outlined in a document entitled "Duties as Assigned," and the allocation of time for driving the pickup truck was precisely stated.

One day the "laboratory assistant" demanded that his title be changed to "truck driver," since driving a truck was the most important part of his job. Making that change would have entailed doubling his pay. It was fortunate for the organization that the written statement of his assigned duties clearly showed his claim to be without merit.

Analytical Judgments Need to Be Made and Substantiated Earlier in this chapter we considered material that belongs in the section on job factors. Therefore, we merely list them here. The job analyst (1) determines what factors are required by the job, e.g., physical effort or analytical ability; (2) provides substantiating data (in written statements, and perhaps also by supplying photographs or by appending forms that are used by the incumbent); and (3) indicates relative degrees of importance or difficulty of the various factors. (In a position description, analysis of job factors is omitted—for obvious reasons.)

If qualifications for incumbents are to be included in this section of the job description, they should be precisely stated. For example, the job descriptions already referred to for two kinds of inspection jobs at Lockheed Aircraft Corporation end with the following paragraphs:

[*Inspector: outside production*] *Knowledge and Ability Required:* Knowledge of all types of outside vendor and subcontractor inspections on casting, forging, tools, all types of parts and assemblies; ability to use precision measuring and layout instruments, to understand outside shop inspection, practice and procedure; to interpret complex blueprints; to use shop trigonometry.

[*Inspector: receiving precision*] *Knowledge and Ability required:* Apply a complete knowledge of Receiving Inspection practice and procedure, A.N., vendor's and company specifications relative to the inspection of machined parts and precision assemblies, welding, and processing techniques, and the machinability of metals.

To read and interpret complex detail assembly blueprints. To use shop mathematics including trigonometry. To make any type of precision instrument surface plate set-up as required.

To manually pull, push or lift over 25 lbs.

Job descriptions and analyses which meet all these criteria are—in theory—useful instruments. Indeed they can be an essential means to a variety of ends—all of which are important in personnel administration. But making job descriptions that are designed to be useful is one thing. The proof of the pudding is in the eating, and the crucial test of job descriptions comes when they are used—by persons with different functions, and for a wide range of purposes. Do they then prove to be as useful as was anticipated? Are they easily understood and readily accepted by everyone who needs this information? In a sense, a job description *is what it does.* But naturally *what is done with* a job description, and by whom, affects *what it can do.*

USES OF JOB DESCRIPTION AND ANALYSIS

Observation and research suggest that not all firms use the procedures of job description and job analysis as effectively as they might. For example, the *National Job Analysis Methods Survey*[16] provided the following statistical data:

However, opportunities to make good use of job descriptions include the following:

For Wage and Salary Administration

Job descriptions are most widely used in connection with wage and salary administration for hourly rated and office employees. Probably every firm that has written job descriptions and analyses uses them to avoid wage and salary inequities and to make sure that pay is in line with going rates for comparable jobs in the industry or in the community (see Chapter 20). An accurate and comprehensive set of job descrip-

tions forms a factual basis for making wage and salary surveys, grading jobs, and developing a fair wage and salary structure.

As a Guide in Every Phase of the Employment Process

Taken separately, or grouped in job families, job descriptions can be helpful to applicants for work, to incumbents, and to supervisors at every stage in the employment relationship, from recruitment to retirement. We shall not go into details here, since that will be done in later chapters, but by taking a quick look at the manifold uses of job descriptions, we can indicate (1) why and how this instrument can be useful for a variety of purposes, (2) the importance of meeting criteria such as those mentioned in the preceding subsection, and (3) what we mean by "integrated" personnel administration (as an art, a method, and a range of skills in which each part needs to be integrally related to every other).

In *recruitment, selection, and placement,* members of the employment department can use job descriptions to get and to give information about the knowledge, training, education, skills, and aptitudes needed for each job (see Chapter 15). A relatively new use of job analysis has been made in companies where management became convinced that psychological tests were screening out persons (with little formal education) whom they felt responsible for trying to employ.[17]

In *orienting and inducting new employees,* job descriptions help to clarify what the employee needs to know about his job and thus prevent avoidable misunderstandings (see Chapter 16). Since they are in writing, job descriptions offer a

---

[16] During the summer of 1968, the Bureau of Business Research, California State College, Long Beach, and the Job Analysis Research Staff of the California State College, Los Angeles Foundation, mailed their questionnaire to a nationwide sample of 1805 firms listed in the 1968 *College Placement Annual.* Size of the firms contacted ranged from under 500 employees to over 100,000 and included all major industrial groups. Responses included 899 completed questionnaires. For a detailed discussion of the findings, see Jean J. Jones, Jr., and Thomas A. DeCotis, "Job Analysis: National Survey Findings," *Personnel Journal,* vol. 48, no. 10, pp. 805–809, October, 1969.

[17] In the Atlantic Refining Company, for example, a successful training program was developed from job analysis which showed "precisely what employees would have to do. This, in turn, gauged the knowledge they would have to acquire." Stephen Habbe, *Company Experience with Negro Employment,* National Industrial Conference Board, Inc., Personnel Policy Study no. 201, vol. 1, New York, 1966, p. 68.

Table 14-1   Ways in Which Respondents to the National Job Analysis Methods Survey (1968) Reportedly Used the Results of the Job Analysis Process

	n=638 Salaried (percent)	n=430 Hourly (percent)
Evaluating	98.0	94.9
Setting wage and salary levels	92.9	88.4
Appraising personnel	58.8	44.0
Establishing incentives	11.3	13.7
Determining profit sharing	6.4	2.1
Other	1.7	1.2
Recruiting and placing	94.8	91.6
Making job specifications	74.3	75.1
Promoting, transferring and rotating	71.5	66.7
Matching men with jobs	64.6	60.5
Structuring jobs	57.7	54.2
Enriching jobs	26.3	24.7
Counseling (vocational)	24.8	25.6
Diluting jobs	19.0	19.3
Indicating sources of employment	17.6	15.6
Placing the handicapped	16.8	25.3
Constructing tests	14.1	17.7
Other	3.0	3.7
Conducting labor and personnel relations	82.8	79.1
Establishing responsibility	70.4	55.6
Establishing accountability	65.7	46.0
Establishing authority	64.3	44.2
Developing performance standards	47.8	42.3
Organizing personnel records	35.3	36.0
Establishing channels of communication	32.0	23.7
Handling grievances	14.6	43.5
Conducting labor negotiations	8.2	33.7
Other	1.1	1.2
Utilizing workers	71.8	67.4
Organizing and planning	55.6	46.5
Avoiding excess task duplication	44.5	40.2
Controlling costs	21.8	28.6
Engineering jobs	16.9	15.6
Controlling quality	13.9	16.0
Predicting changes	12.5	11.2
Other	0.9	0.7
Training	60.5	62.6
Orienting employees	36.2	36.0
Selecting trainees	34.3	33.5
Developing courses	33.4	35.6
Programming teaching machines	1.9	2.3
Other	0.5	0.7

Source: Summary of *National Job Analysis Methods Survey*, pp. 4–5.

reliable, impersonal guide which can be readily referred to during the induction period if a new employee fears that he may have forgotten or misunderstood some requirement, or if his supervisor thinks that the new employee is scanting some part of his job.

For *follow-up and for making performance reviews* (Chapter 16) a job description can provide an excellent checklist, one that can be objectively discussed between an employee and his immediate supervisor during performance appraisals. Without such a guide for realistic thinking, supervisors tend to substitute subjective judgments for verifiable observations of fact. They often rely on emotionally satisfying, but actually meaningless generalizations such as, "In my opinion, Parkman is twice the man Renault is." But if a supervisor knows he is going to center on a job description during a performance appraisal interview, he has a reliable control against making vague character judgments such as: employee N is "stubborn," "uncooperative," or "lazy." Such labeling can be a factor in driving employees toward behavior which seems to justify the label.

Written descriptions and analyses of jobs can be (and have been) used as starting points for free exchange of factual information about job opportunities. When this has been done, many gaps in knowledge have been filled in (on both sides), and many unrealistic expectations have been corrected. Moreover, the frequency and success with which job descriptions are so used by organizational superiors can be regarded as a measure of their ability to supervise.

Duties, expectations, misunderstandings, difficulties, and changes (anticipated or desired) should be freely discussed—as need arises and in relation to clear statements of job duties. Only when this is done can people at work effectively coordinate their efforts to improve their joint performance, working together not only as superiors and subordinates but also as colleagues, with shared objectives.

Job descriptions can also be used to stimulate and direct self-appraisal and self-development. Assuming that the purpose of performance appraisal is to raise the level of performance, job descriptions could be used in performance appraisal to achieve a major goal associated with *position guides.* That use is clarified in the following statement: [18]

> Management Guides . . . also serve to inspire the occupants of the positions . . . to set a goal of achievement and stir the individual to pattern the fulfillment of his position to the ideal as expressed in the guide.

Naturally, a specific job description can't be written in the same style as a position guide. But why shouldn't every supervisor be urged to see to it that every ambitious employee, in effect, has a position guide? Each supervisor could be invited to proceed on the twin hypotheses that every normal human being has a drive for achievement, and that this drive can be harmonized with organizational goals. It would then follow that the issuance of job descriptions should be followed by periodic talks between supervisors and their subordinates. By appraising performance-on-the-job and discussing potentials for employee development, an ordinary performance review can be turned into a progress report. A comparison of the official job description and an incumbent's conception of his own job and work performance can be the subject of a productive interview between the job holder and his supervisor. Such a talk may disclose opportunities for doing better (either in clarifying the written job description or in performance on the job.) And a job holder's will and ability to do his best might be strengthened and re-directed as he thought about job requirements; first by himself, and then during this informal talk with his supervisor.

[18] This statement was taken from a Standard Oil Company of California *Management Manual.*

Job descriptions can be useful in *preventing dissatisfactions or settling complaints* (see Chapter 13). When changes in job content or job context are substantial enough to warrant revising job descriptions, revisions should always be made promptly and supervisors should always review the revised descriptions with incumbents. Doing so may help an employee to understand such matters as why his rate of pay has been altered; such a timely explanation may help to prevent dissatisfaction. Even when revised job descriptions are not reviewed until after complaints have been made, the up-to-date descriptions may serve to settle complaints before they harden into full-fledged official grievances. If grievances cannot be settled short of arbitration, an adequately revised job description supports the company's position.

When *transfer, upgrading, promotion, or downgrading* is contemplated (see Chapter 17), thorough job descriptions provide information needed in deciding whether an employee should be moved up or down (and how far) or whether the nature of his present job fits him for transfer to a vacant position because his proved abilities equip him to meet requirements in other jobs grouped in the same job family. Similarly, if *layoffs* are called for during curtailment of production, job requirements (as outlined in job descriptions) should be considered before senior employees exercise their right to displace junior employees.

If *discipline* (see Chapter 18) is being considered or must be imposed for substandard performance, stated job requirements are of central importance. Is there clear-cut proof that the employee knew what was required, e.g., in regard to quantity and quality of work? Had any failure to meet requirements been reviewed by the supervisor in a friendly talk before a warning or a penalty was imposed? Unless such requirements for constructive discipline are met by supervisors, workers have grounds for dissatisfaction.

Retirement and necessary restriction of activity for health reasons (see Chapter 22) are questions which may be difficult to decide or even to discuss. Feelings in and about people may tend to seem more decisive than objective requirements of the work situation. Yet, many supervisors shrink from mentioning such feelings. Even before the question of retirement arises, increasing physical and mental limitations associated with advancing age may make it impossible for a jobholder to maintain his previous level of performance. If so, the job description (with its careful differentiation between primary and subsidiary duties, and analysis of job factors) can help incumbents and their organizational superiors to think objectively. With a good job description at hand, a supervisor does not need to say to himself (or to the aging job holder): "Bill, I think you're getting too old for this job. You'd better retire." Instead, Bill's current abilities (and disabilities, confirmed by medical examinations, and x-rays, and laboratory tests) can be reviewed in the light of his job description. Perhaps some rearrangement of subsidiary duties will make it possible to retain an employee who is approaching the retirement age but whose experience, reliability, and intelligence still make him an asset to the firm.

Thus, in theory, job descriptions and analyses can be useful for a wide range of purposes. However, to make maximum use of them, they must be widely distributed.

A Suggestion: Wider Distribution for Wider Use

According to the AMA survey, distribution of position descriptions (in companies which responded to the questionnaire) ranged from one set of descriptions to 1,000 copies. The company which had only one set of descriptions kept them in the personnel department. Only members of top management had access to this material for use in organization planning. In some companies, every department head received copies of all position descriptions. In other companies, department heads received copies of position descriptions in their own units. Standard Oil of California issued this policy statement (which we would recommend for application to job descriptions, as well as to descriptions of managerial positions):

> Management of departments and subsidiaries will determine appropriate distribution for Management Guides covering positions in their organizations. This distribution should include a copy to the incumbent of each position for which a management guide [i.e., a position description] is prepared. In general, it is desirable that each member of management be adequately informed with respect to other management positions in the same organization through convenient availability of management guides. [19]

In many organizations, job descriptions are put into manuals, and the theory is that any employee "may" have access to this material. Our own experience, in a few companies, suggests that relatively few employees know that they may see their job descriptions if they wish to. Fewer still have the temerity to ask for them. Obviously, if job descriptions are to serve the purposes listed in the preceding subsection, recruits, candidates, and incumbents should know what is in them.

POSITION DESCRIPTIONS

Anyone who has ever tried to describe and analyze the varied and often somewhat intangible responsibilities of managers and higher-level staff personnel is in a position to recognize the difficulties of doing so. Moreover, a reason for not undertaking this difficult assignment is the risk that precise statements about position requirements might seem inconsistent with salary decisions which usually are—and should be—based largely on the caliber and potential of the

[19] Bennet, *op. cit.,* p. 138.

incumbent (see Chapter 20 for more on this point). However, even as early as 1958, the AMA survey showed that of 140 companies, nearly one-third of the respondents had some kind of description for every job in the organization, nearly two-thirds had descriptions for middle management positions, and slightly over one-half had descriptions for all office and factory jobs including those of first-level supervisors. The present rate of technological advance constitutes a new and compelling reason for practicing the skills needed to analyze duties which are neither invariable nor precisely definable. When technological advances convince top management that a new corporate design should be considered, an essential preliminary step is to review position descriptions which match what management representatives do at all organizational levels.

Profiles of Managerial Jobs

An interesting suggestion for position analysis was presented by Stewart[20] on the basis of diaries by 160 managers in Great Britain in which they kept track of how they had spent their time during a 4-week period. When the individual statements had been grouped (in various ways) by a computer, the following classification was selected as the most meaningful:

> *Group 1: The emissaries,* e.g., field sales managers and general managers. These managers spent most of their time away from the office, attending conferences and other outside events. They were subject to fewer interruptions from colleagues and subordinates than managers in other groups, but including travel time, they worked longer hours.
> *Group 2: The writers,* e.g., payroll managers and computer division managers. These managers devoted about half their time to reading, writing, figuring, and dictating. They spent that time alone, in

[20] Rosemary Stewart, *Managers and Their Jobs: A Study of the Similarities and Differences in the Ways Managers Spend Their Time,* St. Martin's Press, Inc., New York, 1967.

highly specialized activities, and were less subject than managers in most other groups to interruptions occasioned by daily problems and emergencies.

Group 3: The discussers, e.g., production engineers, personnel managers, and chief accountants. These managers spent most of their time with other organizational members, chiefly with colleagues. (For this reason, they might also be classified as belonging to the "horizontal" group.) But they also saw more of their immediate superiors than managers in other groups did. They were subject to many interruptions.

Group 4: The troubleshooters, e.g., works managers and general managers. Members of this group might also be called "man managers" because they spent up to one-third of their time with their subordinates and, unlike other managers, over an hour a day on inspection. Their working day was greatly fragmented.

Group 5: The committeemen, e.g., production managers, production specialists, and works managers. All managers in this group were in large companies. Some of these men had few or no subordinates. Up to half their working day was spent in "multiple discussions," i.e., with more than one person at the same time, usually in committees. Their contacts were both horizontal and vertical. They spent more time on personnel work than managers in other groups did.

This five-group classification illustrates several of the difficulties inherent in making position descriptions. For example, managers in the troubleshooting group apparently spent up to one-third of their time in performing duties which might be classified as essentially supervisory, rather than managerial. Does this fact suggest that the concept of management practiced ("eyeball control," as contrasted with participative management, for instance) may make more difference than his official title in determining what a manager actually does? Another surprising feature of Stewart's classification is that managers with the same function (in theory) were not always classified in the same profile group. For example, several personnel managers turned up

in the "discusser" group, while none was mentioned as being among the "committeemen" (who reportedly spent more time on personnel work than managers in other groups did).

Stewart explains that some apparent inconsistencies are partly due to the fact that persons involved in the general management of a company should really be called "multifunction managers." The responsibilities of a multifunction manager make him spend more time outside his own department than is required of a "single-function" manager. She concludes that any purely functional classification of managerial positions would be inadequate. However, she is convinced that analyzing such key variables as the nature of job contacts and the degree of interruption to which managers are exposed can be useful not only to present managers but also in selecting and training future managers.

A "Ten-dimensional" View of Executive Positions

Another approach to position description, reported in 1959 by Hemphill,[21] also recognizes that standard position descriptions do not adequately portray the complex, varied, and flexible demands made on executives by what are, in effect, "combination jobs." The following sampling indicates the scope and character of dimensions used to identify the variety of demands made on executives by their jobs: *supervising work* (planning, organizing, and controlling the work of other persons); *internal business control* (highly technical, not much contact with general public); *human, community, and social affairs* (for instance, as responsibilites of a district manager who is expected to work effectively with others both inside and outside the enterprise); *exercising broad power and authority* (as a division manager does); and *preservation of assets* (top-man-

---

[21] John K. Hemphill, "Job Descriptions for Executives," *Harvard Business Review,* vol. 37, no. 5, p. 65, September–October, 1959.

agement personnel are responsible for large expenditures and for avoiding unnecessary costs).

Descriptions of Top-level Committee Responsibilities

Some companies have experimented with job descriptions for committees.[22] As technical advances bring increasing need for effective collaboration between men with different functions, different professional backgrounds, and different value attitudes, friction and misunderstanding might be greatly reduced if every such group could work from a blueprint clearly delineating group responsibilities. (Naturally, that description would supplement, not replace, the position descriptions for individual committee members.)

ADVANTAGEOUS USES OF POSITION DESCRIPTIONS

Company experience clearly shows that even at managerial levels there are misunderstandings about what jobs require of incumbents and what incumbents may expect to get from their jobs (in money, status, opportunities for personal growth, and advancement, for instance). These differences can seriously interfere with effective performance.

To Clear Up Misunderstandings

Sometimes when a manager has drafted a description of his own job and his immediate superior studies that draft, serious misunderstandings

come to light.[23] Not all of them can be cleared up, but at least when they are out in the open, there is some possibility of working toward better understanding. With that possibility in mind, the following facts and findings seem significant. Under the auspices of the American Management Association,[24] psychologists conducted patterned interviews in five companies with 58 pairs of executives and their immediate subordinates. (Each man was interviewed separately, and in each pair, the subordinate to be interviewed was selected by the executive, a circumstance which would seem to increase the probability of agreement between the members of each pair.) Here are some of the findings.

Even on the basic question of job content, agreement about all (or almost all) job duties was expressed in only about 8 percent of the interviews, and *almost total disagreement* was disclosed in over 3 percent of these talks. On the more subjective question of the subordinate's qualifications to meet job requirements, *almost no agreement* was revealed in 7 percent of the interviews, while less than half of the pairs interviewed agreed on about half of the subpoints discussed in relation to that topic. In regard to anticipated future changes in the subordinate's jobs, wide differences in expectation were indicated by the fact that in over 35 percent of the interviews there was *almost no agreement*. On the admittedly delicate question of obstacles to effective performance by subordinates, *complete agreement* was indicated in only 1 percent of the interviews.

To Clarify a Manager's Thinking about His Own Job

With reference to managerial positions, it has often been said that a job is what a person makes it. However, it often happens that the results of

---

[22] The Boeing Airplane Company, Seattle Division, is one such company. The following statement is taken from the job description of their planning committee: "To integrate the planning of engineering, manufacturing, sales, and finance into over-all Company plans and objectives to govern the selection of products, the application of effort, and the use of facilities." The main text of that description identifies the scope (its relationship to the policy committee and to the company president), lists seven responsibilities, defines its authority, designates staff support, and indicates membership.

[23] For an excellent case illustration of this point, see Ralph M. Hower and Charles D. Orth, 3d, *Managers and Scientists: Some Human Problems in Industrial Organizations,* Harvard Business School, Division of Research, Boston, 1963, chap. 11, "The Samuel Gross Case," pp. 167-171.

[24] Maier et al., *op. cit.*

this process tend to come about partly by chance. Any manager might feel challenged to make more of his job if he periodically compared what he has actually been doing with what might be expected from a person in his position. Stewart[25] has suggested eight questions by which a manager might evaluate his own performance, in relation to job requirements, needs of the organization, and his own need for continuing self-development. Pondering such questions may reveal possibilities of organizing work more efficiently (to reduce excessively long hours), perhaps reevaluating task priorities in the light of recent changes and/or doing more delegating; reducing unnecessary interruptions; extending the scope of organizational contacts; and setting aside some regular time for professional study.

To Provide a Total Picture

Only when all managerial positions in a given enterprise have been described (with reasonable accuracy and according to a consistent system) is it possible to get an operational view of organizational structure as shown by the organization chart. A complete set of position descriptions mirrors what managers actually do, with whom they are expected to work, and in what relationships, as they meet assigned responsibilities. Moreover, getting a clear picture of what is being done by whom can be helpful as a step toward making needed changes.[26]

SUMMARY

A job description can be a *liability* if it is inaccurate, incomplete, out of date, or if suspicion and antagonism were aroused in making it.

A job description can be an asset if it covers every position in the organization, offering an operational view of the whole, and showing that every job in the enterprise has been designed and analyzed as an integral part of a total effort. Job descriptions can become most valuable as organizational assets if they are suplemented by coaching on the job so that every jobholder, in effect, has a position guide.

A well-made job description meets the following specifications. It is dated and up to date. The job title is apt. The job summary gives a bird's eye view of primary responsibilities. Report relationships and responsibilities for coordinating with other persons are clearly and comprehensively stated. The detailed description of duties is as concise as is compatible with completeness. There is clear-cut differentiation between primary and secondary duties; substantiating data are given to show degrees of difficulty associated with each job factor.

Such job descriptions can be useful for a variety of purposes and at all stages in the employment process. At best, periodic interviews provide every incumbent with what amounts to a position guide.

Position descriptions are more difficult to write because (1) managerial responsibilities are too variable and flexible to lend themselves to precise description and (2) persons at relatively high organizational levels often serve as multifunction managers. However, there are significant advantages in attempting to analyze and define positional requirements. Moreover, only when all managerial positions are defined, with reasonable accuracy, is it possible to get an operational view of the total organizational structure (as pictured in the organization chart).

In the next eight chapters, we consider a wide range of policies, procedures, and practices. In relation to all of them job descriptions can be useful.

---

[25] *Op. cit.,* pp. 146-147.

[26] For a perceptive regional survey of "career ladders" and managerial attitudes toward employee development, see Henry G. Pearson, *Promotional Policies, Structures and Procedures in Greater Boston Manufacturing Firms and the Implications for Career Development,* M.Ed. thesis, Graduate School of Education, Northeastern University, Boston, May, 1972.

SELECTED REFERENCES

Basic Training Course in Position Classification, U.S. Civil Service Commision, Personnel Methods Series, no. 11, parts 1-4, March, 1961, especially part 2, "Classification Process."

Berenson, Conrad, and Henry O. Ruhnke: *Job Descriptions of Production and Research Personnel in the Chemical Process Industries,* Corporate Publications, New York, 1964.

British Institute of Management: *Job Evaluation: A Practical Guide,* The Millbrook Press, Ltd., Southampton, 1961, chap. 3, "Job Description and Specification," pp. 18-22, and chap. 4, "Job Analysis and the Basis of Job Assessment," pp. 23-31.

Corns, Marshall C.: *Organizing Jobs in Banking: The Use of Job Descriptions and Operating Instructions.* Bankers Publishing Company, Boston, 1967.

Evaluating Position Evaluation, The Society for Personnel Administration, Pamphlet no. 10, Washington, D.C., 1962.

Dunn, J. D., and Frank M. Rachel: *Wage and Salary Administration: Total Compensation Systems,* McGraw-Hill Book Company, New York, 1971, "Job Analysis," pp. 133-149.

Fine, Sidney A.: *Guidelines for the Design of New Careers,* The W. E. Upjohn Institute for Employment Research, Kalamazoo, Mich., 1967.

Hanan, Mack, James Cribbin, and Herman Heiser: *Consultative Selling,* American Management Association, Inc., New York, 1970, "Consultative Salesman: Position Description and Analysis," pp. 22-29.

Janger, Allen R.: "Making Titles Meaningful," *Business Management Record,* National Industrial Conference Board, Inc., pp. 43-49, August, 1963.

Lanham, E.: *Job Evaluation,* McGraw-Hill Book Company, New York, 1955, chap. 8, "Job Analysis," pp. 124-175, and chap. 9, "Job Descriptions," pp. 176-215.

Manpower Administration: *Job Descriptions and Organizational Analysis for Hospitals and Related Health Services,* rev. ed., 1971.

Patton, John A., C. L. Littlefield, and Stanley Allen Self: *Job Evaluation: Text and Cases,* 3d ed., Richard D. Irwin, Inc., Homewood, Ill., 1964, part II, "Job Analysis and Description," pp. 65-100.

Prien, Erich P., and William W. Ronan: "Job Analysis: A Review of Research Findings," *Personnel Psychology,* vol. 24, pp. 371-396, 1971.

Rush, Harold M. F.: *Job Design for Motivation: Experiments in Job Enlargement and Job Enrichment, Report no. 515,* The Conference Board, New York, 1971.

Stahl, O. Glenn: *Public Personnel Administration,* 6th ed., Harper & Row, Publishers, Incorporated, New York, 1971, chap. 5, "Classification of Positions," pp. 61-78.

Technical Occupations in Research Design and Development Considered as Directly Supporting to Engineers and Physical Scientists, U.S. Employment Service, Division of Placement Methods, no. E-194, February, 1961.

Trice, Harrison M.: *Effective Hiring in Small Business Organizations,* New York State School of Industrial and Labor Relations, Cornell University, Bulletin 46, Ithaca, N.Y., 1962.

Wells, P. A.: "Recent Developments in the Classification of Scientists in the Federal Service," *Research Management,* vol. 6, no. 1, January, 1963, pp. 73-80.

Chapter 15

Recruitment, Selection, and Placement

The purposes of a recruitment function are patently straightforward: to seek out, evaluate, obtain commitment from, place, and orient new employees to fill positions required for the successful conduct of the work of an organization.

Roger H. Hawk [1]

What is the purpose of the three integrated hiring procedures, recruitment, selection, and placement? From the personnel point of view, management is trying to do far more than merely to fill current vacancies. If this were all that needed to be done, the simplest formula would be vacancy—requisition—fill. But such an oversimplified hiring process would not promote the larger aim of building effective teamwork by achieving a balance between personnel mobility and organizational health. In order to advance this purpose, certain policy decisions have validity for all organizations, despite specific differences in their product or service.

[1] Roger H. Hawk, *The Recruitment Function,* American Management Association, New York, 1967.

CENTRALIZED RECRUITMENT PROCEDURES

In the first place, if the policies of top management are to be consistently and efficiently implemented, all employment activity must center in one place, within a plant or major organizational unit. Only when all requisitions go through one center and all employment records are kept up to date is there a maximum possibility for efficiency and for the type of follow-up that progressively improves employment methods by checking on the success of previous hiring.

If the policy of centralized recruitment and screening is adequately explained by top management, line officials need not feel that, in accepting the services of staff experts, they suffer any loss in prestige or responsibility. It can easily be shown that the work of the employment department (usually a subordinate unit of the personnel division) is a supplement to the judgment of line officials and not a substitute for it. Modern hiring procedures include a type of interviewing that requires familiarity with up-to-date psychological knowledge and various kinds of tests that need to be administered and diagnosed by experts. This expert knowledge can be geared in at various points with the knowledge and training of line officials.

These centralized procedures, properly conceived and administered, are a complement to, and not an invasion of, the line supervisor's responsibilities. The line manager should retain the right to accept or reject the applicant sent to his department by the employment manager. But, since a busy line manager ordinarily has neither the time nor the skill to perform the recruitment and selection process himself, he can benefit by the assistance of a central staff agency. Even smaller firms or organizations can benefit from a centralized employment service, subject to the approval of the supervisor or the manager. [These points are illustrated by the chart on line and staff responsibilities in the employment process (Figure 2-1) in Chapter 2.]

A personnel administrator has an opportunity to advise top management in planning the recruitment procedures that are part of the centralized hiring administered by the employment department. Thus, a centralized hiring policy involves other subsidiary decisions and procedures.

SUBSIDIARY POLICY DECISIONS

First, since the maintenance of individual and organizational stability is a major aim of management, a balance should be kept between the number of people recruited and management's current expectations of hiring needs in the near future. Management ought to know at all times how much and what kind of ability are required.

Only on the basis of such knowledge can recruitment needs be accurately estimated, taking into account the rate of company expansion or contraction, organizational structure, and current data on labor turnover. Newer approaches to manpower planning and projections, which have been dealt with in Chapter 3, are also relevant to the discussion in this chapter.

Second, promises made during recruitment should not oversell either the company or any job in the plant. If they do, employees will inevitably becomes dissatisfied when experience shows them the difference between recruitment talk and employment facts. In whatever form their dissatisfaction is expressed, it militates against organizational stability. Thus any method of high-pressure recruiting salesmanship defeats the long-run aim of the whole hiring process. This is especially applicable to college recruiting.

Third, recruitment procedures should be well adapted to relevant differences in the kind of employees to be hired. Every industrial firm needs a comparatively large number of workers, both men and women, to perform unskilled and semiskilled operations in the factory and also workers skilled in various crafts. Members of this group must usually be able to develop versatility, because in addition to their regular assigned duties, they may be needed as substitutes for other workers, as teachers of new employees, or as understudies for minor supervisory positions (acting as job setters, group leaders, etc.). Employees who are differentiated according to three degrees of skill (skilled, semiskilled, or unskilled) are commonly classified in one main category as hourly rated workers. A second main category is so-called "white-collar" employees, principally in offices, sales, and service operations, and paid by salary periodically. Many of these may be semiskilled or skilled, with separate promotion ladders from the hourly-rated group. Finally, a third category of employees is composed of the comparatively small number of candidates hired primarily for managerial, professional, and technical positions. While small in number, this group has had the most rapid increase of any, as indicated in Chapter 1 (Table 1-1).

Recruiting High-talent Manpower

The last group is usually the most expensive to recruit and often the most difficult to keep, because of the availability of alternative opportunities in shortage occupations represented in this group. Since new recruits to this group are frequently recent college graduates, "college recruiting" is often a specialized function within the corporate or headquarters personnel department, and much preparation goes into the effort.[2] In recent years, especially, the competition for good graduates has been spirited, and even then, many go on to graduate school or take advantage of other opportunities. During a business recession, as in 1971, many firms curtail their college recruitment somewhat.

When high-talent people are recruited from other firms or organizations, as often happens, the recruitment procedure is a little different. No reputable organization wants to be known as "pirating" from others, but because there are such demands for a limited supply of competent people, advertisements in newspapers are used by companies in their own name or to a "blind box" in care of the newspaper. Any Sunday *New*

York Times carries hundreds of these. When a candidate already employed sends his résumé, he may be asked to appear for an interview. As in the case of recent college graduates, the selection procedure is likely to take longer than for other applicants, and if the applicant is a scientist or engineer, the employment interviewer alone will be unable to assess his qualifications. Interviews with company personnel in the specialized area will often be decisive, and problem solving or discussion are often used.[3] (Case 10, "The Rejected Applicant for Employment," illustrates this process.)

For this high-talent group as a whole, two policy requirements are generally valid. Since this type of employee is essential to have and hard to find, some firms recruit on the principle that it is impossible to have too much of a good thing. But this proves quite untrue of top-caliber employees. They become restless if kept too long in subordinate positions where their major capacities remain underutilized. Management's aim to promote individual long-term stability can be fulfilled only when recruitment of this group is limited to the number that can be promoted within a reasonable length of time. High-talent human resources deteriorate if they are hoarded and unused.[4]

A further policy limitation to outside recruitment is imposed by the desirability of leaving room for advancement from the ranks by employees of exceptional ability. This policy has a

---

[2] See Donald J. Petrie, "Holding the Talent You Hire," *Personnel,* vol. 44, no. 5, pp. 22-29, September-October, 1967; George S. Odiorne and A. S. Hann, *Effective College Recruiting,* University of Michigan, Bureau of Industrial Relations, Ann Arbor, Mich., 1961; and "College Graduates: What They Want, What They Have to Offer, Which Ones to Look For, Where, How to Keep Them Once You've Got Them," *Management Review* (American Management Association), vol. 56, no. 6, pp. 4-22, June 1967.

Companies which have made a special effort to hire qualified Negroes have successfully experimented with recruiting at Negro colleges. Some firms have also developed slide talks for use at high schools. For details see Stephen Habbe, *Company Experience with Negro Employment,* National Industrial Conference Board, Studies in Personnel Policy, no. 201, for example as reported on pp. 126-127, with regard to activity by the Du Pont company.

[3] For some examples of this approach, see Jack Pierson, "Interviewing Engineers: How Much Do They Really Know?," *Personnel,* vol. 44, no. 2, pp. 60-67, March-April, 1967.

[4] An experienced employee relations research man has observed, "I'm convinced that we businessmen lose many good people early in their careers simply because we just don't recognize what really able people can do. . . . The result is that we put them into stultifying jobs that offer them no challenge, all too often under mediocre supervisors who are incapable of recognizing unusual ability. No wonder they resign after a year or so." Edwin R. Henry, "What Business Can Learn from Peace Corps Selection and Training," *Personnel,* vol. 42, no. 4, pp. 17-25, July-August, 1965.

healthy effect on employee morale and, when it can be put into practice, promotes organizational vigor. It is important to emphasize that a college degree is not necessarily a measure of a person's worth or potential.

IMPACT OF LABOR MARKET CONDITIONS

The condition of the local labor market, as well as in the nation as a whole, affects the attention which management gives to recruitment, selection, and placement policies and procedures. When there are a greater number of competent employment applicants than jobs waiting to be filled, many organizations feel they need to pay little attention to careful screening, interviewing, testing, and placement. These managements overlook the possibility that there may be a great difference in the competence of applicants and in their capacity to fit into the particular organization.

During most of the period since the Second World War the American labor market generally and many local labor markets have faced shortages of high-talent manpower. (An exception can be made for the 1970–1972 period.) Employers have thus been forced to pay more attention to effective recruiting and to careful selection designed to maximize the prospect of the kind of job placement which will induce the new employee to remain with the organization.

As labor-force and labor-market projections are made for the period ahead to 1980, labor shortages in almost all but the unskilled occupations are likely to continue. In some occupations, such as technical, professional, and managerial, the shortages will again become severe. (See Table 1-1 in Chapter 1.) The prospect, therefore, is that managements will be forced to tap wider resources in the labor market by using a variety of recruitment channels, by hiring more people from the so-called minority groups (Negroes, older workers, women, handicapped workers,

etc.) and by more effective utilization on the job of the existing work force. There will also be continuing pressures to employ persons who are relatively disadvantaged, in terms of poor education, lack of work experience, or past or present discrimination in employment.

POLICY DECISIONS IN RECRUITING AND HIRING THE DISADVANTAGED

Not all the disadvantaged are Negroes, but many of them are. Some are whites who have inadequate education and work experience, like many Negroes, Puerto Ricans, and Mexican-Americans, as we have already noted in Chapter 4. In this broad group are men, women, older people, and teen-agers (many of them school dropouts)—all characterized by an inability to find jobs except in very tight labor markets. Measured in individual or family incomes, nearly all are poor. Some appear to lack a motivation to work and leave a job a few days after they show up for the first time.

Except during the wartime labor shortages of the Second World War, when 12 million young men were in the armed forces, private industry has not hired many of these people until recently. During the past several years there has been increasing pressure to employ the disadvantaged. This has led, in part, to more jobs for better-educated Negroes, who had been the victims of discriminatory policies in the past. State Fair Employment Practice laws and the Civil Rights Act of 1964 make nondiscrimination in employment our national policy, enforced by the Equal Employment Opportunity Commission and the Office of Federal Contracts Compliance. In addition, the Age Discrimination in Employment Act bans employers with 25 or more workers from firing or refusing to hire an individual between forty and sixty-five simply because of his or her age. The Department of Labor also enforces an order banning discrimination in employment on the basis of sex. Nondiscrimination of all types should be clearly stated as a part of any organization's recruitment policy.

As suggested in Chapter 4, the problem of the really disadvantaged persists and presents policy decisions for employers on a number of questions:

1 Should an active effort be made to seek out the disadvantaged in their home areas (often the urban ghettos), rather than expecting them to come to the employment office looking for work?

2 Will extra effort be required from management if recruitment of minority-group members brings them into a community where local prejudice creates difficulties in housing, education, and recreation for the new employee and his family?

3 Should adjustments be made in normal hiring standards (such as the requirement of a high school diploma)?

4 If so, should special preemployment and on-the-job training be supplied?

5 Can it be said that some employment tests are culturally-biased or otherwise inapplicable to disadvantaged persons? What changes, if any, are needed?

6 Will special follow-up be necessary or desirable for disadvantaged job applicants?

7 Will special supervisory qualities and skills be needed to induct and supervise these new employees, and if so, what are they?

8 Since there are additional costs in recruiting, hiring, and training disadvantaged persons, should a government subsidy be made available to induce employers to hire them?

In our opinion, all these questions should be answered in the affirmative by managers concerned with the social implications of leaving disadvantaged minorities out of productive private employment. The alternative is some form of guaranteed income maintenance or subsidized public service employment, both of which may still be necessary for some of this group. There is a growing literature on practical company experience with hiring and training members of minority groups and those whose labor market disadvantages would normally exclude them from private employment.[5]

Probably the most publicized national effort has been that of the National Alliance of Businessmen's Job Opportunities in the Business Sector (JOBS) program, launched early in 1968 with funding by the U.S. Department of Labor and supported by businessmen's committees in more than 50 major cities. While actual retentions fell short of the goal of about 600,000 jobs for the disadvantaged by June 30, 1971 (in part because of the business recession), the effort made an increasing number of managers aware of the managerial and organizational changes necessary to bring these people into meaningful employment. Among other organizations, the Opportunities Industrialization Centers and the National Urban League have worked effectively with business in opening opportunities to disadvantaged minorities.

However, for most of the organization's manpower needs, the recruitment, selection, and

---

[5] See, for example, the 16 volumes in the *Studies in Negro Employment,* under the direction of Herbert R. Northrup of the Industrial Research United of the Wharton School of Finance and Commerce, University of Pennsylvania, Philadelphia, 1970-1971; Peter B. Doeringer (ed.), *Programs to Employ the Disadvantaged,* Prentice-Hall, Inc., Englewood Cliffs, N.J., 1970; Allen R. Janger and Ruth G. Shaeffer, *Managing Programs to Employ the Disadvantaged,* Studies in Personnel Policy no. 219, National Industrial Conference Board, New York, 1970; and Charles A. Myers, *The Role of the Private Sector in Manpower Development,* The Johns Hopkins Press, Baltimore, 1971, especially chap. 3. (This is a review of research and experience, with some unanswered questions.) See also Paul S. Goodman, "Hiring, Training, and Retraining the Hard-core," *Industrial Relations,* vol. 9, no. 1, pp. 54-66, October, 1969 (also reprinted in Paul Pigors, Charles A. Myers, and F. T. Malm, *Management of Human Resources: Readings in Personnel Administration,* 3d ed., McGraw-Hill Book Company, New York, 1973, selection 31).

placement processes that are widely used will be adequate. Increasingly, as we noted in Chapter 3 for managerial manpower, advance manpower planning and forecasting is an important part of the recruitment process generally.

MANPOWER PLANNING AND FORECASTING

How does a firm or organization determine what its future manpower requirements will be? The longer the period of advance planning, the greater the possible margin of error in forecasting. But whatever the period—1 year, 2 years, or 5 years—the forecast has to be based on some estimate of the future demand for final products or services produced (a market forecast); changes in technology and financial resources which may affect the organization's capacity to meet the market forecast; the probable condition of the external labor market and internal manpower capabilities; and then the total staffing requirements to achieve the organizational objectives indicated by the other forecasts, taking into account replacements for normal attrition.

The extent to which overall manpower forecasts can be subdivided by occupational groups in the organization depends in part on the usefulness of more detailed breakdowns. We have already noted the importance of forecasting managerial requirements. Other high-talent manpower requirements such as for technical and professional personnel, may also be desirable. In any case, some "model" of the manpower forecasting process is necessary. It is also useful to consider forecasting and manpower planning as part of a larger system of manpower resources management. Figures 15-1 and 15-2 illustrate these two approaches.

Both these models have a place for an "inventory" of internal manpower resources or labor supplies. Increasingly, firms and organizations are developing computer-based personnel inventories to assist the personnel department and line managers in better internal manpower deploy-

ment. For example, IBM has a Personnel Data System (PDS), primarily for its technical and professional personnel, which contains the following principal items on each employee: (1) personnel data such as home address, marital status, number of dependents, etc.; (2) employment history, showing jobs held within the company, salary changes, and appraisals; (3) previous employment, publications, patents, etc.; (4) educational achievement, with major and minor fields of concentration; and (5) specific skills. The file is updated as changes occur. This data base can be used for many retrieval purposes, among which are simulation in manpower planning and as an inventory which can be drawn on by the manager seeking a person with particular qualifications when an opening occurs.[6]

The application of electronic data processing to the personnel function has been spreading in the last 5 years. A 1969 survey of 900 companies showed that 408 (about 45 percent) were making some use of computer-based personnel systems, and that 139 (34 percent of the 408) had computer-based employment and staffing records. But only 8.6 percent used them for manpower forecasts and manning studies.[7] The armed ser-

---

[6] John J. Bricker, *The Systems Approach to Personnel Management,* American Management Association, Inc., New York, 1965. The author concludes: "It is not technology that is holding us back; it is our own vision and imagination. If we are really serious about turning personnel into a profession, then we should adopt a more professional attitude, tools and techniques. I believe that if personnel is to accomplish its basic mission, it must create and use a personnel system." For another account of the IBM system, see W. J. Peddicord, "Advanced Data Systems for Personnel Planning and Placement," *Computers and Automation,* vol. 15, no. 9, pp. 1-4, September, 1966. See also Glenn A. Bassett, "Manpower Forecasting and Planning: Problems and Solutions," *Personnel,* vol. 47, no. 5, pp. 8-16, September–October, 1970 (also reprinted in Pigors, Myers, and Malm, *op. cit.,* selection 27).

[7] Edward J. Morrison, *Developing Computer-based Employee Information Systems,* AMA Research Study 99, American Management Association, Inc., New York, 1969, p. 14. This study has illustrations of employee information systems in the Ford Motor Company, IBM (the actual input and code sheet used), Standard Oil (Ohio), Polaroid, and

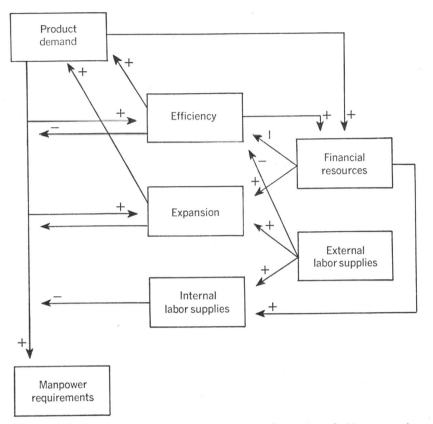

Figure 15-1 A model of manpower forecasting. (*Source: H. G. Heneman, Jr., and George Seltzer,* Employer Manpower Forecasting, *Manpower Research Monograph no. 19, U.S. Department of Labor, Washington, D.C., 1970, p. 10. For a full explanation of each of the boxes, see pp. 9–11.*)

vices are probably far in advance of much of private industry, because of the larger numbers of personnel involved. For example, during the mid-1960s, the Army Air Force developed a computer-based personnel data system for its 135,000 officers, to assist managers in carrying out their specific missions.

Within the framework of longer-run manpower requirements, most actual recruitment be-

gins with the employee requisition filed by a manager or supervisor for an immediate or anticipated manpower need.

REQUISITIONING EMPLOYEES

The supervisor's hiring activity begins with the requisition. In larger organizations with many different jobs, the requisition should be made on the basis of accurate job specifications to be drawn up by the first-line supervisor in cooperation with a specially trained job analyst (usually from the employment department). The principles discussed in Chapter 14 apply here. Two

Honeywell, Inc., among others. For a more recent account of computer-based skills inventories, see Thomas H. Patten, Jr., *Manpower Planning and the Development of Human Resources,* John Wiley & Sons, Inc., New York, 1971, chap. 6, especially pp. 226–251.

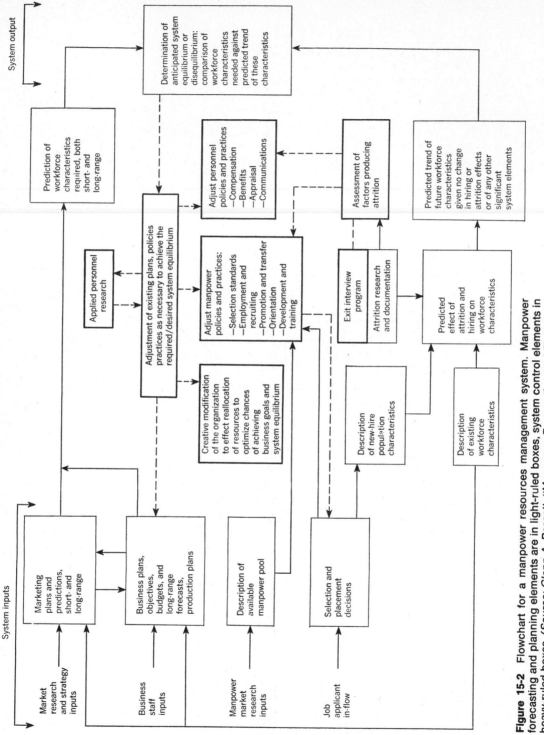

Figure 15-2 Flowchart for a manpower resources management system. Manpower forecasting and planning elements are in light-ruled boxes, system control elements in heavy-ruled boxes. *(Source: Glenn A. Bassett, "Manpower Forecasting and Planning," Personnel, vol 47, no. 5, p. 12, September–October, 1971.)*

points of importance about the requisition are that it be clear-cut regarding the exact demands of the job (the technical job content being in conformity to that stated in the job description) and that it be definite and realistic regarding what the first-level supervisor wants. Some supervisors submit requisitions that call for supermen. This is apparently done on the theory that, allowing a due margin for errors by "those guys in the employment department," such requisitions will produce candidates somewhere above the level of a moron.

Effective collaboration between supervisors and the employment section of the personnel department is important at this point, as at others. If supervisors are cooperative and personnel people have in the past proved efficient and not officious, good teamwork between line and staff should not be difficult to obtain, and each official can make a special contribution to an employment process that will attract and develop qualified employees.

RECRUITMENT

Chronologically, of course, recruitment may come before requisition in filling any given vacancy, because the employment office may take applications for employment in advance of actual hiring requisitions. Thus it is to be expected that, except in periods of extreme labor shortage, an appropriate number of promising candidates to fill future vacancies will always be on file in the employment department.[8] This list is gathered from a variety of sources and includes qualified former employees who have been laid off or who for some reason have voluntarily left the company. The employment manager keeps in touch with former employees so that he may inform them when suitable openings occur. As former company members in good standing,

they will naturally be given preference over strangers. Recruitment is a continuous process.[9]

Contact with potential candidates not previously employed by the company is established by what amounts to advertising in one form or another. The best means of advertising, because it is both the most effective and the cheapest, is not done by the employment manager at all but is carried on by present or former employees who tell their friends that the firm is a desirable place to work.[10]

The employment manager may usefully make the same point, though obviously with less force. In written advertisements and by personal contacts (formal or informal), he reaches the leaders of a variety of local groups such as schools, trade unions, churches, private employment agencies, clubs, the prison association, etc. These leaders are usually interested in knowing that a reputable company in the community is looking for prospective candidates to fill permanent positions. Obviously, no written or spoken words to this effect will carry weight in the long run except as supported by the testimony of satisfied employees.

In addition to these private groups, the employment manager should also keep in touch with the local office of the public employment service. As a central clearinghouse for the local labor-market area, the public employment service knows more about the supply of various types of labor, relative to the demand, than the average employer does. It is in a position to assist him in recruiting applicants for jobs according to

---

[8] This assumes, of course, that *present* employees have preference over new recruits for jobs involving promotions. We shall consider this policy in the next chapter.

[9] For part-time professional, office, and even factory employees, a growing recruitment source is the part-time employment agencies, e.g., as Manpower, Inc., Kelly Girls, and Snelling & Snelling.

[10] For a discussion of this and other recruitment practices used by employers in the San Francisco Bay area for various groups of employees, see F. T. Malm, "Recruiting Patterns and the Functioning of Labor Markets," *Industrial and Labor Relations Review,* vol. 7, no. 4, pp. 507–525, July, 1954 (reprinted in Pigors, Myers, and Malm, *op. cit.,* selection 28). See also Hawk, *op. cit.,* chap. 2.

his own specifications. Also, through its inter-area clearance system, the public employment service can tap a wider labor market than can ordinarily be reached by a single employer. It can also be useful in a manpower-mobilization program. However, its continued value will be determined in large part by the use that employers make of it voluntarily as an aid in recruitment and selection.

Recruitment procedures may be improved if the personnel administrator carefully studies the correlation among sources of labor, methods of recruitment, and subsequent job performance. He should be able to answer the question: From what sources and by what methods have we secured our most satisfactory employees?

A 1968 study of a large number of San Francisco Bay area employers showed the variety of recruitment channels used for "white-collar workers"—professional, managerial, clerical, and sales. Table 15-1 indicates that formal channels were more frequently used, but similar stud-

Table 15–1   Most Important Recruitment Channel Used by Survey Establishments for White-collar Workers, by Major Occupation Group— Bay Area Employer Policy Survey, 1967

Most important channel	Professional	Managerial	Clerical	Sales
All establishments*				
Number	251	302	304	166
Percent	100.0	100.0	100.0	100.0
Informal channels	35.9	82.3	22.3	59.7
Direct hiring	15.5	5.6	15.8	23.6
Recommendations of own employees or "word of mouth"	4.8	1.0	3.6	8.4
From within the establishment	10.0	72.4	1.6	21.7
Referrals from clients, suppliers, and associates	1.2	1.3	—	4.8
Headquarters or divisional employment office, transfers	4.4	2.0	1.3	1.2
Formal channels	58.1	15.0	77.0	37.3
Private employment agencies	20.7	5.6	40.5	13.3
California Department of Employment	—	—	15.5	4.2
School or college placement services	14.3	1.7	1.0	2.4
Unions	1.6	—	4.9	6.6
Newspaper advertising	12.3	2.7	11.8	10.8
Trade or professional journals	4.4	2.0		
Professional or management associations	2.8	1.3		
Civil service lists	4.0	1.7	3.3	
Other	4.0	2.7	0.7	3.0

*Totals exclude establishments not employing workers in a given occupation group and three others with incomplete returns.

Source: Margaret S. Gordon and Margaret Thal-Larsen, *Employer Policies in a Changing Labor Market,* Institute of Industrial Relations, University of California, Berkeley, Calif. July, 1969, p. 197.

ies of recruitment of blue-collar workers support the greater use of informal channels mentioned earlier. Note, however, the infrequent use of the state employment service, which is a part of the federally funded federal-state employment service system. Some firms have made extensive use of this system, especially when they need help in filling hard-to-fill jobs. With the spread of the computer-based Job Bank system, in which all employer openings are listed daily, employer use of the public employment service may increase. When a national system of computer-based job-man matching is developed, the service could become the central clearinghouse for local, regional, and national labor markets.

However efficient recruitment becomes, not all the candidates will prove acceptable as regular employees. The next phase, selection, is a more careful screening of potential candidates from the lists made up by recruitment.

SELECTION

In selection, instead of ending with the name of a potential candidate in a file, we are moving toward actual placement on a job. If this is to be successful, management needs to learn and to weigh a number of factors about the potential employee. How shall it be judged whether his employment in this company, under present conditions, in a current opening will actually work out to the advantage both of the company and of the candidate?

In seeking information on all relevant factors, the employment manager may make use of the following techniques,[11] though not necessarily in the order given here.

[11] The reception of applicants in the employment office is not discussed here, since it is not a fact-finding technique. It is, however, important that this reception be in keeping with management's personnel point of view, since this first contact may go a long way toward answering the applicant's unspoken question: Is this a good place to work? A dirty or unattractive employment office or one that is hard to find means that this question is likely to be answered in the negative.

Preliminary Interview

The first interview may be conducted by an assistant in the employment department and is management's opportunity for a preliminary decision as to the applicant's suitability. It may be obvious at once that a given individual is not suited to the kind of job for which there are current or expected openings, since he or she does not meet certain requirements as to size, physical strength, or age. Or it may be apparent that the person will not fit in well with the company's present personnel. Such a decision may lay management open to an accusation of "discrimination," unless it can be shown that the applicant lacked the qualifications essential to performance of the job.

Many companies modified their application forms, hiring procedures, hiring standards, and personnel practices after the establishment of the Federal Fair Employment Practice Committee (FEPC) "to promote the fullest utilization of manpower and eliminate discriminatory employment practices." Many states have subsequently enacted antidiscrimination laws. In order to conform to the spirit of these laws and the directives of the Equal Employment Opportunity Commission established after the passage of the Civil Rights Act of 1964, management must make sure that no applicant will be discriminated against because of race, color, religion, and, since 1966, because of sex. On the other hand, a candidate may be "undesirable" for a routine job because he or she has too much education or intelligence to be contented and acceptable on a work team where there is a current vacancy.[12]

If the applicant seems to be a likely candidate, the preliminary interview should conclude with reassurance about the various tests to be taken (if

[12] A study of the predictive value of weighted application blanks showed that male recruits for assembly-line jobs tended to quit if they had higher-middle-class aspirations, were married, young, and restless. Harrison M. Trice, "The Weighted Application Blank—A Caution," *The Personnel Administrator*, vol. 9, no. 3, pp. 17–19, May–June, 1964.

any are used). It should be made clear that tests are administered to determine just how good the candidate is and where his special abilities lie, rather than to trick him into making mistakes. Tests are so commonly regarded as mantraps that employees almost always need reassurance on this point. When the preliminary interview precedes the filling out of the application blank, some explanation may also be offered about the blank itself.

The Application Blank

Although there is no one best or standard form, a properly designed application blank has the following advantages:

1 It constitutes a simple test of the candidate's ability to spell, to write legibly, and to answer factual questions rapidly and accurately. [13]

2 Combined with material gathered later during testing, it gives the employment manager a line on the candidate before the main employment interview begins.

3 Some candidates find it easier to think out the answers alone than if the same questions are asked during an interview.

4 It gives the candidate assurance that his desire for work and some of his qualifications are on record with the company.

These advantages are to be realized only under certain conditions. The application blanks should conform to the following pattern:

1 They should be brief, in order not to discourage employees who are unaccustomed to doing much writing.

2 They should contain only items that, according to company experience, are correlated with job success. It follows from this that each company should develop its own application

[13] In companies hiring hard-core unemployed minority applicants who have difficulties, the application blank must be filled out with the help of an employment interviewer.

form, preferably after studying blanks used by other companies.

For example, among the characteristics which might be listed on an employment application blank, to be filled out by the applicant, are the following: [14]

Date of birth
Marital status
Number of children or other dependents
Height and weight
Years of education (and grades or degrees completed)
Other special schooling or training
Previous jobs held
Average earnings on prior jobs
Reasons for leaving last job

Why is each of these items important in considering applicants for employment? Some are of obvious significance for placement: age, height, and weight; years of education and other special schooling or training; and previous jobs held. Prior employment experience may also be checked to see how the applicant was regarded by his former employers. Reasons for leaving last job tell something about an applicant's aspirations as well as factors beyond his control (layoff for lack of work). Marital status and number of dependents indicate the applicant's responsibilities and obligations.

[14] Most of these items should be in the simplest application blank used by small firms; more detail would be included in the typical blank used by larger companies, especially for white-collar, technical, and professional personnel. See Harrison M. Trice and William J. Wasmuth, *Effective Hiring in Small Business Organizations,* New York State School of Industrial and Labor Relations, Cornell University, Bulletin 46, Ithaca, N.Y., July, 1962, pp. 18-23. Sample application blanks for different types of personnel are found in *Forms and Records in Personnel Administration,* National Industrial Conference Board, Inc., Studies in Personnel Policy, no. 175, New York, 1960, pp. 11-32, and Elizabeth Marting (ed.), *AMA Book of Employment Forms, American Management Association,* New York, 1967. For a discussion of a special type, see George W. England, *Development and Use of Weighted Application Blanks,* W. C. Brown Co., Dubuque, Iowa, 1961.

Investigation of Previous Employment History

By checking the information given on the application blank and that gained from other sources, the employment manager has an opportunity not only to double-check on facts but also to test the applicant's candor and accuracy. Except perhaps for professional employees, letters of recommendation do not seem to be a sound device for getting reliable information. The writers are sometimes more concerned with avoiding disagreeableness than with stating their considered opinion or describing their experience with the candidate. When previous employers are consulted, it is desirable to do so over the telephone or, if necessary, by calling on them. This step is obviously not necessary for those applicants who have had no previous jobs, as in the case of young people or the "disadvantaged" discussed earlier.

The Physical Examination

Before the physical examination is made, special reassurance should be given that, like other tests, it is used to help both the applicant and the company rather than to spy out weaknesses. Applicants with some physical handicaps, for example, may be perfectly capable of handling certain types of work, and their motivation to work may be very high because of their handicaps. (For an example, see Case 4, "The Girl and the Computer.")

It should be recognized, however, that the company must protect itself against the risk of claims for compensation from individuals who are afflicted with disabilities such as hernia, for instance. The medical examination should be both general and thorough. If no company doctor is available, it may be given by any qualified physician who has adequate knowledge of the company's job requirements. Data disclosed by examination and questioning may be supplemented, if necessary, by x-ray and laboratory tests. The findings should be carefully recorded so as to give a complete medical history, the scope of current physical capacities, and the nature of disabilities, if any. Information should be confidential.

Employment Tests

Before a given company decides whether or not to use employment tests, it is well to heed the counsel of experience. "Buying and installing a test program is not like buying an electric typewriter—a relatively discrete, independent, and useful unit. Instead it is more like installing a complex accounting machine whose work means changes throughout the organization." [15] The following general questions should be answered:

1 Is top management prepared to spend the money required to develop tests that are well suited to the specific company and to hire the experts needed to administer them? Tests are useful for the most part in larger organizations which do a lot of hiring. No adequate estimation of their worth can be made in any organization until considerable evidence has been collected and correlated with its job specifications resulting from job evaluation, production standards, employee rating, and labor turnover. This kind of work cannot properly be done by amateurs. Such tests can actually be misleading unless expertly administered and diagnosed.

2 Does everyone concerned recognize the limitations of tests, and will their pitfalls be avoided? Test results are not guarantees of performance. Special dangers to be avoided are the suppositions that a single brief test can provide significant results and that standard tests are necessarily useful for a given company's requirements. [16]

[15] Mason Haire, "Use of Tests in Employee Selection," *Harvard Business Review,* vol. 28, no. 1, p. 50, January, 1950 (reprinted in Pigors, Myers, and Malm, *op. cit.,* selection 29).

[16] As noted earlier in the discussion of hiring the disadvantaged, some employment tests may discriminate against this group. See Richard S. Barrett, "Gray Areas in Black and White Testing," *Harvard Business Review,* vol. 46, no. 1, pp. 92–95, January-February, 1968. On Mar. 8, 1971, the U.S.

3 Are supervisors ready to accept tests as an improvement in hiring procedure? Unless department heads believe that tests are worth experimenting with, they will probably not support test findings. In that case, tests will neither promote line and staff collaboration nor reduce labor turnover.

If, knowing all these limitations, line managers from the top down want to cooperate with the personnel administrator and the safety director in experimenting with tests, the results may be of great value (1) as a measurement of the extent to which an applicant's abilities and disabilities fit or unfit him for job demands; (2) as a check on reported experience; (3) as a basis for objective comparisons between applicants; and (4) as an aid in setting up standards for employment procedures so that predictions can be traced, checked, and progressively improved.

There has been considerable experimentation with tests of numerous kinds.[17] What are their reliability and validity in the sense that test results consistently measure what we wish to measure? In the selection of hourly rated workers, mechanical, clerical, and trade tests have proved to be most satisfactory. Tests of this type are generally classified as *performance tests*. They are a refinement of the work-sample technique and are used to measure what an employee actually can do.

For factory jobs, management is concerned not only with what an employee can do but also with his safety. Jobs differ according to their rate of accident liability, i.e., whether or not there are special job risks. People differ according to their accident-proneness; i.e., in an unselected group, whatever the job, some individuals have a disproportionate number of accidents. For the safety of accident-prone persons and for the sake of others who work with them, it is important to keep these individuals away from jobs where the rate of accident liability is high, especially if this rate is associated with a high rate of accident severity. In order to protect workers, there has been considerable experimentation with tests to appraise accident-proneness. In relation to skilled work, it has been possible to measure one factor that has considerable prediction value: hand-eye coordination. Those who do well in tests of hand-eye coordination have a lower accident rate and a higher rate of productive efficiency than those who do badly.

For example, 128 London bus drivers were given hand-eye coordination tests at the time of their employment. Subsequently, their progress was followed for 5 years. A review of the individual accident records showed that 260 (25 percent) of 1,052 accidents were contributed by only 14 of the drivers. Of these 14 drivers, at least 5 (35 percent) could have been eliminated before employment on the basis of their coordination test.[18]

In relation to unskilled work, this factor seems not to have the same validity, and no tests have yet been developed that enable advance predictions of accident-proneness among unskilled workers. To the extent that it is possible to detect accident-proneness in certain types of work, proper placement involves putting employees on jobs where the accident potential is minimal.

Performance tests in general are subject to the limitation that other factors are responsible for a large percentage of job failures. The general level

---

Supreme Court unanimously struck down the Duke Power Company's requirement that laborers could advance only if they had a high school diploma or passed two standard achievement tests, on the grounds that these do not relate to qualifications to perform the work. *New York Times,* Mar. 9, 1967, p. 1, and *Business Week,* p. 34, Mar. 20, 1971.

[17] Marvin D. Dunnette, *Personnel Selection and Placement,* Wadsworth Publishing Company, Belmont, Calif., 1966, especially chaps. 3 and 7. Also, C. H. Lawshe and Michael J. Balma, *Principles of Personnel Testing,* 2d ed., McGraw-Hill Book Company, New York, 1966; and Robert M. Guion, *Personnel Testing,* McGraw-Hill Book Company, New York, 1965.

[18] E. G. Chambers, *Memorandum on Accident Proneness amongst the Drivers of Road Vehicles,* Cambridge University, Medical Research Council, Unit of Applied Psychology, Report 47/385, 1946.

of intelligence is one other item about which the employment manager needs information. Thus another group of tests is used to forecast an employee's ability to learn. Such *aptitude tests* are more difficult to validate since they are used to forecast future performance after training.[19] Furthermore, they usually measure general ability, which is expected to be applied to particular jobs. They are also open to the objection that differences in background may account for differences in test results. When a battery of tests is used, something about intelligence can probably be deduced, although it is sometimes doubtful whether the results are as pertinent to the job situation as data to be gained by careful interviewing. It should in any case be noted that test objectives must be formulated with care. The objective is not always to find individuals who demonstrate superior ability. Sound placement is as important as selection. For instance, in placing routine workers, especially for repetitive factory jobs, the most intelligent candidates are not necessarily the most acceptable. Study of employees making good on the kinds of jobs currently available usually shows that people with a specific level of intelligence, not always the highest, are most successful. On that same job, an employee who has much more or much less intelligence is liable to boredom or overstrain. Furthermore, since he is to work in a group whose regular members have one general level of intelligence, he will more easily be assimilated as a teammate if his intelligence is at about the same level. If he gives evidence of superior intelligence, fellow employees are apt to deride him as a "brain" or "quiz kid."

It is generally known that interest in, and ability to get along with, other people are important factors in job success. With this in mind, psychologists have devised a third group of tests to measure the more complex aspects of *temperament and personality*. When used as a supplement to performance and aptitude tests, they have a negative value in weeding out candidates who have the required skills but are likely to become misfits because of personal conflicts or maladjustments. The whole field of personality tests needs development and doubtless will be carried further. At the present time, personality tests may be useful to the employment manager not primarily as a substitute for the diagnostic skills used in interviewing but chiefly because they give clues that often lead to significant insight when followed up in the employment interview.[20]

However, even in the case of so-called "normal" and able people, the employment manager still needs, most of all, to know about each job applicant: *Will* this person do all that he *can?*

In hiring workers who are expected to fill or to prepare themselves for skilled jobs, a tentative answer to this question is usually sought in the main employment interview. In regard to applicants for unskilled and semiskilled jobs, on the other hand, judgment on this matter is made later by the first-level supervisor during the employees' probationary period.

The Employment Interview

In many companies, this interview is the only tool used in selecting new employees, particularly for skilled and technical positions. In all companies, it is an essential step in the recruitment and selection procedure. Pitfalls to be avoided by the interviewer are:

---

[19] See Edwin E. Ghiselli, *The Validity of Occupational Aptitude Tests,* John Wiley & Sons, Inc., New York, 1966.

[20] Some personality and other tests have not been validated, yet are sold widely. "Many a personnel man continues to rush to be first in line to purchase employee selection devices despite the absence of supporting research or even in the presence of negating research." Bernard L. Rosenbaum, "Are Psychological Tests Perishables?" *Personnel Journal,* vol. 46, no. 9, pp. 576-579, October, 1967. See also Robert M. Guion and Richard F. Gottier, "Validity of Personality Measures in Personnel Selection," *Personnel Psychology,* vol. 18, no. 2, pp. 135-164, Summer, 1965.

1 Thinking that in one brief interview anyone can make a complete and reliable diagnosis of a person's character or clearly forecast his future achievements.

2 Overselling the job or the company on the basis of what is offered to exceptional employees. For the average new employee, this inevitably leads to disappointment.

3 Being so familiar with job and company requirements, or having repeated them so often, that many points are carelessly described or even omitted.

4 Being unduly influenced by trivial mannerisms or by resemblance or dissimilarity to people whom the interviewer likes or dislikes.

5 Assuming that the interviewer's uncorroborated judgment is more valid than any or all other evidence gathered about the candidate.

6 Assuming that the sole function of the interviewer is to accept or reject the candidate. Every type of interview can succeed as a human experience if courtesy is preserved throughout. If a candidate must be rejected at the end of this talk, courtesy is of special importance, because this one interview may determine the applicant's opinion of the company. It may also play a part in conditioning his attitude toward other companies and toward his own future. (For a case illustrating some of these pitfalls, see Case 10, "The Rejected Applicant for Employment.")

In order to avoid these risks, an employment interviewer should be personnel-minded and have certain other qualifications. He should be skilled in interview techniques, able to talk and understand the language of the majority of applicants, be thoroughly familiar with the company's range of job opportunities and with the wages paid for similar jobs in local industry, and a perennial student of local labor conditions, labor policies, relevant legislation, and current developments in his own industry. For these reasons, the main interview should usually be conducted by the employment manager himself, supplemented by specialists in areas where his knowledge of job requirements may not be suf-

ficient, as in the interviewing of engineers, scientists, and managerial candidates.

The primary function of the employment interview (when used in conjunction with the other techniques previously described) is to complete or to correct the picture whose outlines have been blocked in by the other selection procedures. Details of personality are filled in during an interview by frankly depending on the personal impressions that, by the use of objective standards and tests, have been subordinated during other preemployment procedures. Since interviewing is the most costly of selection techniques, it cannot be done haphazardly.[21]

Conducting the Employment Interview Much of what was said about interviewing in Chapter 10 applies to the employment interview. But planning can be more definite when the subject matter is known in advance than when the direction of talk cannot be predicted.

In preparing for this interview, the employment manager may either use a checklist or merely go over in his mind the material already gathered about the applicant. He will also want to do some preliminary thinking about the job for which this individual seems best fitted. Such preparation enables the employment manager to make a tentative schedule, mental or written, of the topics to be covered during the interview according to the order of importance and the sequence in which they can most easily be introduced. He also thinks out in advance the kind of

[21] A study of interviews with Canadian army recruits revealed that interviewers developed stereotypes of good candidates, showed early biases, used favorable tones with a good candidate and unfavorable ones with one likely to be rejected, and were influenced more by unfavorable information than by favorable. E. C. Webster, *Decision Making in the Employment Interview,* McGill University, Montreal, 1964. Lyman W. Porter has pointed out "that very few studies have isolated the validity of the interview by itself rather than as part of a selection situation which includes tests and background data." "Personnel Management: A Review of the Recent Psychological Literature," *Annual Review of Psychology,* vol. 17, p. 405, 1966.

observation that it seems most important to make, either because of inconsistencies in data previously gathered or because there are indications of unusual qualifications or possible disabilities.

During the interview itself, the employment manager has in mind certain questions that he usually does not put directly to the applicant. For instance, he may be interested to know: Why is this person applying for work in this company? What values does he expect to get here besides money? Will his needs and values fit in with what we can give him? What seem to be his job qualifications? How will he work out on the job? What are his potentialities? Is he a stable person?

Using such mental questions as guides, a progressive evaluation can be made of information obtained during the interview, correlated both with data previously gathered about this person and with knowledge of company practice and specific jobs. Some of these judgments are obviously more difficult to make than others. For instance, in interviewing an applicant for the job of telephone operator, it is easy to decide whether or not she has a "good voice" but far more difficult to judge her emotional stability.

Some of the necessary information is obtained by asking direct questions. In doing this, the interviewer should exercise some caution.[22] The questions should be stated in words whose meaning will be clear to the applicant, i.e., insofar as possible in terms of the individual's context of experience. Second, inquiries should not be put in the form of leading questions, i.e., suggesting a specific answer. For instance, the question, "How do you feel about the work I have outlined?" is preferable to "Don't you think the work I have outlined is interesting?" Trick questions should never be used. They often confuse and antagonize the applicant. Thus they are out of keeping with the relation into which management wants to enter with every employee, beginning with preliminary contacts. Other precautions to be observed are that questions should be asked one at a time and not be so rapid or so numerous as to confuse the applicant. All should be pertinent to the work situation.

This last point needs further comment. Sometimes questions are relevant to the work situation although not directly connected with the job itself. For instance, if a married woman is applying for a job, the interviewer needs to know whether she has young children and, if so, what arrangements can be made for their care. Experience shows that no mother should undertake to work on the night shift if she is entirely responsible for the care of young children during the whole day. When such a situation is revealed during an interview, tact is needed to help the applicant understand that it is a sense of responsibility toward employees and not indifference to their needs that prevents management from employing a person who would inevitably be subjected to overstrain.

During the interview, the employment manager may come to feel that the candidate, although a desirable person, is not likely to succeed in the job for which he has applied and has been tested. In this case, the employment interview is an opportunity to steer the candidate toward another job in which he may excel. The aim here is, if possible, to make assets out of liabilities by matching some special lack or idiosyncrasy with a specific company condition.[23] For example, a

[22] Milton M. Mandell, *The Employment Interview,* American Management Association, Research Study no. 47, 1961; Felix M. Lopez, Jr., *Personnel Interviewing,* McGraw-Hill Book Company, New York, 1965; and Elizabeth Sidney and Margaret Brown, *The Skills of Interviewing,* Tavistock Publications, London, 1961.

[23] In this connection, for a study on the need and possibilities of employing physically impaired workers, see *The Company and the Physically Impaired Worker,* National Industrial Conference Board, Inc., Studies in Personnel Policy, no. 163, New York, 1957; and "Personnel Practices Relating to the Handicapped in Small Companies," *Management Record* (National Industrial Conference Board, Inc.), vol. 22, nos. 7-8, pp. 28-32, July-August, 1960.

person who is shy and introvertive may not mind working on a single-machine job or on the "graveyard" shift. In a large Eastern corporation, it was found that a special type of inspection caused headaches and eyestrain to people who had inadequate muscular control or far-sighted vision but not to nearsighted people. Thereafter, nearsighted girls or women were steered toward this work.

Utilization of Older Employees Another group that deserves special consideration is made up of older workers. In the United States, the proportion of older people is increasing. Many of them are still willing and able to work. These facts raise an important question for employment policy: Is it worthwhile for management to try to utilize the services of people who have reached the customary retirement age?[24]

The answer to this question, for any given company, may well depend on where these older people have been employed. When a person with a good employment record wants to continue working in a company after the customary retirement age, there are good reasons for continuing his employment, provided that he has the skill, ability, and stamina needed for an available job. In such a case, a worker's long membership in the organization, his willingness to assume responsibility without close supervision, and his job experience may be assets that more than counterbalance some decline in dexterity and strength. Moreover, the offer of continuing employment is fitting recognition of what a company owes an employee who for many years has been a "worthy citizen" of the organization. Of course, there is the risk that such special consideration may lead to complaints of discrimination from less effective employees who are retired. But this objection can be met by treating selected candidates as "contingents." As pointed out by J. Douglas Brown,

> A necessary step in the solution of the problems of industry's role in respect to the older worker is the firm acceptance of the need for a fixed age at which the worker's expectancy of continued employment ends. Attainment of this age should terminate all seniority rights and all further accumulation of pension credits, whatever future employment relations may develop.[25]

Specially selected employees should be reemployed annually on a system like probation.

The question of employing older workers is more difficult when these people have already been retired from some other organization. Regardless of their technical skills and knowledge, such people have a difficult adjustment to make when they start work in a new place. For example, in a new work environment, it is not easy for an "oldster" in years and in outlook to be a "youngster" in length of service. Nor can all the necessary adjustments be made by the older worker alone. The friction caused by a "generation gap" is something that has to be reckoned with. For these reasons it is more difficult to tell whether or not mutually satisfactory adjustments can be made when people past the usual retirement age are taken on as new hires.

Concluding the Employment Interview An important step to be taken with all candidates for employment, either at the end of the employment interview or at some other time before

---

[24] For a stimulating analysis of this whole question, see Harland Fox, "Utilization of Older Manpower," *Harvard Business Review,* vol. 29, no. 6, pp. 40–54, November, 1951. See also Donald M. Smith, "Help Wanted: Older Workers for Special Jobs," *Personnel Administration,* vol. 21, no. 4, pp. 35–38, July–August, 1958; and B. V. H. Schneider, *The Older Worker,* University of California, Institute of Industrial Relations, Berkeley, Calif., 1962; and U.S. Bureau of Labor Statistics, *Industrial Retraining Programs for Technological Change: A Study of the Performance of Older Workers,* Bulletin no. 1368, 1963.

[25] J. Douglas Brown, "The Role of Industry in Relation to the Older Worker," in *The Aged and Society: A Symposium on the Problems of an Aging Population,* Industrial Relations Research Association, December, 1950, pp. 70–71.

placement, is to give an accurate picture of job requirements and company standards. In most companies, some explanations are offered during the employment interview about what the company expects from its employees. (More detailed information on the induction process is found in Chapter 16.) During talk about the job, it may be possible to predict whether a given applicant will find his work monotonous. (Monotony is often spoken of as though it were a feature of the job itself, but it may also describe an individual's attitude toward a job.) When candidates during selection can be steered away from the type of work that seems to them monotonous, time, money, and nervous strain are saved at the stages of placement and follow-up.

If for any reason the interviewer concludes during the conversation that the applicant cannot be accepted, a tactful but clear statement of this fact should be made. It is tempting to let the rejected applicant leave without putting the unpalatable truth into words, but it is kinder to reject an applicant promptly than to allow him to realize gradually why he has received no word about the job for which he is waiting. The interviewer should also give the grounds for the rejection if he thinks that there is a reasonable expectation that this might be used constructively by the applicant.

Even when an interview confirms the favorable impression gained from other sources of information, the applicant is not definitely accepted as a regular worker at this point. He is only classified as apparently desirable. This tentative judgment needs to be confirmed by actual tryout and approved by the supervisor who will be responsible for the candidate's work if he is accepted at the end of the probationary period. Thus the successful employment interview is followed by introducing the candidate to his future supervisor, who, if he decides to accept him, will show the new employee his workplace, acquaint him with his fellow employees, and explain exactly what the job requirements are.

PLACEMENT: AN EXPERIMENTAL DECISION

Placement has an experimental element. But for most employees it is a decisive step and should consist in matching what the supervisor has reason to think the new employee can do with what the job *demands* (job requirements), *imposes* (in strain, working conditions, etc.), and *offers* (in the form of pay rate, interest, companionship with others, promotional possibilities, etc.). It is not easy to match all these factors for a new worker who is still in many ways an unknown quantity. For this reason, the first placement usually carries with it the status of probationer.

If the company is unionized, probation is specifically defined as a trial period, usually 1 to 3 months, at the end of which period the worker who makes good becomes a regular employee. During this time, the union will usually accept without question management's decision to discharge an unsatisfactory probationer. But, once a worker has achieved the status of a regular employee, management can discharge only for cause. It is therefore obvious that the supervisor who authorizes the transition from probationer to regular employee makes a decision that is of great importance to management. This decision is especially important in those cases where normal hiring standards have been relaxed, as in the hiring of disadvantaged people with labor-market or physical handicaps.

The Question of Interim Placements

If there is no current opening that seems suitable for a specific worker, some companies seek to hold a desirable employee by offering temporary placement in any available job no matter how unsuitable. The excuse made for such a sacrifice to expediency is that the candidate is placed with the company and may be transferred to the desired position as soon as an opening occurs. From the viewpoint of employment policy, such placement is ill-advised, because it leaves too much room for misunderstanding and for development of individual and organizational instability. The following is a case in point.

A Case Example: The Demoralized Apprentice

A likely looking boy applied for the opportunity of becoming a machinist apprentice. Unfortunately, the class was full and the next one was not due to start for 6 months. In the meantime, the boy was placed as a helper to an elderly rough grinder who had been with the company 20 years and who therefore was presumably a well-satisfied and stable employee. A month later, the boy was slated for discharge on the ground that he was uncooperative and slovenly in his work.

Only during an exit interview was the root of the difficulty uncovered, so that the new employee could be spared the humiliation of having failed on his first job. During the interview, it was brought out that the worker whom the boy was helping had jeered at his aspirations to make something of himself and scoffed at the idea that the company would actually train him as an apprentice. He assured the boy that the talk of training was only "a come-on game." "Why not get wise to yourself? I used to think I could make something of myself, too. And look at me! What have I got to show for 20 years of faithful service?" Exposed to such defeatism and without the encouragement that he should have received in follow-up interviews, the boy had become discouraged and demoralized. After the talk, he was placed as a helper to a more satisfied worker and was reassured at intervals until the time came for him to start his apprentice training.

Although interim placements can, of course, be more skillfully handled than this one, they are unsound in principle because they ask too much of everyone concerned. Marking time is always a strain, the ill effects of which are usually communicated to others in the work group. Normally, the newly hired employee is placed on the job for which he is thought fit and for which a requisition was made. If he proves satisfactory after adequate induction, training, and probation, he is accepted as a regular employee.

SUMMARY

The interrelated steps of recruitment, hiring, and placement reviewed in this chapter illustrate the systems approach to personnel policies in building an effective work force in any organization.

The broad purposes of top management can be an effective force at the work level only when procedures growing out of these policies are centralized at the beginning. Recruitment, employment interviews, testing, special efforts in reaching the disadvantaged, manpower planning, and forecasting (including computer applications) are all methods which require expert knowledge of the type found in effective personnel departments. When these aspects of recruitment, selection, and placement are all seen as steps toward an enduring employment relationship and are progressively improved by subsequent evaluation of successes and failures on the job, excessive labor turnover can be reduced and new employees more rapidly come to feel a sense of membership in the organization.

The condition of the labor market for different occupational groups affects the quality of applicants, and during periods of labor shortage, hiring standards may have to be relaxed. Social pressures to provide employment opportunities for those with various disadvantages (particularly in minority groups) also require new policy decisions and modifications in established hiring standards and procedures.

Staff services support top management's objective of securing applicants who can become productive employees. The key management representative during an initial placement is the first-level supervisor, whose responsibility it is to determine which probationers are acceptable as regular employees. Once placement occurs, on-the-job training or other types of training may begin, along with appraisal of subsequent performance.

SELECTED REFERENCES

Ace, Merle E.: "Psychological Testing: Unfair Discrimination?" Industrial Relations, vol. 10, no. 3, pp. 301–315, October, 1971 (also reprinted in Paul Pigors, Charles A. Myers, and F. T. Malm, *Management of Human Resources: Readings in Personnel Administration,* 3d ed., McGraw-Hill Book Company, New York, 1973, selection 30).

Doeringer, Peter B. (ed.): *Programs to Employ the Disadvantaged,* Prentice-Hall, Inc., Englewood Cliffs, N.J., 1970.

Dunnette, Marvin D.: *Personnel Selection and Placement,* Wadsworth Publishing Company, Inc., Belmont, Calif., 1966.

England, George W., and Donald G. Paterson: "Selection and Placement: The Past Ten Years," in Herbert G. Heneman, Jr., et al. (eds.): *Employment Relations Research,* Harper & Row, Publishers, Incorporated, New York, 1960 (for the Industrial Relations Research Association).

Ghiselli, Edwin E.: *The Validity of Occupational Aptitude Tests,* John Wiley & Sons, Inc., New York, 1966.

Goodman, Paul S.: "Hiring, Training, and Retraining the Hard-core," *Industrial Relations,* vol. 9, no. 1, pp. 54–66, October, 1969 (reprinted in Pigors, Myers, and Malm, *op cit.,* selection 31).

Guion, Robert: *Personnel Testing,* McGraw-Hill Book Company, New York, 1965.

Haire, Mason: "Uses of Tests in Employee Selection," *Harvard Business Review,* vol. 28, no. 1, pp. 42–51, January, 1950 (reprinted in Pigors, Myers, and Malm, *op. cit.,* selection 29).

Hawk, Roger H.: *The Recruitment Function,* American Management Association, New York, 1967.

Heneman, Herbert G., Jr., and George Seltzer: *Employer Manpower Forecasting,* Manpower Research Monograph no. 19, U.S. Department of Labor, Washington, D.C., 1970.

Janger, Allen R., and Ruth G. Sheaffer: *Managing Programs to Employ the Disadvantaged,* Studies in Personnel Policy no. 219, National Industrial Conference Board, New York, 1970.

Malm, F. T.: "Recruiting Patterns and the Functioning of Labor Markets," *Industrial and Labor Relations Review,* vol. 7, no. 4, pp. 507–525, July, 1954 (reprinted in Pigors, Myers, and Malm, *op. cit.,* selection 28).

"Methods of Recruiting Engineers," in *Optimum Use of Engineering Talent: Meeting the Need for Technical Personnel,* American Management Association, Management Report no. 58, New York, 1961.

Miller, Robert B.: *Tests and the Selection Process,* Science Research Associates, Inc., Chicago, 1966.

Morrison, Edward J.: *Developing Computer-based Employee Information Systems,* American Management Association Research Study no. 99, American Management Association, Inc., New York, 1971.

Odiorne, George S., and A. S. Hann: *Effective College Recruiting,* University of Michigan, Bureau of Industrial Relations, Report no. 13, Ann Arbor, Mich., 1961.

Peskin, Dean B.: *Human Behavior and Employment Interviewing,* American Management Association, Inc., New York, 1971, esp. chap. 5, "Evaluating Success and Failure."

Tracey, William R.: *Designing, Training and Development Systems,* American Management Association, New York, 1971. (Also, *Evaluating Training and Development Systems,* AMA, 1968.)

Trice, Harrison M., and William J. Wasmuth: *Effective Hiring in Small Business Organizations,* New York State School of Industrial and Labor Relations, Cornell University Bulletin 46, Ithaca, N.Y., July, 1962.

Wikstrom, Walter S.: *Manpower Planning: Evolving Systems,* The Conference Board, New York, 1971. [Includes case examples from Standard Oil Company (New Jersey), Hewlett-Packard, 3M Company, Bell Telephone System, Scott Paper, IBM, Union Oil, and Lockheed.]

Chapter 16

Training and
Performance Appraisal

Training is not something that is done once to new employees—it is used continuously in every well-run establishment. Every time you get someone to do work the way you want it done, you are training. Every time you give directions or discuss a procedure, you are training.

C. R. Dooley[1]

No organization can choose whether or not to train employees. Every new employee, regardless of his previous training, education, and experience, needs to be introduced to the work environment of his new employer and to be taught how to perform specific tasks. Moreover, specific occasions for retraining arise when an employee is transferred or promoted, or when jobs change and new skills must be learned, perhaps because of changes introduced by advancing automation. Even when responsibilities for orientation, induction, and retraining are not regarded by managers as calling for planned procedures, they will be met in some way or other, by someone in the work situation. Thus the only choice left to management is whether training shall be haphazard, casual, and possibly misdirected, or whether it shall be made a carefully planned part of an integrated program of personnel administration.

Furthermore, training does not end with the initial induction of an employee, nor is it to be limited to retraining for new jobs or altered work methods. People are constantly being "trained" and retrained by the way organizational superiors and long-service employees treat them, and by the opportunity—or lack of it—to find how their work performance is appraised, formally

[1] C. R. Dooley, "Training Within Industry in the United States," *International Labour Review,* vol. 54, nos. 3-4, p. 161, September-October, 1946.

and informally, by supervisors and teammates. The supervisor's appraisal may be informal, on a now-and-then basis; it may not be part of any systematic plan. Or it may be formalized, carried out at regular intervals, in progress reviews based on careful job descriptions or position guides. It may be followed through by efforts to help an employee progressively raise the level of his performance. Appraisal can be, and should be, a form of training, using the term "training" in its widest sense—as an aid to self-development.

In Chapter 3, we considered some aspects of training and appraisal in connection with management development. Much of what we said there is relevant to training and performance appraisal of all employees. Effective managers are those who can best develop *all* human resources in the organization, for the purpose of achieving organizational objectives. If employees see training and appraisal as ways to achieve better personal goals at work, they will welcome these opportunities. Otherwise, training courses and appraisal procedures are virtually worthless. For training and appraisal to be successful, therefore, employees must *want* to learn and to improve their performance, and supervisors must *be able* to teach and to help subordinates raise the level of their performance. We noted in Chapter 7 that this is an important responsibility of supervisors.

BENEFITS OF WELL-PLANNED INDUCTION AND TRAINING PROGRAMS

How should induction and training programs be carried out in order to be fully effective? What are the chief benefits to be derived? A summary listing may be helpful:

1 Orientation and induction provide a new employee with general information that he needs about the organization—about policies, procedures, practices, and rules that will affect him, and also about the job on which he will work. All this information should be communicated to him in a way that can help him to feel at home in his new work environment as quickly as possible.

2 A new employee is instructed in the requirements of the specific job he is to perform, as outlined in an accurate and comprehensive job description. In this way he can rapidly learn to measure up to standards for performance, thus increasing his value to the organization and satisfying his human need for personal growth on the job.

3 An advantageous by-product of training is that accidents, spoiled work, and damage to machinery and equipment can be kept to a minimum by well-trained employees.

4 Dissatisfactions, complaints, absenteeism, and turnover can be greatly reduced when employees are so well trained that they can experience the direct satisfactions associated with a sense of achievement and the knowledge that they are developing their inherent capabilities at work.

5 As an employee responds to continued training, he can progressively increase his value to the organization and thus prepare himself for promotion.

6 Continued training can help an employee to develop his ability to learn—adapting himself to new work methods, learning to use new kinds of equipment, and adjusting to major changes in job content and work relationships. In the years ahead, when technological advances will doubtless continue to change many work situations rapidly, versatility and adaptability may well be the most important advantages that can be derived from training. Training constitutes an *investment* in human resources, and can be measured in the human asset accounting approach discussed in Chapter 1.[2]

Thus, training that fosters employee self-development and versatility should be planned, ad-

[2] For another specific example of this approach, see John Douthat, "Accounting for Personnel Training and Development Costs," *Training and Development Journal,* vol. 24, no. 6, pp. 2-6, June, 1970. Training costs are capitalized, to avoid the distortions of treating training costs as expenses when incurred.

ministered, and accepted as a never-ending process. It can be continued until the day of retirement with every employee who is interested in learning and in teaching. Even when a given employee has passed the stage where he can easily learn a new job or a new skill, he may still participate in the training program; perhaps offering valuable service in helping to orient and induct new employees.

The responsibility for final results clearly rests with line management—with supervisors in the department in which employees are trained and evaluated. Since the supervisor is responsible for the results in his department, he is also clearly responsible for the proper induction, training, and approach of the employees whom he supervises. He may have assistance in this, but he cannot escape the responsibility.

In most large and medium-sized organizations, however, it has been found advisable to place staff responsibility for planning and developing these programs in the hands of a specialist. This person may be a personnel administrator or a training director who is either in a separate department or (preferably) subordinate to the personnel administrator. Unless there is a staff man primarily concerned with assisting line management in developing and administering these programs, they are likely to be neglected by managers who are confronted with what seem to them to be more urgent problems.

For example, in some firms new employees are hustled from the employment office to their new jobs without so much as a word about the company for which they are going to work. If the supervisor is busy when they report for work, as he usually is, the new employees are assigned to some of the "older hands" for training. The results are sometimes unsatisfactory, for the older worker may not be a good teacher and may also be preoccupied with his own work. Furthermore, if there is a union steward in the department, he will probably be more interested in the new employee than will the busy supervisor.

INDUCTION AS A PART OF TRAINING

Before a newly hired employee is trained for a specific job, he should be welcomed as a new member of the organization. The first day of employment is long remembered by most people. Initial impressions and information count heavily in later attitudes toward the job and the company. Proper induction is therefore an integral part of the training process. Helping new employees to feel at home more quickly enables them to get the full benefit of specific job training. The new employee is often highly motivated to do a good job, and his introduction to the new organization should build on this attitude toward work.

A friendly welcome to the organization is not the only purpose of good induction, however. An equally important objective is to give the new employee accurate and useful information about the company, the employee services it offers, and the personnel policies that will affect him as well as all other employees.

Elements of an Induction Program

A good induction program has three parts:

1 Introductory information given informally or in group sessions in the personnel department.
2 Further information given by the new employee's supervisor in the department about departmental facilities and requirements.
3 A follow-up interview several weeks after the employee has been on the job, given by either the supervisor or a representative of the personnel department, to answer further questions that the new employee may have and to repeat some of the earlier information for emphasis.

The actual information provided in a well-planned induction program will vary with each organization, but it should cover all matters which may affect the new employee during his first months with his new employer. The checklist of steps shown in Exhibit 16-1 is illustrative; some of these steps would normally be covered in an employee handbook and, in unionized firms, in the union agreement, but many would have to be handled orally, some by a personnel staff representative and some by the new employee's supervisor.

Exhibit 16-1 Checklist of Steps in an Induction Program for New Employees

---

The company (or organization)—its history, development, management, product or service

Personnel Policies—what the new employee can expect of the company and what it expects of him

Terms of employment—including general disciplinary rules and (if unionized) provisions of union agreement

Employee activities—benefits and services available

Physical facilities—cafeteria, washrooms, parking lot, etc.

The job or department for which the new employee is hired—general nature of the work, hours, wages, opportunities for promotion

The supervisor of the new employee—introduction to him, to other supervisors in the department, and to union stewards, if any

Departmental rules and regulations—safety measures

Relation of employee's new job to other jobs in department, and to work of related departments

Detailed description of job—its duties, standards, hours, wage rate or incentive, workplace, tools, equipment (merging into actual on-the-job training)

Introduction to fellow workers

Subsequent follow-up (several weeks later) to answer further questions; reviewing key information; and checking on success of initial job placement during the probationary period of employment

---

In short, the whole induction program should be directed toward giving the new employee a real feeling that he is welcomed as a member of the organization. A good deal of the success of subsequent training and performance on the job depends on good prior orientation and induction to the organization. Failure is measured in dis-

satisfaction, poor work, and often labor turnover.[3]

TYPES OF EMPLOYEE TRAINING

The types of employee training best suited to a specific organization depend upon a number of factors, such as skills called for in jobs to be filled, qualifications of candidates applying for jobs, and the kinds of operating problems confronted by the organization. Although it is important that the training program be developed to meet specific needs, the personnel administrator or training director should also be familiar with the whole range of training as practiced in other firms and organizations so that he can advise managers on training methods best suited to their needs.

Various types of employee training and their relative advantages may be outlined as follows (management development has already been discussed in Chapter 3).

Public Vocational School Training or "Refresher Courses"

Public vocational school training or "refresher courses" may be arranged by the training director in cooperation with public or trade school authorities, to provide training for prospective employment applicants in shop mathematics, blueprint reading, stenography, computer programming, etc. In some cases, this type of training precedes employment, although it is likely to be more effective if it is closely geared to the needs of a specific company. Too often, vocational schools have been a dumping ground for less able students, but there is no reason why good teaching related to employment opportunities cannot make vocational training a real ser-

---

[3] For a research study on the effect of a good induction program in a supermarket chain, see B. W. Marion and S. E. Trico, "Job Orientation—A Factor in Employee Performance and Turnover," *Personnel Journal*, vol. 48, no. 10, pp. 799-804, 831, October, 1969.

vice to employing organizations, as well as to efforts to retrain displaced employees. [4]

Apprentice Training

Apprentice training is desirable in industries such as the metal trades, printing trades, and building construction, which require a constant flow of new employees who expect to become all-around craftsmen. Since the training program is long and requires continual supervision, this method of training is expensive. Standards are rigid and are defined in an apprenticeship agreement that, in unionized firms, involves union acceptance. Furthermore, after the long period of apprenticeship is completed, there is no assurance that the man will remain with the firm that trained him. Nevertheless, there is a continuing need for apprentices to skilled crafts, and access to apprenticeship lists should *not* be discriminatory. Qualified applicants should be acceptable regardless of color or race, or whether they are related to present craftsmen. [5]

There have been some notable examples of union-sponsored apprenticeship training programs, in cooperation with employers. One is the program started many years ago by the International Printing Pressmen and Assistants' Union. This union has also had an extensive program of

retraining present craftsmen for new jobs resulting from changing technology and materials, such as the newer types of packaging on which product labels and descriptive materials are printed.

Vestibule Training

Vestibule training is used primarily when large numbers of employees must be trained quickly, as during rapid expansion of employment in some firms or industries, although it is also helpful as a preliminary to on-the-job training. New workers are trained for specific jobs on special machines or equipment in a separate location. In some cases, an attempt may be made to duplicate as closely as possible the actual workroom conditions, but one of the advantages of vestibule training is that it permits more emphasis on teaching the best method than on getting out production. Furthermore, trainees have an opportunity to get accustomed to work routine and recover from their initial nervousness before going on to actual jobs.

The artificial atmosphere usually associated with this type of training, however, may actually increase the adjustment problem for trainees. In one company known to the authors, the vestibule school became increasingly different from the manufacturing department that it was supposed to duplicate, because the school lagged behind the shop in manufacturing technique and equipment. Moreover, trainees who had been constantly helped by the teacher missed his encouragement when they moved into the shop, and they became easily discouraged. The supervisor had to retrain these workers, yet pressing production demands forced him to leave them alone much of the time, thus increasing their sense of failure. Many quit voluntarily. Management finally decided to assign staff instructors to do training on the job, and eventually the vestibule school was discontinued.

Another firm succeeded in meeting this difficulty by making the vestibule training period

[4] George P. Shultz and Arnold R. Weber, *Strategies for the Displaced Worker,* Harper & Row, Publishers, Incorporated, New York, 1966. The use of public vocational schools was only one of many programs developed to help displaced Armour employees, described and evaluated in this book.

[5] Unions, particularly local unions, have more often been guilty of this than employers in apprenticeable crafts. Within recent years, a number of unions, however, have admitted Negro apprentices or provided preapprenticeship programs. F. Ray Marshall and Vernon M. Briggs, Jr., *The Negro and Apprenticeship,* Johns Hopkins University Press, Baltimore, 1967. The Workers Defense League has been active in preparing young minority males for craft apprenticeship tests and getting a number into apprenticeship programs. F. Ray Marshall and Vernon M. Briggs, Jr., *Equal Apprenticeship Opportunities: The Nature of the Issue and the New York Experience,* Policy Papers in Human Resources and Industrial Relations no. 10, Institute of Labor and Industrial Relations, The University of Michigan-Wayne State University, Ann Arbor, Mich., 1968.

relatively short (about 1 week); the instructors in the vestibule school then visited trainees on the job during the succeeding weeks. The continued interest and encouragement of their former instructors helped the trainees to do better work, yet it did not interfere with the responsibility of the departmental foreman to offer encouragement during the same period.

On-the-Job Training

In contrast to vestibule or off-the-job training, the new employee is assigned, in on-the-job training, to a specific job at a machine or workplace in the shop, office, or laboratory. He is instructed by an experienced employee, a special instructor, or his supervisor. Effective on-the-job training depends primarily upon qualified trainers. Without them, it is simply the old haphazard practice of putting new workers with "old hands" who may have neither the inclination nor the ability to teach the newcomer properly.

With competent instruction, however, this type of training may be most effective for rapid training of large numbers of unskilled and semiskilled workers. It was the method by which, during the Second World War, millions of persons, many of whom had never been in the labor market before, were trained to do thousands of different jobs in war plants. The value of adequate on-the-job training was one of the war's great lessons in the development of human resources.

While this experience was impressive, it is not likely to be repeated on the same scale. As we have seen in Chapter 4, the nature of work has changed during the last two decades, and especially within the past 10 years, in the direction of jobs which require more education. Increasingly, secondary school work in science and mathematics is a minimum requirement for entry into many of the jobs which involve subsequent on-the-job training. In fact, it is evident that on-the-job training will be more effective if the new employee has a sound basic secondary education

prior to employment.[6] Many skills are learned on the job, and this type of training is probably the most frequent way in which people are trained, especially for jobs which are more specific to the organization. For the disadvantaged employee, preemployment training may need to precede on-the-job training, although both may be organized by the firm with or without a government subsidy.[7]

Programmed Instruction

A more recent training method is based on the earlier work of psychologists in developing teaching machines. Programmed instruction uses teaching machines, programmed books, or filmstrips. It differs from conventional forms of training in which the trainer guides the learning process, because the material to be learned is presented in a manner which the student himself can control. Learning proceeds in "bits," to which the individual student responds with correct or incorrect answers or solutions, and he moves ahead only as fast as he learns and understands each step or bit. Some standardized programs are available for such fields as calculus, spelling, and blueprint reading, but others have been developed by industrial firms for their own needs. Among these are Chase Manhattan Bank (keypunch and other office machine operations),

[6] If the labor market tightens, of course, employers tend to lower hiring standards and do more on-the-job training coupled with job redesign. For a survey and analysis of experience, see Peter B. Doeringer and Michael J. Piore, *Internal Labor Markets and Manpower Analysis,* D. C. Heath and Company, Lexington, Mass., 1970, pp. 17–22.

[7] There have been many such programs with support from the Manpower Training and Development Act administered by the U.S. Department of Labor. An example of a city-supported program in the Port of New York Authority is described by its executive director, Thomas J. Riley, "The 'BEST' Program for Unemployed and Unskilled," *Training and Development Journal,* vol. 20, no. 3, pp. 40–44, March, 1966. Over 4,500 disadvantaged people were in training in this program at the end of 1965. For later experience, see Charles A. Myers, *The Role of the Private Sector in Manpower Development,* The Johns Hopkins Press, Baltimore, 1971, chap. 3, "Hiring and Training the Disadvantaged."

Lever Brothers Company (product knowledge and completion of sales forms), Halle Brothers Company (retail sales training), and Arthur Wiesenberger and Company (basic finance for security salesmen).[8] Programmed instruction may also be useful in the retraining process as old skills become obsolete.

THE NEED FOR CONTINUAL RETRAINING

The impact of rapid technological change and automation on existing skills and jobs has been mentioned in earlier chapters. This means that *training is a continuing function* and that programs for retraining employees for new occupations and jobs in the same organization will be increasingly necessary. As the repetitive, routine, and clerical jobs are eliminated by electronic data processing installations, for example, some of the displaced workers (the ones who have the requisite educational qualifications) can be retrained as programmers, console operators, etc. It will be necessary for management to give considerably more attention to retraining employees for changed jobs than it has in the past.[9] In some cases, retraining programs can be developed jointly with unions representing affected employees.

An outstanding example of a union-sponsored retraining program to qualify craftsmen for new jobs created by the atomic energy and space programs is the 5 year part time course for journeymen (craftsmen) started in 1953 by the United Association of Journeymen and Apprentices of the Plumbing and Pipe Fitting Industry, with the assistance of contributions from the national contractors in the industry. This program has helped members to qualify for highly skilled jobs in the construction and maintenance of atomic plants, missile bases, automatic refineries, chemical plants, and many other modern industries. The old concept of "the plumber" has been supplanted by a variety of skills adapted to changing technology.

Employee education provided off the employer's premises is also often helpful in preparing for new or better jobs. Many firms provide tuition refunds or supplements.[10]

DEVELOPING A TRAINING PROGRAM

It is impossible to recommend a training program that would be equally good for every organization, because there are so many special features in each one to which the program should be adapted. Training is usually needed where there is a special problem interfering with production or service, such as excessive turnover among new

[8] Ned A. Rosen and Emil A. Mesics, *Programmed Instruction: What It Is and Where It Is Going,* Cornell University, New York State School of Industrial and Labor Relations, Reprint Series, no. 141, Ithaca, N.Y., 1963 (reprinted from *The Business Quarterly,* vol. 28, no. 2, pp. 39-48, Summer, 1963. For other company case histories, see Gabriel D. Ofiesh, *Programmed Instruction: A Guide for Management,* American Management Association, New York, 1965. Costs of programmed learning are discussed by Joseph P. Yaney, "Programmed Learning: Costs and Cost Reduction," *Training and Development Journal,* vol. 20, no. 3, pp. 16-20, March, 1966; Robert B. Nordberg, "Teaching Machines: Six Dangers and One Advantage," in Joseph S. Roucek (ed.), *Programmed Teaching: A Symposium on Automation in Education,* Philosophical Library, New York, 1965, pp. 1-7; and Ralph A. Dreckman, "Programmed Learning: The State of the Art for Training Practioners," *Training and Development Journal,* vol. 22, no. 3, pp. 51-60, March, 1968.

[9] For a case study of an early successful experience, see F. F. Foltman, "Xerox Corporation: A Case Study in Re-

training," *Management of Personnel Quarterly,* vol. 1, no. 5, pp. 8-20, Autumn-Winter, 1962; and a later follow-up, Ned A. Rosen, Lawrence K. Williams, and F. F. Foltman, "Motivational Constraints in an Industrial Retraining Program," *Personnel Psychology,* vol. 18, no. 1, pp. 65-79, Spring, 1965. Those who volunteered for retraining to avoid layoffs were the better-educated younger employees. Older employees had less confidence in their ability to learn new jobs and felt they were protected by seniority provisions. Other company retraining programs are discussed in Ida R. Hoos, *Retraining the Work Force: An Analysis of Current Experience,* University of California Press, Berkeley, 1967, Chap. 3.

[10] See Edward A. C. Dubois, *The Case for Employee Education,* American Management Association, Management Bulletin 100, New York, 1967.

employees, considerable absenteeism, a high accident rate, excessive spoilage of work, or a serious shortage of adequate replacements for a given job. These are examples of training needs which specially developed training programs are designed to meet. Usually supervisors are glad to talk about their problems and are anxious to have help in solving them. A training program developed in this way is bound to have the support of supervisors, because they recognize its usefulness to them and therefore do not regard it as just something that a personnel administrator or training director thinks would be helpful in a general way.

Once training needs have been determined, the training director in consultation with the line officials involved should consider the following points: (1) who is to be trained, (2) the content of the training program, (3) who is to do the training, and (4) when, for how long, and where it should be done. [11]

Evaluating Results

Finally, as the program is put into operation with the support of top management, and as experience regarding it accumulates, the results should be checked and evaluated. Has production increased? Were former training periods reduced for certain jobs? Are new workers able to reach expected earnings more quickly? Are there fewer accidents? Is there less spoilage and less damage to machines and equipment? Have turnover rates been reduced? Answers to these questions, applying to the same or comparable groups of workers before and after the new training program, will indicate the degree of its success and perhaps suggest changes that would make training even more effective. [12]

A Case Example: How a Training Need Was Met

The steps in developing a training program are illustrated in part by the experience of a cotton-goods mill in establishing a "loom-fixers' school" [13] Supervisors of the weaving departments had felt that the old method of training loom fixers was not getting sufficiently good results. It was traditional in the industry for "learner fixers" to pick up what they could by working with older men. All the old-timers had learned this way, yet the supervisors had difficulty with them when new types of looms were introduced or when it was necessary to make transfers to different types of looms for production reasons. The old-timers lacked versatility and frequently had no adequate understanding of the way in which a loom functions.

This company lacked a training director, but the superintendent and the employment manager, with the supervisors' help, established a loom-fixers' school—one of the first to be set up in any textile firm. Various looms in different stages of assembly were put in a special room, and a loom expert who was also an excellent teacher was secured as the instructor. Weavingroom supervisors urged their older loom fixers as well as learners to attend classes before or after their shifts. In

[11] See F. T. Malm, "Analyzing Training Needs and Results," adapted from "Comment rendre la formation plus efficace: analyse des besoins et des résultats en matière de formation," *Hommes et Techniques,* no. 204, pp. 1293-1305, November, 1961 (reprinted in Paul Pigors, Charles A. Myers, and F. T. Malm, *Management of Human Recources: Readings in Personnel Administration,* 3d ed., McGraw-Hill Book Company, New York, 1973, selection 33).

[12] For an evaluation of a combined induction and training program for new employees, designed to reduce anxiety on the first job, compared to a control group handled in the old way, see Earl R. Gomersall and M. Scott Myers, "Breakthrough in On-the-job Training," *Harvard Business Review,* vol. 44, no. 4, pp. 62-72, July-August, 1966. The experiment and evaluation were conducted at Texas Instruments Incorporated. For a more general discussion of evaluation methods, see D. L. Kirkpatrick, "Evaluation of Training," chap. 5 in *Training and Development Handbook,* American Society of Training and Development, McGraw-Hill Book Company, New York, 1967; and William R. Tracey, *Evaluating Training and Development Systems,* American Management Association, Inc., New York, 1968.

[13] Case drawn from the industrial experience of one of the authors.

addition, difficult problems in fixing looms were brought to the school by loom fixers and worked out with the assistance of the instructor.

The results were excellent. Many men took the courses each year, spurred on by the prospect of more rapid promotions. Supervisors reported that their loom fixers were better trained and more versatile in meeting new types of mechanical problems. New men learned loom fixing more quickly than had been thought possible, because in the school they were able to take apart and reassemble a loom under the guidance of an expert instructor.

Only one instructor was needed in this school, and he proved to be an excellent teacher. Not every organization is so fortunate in meeting specific training needs, however. No matter how well the training program looks on paper, it cannot succeed without competent instruction.[14]

TRAINING PRINCIPLES AND TECHNIQUES

The best-planned training programs are likely to be ineffective if the trainers are poorly qualified. A well-qualified trainer is one who not only has mastery of the technical details of the particular job, but knows how to train, i.e., to teach. Certain principles of learning, developed by the work of psychologists, are applicable here.[15]

These principles can be briefly summarized. (1) The student or trainee must *want* to learn; his motivation to improve his job performance or to learn a new skill must be high. (2) Motivation is increased by the prospect of some reward at the conclusion of the learning process, for example, a promotion or a better job. (3) The consequences of his learning need to be checked by the teacher or trainer, as the latter tells him when he is learning correctly or incorrectly and why. This is known as "feedback." (4) This is best accomplished through learning by doing, rather than by listening. (5) The material to be learned should be developed in stages, with feedback correction at each stage, if necessary. (6) When the learner has made the correct responses to the learning process, *he has learned.* Whether his new knowledge survives can be tested periodically again by the feedback process.

While learning theory is much more complex than this brief summary indicates, these principles underlie effective teaching and training. We have referred earlier to the World War II training experience, under the Training Within Industry program. The Job Instructor Training program (JIT), under which more than a million supervisors were given instruction in how to train new employees, was based on the principle summarized above. It suggested that before actual training begins, the instructor must get ready to instruct. Four steps were recommended; and these have applicability today in training programs for unskilled as well as skilled workers:

> **1** *Have a timetable.* How much skill do you expect the trainee to have, and how soon? This gives both the trainee and the instructor a series of goals at which to aim.

[14] For evidence of the difference in results between trained and untrained job instructors, see Norman R. F. Maier, *Psychology in Industry,* 2d ed., Houghton Mifflin Company, Boston, 1955, pp. 347–350. After 12 days of training, beginners who were trained by instructors with no special training themselves performed 25 units of work, while those taught by trained instructors performed 38 units.

[15] As examples, see Richard Bugelski, *The Psychology of Learning,* Holt, Rinehart and Winston, Inc., New York, 1956; Nathaniel F. Cantor, *The Teaching-Learning Process,* Holt, Rinehart and Winston, Inc., New York, 1953; Ernest R. Hilgard, *Theories of Learning,* 2d ed., Appleton-Century-Crofts, Inc., New York, 1956; and William McGehee, "Are We Using What We Know about Training? Learning Theory and Training," *Personnel Psychology,* vol. 11, pp. 1–12, 1958 (reprinted in Harry W. Karn and B. von Haller Gilmer, *Readings in Industrial and Business Psychology,* 2d ed., McGraw-Hill Book Company, New York, 1962, pp. 159–167). For a useful summary of learning theory as applied

to training, as well as for a clear presentation of other aspects of the training function in industry, see Bernard M. Bass and James A. Vaughn, *Training in Industry: The Management of Learning,* Wadsworth Publishing Company, Inc., Belmont, Calif., 1966. Also, Len S. Powell, *Communication and Learning,* Sir Isaac Pitman and Sons, Ltd., London, 1969.

2 *Break down the job.* List the principal steps. Job description and analysis are a necessary preliminary to training. The working sequence of operations should be listed, and even the exact motion sequence may be useful. "Key points," such as special knacks of doing an operation, quality requirements, safety and health precautions, and factors requiring careful judgment on the part of the operator, should be listed. Experienced workers may think they "know their job by heart," but usually they omit important points in the first listing. Consequently, a written job analysis is usually necessary if training is to be efficient.

3 *Have everything ready.* Have the right equipment, materials, and supplies ready. This is an important preparatory step, so that there need be no delays when actual training begins.

4 *Have the workplace properly arranged.* Have the workplace properly arranged just as the worker will be expected to keep it.

The instructor is now ready to begin the actual training process, which was divided into four steps under the JIT program:

1 *Prepare the worker.* Put the worker at ease. Find out what he already knows about the job. Get him interested in learning the job by explaining its relationship to other jobs and to the company's product. Place him in the correct working position.

2 *Present the operation.* Tell, show, illustrate, and question carefully and patiently. Stress the key points as listed on the job breakdown sheet. Instruct clearly and completely, taking up one point at a time—but no more than he can master.

3 *Try out performance.* Test the trainee by having him perform the job. Have him tell and show you what he does; have him explain the key points. Ask questions and correct his errors. Continue until you know he knows how to do the job.

4 *Follow-up.* Put the trainee on his own. Designate to whom he goes for help. Check him frequently and encourage further questions. Get him to look for key points as he progresses. Be sure that he understands the *reason* for his job and its relationship to other jobs in the department or plant. As he acquires skill and understanding, taper off the extra coaching and finally close your follow-up.

All this was summed up in the sentence, "If the worker hasn't learned, the instructor hasn't taught." This conclusion might well apply to a different type of training: "economic education."

"ECONOMIC EDUCATION" AS PART OF "TRAINING"

Some top executives have shown increasing interest in "economic education" programs for employees as a part of their training. Such interest seems to rest on the assumption that employees will be more productive and understanding of the problems facing management and owners if they are given some exposure in formal sessions to the "fundamentals" of our free-enterprise system. Packaged programs, such as "How Our Business System Operates," have been developed for widespread use by trained instructors with small groups of employees. Many companies have also installed "information racks" in which free pamphlets on hobbies, health, and other topics of general interest are included with others on economic problems.

How effective are these programs and devices as training (or indoctrination) procedures? Should the personnel administrator encourage top-management officials to introduce or to continue them? There is little objective evaluation of the results obtained by such means, and management itself is divided in its opinion on their effectiveness.[16] In one company, an evaluation of the results of a packaged program on the American economy revealed that employees were much less interested in general economics than in the specific economic problems facing their own firm

[16] See "Changing Fashions in Economic Education," *Management Record* (National Industrial Conference Board, Inc.), vol. 13, no. 10, pp. 18–21, October, 1960; William H. Whyte, *Is Anybody Listening? How and Why U.S. Business Fumbles when It Talks with Human Beings,* Simon and Schuster, Inc., New York, 1952, chap. 1, "The Great Free Enterprise Campaign," pp. 1–20, and J. Roger O'Meara, "Helping Employees Understand Economic Realities," *The Conference Board Record,* vol. 5, no. 12, pp. 44–51, December, 1968.

and affecting their own job. Where there is an atmosphere of suspicion of management's motives in providing "economic education," the results may even be negative. Informal communication, through the foreman, on specific economic conditions affecting the volume of work may be more effective if top management has been in the habit of bringing the foreman in on discussions of these problems. Information sharing, through the line organization and in union-management committees, on problems facing the firm is likely to prove superior to more formal programs because it gets down to brass tacks, answers questions that are actually being asked, and avoids generalities about the economic system which have overtones of propaganda.

THE NEED FOR PERFORMANCE APPRAISAL

We emphasized at the outset of this chapter that employees are also trained and retrained by the way their organizational superiors treat them at work. Part of this is the way their performance is appraised from time to time by their immediate supervisor, who is responsible for giving them this information.

Systematic performance appraisal (also called "merit rating" or "employee rating") has been adopted by many organizations as a means of helping supervisors to evaluate the work of each employee. These appraisals have been used most frequently as a basis for selecting candidates for promotion to better jobs or for making "merit" increases in hourly rates or salaries. They are also useful as a check on the success of recruitment, selection, placement, and training procedures.

Informal appraisals of employee performance take place whenever a supervisor says, "I think Bill's a better man than John, so I'm going to promote him." What are the objections to this kind of informal appraisal? One difficulty is that, without systematic information, regularly gathered and periodically reviewed with the employee, it is hard for a supervisor to be fair. Moreover, it is impossible for him to prove that he is fair. Employees have no satisfactory basis on which to build their expectations. The charges of favoritism and the inevitable disappointments that ensue have a bad effect on supervisory-employee relationships.

Formal appraisal plans have been developed to reduce the element of favoritism and snap judgment in personnel decisions. But performance appraisal is not a substitute for objective records of output, quality, piecework or incentive earnings, and other concrete data that indicate relative employee performance. Appraisal is essentially subjective and therefore cannot be exact, but if it is based on pooled judgments periodically rendered by supervisors when each employee is compared with every other employee in the same work group or rated against specified standards of performance for such factors as "supervision required," "job knowledge," "quantity of work," "quality of work," "adaptability," etc., these results are certainly better than the individual judgments and hasty opinions that might otherwise be used.

DEVELOPING AND ADMINISTERING AN APPRAISAL PLAN

Should the personnel department consider the development and administration of an employee-appraisal plan as one of its exclusive functions? The answer is clearly "no." Like so many other parts of the personnel program, performance appraisal is ultimately a line responsibility, to be met with the assistance of the personnel administrator and his staff. Moreover, almost any plan will be worthless if it lacks the support of top management, if supervisors are poorly trained in systematic appraisal or unconvinced of its value, if discussion of results with employees is badly handled, or if appraisals are not honestly used for the purposes intended. These and other difficulties often prevent the successful operation of a systematic program. They may be avoided if the personnel administrator helps management by taking the following steps:

1 Secures full agreement of line management on the need for a formal performance-appraisal plan and on the purposes for which it will be used. A choice has to be made among several types of appraisal plans: (*a*) point system with weights for each factor; (*b*) nonpoint system with a chart or form describing the factors to be appraised; (*c*) the rank-order or forced-distribution method, in which each supervisor ranks his employees on overall performance or divides them into groups such as the top 10 percent, the next 20 percent, etc.; (*d*) the field-review method, in which the performance of each employee is reviewed in detail by the supervisor with the help of the personnel department; (*e*) the critical incident method in which supervisors note "good" and "bad" incidents about the performance of each of their employees; or (*f*) appraisal by results or objectives.[17]

2 Studies plans of other companies and existing literature on the subject, to develop a plan best suited to the needs of the particular organization.[18] Complicated plans should be avoided; in our judgment, point systems are open to criticism because of their complexity. Ratings in not more than five classes, such as *A, B, C, D,* and *E,* are preferable, because points and numerical weights suggest a degree of accuracy that is not

possible in subjective employee performance appraisal.[19] Much depends, however, on how the appraisal plan has been developed and how carefully the raters have been trained. For illustrative forms representing two different approaches see Exhibits 16-2 and 16-3 at the end of this chapter.

3 Enlists the cooperation of supervisors in drawing up the appraisal form, including discussion of factors to be used, weights and points (if any) to be assigned to each factor, and uniform descriptions or instructions to be followed.

4 Makes sure that the purpose and nature of the performance-appraisal plan are explained to those who will make the appraisals (first-level supervisors and department heads) and to those who will be affected by the appraisals. For example, where there is a union, there should be full discussion of the proposed appraisal plan with union representatives, and subsequently it should be explained to all employees.

5 Provides or secures careful training of the supervisors, in order to get unbiased, uniform appraisals of all employees. "Progress in rating," according to the training director of a company with successful employee rating, "will be almost directly proportionate, at least in the early stages of the program, to the amount of intelligent effort expended to improve the ability of the individual raters."

6 Achieves line and staff coordination and mutual checking of employee-performance appraisal, in order to get consistency and uniformity within and between departments. In a large metal-trades company, there was much employee dissatisfaction because, in one department, a point rating of 75 was "excellent," whereas it took 90 in another department to be considered excellent. Coordination of appraisals through

[17] For a review of several of these types, see John F. Wetjen, "Performance Appraisals: A Study of Systems Used to Appraise Employee Performance," *Training and Development Journal,* vol. 22, no. 3, pp. 46-63, March, 1968.

[18] Excellent suggestions on performance appraisal and actual plans from a number of well-known companies are found in *Appraisal of Job Performance: Rating or Merit Rating Programs for Employees and Managers,* National Industrial Conference Board, Inc., Studies in Personnel Policy, no. 121, New York, October, 1951 (second printing, 1959). See also Thomas L. Whisler and Shirley F. Harper (eds.), *Performance Appraisal: Research and Practice,* Holt, Rinehart and Winston, Inc., New York, 1962. For practical suggestions to the operating manager, see Marion S. Kellogg, *What to Do about Performance Appraisal,* American Management Association, New York, 1965.

[19] For a discussion of the reliability of ratings, see Joseph Tiffin, and E. J. McCormick, *Industrial Psychology,* Prentice-Hall, Inc., Englewood Cliffs, N.J., 1965; and Richard S. Barrett, *Performance Rating,* Science Research Associates, Inc., Chicago, 1966. Tiffin and McCormick point out a number of other pitfalls in achieving uniformity in rating, requiring substantial training of raters. See also Stanley Sloan and Alton C. Johnson, "Performance Appraisal: Where Are We Headed?" *The Personnel Administrator,* vol. 14, no. 5, pp. 12-19, September-October, 1969.

group discussions with the personnel administrator and superintendents can help to minimize such discrepancies.

7 Arranges for periodic discussion of performance appraisals by the supervisor with each of his employees. Good points should be stressed, difficulties pointed out, and better performance encouraged. [20] If these interviews are poorly handled, much harm can be done, but unless there is adequate discussion of appraisals with employees, the plan may be regarded as a blacklist by employees. Every employee has a right to know from his supervisor how he is getting along, and a good superivsor will let him know from day to day. The appraisal discussion should be in the nature of a progress review, with an opportunity for the employee to respond if he feels differently about his own job performance.

The difficulties of discussing performance appraisals with employees, however, should not be minimized. Some programs have failed because supervisors were unwilling to discuss appraisals with employees, rated everyone high to avoid unpleasantness, or botched the discussions with employees.

8 Recommends careful use of the appraisals in selecting employees for promotion to better jobs, as discussed in the next chapter.

9 Provides for challenge and review of performance appraisals through the complaint and grievance procedure if employees or their union representatives are dissatisfied with management's decisions based on the appraisals. Union representatives are entitled to challenge these personnel decisions, and this is clearly preferable to a situation in which joint appraisal would put the union in a position of passing on the performance of its own members.

In summary, a systematic performance appraisal plan helps supervisors to review more

carefully the performance of their employees, and this is probably its greatest value to any organization. Line management should participate from the start in the development of the program, for it is the line's responsibility to evaluate employee performance. The personnel man should clearly remain in his staff capacity.

LIMITATIONS OF PERFORMANCE APPRAISAL SYSTEMS

Some of the limitations of formal performance appraisal systems have been suggested in the preceding discussion. They are similar to those noted in the earlier discussion of appraising management performance in Chapter 3. Perhaps most important is the reluctance of supervisors to take the time and trouble to prepare the periodic appraisals of each of their subordinates and, especially, to discuss the results with them. As Douglas McGregor has pointed out, [21] there may be a sound reason for this reluctance, as many supervisors "are uncomfortable when they are put in the position of 'playing God.'" But the alternative is to develop with nonmanagerial employees the type of approach suggested by Theory Y—"management by objectives." Do all employees below the managerial or professional level desire to establish, with their supervisors, their own goals in their jobs, and to be evaluated on these goals or objectives? One program, called Work Planning and Review, was substituted for traditional appraisal methods in a General Electric plant, with better results in improved job performance. [22] Despite such successes, however, it seems more likely that the

---

[20] See Norman R. F. Maier, *The Appraisal Interview,* John Wiley & Sons, Inc., New York, 1958, chap. 1, "Three Types of Appraisal Interview"; also appears in *Personnel,* vol. 54, no. 5, pp. 27-40, March-April, 1958; and in Pigors, Myers, and Malm, *op. cit.,* selection 33. For specific suggestions, see Kellogg, *op. cit.,* chaps. 3-5.

[21] Douglas McGregor, "An Uneasy Look at Performance Appraisal," *Harvard Business Review,* vol. 35, no. 3, pp. 89-94, May-June, 1957.

[22] H. H. Meyer, E. Kay, and J. R. P. French, Jr., "Split Roles in Performance Appraisal," *Harvard Business Review,* vol. 43, no. 1, pp. 123-129, January-February, 1965. Also by the same authors, "Effects of Threat in a Performance Appraisal Interview," *Journal of Applied Psychology,* vol. 49, no. 5, pp. 311-317, October, 1965.

traditional methods of performance appraisal will continue to be used more widely among blue-collar and white-collar employees below the managerial and professional levels.[23]

Another limitation in practice is that performance appraisals "are so often made, recorded, filed and forgotten."[24] Later personnel decisions are then made without reference to these appraisals, despite the fact that the whole purpose of performance appraisal is to improve employee performance and to reward such improved performance by promotions, favorable transfers, merit wage and salary increases, etc. On the other hand, the attempt of some appraisal systems to make fine distinctions between individuals by means of weights attached to traits or factors is likely to run afoul of charges that length of service is being ignored. Simpler rating forms, such as the one illustrated in Exhibit 16-3, may well be more practical, both because supervisors are more willing to fill them out and because they are useful in making distinctions between employees in subsequent personnel decisions. If performance appraisal can be more clearly related to performance *standards* expected on each job, it is also less likely to be criticized as wholly subjective because such traits as "dependability," "initiative," etc., are being evaluated.

Establishing performance standards for professional and technical employees, such as scientists and engineers, is particularly difficult. It is possible, however, to develop some broad classifications which describe the difference between the individual who contributes creatively to the work of a research group, for example, and one who does not pull his weight. Again, the emphasis is on a fairly simple system, rather than on a detailed analysis of traits, with arbitrary weights attached to each.[25]

The only alternatives to systematic performance appraisal are (1) informal judgments of supervisors and (2) acceptance of length of service or seniority as the sole criterion in making promotions, salary increases, etc. Since few managers would willingly agree that seniority *should* be the sole criterion, then they must ask: Are informal judgments sufficient? We believe that the answer is that they are not, that they cannot be defended against charges of discrimination, and that consequently, some method of performance appraisal (preferably a simple one) is a necessary part of the manager's task of developing the human resources in his organization. It must be emphasized, however, that the appraisal of one human being by another is not "scientific" but subjective and that the process involves some important ethical questions.[26] Two-way appraisal, in which the subordinate "evaluates" the manager's performance also, and even wider "power network" collaborative problem solving may also be worth further experimentation.[27]

[23] See Harold Mayfield, "In Defense of Performance Appraisal," *Harvard Business Review,* vol. 38, no. 2, pp. 81-87, March-April, 1960. For a contrary view, suggesting a Theory Y approach in appraising the performance of salesmen, for example, see Alva F. Kindall and James Gatza, "Positive Program for Performance Appraisal," *Harvard Business Review,* vol. 41, no. 6, pp. 153-167, November-December, 1963. For a review of recent literature, see Stanley Sloan and Alton C. Johnson, "New Context of Personnel Appraisal," *Harvard Business Review,* vol. 46, no. 6, pp. 14-20, 29-30, and 194, November-December, 1968.

[24] Thomas L. Whisler, "Appraisal as a Management Tool," in Whisler and Harper, *op. cit.,* p. 476.

[25] For an example of a simple system developed in the Kordite Corporation, a subsidiary of the Mobil Chemical Company, see Irwin W. Krantz, "Evaluating the Technical Employee: A Results Approach," *Personnel,* vol. 41, no. 1, pp. 47-58, January-February, 1964. Some of the difficulties in appraising research and development personnel are discussed by R. F. Moore, "Appraisal at Its Apogee," *Research Management,* vol. 10, no. 1, pp. 61-72, January, 1967.

[26] See Kellogg, *op cit.,* chap. 2, "The Ethics of Employee Appraisal," also in *Personnel,* vol. 42, no. 4, pp. 33-39, July-August, 1956.

[27] For an illustrative case in a regional office of the Internal Revenue Service, see B. Frank White and Louis B. Barnes, "Power Networks in the Appraisal Process," *Harvard Business Review,* vol. 49, no. 3, pp. 101-109, May-June, 1971.

302

Exhibit 16-2 A Performance Appraisal Form with Seven Items Rated on 5-point Scale; Comments Can Be Added on Reverse Side

Performance appraisal	Salaried employees-nonexempt

Name	Division	Date	Position	Department	Date of last review

Instructions

Evaluate the employee on the job *now being performed.* **Circle the dot in the space above the horizontal line which most nearly expresses your over-all judgment on each quality. The care and accuracy with which this appraisal is made will determine its value to you, to the employee and to the organization.**

Consider the employee's performance since the last appraisal and show by a check (√) whether he has gone back, remained stationary or gone ahead in each of the qualities listed to the left.

						Has improved	Little or no change	Has gone back
Knowledge of work Consider knowledge of his job gained through experience; general education; specialized training.	Well informed on all phases of work	Knowledge thorough enough to perform without assistance	Adequate grasp of essentials. Some assistance	Requires considerable assistance	Inadequate knowledge	Comments		
Quality of work Consider the volume of work produced under normal conditions. Disregard errors.	Rapid worker. Unusually big producer	Turns out good volume	Average	Volume below average	Very slow worker	Comments		
Quality of work Consider neatness, accuracy and dependability of results regardless of volume.	Exceptionally accurate, practically no mistakes	Seldom necessary to check work	Acceptable, usually neat, occasional errors or rejections	Often unacceptable, frequent errors or rejections	Too many errors or rejections	Comments		
Ability to learn new duties Consider the speed with which he masters new routine and grasps explanations. Consider also ability to retain this knowledge.	Exceptionally fast to learn and adjust to changed conditions	Learns rapidly. Retains instructions	Average instruction required	Requires a great deal of instruction	Very slow to absorb. Poor memory	Comments		
Initiative Consider the tendency to contribute, develop and/or carry out new ideas or methods.	Initiative resulting in frequent saving in time and money	Very resourceful	Shows initiative occasionally	Rarely shows any initiative	Needs constant prodding	Comments		
Cooperation Consider manner of handling business relationships	Goes out of the way to cooperate	Gets along well with associates	Acceptable	Shows reluctance to cooperate	Very poor cooperation	Comments		
Judgment and common sense Does he think intelligently and make his decisions logically.	Thinks quickly, logically. Outstanding	Judgment usually logical	Fairly reliable	Inclined to be illogical	Poor, unreliable	Comments		

Source: Olin Mathieson Chemical Corporation.

Instructions: Based on the appraisal you have made on the reverse side please answer the following questions in your own words.

Do you see any need for improvement? ☐ Yes ☐ **No** (If "yes" please explain)

_____

Is employee well suited for type of work he is now doing? ☐ Yes ☐ No (If "no" indicate type of work for which he is suited)

_____

What contribution has employee made to company, department or division beyond normal requirements of position?

_____

What would be your over-all evaluation of employee? (Place check (√) above horizontal line)

Excellent   Good   Satisfactory   Fair   Poor

Any difference of opinion between the immediate supervisor and the reviewing supervisor should be reconciled if possible. If not possible, the points of difference should be noted in this space.

_____

_____

Reviewed by _____   Date _____

Questions to be answered after discussion of appraisal with employee

What was the attitude of the employee toward the discussion of his appraisal?

_____

_____

If improvement is indicated, what suggestions have you made?

_____

_____

Remarks or any further comments you may have for improvement

_____

Completed by _____ Date _____ This appraisal was discussed with employee on: Date _____

303

PREPARATION AND FOLLOW UP NOTES ON A WORK PERFORMANCE DISCUSSION

Employee Name	Department
What do the individual's raters think he does well?	What does he believe he does well?
In what areas do the raters think he can improve?	In what areas does he believe he should improve?

Since the last evaluation, in what ways does the individual feel he has improved?

Do you agree?

What specifically can you do to help the individual develop or improve?	What are his plans for helping himself?

Rating Review Sheet of the Standard Oil Company (New Jersey) 8½ x 11. Notes are recorded in the left-hand column of this form prior to the follow-up interview between the supervisor and the individual whom he has rated. The other column is filled out during or after the interview, and then the form is sent to the personnel department.

What follow-up action on this discussion will be taken?	What seemed to be the general reaction of the individual to this discussion?
When?	
Date of Discussion:	Signature of Reporting Supervisor:

SNJ-PER-33B (2-59)

PLEASE RETURN THIS FORM COMPLETED TO THE PERSONNEL DEPARTMENT

Exhibit 16-3 A simplified performance appraisal form, with questions which put considerable responsibility on the raters, and spaces for employee feedback. (*Source: Forms and Records in Personnel Administration, Studies in Personnel Policy, no. 175, National Industrial Conference Board, Inc., New York, 1960, p. 174.*)

SUMMARY

Employee induction and training are important procedures in building an effective work team that will reach a high level of productive efficiency. They are not separate from the job of getting out production but are part of that job and hence a responsibility of line management. Generally, however, a staff man—a training director or the personnel administrator—is used by line management to develop the training program in the light of the needs of the organization and in cooperation with line supervision. He can also assist in developing instructors who have a grasp of sound training techniques. "Economic education" as part of a formal training program is open to question unless closely related to employees' experience in the company.

Both induction and training are integral parts of a personnel program which also includes such features as job description and analysis, recruitment, selection, promotion, transfer, discipline, changes in job assignments, job evaluation, and accident prevention. The success of training is measured by subsequent performance on the job, and one method of assessing job performance is a formal system of performance appraisal.

While there are many performance appraisal systems, and many limitations to formal procedures, there is no adequate alternative to some systematic and uniform method if management wishes to avoid charges of discrimination or arbitrary managerial action. Furthermore, the increasing pressure for seniority as a criterion in promotions, transfers, and separations makes it imperative that management have defensible reasons for departing from seniority. We shall turn in the next chapter to a further discussion of the problems and policy choices which face managers in making these personnel decisions.

SELECTED REFERENCES

Induction

Employee Induction, National Industrial Conference Board, Inc., Studies in Personnel Policy, no. 131, New York, 1953.

Marks, W. R.: *Induction—Acclimatizing People to Work,* Institute of Personnel Management, London, 1970.

Training

Bass, Bernard M., and James A. Vaughn: *Training in Industry: The Management of Learning,* Wadsworth Publishing Company, Inc., Belmont, Calif., 1966.

Cantor, Nathaniel F.: *The Teaching-Learning Process,* Holt, Rinehart and Winston, Inc., New York, 1953.

Ghiselli, Edwin E., and Clarence W. Brown: *Personnel and Industrial Psychology,* 2d ed., McGraw-Hill Book Company, New York, 1955, chap. 13, "Training in Industry."

Haire, Mason: *Psychology of Management,* 2d ed., McGraw-Hill Book Company, New York, 1964, chap. 5, "Training."

Malm, F. T.: "Analyzing Training Needs and Results," adapted from "Comment rendre la formation plus efficace: analyse des besoins et des résultats en matière de formation," *Hommes et Techniques,* no. 204, pp. 1293-1305, November, 1961 (reprinted in Pigors, Myers, and Malm, *Management of Human Resources: Readings in Personnel Administration,* 3d ed., McGraw-Hill Book Company, New York, 1973, selection 32.)

Otto, Calvin P., and Rollin O. Glaser: *The Management of Training,* Addison-Wesley Publishing Company, Inc., Reading, Mass., 1970.

Stokes, Paul M.: *Total Job Training: A Manual for the Working Manager,* American Management Association, New York, 1966.

Tracey, William R.: *Evaluating Training and Development Systems,* American Management Association, Inc., New York, 1968.

Performance Appraisal

Barrett, Richard S.: *Performance Rating,* Science Research Associates, Chicago, 1966.

Evaluating Engineering Performance: Specific Programs for Individual and Group Evaluation, National Society of Professional Engineers, Washington, D.C., 1963.

Kellogg, Marion S.: *What to Do about Performance Appraisal,* American Management Association, New York, 1965.

Kindall, Alva F., and James Gatza: "Positive Program for Performance Appraisal," *Harvard Business Review,* vol. 41, no. 6, pp. 153-167, November–December, 1963.

Krantz, Irwin W.: "Evaluating the Technical Employee: A Results Approach," *Personnel,* vol. 41, no. 1, pp. 47-58, January–February, 1964.

Lopez, Felix M., Jr.: *Evaluating Employee Performance,* Public Personnel Association, Chicago, 1968.

McGregor, Douglas: "An Uneasy Look at Performance Appraisal," *Harvard Business Review,* vol. 35, no. 3, pp. 89–94, May–June, 1957.

Maier, Norman R. F.: *The Appraisal Interview,* John Wiley & Sons, Inc., New York, 1958.

Mayfield, Harold: "In Defense of Performance Appraisal," *Harvard Business Review,* vol. 38, no. 2, pp. 81–87, March–April, 1960.

Meyer, Herbert H., Emanuel Kay, and John R. P. French, Jr.: "Split Roles in Performance Appraisal," *Harvard Business Review,* vol. 43, no. 1, pp. 123–129, January–February, 1965.

Schinagl, Mary S.: History of Efficiency Ratings in the Federal Government, Bookman Associates, Inc., New York, 1966.

Sloan, Stanley, and Alton C. Johnson: "New Context of Personnel Appraisal," *Harvard Business Review,* vol. 46, no. 6, pp. 14–20, 29–30, and 194, November–December, 1968.

Thompson, Paul H., and Gene W. Dalton: "Performance Appraisal: Managers Beware," *Harvard Business Review,* vol. 48, no. 1, pp. 149–157, January–February, 1970.

Whisler, Thomas L., and Shirley F. Harper (eds.): *Performance Appraisal: Research and Practice,* Holt, Rinehart, and Winston, Inc., New York, 1962.

Zander, Alvin (ed.): *Performance Appraisals: Effects on Employees and Their Performance,* Foundation for Research on Human Behavior, Ann Arbor, Mich., 1963.

Chapter 17

Promotions, Transfers, and Separations

Most promotions and lateral transfers . . . are determined by ability factors as well as seniority. The emphasis on ability varies from complete reliance on merit and ability to automatic promotion of the most senior employee, subject only to his ability to perform the job after a trial period.

Peter B. Doeringer and Michael J. Piore[1]

Most managers proceed on the generally valid assumption that most (but not all) employees want to qualify for better jobs in the course of their work lives. Thus a promotion-from-within policy helps to meet these aspirations and provides the organization with a continuing supply of better-qualified human resources. Promotions, however, are not the only personnel decisions which concern managers and employees; transfers and layoffs are also ways in which the changing fortunes of the organization are ad-

justed to the human resources which it employs. Each of these managerial decisions involves *human* problems, and where unions are involved, labor-management relations problems. This chapter will consider some of the ramifications of these problems, which concern managers as well as their personnel specialists.

SOME DEFINITIONS

What is a promotion? If an employee moves from the second shift to the preferred first shift on the same job, or if he moves into a room where working conditions are better although

[1] Peter B. Doeringer and Michael J. Piore, *Internal Labor Markets and Manpower Analysis,* D.C. Heath and Company, Lexington, Mass., 1971, p. 54.

other features on the job are the same, is this a promotion—or a transfer?

We shall consider that a *promotion* is the advancement of an employee to a better job—better in terms of greater responsibilities, more prestige or "status," greater skill, and especially, increased rate of pay or salary. Better hours or better location or working conditions may also characterize the "better job" to which an employee seeks "promotion," but if the job does not involve greater skill or responsibilities and higher pay, it should not be considered a promotion.

The term "upgrading" refers to a practice closely related to promotion. In fact, it amounts to a small-scale (or limited) promotion. Upgrading is the movement of an employee to a more responsible job within the same occupational unit and with a corresponding increase in pay. When a second-class machinist is moved up to the job of a first-class machinist, he has been upgraded. Similar upgradings take place among office employees. For example, in the claims department of an insurance company, a "junior approver" moves up to the position of "approver."

Both upgrading and promotion are ways of recognizing and developing the abilities of employees within the organization, instead of filling skilled and responsible positions from outside. However, for certain highly skilled or professional jobs, it is often necessary to recruit specifically for openings. Apart from the lowest entry jobs, there are often other "ports of entry" in the internal labor market.[2]

Promotion and upgrading should be distinguished from *transfer,* which is the movement of an employee from one job to another on the same occupational level and on about the same level of wages or salary. No appreciable increase or decrease in duties and responsibilities is in-

volved, although there may be a change in their specific nature and in working conditions.

Some transfers may appear to involve a decrease in job duties and especially in pay. This type of transfer is more accurately described as *downgrading* or *bumping,* because it is most frequently used to protect employment opportunities for employees (usually blue-collar) displaced from higher-rated jobs. They are downgraded to less desirable jobs, bumping less qualified or junior employees, who in turn may displace others or be laid off, often in reverse order of seniority.

Finally, *layoff* occurs when lack of business or budget curtailments (in nonprofit organizations) force a reduction in the number of employees. Layoffs are the most frequent type of *separation* of employees from the employed work force, but unlike quits, retirements, or deaths, they do not always involve a permanent separation from the payroll. Laid-off employees often expect to be rehired by their employer when conditions improve. A negotiated collective bargaining agreement usually establishes specific recall rights, almost always on the basis of seniority.

All these types of personnel decision involve policy choices and problems. We shall consider them in the order presented above.

SENIORITY AND COMPETENCE IN PROMOTIONS

The most important policy question in promotion is the relative significance of seniority and competence. There is an increasing tendency, especially in unionized firms, to give more weight to seniority in making promotions within the bargaining unit, because of the great importance that workers attach to length of service. This raises two basic questions: Is the employee with the longest service necessarily the most competent? If workers automatically qualify for better jobs by accumulating seniority, will new employees be motivated to improve their performance?

The answers to these questions, particularly the second, are so often in the negative that *man-*

[2] For illustrative examples see *ibid.,* chap. 3, especially fig. 3, p. 46.

agement should stress competence above seniority in promotion when two or more candidates are being considered. No supervisor can get effective results with people if he is limited in his opportunity to make the best use of each person's capacities. Promotions should be fairly and capably used by management to place on each job the most competent and productive workers available. Promotions should be a reward to encourage those employees who make a successful effort to increase their knowledge or skill and who maintain a high level of productivity. When seniority is made the *sole* basis for promotion, it becomes a straitjacket. Seniority should be considered, but only when the qualifications of two candidates for a better job are, for practical purposes, substantially equal.[3]

In Unionized Firms

Management will not be able to win acceptance for this kind of promotion policy, however, unless it succeeds in establishing confidence in the fairness of its procedure for selecting the employee to be promoted. The difficulties are especially obvious in unionized firms. Certainly, one of the reasons for the demand for strict seniority in promotions was the abuse by some managements of the privilege of selecting the best man. Too often, this was influenced by personal acquaintance, favors performed, and recent events, rather than by objective records of output, or a systematic subjective procedure for appraising employees, or after careful interviews with several candidates for higher positions.

Clearly, management needs these records and performance appraisal procedures if it is fairly to administer a promotion policy based upon employee competence. The only way that management can meet increasing union demands for

straight seniority in promotions is to insist that competence be considered the most important factor and then to demonstrate its fairness and objectivity by selecting for promotion those employees who, on the basis of records and performance appraisals, are clearly superior to their fellow employees. This means that, in most cases, slight differences in competence should not be considered. In the agreement between a union and a large automobile manufacturing firm, the following clause appeared: "In the advancement of employees to higher paid jobs when ability, merit, and capacity are equal, employees with the largest seniority will be given preference." The impartial umpire (arbitrator) under the agreement ruled in a series of cases that seniority should be disregarded only where an employee with less seniority stands "head and shoulders" above the employees with greater seniority. Other arbitrators have followed this concept.[4]

A personnel-minded management is willing to go more than halfway to meet the union on this difficult question. For example, one company, operating under a union agreement that retained management authority to make promotions on the basis of competence, nevertheless instructed its supervisors to consider the senior employee first when a promotion was to be made. If the senior employee was clearly unqualified for the job, as evidenced by records of performance and other information such as attendance, safety record, etc., the supervisor could then promote a more capable junior employee. He was asked, however, to make a full report to the superintendent on his reasons for not following seniority. If the superintendent approved this departure from the seniority principle, he sent the report to the personnel administrator, who in turn notified the union of the reasons for promoting the junior

[3] The adverse effects of seniority on efficiency are described by Dan H. Mater, "A Statistical Study of the Effect of Seniority upon Employee Efficiency," *Journal of Business,* The University of Chicago, pp. 169-204, April, 1941. This is still the only careful study of this subject in the literature.

[4] James J. Healy, "The Factor of Ability in Labor Relations," in *Arbitration Today, Proceedings of the Eighth Annual Meeting of the National Academy of Arbitrators,* 1955, pp. 45-54.

man. If the supervisor had a reasonable doubt about the qualifications of the employee with greatest seniority, he was instructed to put the employee on the job for a trial period of 6 weeks. This procedure tended to reduce the number of complaints about promotions.

In Nonunion Firms

In nonunion firms and organizations, these difficulties over promotion decisions are not usually serious. Presumably, management has more latitude in selecting the most competent employee for promotion to a better job, and the decision is not likely to be openly challenged. But senior employees who have been passed over may nurse grievances unless the grounds for the decision are understood by those affected by it. The importance of having good reasons for personnel decisions is hardly less necessary in nonunion situations than when a union can challenge management's decisions. Length of service (seniority) may still be an important consideration.

Even in firms in which blue-collar workers are unionized, there are substantial groups of employees not represented by the union: white-collar, technical, and professional employees. These employees are typically less concerned with seniority than with merit as a basis for promotions. This has often been made evident by research and development personnel, who seem to place high value on "advancement on merit," "merit-based salary increases," and a "supervisor who is objective in his evaluation" of their performance.[5] When managers are preoccupied with union demands for more emphasis on seniority, they tend to overlook the different motivations of this increasingly important group of employees.

Nondiscrimination in Promotions

It should not be necessary to stress that when promotions are made on the basis of competence and ability, rather than primarily on length of

[5] Hjalmar Rosen, "Occupational Motivation of Research and Development Personnel," *Personnel Administration,* vol. 26, no. 2, pp. 37–43, March–April, 1963.

service, there should be no discrimination among candidates because of sex, race, religion, or national origin. We have already stressed the importance of *selecting* new employees without discrimination on the basis of these factors, and the point applies with equal force to decisions on promotion. The fact is that in the past, many firms and organizations have *not* made these decisions on the basis of competence alone, and in the case of the American Negro, the result has been the nationwide drive for "equal rights" in employment as well as in other areas of American life.

The handicap which faces minority groups of employees in seeking promotions is, in some cases, the lack of an adequate educational background. But this is not true of all such candidates for promotion, and management needs to pay more attention to seeking out qualified blacks and other members of minority groups for promotions, as well as to develop training programs and upgrading which might prepare them for subsequent promotions. But should these employees be given "preference" in promotions, as some Negro civil rights spokesmen have argued? This would appear to be "discrimination in reverse" even though it might be considered redress for past discrimination. If management has a policy of promotion on the basis of competence, fairly administered without respect to other considerations, and it can prove the fairness of application in each case, pressure for a policy of "discrimination in reverse" should be firmly resisted.[6]

Problems in Determining Seniority

If seniority is to be given some weight in promotions for certain groups of employees, however, the problem still remains: How is an employee's

[6] The Civil Rights Act of 1964, Title VII, specifically states: "Nothing in this title shall be interpreted to require any employer . . . to grant preferential treatment to any individual or any group . . . on account of an imbalance which may exist with respect to the total number or percentage of persons of any race . . . employed by any employer." Nonetheless, there are pressures on employers to hire more blacks and other minority groups than before.

"seniority" determined? We have been using the term as if seniority were a readily definable and measurable factor, but this is possible only if certain basic questions are first answered:

1 What is the seniority unit—occupation, department, plant, or company?

2 Within this unit, how is seniority to be computed, and when is it broken?

Occupational or job seniority is likely to be easier to defend as a basis for promotion to a better job when there is a functional relationship between the two jobs. If the choice is between an employee who has been on a certain job 2 years and with the department (or plant or company) for 15, and an employee who has been on the job for 10 years and with the department (or plant or company) for 12, the latter is likely to feel that he is "next in line" for advancement to a more skilled and related job. Occupational seniority, however, tends to restrict mobility within the organization and may be less appropriate for certain other purposes, such as transfer and layoff.

Computation of seniority, or length of service, within the seniority unit can be made in several ways. An employee's seniority can start when he is first employed in the company (or in the plant, department, or job), regardless of subsequent transfers, layoffs, leaves of absence, etc. Or these interruptions may be deducted to compute a net length of service. Another possibility is to compute seniority from the date when the employee was *last* hired. This would be his length of continuous service, although in practice exceptions are often made for interruptions due to temporary layoffs and leaves of absence. Occupational seniority is usually broken with transfers to a different job, and all types of seniority are broken when an employee quits or is discharged.

Increasing emphasis on seniority in personnel decisions requires that management, with the assistance of the personnel administrator, establish clear policies on these questions. In unionized firms, such matters will obviously be negotiated

with union representatives. In either case, when decisions have been reached, the seniority of each employee should be computed and posted, so that employees can be informed of their relative seniority standings and any errors corrected before the seniority lists are actually used.

OTHER POLICY ELEMENTS IN PROMOTION

In addition to the relative emphasis on competence over seniority, there are other elements of a sound promotion policy. A few of these elements are:

1 A statement of management's intention that higher-paid and better jobs will be filled by *promotion from within* whenever possible, rather than by hiring from outside the organization. Obviously, the statement will be worthless if it is not faithfully followed. If it is necessary to go outside to fill specific skilled or professional jobs, these should be identified in advance.

2 Encouragement for supervisors to *permit capable employees to leave the department or plant if better opportunities are available elsewhere.* If a good man is held back, he is not likely to remain a satisfied employee. An open job-bidding system encourages this internal mobility.

3 *Establishment of lines of progression—ladders of promotion—*within the organization. It is desirable to use job analysis to develop a chart showing basic job requirements (in competence, experience, formal education, etc.) and how each job leads to another. Employees need to know what is expected on higher-rated jobs to prepare themselves for advancement. As an example, the Cooperative Wage System (CWS) developed by the basic steel companies and the steelworkers' union provides such job descriptions, and in specific plants there are ladders of promotion for departments or production units within the plant or mill. See Figure 17-1 for an illustration. In other industries, lines of progression or promotion ladders may be much shorter and have a number of "ports of entry" where applicants are hired directly for higher-skilled jobs.[7]

[7] See Doeringer and Piore, *op. cit.,* for additional examples, especially pp. 45 and 46.

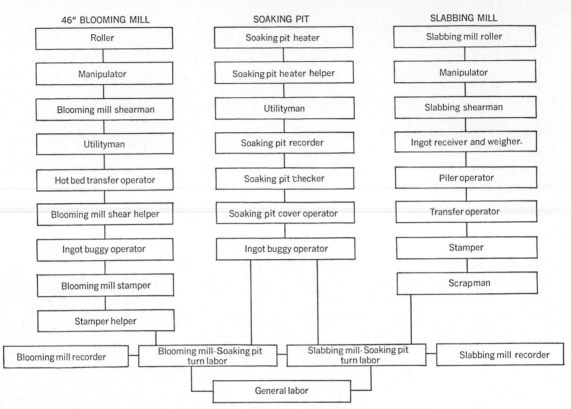

Figure 17-1 Line of progression: 46-inch blooming mill, soaking pit, slabbing mill. (*Source:* Peter B. Doeringer and Michael J. Piore, *Internal Labor Markets and Manpower Analysis,* D. C. Heath and Company, Lexington, Mass., 1971, p. 44.)

4 *Posting of openings for promotions,* so that interested employees may apply within a specified period, usually several days or a week.[8] If possible, the opening should be posted and the candidate selected before the job actually becomes vacant. If the job is temporarily filled by an employee who is subsequently advanced to the job permanently, the other applicants are likely to feel that the posting procedure is a farce.

[8] For an example of such a system applied throughout a company, including the management group, see Theodore M. Alfred, "Checkers or Choice in Manpower Management," *Harvard Business Review,* vol. 45, no. 1, pp. 157–167, January–February, 1967 (reprinted in Paul Pigors, Charles A. Myers, and F. T. Malm, *Management of Human Resources: Readings in Personnel Administration,* 3d ed., McGraw-Hill Book Company, New York, 1973, selection 11).

5 *Provision for training as a means of preparation for promotion.* Special on-the-job training, vestibule schools, night classes, or vocational courses should be available, as well as special retraining programs. The changing job requirements which an age of science and technology brings will necessitate more extensive retraining of employees if they are to qualify for better jobs.

6 *Line responsibility for making promotions,* with the advice and assistance of the personnel department in a staff capacity. The supervisor should propose promotions, which should then be subject to approval by his immediate superior in the line organization. This serves as a check on the fairness of promotions and ensures that the policy will be consistently administered. In unionized firms, joint responsibility of management and the union is neither a wise nor a workable procedure.

7 *Provision for employee or union challenge of a particular promotion in the bargaining unit, within the limits of the promotion policy* and the union agreement. Some firms have taken the position that "questions as to the correctness of management's selection will be heard by management but will not be arbitrable." Where management has demonstrated its fairness over a considerable period, it may be possible to secure this type of provision in union negotiations, but ordinarily a management that has consistently adhered to a sound promotion policy should have little to fear from a commitment to arbitrate grievances about promotions. (See Case 13, "Factors in Promotion Policy," for a dispute settled prior to arbitration.)

Finally, it should be noted that not all employees want promotions, particularly if they will leave a congenial work group, or if they have feelings of inadequacy for a more responsible job. Promotions should not be forced on reluctant employees.

HANDLING PROMOTIONS

The actual handling of promotions by line officials offers the personnel administrator an excellent opportunity to develop understanding and acceptance of management policy. In his contacts with supervisors, he can emphasize the importance of skillful policy administration.

Communication of the firm's promotion policy is important. Employees expect to be informed about ladders of promotion, how they can prepare themselves for advancement, and what will be expected of them on the higher-rated jobs. In selecting candidates for promotion, careful review of any objective records of performance as well as appraisal is necessary. The man to be promoted should not be selected casually or on the basis of something that happened last week. Senior employees who have been bypassed in the selection of a better man are entitled to an explanation of the reasons. People have a right to know in advance about the changes that will affect them, even if the results for them are negative. Employees who are unable to handle more skilled and responsible jobs should not be falsely encouraged.

When a management decision on promotion is disputed, however, the resulting discussions with aggrieved employees (and union representatives) offer a further opportunity to achieve understanding. If management itself has departed from established policy or lacks adequate reasons for its action, the conference may still be a fruitful one if errors are admitted and adjustments made. On the other hand, if after investigation the promotion appears to be fully justified, reasons can be more thoroughly explained, records produced, and the consequences of a departure from sound policy pointed out.

In one dispute over a promotion, for example, the union representatives argued that management had unfairly ignored seniority in selecting a younger carpenter's helper for promotion to the job of "outside carpenter." Management maintained that the younger man was more competent and that the older man (sixty-five years of age) was physically unable to do the work because his eyes were poor and he had once fallen off a ladder when assigned to temporary outside work. Unfortunately, it was not until the dispute had advanced to the last stage of the grievance procedure—between top management and the regional officer of the union—that management convincingly stressed the point that, in bypassing the older man, it was also protecting him by not putting him on a job in which his own safety and that of others would be endangered.

The presence of a union serves as a check on the fairness and correctness of management's decisions in promotions. Of course, strong unions may push weaker managements in the direction of unwise and exclusive reliance on seniority in promoting employees to jobs of higher responsibility and earnings. In one large company, for example, plant management had accepted, under the pressure for continuous production, a procedure for "instantaneous seniority" in filling even temporary openings in more skilled and better-paid jobs. Where a senior employee could not initially perform the job, he expected that a trainer would be put with him, and this was often done. Eventually, a different and more workable system was put into effect through arbitration, to which both management and the union had submitted a dispute over the continuance of the old system and the substitution of a new one.

In the absence of a union, and for employees such as clerical, technical, and professional employees who are not normally unionized, a fair, consistent handling of promotions is obviously no less necessary than when a union is present.

THE NEED FOR A TRANSFER POLICY

Like promotion, transfer is used to place employees in positions where they may get greater job satisfaction and contribute their best efforts to the organization. If a newly hired employee is assigned to a certain job and left there despite his desire to transfer to a different kind of work or to advance to a better job, he will not be satisfied. His resentment will probably express itself in reduced work effectiveness and perhaps in formal complaints. When better job opportunities are available outside the organization, his dissatisfaction is frequently registered in labor-turnover statistics.

Every organization, therefore, needs sound policies of transfer as well as of promotion. A personnel administrator should be prepared to make recommendations for these policies and to help line managers administer them effectively. He should also make sure that these policies are supported by other features of the personnel program. For example, careful job description and analysis are needed to establish avenues of transfer as well as ladders of promotion. Sound pro-

cedures of selection and placement are required to prevent an excessive number of subsequent transfers. Systematic training of employees and supervisors helps to prepare workers to make successful transfers as well as to be promoted and enables supervisors to administer transfer and promotion policies effectively.

Before turning to a discussion of requirements in transfer policy, it is worthwhile to distinguish among the different types of transfer. Transfers differ in terms of (1) the unit within which each personnel change takes place and (2) the purpose for which each is made. The transfer unit may be the work group or section, the department, the plant, or the entire company or organization when there is more than one plant or location. The nature of the operation or the industry has an important bearing on the appropriate unit for transfer. For example, interdepartmental or interplant transfers are easier to arrange and require less training if job skills are roughly comparable in each department or plant than if the work is entirely different.

When we consider transfers from the standpoint of their purpose, five types may be distinguished, although these are not always mutually exclusive.

Production Transfers

Production transfers are transfers from jobs in which labor requirements are declining to jobs in which they are increasing or in which vacancies have occurred through separations. This type of transfer is made to avoid layoffs on one job at the same time that employees are being hired for a similar type of work. Production transfers at approximately the same occupational level are an essential part of a program to stabilize company employment, and they require some form of centralized employment control. The personnel department may act as a clearinghouse through which all layoffs and hirings are funneled. In some cases, production transfers may of necessity be to less skilled jobs, so that downgrading is involved. What we call "production transfers" here would also apply to similar situations in nonmanufacturing enterprises and organizations. This type of transfer is becoming increasingly important as technical changes affect a growing number of jobs and skills.

Replacement Transfers

Replacement transfers are similar to production transfers in their intent, i.e., to avoid layoffs. However, in replacement transfers, a long-service employee is transferred to a similar job, usually in another department, where he replaces or "bumps" an employee with shorter service. A replacement-transfer program is used when all operations are declining and is designed to retain the long-service employees as long as possible.

Versatility Transfers

The versatility transfer is for the purpose of providing management with a more versatile group of employees. This type of transfer may be used as preparation for production or replacement transfers. The versatility transfer is also necessary for flexibility of operation in a small shop where there is not enough work on a particular job to keep a man busy. A small gear plant, for example, had to use its milling-machine operator on a number of other jobs; in fact, he practically had to be an all-round machinist. This type of transfer will be increasingly necessary as part of a continued retraining program.

Shift Transfers

Where there is more than one shift and shift assignments are not rotating, transfers may be made from one shift to another on the same type of work. Generally, transfers are from the late shifts (the second and third) to the day (first) shift. Many workers dislike a second-shift assignment because it interferes with their participation in the afternoon and evening life of the community. Others object to the third shift because

it requires a reversal of the normal processes of working and sleeping. Yet there are always some people who have special reasons for preferring the second or third shift to the first. For example, a mother may prefer second-shift employment if her husband already works on the first, so that someone is at home with the children most of the day.

Remedial Transfers

This type of transfer is made for various reasons primarily concerning the person on the job. *Initial* placement may have been faulty, or the worker may not get along with his supervisor or with other workers in the department. He may be getting too old to continue on his regular job, or the type of job or working conditions may not be well adapted to his present health or accident record. If the job is repetitive, the worker may have gone stale and would benefit by transfer to a different kind of work.

One of the key principles of good personnel administration is the treatment of employees as individuals, within the framework of broad policies. Remedial transfers offer an excellent opportunity for management, working with the personnel department, to practice this principle.

A large textile company, for example, introduced a formal induction program for new employees during a period of severe wartime labor shortages. An important part of the program was the follow-up interview with the new employee after the first 6 weeks of employment. In a number of cases, remedial transfers were recommended by the personnel department and made with the approval of the supervisors concerned. These transfers resulted in better placement and improved employee morale.

ELEMENTS OF A TRANSFER POLICY

If the responsibility for interdepartmental transfer is left with the individual supervisor, his employees may hesitate to ask for transfers out of the department. Some supervisors may be more lenient than others, or they may recommend transfer to get rid of poor workers rather than attempting to improve them or discharge them. Without a policy, there are no bench marks to follow in making other types of transfer, such as production and replacement transfers.

A systematic transfer policy, therefore, is needed to get reasonable consistency of treatment throughout the organization. In formulating this policy, information and decisions are needed on the following:

1 *The circumstances under which transfers will be made.* Are operations in different departments sufficiently alike to permit production and replacement transfers? What other types of transfers should the organization encourage?

2 *Responsibility for initiating and approving transfers.* Should the first-level supervisor have the entire responsibility, or should his decision be subject to review by his immediate superior or by the personnel administrator?

3 *Jobs to which transfers will be made,* as shown by job description and analysis. How much retraining, if any, will be required, and how much time should a transferee be given to demonstrate that he can satisfactorily perform the new job? What rate of pay will he be given during the training period?

4 *The area or unit over which transfer will take place.* Should transfers be made between departments, divisions, and plants, or only within one subunit? When an employee is transferred, does he carry his previous seniority credit with him, retain it for a temporary period, or lose it altogether?

5 *Basis for transfers,* when two or more persons desire transfer to the same job or same shift. Should seniority (length of service) be the sole determinant, assuming minimum capacity to handle the job? Or should skill or competence be the deciding factor? What importance, if any, should be given to marital status and dependency?

6 *The rate of pay* or salary to be received by the transferee on the job to which he is transferred. Under what circumstances should he get the rate of his previous or regular job (assuming it is higher), and when should he get the rate of the new job (assuming it is lower)?

Most organizations need, at one time or another, all the types of transfers we have discussed. These transfers should either be initiated by the immediate supervisor or recommended by the personnel department, subject to review, if disagreement arises, by a representative of higher line management. A new and inexperienced personnel administrator may be tempted to take upon himself the authority to decide about transfers. But to do so would be to assume line responsibilities not appropriate for his staff role.

Whether transfers are to be made only within departments or between departments, divisions, and plants depends largely on the similarity of operations and how much retraining is necessary. If the transfer unit is too wide, e.g., in replacement transfers, excessive bumping of shorter-service employees will be necessary, particularly where seniority is the sole basis for transfer. To avoid this, the transferee may be required to possess the necessary ability to do the job or to demonstrate his competence within a short trial period. As in promotions, records of employee performance and appraisal procedures are of great assistance to management in making these transfers. If interdepartmental or interplant transfers are used as a means of keeping experienced employees in the organization, it will be necessary to adopt some form of plant-wide or company-wide seniority so that experienced employees do not lose accumulated rights if they are later returned to their former jobs. This is one of the thorniest questions in the whole seniority problem.

Finally, in production or replacement transfer to prevent layoff or in a remedial transfer to correct faulty placement, the transferee should ordinarily get the pay rate of the new job, not that of his previous job. The same is true of shift transfers, which are ordinarily desired by employees who wish to get on a preferred shift. When transfers are made to accommodate management and to balance operations, as in many versatility and some shift transfers, the transferee should be paid his old rate or the new rate, whichever is higher.

FORMULATING A LAYOFF POLICY

Nearly every organization, at one time or another, is faced with the necessity of laying off employees for lack of work. Some layoffs are temporary and expected by employees because of the nature of the job. These can be planned for and are not so serious. When a change in operations or a decline in business necessitates permanent layoffs, however, the problem is more difficult.

In both types of layoffs, but especially in the latter when long-service employees will be affected, there is need for a definite layoff policy. Union seniority rules are in part a response to the demand of workers for some certainty as to the order of layoffs. Then long-service employees know, at least, that they will not be the first to be laid off if operations decline, and they have a pretty good idea how many others will precede them.

Granting the need for a sound policy, its formulation is not easy because of various possible alternatives and the conflicting demands of seniority and efficiency. These apply with almost equal force to unionized and nonunion firms and organizations.[9] Three major problems must have

the full consideration of top management in formulating a layoff policy and procedure.

Will Hours of Work Be Reduced Before Any Employees—or Certain Groups—Are Laid Off? It is common to lay off probationary (new) employees first and, after this, to reduce hours, but experience has demonstrated the undesirability of excessive work sharing. When workers were getting only 2 or 3 days of work each week, nearly all were dissatisfied. From the standpoint of the individual firm, it is better to lay off the junior employees in order to give the remaining senior employees at least 4 days (or 32 hours) of work a week. Generally, however, some work sharing should precede the layoff of employees (excluding probationers) if it becomes necessary to lay off workers who have seniority standing. Union contracts frequently spell out the procedure to be followed.

What Factors Shall Determine Who Will Be Laid Off First? As we have seen, in unionized firms seniority is increasingly accepted as important and in many cases is considered the sole factor. The strong desire of employees for recognition of length of service[10] and for a definite order in layoffs is met in some firms by following strict seniority in layoffs. Efficiency is then protected by (1) careful selection when new employees are hired, (2) weeding out clearly incompetent employees by discharge, and (3) promotion on the basis of competence, when the junior employee is clearly more competent than the senior employee.

Some union contracts, however, provide that consideration also be given to skill and competence or that the seniority clause not be applied strictly in all cases. Layoff policies in nonunion firms generally give some consideration to family status and when the firm is dominant in a small

---

[9] For a discussion of the layoff procedures developed prior to the layoff of over a thousand employees in an electronics firm in 1963, see Thomas H. Sebring, "Planning for a Personnel Reduction," *Personnel Journal*, vol. 44, no. 4, pp. 179-183, April, 1965. See also Joseph D. Mooney, "An Analysis of Unemployment among Professional Engineers and Scientists," *Industrial and Labor Relations Review*, vol. 19, no. 4, pp. 517-528, July, 1966.

[10] For a discussion of this aspect of "job rights," see Frederic Meyers, *Ownership of Jobs: A Comparative Study*, University of California, Institute of Industrial Relations, Los Angeles, 1964.

community, take into consideration whether or not the employee is a local resident. More weight is also given to the relative competence of employees. Another alternative to straight seniority in layoffs is to exempt a certain percentage of the ablest employees, usually 10 to 15 percent, in each job classification from the application of seniority rules. This group of clearly "exceptional" employees may be retained regardless of seniority, and the others laid off on a straight seniority basis. If management has freedom in making promotions on the basis of competence, however, perhaps it would be well for management to follow straight seniority in layoffs (when competence is adequate for the job) as a means of providing a greater degree of employment security to long-service employees. This is certainly a persistent union demand, reflecting strong pressure from workers.

How Should Seniority Be Determined? This involves two points, as we have seen earlier in this chapter: (1) the seniority unit—occupation, department, plant, or entire company—and (2) interruptions in length of service that might abrogate seniority rights. The first problem is particularly troublesome, for whatever decision is reached, someone is likely to consider it unfair. For example, if long-service employees are transferred from another department to avoid laying them off, considerable training may be necessary, and the younger employees they displace may be resentful because "outsiders" are taking their jobs. On the other hand, a narrow departmental or occupational unit will lead to layoff of long-service people in one department while employees with short seniority who are fortunate enough to be in a stationary or expanding department are retained. The second problem requires decisions on whether seniority is broken by transfers, layoffs, and extended absences due to illness, family problems, etc. In unionized organizations, both require negotiations with unions in unionized firms.

Other Features of Layoff Policy

In formulating layoff policy, consideration should be given to still other questions. Should leaves of absence or advance rehiring commitments be given to key employees whose services will be needed within the foreseeable future? Should advance notice of layoff be given? Or would paying some form of dismissal compensation in lieu of notice be preferable? What part should exit interviews play in the layoff program? What should be done to place laid-off employees with other firms in the area?

Advance hiring commitments offer another means of cushioning the shock of layoff. Under a straight seniority policy, the last employee laid off is the first one recalled, and to some extent this removes the uncertainty, "When shall I get back to work?" But management should be able to do more than this. Commitments are made in advance for materials and equipment; why not for key men? To the degree that it is possible to estimate future labor requirements following a temporary curtailment or shutdown, it should be possible to specify approximate dates on which groups of key employees will be rehired.

When permanent layoffs are necessary, they should be planned as far in advance as possible, in order to give adequate notice to the employees affected. Steelworkers at one mill bitterly remembered the cold formal notice that they found in their pay envelopes on a Saturday: "Effective Monday, your services will no longer be required." At least 1 week's advance notice of layoff should be given, and a longer notice to long-service employees.[11] Some firms fear that this will result in a "slowing down" during the last week and consequently prefer to give a week's pay in lieu of notice. If a slowdown oc-

[11] Arnold R. Weber and David P. Taylor, "Procedures for Employee Displacement: Advance Notice of Plant Shutdown," *Journal of Business*, vol. 36, no. 3, pp. 302–315, July, 1963. For other experiences, see "Strategy for an Employee Cutback," *Business Management*, September, 1965, pp. 54-62.

curs, however, it is an evidence of poor morale that no layoff policy will cure.

Severance pay is provided by some firms,[12] but more companies and organizations should consider the possibility of some compensation for permanent displacements caused by technological change, shutting down of less efficient plants, etc. The amount of compensation should vary with the employee's earnings and length of service, and it should be regarded as a payment to which a permanently displaced worker is entitled as a consequence of the loss of his job. The availability of severance pay may discourage employer placement efforts, but if so, this is unfortunate and shortsighted.

Finally, each company or organization should make an effort to place laid-off employees with other firms in the community. The first approach might well be through the public employment service. In planning layoffs, it is desirable that each company notify the service as far in advance as possible of the probable number of employees who will be laid off on an approximate future date in each job classification. The personnel administrator can thus help to fulfill the broad obligation that his company has in working closely with agencies in the labor market that are seeking to place workers in new jobs. As we said in Chapter 15, the public employment service can become an effective clearinghouse for workers and jobs only when it is fully used by employers and job seekers.[13]

EMPLOYMENT STABILIZATION

Although some layoffs are inevitable in certain industries, no organization should neglect serious study of how it can minimize layoffs by employment-stablization methods. The experience of many pioneering firms in various industries has conclusively demonstrated that seasonal and intermittent unemployment can be reduced by management action. Managers need to acquaint themselves with the methods that have been successfully used to stabilize employment in other firms, and to consider what methods are applicable in their own organization.[14]

Many of the personnel policies and procedures that we have already discussed are essential in a program to stabilize company employment. A centralized hiring and placement process is needed to avoid the wasteful practice of hiring workers in one department while they are being laid off in another. Replacement transfers and production transfers can also be used to avoid this, and workers should be trained to do several jobs so that they can be transferred rather than laid off. Some work sharing is also necessary and desirable, if not carried too far.

Firms with seasonal sales have sought to even out their production by manufacturing standard products for stock during the slack periods or by standardizing or simplifying their line of products so that manufacture for stock becomes feasible. Other firms have changed the pattern of their sales by stimulating off-season orders through advertising and through increased sales efforts that tap new markets or change the buying habits of consumers. Some particularly ingenious companies have developed sidelines or fill-

[12] *Severance Pay Patterns in Manufacturing,* National Industrial Conference Board, Studies in Personnel Policy, no. 174, New York, 1959 and *Severance Pay Patterns in Nonmanufacturing,* National Industrial Conference Board, Studies in Personnel Policy no. 178, New York, 1960; *Major Collective Bargaining Agreements: Severance Pay and Layoff Benefit Plans,* Department of Labor, U.S. Bureau of Labor Statistics, Bulletin no. 1425-2, Washington, D.C., 1965.

[13] For a comprehensive discussion of the experience under the Armour Automation Fund Committee, see George P. Shultz and Arnold. R. Weber, *Strategies for the Displaced Worker,* Harper & Row, Publishers, Incorporated, New York, 1966. This involved interplant transfers, severance pay, and retirement benefits, placement efforts, and retraining.

[14] Suggestions will be found in *Steadier Jobs: A Handbook for Management on Stabilizing Employment,* Industrial Relations Counselors, Inc., New York, 1954; and Joseph L. Snider, *The Guarantee of Work and Wages,* Harvard Graduate School of Business Administration, Boston, 1964. See also Robert S. Eckley, "Company Action to Stabilize Employment," *Harvard Business Review,* vol. 44, no. 4, pp. 51-61, July-August, 1966.

ers that diversify their line of products and provide orders sufficient to maintain factory employment on a more even keel throughout the year.

Stabilization of employment also has costs. If present employees are worked overtime to avoid hiring temporary employees, overtime premium payments will have to be made. Production for inventory in slack periods increases inventory costs, which may be offset by better utilization of equipment. Personnel costs and benefits must be balanced against these other costs and savings to determine the net costs of an employment stabilization program.

SUMMARY

A promotion-from-within policy requires primary emphasis on competence, as an incentive for employees to qualify for better jobs and to utilize most effectively the human resources in an organization. But management will have to demonstrate in practice that its decisions are fair, rather than the result of "pull," "influence," or discrimination. Otherwise, it may be unable to resist the demand that seniority be the governing factor or that certain minority groups be given preference in promotions.

Transfers are also helpful in utilizing human resources. They help to retain long-service employees as operations shift or decline, to develop versatility in employees, to permit movement between shifts, and to remedy unsatisfactory placements. Policies and procedures must be developed to cover these types of transfers and to meet such other issues as the basis on which transfers will be made and the location of responsibility for making them.

Policies and clearly stated procedures are also needed for downgrading and layoff. Seniority is an increasingly important factor in downgrading and layoff, but this raises difficult questions that must be answered in a policy statement. What is

the seniority unit? How is seniority computed? Other features of layoff policy, such as reducing hours of work for all employees before layoff and giving advance notice of layoff, must also be considered. It is the concern of a personnel administrator to bring these issues to the attention of top management in formulating and administering policies and procedure, and to assist the company in reducing the need for layoff by employment stabilization.

Downgrading and layoff have sometimes been used as disciplinary measures, and in some firms "layoff" is frequently confused with "discharge." A clear distinction should be made, however, because discharge and disciplinary measures are usually with prejudice to the employee. We shall consider the features of a constructive disciplinary policy in the next chapter.

SELECTED REFERENCES

Belzung, L. D., John P. Owen, and John F. MacNaughton: *The Anatomy of a Workforce Reduction: A Study of Workers Affected by a 1962 Reduction in Force at the Humble Oil & Refining Company, Baytown, Texas, Refinery,* University of Houston, College of Business Administration, Center for Research in Business and Economics, Houston, Texas, 1966.

Building Better Promotion Programs, U.S. Civil Service Commission, Personnel Management Series, no. 2, 1952.

Chamberlain, Neil W.: *Management in Motion: The Corporate Decision-making Process as Applied to the Transfer of Employees,* Yale University, Labor and Management Center, New Haven, Conn., 1950.

Doeringer, Peter B., and Michael J. Piore: *Internal Labor Markets and Manpower Analysis,* D.C. Heath and Company, Lexington, Mass., 1971, especially chaps. 3 and 7.

Elliott, John M.: "Promotion from Within: Fact or Farce?," *Personnel,* vol. 29, no. 3, pp. 227–233, 1952.

Haas, George H., and Elizabeth R. Floyd: *Company Severance Pay Plans,* American Management Association, Research Report 29, New York, 1957.

McConkey, Dale D.: "Ability vs. Seniority in Promotion and Layoff," *Personnel,* vol. 37, no. 3, pp. 51-57, May-June, 1960.

Olson, Ruth L.: "The Design and Installation of Promotion Policies and Procedures," *Personnel Administration,* vol. 13, no. 1, pp. 19-22, 1950.

Sebring, Thomas H.: "Planning for a Personnel Reduction," *Personnel Journal,* vol. 44, no. 4, pp. 179-183, April, 1965.

Shultz, George P., and Arnold R. Weber: *Strategies for the Displaced Worker,* Harper & Row, Publishers, Incorporated, New York, 1966.

Slichter, Sumner N., James J. Healy, and E. R. Livernash: *The Impact of Collective Bargaining on Management,* The Brookings Institution, Washington, D.C., 1960, chaps. 5-7.

Steadier Jobs: A Handbook for Management on Stabilizing Employment, Industrial Relations Counselors, Inc., New York, 1954.

Varela, Jacobo A.: "Why Promotions Cause Trouble—And How to Avoid It," *Personnel,* vol. 41, no. 6, pp. 17-21, November-December, 1964.

Weber, Arnold R., and David P. Taylor: "Procedures for Employee Displacement: Advance Notice of Plant Shutdown," *The Journal of Business* (University of Chicago), vol. 36, no. 2, pp. 302-315, July, 1963.

Chapter 18

Constructive Discipline

Discipline in the broad sense means orderliness—the opposite of confusion. It is a fundamental requirement for the people working in a plant just as it is for other segments of society. . . . Shop discipline, as we use the term, does not mean strict and technical observance of rigid rules and regulations. It simply means working, cooperating, and behaving in a normal and orderly way, as any reasonable person would expect an employee to do.

Earl R. Bramblett[1]

In this chapter, we consider the following questions: How can discipline contribute most effectively to "normal and orderly" behavior? Why have unions so often been dissatisfied with managerial decisions and actions for purposes of discipline? Why might a manager plan for disci-

[1] Earl R. Bramblett, "Maintenance of Discipline," p. 10, *Management of Personnel Quarterly,* vol. 1, no. 1, Autumn, 1961 (reprinted in Paul Pigors, Charles A. Myers, and F. T. Malm, *Management of Human Resources: Readings in Personnel Administration,* 3d ed., McGraw-Hill Book Company, New York, 1973, selection 35). (Mr. Bramblett, ret. 1971, was director of labor relations for the General Motors Corporation.)

plinary action, even if he believes in participative management? What might be said in a corporate policy on discipline? What makes an organizational disciplinary procedure acceptable and workable? What steps are needed in a constructive disciplinary process?

TWO VIEWS OF DISCIPLINE

A manager's answers to such questions naturally depend in large measure on whether his general concept of managing is closer to System 2 (Theory X) or System 4 (Theory Y).

A Negative View (System 2)

Traditionally, managers have thought of discipline only as punishment. Even today, many managers and supervisors see discipline primarily as a means to enforce external demands for responsible behavior. They do not place any reliance on spontaneous self-discipline. Instead, they expect orderly behavior to depend primarily on fear of penalties.[2] Thus they exercise discipline—as punishment—partly as a deterrent and partly as retributive justice. And in investigating instances of employee misconduct, many managers rely on methods of detection that are in violation of an individual's right to privacy and human dignity.[3]

In the "good old days," this negative view of discipline was often carried to extremes. "Industrial discipline has traditionally been both severe and irresponsible."[4] Especially as exercised by old-time foremen, who had authority to administer discipline up to and including discharge, discipline often failed to meet standards of fairness. The following example illustrates these general statements.

A Case Example: Peremptory Discharge

Albert Prestorato was an experienced heeler in a firm manufacturing canvas footwear. The department had been having trouble with "started, or sprung, heels." This defect was often caused by improper hand rolling but might also be brought about by atmospheric conditions or improper mixing of cement in another section. The department superintendent brought pressure on his foremen to eliminate this defect. One of the foremen, who had been raked over the coals, relieved his annoyance by taking it out on his workers. He threatened: "The next man who has any started heels is fired. That's all!"

That same day, 50 pairs of shoes with sprung heels were traced to Prestorato, who had been in the department 10 years and was one of the most efficient operators. The foreman doubtless realized the trouble could not be wholly Prestorato's fault, but he feared loss of face if he failed to carry out his threat. He discharged Prestorato on the spot. However, in order not to lose the services of this valuable employee, he rehired Prestorato the next day. Unfortunately, neither the foreman nor Prestorato remembered the company rule that discharge automatically broke an employee's service record, and 15 years later Prestorato claimed that his 25-year service record made him eligible for an extra week's vacation. He then discovered that his continuous-service record dated only from the time when he was rehired after his peremptory discharge.

Revolt against such arbitrary exercise of power and its unfortunate consequences was a prime reason why workers formed unions. Today, unions have been successful in making "due process" a part of every labor agreement. However, unionization has not removed feelings of dissatisfaction with regard to disciplinary actions taken by management. Instead, it has made that dissatisfaction articulate.

Union Dissatisfaction with Disciplinary Action by Management

The largest single occasion for arbitration has been dissatisfaction with disciplinary action

[2] In a study utilizing role playing as a method of determining how supervisors would handle a disciplinary problem, observers found that 35 percent of the participants followed a strict judicial approach. See Norman R. F. Maier and Lee E. Danielson, "An Evaluation of Two Approaches to Discipline in Industry," *Journal of Applied Psychology,* vol. 40, no. 5, pp. 319–323, October, 1956.

[3] See Mary Ann Coghill, "The Lie Detector in Employment: An Examination of Some of the Problems," *Key Issues: Background Reports on Current Topics and Trends in Labor-Management Relations,* no. 2, July, 1968, New York State School of Industrial and Labor Relations, Cornell University, Ithaca, N.Y. See also Bruce Gunn, "The Polygraph and Personnel," *Personnel Administration,* vol. 33, no. 2, pp. 32–37, May-June, 1970, and Martin Markson, "A reexamination of the role of lie detectors in labor relations," *Labor Law Journal,* vol. 22, no. 7, pp. 394–407, July, 1971.

[4] Orme W. Phelps, *Discipline and Discharge in the Unionized Firm,* University of California Press, Berkeley, Calif., 1959, p. 4.

taken by supervisors. For example, in a study of 1,728 grievances which in 1954 had been brought to arbitration and processed under the rules of the American Arbitration Association, 456 cases (26.4 percent) were concerned with discipline and discharge.[5] A special 14-year follow-up study made available by J. Murphy, Director of the Education Department, American Arbitration Association, New York, showed that the year-to-year variation was slight. In 1967 there were 757 cases (27.2 percent) concerning discipline and discharge. For the first 6 months of 1968 the figures were 404 cases (27 percent).

A similar study of grievance arbitration in *one company* showed that during the 10 years from 1942 to 1952, which were covered by the study, disciplinary action by the company was the cause of 89 disputes brought before arbitrators. Discharge was challenged as unjust and improper in 18 cases; demotion, less drastic than discharge, was contested as unfair in 6 cases. Most of the remaining cases entailed the imposition of disciplinary layoff.[6]

Many employees who were discharged and protested this disciplinary action were reinstated by impartial arbitrators. It may be expected that in such cases, employers took a close second look. Consequently, it is encouraging to note that many reinstated employees made satisfac-

Table 18-1   Disposition of 456 Cases of Disciplinary Action (1954)

Disposition	Number	Percentage
A Discharge cases		
Discharge sustained	149	46.4
Reinstatement with full back pay	60	18.7
Divided (generally reinstatement without full back pay)	112	34.9
Total	321	100.0
B Discipline cases other than discharge		
Discipline sustained	76	56.3
Grievance sustained	45	33.3
Divided	14	10.4
Total	135	100.0
Grand total	456	

tory progress. The following responses from their employers, to a follow-up survey, are significant:

Has the grievant been a satisfactory employee since reinstatement?
"Yes": 65 percent. "No": 35 percent.
Has the grievant made normal occupational progress?
"Yes": 65 percent. "No": 35 percent.[7]

The questions were also asked: *"Has there been a recurrence of disciplinary problems? Have any disciplinary penalities been imposed since reinstatement?"* Of a total of 123 reinstated employees who were covered by the survey, information on subsequent disciplinary history was made available in 96 cases, of whom 67 (or 70 percent) had presented no subsequent disciplinary prob-

[5] *Procedural and Substantive Aspects of Labor-Management Arbitration: An AAA Research Report,* American Arbitration Association, New York, 1957, p. 23. See Table 18-1.

[6] See "Arbitration of Discipline Grievances in Bethlehem Steel," *Monthly Labor Review,* vol. 77, no. 6, pp. 623-628, June, 1954. This article was based on a more complete report, *Arbitration of Labor-Management Grievances—Bethlehem Steel Company and United Steelworkers of America, 1942-1952,* U.S. Bureau of Labor Statistics, Bulletin 1159, 1954. For other experience from the arbitrator's point of view, see Lloyd H. Bailer, "The Discipline Issue in Arbitration: Individual Differences and Shop Practices"; Louis Yagoda, "Employer Rules," *Labor Law Journal,* vol. 15, no. 9, pp. 567-576, September, 1964; and Morris Stone, "Why Arbitrators Reinstate Discharged Employees," *Monthly Labor Review,* vol. 92, no. 10, pp. 47-50, October, 1969.

[7] These data were taken from a study by Arthur M. Ross, "The Arbitration of Discharge Cases: What Happens after Reinstatement?," in National Academy of Arbitrators, *Critical Issues in Labor Arbitration,* Proceedings of the Tenth Annual Meeting, Bureau of National Affairs, Inc., Washington, D.C., 1957, pp. 34-36.

lem. Eight employees repeated the same offense for which they were originally terminated, and four of these had been discharged again. Another 21 employees subsequently committed some different offense, the employer stated, and 11 of these individuals were again discharged.

Finally, *"What has been the grievant's attitude since reinstatement?"* The responses were as follows:

"Attitude good": 54 percent—mostly still employed. In 28 cases, employers stated definitely that the disciplinary crisis had a favorable effect on the grievant's behavior.

"Attitude unchanged": 14 percent—most still employed. The significance of this response is not clear. Presumably what is meant is that the attitude continued unsatisfactory or else that the original problem was not one of attitude.

"Attitude poor": 30 percent—about half still employed. Some employers reported that the reinstated employees now considered themselves above the law. Possibly in these cases the arbitrator's decision turned out to be "wrong" (for plant efficiency) even though it may have been "right" (on the basis of testimony presented at the hearing, and in the context of the existing labor agreement).

Such findings suggest that first-level supervisors need a better understanding of how a constructive discipline process can help a "problem" employee to reorient himself.

A more recent investigation of company experience with reinstated employees supports the above findings and conclusion.[8] Of the 53 employees covered in this study, only 3 were discharged a second time and only 5 did not return to work after reinstatement. Of the 45 employees who reestablished their employment status, 32 were considered by management as good, satisfactory, or improved workers.

[8] Thomas J. McDermott and Thomas H. Newhams, "Discharge-Reinstatement: What Happens Thereafter?" *Industrial and Labor Relations Review,* vol. 24, no. 4, pp. 526–540, July, 1971.

A Positive View (System 4)

An executive who believes in participative management and has been convinced by findings of behavioral scientists[9] is not satisfied merely to keep disciplinary procedures within limits which can be policed by a union or confirmed by an impartial arbitrator as justified under the provisions of a current labor agreement.[10] Instead, such a forward-looking executive wants to make sure that disciplinary action:

- Starts with an effort to foster mutual understanding and an organization-centered view.
- Is fair.
- Is demonstrably consistent with sound principles of human relations (including "due process" and the right of appeal).
- Is in accord with a policy statement on discipline which is clear and well known to all.
- Implements ideas that have been worked out by conferring with representatives of those who are subject to discipline.
- Takes account of any extenuating features in each situation where someone feels that discipline is called for.

Only when disciplinary action meets such specifications can it play a part in the kind of mutually responsible behavior which contributes to peak efficiency.

This kind of discipline can be achieved in nonunionized enterprises (as was mentioned in Chapter 13), although formal procedures for processing grievances and for terminal arbitra-

[9] See Gene S. Booker, "Behavioral Aspects of Disciplinary Action," *Personnel Journal,* vol. 48, no. 7, pp. 525–529, 1969.

[10] See Harry Seligson, "Minority Group Employees, Discipline and the Arbitrators," *Labor Law Journal,* vol. 19, no. 9, pp. 544–554, September, 1968, for a comprehensive statement of traditional criteria applied by an impartial arbitrator in his review of disputed discipline cases. The author suggests that to match industry's current obligation as an institution of social change, the arbitration process needs to be liberalized by adopting a more flexible set of guidelines or limits of tolerance in appropriate situations.

tion are less frequently found there.[11] Nevertheless, it should be noted that major aims of personnel administration remain unmet unless constructive discipline—achieved primarily by participative management—can be relied upon to supplement and reenforce self-disciplined behavior by a majority of employees.

WHY PLAN FOR DISCIPLINARY ACTION?

Many managers now believe that peak performance depends on action by which employees in subordinate positions voluntarily (1) carry out instructions issued by supervisors and (2) abide by rules of conduct and standards of work which have been established to ensure successful attainment of organizational objectives. According to this concept, effective discipline is a by-product of positive and intelligent leadership and of willing cooperation by subordinates, within the framework provided by policies and procedures established and accepted for the organization as a whole. The strongest basis for discipline is voluntary self-discipline.

If all employees, at all times, could be counted on to behave reasonably, there would be no need for supervisors to take any disciplinary action. If all supervisors could be counted on to be reasonable in imposing corrective discipline, there would be no need to set up any procedure to implement the right of appeal. However, human nature being what it is, neither of these expectations is realistic. Nevertheless, experience suggests that most employees want to do what needs to be done, at work and in their other conduct, to meet organizational needs and accepted standards of behavior. Even before they start to work in a business or industrial organization, mature persons have accepted the idea that following instructions and abiding by fair rules of conduct are responsibilities of every member in any organization. Therefore, if the employment relationship is good, in other respects, most employees can be counted on to exercise a considerable degree of self-discipline. They will respond to positive leadership and need not be threatened or punished.[12] Also, wherever effective teamwork exists, group discipline can be counted on to supplement self-discipline. (However, as noted in Chapter 6, teamwork in small work groups can also be exercised as a counterforce to management objectives and discipline.)[13]

Unfortunately, in any large organization there are likely to be a few employees who, for various reasons, fail to observe established rules and standards, even after having been informed of them. In periods of extreme labor shortage, the number of these intransigent employees is apt to increase, but it is usually not larger than a very small minority of all employees.

A Special Need

Recently, however, in some organizations, constructive discipline, first of all as orientation, has been especially needed by new employees recruited from among the hard-core unemployed. Absenteeism has been a problem with some of them. Why? "Many have been so crippled in every way, emotionally and economically, with

[11] See *Personnel Practices in Factory and Office,* National Industrial Conference Board, Inc., Studies in Personnel Policy, no. 145, New York, 1954, p. 56. A survey covering 284 companies revealed grievance procedures for hourly workers not represented by unions in 61 cases (21.5 percent) as against 211 firms (74.3 percent) who did not have such procedures. Arbitration was provided for in 17 (27.9 percent) of the 61 companies which heard employee complaints. Another survey, *Employee Communications: Policy and Tools,* National Industrial Conference Board, Inc., Personnel Policy Study, no. 200, New York, 1966, p. 57, reports that in nonunion companies that have a grievance procedure management permits the complainant to be accompanied by a fellow employee when he presents his complaint.

[12] For a case example of a firm which moved from a punitive disciplinary policy to one in the direction of Theory Y, see John Huberman, "Discipline without Punishment," *Harvard Business Review,* vol. 42, no. 4, pp. 62–68, July–August, 1964. Additional information and case illustrations were provided in Huberman's talk at the Nineteenth Annual Conference, March 4–5, 1970, McGill University Industrial Relations Center. See Frances Bairstow (ed.), *Innovations in Industrial Organization and Labour Relations,* pp. 133–143.

[13] As an example, see Case 2, "Who Owns the Improved Tool?"

criminal records, or on drugs, that the new-found responsibilities were just too much for them. They've been out of work so long that the work habit has been destroyed."[14] Or, as John M. Roche, Chairman of General Motors, put it, "Many have never observed a single regulation in their lives. They don't realize the meaning of punctuality."[15]

New employees with this background and these attitudes impose special requirements for effective supervision and constructive discipline. The first requirement for supervision is understanding: of corporate purpose and policy (with regard to the employment of persons previously regarded as unemployable), of reasons for undisciplined behavior, and of effective ways to help these individuals reorient themselves. Only the last two points need any elaboration.

Particularly in relationships with nonwhites, a person-centered approach is needed to replace stereotyped thinking. It is reasonable to recognize that "The way employees behave depends on their home environment, their economic status, and their education. It has nothing to do with the color of their skin."[16]

A supervisor with a positive approach to discipline needs support from higher managers. Then he is in a position to make an intelligent and cooperative start in working with disadvantaged persons whose behavior is likely to be somewhat undisciplined at first. Certainly he cannot overlook such behavior. To do so would be unfair to other employees, as well as to those who need reorientation. It would tend to weaken morale. And undisciplined behavior is likely to be contagious for those whose self-discipline is at all shaky. Questions for the supervisor therefore become: How can such behavior best be coped with? Whose cooperation can be enlisted? What unusual, or innovative, measures might be effective?

At General Motors, the so-called "buddy system" was instituted[17] to help reduce absenteeism among recently recruited Negroes from poverty areas. Members of the Negro community, most of them regular GM employees, worked with the absentees to help them develop a greater sense of responsibility toward their employer. Early reports indicate that a considerable measure of success has been achieved in this way.

Naturally, a supervisor cannot delegate his disciplinary responsibilities to anyone. But it seems intelligent to have his activities supplemented by insiders who can communicate more effectively with persons who have a similar cultural background. However, it should be made clear that supervisors cannot adjust to and accept unsatisfactory performance indefinitely on the ground that the person concerned is disadvantaged.

A Special Case: Needs for Discipline on Campus

Appropriate response to undisciplined behavior by students requires situational analysis. (See Chapter 9, for details.) In thinking about discipline needed on campus, it is useful to distin-

---

[14] Gertrude Samuels, "Help Wanted: The Hard-core Unemployed," *The New York Times Magazine,* Jan. 28, 1968, p. 47. She was quoting a spokesman for the Mayor's Committee for Human Resources, in Detroit. The managing editor of an influential Negro Weekly in Detroit said: "Much of the problem here is the migrants from the South, who know nothing but working for the white-man boss. These are people who for three and four generations have been on welfare. . . . Psychologically, many of them are 'getting even with Whitey.'"

[15] *Ibid.,* p. 48.

[16] This statement was made by a quality control analyst and chief inspector at the Cook Electric Company's Wirecom Division. (He happened to be a Negro.) The vice-president and general manager of that division (who happened to be a white man) expressed general satisfaction with performance of Negroes but added, "They require somewhat more supervision and their absenteeism is higher." Stephen Habbe, *Company Experience with Negro Employment,* Studies in Personnel Policy, No. 101, National Industrial Conference Board, Inc., New York, 1966, vol. 1, p. 122. (For a later review of experience, see Charles A. Myers, *The Role of the Private Sector in Manpower Development,* The Johns Hopkins Press, Baltimore and London, 1971, chap. 3.)

[17] Samuels, *op. cit.,* p. 48.

guish between (1) occasional outbreaks of rowdyism, such as have been traditional on many campuses in spring; (2) the undisciplined behavior that has always been characteristic of a relatively small proportion of students (the experimental misconduct of young people aspiring to establish their identity);[18] and (3) militant behavior of revolutionary activists who belong to such organizations as Students for a Democratic Society and Youth Against War and Fascism.

The first type of undisciplined behavior rarely needs to be taken seriously except during the brief intervals while it is occurring. Aggressive individuals in the second group have always tended to react explosively against what they see as paternalism or arbitrary enforcement of senseless rules. Nevertheless, they readily identify with the Establishment and merely wish to have some recognition as individuals and some share in the decisions that affect their life on campus. Instances of overenthusiastic self-expression ("misconduct") can be handled by following the principles of constructive discipline. As emphasized by Frederick Harbison,[19] rules of conduct governing campus activities easily lend themselves to joint negotiations. And effective two-way communication between representatives of the student body and the administration are essential prerequisites for establishing mutually satisfactory relationships.

Militant activists, on the other hand, perceiving themselves as moral crusaders, readily resort to violence, confronting the Establishment with "nonnegotiable demands." No such coercive action, designed to shatter the foundations of campus life (and possibly also of related community activities), can be tolerated without jeopardizing the integrity of the academic institution. However, any firm attempt to retain control presupposes internal unity of purpose—within the faculty and between faculty members and administrative officials, and mutual confidence between members of the administration, faculty, and different age groups of the student body. The former can be achieved only by continuing two-way communication at the level of principles and policy. The second requires, in addition, establishing and maintaining effective procedures for handling dissatisfactions and complaints. Voluntary abdication of authority by administrative officials in favor of intervention by armed police or units of the National Guard tends to do more harm than good. It alienates dissatisfied faculty members and arouses otherwise apathetic or uncommitted students, who begin to believe that the revolutionary activists may be right.

Principles and procedures of personnel administration may not seem directly applicable to relationships between administration officials, faculty members, and students. However, many of the principles clarified by enlightened managers in policy thinking offer useful guidelines for university administrators who wish to cope constructively with occasionally rowdy behavior on the part of normally well-behaved students or more serious misconduct by experimentally minded individuals. Moreover, participative management,[20] (considered at some length in

[18] "Students come to the university in the most rootless and tumultuous phase of their lives. Typically, they have outgrown the families of their childhood but have not yet established the families of their adulthood. The more promising the student, the more his ideas and values are in ferment. A student body, consequently, is a self-renewing whirlpool of energy, idealism, confusion, and discontent." Arthur M. Ross, "Industrial Jurisprudence and the Campus," *Educational Record,* vol. 51, no. 1, pp. 28-33, Winter, 1970. Quotation on pages 28-29.

[19] Frederick H. Harbison, "The Campus Revolt from an Industrial Relations Perspective," in Gerald G. Somers (ed.), *Proceedings of the Twenty-second Annual Winter Meeting, Industrial Relations Research Association,* Dec. 29-30, 1969, New York City, Madison, Wis., February, 1970, pp. 2-14.

[20] See John Hersey, *Letter to the Alumni* (of Yale University), Alfred A. Knopf, Inc., New York, 1970, for an example of exceptionally effective group discipline by members of the student body at Yale University. Especially in the role of marshal, student activity was a major factor in preventing anticipated violence on the Mayday weekend of 1970 and in making unnecessary any intervention by the police.

Chapters 1, 5, 6, and 7) is just as much needed—and just as appropriate—on campus as it is in any organization all of whose members are mature persons.

On the other hand, preventive discipline may be fruitless when used to establish cooperative relationships with militant advocates of an "alternative society" (or counterculture). And permissiveness is likely to be perceived, and reacted to, as weakness. With militant activists, as with disruptively inclined members of any other community (or organization), the final step in the disciplinary process—dismissal—may be necessary. After careful investigation of all the relevant circumstances by an academic disciplinary committee and upon proof of unacceptable misconduct, they should be expelled, thus ceasing to be members of the academic community.

POLICY THINKING ABOUT DISCIPLINE

Many managers see the primary purpose of discipline as being to supplement and strengthen self-discipline within each individual and within each work group. The following statement of policy expresses that view (in the kind of language that distinguishes a policy from a procedure or rule).

A Sample Statement of Policy and Procedure on Discipline

Overall purpose. It is management's intention to foster, at all times, and throughout the whole employment relationship, the high morale that makes for self-discipline in every employee and group discipline within every work team. When it is necessary for management representatives to take disciplinary action, their behavior should demonstrably implement two related purposes:

1 To inform or remind employees about accepted standards of work and of conduct.
2 To prevent undisciplined behavior by an unruly minority from exercising an undue influence.

Our disciplinary procedure should be used, whenever possible, in such a way and at such times as to reinforce in employees the desire to meet standards accepted for the organization.

This policy is to be implemented by the attached procedure and by the established disciplinary process, both of which shall be made known to all employees when they are hired.

Rules. The responsibilities which all employees are expected to meet are summarized in a minimum of rules[21] for efficiency, safety, and good conduct. These rules are to be carefully explained to every new employee. If necessary, they are to be reemphasized by supervisors in follow-up interviews. Each of these rules is to be promptly and impartially enforced.

Responsibilities. No management representative should ever overlook disobedience, either of plant rules or of a supervisor's order. If an employee should ever feel that either a rule or an order is unsuitable, he should still obey it. He has recourse to the grievance procedure by entering a complaint with his representative on the grievance committee.[22]

Disciplinary procedure. Any act of clear-cut disobedience (where the facts have been established) shall be considered ground for disciplinary action. The scope of such action shall depend on the supervisor's judgment as to the seriousness of the offense (in relation to the various rules, or to the gravity of the situation) and the possibility of misunderstanding by an offender. Disciplinary action should be set in motion by the supervisor in charge. Its nature should depend on what disciplinary steps, if any, have previously been taken with the employee. Punitive action, especially discharge, should be taken only after due warning [except in extreme cases—see rules, p. 331]. In case of reasonable doubt as to facts, the employee should be suspended from work pending further investigation.

---

[21] In our opinion, it is good practice to have as few rules as possible. A multiplicity of rules often breeds contempt for the very idea of law. Such contempt is usually expressed in nonobservance and even in nonenforcement of whatever rules are regarded as unimportant. Whenever this happens, management authority is weakened.

[22] In a nonunion firm, this provision would naturally be worded differently, but the right of appeal, and its implementing procedure, should be specifically referred to.

AN ORGANIZATIONAL DISCIPLINARY PROCEDURE

What Makes It Acceptable and Workable?

The character of a disciplinary procedure, like that of a policy, should reflect the general principles and purposes of top management. For example, does the procedure consist only (or primarily) in a list of offenses and rules as prohibitions, forbidding certain kinds of action? Or does it give positive directions, prescribing what employees are expected to do?

Whatever else is aimed at in a written statement of disciplinary procedure, two objectives are commonly agreed upon. First, the official statement should inform everyone concerned what top management expects (positively or negatively) *in general,* of all employees. Employees cannot reasonably be asked to meet standards or to obey rules unless they know what the standards and rules are. Nor can supervisors be expected to represent top management, in explaining and enforcing regulations, without specific guidance. Yet both these points are overlooked by those managers who insist that, since it is impossible to anticipate everything that might occur, each offense "should be considered on its own merits." Without uniformity of definition, the same offense is almost certain to get different treatment at different times and in different parts of the organization. Naturally, to formulate such a procedure is a responsibility of higher management, but its effectiveness depends on understanding and agreement at every organizational level.

Consultation That Evokes Participation

Managers (and personnel administrators) who take a positive view of discipline—as a form of education and of reinforcement—naturally wish to secure participation from all employees in all stages of working toward self-discipline. In many concerns, such participation is invited by consulting with all supervisors *before* the procedure

for discipline is put into final form. In some companies, representative employees are also asked to contribute their opinions about what kinds of behavior should be specified as desirable, or as undesirable and therefore as meriting disciplinary action. Unless all supervisors have a chance to express their opinions, how can it be expected either that the rules will represent a broad base of experience or that supervisors can effectively represent top management in administering discipline? Unless employees get a hearing, how can they be expected to feel that managers want to take account of all relevant experience before making final decisions about disciplinary procedure? The personnel administrator may usefully serve as moderator during such discussions and should report the consensus to top management.

The question has been raised: In unionized firms, should the formulation of plant rules be a matter for joint decision with union representatives? Union contracts usually provide that workers may be discharged for "just cause," and, either directly or by implication, they recognize management's responsibility for promulgating reasonable plant rules. It is not necessary to take sides in the controversy over "management prerogatives" to assert that it is sound practice to give union officials copies of the policy statement on discipline, to invite participation by union representatives in initial discussions of disciplinary procedure, to consult them if any changes are contemplated, and to notify them of all decisions in regard to proposed disciplinary action.

In talking with union representatives about management's responsibility for discipline, it is important to make clear that such discussions are intended to be informational and educational for all concerned. They do not—at this stage—form part of collective bargaining. Full and friendly discussion about needs and plans for discipline can be useful in preventing many dissatisfactions with might otherwise develop into grievances and even into full-fledged disputes. When union officials understand management thinking about plant rules and disciplinary action, they may be able to accept as reasonable ideas that they would condemn as arbitrary if they were put into effect unannounced. Moreover, during advance discussion, management representatives have a chance to consider any objections that union representatives may have to proposed disciplinary measures.

What Should Be Said in the Written Procedure?

Naturally, no list of offenses or rules can be comprehensive. A company-wide procedure resembles a company policy to the extent that its reference is necessarily general (although a procedure should be less general than a policy). For example, behavior that shall subject an employee to some measure of discipline varies, to some extent, between different companies or industries. Most companies regulate smoking on company premises, but chemical companies place such a premium on safety that "bringing matches or lighters into the plant" is defined as sufficient cause for immediate discharge. The relative seriousness of infractions of rules may even vary according to specific circumstances and needs in different parts of the same company.

The following list of offenses (formulated in one company after discussions with supervisors and union representatives) may serve to indicate the kind of behavior that has often been specified in disciplinary procedures. (The items in this list are not arranged in the order of their seriousness, nor are specific penalties for violations listed.)[23]

> Using liquor on the premises; drunkenness
> Fighting or attempting to injure others (aggressor only)
> Stealing from company or from any employee

Falsifying time cards and production records
Immoral behavior
Unauthorized possession of weapons
Engaging in a strike or group stoppage of work of any kind, slowdown, sabotage, picketing, or failure to abide by the terms of the union agreement or by the award of an impartial arbitrator
Willful destruction of company property
Insubordination or willful disobedience in carrying out reasonable requests of the supervisor
Gambling and bookmaking on the premises
Refusing to accept job assignments
Unexcused absence for a period of 3 consecutive working days without notification of the supervisor or the employment department
Inefficiency, i.e., failing to do the amount and quality of work that were expected of the employee when he was hired
Defacing company property
Violation of safety rules
Continued unexcused tardiness and absenteeism
Horseplay and practical joking
Smoking in prohibited areas

In developing a disciplinary procedure on the basis of such a list it is important to distinguish between major and minor offenses. One labor relations director has suggested as examples of major offenses: "assault on a member of supervision; assault with a weapon on fellow-workers, . . . leadership and direction of a strike in violation of the labor agreement; theft and sabotage."[24] Discharge is the customary penalty for these. All minor offenses merit less severe penalties, depending upon such variables as the specific offense, extenuating circumstances, prior conduct of the offender, length of service, and elapsed time since last infraction.

Rules Should Be Stated Positively

In companies where top management has a positive policy for discipline, the written procedure can suitably be stated as a general description of *what employees are expected to do.* For example:

---

[23] For a somewhat different list, with suggested penalties, see Joseph B. Wollenberger, "Acceptable Work Rules and Penalties: A Company Guide," *Personnel,* vol. 40, no. 4, pp. 23-29, July-August, 1963.

[24] Bramblett, *op. cit.,* pp. 12-13.

1 Everyone is expected to abide by all safety regulations and to be safety-minded at all times—not only for himself but also in relation to his fellow employees.

2 Every subordinate is expected to support management authority by following the instructions issued by his immediate supervisor. (If any employee feels that an instruction or an order is unreasonable, he should obey under protest and then file a complaint. The only exception is an order or instruction that may jeopardize the employee's safety or health. In such a case, the employee should ask for a written order so that the reason for his prudent noncompliance is a matter of record and can subsequently be investigated.)

3 Every employee should respect the property rights of the company and of all other employees.

4 Every employee should always show a responsible attitude toward his work and toward other employees. He should report for work promptly and regularly and not leave early; meet established standards for quantity and quality of work; refrain from drinking intoxicating liquor and from offering liquor to another employee on company premises; exercise self-control, even under provocation, and refrain from practical jokes or horseplay.

Employees Should Be Informed about Rules

Employees should be familiar with all company rules. In unionized firms, some of this information may be included in the discipline-discharge clause of the labor agreement. Usually, however, such a clause is concerned with establishing the employee's right of appeal if he thinks that he has been unjustly disciplined or discharged. It seldom includes details on all rules and consequences of violation.

It is therefore necessary for management, or the union and management jointly, to provide this important information to all employees in some other manner. Bulletin-board announcements are sometimes used, but they suffer from the coldly formal nature of that medium. A more effective, and more widely used, kind of written

communication is the employee handbook, in which a section can be devoted to summarizing or listing rules of conduct, the reasons for them, and—if desired—the penalties that will follow violations.

Oral communication can supplement written material about disciplinary policy. One timely occasion for it is during induction. At this time a representative of the personnel department or the supervisor (preferably the latter) can tell new employees about standards of work and rules of conduct, as listed in the employee handbook. Second, as part of subsequent follow-up, or in answer to questions, a supervisor can give further explanation of new rules or of any which were not clearly understood before.

Such changes in plant or office rules as may be necessary from time to time should also be explained orally by supervisors. Bulletin board announcements have often proved inadequate. A member of the personnel department may help to clarify reasons for certain rules and the need for prompt and consistent action on them.

Penalties

A statement of disciplinary procedure should specify kinds of disciplinary action that will be taken as a last resort. Before he can become subject to discipline, every employee is entitled to know that undisciplined behavior will be penalized. However, experience suggests that it is unwise for the general statement to spell out an invariable set of penalties. Such a "shopping list" may actually invite misbehavior. To an irresponsible employee a minor penalty may be a small price to pay for the pleasure of indulging in forbidden behavior.

THE DISCIPLINARY PROCESS

What does belong in the written procedure is a list of disciplinary steps, showing that action—when necessary—will proceed in an orderly sequence from an informal talk, through official warning, and into a graded series of penalties.

Some employers specifiy certain offenses for which the penalty is immediate discharge or suspension leading to discharge.[25] The following table is based on a survey of 473 companies ranging in size from 250 employees to 5,000 employees and over.

Table 18-2 Survey of 473 Companies: Offenses Listed as Meriting an Extreme Penalty

Type of Offense	Immediate discharge, percent	Suspension, subject to discharge, percent
Dishonesty	77	?
Malicious damage	75	2
Fighting	56	3
Intoxication	56	2
Insubordination	35	4
Carelessness	1	5
Safety violation	1	8

The question: "What is disciplinary action?" is one which is answered differently in different companies, even today. But in an increasing number of concerns, managers, supervisors, personnel administrators, and directors of labor relations accept the idea that the disciplinary process should not be limited to official reprimands and penalties. Instead it should implement the clinical approach and include all the following steps:

1 Preliminary investigation
2 An informal, friendly talk
3 An oral warning or reprimand
4 A written or official warning
5 A graduated series of penalties, such as disciplinary layoff, demotional downgrading or transfer, and—as a last resort—discharge

---

[25] *Personnel Practices in Factory and Office: Manufacturing,* Studies in Personnel Policy no. 194, National Industrial Conference Board, New York, 1964, pp. 133-138.

In addition to these steps, which always need to be taken (except when immediate discharge is warranted), another procedure which is sometimes desirable is *suspension* (pending investigation). All these steps are important for personnel relations and for labor relations. We therefore consider each of them further.

Preliminary Investigation: Getting the Facts

When an employee fails to meet established standards of work or of conduct, his immediate supervisor cannot afford to ignore such unsatisfactory behavior. A supervisor who accepts substandard work performance or condones a breach of good conduct communicates to employees that announced rules are meaningless words. In fact, prevailing laxity of rule enforcement has often been cited by offenders as an excuse.

On the other hand, a supervisor should also refrain from taking hasty corrective action. Instead, when a breach of discipline occurs, an alert supervisor investigates. Has the offender's past record been spotty, or is this his first offense? Are there any extenuating circumstances, such as ill health, family troubles, or another unsettled grievance, which may explain his action? Here, the supervisor is applying situational thinking (described in Chapter 9).

A Case Example

Failure to get all the relevant background facts can lead to ill-advised disciplinary action, often with serious consequences. This point was driven home to the half-million wartime supervisors who received instruction in Job Relations Training through the Training Within Industry program. They were told of the case of Joe Smith, who was absent from work the day after a general wage increase. His foreman concluded that he had taken the day off. Since this was not the first time, he decided to lay Joe off for a week when he returned. Later, another foreman asked him why he had been so rough on Joe and explained that the whole department knew that Joe's father had been in an automobile accident that day and that Joe had to look after him. He told a neighbor to tell his foreman why he could not be at work, but the neighbor had forgotten to do so. When Joe appeared for work, he assumed that his foreman knew the whole story. The foreman got in the first word, however, and Joe had no further chance to explain.

In this case, giving the employee a chance to explain would have prevented the damage done by unjust treatment. But many breaches of discipline are not so easily explained. Rational and logical explanations may not always be forthcoming. In interviewing an employee, the supervisor often has to probe more deeply to get at hidden causes or motivations. Skillful interviewing is needed, not in a spirit of cross examination, but in an effort to understand *why* the employee acted as he did. Objective facts in themselves seldom provide the answer; sentiments and feelings are frequently at the root of undisciplined behavior.

If initial investigation does not promptly reveal all the facts needed to decide whether or not disciplinary action is called for, the special procedure of suspension is appropriate.

A Possible Step: Suspend the Employee and Suspend Judgment

If temporary suspension were used more often as a means to gain time for thorough investigation, there would be fewer arbitration cases and a corresponding decrease in awards that reverse or modify managerial decisions. Among the chief advantages of temporary suspension is that it enables a supervisor to act promptly, perhaps in a situation that could become explosive and where a serious penalty may prove to be justified but where key facts have not yet been established. While the suspect is suspended, there is time to look into facts calmly and systematically. The mechanism of suspension thus protects both

management and the employee. If investigation shows that the suspended employee should not be punished, he has no ground for a grievance, since he will suffer no loss of pay. If, however, a penalty—such as a disciplinary layoff—does seem warranted after investigation, then the time of suspension becomes part of the disciplinary layoff. A suspension is not in itself a punishment. Thus there is no risk that a hasty decision would have to be reversed if subsequent investigation should show that a suspected employee had not been at fault.

Suspension would have been appropriate in the case (cited earlier in this chapter) involving Albert Prestorato. If the foreman had suspended him instead of discharging him, there would have been no serious consequences for anyone.

Every supervisor, employee, and union official should know in advance about the duties and rights of an employee who is suspended. The employee's *duties* are these: He should promptly leave the company's premises. (Failure to do so in an orderly manner is commonly accepted as sufficient ground for discharge, regardless of the reasons for suspension.) During further investigation of the case, and before a final decision by higher management, the employee should not report for work. However, the employee has the *right* to appeal his case through the grievance procedure. If a representative of the union is available, the suspension should take place in his presence. If subsequent investigation clears the employee, he is entitled to reinstatement, without prejudice and without loss of pay or any other privileges.

In most cases where discipline seems called for, however, a brief preliminary investigation by the supervisor in charge is all that is needed before the second step which is a regular part of a constructive procedure.

The Informal, Friendly Talk

The informal, friendly talk is closely related to other supervisory techniques, for example, counseling[26] and performance appraisal, by which a foreman helps his subordinates to evaluate their own current behavior in relation to agreed-upon standards and tasks. When such an interview is part of the disciplinary process, aims should include getting at the reasons behind undesirable behavior, stimulating the sense of responsibility (which has not been evidenced by the employee), and perhaps strengthening or reestablishing the cooperative relationship which has temporarily been weakened or broken.[27]

Such objectives are not always possible to achieve, but whatever the immediate outcome of the interview, the supervisor should never lose his temper or use abusive or profane language. To do so is conduct unbecoming of a management representative.

If a friendly talk is not enough to bring a needed correction in employee behavior, then the next step must be taken.

An Oral Warning or Reprimand

At this stage the possibility of imposing a penalty is specifically mentioned. However, even now, disciplinary action remains *unofficial* because it does not become a matter of written record (except in the supervisor's notes on performance appraisal). The preventive purpose of discipline should still be stressed, for example, by the manner, tone, and wording of what needs to be said. If a supervisor still hopes that no penalty need be imposed, that attitude can usually be communicated. If, on the other hand, he looks forward to "getting" a subordinate whose behavior has

been annoying him, that feeling is almost certain to be understood—and resented—by the employee.

A tactful, friendly supervisor looks for a favorable time and place for such a talk, which should always be private. The aim is to help the employee correct his behavior by putting him on notice that his poor work or undesirable conduct cannot be tolerated. Unless he improves, he will be subject to official disciplinary action.

Many old-line foremen, who have been accustomed to "give a man a few days off to think it over" as the first disciplinary step, find it hard to believe that an oral reprimand could be effective. But experience suggests that if skillfully given, such a word of warning can help employees to straighten themselves out.

However, when given in an unfriendly manner, hurriedly, and in public, reprimands not only tend to be ineffective but may actually provoke employee hostility and defensive behavior.[28] The following example may be used as a case in point:

A Case Example: Mary and the "Fussbudget"

A section supervisor in the payroll department had observed that Mary Ahern, the senior clerk, was in the habit of taking a prolonged coffee break. Instead of the customary 15 minutes, Mary would absent herself from work for as long as half an hour. One day, when the supervisor was under pressure (because two girls were out on sick leave), he spoke to Mary, on her way to the canteen, and told her to stop abusing this privilege. He said, "I shall expect you back in exactly 15 minutes." The order was given in the hall, near the reception desk, and in front of several visitors and employees. Mary obviously resented this reprimand, but she made no reply.

---

[26] See Chap. 10. The effectiveness of the nondirected interview in bringing corrective action has been demonstrated in psychotherapy and in employee counseling. See Carl R. Rogers, *Counseling and Psychotherapy,* Houghton Mifflin Company, Boston, 1942. Of course, serious and deep-rooted cases of employee maladjustment cannot adequately be handled by supervisors. An employee who has such a maladjustment should, if possible, be referred to a psychiatrist for diagnosis and treatment.

[27] For three sample interviews, with analysis, see John D. Staley, *The Disciplinary Interview,* American Management Association, New York, 1965.

[28] See David Kipnis and Joseph Kosentino, "Use of Leadership Powers in Industry," *Journal of Applied Psychology,* vol. 53, no. 6, pp. 460-466, 1969, for a stimulating analysis of the subordinate's response to misuse of supervisory powers.

Half an hour later she returned at a leisurely pace ostentatiously ignoring her supervisor, who was sitting at his desk, watch in hand. As she passed by, he challenged her, "Look here, Mary. Half an hour ago, I told you to be back in 15 minutes. I cannot tolerate such disregard of my orders!" Mary snapped back, "Oh, you're an old fussbudget!" and continued to saunter toward her machine.

The section supervisor felt angry and humiliated. Shortly afterward, he left his desk and went to the assistant treasurer's office, demanding that Mary be disciplined. When the assistant treasurer investigated the facts, he concluded that the section supervisor needed counseling on how to discipline an employee in private.

A Written Reprimand and/or Warning

If an employee does not respond to preliminary and unofficial talks in private, then a formal written warning is called for. In a unionized concern, such an official document should be issued, if possible, in the presence of the shop steward. The warning notice contains a statement of the offense and is to be signed by the employee or the shop steward. Refusal to sign represents a protest against the disciplinary action and automatically sets the grievance machinery in motion. In addition to the copy which is given to the employee, copies are sent to the personnel department and to the labor relations department, where they become part of the offender's employment record for 6 months to 1 year. A copy should also be provided for the union records. Naturally, the supervisor also keeps a copy for his own records. Exhibit 18-1 shows the disciplinary action report used by the Ford Motor Company. This report can also be used for more serious disciplinary action.

(At this stage, as at all other stages of the disciplinary process, the supervisor's manner, attitude, and aims are important. These are all illustrated in Case 17, "Difficulties Connected

with Work Scheduling," which took place in a hospital. Case 15, "Discharge for Insubordination,"[29] is another case in point.)

The written warning should not be issued until after both a friendly talk and an oral warning have been tried. It should never be used to establish a blacklist. This is poor personnel practice. In addition, any discriminatory use of disciplinary procedures may expose the company to a union charge of having violated Sec. 8(*a*) (3) of the Taft-Hartley Act, which states that it is an unfair labor practice for an employer "by discrimination in regard to hire or tenure of employment or any term or condition of employment to encourage or discourage membership in any labor organization."

Penalties up to and Including Demotion

In case of repeated or continued offenses or continued failure to meet work standards, the supervisor is responsible for deciding what penalty is appropriate. A suitable penalty should be selected according to (1) the seriousness of the offense and (2) whether the undesirable action is a first, second, or third offense, or perhaps merely a continuation of behavior about which the employee has been warned. The supervisor should be guided by experience elsewhere in the organization with similar offenses, and he may have suggested penalties or ranges to choose from.[30] Here is where he may be expected again to confer with the personnel or labor relations specialist for guidance on difficult cases.

Disciplinary layoff, for a period which corresponds to the seriousness of the offense, has sometimes proved useful in helping a thoughtless

[29] For insubordination cases that were arbitrated, see Maurice S. Trotta, "Insubordination," *Management of Personnel Quarterly,* vol. 4, no. 1, pp. 20-25, Spring, 1965. See also Harold E. Wallace, "Insubordination because of Fear: A Survey of Arbitral Findings," *Management of Personnel Quarterly,* vol. 9, no. 2, pp. 33-39, Summer, 1970.

[30] For a specific list, drawn from a variety of company experiences, see Wollenberger, *op. cit.*

Exhibit 18-1   A Disciplinary Action Report Which Can Also Serve as a Warning Notice*

Disciplinary action report	Shift	Disposition by: Foreman ☐ Labor relations ☐	Date
Social Security no.	Name	Badge no.	Dept.
Company seniority	Classification		

Previous disciplinary action	Date	Charge	Penalty

Present charge	Employee desires Yes No Employee's signature (if no) Union→ Representation
Penalty and date assessed	Committeeman should sign here if he received notification of this action
Foreman's signature	Labor relations representative signature

Facts supporting charge (list in detail)—attach additional form if more space needed

Character of service	Excellent	Good	Fair	Unsatis-factory
Workmanship				
Conduct				
Application				
Attendance				
Safety				

Labor relations copy

*Note that this form must be completed when any disciplinary action is taken against an employee, and reference is also made to previous disciplinary action. The employee must sign if he does not desire union representation; otherwise the union committeeman signs, along with the foreman. The original copy is sent to the labor relations office, and carbon copies are retained by the foreman, the timekeeping office, and the union.

employee to make a new start. But, especially in periods of labor surplus, disciplinary layoffs have sometimes been used too readily. One foreman admitted this in discussions leading to the formulation of a new disciplinary procedure when he said: "The fellow you lay off is often glad to take the time off, and in the meantime you've lost the services of one of your regular hands. And if he isn't glad for the loaf, he's sore at you when he's allowed to come back."

Another penalty whose usefulness may be questioned is downgrading or demotion. Such discipline may be the only alternative to discharge when there is continued failure to meet job standards. However there are serious disadvantages to demotion as a disciplinary measure, e.g., the likelihood that the employee will be dissatisfied and discouraged with his lower-rated job and that his dissatisfaction may spread to others in his new work group.

Termination of Employment Is the Ultimate Penalty

Discharge is such a drastic form of action that it should be reserved only for the most serious offenses or for people who will respond to no lesser penalty. We have already noted the few serious offenses which may call for immediate discharge.

From the employee's standpoint, discharge represents a serious setback. It wipes out his seniority standing as well as other rights associated with continued employment and makes it difficult to secure new employment if the prospective employer learns why he left his last job. Moreover, since it reduces his chances of earning a livelihood, it may affect his personal equilibrium and family relationships. Of course, this may not always happen. Discharge may bring greater maturity to an immature employee. Thus it may turn out to be the best thing that could have happened to him.

For the organization, discharge always involves serious losses and wastes. Some of these costs can be reckoned in dollars. They represent time and money spent in hiring, training, and supervising an employee who now leaves the company. What can be even more costly is the disruption of work teams and the damage to morale occasioned by any discharge, especially if it is challenged. Further costs in money and morale must be paid if a discharge results in a grievance which is processed all the way up to and through arbitration.

In a discharge case, arbitration hearings are apt to be unpleasant. They entail personal criticisms and often admission of mistakes all around. They always require the discussion of painful issues. Moreover, talk that necessarily centers on failure to meet requirements is apt to degenerate into bitter recriminations which evoke immediate resentment and may leave lasting scars.

Nowadays, recognition of such costs and consequences, as well as pressure from unions, has greatly reduced the ratio of discharge as compared with earlier times. In many companies, especially in unionized concerns, first-level supervisors now have authority only to *recommend discharge,* although most supervisors are empowered to demand that an undesirable employee be transferred out of their department or section.

Sometimes discharge for "just cause" is necessary. When this ultimate penalty has been arrived at by "due process," even the union does not always protest it. For example, in some cases unions have agreed with management, notably when a discharge followed drunkenness, fighting, or unauthorized work stoppage when such conduct has been specified in the labor agreement as meriting immediate discharge. In other cases, when discharge has been imposed after due warning, unions have been unwilling to process a grievance filed by the employee whose employment has been terminated. For instance, in one firm, a skilled employee with 5 years' seniority was discharged for bringing liquor into the plant, drinking it, and offering it to other employees. When the union business agent protested the discharge, the personnel administrator called his attention to previous warnings for the same offense and pointed out the danger of permitting such a practice in the vicinity of high-speed machinery. The union dropped the case.

In another firm, the personnel administrator notified the union business agent that a male worker had been warned by the foreman about using abusive language toward women employees in the department. The business agent checked the statement and found it to be accurate. Two weeks later when the employee was discharged for continued and excessive swearing, the union declined to press the case.

Advance notification does not mean, however, that union representatives ought to participate jointly with management in *taking disciplinary action.* Such a practice would dilute management's responsibility for discipline and put union officials in an awkward position. The union's role is to challenge any management decision which it considers unfair.

Procedure in Discharge   Discharge is such a serious step that correct procedure on both sides is important. For example, the supervisor should be able to prove that he followed "due process." The dismissal notice should state and explain all charges, based on the records and the written memoranda which the supervisor has kept and put in the employee's file. Regard for "just cause" requires that management be in a position to establish the employee's guilt, thus justifying disciplinary action. In companies where the first-level supervisor lacks authority to discharge, clearing with the next higher management representative is mandatory. Furthermore, the personnel administrator (and/or the labor relations director) should be consulted.

Arbitrators agree that management should also consistently follow an announced disciplinary procedure.[31] A supervisor is in an unassailable position if the record shows that his action was based on established facts, that he has made a genuine effort to help an offender, given ample warning, and finally put a hardened offender on notice that his unsatisfactory behavior would no longer be tolerated.

The employee, in turn, is responsible for the timely and proper exercise of his right to protest and to appeal any disciplinary action that, in his opinion, is unjustified. However, he must do so in an orderly and peaceful manner. Any resort to direct action or concerted group pressure, such as inciting a work stoppage by sympathetic fellow employees, is in itself a recognized ground for discharge not only for the employee who instigated the illegal work stoppage but for all participants.

SUMMARY

Ideas about organizational discipline have changed considerably since "the good old days." Nowadays, arbitrary exercise of managerial authority is challenged.

Progressive managers intend, as a matter of policy, that disciplinary action should always incorporate consideration of "just cause" and "due process." They are convinced that *discipline should be used primarily to reenforce self-discipline within individuals and in work groups, penalties being applied only after educational methods have failed.*

A chief executive who believes that high morale and voluntary participation are prerequisites for peak efficiency naturally wishes to have a positive policy for discipline. Such a policy (which should be in writing) can state manage-

[31] Morrison Handsaker, "The Arbitration of Discipline Cases," *Personnel Journal,* vol. 46, no. 3, pp. 153–156, March, 1967. For a case involving arbitration of a discharge, see Case 14, "Discharge for Proper Cause?"

ment's purpose *to supplement self-discipline* by the cooperative majority and *to reenforce* a necessary minimum of rules.

Steps in a disciplinary process (designed primarily to reorient and correct employees) should be as follows: preliminary investigation (possibly followed by suspension if facts cannot promptly be established); then a friendly talk, followed, if necessary, with an unofficial warning. If these informal steps prove inadequate, official disciplinary action is not only justifiable but obligatory. According to "due process," the first formal disciplinary step is issuing an official, written warning. If this warning is flouted, the stage of penalties has been reached. These customarily start with disciplinary layoff and may end with discharge.

The climate in which self-discipline flourishes is also one in which needs for job changes can be, and are, freely discussed and fully understood. In the next chapter we turn to ways of managing these changes.

SELECTED REFERENCES

Black, James Menzies: *Positive Discipline,* American Management Association, Inc., New York, 1970.

Bramblett, Earl R.: "Maintenance of Discipline," *Management of Personnel Quarterly,* vol. 1, no. 1, Autumn, 1961 (reprinted in Paul Pigors, Charles A. Myers, and F. T. Malm: *Management of Human Resources: Readings in Personnel Administration,* 3d ed., McGraw-Hill Book Company, New York, 1973, selection 35).

Handsaker, Morrison: "The Arbitration of Discipline Cases," *Personnel Journal,* vol. 46, no. 3, pp. 153-156, March, 1967.

Huberman, John: "Discipline without Punishment," *Harvard Business Review,* vol. 42, no. 4, pp. 62-68, July-August, 1964.

Jones, Dallas, *Arbitration and Industrial Discipline,* University of Michigan, Bureau of Industrial Relations, Ann Arbor, Mich., 1961.

Ross, Arthur M.: "The Arbitration of Discharge Cases: What Happens after Reinstatement?," in National Academy of Arbitrators, *Critical Issues in Labor Arbitration, Proceedings of the Tenth Annual Meeting,* Bureau of National Affairs, Inc., Washington, D.C., 1957, chap. 2, pp. 21-60.

Seligson, Harry: "Minority Group Employees, Discipline and the Arbitrator," *Labor Law Journal,* vol. 19, no. 9, pp. 544-554, September, 1968.

Slichter, Summer H., James J. Healy, and E. Robert Livernash: *The Impact of Collective Bargaining on Management,* The Brookings Institution, Washington, D.C., 1960, chap. 21.

Staley, John D.: *The Disciplinary Interview,* American Management Association, New York, 1965.

Stessin, Lawrence: *Employee Discipline,* Bureau of National Affairs, Inc., Washington, D.C., 1960.

Tead, Ordway: *Human Nature and Management,* 2d ed., McGraw-Hill Book Company, New York, 1933, chap. 18, "The New Discipline."

Wollenberger, Joseph B.: "Acceptable Work Rules and Penalties: A Company Guide," *Personnel,* vol. 40, no. 4, pp. 23-29, July-August, 1963.

Zimpel, Lloyd, and Daniel Panger: *Business and the Hardcore Unemployed: A Management Guide to Hiring, Training and Motivating Minority Workers,* Frederick Fell, Inc., New York, 1970, chap. 10, "'For the Good of the Company': Discipline and Dismissal," pp. 218-234.

Chapter 19

Managing Changes in Jobs and Work Schedules

Every organization is in a continuous state of change. Sometimes the changes are great, sometimes small, but change is always taking place. The conditions requiring these changes arise from both within and without. As a consequence, there is never-ending need for decisions which guide adjustments to change. The adequacy of these decisions for meeting an organization's current and developing internal and external situations determines the well-being, power, and future of that organization.

Rensis Likert [1]

In our dynamic industrial economy, managers constantly make decisions that involve changes in the investment pattern, organization structure, work process, and methods of utilizing the human resources of a firm or organization to obtain increased efficiency. But management does not have complete freedom of decision making; it must operate within certain prescribed limits established by public policies and sometimes by union agreements. Further, progressive managements must also pay serious attention to the *human* aspects of change. However well-designed the change may be technically, there will be difficulties in implementing it if employees resist it.

Changes in the work environment need not be spectacular to have important ramifications for a firm or other type of organization. Every modification in the existing technical-social system should be carefully considered before management initiates action. Often planning how to in-

[1] Rensis Likert, *The Human Organization,* McGraw-Hill Book Company, New York, 1967, p. 128.

341

troduce a change may require greater skill and more time on the part of management than designing the change itself.

The human problems created by technical and social changes are equally serious in office and plant situations and equally applicable to employees of every level and status within the organization. A new machine or piece of equipment, a new method of using old machines or equipment, the use of new materials, a change in the organization structure, a rearrangement of tasks—these have in the past brought lower costs and higher output of new products or services, as well as, in some cases, fewer employees.

The current interest in automation and the concern for its economic and social consequences focus attention on a new aspect of human adaptation to change. What is new is the *rate* at which technical and social changes are taking place not only in a firm, but in our society in general.[2] The changes resulting from automation, for example, are more rapid and dramatic than the smaller, successive improvements that have been made in nearly every firm or industry heretofore. The problems of automation are not dissimilar to the problems that have faced managements before this new word entered our everyday vocabulary, but the policies and procedures that result may very well be different.[3]

For example, in a more automated plant or office, seniority rights to particular jobs are destroyed and seniority units may have to be wider. As we have noted earlier, considerable retraining will be necessary. Promotion ladders are changed, and there may be more hiring from

outside for skilled jobs. Finally, as we shall see in later chapters, wage and salary classifications are changed, and greater emphasis may be given to the factor of "responsibility" in job-evaluation programs.

The management of changes that affect the human resources of a firm often leads to varying forms and degrees of resistance and hostility. In this chapter we shall consider ways of handling changes to minimize friction. The emphasis will be on more effective communication and more active participation as the most useful means to accomplish this objective.

Changes in working schedules and hours also result from technical changes, as well as from the changing fortunes of a business or other organization. These are sometimes resisted by employees whose customary routine is thus disturbed, and management is faced with the task of effectively planning these changes in job assignments.

RESISTANCE TO CHANGE

When employees resist new methods or new equipment, the reaction of technically trained managers is frequently that "these people are unwilling to face the facts" of the necessity for the change or that they are acting "emotionally." But employee attitudes toward change are *facts* to be understood before constructive action can be taken by line management with the help of the personnel administrator. Why do employees resist change?

Resistance to change is not new. People have always objected to changes which threatened their accustomed way of life. This generalization applies just as much to employers and managers (who often object to and resent changes initiated by government or by labor unions) as it does to employees. In an industrial environment, resistance to change has usually been associated with attempts of employees to resort to overt or subtle measures to impede technological changes that upset the customary work process and threaten

---

[2] However, these changes have not dramatically increased productivity in the entire economy only in certain industries. See *Technology and the American Economy,* Report of the National Commission on Automation and Economic Progress, vol. 1, Government Printing Office, Washington, D.C., 1966.

[3] For a review based on research in a number of firms, see Richard A. Beaumont and Roy B. Helfgott, *Management, Automation and People,* Industrial Relations Counselors, New York, 1964.

loss of skills, earnings, or jobs. Managers tend to view this as "resistance to progress" by employees who are oblivious to the needs of innovative management and the needs of business organizations to be competitive.

The Effect of Unions

The advent of labor unions merely institutionalizes worker resistance to technological change, in the traditional view. Today, however, few unions are opposed to technical changes as such; unions are an effective device for controlling the introduction of new machinery and new methods, by mitigating the impact on workers and making the best bargain possible under the circumstances.[4] Management also often feels that work rules which must be negotiated with a union, rather than instituted unilaterally, impede efficiency by restricting managerial flexibility. This overlooks the fact that people affected by managerial decisions must willingly accept them and implement them if the long-run efficiency of the organization is to be maintained and improved. Sudden, arbitrary, and unexplained changes resulting from managerial decisions are often resisted because communication has been inadequate, even though no economic loss is threatened by the change.

When job opportunities are shrinking in a particular industry such as railroads or in an occupation such as a musician, unions representing the employees affected may resort to restrictive work rules or make-work practices designed to

protect existing jobs as long as possible. The work-rules controversy involving the diesel firemen on railroads began in 1959, and three successive presidential boards have attempted to deal with it. The resistance of the firemen and their union was probably strengthened by the knowledge that alternative job opportunities were not readily available in an economy with substantial general unemployment (5 to 6 percent), even though generous job protection for most of the existing firemen was recommended by the boards and accepted by railroad management. It seemed that the issue was finally settled in April, 1964, for at least 2 years, when the Supreme Court upheld the validity of the arbitration board's award of November, 1963, effective for 2 years. The award provided for the immediate layoff of some firemen, transfers for others, job protection for long-service ones until retirement or death, and the right of the union to designate 10 percent of the jobs as always requiring a fireman. However, after the expiration of the arbitration award, negotiations have continued but no further changes have occurred.

Studies of Resistance to Change

Experimental and field research on resistance to industrial and social change indicates that the reaction of employees to those initiating the change (in this context, management) affects the degree of resistance.[5] If employees have confidence in management's fairness, resistance is likely to be much less than if they suspect management of a cold-blooded unconcern for the human consequences of a technical change. Thus, the heritage of good or bad personnel and labor relations has a tremendous bearing on the success of a change. In other words, "it is clear,

---

[4] Various union policies toward technological change are discussed by Summer H. Slichter, James J. Healy, and E. Robert Livernash, *The Impact of Collective Bargaining on Management,* The Brookings Institution, Washington, D.C., 1960, chap. 12. They conclude that union policies may have increased relative wages on the changed jobs and required excessive crews in some cases. Also (p. 371): "They have considerably eased the hardship of displacement, partly by forcing managements to do advance planning in the introduction of technological changes, partly by encouraging more gradual introduction of technological changes and partly by giving displaced workmen an opportunity to qualify for other jobs."

[5] Alvin Zander, "Resistance to Change—Its Analysis and Prevention," *Advanced Management,* vol. 15, no. 1, pp. 9-11, 1950 [reprinted in Warren G. Bennis, Kenneth D. Benne, and Robert Chin (eds.), *The Planning of Change: Readings in Applied Behavioral Sciences,* Holt, Rinehart, and Winston, Inc., New York, 1961, pp. 543-548].

therefore, that the motivational and communication techniques used by the manager have as much impact as the character of the change itself. Change must be preceded by preparation for change."[6] This preparation will obviously be affected by the personnel concepts of management discussed in Chapter 1. Traditional management has to "change" first if it hopes to gain wholehearted acceptance of change.

For example, the impact of participation by employees in introducing change, and therefore reducing their resistance to it, is illustrated by a controlled experiment in a garment factory.[7] The reader will recall (from Chapter 1) that a cost-reduction change was introduced by management in the "control" group and was developed more slowly by agreement with the three "experimental" groups. Productivity actually dropped in the control group, as the members reacted to the imposed change by restricting output. In the three experimental and participative groups, however, production increased.

A later similar experimental study in a large multidivision corporation showed less striking differences between the "participative" and the "hierarchically controlled" groups of clerical employees. In fact, the latter group got higher productivity initially by a management-imposed staff cut of 25 percent. But employee feelings of responsibility for good work, attitudes toward supervision, and other employee attitudes deteriorated. The researchers concluded that if the experiment had been continued longer, "productivity and the quality of work would have continued to increase in the participative program,

while in the hierarchically controlled program productivity and quality of work would have declined."[8]

Studies have also shown that resistance to change often results from a conflict of individual and group loyalties. An individual may want to "please the boss," but he may be restrained by group pressure to protect the slower members of the group who would be hurt most by a change. Restriction of output in nonunion plants is well known; it did not originate with unions.[9] Group loyalties may also be outraged when the initiators of change fail to consult the group in advance about the proposed change or do not permit the group members to participate in planning the change.[10] Unions have increasingly insisted upon the right to participate in discussions about technical changes affecting their members.

A Case Example

A simple example in a company known to the authors will illustrate the kinds of reactions engendered by change. One morning the labor relations director of a blanket mill got word from the shop steward in the folding room that "the girls were so mad they were ready to walk out."

[6] Leo B. Moore, "How to Manage Improvement," *Harvard Business Review,* vol. 36, no. 4, p. 78, July–August, 1958.

[7] Lester Coch and John R. P. French, Jr., "Overcoming Resistance to Change," *Human Relations,* vol. 1, no. 4, pp. 512–532, 1948. This experiment was replicated in a Norwegian factory in 1956, with similar results. See John R. P. French, Jr., J. Israel, and D. As, "An Experiment on Participation in a Norwegian Factory," *Human Relations,* vol. 13, no. 1, pp. 3–19, February, 1960.

[8] Rensis Likert, "Measuring Organizational Performance," *Harvard Business Review,* vol. 36, no. 2, pp. 41–50, March–April, 1958 (reprinted in Paul Pigors, Charles A. Myers, and F. T. Malm, *Management of Human Resources: Readings in Personnel Administration,* 3d ed., McGraw-Hill Book Company, New York, 1973, selection 2). This experiment is also discussed in Likert, *New Patterns of Management,* McGraw-Hill Book Company, New York, 1960, and summarized in Chap. 1 of this book.

[9] Stanley B. Mathewson, *Restricting of Output among Unorganized Workers,* The Viking Press, Inc., New York, 1931. For a detailed example, see F. J. Roethlisberger and W. J. Dickson, *Management and the Worker,* Harvard University Press, Cambridge, Mass., 1939, pp. 409–477.

[10] For two other case studies, see Harriet O. Ronken and Paul R. Lawrence, *Administering Changes: A Case Study of Human Relations in a Factory,* Harvard Business School, Division of Research, Boston, 1952; and Paul R. Lawrence, *The Changing of Organizational Behavior Patterns: A Case Study of Decentralization,* Harvard Business School, Division of Research, Boston, 1958.

During the night, 6 or 8 inches had been sawed off the end of each girl's folding table, despite the fact that on the day before they had assured the boss that the old tables were "just right."

The full story came out after the department supervisor was called in. His explanation was that the truckers had complained that the narrow aisles between the tables caused them to knock blankets onto the floor and soil them. Consequently, he had decided, after measuring, that the tables could be shortened without any inconvenience to the girls. "Just to be friendly," he asked some of the girls how they liked their old tables. At the end of the shift he arranged with the carpenters to do the necessary work. His reaction to the whole thing was: "Why should such a little thing raise such a big fuss? Girls are so unreasonable. The tables are still big enough to fold blankets on."

This example illustrates the importance of the social aspect of change. The action by the superintendent did not threaten the girls' jobs, skills, or even earnings, but they were outraged by the lack of concern for their feelings and ideas. "Participation" in making changes involves more than "being friendly"; it means working with the people affected to develop the most satisfactory adaptation to the change from the standpoint both of the employees involved and of the organization as a whole.[11]

Managers in most organizations are the initiators of change, as we said at the outset of this chapter. However, this does not mean that when they are affected by changes initiated higher in the organization, or even from subordinates,

they accept changes willingly. Two case examples will illustrate the kind of resistance that occurs when managers react to proposals for change or actual changes in which they have had no part.

Case Examples: Managers Also Sometimes Resist Change

The first concerns the introduction of computers in managerial work. The computer revolution in management has affected accounting, inventory control, and production planning and control, and it has moved into other types of structured managerial work. The introduction of a computerized information and control system involves systems design and program development, largely the work of specialists in the computer center. When they fail to involve the managers in the departments affected in the planning of the new system, resistance often results. Some years ago a large manufacturing firm began to develop an integrated information system that would process orders for original equipment and spare parts into the manufacturing operation, schedule assembly and spare-parts requirements, prepare schedules for assembly and manufacturing, control inventory, predict man and machine requirements, and measure performance vs. commitments for marketing, manufacturing, and purchasing departments. Many benefits and cost savings were anticipated. During the first 2 years of the development of the new system, considerable resistance arose, particularly among the affected middle managers. As one member of the task force working on the project explained later, "If we had it to do over again, we should have done a better job of bringing the operating people into the team. It was never *their* responsibility, always *ours*." In other words, the involvement, cooperation, and support of the affected managers were essential for

---

[11] For further discussion of the importance of this aspect of change, see Paul R. Lawrence, "How to Deal with Resistance to Change," *Harvard Business Review,* vol. 32, no. 3, pp. 49–57, May–June, 1954. See also Floyd C. Mann and Franklin W. Neff, *Managing Major Change in Organizations,* Foundation for Research on Human Behavior, Ann Arbor, Mich., 1961, especially "Toward an Understanding of the Management of Change," pp. 61–86.

the new program to succeed, eventually.[12] There are other similar examples in the experience with computer introduction.

The second example involves the proposal to introduce a more accurate gunnery system, continuous-aim firing, on warships of the U.S. Navy early in this century. The proposal was made by a young naval officer serving in the Pacific, after he had seen a device developed by a young British naval officer in that area. He sent memos to the Naval Bureau of Ordnance in Washington but got no answer. After further insistent inquiries, the reply came that the device was impractical, even though the young captain had seen it in successful operation! Convinced of the correctness of his views, he took an unusual step: he went over the heads of his superiors in the Navy and wrote directly to President Theodore Roosevelt. The President, perhaps impatient with Navy "brass," brought the young officer to Washington to work on this project, and eventually it became a standard part of the equipment on every naval vessel. Here there had been resistance to change at the very highest levels of an organization, partly because a large bureaucratic organization tends to resist change anyway, and partly because the senior officers had been brought up to believe that existing fire-power mechanisms aboard ship were adequate.[13]

Some Employees Welcome Change

Preoccupation with "resistance" to change overlooks the willingness of many employees (as well as managers) to welcome change if it *benefits*

them. Perhaps a particular change will relieve an employee of repetitive and boring or physically difficult and unpleasant work. A change that gives an employee a better opportunity to utilize his own capacities by training for, and transferring to, a better job may be welcomed.[14] The manager who emphasizes the *positive* aspects of change for the affected employees and welcomes their ideas has put change in its proper perspective. "Where he makes his mistake . . . is in assuming that resentment is the *necessary* price of seeking change and improvement. For under certain conditions people do *not* react negatively to the idea of improvement and its installation. . . . People do not resist change or resent criticism; but they do resist *being* changed and do resent *being* criticized."[15] (For an illustration, see Case 4, "The Girl and the Computer.")

STEPS IN INTRODUCING JOB CHANGES

Some elements in successful handling of job changes have already been indicated. Experience suggests the following steps, some of which are more obviously needed when employees are represented by a union.[16]

---

[12] Edgar F. Huse, "The Impact of Computerized Programs on Managers and Organization: A Case Study in an Integrated Manufacturing Company," in Charles A. Myers (ed.), *The Impact of Computers on Management,* The M.I.T. Press, Cambridge, Massachusetts, 1967, pp. 282-302. For supporting evidence from another study, see Mann and Neff, *op. cit.,* Case 1, pp. 5-13.

[13] For a full account of this interesting case, see Elting E. Morison, *Men, Machines and Modern Times,* The M.I.T. Press, Cambridge, Mass., 1966, chap. 2, "Gunfire at Sea: A Case Study of Innovation." The young naval officer later became Admiral Sims of the U.S. Navy.

[14] For results of a study indicating that under certain conditions most employees think that management should put in new machinery and that employees benefit from change, see W. H. Scott and Others, *Technical Change and Industrial Relations,* Liverpool University Press, Liverpool, England, 1958, chap. 4, "Attitudes to Change."

[15] Moore, *op. cit.,* p. 77. Another writer has observed: "I believe that behavioral scientists acting as organizational consultants have tended to place overmuch emphasis on overcoming resistance to change and have underemphasized the importance of enlisting in the service of change the energies and resources which the client can consciously direct and willingly devote to problem solving." Roger Harrison, "Choosing the Depth of Organizational Intervention," *The Journal of Applied Behavioral Science,* vol. 6, no. 2, pp. 181-202, April-May-June, 1970. Quotation on p. 197.

[16] For a full discussion of this experience, see Solomon Barkin, "Handling Work Assignment Changes," *Harvard Business Review,* vol. 25, no. 4, p. 473, Summer, 1947; and Richard A. Lester and Robert L. Aronson, *Job Modifications under Collective Bargaining: A Survey of Company Experience and Four Case Studies,* Princeton University, Industrial Relations Section, Princeton, N.J., 1950. More recent discus-

There should be advance explanation and consultation with the employees concerned and (if there is a union) the union representatives. This consultation should take place well in advance of the changes, and there should be full discussion of competitive conditions and other reasons that made the change necessary. In general, employees are more inclined to accept changed job assignments willingly if they know *why* these are necessary. It is not unlikely, furthermore, that employee and union reactions to proposed changes will reveal factors overlooked by management in the initial proposal. Genuine two-way communication is an essential part of this advance consultation, which can become genuinely participative.

In unionized firms management should discuss specific changes with the union in advance and negotiate modifications following a trial period if any grievances arise under it. Many managements regard the determination of output standards and new work assignments as a managerial prerogative, and they insist that timestudy data should not be the subject of bargaining. There is ample evidence, however, that the firms most successful in winning employee and union acceptance of changes in work assignments are those which use job evaluation and timestudy data (considered in greater detail in Chapters 20 and 21) as a basis for discussion with union representatives. This discussion may reveal the need for modifications in the technical approach in order to gain understanding and reduce resistance to the change. Only in this way can the needs of employees and their union for job security be reconciled with the firm's needs for lower costs.

This view was well expressed by Professor J. Douglas Brown, founder and for many years director of Princeton University's Industrial Relations Section:

> Under collective bargaining, job modifications are no longer the private preserve of the engineer and the timestudy man. A blunt presentation of engineering data may transmit facts, but at the same time create such a fog of sudden fear and frustration that a reasonable adjustment may be delayed for months and attended by burdensome wage costs. From the cases studied in the following report, successful change occurs when, by far-sighted planning, advance knowledge and discussion, and a willingness to compromise *ex parte* judgments, the change is treated as a readjustment of minds as much as a readjustment of technical methods. . . . It is fortunate for the American consumer that the same institution—the trade union—which can translate the workers' fear of adverse consequences of technological change into a powerful brake, can also, as an instrument of communication and participation, aid greatly in assuring willing and understanding adjustment. [17]

A different view, however, is held by the automobile companies, which have insisted on management's right to establish production standards without bargaining, letting the union bring grievances. Unsettled grievances over production standards have been specifically nonarbitrable under the collective agreements in the automobile industry, except when it is claimed that employees' health or safety is endangered. Otherwise, strikes are possible in the event of disagreements. One reason for this management position was that with as many as 5,000 operations subject to change periodically, "bargaining would be never-ending, leaving many operations without standards and therefore with no control." [18] In these cases, management must be very sure of the rightness and fairness of its standards

---

sions center on the manager as "a change agent" utilizing some of the skills growing out of the "organization development" (OD) approach. See Michael Hill, "The Manager as a Change Agent," *Personnel Journal*, vol. 50, no. 1, pp. 60-63, January, 1971. Refer back to Chap. 3 for discussion of the OD approach.

[17] Lester and Aronson, *op. cit.,* foreword.
[18] W. W. Aulepp. *The Union's Role in Production Management,* American Management Association, Production Series, no. 189, New York, 1950, "Who Shall Determine Work Standards: A Management View," p. 12.

or be prepared to face a spate of grievances and perhaps work stoppages. A number of the latter have occurred over the years.

Advance planning of changes should make it unnecessary to introduce them so rapidly that employees' resistance is increased. Gradual introduction is essential for thorough advance discussion with employees (and their union representatives) and for their understanding and acceptance of the need for change. [19] Gradual introduction also makes it possible to transfer displaced employees to other jobs where their skills can be utilized (possibly after some retraining) and where they can expect to make approximately the same earnings as on the old job.

Changes should be timed, if possible, to coincide with periods of expanding business activity in the firm and in the community, so that displaced workers may be transferred to other jobs in the plant without loss of seniority or find jobs in other firms. Technological changes that coincide with substantial layoffs and wage reductions, as in a period of business depression and high general unemployment, may arouse strong resistance although there is some evidence that job insecurity may convince workers of the necessity of accepting changes to preserve the remaining jobs in a firm facing severe competition. If some layoffs are necessary, advance notice should be given and dismissal compensation or severance pay should be considered as a means of mitigating

the effects of displacement. [20] The displacement effects of technological changes in automating industries currently present a major challenge to both unions and managements. The responsibility of both parties to develop programs that will meet this challenge through joint action should receive top priority if the full potential of technological changes is to be realized for a firm and the economic and social costs are to be minimized for employees. For instance, the "supplementary unemployment benefit plans," developed through collective bargaining in the automobile and steel industries as a result of original union pressure for a "guaranteed annual wage," help to ease the adjustment to change and force management to plan it more carefully (see Chapter 20 for a fuller discussion of these plans). Government programs of unemployment insurance, old-age benefits permitting retirement, and aid to distressed areas also ease the impact of technical dislocations.

Two agreements in longshoring and meat packing illustrate other approaches to this problem. The 1959 Armour agreement established a nine-man committee with an impartial chairman to study the problems of automation and made recommendations for retraining and relocating programs for workers whose jobs were eliminated by technological changes and plant closures. The work of the committee was financed from a fund established by the company. [21] The 1961 Pacific Maritime Association agreement established a fund to stablize temporarily the earnings and employment opportunities of the registered work force. It worked well for more than a decade.

[19] In his study of technological changes in 18 cotton mills, Elliott Dunlop Smith concluded: "In some of the strikes with which we came in contact, the flatness of union refusals seemed to arise less from the unwillingness of the union to consider the management's proposals than from the haste and abruptness of the management's action." *Technology and Labor,* Yale University Press, New Haven, Conn., 1939, p. 157. A much later study has shown the importance of communication with employees about the reasons for mergers and their probable impact. See Geneva Seybold, *Communicating with Employees about Mergers,* Personnel Policy Study no. 211, National Industrial Conference Board, Inc., New York, 1968.

[20] See references in Chap. 17 and George H. Haas and Elizabeth R. Floyd, *Company Severance Pay Plans,* American Management Association, Research Report 29, New York, 1957.

[21] For a discussion of the work of this committee, see George P. Shultz and Arnold R. Weber, *Strategies for the Displaced Worker,* Harper & Row, Publishers, Incorporated, New York, 1966.

Careful advance preparation and standardization of the new job and all auxiliary operations are important. These steps help employees affected by the change to attain the new work standard without additional strain and to make expected earnings on the job. Many technical changes that looked well on paper have failed because management has not adequately improved the other operations that feed the jobs affected by the changes.

During the trial period for the change, tentative standards and rates should be established. Employees may be guaranteed either their average straight-time hourly earnings in some past period or their (lower) base rates. A full guarantee of previous earnings protects them against losses that are the result of mechanical or materials difficulties during the trial period. But if employee cooperation is already poor, this guarantee may cause the operators "to take it easy" and not give the new standard a fair trial. A better plan may be to provide a flat bonus or guarantee in addition to actual earnings under the new tentative rate, thus providing some incentive. Another possibility is supplying helpers during the trial period, until the "bugs" have been removed from the new operation.

At the end of the trial period, all data on the change should be reviewed with employees and their union representatives, for the purpose of reaching agreement on new output standards. Responsible union officials can be helpful here, as they were in one firm when employees slowed down on a newly introduced machine. After reviewing the data with company representatives, the union convinced the workers that they should give the new output a fair trial. The result was that the new standard proved to be a fair one and yielded earnings that were in line with those on jobs of comparable skill and difficulty.

Sharing the gains from technological change with workers affected, in part directly and in part indirectly through generalized wage and salary increases, may also facilitate positive acceptance of the change. The economic aspects of sharing the gains, and the problems associated with them, are among the most complex in labor-manage-

ment relations and are discussed more fully in Chapter 21.

Finally, if agreement cannot be reached on specific aspects of the change, the unresolved dispute should be submitted to arbitration, like any other unsettled grievance, with the understanding that both parties will abide by the arbitrator's decision. The knowledge that the grievance procedure and arbitration are available provides employees with an element of stability as a counterbalance to the uncertainty created by technological changes.

In administering these changes, line management has the primary responsibility. Some of the decisions on the nature of a change, its timing, and the manner of its introduction must be made by top management, with the advice and counsel of the personnel administrator and, in unionized firms, following discussions with union representatives. Furthermore, superintendents and supervisors need to be kept informed of the necessity for the change and the way in which it is to be introduced, for the latter will be primarily their responsibility. It is also important for managers and personnel administrators to follow up the adjustment of employees to the change after it is completed.[22]

For a case which involves the application of some of these points, see Case 16, "Approaches to Introducing Job Changes." The reader may also consider the extent to which these steps apply to changes affecting management itself.

A Case Example: The General Foods Plant Relocation

The experience of the General Foods Corporation in closing four plants and combining all operations in one new larger plant in another

[22] For a case example of automation in a bakery, in which the follow-up was deficient, see Otis Lipstreu, "The Automation Anxiety Syndrome: Symptoms and Treatment," *Management of Personnel Quarterly,* vol. 5, no. 1, pp. 31-35, Spring, 1966.

state illustrates the importance of advance communication with employees (and union representatives in unionized plants). It also shows the value of clear policies on how people will be affected by the move.

Some 1,800 employees (including supervisory and managerial staff) were notified by letter on March 7, 1962, of the General Foods Board of Directors decision to make the move a year hence.[23] The news release accompanying the letter was a detailed announcement of the company's plans and the reasons behind them.

On May 3, 1962, a policy on transfer and termination was circulated to employees at all four plants, indicating the company's intention to transfer to the new plant those employees who wished to go and who qualified for job openings. For those who decided not to transfer, assistance in finding other employment was offered and termination allowances were promised. For those intending to transfer, a detailed statement was made on reimbursement of moving expenses. Subsequently, as the manning schedule for the new plant developed, specific job openings were offered, and transferring employees had preference over newly hired employees at the new location.

When the new plant opened in Dover, Delaware, some 555 employees decided to transfer as a result of the program. Of these, 423 moved to Dover from the four plants scheduled for closing; 83 transferred to other plants of General Foods, and 49 moved to Dover from General Foods headquarters and other plants. Many of those who elected not to transfer and take termination allowances were evidently reluctant to leave their home communities, and some undoubtedly found other employment. Despite the

[23] For the full text of the letter sent to all employees, and for other data on the move, see Edmund S. Whitman and W. James Schmidt, *Plant Relocation: A Case History of a Move,* American Management Association, Inc., New York, 1966. See also David B. Lipsky, "Interplant Transfer and Terminated Workers: A Case Study," *Industrial and Labor Relations Review,* vol. 23, no. 2, pp. 191–206, January, 1970.

forward-looking program developed to meet this move, the closing of the plants did have some human costs in confronting many older displaced workers with a change in their established work environment.

DETERMINING HOURS OF WORK: WORK SCHEDULES

Just as changes in job assignments sometimes involve difficult human problems, so changes in hours and work schedules require an adjustment between the technical requirements of the organization and the human requirements of the work force. The task of management here, with the help of the personnel administrator, is to develop policies that integrate the need of the enterprise for maximum production at lowest cost with the need of employees for satisfactory working hours and work schedules. In unionized plants, of course, discussions with union representatives would be part of this policy development.

Some industries must be operated continuously, day and night—for technical reasons in continuous-process industries, such as chemicals; for cost reasons when expensive capital equipment must be fully utilized; or because the public requires uninterrupted service, as in the case of public utilities, hospitals and some forms of transportation. Some new occupations, e.g., computer operator and computer programmer, are on three shifts because of the cost of computer equipment and the backlog of work for computer use. When this necessity does not exist, the decision on the number of hours per day and per week to operate the present facilities of an organization will depend upon (1) the demand for the product or service relative to existing capacity and the investment it represents, (2) the availability of additional labor or the willingness of present employees to work longer hours, (3) federal and state legislation on hours of work, and

(4) union contracts regulating hours of work. Within this framework, the decision on the length of work schedules for individual employees will be affected primarily by judgments on the optimum workday and workweek. What are the optimum hours of work for human beings?

No general answer can be given to fit all work situations. Experience with long working hours in this country during the Second World War indicates that "on the whole, the 5-day week and the 8-hour day are more efficient than a work schedule with longer hours." [24] When a sixth day of 8 hours or less is added, there is some loss in hourly efficiency, and it is seldom that more than a 46- or 48-hour week should be recommended in any regularly scheduled work weeks. Furthermore, 1 day of rest in 7 is considered essential. Longer hours may bring greater total weekly output, but at the expense of lower hourly efficiency, increased absenteeism, more accidents, and lower morale.

These comments apply principally to production or craft work. They are less applicable to the work of professional and technical employees or managers. In research and development groups, members may work longer than the regular working schedules of the rest of the organization, because of their interest in completing a particular experiment or assignment. Sometimes they work late at night and prefer to come in later in the morning, with an irregular schedule which often disturbs those managers who insist, literally or figuratively, that everyone "punch a time clock." Indeed, top and middle managers are often poor examples of this, for they too work long hours, often in the evening at the office or taking work home. Perhaps it is ironical that at a time when production, craft, and office workers

and their labor organizations are pressing for a shorter work week (at least at regular rates of pay, with overtime pay beyond this), professional employees and managers are working longer hours. [25]

Proposals for a Shorter Workweek or Work Year

Organized labor has long favored a compulsory shorter workweek, through overtime payment after 35 or even 30 hours, as a means of increasing employment. The proposal involves maintaining existing weekly wages, so that a general reduction in the average workweek from 40 to 35 hours, at 40 hours' pay, would mean a 14 percent increase in average hourly earnings. Most economists believe that this increase in labor costs would not be offset by an increase in *worker* productivity *as a result of* the shorter hours. They point out that shorter hours have been possible over the past 50 years because of higher productivity resulting from increased capital investment per worker, although it is also admitted that legislation and union pressure have been necessary to push management in the direction of shorter hours. The steel industry had the 12-hour day until about 1920.

If workers represented by unions prefer to take productivity gains in the form of shorter hours, including longer vacations, as the Steelworkers' Union did in the 1963 negotiations resulting in 13-week vacations every 5 years for senior employees, then they have a right to make that choice. But shorter hours as a remedy for unemployment has not won widespread support outside union circles. It is generally believed that a 40-hour workweek is essential to meet this country's domestic and international obligations

---

[24] Max D. Kossoris, *Studies of the Effects of Long Working Hours,* U.S. Bureau of Labor Statistics, Bulletin 791-A, 1944, part 2, p. 2. This conclusion was based upon 12 careful studies in various types of metalworking industries. See also *Hours of Work and Output,* U.S. Bureau of Labor Statistics, Bulletin 917, 1948.

[25] See Peter Henle, "Leisure and the Long Workweek," *Monthly Labor Review,* vol. 89, no. 7, July, 1966, p. 722. When other employees work longer hours, sometimes at two different jobs, the reason is the desire for additional income.

and that more rapid economic growth is the best way of dealing with high general unemployment.[26]

An exception, of course, is the case of shorter workweek schedules to accommodate part-time workers, particularly in the service industries, where teenagers, married women with children in school, etc., want only short workweeks. Furthermore, when full-time employees do work shorter hours, as the rubber workers did for some years, they often take second jobs to increase their income. Even among full-time workers, it is estimated that as many as 4 million "moonlight" (hold multiple jobs) and about 15 percent of lower-middle-income males are said to be moonlighters, mainly to meet regular expenses or pay off debts.[27]

The 4-day 40-hour Workweek

A more recent development is the apparent desire of workers for more weekend leisure rather than additional moonlighting income. A growing number of companies in industries which do not require much if any weekend operation have adopted the 4-day, 40-hour workweek.[28] Another interpretation of this is the "flexible" or "rearranged" workweek, since one possibility is a 4-day week at 10 hours a day, and in others

[26] For a discussion of this and related issues in shorter hours, see Clyde E. Dankert, Floyd C. Mann, and Herbert R. Northrup (eds.), *Hours of Work,* Harper & Row, Publishers, Incorporated, New York, 1965.

[27] "Moonlighting—An American Tradition," *Manpower,* vol. 3, no. 8, pp. 11-14, August, 1971.

[28] Riva Poor (ed.), *4 Days, 40 Hours: Reporting a Revolution in Work and Leisure,* Bursk and Poor Publishing, Cambridge, Mass., 1970. Mrs. Poor notes (p. 15): "4 days, 40 hours is not the 4 days, 32 hours that the unions are beginning to talk about again, although it is possible that 4-40 could lead to 4-32, and will probably do so *in the long run."*

For a survey on the status of the 4-day week in 1,056 companies see Kenneth E. Wheeler, Richard Gurman, and Dale Tarnowieski: *The Four-day Week: An AMA Research Report,* American Management Association, Inc., New York, 1972.

(with less than 40 hours), 9½ hours a day Monday through Thursday (with overtime pay after 8 hours) or 12 hours a day for 3 days for computer operators on continuous shifts in a large insurance company. However, many are relatively small firms, often in manufacturing.

One of the advantages claimed for the shorter workweek with longer workdays is that absenteeism (either Mondays or Fridays) is reduced with no loss of production and even a possible productivity increase. Turnover may be less. Commuting time is reduced also, not only by one day but also at off-hours during the workweek. These advantages can be realized only with careful advance planning, including consultation with employees whose prior work patterns are changed.[29]

Payment for Overtime Work

The federal Fair Labor Standards Act of 1938 established the 40-hour week as the standard workweek for all personnel in industries involved in interstate commerce, with certain minor exceptions. However, there is no absolute limitation on working hours; the only requirement is that hours worked above 40 must be paid for at not less than 1½ times the regular rate of pay. This public expression of socially desirable hours of work was partly a result of depression conditions, when a penalty on overtime work was designed to spread available employment. The 8-hour day and 40-hour week at straight-

[29] For other accounts and evaluations, see Kenneth E. Wheeler, "Small Business Eyes the Four-day Workweek," *Harvard Business Review,* vol. 48, no. 4, pp. 142-147, May-June 1970; "Why the Work Week Pattern Is Changing," *Business Week,* pp. 108-109, Mar. 13, 1971; and John Wittman, "The Compressed Workweek: More Questions than Answers," *Manpower* (U.S. Department of Labor), vol. 3, no. 1, pp. 18-19, July, 1971. The Gallup Poll reported in March, 1971, that married women opposed the 10-hour days in the 4-day, 40-hour week by a two-to-one majority because it would be "too tough" on their husbands or they would not have sufficient time for household chores. *The New York Times,* Mar. 25, 1971, p. 65.

time rates are now standard practice in most industries except purely local ones. Collective-bargaining agreements between employers and unions have further strengthened this practice and, in some cases, specified the payment of overtime rates after only 35 or 36 hours a week. Office work schedules, usually not covered by union agreements, are often less than 40 hours.

Under many collective-bargaining agreements, work on Saturday and Sunday is compensated at time and a half and double time, respectively, regardless of whether or not the employee has worked 40 hours. Again, this is an expression of the undesirability of work at times that are generally regarded as days of recreation and rest. When public convenience or necessity demands that work be done on Saturdays and Sundays, the payment of higher rates can be considered as a legitimate bonus.

The payment of premium rates for work beyond 8 hours a day and 40 hours a week, and for Saturday and Sunday work, is desirable from another standpoint. It is difficult to recruit workers for these schedules except in periods of great surplus, and premium rates serve, therefore, as a means of attracting the necessary labor. The same is also true of work on late shifts, as we shall point out later. Moreover, some employees, as we have noted earlier, prefer overtime work at premium pay as a way of earning more money.

Scheduling Changes in Hours

When management has determined the hours of work per day and per week, it faces the further responsibility of scheduling the hours to be worked by different groups of employees. Frequently, in order to achieve or maintain balanced operations, it is necessary for some "bottleneck" department to work longer than others; or, for production reasons, management may be forced temporarily to reduce the hours of work in certain departments as an alternative to layoffs. It is sound practice here to tell employees in advance about the proposed change in work-

ing hours and the reasons for it. In unionized concerns, this notification will involve discussions with union representatives.

Arbitrary and unexplained changes in work hours will not secure full cooperation of employees any more than arbitrary actions in making other changes in work. Some managements resent the necessity of discussing these changes in advance with employees and their representatives as an encroachment on management's "rights," but this is shortsighted. Not only have employees a legitimate concern about the hours they are expected to work, but as human beings they have a right to know in advance about changes that will affect them.

Overtime Work

Another problem concerns fair assignment of overtime work when there is not enough for every worker. If overtime is paid at premium rates, employees may welcome this additional income and actively seek more overtime work. Equal division of the available overtime among those requesting it is the fairest practice and the only one that will preclude charges of favoritism. When those offered overtime decline to accept it, this should count as "overtime worked" for purposes of equitable distribution.

When overtime work is necessary, a schedule should be prepared and posted, listing the overtime assignments for each employee. Employees then know clearly when they are expected to work longer than normal hours, and they can plan accordingly. In a stitching room, for example, considerable confusion and dissatisfaction resulted from the practice of asking the girls in the morning whether they wanted to work overtime the same afternoon. Many complained that their recreational plans were often upset by this practice. Dissatisfaction was eliminated by the posting of definite schedules.

For a case illustrating other aspects of scheduling work assignments, see Case 17, "Difficulties Connected with Work Scheduling."

Shift Operations

Adding another shift is one alternative to lengthening the hours of work for present employees if it is necessary to expand output. Shift operations, however, may also be necessary for other reasons. The availability of additional labor and state laws governing hours and night work will also determine the feasibility of extra shifts in periods of high production. Even when it is not necessary to expand output, automated plants and continuous-process industries, such as steel, chemicals, and many public utilities, must operate around the clock. So must hospitals.

Each shift has its own characteristics, which must be appreciated by line officials and by the personnel administrator if problems arising under shift assignments are to be met successfully. What situations are created for employees by the different shifts?[30]

First (Day) Shift   The first shift is almost universally preferred by employees because it is the only one that fits the traditional pattern of work, rest or recreation, and sleep. Nevertheless, some workers prefer later shifts for a number of reasons. Since supervision is closer and the pace of the work is generally faster on the first shift, the easygoing type of worker may therefore wish to avoid it. Working mothers may also prefer second-shift work if their husbands already work on the first shift.

Second (Evening) Shift   Work on the second shift conflicts squarely with the routines of family living and with late afternoon and evening

---

[30] Much of the following is taken from a report on extensive research in the human aspects of shift problems by one of the authors. Paul Pigors and Faith Pigors, *Human Aspects of Multiple Shift Operation,* Massachusetts Institute of Technology, Department of Economics and Social Science, ser. 2, no. 13, Cambridge, Mass., May, 1943, chap. 1. For later corroborating studies, see P. E. Mott, Floyd C. Mann, Q. McLoughlin, and D. Warwick, *Shift Work: Social, Psychological and Physical Consequences,* The University of Michigan Press, Ann Arbor, Mich., 1965.

recreation. The married male worker on a second-shift schedule from 3 to 11 P.M., for example, may want a later breakfast than children or other workers in the household who are accustomed to rising earlier. The midday meal for children at school may be too early for the male worker, who usually wants something to eat before he goes to work. With the exception of the noon hour, the father seldom sees his older children during the week, for they are at school before he awakes and asleep when he returns home from work at night. His wife is faced with an evening at home alone, for except on the day off, evening recreation is out of the question for the second-shift worker. Opportunities for a night out "with the boys" or at a social club are also restricted.

Single employees on the second shift complain particularly about the loss of afternoon and evening recreation. Beginning the day with leisure and ending with work does not appeal to many persons. With the exceptions mentioned earlier, probably most of the "contented" second-shift employees are those, especially older ones, who have become resigned to this schedule because they do not expect much fun out of life anyway.

Third (Night, or "Graveyard") Shift   Employees assigned to the third shift face a reversal of the normal sequence of working, sleeping, and eating. The third shift worker's "day" is other people's night, and he must try to sleep when the community is going about its daily tasks. As one employee said, "It's hard to live a night-shift life in a day-shift neighborhood." Furthermore, normal eating habits are upset. The night employee generally eats when he comes home from work in the morning before he goes to bed: then he may have his "breakfast" when he awakes sometime in the late afternoon. Finally, if he has to be at work by 10:30 or 11 P.M. and must travel a considerable distance, his opportunities for evening recreation are almost as limited as those of second-shift workers. The psychological and physical adjustments necessary for night work are therefore considerable. A number of studies have shown a higher incidence of ulcers on evening and night shifts.

Additional problems may face the night employee on the job. His opportunities for a hot meal at work around 2 A.M. may be poor unless there is an all-night cafeteria or lunchroom. Technical services provided by maintenance crews, nurses, child-care centers, and the personnel department are frequently poorer on the night shift than on the other shifts, and the same is often true of supervision. In fact, the night-shift employee sees his department head only if the latter arrives for work as the night shift is leaving. As in the case of the second shift, there are some employees who either prefer the night shift for personal reasons or who seem to be resigned to it, but most workers hope eventually for transfer to an earlier shift.

An important responsibility of the personnel administrator is helping management to make second and third shifts as attractive as possible. Various methods have been used at different times, principally the following:

1 Premium pay for second- and third-shift assignments, as specified in many union contracts.
2 Cooperation with community officials and local businessmen in providing morning and late-evening recreation, better schedules on public transportation systems, and evening hours in banks, stores, beauty parlors, etc.
3 Improving in-plant services on the late shifts, such as cafeterias, first aid, and supervision.

Employees on these late shifts have many personal problems arising from the necessary adjustments, and these require sympathetic consideration. Supervisors, therefore, need to be especially understanding of these difficulties.

Another type of problem arising under shift operations is intershift conflict. When each crew uses the same tools and machines, the previous crew may not leave work in proper order or machines in proper condition. Undesirable jobs or duties are left for the next shift, and this process can become progressively worse unless it is checked at the start. If supervision is overlapped at shift-change time, much of this buck-passing can be prevented. Each conflict, however, is a product of local factors, such as employee attitudes, method of wage payment, composition of work groups, etc. But intershift cooperation is possible when employees realize their independence.

Rotating shifts are found in some companies and industries, partly because of employee and union preference. Possibly because the late shifts are less desirable than the first or daytime shift, employees feel that it is fairer to share the good with the less desirable among all the regular employees. Rotation of shifts may occur once every week, although this has the disadvantage that physiologically it is difficult for some employees to adjust to such frequent *changes* in shifts. If there is some break between shift changes, perhaps this objection has less force; but rotation of shifts every 4 weeks, or even less often, is found in some plants because of the difficulties of too frequent shift changes.[31]

The equity principle sought by rotation of shifts conflicts with the seniority principle found, for example, in the textile industry. Here shift assignments are made on the basis of seniority, and workers whose lower seniority confines them to night shifts look forward to the time when they can qualify by seniority for a permanent day-shift assignment. No such hope is held out to the older employee under rotating shifts for all

[31] For a study of group preferences for rotating shifts, see A. A. I. Wedderburn, "Social Factors in Satisfaction with Swiftly Rotating Shifts," *Occupational Psychology*, vol. 41, nos. 2 and 3, pp. 85-107, April–July, 1967. This study of employees in a new steelworks in South Wales indicated that those in the age group from thirty-one to forty, married, and with dependents showed the highest satisfaction with swiftly rotating shifts.

employees. On the other hand, rotation assures experienced employees on all shifts which the seniority principle does not. Under shift assignment by seniority, the late shifts are apt to be staffed by less experienced employees with low seniority, and production may suffer.

Shift assignments by management must take into account the technical needs of the industry and the human needs of employees as expressed by them and by their union representatives.

SUMMARY

Management must be capable of adapting the organization to dynamic conditions if a firm is to compete effectively in an economy which demands constant innovation and if an organization is to grow effectively. These managerial decisions affect the human resources of the organization, and their implementation requires willing cooperation from employees. Job changes involve some of the most difficult human problems facing managers and personnel administrators.

A personnel administrator can make a substantial contribution by advising line managers on ways to reduce employee resistance to change and by encouraging the desire of some employees *for* change. He can also assist the line by participating in the formulation of policies that reconcile the human needs for security and for reasonable working schedules with technical demands for efficiency. Other ways to work toward this objective are by careful planning, consultation, and explanation to invite meaningful participation. All these practices can help employees adjust to job changes. Finally, managers, with the help of their personnel advisers, can recognize and utilize positive attitudes that employees have toward progressive changes.

Thus, by stressing the positive aspects of change and minimizing the negative ones, management can go a long way toward achieving its goal of flexibility by recognizing human needs

and by helping people to meet these needs even under the stress of technological changes. The same is generally true of changes in working hours and shifts, which also involve changes in employees' preexisting work and living habits.

SELECTED REFERENCES

Baldwin, George B., and George P. Shultz: "Automation: A New Dimension to Old Problems," *Proceedings of the Seventh Annual Meeting,* Industrial Relations Research Association, Detroit, Mich., December, 1954, pp. 117–128.

Beaumont, Richard A., and Roy B. Helfgott: *Management, Automation, and People,* Industrial Relations Counselors, New York, 1964.

Bennis, Warren G.: *Changing Organizations,* McGraw-Hill Book Company, New York, 1966.

Coch, Lester, and John R. R. French, Jr.: "Overcoming Resistance to Change," *Human Relations,* vol. 1, no. 4, pp. 512–532, 1948.

Croome, Honor: *Human Problems of Innovation,* H. M. Stationery Office, Department of Scientific and Industrial Research, London, 1960.

Lester, Richard A., and Robert L. Aronson: *Job Modifications under Collective Bargaining: A Survey of Company Experience and Four Case Studies,* Princeton University, Industrial Relations Section, Princeton, N.J., 1950.

Likert, Rensis: "Measuring Organizational Performance," *Harvard Business Review,* vol. 36, no. 2, pp. 41–50, March–April, 1958 (reprinted in Paul A. Pigors, Charles A. Myers, and F. T. Malm: *Management of Human Resources: Readings in Personnel Administration,* 3d ed., McGraw-Hill Book Company, New York, 1973, selection 2).

Mann, Floyd C., and Franklin W. Neff: *Managing Major Change in Foundation for Research on Human Behavior,* Ann Arbor, Mich.,

Moore, Leo B.: "How to Manage Improvement," *Harvard Business Review,* vol. 36, no. 4, pp. 75–84, 1958.

Morison, Elting E.: *Men, Machines and Modern Times,* The M.I.T. Press, Cambridge, Mass., 1966.

Scott, W. H., and others: *Technical Change and Industrial Relations,* Liverpool University, Department of Social Science, Social Science Series, Liverpool, England, 1956.

Slichter, Summer H., James J. Healy, and E. Robert Livernash: *The Impact of Collective Bargaining on Management,* The Brookings Institution, Washington, D.C., 1960, chap. 12, "Union Policies toward Technological Change," pp. 342-371.

Somers, Gerald G., Edward L. Cushman, and Nat Weinberg (eds.): *Adjusting to Technological Change,* Harper & Row, Publishers, Incorporated, New York, 1963 (for the Industrial Relations Research Association).

Zander, Alvin: "Resistance to Change: Its Analysis and Prevention," *Advanced Management,* vol. 15, no. 1, pp. 9-11, 1950.

Hours and Shifts

Dankert, Clyde E., Floyd C. Mann, and Herbert R. Northrup (ed.): *Hours of Work,* Harper & Row, Publishers, Incorporated, New York, 1965 (for the Industrial Relations Research Association).

Mott, P. E., Floyd C. Mann, Q. McLoughlin, and D. Warwick: *Shift Work: Social, Psychological and Physical Consequences,* The University of Michigan Press, Ann Arbor, Mich., 1965.

Wheeler, Kenneth E., Richard Gurman and Dale Tarnowieski: *The Four-day Week,* An AMA Research Report, American Management Association, Inc., New York, 1972.

Providing Pay and Services

INTRODUCTION

Money makes a difference to employees—not only for what it can buy, but also for what it may seem to show. Does it show that management intends to treat every employee fairly, to offer incentives that appeal to an inner-directed individual, and equitably to share the gains derived from higher productivity?

Like money, employee benefits and services relate to job context rather than to job content. However, like money, these peripheral rewards matter to many employees and to the union representatives who bargain for them. In regard to benefits and services, a chief executive's area of freedom is not as large as it used to be. Nowadays, it consists chiefly in deciding whether to do more than is legally required and in hunting for new ways to work *with* employees, so that both "the whole man" and the whole organization may benefit.

Chapter 20, Wage and Salary Policies and Administration, centers on wage and salary surveys, factors that affect wage and salary levels in the particular firm, and job evaluation. Administration of these procedures as jobs and conditions change is a continuing problem.

Chapter 21, Pay Incentive Systems; Sharing Productivity Gains, considers the assumption that employees can be induced to work harder than they normally would if they can count on getting more money for a larger output of acceptable quality. The difficulties associated with making equitable timestudies, concealed losses brought about by resentment, and the ingenuity displayed by employees in trying to "beat the system" have made some managers wonder whether individual incentive plans are worthwhile. Group and plant-wide incentives offer a possible alternative, as does measured day-work. For executives, however, incentive compensation has grown in recent years.

Sharing the gains from higher productivity entails measuring the productivity increase or the savings in costs. The difficulties are substantial, but some firms have found ways of reconciling apparently incompatible aims. Several of these experiences are considered, along with profit sharing, suggestion systems, and a plan (the Scanlon Plan) for increasing employee participation in solving production problems and reducing costs by providing bonus payments based on measured savings.

Chapter 22, Programs for Employee Health and Safety: An Ecological Approach, calls attention to the need for reappraising and possibly reorganizing a company's safety and health function. A brief review of the historical background and of such recent legislation as The Occupational Safety and Health Act (1971) and of relevant modern knowledge is offered to help achieve a unified view of what remains to be done. Policy statements can express top management's continuing interest in the well-being of every organizational member and belief in the principle of mutual responsibility. In planning and administering procedures, practices, and rules for health and safety, there is need for collaboration between staff specialists, representatives of line management, nonsupervisory employees, and their union representatives. Widespread participation in intradepartmental and interdepartmental committees can ensure full implementation of top management's purpose to help themselves and one another in preserving the priceless organizational assets of safety and health. An analysis of the accident process and the accident context focuses attention on the importance of education and prevention in successful safety management. Effective safety and health services are integral parts of a total personnel policy system.

CASES IN PART 2 THAT RELATE TO SECTION E

3 Dissatisfactions of an Expatriate Engineer
4 The Girl and the Computer
6 Conflict of Interest?
7 The Good-neighbor Policy
11 Will More Money Be a Motivator?
19 Fear? Or Featherbedding?

Chapter 20

Wage and Salary Policies and Administration

Pay, in one form or another is certainly one of the mainsprings of motivation in our society. ... The most evangelical Human Relationist insists it is important, while protesting that other things are too (and are, perhaps in his view, nobler). It would be unnecessary to belabor the point if it were not for a tendency for money drives to slip out of focus in a miasma of other values and other practices. As it is, it must be repeated: pay is the most important single motivator used in our organized society. As a motivator, it becomes part of general psychological problems.

Mason Haire, Edwin E. Ghiselli, and Lyman W. Porter[1]

In some firms, good wages and salaries have probably been overemphasized as the key to satisfactory personnel relations. Occasionally an employer asserts that "workers are *only* interested in the size of their paychecks." The onesidedness of this view has been demonstrated by recent research which shows clearly that workers are not motivated solely by financial incentives. Other goals and job satisfactions are important, and, for some individuals, more important than pay (see Chapters 1 and 6).

Still, "fair" wages and salaries are important to most employees, despite "morale studies" which show that wages are fifth or sixth in a scale of job satisfactions. If wages or salaries are adequate, other needs are felt to be more important; if wages or salaries are considered inadequate or unfair, they tend to become first in importance to

[1] Mason Haire, Edwin E. Ghiselli, and Lyman W. Porter, "Psychological Research on Pay: An Overview," *Industrial Relations,* vol. 3, no. 1, p. 3, October, 1963 (reprinted in Paul Pigors, Charles A. Myers, and F. T. Malm, *Management of Human Resources: Readings in Personnel Administration,* 3d ed., McGraw-Hill Book Company, New York, 1973, selection 37).

many people.[2] The equity or fairness of wage and salary *increases* is also important to employees.[3] When pay is tied to performance, furthermore, money is an important motivator; when it is not so tied, it does not motivate and satisfaction is low, turnover and absenteeism high.[4] Thus, a fair wage and salary policy and consistent internal wage and salary relationships are vital to the achievement of individual and group effort in any organization.

Relationship to Other Personnel Policies: A Systems View

If the general level of wages and salaries in the organization is too low in relation to other comparable firms, management will find it difficult to attract and hold qualified personnel, particularly those in short supply such as technical, professional, and managerial personnel. But recruitment is not the only phase of the personnel program in which wages and salaries are important. A good promotion policy requires that earnings on each job be related to the worth of the job, so that promotions will bring an increase in pay as well as in status. Furthermore, the establishment of these sound internal wage and salary relationships is necessary to avoid the dissatisfactions that would otherwise develop over inequities between similar jobs. Finally, methods of wage payment and particularly the manner in which a wage-incentive plan is handled also affect the ability of management to get effective results with people on those types of jobs. These are all interrelated parts of a personnel policy system.

Managers, therefore, must give considerable attention to sound wage and salary policies. They can get help from the personnel administrator, as an adviser to top management in policy formulation and as one who assists the line organization in developing and utilizing effective procedures. Managerial responsibility covers the following points:

1 *The general level of wages and salaries* in the firm or organization, as compared with levels in competing firms or comparable organizations in the area or in the industry. Changes in the level over time must also be considered.
2 *Wage and salary administration:*
  a Establishing and maintaining satisfactory internal relationships between the earnings on each job and
  b Advancing individuals within rate ranges.
3 *Methods of wage payments,* by time or by output, and the characteristics of a good wage-incentive plan. Sharing the gains from productivity (Chapter 21).

It is evident that these points are interrelated, particularly the first two, which are the subject matter of this chapter. Furthermore, the factors that influence determination of the general level of wages and salaries and changes in it are also relevant to establishment of internal wage and salary relationships. Thus, there is also a wage and salary system.

WAGE AND SALARY LEVELS AND CHANGES

The level of wages and salaries in some organizations, e.g., the federal government, is established by law and by Civil Service regulations; but other organizations, including profit-making

---

[2] This conclusion is based on a study conducted by the MIT Industrial Relations Section of worker job satisfactions in a New England city, following a partial mill shutdown in 1948; see Charles A. Myers and George P. Shultz, *The Dynamics of a Labor Market,* Prentice-Hall, Inc., Englewood Cliffs, N.J., 1951. Similar conclusions were reached in another labor-market study by Lloyd G. Reynolds, *Structure of Labor Markets,* Harper & Row, Publishers, Incorporated, New York, 1951. As noted in Chap. 1, social psychologists have also pointed out the importance of a hierarchy of needs, the urgency of which varies with the degree of fulfillment. See, for example, Mason Haire, *Psychology in Management,* 2d ed., McGraw-Hill Book Company, New York, 1964, chap. 2.

[3] "Satisfaction from money results primarily from an *increase* in income, not from income itself," Saul W. Gellerman, "Motivating Men with Money," *Fortune,* March, 1968, p. 145.

[4] Edward E. Lawler III, *Pay and Organizational Effectiveness: A Psychological View,* McGraw-Hill Book Company, New York, 1971, especially part III. This relation of pay to performance may explain the apparent contradiction between some of the discussion in Chap. 6 and this chapter, particularly the quotation at the beginning.

firms as well as nonprofit organizations, may have more flexibility in deciding what level of wages and salaries they can pay. This decision (even for the federal government) is affected by (1) the quality of employees the organization needs for effective operation, (2) the competition of other organizations for employees of this quality, and (3) the ability of the organization to pay sufficient wages and salaries to attract and hold the people it needs. This last point is influenced by the financial condition ("ability to pay") of the firm or organization, including budget limitations imposed on governmental and nonprofit organizations. Government, through minimum-wage laws, places a lower limit on wage levels that can legally be paid.

Changes in the level of wages and salaries are influenced by some of the same external forces, e.g., what other firms and organizations are doing to meet competition in the labor market, and ability of the firm or organization to pay for the changes in order to maintain the same quality of recruits. Other factors are also important, since employee satisfaction and dissatisfaction with existing levels are importantly affected by (1) wage and salary changes made by comparable firms and organizations or in comparable jobs and occupations and (2) changes in the cost of living since the last wage-salary change. Finally, upward changes in minimum wages established by law may require upward changes in other wages and salaries above the minimum.

Both the level and changes in the level will also be affected by the pressure of labor organizations through collective bargaining and the tightness or looseness of the labor market generally and for particular occupational groups. When unemployment is 6 percent, wage and salary changes through collective bargaining or in nonunion firms and organizations are likely to be less than when unemployment averages under 4 percent. Even then, the market for skilled workers and for technical, professional, and managerial people is likely to be much tighter than the average, and the level of salaries established for

these groups may be relatively higher. In part, this is a matter of internal wage and salary relationships, which we shall consider later in this chapter.

Wages and Salaries Paid by Comparable Firms or in Comparable Occupations

In many respects, as the preceding section indicated, both the level of wages and salaries and changes in it are most importantly affected by what is happening elsewhere. The spread of collective bargaining has accentuated these external comparisons.[5] And, as we know, nonunion firms and organizations "look over their shoulders" to see what unions are getting through collective bargaining in comparable firms, organizations, occupations, and localities.

If a firm or organization decides it is necessary to pay "the going rates" for comparable jobs, it is imperative to establish a basis for this comparison and then collect relevant data. Even if the decision is to pay more than the average, or less, comparisons are still necessary. Wage and salary surveys, therefore, are essential.

Making Wage and Salary Surveys

Systematic wage and salary surveys are conducted by leading firms, employer associations, and governmental agencies.[6] They include the following steps:

[5] For a fuller discussion, see Arthur M. Ross, *Trade Union Wage Policy,* University of California Press, Berkeley, Calif., 1948; John T. Dunlop, *Wage Determination under Trade Unions,* The Macmillan Company, New York, 1944; George P. Shultz, *Pressures on Wage Decisions,* The M.I.T. Press, Cambridge, Mass., and John Wiley & Sons, Inc., New York, 1951; and Richard A. Lester, *Company Wage Policies: A Survey of Patterns and Experience,* Princeton University, Industrial Relations Section, Princeton, N.J., 1948, pp. 18-20. Lester found that half of the 104 companies studied adjusted their wage scales to community levels, a fourth were guided by some combination of community and industry levels, and the remaining fourth were equally divided between industry orientation and the application of a uniform scale in all plants of a multiplant company (p. 42).

[6] See Arnold N. Tolles and Robert Raimon, *Sources of Wage Information: Employer Associations,* Cornell University, Studies in Industrial Relations, Ithaca, N.Y., 1952, vol. 3.

1 *Selection of area, industry, or firms to be included in the survey.* This is frequently a point of difference with unions, since the inclusion of low wage, nonunion firms in the sample will usually cause a particular firm's wage level to compare "favorably" with the average for the community or industry.

2 *Listing key jobs and positions common to most firms in the survey. Detailed descriptions of these jobs,* so that valid comparisons can be made. (Job description and analysis were discussed in Chapter 14.)

3 *Making a schedule of information to be obtained,* e.g., hourly rates or earnings, weekly earnings or salaries, hours worked, shift premiums, other wage and salary supplements and methods of wage payment. These are necessary since the content of the terms "wages" and "salaries" often varies in different firms.

4 *Collection of accurate wage and salary data* on jobs that are essentially similar, by questionnaires, or preferably, interviews in each firm.

5 *Compilation of the wage and salary data for each job,* showing the mean or arithmetical average, the median, the range of rates paid, and supplementary wage and salary data. The data may also be reported by companies, labeled A, B, C, etc.

6 *Finally, presentation of results and recommendations* to management.

In collecting and compiling wage and salary information, it is vital that the data refer to jobs with essentially similar content and that for each job the data be essentially comparable. In other words, it is downright misleading to learn that Firm A pays machinists $4 an hour and Firm B pays them $3.50, when further investigation would reveal that Firm B's machinists do their own setup work and are paid on an incentive basis, while machinists in Firm A do not do setups and receive only an hourly rate. Clearly, *two* different jobs are involved, and they cannot fairly be compared. Yet this is often what happens when an executive in Firm A telephones to one in Firm B "to find out what you're paying machinists."

If wage and salary data are to be useful in helping to determine a firm's general level of wages and salaries, they must be collected systematically and thoroughly.[7] Detailed data will be helpful in explaining to employees or union representatives whether class 1 machinists (the most skilled) in Firm A are paid a higher hourly rate than class 1 machinsts in Firm B, or whether stenographers receive different starting salaries in each firm. The personnel department in many firms performs a valuable service by making these periodic wage and salary surveys, which are frequently undertaken in cooperation with a local association or a local branch of a national association.

An example of an association-wide salary survey is shown in Table 20-1. The Administrative Management Society (formerly National Office Management Association) conducts an office salary survey for 145 cities in the United States and Canada. Participating companies in these cities are provided with a guide which describes the survey and the descriptions of the jobs surveyed and then presents the national and area averages for each job for the two latest years (as shown in Table 20-1). The annual report is careful to point out that the rates for individual jobs vary from city to city, and that employer competition for clerical employees is largely limited to local areas.

Other Factors Affecting Wage and Salary Levels and Changes

Usually there is a considerable range of wage rates and salaries for comparable jobs. This permits a company to include in its policy considerations the other factors that affect the general wage level. Some firms in each community gen-

[7] For some further suggestions, see William A. Groenkamp, "How Reliable Are Wage and Salary Surveys," *Personnel,* vol. 44, no. 1, pp. 32–37, January–February, 1967. See also J. D. Dunn and Frank M. Rachel, *Wage and Salary Administration: Total Compensation Systems,* McGraw-Hill Book Company, New York, 1971, chap. 11.

Table 20-1 A National Survey of Office Salaries, by Areas,* of 17 Most Common Clerical and Data Processing Jobs (in Dollars per Week, Arithmetic Means, Weighted, by Number of Employees, Reported for Each Job)

	Mail clerk-file clerk	General clerk-B	General clerk-A	Accounting clerk-B	Accounting clerk-A	Bookkeeping machine operator	Offset duplicating machine operator	Telephone Switchboard operator	Typist-clerk	Stenographer	Secretary-B	Secretary-A	Key punch operator-B	Key punch operator-A	Tabulating machine operator	Computer operator-B	Computer operator-A
Total U.S., 1969	79	88	105	98	122	92	102	94	86	N.A.†	111	129	90	99	N.A.†	N.A.†	N.A.†
Total U.S., 1970	84	93	112	103	127	99	108	97	93	102	117	135	96	106	116	125	146
Eastern U.S.	87	94	114	105	130	99	110	99	91	101	120	139	96	107	116	128	146
E. Central	81	90	110	101	126	96	105	98	90	103	116	133	92	105	114	125	148
W. Central	79	88	106	97	123	96	105	93	88	97	110	128	92	101	113	120	142
Southern	81	90	107	102	126	93	102	92	91	100	112	131	93	103	114	120	142
Western	92	105	119	109	132	111	119	108	104	114	127	144	109	117	124	134	159
Canada	70	79	104	94	118	78	92	77	76	83	95	112	83	90	111	108	129

*Note the regional differentials, as well as the spread between the different office jobs within a region. Despite the job descriptions supplied, it is possible that these jobs are not always comparable, so that averages should be treated with caution.

†Not available.

Source: "Administrative Management Society Report," Administrative Management, vol. 31, no. 9, pp. 61–62, September, 1970, based on the 24th annual survey for 1970–1971.

erally pay higher wages and salaries and are the "wage and salary leaders" on the basis of the first consideration below.

The financial condition of the firm, or its "ability to pay," determines whether it can make a choice between (1) paying above the community or industry average in an effort to attract better employees, (2) keeping in line with comparable firms, or (3) paying lower wages and possibly using other means to attract and hold employees. Ability to pay is also a factor in wage and salary changes. If the firm is losing money or making less than it considers an adequate profit, management will naturally be reluctant to follow patterns established by other firms. Wages as costs are always important to management, while employees and unions tend to think of wages as incomes. "Ability to pay" has frequently been injected into collective-bargaining discussions by management as a reason for opposing a union wage demand. Conversely, it has often been introduced by union officials as a proof that the company can afford to meet the union's demands for a wage increase.

Financial condition may be affected by the level of *labor productivity* (output per man-hour) in the firm. However, in any given company productivity can seldom be measured accurately enough to be a valid factor in determining its general level of wages. Nonetheless, increased labor productivity in the economy as a whole is the soundest basis for increases in real wages and salaries. Money wage increases that cannot be absorbed by lower unit costs resulting from greater output per man-hour will eventually be offset by increases in product prices and hence in the cost of living, although this will vary among industries. The wage-price guideposts suggested in the President's Economic Report in 1962 spelled out these points, even though the guideposts were later dropped officially.

Changes in labor productivity occur at different rates in different firms and industries. This variation is due primarily to technological changes, and to some extent it is reflected in long-run wage differentials. The firm which is more efficient because of greater productivity should be prepared to face union demands that gains be shared with workers as well as with owners and consumers. We shall discuss this question in greater detail in Chapter 21, but here it should be noted that sharing these gains with employees through general changes in the wage and salary level is preferable to making job-rate increases which distort the wage and salary structure.

However, financial condition is also a function of *managerial efficiency* in reducing other costs. Thus there is serious doubt whether nonlabor economies that a superior management is able to effect should be the basis for a substantially higher level of wages, or whether wasteful management practices should be the basis for paying lower wages. Some unions try to make "ability to pay" an important factor in wage negotiations. But these issues are not always squarely faced. Usually, the large national unions are reluctant to subsidize an inefficient management by accepting lower than standard wage scales, although in the past they have made concessions in marginal firms when job security was involved. They are apt to be more anxious to use ability to pay as a factor in negotiations when profits are good, just as management tends to rely on it in periods of financial stringency. However, financial condition is always an important underlying factor. Therefore, managements and unions that are realistic will recognize it as such under both sets of conditions.

Whenever management relies on financial condition and ability to pay in union negotiations, it should be prepared to buttress its position by presenting factual information on costs, prices, and profits. The personnel administrator can bring his influence to bear in urging top management to put forward objective reasons for its ability or inability to meet wage and salary requests from employees, whether union or nonunion. If management hopes to develop understanding, it is not wise to keep employees and their representatives in the dark about the financial condition of the enterprise of which they are a part. Indeed, the National Labor Relations Board may order an employer to provide such information to a union if a refusal-to-bargain charge is involved.

Changes in the Consumer Price Index (popularly called "cost-of-living index"), as reported by the U.S. Bureau of Labor Statistics, should also be considered as a factor in a firm's general level of wages and salaries, particularly in relation to upward revisions. The Consumer Price Index is compiled by the Bureau of Labor Statistics to measure average changes in prices of a "market basket" of goods and services bought in various-size cities by urban wage earners and clerical-worker families. The essential objective of this index is to measure average changes in the *price* of the same market basket of goods and services from month to month and year to year. If money wages and salaries fail to keep pace with the increase in consumer prices, employees have cause for dissatisfaction over the increasing difficulty of making ends meet. Firms that have been most successful in avoiding this sort of discontent have been leaders in making wage and salary increases during periods of rising retail prices. If a company has a policy of following the leader in wage changes, the cost of living will not usually be a separate consideration.

A number of firms and unions have adopted "escalator" clauses, providing for *automatic wage and salary increases* as the cost-of-living index rises. The outstanding example, of course, is the General Motors—United Automobile Workers (CIO) agreement, which has been widely copied by other firms and unions. This agreement, first signed in May, 1948, provided for quarterly wage adjustments of 1 cent an hour for each increase or decrease of 1.14 points in the BLS Consumer Price Index, except that decreases were limited to a total of 5 cents an hour. Essentially the same clause was continued in the 5-year agreement signed in May, 1950. In 1955, the ratio was changed to 1 cent for each 0.5 point change in the index, later reduced to 0.4. The 1967 agreement, which contained substantial wage increases and other benefits, provided for

no new cost-of-living increase during the first year of the 3-year agreement and 3-cent minimums and 8-cent maximums in the second and third years. The 1970 agreement, following the General Motors strike, removed the maximum limit on the cost-of-living escalator which had limited adjustments during the inflationary period. This "escalator" principle is now found in contracts in the transportation, machinery, chemical, textile, and primary metal industries, although many managements and some unions oppose the clause.

A more frequent practice is to provide for a wage-reopening clause in the agreement, so that wage adjustments can be negotiated in the light of subsequent changes in the cost of living. It should be noted, however, that the "cost of living" is not the same as "a living wage." The latter implies a wage income sufficient to achieve a certain *standard* of living. The former simply measures changes in the cost of a given list of goods and services consumed by middle-income families in large cities. The list is revised after some years to reflect changes in consumer tastes, such as in consumer durables or leisure-time activities.

Finally, federal and state *minimum-wage laws* place an absolute lower limit on the level of wages and salaries that can be paid by any firm subject to these laws. The principal federal laws are the Fair Labor Standards (Wage-Hour) Act of 1938, as amended, under which there is a $1.60 an hour minimum wage (effective Feb. 1, 1968), except for workers in certain industries;[8] and the Public Contracts (Walsh-Healey) Act of 1936, which permits the Secretary of Labor to specify minimum wages to be paid in various industries holding government contracts. A number of states also have laws providing for a flat minimum wage or for commissions to recom-

---

[8] A minimum of $1.15 an hour applies to employees in hospitals, nursing homes, schools, federal employment, construction, laundries, restaurants, hotels, and farming, all of which were brought under the act in the 1966 amendments. Overtime pay begins after 42 hours in these industries; after 40 in all other industries covered by the act.

mend minimum wages for certain industries. The legal minimum is theoretically based on the concept of "a living wage," although in practice the ability of firms to pay the minimum is also considered. When, owing to a minimum-wage law, a firm is forced to raise its starting rate, it usually also raises wages and salaries on jobs above the minimum in order to preserve differentials for skill and to maintain a balanced wage and salary structure.

During wartime and in emergency periods, *governmental action* may affect a firm's wage level in other ways also. Orders of the National War Labor Board, and subsequently of the National Wage Stabilization Board and the Fact-finding Board, had a tremendous effect on wage-level changes in the war and postwar periods, as did the 90-day wage-price freeze ordered by President Nixon on August 15, 1971, and the subsequent wage-price controls. Some states now require compulsory arbitration of wage and other disputes in public utilities. In other states, voluntary arbitration of wage disputes in these industries is not uncommon. Arbitrators usually base their decisions on an analysis of all the factors that we have reviewed.

Arbitration of wages in contract disputes is fairly rare in the United States, probably covering only about 2 percent of the wage settlements. But the ranking of wage criteria used by arbitrators in making decisions is of some significance. According to one study, arbitrators used wage comparisons as a basis for their decisions in 60 percent of the cases, and over 80 percent of these were intraindustry comparisons. Cost-of-living data were given first weight in 34 percent of the cases studied for the period from 1945 to 1950, financial condition of the employer in 3.5 percent, substandard wage levels in 1.8 percent, and differential features of the work in 0.9 percent.[9]

This discussion of criteria for wage levels and

wage changes should not be concluded without again stressing the difficulties of securing agreement on which criteria to use.[10] In many collective bargaining negotiations, managements and unions tend to use those arguments which best support their preconceived positions, and the arguments that they use vary with business conditions. If management hopes to place wage determination on a more objective basis, it should be prepared to discuss fully all the facts affecting the enterprise. It should also frankly recognize the validity of relevant facts presented by the union, including the pressures that a union faces. Wage negotiations today usually involve a balancing of pressures confronting the company and the union—pressures from the product market, the local market, the union membership, and rival unions. At certain times, some of these will seem more important than others, and the wage settlement often represents a compromise between the positions originally maintained by each party.

Many of the preceding points, as well as those which follow, are illustrated in Case 18, "A Dispute over Rates on Three Jobs."

Internal Wage and Salary Relationships

The relationship of wages and salaries paid on different jobs is just as important for good personnel relations as the firm's general level of wages.[11] An adequate wage and salary structure tends to attract high-grade employees and to be accepted by them as fair and equitable. They may be dissatisfied if workers in a firm across the street, or in another community, are earning more money for comparable work, but more se-

[9] Irving Bernstein, *Arbitration of Wages,* University of California Press, Berkeley, Calif., 1954, pp. 14, 31.

[10] See Sylvia Wiseman, "Wage Criteria for Collective Bargaining," *Industrial and Labor Relations Review,* vol. 9, no. 2, pp. 252–267, January, 1956.

[11] E. Robert Livernash, "Wage Administration and Production Standards," in Arthur Kornhauser, Robert Dubin, and Arthur M. Ross (eds.), *Industrial Conflict,* McGraw-Hill Book Company, New York, 1954 (reprinted in Pigors, Myers, and Malm, *op. cit.,* selection 39).

rious individual dissatisfactions are likely to arise over wage inequities within the firm. Possibly with some exaggeration, the National War Labor Board in one case observed: "There is no single factor in the whole field of labor relations that does more to break down morale, create individual dissatisfaction, encourage absenteeism, increase labor turnover, and hamper production than obviously unjust inequalities in the wage rates paid to different individuals in the same labor group within the same plant." [12]

The truth in this statement is evident to anyone who has talked with wage earners and salaried employees. If Bill is earning less money than Jim on a job that he firmly believes is more difficult or more skilled than Jim's, he is dissatisfied and unlikely to do his best work. Wage and salary differentials are a mark of social status in almost every organization. If they do not correspond with the relative significance of jobs, as employees view them, the employees' sense of justice is outraged.

Psychologists have called this feeling an example of "cognitive dissonance." Employees who "choose objectively dissonant comparisons (e.g., comparison persons of *similar* status who earn more than themselves) will be more often dissatisfied with (wage) comparisons than will men who choose objectively consonant comparisons (e.g., comparison persons of *different* status who earn more than themselves)." [13] Satisfaction is expressed in terms of some other difference with the comparison person: skill, seniority, type of work, or place of work. Dissatisfaction occurs when the person feels that he is equal or superior to the higher earner in any of these respects. It is also generally true that employees whose earnings are relatively low tend to be more dissatisfied than others with the comparisons they make. Understandably, very low wages are a source of absolute dissatisfaction because they make living difficult. These people are often in the "poverty" group, especially if employment is irregular.

Some of the comparisons people make concerning their pay involve groups outside the company, especially if there are opportunities to move to another comparable job outside. It has been suggested that "at the two extremes of the hierarchy—the hourly paid worker and the chief executive—there is the clearest awareness of being a member of a broad extracompany group." [14] Perhaps the same is true of technical and professional people generally. But in a study of managers, "middle and lower managers tended to compare themselves with groups inside the company," [15] and this is probably true also of employees on many other jobs.

Consequently, dissatisfaction with wage and salary comparisons within the organization is especially strong when there appear to be no valid reasons for the differentials that exist. When management uses haphazard methods to set rates for different jobs, inequities are bound to arise. One job rate may be changed without making corresponding changes in the rates on related jobs. Or a key employee on a particular job may threaten to quit unless he is given a raise; then others on that job may claim similar treatment, particularly in a labor-shortage period. Gradually, a chaotic wage and salary structure develops, with destructive effects on employee morale.

An increasing number of firms have found that a formal job-evaluation procedure can reduce these inequities to a minimum by helping to

[12] William H. Davis (chairman), "West Coast Airframe Companies Case," in *War Labor Reports,* National War Labor Board, Mar. 3, 1943, vol. 6, p. 594 (majority opinion). A social psychologist has more recently pointed out, "In the long run, an anachronistic or inappropriate pay system can be a powerfully retarding force." Edward E. Lawler III, *Pay and Organizational Effectiveness,* p. 283. This is why Herzberg classified pay as "a dissatisfier," as we discussed in Chap. 6.

[13] Martin Patchen, *The Choice of Wage Comparisons,* Prentice-Hall, Inc., Englewood Cliffs, N.J., 1961. p. 103.

[14] Haire, Ghiselli, and Porter, *op. cit.,* p. 7.

[15] *Ibid.* See I. R. Andrews and Mildred M. Henry, "Management Attitudes toward Pay," and Edward E. Lawler III and Lyman W. Porter, "Perceptions regarding Management Compensation," *ibid.,* pp. 29-49.

establish acceptable internal wage and salary relationships. The "acceptability" refers to the employees, for it is important that employees believe that wage and salary differentials are equitable. What a job is worth to the company or organization is not easily determined by this method, but it does help to answer the question: What do we have to pay for different jobs?

ELEMENTS OF JOB EVALUATION

After a careful, detailed description and analysis have been prepared for each job in the organization (as outlined in Chapter 14), the evaluation process can begin. Job evaluation is a systematic method of appraising the worth of each job in relation to other jobs in the organization. It cannot be completely accurate, since it depends upon the judgments of the evaluators. But these are informed judgments based upon detailed studies of the jobs and comparisons of their contents, and for this reason relative evaluations are likely to be more reliable and acceptable to employees than are haphazard determinations. Furthermore, job evaluation rates the *jobs,* not the *men and women* on the jobs, which, as we have seen, is the task of performance appraisal.

Job evaluation is used to determine the relative compensation of salaried jobs as well as of hourly rated jobs, although usually the list of factors is somewhat different, as we shall see. For example, "responsibility for confidential data" might be appropriate in the evaluation of the former but not in the latter. One method of job evaluation is to rank all jobs in their order of difficulty or importance and then assign them to broad job classifications, as in government jobs covered by Civil Service.[16] The principal methods of job evaluation, however, are (1) point rat-

ing and (2) factor comparison,[17] although some plans combine features of both. No one plan can be recommended as best for every organization. The development of a suitable plan in a given company requires careful preliminary thought and discussion by a management committee or a management-labor committee, with the advice of the personnel administrator.

Selecting Job Factors Job evaluation plans differ in the nature and number of job factors they use. The management committee, with staff advice, may make its own selection, or adopt one of the standard plans developed by large employer associations such as the National Metal Trades Association or the National Electrical Manufacturers Association. These plans, which are widely used by firms in these industries, include job factors grouped under headings such as *skill, effort, responsibility,* and *job conditions,* when hourly rated jobs are involved. A somewhat different set of factors is often used for evaluating salaried jobs, e.g., *education, experience, complexity of duties, monetary responsibility, contacts, working conditions,* and (in the case of supervisory jobs) *type and extent of supervision.* Table 20-2 shows a comparison of these two sets of job factors, with the percentage weights assigned to each factor in one of the standard plans. Plans also differ in the weights they assign such factors as "responsibility."[18]

---

[16] A modified factor plan is used to grade supervisory positions in the U.S. Civil Service. See *Supervisory Grade Evaluation Guide,* U.S. Civil Service Commission, September, 1965. The Federal Pay Comparability Act of 1970 assures federal employees pay boosts in line with those in private industry, and most federal jobs except those at the top pay as much as comparable jobs in private industry.

[17] For a full discussion of these methods, see Jay L. Otis and Richard H. Leukart, *Job Evaluation: A Basis for Wage Administration,* 2d ed., Prentice-Hall, Inc., Englewood Cliffs, N.J., 1954; Charles W. Lytle, *Job Evaluation Methods,* 2d ed., The Ronald Press Company, New York, 1954; E. Lanham, *Job Evaluation,* McGraw-Hill Book Company, New York, 1955; *Job Evaluation,* International Labour Office, Studies and Reports, New Series, no. 56, 1960, and Dunn and Rachel, *op. cit.,* chaps. 10 and 11.

[18] The Cooperative Wage System (CWS) developed jointly by the Steelworkers Union and the steel companies assigns 52 percent of the points to "responsibility" (4 categories), while the National Metal Trades and National Electrical Manufacturers Association plans assign only 20 percent, giving relatively more weight to the skill factors. See Robert L. Sauer, "Selecting the Best Job Evaluation Plan," *Industrial Engineering,* vol. 9, no. 3, pp. 16–20, March, 1971.

Table 20-2   Relative Weights for Job Factors in Hourly Rated and Salaried Jobs in Comparable Job Evaluation Plans.

Hourly rated jobs		Salaried jobs* (clerical, supervisory, and technical)	
Factors	**Percent of total points**	**Factors**	**Percent of total points**
Skill		**1** Education	25
1 Education	14	**2** Experience	31.25
2 Experience	22	**3** Complexity of duties	25
3 Initative and ingenuity	14		81.25
Effort	50	**4** Monetary responsibility	6.25
4 Physical demand	10	**5** Contacts	6.25
5 Mental-visual demand	5	**6** Working conditions	6.25
Responsibility	15	(For supervisory jobs, additional points are added for "types of supervision" and "extent of supervision," with other percentages reduced correspondingly.)	
6 For equipment or process	5		
7 Material or product	5		
8 Safety of others	5		
9 Work of others	5		
Job conditions	20		
10 Working conditions	10		
11 Hazards	5		
	15		
Total	100		

*Note the greater percentage weights for "education" and "experience" for salaried jobs. the higher weight for "complexity of duties" as compared to "initiative and ingenuity" (for hourly rated jobs) and the lower weight for "working conditions" for salaried jobs.

Source: Computed from tables in manuals prepared by the Industrial Relations Department of the National Electrical Manufacturers Association, New York: *Job Rating Manual, Definitions of Factors Used in Evaluating Hourly-rated Jobs* (1946 ed.), and *NEMA Salaried Job Rating Plan: Definitions of Factors Used in Evaluating Clerical, Supervisory and Technical Positions* (1949, reprinted in 1956).

It may be unnecessary to use a large number of factors and subfactors. Studies show that, in practice, ratings are often controlled by a few factors and that a simple list of factors will yield about the same results as a more complicated system.[19]

[19] C. H. Lawshe. Jr., "Studies in Job Evaluation. II. The Adequacy of Abbreviated Point Ratings for Hourly-paid Jobs in Three Industrial Plants," *Journal of Applied Psychology,* vol. 29, no. 3, pp. 177–184, 1945. A more recent unpublished study of the relationship between 12 job factors and wages paid indicates that a few (such as skill and working conditions) show a significant correlation, and even these vary with the kind of plant involved and the membership on the job evaluation committee. Nicholas Perna, *Wage Determination in a Non-union Firm,* doctoral dissertation in economics, Massachusetts Institute of Technology, Cambridge, Mass., 1969.

Steps in the Evaluation Process

After job factors have been selected and jobs described and analyzed in terms of these factors, the usual steps in a point-rating plan of job evaluation, using some aspects of the factor-comparison system, are as follows:

1 Assigning "weights" in terms of total points to each of the factors, so that, for example, "skill" may have a maximum of 90 points, while "physical effort" is assigned a maximum of only 50. Sometimes the factors are subdivided, as in "responsibility for tools and equipment" and "responsibility for materials and products." Weights for each factor may properly vary with the firm and the industry, depending on the nature of the jobs. Table 20-2 shows the *relative* weights used by well-known plans for hourly rated and salaried jobs.

2 Selecting from 15 to 25 "key jobs," including representative unskilled, semiskilled, and skilled jobs on which there are a fairly large number of workers. These jobs are usually well known and easily identified by employees and supervisors. They constitute the "yardstick" against which the other jobs are later measured.

3 Evaluating the key jobs by assigning points to each factor. This is the heart of the evaluation process, because the point totals for each factor for each job should represent the best judgment of the evaluation committee on the *relative* importance of each factor in job *A* as compared with job *B,* job *C,* etc. In some plans, this step is shortened by deciding which "degree" (first, second, third, etc.) of a factor is appropriate, and each "degree" then carries a fixed range of points. For an example of this, see the National

Electrical Manufacturers Association plans referred to in the note to Table 20-2.

4 Evaluating all the other jobs, department by department, in relation to the evaluations already placed on the "key jobs." When the number of jobs is large, the evaluation must constantly be checked by reference to a growing catalogue that lists for each factor the job which has been assigned the most points or highest degree, which second, third, etc. In this way, the *relative* character of the evaluation process is maintained.

5 Determining a wage or salary "curve" by means of a wage or salary survey of the key jobs (the survey method was described earlier in this chapter). The curve (which may be a straight line) is based upon the present rates paid on those key jobs whose rates are in line with those paid by other firms in the labor market or in the industry. It is derived from a scatter diagram of points whose coordinates represent for each key

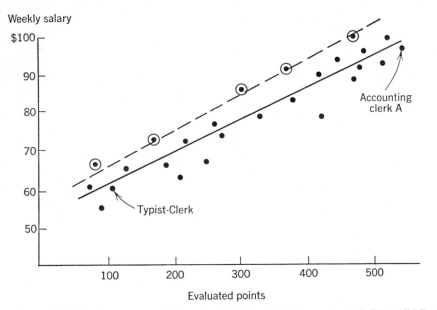

Figure 20-1 A salary curve with key clerical jobs plotted as evaluated. The solid line (salary curve) represents the "best fit" of the plotted rates. The broken line suggests a possible general increase in salaries, which would avoid a number of "red circle" rates above the salary curve for present incumbents on jobs with out-of-line rates. The proposed curve represents a percentage increase; a parallel line would represent a flat dollars-per-week increase.

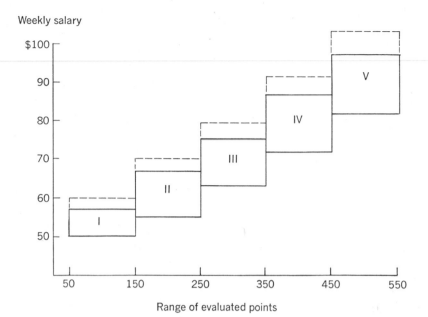

Figure 20-2 Possible clerical salary grades, based on salary curves and evaluated jobs. Note the overlap between the top of the lower grade and the bottom of the next higher grade. The dotted portion at the top of each grade indicates the additional range for "merit" increases, based on performance appraisal, automatic length-of-service increases, or both. (See page 367.)

job (1) rate paid and (2) point-evaluation total. Figure 20-1 shows a scatter diagram with a salary curve for clerical jobs.

6 Interpolating from the curve the single rates (or rate ranges)[20] for other jobs, considered either singly or in groups called "grades." (An example of salary grades is shown in Figure 20-2. For piecework or incentive jobs, the curve gives the base rate.) Assuming that job rates above the curve are lowered to the curve and that job rates below are raised to the curve, the decreases and increases, weighted by the number of employees on each job, should roughly cancel out, leaving the total payroll unchanged. Job evaluation is not a method of increasing or decreasing total payroll; rather it is a procedure for distributing a given payroll among various jobs in accordance with their relative job contents.

7 Putting the new rates into effect, by raising job rates below the curve but not reducing present incumbents on jobs whose present rates are above the curve. These employees have "red circle" rates, as shown on Figure 20-1. By transfers and upgrading, or as job contents change, or through turnover as new employees are hired at the proper job rates, these above-the-line present-incumbent rates will gradually be eliminated. This process may be a lengthy one, however, giving rise to many complaints. A better method is to put the results of the job evaluation into effect at the time of a general wage or salary increase, as indicated by the dotted line on Figure 20-1. Then it may be possible to achieve a balanced wage and salary structure immediately by not raising, or by raising in lesser amounts, the rates of employees on jobs that have been overpaid according to the evaluation.

8 Continuing administration of the program, by analyzing and evaluating changed jobs and new jobs to establish rates that will bear a proper

[20] See Walter Fogel, "Wage Administration and Job Rate Ranges," *California Management Review,* vol. 7, no. 3, pp. 77–84, Spring, 1965.

relationship to the rates on existing jobs. If existing rates are challenged, reevaluations should be made. Job evaluation must be kept up to date if it is to be worthwhile. This will also involve periodic wage surveys to assist in keeping key-job rates in line with prevailing or "market" rates for similar jobs.[21]

Advantages of Job Evaluation

A well-developed plan of job evaluation has clear advantages in achieving a more rational and consistent internal wage and salary structure. If key-job rates are carefully kept in line with market rates on similar jobs, the firm's general wage level will also be more satisfactory. Finally, and most important, when there are a number of jobs that are peculiar to the firm, job evaluation provides a means of determining rates for these jobs that will be consistent with rates on jobs that are more common in the community or industry.

These wage- or salary-setting advantages of job evaluation are clear, but the "administrative" purposes or advantages of job evaluation have not received enough emphasis.[22] These are especially important when a committee has responsibility for job evaluation:

[21] These same curves apply to salaried jobs and, with modifications we shall discuss later in the chapter, to professional and managerial positions. See Robert E. Sibson, *Wages and Salaries: A Handbook for Line Managers*, rev. ed., American Management Association, New York, 1967. Some salary "curves" are based on years of experience of members of a given group. See Robert L. McCornack, "A New Method for Fitting Salary Curves," *Personnel Journal*, vol. 46, no. 9, pp. 589-595, October, 1967.

[22] These purposes are stressed and ably discussed by E. Robert Livernash, "Job Evaluation," in W. Woytinsky and Associates, *Employment and Wages in the United States*, The Twentieth Century Fund, New York, 1953, chap. 35, pp. 427-435. For further discussion of the advantages and limitations of job evaluation, see Livernash, "Wage Administration and Production Standards," in Arthur Kornhauser, Robert Dubin, and Arthur M. Ross (eds.), *Industrial Conflict*, McGraw-Hill Book Company, New York, 1954, pp. 330-334 (reprinted in Pigors, Myers, and Malm, *op. cit.*, selection 39).

1 Specializing and centralizing the process of determining wage and salary differentials in the committee, with staff analysts to assist it.

2 Securing agreement among the various management officials in the organization and among union representatives in unionized plants on the question of proper wage and salary differentials.

3 Establishing a frame of reference for the settlement of grievances over individual job rates and for negotiations with the union over internal wage differentials.

4 Developing procedures for systematically reviewing job rates as job contents change with technological and process improvements or as variations occur among market rates for particular jobs.

These advantages of job evaluation as a part of wage and salary administration, however, will not be realized unless there is full *communication* of the purposes of a systematic approach to all affected employees. Where blue-collar jobs are involved and there is a union, employees will generally know what the plan is. But salaried employees also need to know, and the time is past when salary ranges are "top-secret" information known only to the chief executive. Progressive managements believe that each employee is entitled to know where he stands in the salary scale and how salary policies affect him. Without this knowledge, it is much less likely that pay increases will motivate employees to achieve higher standards of performance.

Limitations and Problems of Job Evaluation

Although job evaluation does have clear advantages over haphazard procedures of wage and salary determination, its proponents and practitioners have sometimes overlooked its limitations. It is inaccurate to claim scientific exactness for the results of job evaluation. No judgment, however well informed, is exact in a scientific sense; yet some managements have maintained that the rates set by job evaluation should not be open to question or discussion by union representatives. This position is difficult to defend. If adopted, it denies management an opportunity to explain its own valid methods directly to union officials.

Another limitation of job evaluation is that jobs of equal content in terms of the usual factors may not necessarily be of equal attractiveness to workers. For example, it is not uncommon to find that one job in a plant is more or less a "blind-alley" job, whereas another is recognized by workers as a steppingstone to a better job. Yet the two jobs may be equal in terms of skill, responsibility, physical effort, mental effort, and working conditions. Traditionally, the rate on the blind-alley job may have been higher than on the other, yet a job-evaluation program can upset this relationship and create a new kind of inequity.

Career prospects outside the company are also important. Some jobs are highly specialized in a particular firm, whereas others develop skills that are marketable in other firms and industries. Despite similarity in job content, it may be necessary to pay more for the first type of job than for the second in order to attract and hold capable workers. The same comment can be made with respect to two jobs equal in content but different in continuity of employment. It is traditional, for example, that maintenance carpenters in a factory have traditionally steadier employment than construction carpenters outside, and the higher hourly rates of the latter generally reflect this important difference. In short, *unless the results of job evaluation approximate in practice the relative social evaluations that workers place on the jobs, dissatisfactions are apt to be created by the system itself.*

Inflexibility and overreliance on internal standards of job comparison are other limitations of job evaluation. In some labor markets, the supply and demand for a particular type of labor or occupation have an important bearing on the rates paid, and a job evaluation plan that seeks to determine wage differentials largely on the basis of factors and points, without reference to market rates, is likely to breed opposition, especially in unionized situations. This difficulty can be minimized if the plan has a relatively large number of key jobs which are related to market rates and if changes are made in pay rates on these key jobs as market rates change, regardless of changes in job content. A simple plan is likely to be more flexible, and flexibility is vital if market forces are important

If the market rate that must be paid on a certain job to attract and retain good workers is much higher than the job-evaluation system would justify, it may be better to make this job an "exception" and have it recognized as such by everybody. Juggling points to "justify" a high rate, which has been done in some cases, is less defensible, although a "balancing factor" may be added to the standard factors to take into account these variables. Obviously, in isolated labor markets and in certain types of firms where jobs are unique, this problem of adjustment to market forces is not so great.

In view of these limitations, common sense, more than devotion to "a system," is needed in developing and applying job evaluation. Its principal usefulness is in relating rates on jobs that are more or less specialized in the particular firm to the established or market rates on jobs that are common to the industry or the area.

Two other problems in job evaluation should be mentioned, problems that are particularly important in unionized plants. First, as we have seen, the process of job evaluation may result in the *reduction* of some job rates, as well as in the increase of others. This is to be expected if a greater internal consistency is desired in a previously chaotic wage structure. Even though the rates of present incumbents on those jobs are not reduced and even though the new lower rate is to be paid only to new employees, the idea of any rate reduction is opposed by some unions. Failure to understand and accept the principle of job-rate reductions as well as increases, however, will eventually result in an "out-of-line" rate structure. This is particularly likely when changes in job content result from technological or process changes. A simplified job should carry a lower rate relative to unchanged jobs, and the gains from technological change should be shared with *all* employees through general wage increases rather than only with particular employees on the affected jobs.[23]

Second, in unionized plants, management must accept realistically the fact that rates on important or key jobs will be negotiated with the union and not determined precisely by factors and points under a formal job-evaluation system. In fact, this very process of negotiation may give the plan the flexibility that it needs with reference to market forces and the social evaluations of workers. In saying this, we do not intend to minimize the danger that unions may bring pressure for job-rate changes that would unbalance the rate structure. If there are several unions in a plant, some of them representing small groups of skilled workers, there is frequent pressure to get increases for a particular group.

Impact of Automation　　The last, but not least important, problem of job evaluation is the tendency for automation of factory and office jobs to change the whole concept of job duties and requirements in relation to the job evaluation process. For example, not much "effort" may be required to watch control panels for automated processes, and skill may even be less than for semiautomatic jobs; but responsibility is likely to be greater, and there is a good deal of "watching" and "waiting time" which does not appear to be "work." Job factors such as "machinery utilization," "time span of employee discretion,"

[23] For further discussion of this point, see Chap. 22.

and "isolation from fellow workers" may become important.[24] The emphasis may be more on the potential skill needed in emergencies than on the daily application of a skill to a job which is within the control of the employee. All this suggests the great importance of continuing study and revision of job evaluation plans to keep them abreast of changes in the nature of work itself.

Difficulties in Evaluating Professional and Managerial Jobs

Another major limitation of traditional job evaluation is that it is not well suited to determining the relative worth of such professional jobs as those held by engineers and scientists or of managerial jobs. The reason is that these are much more difficult to describe and analyze in terms of the usual job content and job factors. Job assignments to many professional people are given on the basis of their individual professional qualifications, and only in large organizations is it possible to describe broad categories of engineering or scientific jobs. This has been called the "generic" approach, which is used in place of either the individual approach or the "career-curve" approach based on professional degrees and years of service.[25] In the latter, the more advanced professional degrees a man has and the longer his service, the higher his salary. Public school teachers are often paid on this basis.

[24] William A. Faunce, "The Automobile Industry: A Case Study in Automation," in H. B. Jacobson and J. S. Roucek (eds.), *Automation and Society,* Philosophical Library, Inc., New York, 1959, chap. 4; Robert L. Aronson, "Automation—Challenge to Collective Bargaining?," in Harold W. Davey, Howard S. Kaltenborn, and Stanley H. Ruttenberg (eds.), *New Dimensions in Collective Bargaining,* Harper & Row, Publishers, Incorporated, New York, 1959, chap. 3; and Edward B. Shils, *Automation and Industrial Relations,* Holt, Rinehart and Winston, Inc., New York, 1963, chap. 12, "Problems of Wage Administration in an Automated Era."

[25] See Sibson, *op. cit.* For a defense of separate plans, see Thomas C. Rodney, "Do R&D Positions Call for Separate Job Evaluation Plans?," *Personnel,* vol. 42, no. 3, pp. 37-43, May-June, 1965.

Several other approaches have been suggested for managerial and professional personnel. One, which could apply to blue-collar and lower white-collar jobs as well, entails utilizing the "time span of discretion" on each job, the shorter applying to the manual job and the longer to the executive position.[26] A more widely used approach in this country for managerial and professional positions is one called the "guide-chart profile method."[27] Positions are described and evaluated in three areas (1) know-how, (2) problem solving, and (3) accountability. The charts used in this approach have various degrees and categories, each of which has point values or weights, adding up to a total which places a particular position relative to others. Salary comparisons with other comparable firms establish the slope of the salary curve. A somewhat similar approach has been developed out of the experience of the British Broadcasting Company, emphasizing related factors with different titles but avoiding specific weights, to place positions in various salary grades.[28]

Some authorities believe that managerial positions at the higher levels are difficult to evaluate because the worth of the job is so much a function of the individual in it. As one management consultant has said, "It is pointless to talk about evaluating an executive job, when the real evaluation relates to what an individual has made of his job, compared with what others have made of their jobs. In the final analysis, an executive is 'worth' what his superiors believe he is worth."[29] He might have added, and what the market, i.e., other firms might pay him if he left. Top managers, like movie stars and outstanding professional athletes, are often paid as individuals for the job they do.

Supplementary Systems of Pay for Managers
Management salary levels established by individual contracts or through job (position) evaluation are increasingly supplemented by various forms of compensation which have incentive aspects. Bonus plans based on company profits usually involve top-management decisions on the actual individual distribution, so that superior performance is rewarded more generously. The General Motors bonus plan developed by Alfred P. Sloan, Jr., is one of the oldest and best known. In 1969, 65 percent of a large sample of manufacturing firms paid executive bonuses, 40 percent of retail firms did so, and lower percentages were found in the other major industry groups.[30] The median bonus award paid to the three highest-paid executives in manufacturing firms was 37 percent of base salary, a substantial financial incentive. The same percentage applied in retail trade, but the bonus award in life insurance firms averaged only 8 percent of base salaries.

[26] This approach was developed in Glacier Metals Company, Ltd., in Great Britain, by a consultant, Elliot Jacques. See his *Equitable Payment,* John Wiley & Sons, Inc., New York, 1961, and *Time Span Handbook,* William Heinemann, Ltd., London, 1964. For an evaluation of this approach relative to others, see Thomas Atchison and Wendell French, "Pay Systems for Scientists and Engineers," *Industrial Relations* vol. 7, no. 1, pp. 44-56, October, 1967; and Edwin F. Beal, "In Praise of Job Evaluation," *California Management Review,* vol. 5, no. 3, pp. 8-17, Summer, 1963 (reprinted in Pigors, Myers, and Malm, *op. cit.,* selection 38).

[27] This has been developed by Edward N. Hay & Associates, of Philadelphia, and has been used by manufacturing firms, banks, and many other organizations for professional and managerial positions. Two examples are the Officer Salary Administration Plan of the Chemical Bank New York Trust Company and the Mead Corporation's Salary Administration Plan for Exempt Employees (booklets). For further discussion, see William F. Dinsmore, "The Case for Evaluating Professional Jobs," *Personnel,* vol. 41, no. 6, pp. 54-60, November-December, 1964.

[28] Joan Doulton and David Hay, *Managerial and Professional Staff Grading,* George Allen & Unwin, Ltd., London, 1962, especially chap. 2.

[29] See Arch Patton, "What is an Executive Worth?," *Harvard Business Review,* vol. 39, no. 2, pp. 65-73, March-April, 1961. There also seems to be a relationship between executive salaries, the profitability, and size (in sales volume) of the firm. See data in Harland Fox, *Top Executive Compensation,* The Conference Board, Report no. 501, 1970.

[30] Harland Fox, *op. cit.,* pp. 10 and 51. See also David W. Ewing and Don H. Fenn, Jr. (eds.), *Incentives for Executives,* McGraw-Hill Book Company, New York, 1962.

Stock options are another type of managerial incentive. Boards of directors give key managers rights to purchase company stock at the market price on a given date, and if the stock price rises, the rights can be exercised (under the new Internal Revenue rules) up to 5 years after the date the options were granted. Capital gains from the sale of the stock (at lower tax rates than would apply to salaries) can be realized 3 years after the stock is purchased. Almost 90 percent of the manufacturing firms in the NICB survey had these restricted stock option plans in 1969.

Finally, there are various forms of deferred executive compensation, including pensions, bonus plans, salary payments, and profit-sharing increments, usually after retirement. These have been developed because of high marginal income tax rates on executive salaries, but they constitute a form of incentive for the executive to remain with the firm and seek to increase its profits.

In short, these plans do have the incentive value of identifying top management's personal financial gain with the profitability of the company. Most of the increase in total managerial compensation since the end of the Second World War has been in these supplements to base salaries. The incentive significance of this fact has been summarized in a recent study in these words: "Since all stock options and many deferred pay contracts and profit-sharing arrangements use the corporation's common stock as the compensation medium, their top officers' economic fortunes are closely linked with those of shareholders. . . . The alleged separation of present-day ownership and management objectives seems, in short, to be vastly overstated."[31]

When stock prices go down, however, stock options issued at higher prices lose some of their appeal. Nevertheless, about 90 percent of the 100 largest United States corporations give stock op-

tions to their executives; fewer have profit sharing, and still fewer have executive cash bonuses. If payouts are based on yearly company or division profits, however, they may reward hard-driving executives who increase short-run profits at the expense of maintaining the loyalty and motivation of the "human assets" of the organization. This is the point made by Rensis Likert in calling for some form of "human resource accounting," mentioned in earlier chapters.

Advancing Individuals within Rate Ranges or Salary Grades

Leaving aside the exceptional individual salaries and additional increments for exceptional people, most jobs and positions carry *ranges* instead of single rates. Rate ranges are needed where jobs and positions are grouped in broad grades or classifications, and some procedure is used for advancing the wages or salaries of individuals within these ranges. In other words, if the rate range for all-round machinists is $3.50 to $4 an hour, how can John Jones, who now receives $3.65, get a higher rate within the range? Or, how can Mary Smith, a keypunch operator whose job is in salary grade III, get an increase (see Figure 20-2)? On what basis can William Green, a production manager, expect an increase within his job's salary range?

There are two bases for making individual increases within these ranges, merit and length of service. The latter is subject to the same objection that has been made against seniority as the sole factor in promotions: the reward for superior performance is reduced. However, if merit or performance is to be the sole or major factor in making individual increases decisions ought to be based on something more reliable than the supervisor's offhand opinion

Most firms faced with this problem have adopted a performance-appraisal plan, which was discussed in Chapter 16. A poorly conceived and poorly administered appraisal plan, however, can be only a slight improvement on haphazard judgments, and it may be worse. If the fairness of merit increases is widely questioned, it

[31] Wilbur G. Lewellen, "Executives Lose Out, Even with Options," *Harvard Business Review,* vol. 46, no. 1, p. 134, January–February, 1968. See also Lewellen, *Executive Compensation in Large Industrial Corporations,* National Bureau of Economic Research, Inc., New York, 1968.

may be expected that employees (and their union representatives) will press for automatic length-of-service increases of single rates for everyone on the job.

Faced with a demand for length-of-service increases to the top of each rate range, some companies have negotiated a compromise that takes into account the advantage of partial recognition of seniority and yet retains a merit incentive. Under this plan, increases to the midpoint of the range are made automatically on a length-of-service basis, and increases above the midpoint are made on a merit basis.

Rate ranges for different jobs are usually known and communicated, especially in unionized firms; but salary grade ranges, particularly for professional and managerial jobs, are less widely known. However, secrecy would seem to defeat the very purpose of establishing equitable salary relationships.

Rates on "Women's Jobs"

The matter of "women's rates" is also a problem in wage and salary administration. Should women be paid less than men on the same jobs? Job evaluation helps to answer this question. If the content of the job as performed by women is identical with the content of the job as performed by men, there should be no difference whatever in their rates. Discrimination on the basis of sex, in other words, has no place in good wage and salary administration.[32] If certain adjustments are made in the job to accommodate women employees, such as special lifting devices, etc., then the rate should be based on the job content as evaluated in relation to the con-

tent of other jobs. In this sense, "women's jobs" may carry a lower rate than "men's jobs," but these exceptions are becoming less frequent. While there may be some jobs on which women should not be employed, women are working on more and more jobs, formerly held only by men.

THE GROWING IMPORTANCE OF WAGE AND SALARY SUPPLEMENTS

An important part of wage and salary administration is keeping some control over the growth of wage and salary supplements, popularly known as "fringe benefits." We have already noted that wage and salary surveys must take into account differences in fringe-benefit payments between companies. A firm which pays generous benefits may also pay lower basic rates, although generally the relationship is a positive rather than a negative one. Employers able to pay higher wages also often provide generous wage and salary supplements.

In addition to legally required payments (such as unemployment compensation and old-age insurance contributions), there is a growing trend toward employer-financed sickness, accident, and hospitalization benefits, life insurance, and retirement pensions. Then there are paid rest periods, lunch periods, washup time, travel time to and from work, etc.; and specific payments for time not worked such as vacations, holidays, jury juty, etc. Finally, some reports on wage and salary supplements include profit sharing, Christmas bonuses, company payments for union steward time in settling grievances, etc. Figure 20-3 shows the trend in these fringe benefits every two years, 1949–1969, as reported for 146 identical companies by the Chamber of Commerce of the United States.

As a percentage of the payroll, these supplementary payments have increased from nearly 18 percent to nearly 32 percent—a *percentage* increase of about 60 percent since 1949. The reasons for this are complex. Employees pay no income taxes on these benefits, and even if they contribute partly to the cost by direct contribu-

[32] Many union agreements provide for "equal pay for equal work" in an attempt to prevent discrimination in wages between men and women on comparable jobs. Some states have also passed laws requiring equal pay for equal work, designed to eliminate this discrimination, and a federal "equal pay for equal work" act was passed in 1963 effective June 11, 1964. Within a given plant, the principle can be defended, but if it is applied more broadly to all firms in an industry, other questions arise. What is "equal work"? Should financial condition or the local labor market have no influence on rates paid for similar jobs in different localities?

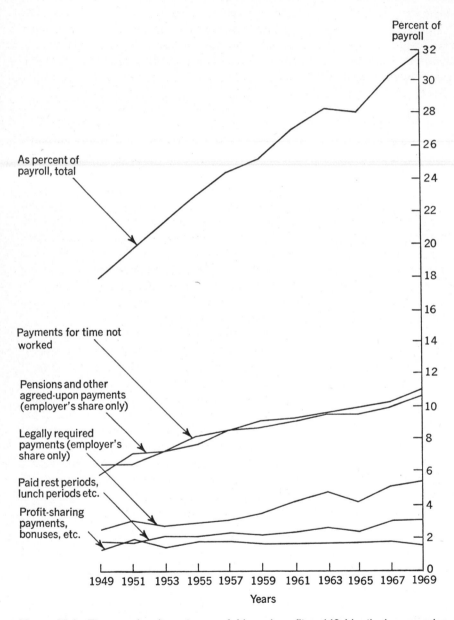

Figure 20-3 The growing importance of fringe benefits—146 identical companies. (*Source:* Employee Benefits, 1969, *research study prepared by Economic Analysis Study Group, Chamber of Commerce of the United States, Washington, D.C., 1970. The report is published every two years; 1971 data were not available in time for inclusion in the chart.*)

tions or by receiving these benefits in lieu of wage and salary increases, they get more for their money in group plans than they could buy in protection individually. Individual employees may also have different reasons for preferring various types of fringe benefits to money in the paycheck.[33] Employers also benefit because fringes do not enter into basic rates and thus do not increase overtime payments, holiday and Saturday or Sunday premium pay, etc.

Most managers try to keep wage and salary supplements in line through surveys of what other comparable firms and industries pay. But some are always in the forefront, providing more generous benefits than their competitors. In part, this may be an attempt to attract better employees to the company and to keep good ones from leaving. In part, it may be a kind of "new paternalism," especially in nonunion firms which hope to remain unorganized. It is a curious fact that the large firms, which have higher wage and salary levels than smaller ones, also provide more generous wage and salary supplements. Are these really necessary to attract and hold superior employees? Whether they are or not, the prospect is that fringe benefits will grow and spread in the next decade.[34]

RESPONSIBILITY FOR WAGE AND SALARY ADMINISTRATION

The responsibility of line management for getting effective results with people obviously includes the responsibility for establishing equitable wage and salary relationships. It should not be delegated exclusively to a staff group. Line managers are vitally concerned with the wages and salaries that are paid to the people they supervise, so that permanent or rotating membership on a job evaluation or salary administration committee is an important managerial commitment.

The personnel department or the wage and salary administrator and job analysts on his staff may train and assist the evaluation committee in its work, but they should not perform the line function of actually evaluating jobs and setting proper rates. Continuing administration of the program should also be a committee responsibility, assisted by the personnel department in calling attention to new and changed jobs and by providing necessary data.[35]

When wage and salary administration involves individual merit increases within rate ranges established by job evaluation, it is also important that the personnel department not usurp line authority. In one firm, for example, all increases within rate ranges had to be approved by the personnel department, and supervisors soon acquired the habit of telling an employee who sought a raise, "Well, Fred, I'd like to give one to you, but it has to have the OK of the personnel department, and they've been turning me down lately." The proper role of the personnel department should be to assist management in developing and administering a performance appraisal program on which individual merit increases may be based. But each supervisor and

[33] For a review of various studies, see Richard A. Lester, "Benefits as a Preferred Form of Compensation," *Southern Economic Journal,* vol. 33, no. 4, pp. 488–495, April, 1967 (reprinted in Pigors, Myers, and Malm, *op. cit.,* selection 42). The implications are discussed in Haire, Ghiselli, and Porter, *op. cit.,* pp. 5–6 (reprinted in Pigors, Myers, and Malm, *op. cit.,* selection 37). For another study, see Jay R. Schuster, "Another Look at Compensation Preferences," *Industrial Management Review,* vol. 10, no. 3, pp. 1–18, Spring, 1969.

[34] See Glenn A. Bassett and Harlow A. Nelson, "Keys to Better Salary Administration," *Personnel,* vol. 44, no. 2, pp. 23–30, March–April, 1967.

[35] For a detailed prediction, see T. J. Gordon and R. E. LeBlue, "Employee Benefits, 1970–1985," *Harvard Business Review,* vol. 48, no. 1, pp. 93–107, January–February, 1970. (A summary is reprinted in Pigors, Myers, and Malm, *op. cit.,* selection 43.) A careful study of private pensions plans showed that in 1965 only 13 to 14 percent of persons over 65 received income support from this source and predicted that by 1980 only 15 percent of males and 15 to 18 percent of females would receive private pensions. See Daniel M. Holland, *Private Pension Funds: Projected Growth,* Occasional Paper 97, National Bureau of Economic Research, New York, 1966.

manager should know the limits of his authority to make these increases and which are subject to the approval of his own superior in the line organization. The wage and salary administration unit in the personnel department may perform a coordinating function, but it should not exercise control directly.[36] This is a line responsibility.

Whether union representatives should participate directly and have joint responsibility for determining relative job rates on jobs within the bargaining unit and for putting them into effect is a moot question. Some unions actively oppose the introduction and continuance of job evaluation. Most unions take the position that they should be consulted on the basic principles of the plan and that they should be kept informed of each step, but they oppose full joint participation. They feel this would put union representatives in the position of having to argue against their own constituents if union members subsequently objected to rates set under the plan. These unions prefer to retain their position as critics and present complaints against specific results of the program.

On the other hand, a few unions have supported joint union-management job evaluation. These have involved successful attempts to establish mutually determined job classification systems through contract negotiations and joint committees.[37]

[36] One personnel department used PERT (Program Evaluation and Review Technique) to install more quickly a job evaluation program for 1,110 salaried positions in a technically based firm. The final PERT network was used in meetings with division and department heads to explain the steps in the program. Glenn H. Varney and Gerard F. Carvalho, "PERT in the Personnel Department," *Personnel,* vol. 45, no. 1, pp. 48–53, January–February, 1968.

[37] For an account of a negotiated classification structure in an automated plant, see Ken Bannon and Nelson Samp, "The Impact of Automation on Wages and Working Conditions in Ford Motor Company-UAW Relationship," in *Automation and Major Technological Change,* AFL-CIO, Industrial Union Department, Washington, D.C., 1958, pp. 13–27. The Tennessee Valley Authority handles job classification problems through a joint union-management committee prior to negotiations. James D. Schneider, "Collective Bargain-

SUMMARY

Two principal aspects of the wage and salary question have been considered in this chapter: (1) determination of the general level of wages and salaries and (2) internal wage and salary relationships. The first is an important top-management responsibility; in unionized firms, periodic negotiations on wages with union representatives are necessary. The second also requires the attention of line officials, with the personnel department acting as a service and advisory agency in securing the job descriptions and analyses that are necessary for thoroughgoing job evaluation.

Four factors are important in determining the general level of wages and changes in it: (1) wages paid for comparable work by other firms in the community or in the industry; (2) financial condition of the firm, particularly as affected by managerial efficiency and labor productivity; (3) "cost of living"; and (4) governmental intervention, such as minimum-wage laws or governmental dispute settlement. The personnel department is expected to keep informed on these factors and especially to assist management in making periodic wage and salary surveys.

Internal wage and salary relationships affect employee morale and performance and some systematic policies and methods of determining differentials between jobs are needed to avoid a chaotic wage and salary structure. Increasing use is being made, therefore, of job evaluation, although sometimes its basic limitations are overlooked. These limitations are particularly impor-

ing in the Field of Job Classification," *Personnel,* vol. 30, no. 1, pp. 49–53, July, 1954. See also Jack Stieber, *The Steel Industry Wage Structure: A Study of the Joint Union-Management Job Evaluation Program in the Basic Steel Industry,* Harvard University Press, Cambridge, Mass., 1959; and Sumner H. Slichter, James J. Healy, and E. Robert Livernash, *The Impact of Collective Bargaining on Management,* The Brookings Institution, Washington, D.C., 1960, chap. 19, "Evaluated Rate Structures," pp. 558–590.

tant when an attempt is made to apply job evaluation to professional and managerial jobs, which do not easily lend themselves to standard job evaluation procedures. There are special problems in executive compensation.

Finally, wage and salary supplements (fringe benefits) are an important part of the process of wage and salary administration. So are incentive systems of payment and other ways of sharing productivity gains. These are considered in the next chapter.

SELECTED REFERENCES

Beal, Edwin F.: "In Praise of Job Evaluation," *California Management Review,* vol. 5, no. 3, pp. 8-17, Summer, 1963 (reprinted in Paul Pigors, Charles A. Myers, and F. T. Malm, *Management of Human Resources: Readings in Personnel Administration,* 3d ed., McGraw-Hill Book Company, 1973, selection 38).

Belcher, David W.: *Wage and Salary Administration,* 2d ed., Prentice-Hall, Inc., Englewood Cliffs, N.J., 1962.

Dunn, J. D., and Frank M. Rachel: *Wage and Salary Administration: Total Compensation Systems,* McGraw-Hill Book Company, New York, 1971.

Gray, Robert D.: *A Guide to Systematic Wage and Salary Administration,* California Institute of Technology, Industrial Relations Section, Bulletin 29, Pasadena, Calif., 1959.

Haire, Mason, Edwin E. Ghiselli, and Lyman W. Porter: "Psychological Research on Pay: An Overview," *Industrial Relations,* vol. 3, no. 1, pp. 3-8, October, 1963 (reprinted in Pigors, Myers, and Malm, *op. cit.,* selection 37).

Lanham, Elizabeth: *Administration of Wages and Salaries,* Harper & Row, Publishers, Incorporated, New York, 1963.

Lawler, Edward E. III: *Pay and Organizational Effectiveness: A Psychological View,* McGraw-Hill Book Company, New York, 1971.

Lester, Richard A.: "Benefits as a Preferred Form of Compensation," *Southern Economic Journal,* vol. 33, no. 4, April, 1967 (reprinted in Pigors, Myers, and Malm, *op. cit.,* selection 42).

———:*Company Wage Policies: A Survey of Patterns and Experience,* Princeton University, Industrial Relations Section, Princeton, N.J., 1948.

Livernash, E. Robert: "Wage Administration and Production Standards," in Arthur Kornhauser, Robert Dubin, and Arthur M. Ross (eds.), *Industrial Conflict,* McGraw-Hill Book Company, New York, 1954, pp. 330-334 (reprinted in Pigors, Myers, and Malm, *op. cit.,* selection 39).

Nealey, Stanley M.: "Pay and Benefit Preference," *Industrial Relations,* vol. 3, no. 1, pp. 17-28, October, 1963.

Opsahl, Robert L., and Marvin D. Dunnette: "The Role of Financial Compensation in Industrial Motivation," *Psychological Bulletin,* vol. 66, no. 2, pp. 94-118, August, 1966.

Otis, Jay L., and Richard H. Leukart: *Job Evaluation,* 2d ed., Prentice-Hall, Inc., Englewood Cliffs, N.J., 1954.

Patton, John A., C. L. Littlefield, and Stanley A. Self: *Job Evaluation: Text and Cases,* 3rd ed., Richard D. Irwin, Inc., Homewood, Ill., 1964.

Riegel, John W.: *Administration of Salaries for Engineers and Scientists;* and *Intangible Rewards for Engineers and Scientists,* University of Michigan, Bureau of Industrial Relations, Ann Arbor, Mich., 1958.

Sibson, Robert E.: *Wages and Salaries: A Handbook for Line Managers,* rev. ed., American Management Association, New York, 1967.

Slichter, Sumner H., James J. Healy, and E. Robert Livernash: *The Impact of Collective Bargaining on Management,* The Brookings Institution, Washington, D.C., 1960, chaps. 19 and 20.

Wiseman, Sylvia: "Wage Criteria for Collective Bargaining," *Industrial and Labor Relations Review,* vol. 9, no. 2, pp. 252-267, 1956.

Chapter 21

Pay Incentive Systems; Sharing Productivity Gains

The challenging opportunities that are inherent in every industrial organization for people to assume responsibility, achieve status, acquire new skills, learn, develop, exercise creativity become apparent once this area of collaboration is carved out. The idea that workers are paid to do what they are told and management is paid to tell them not only prevents effective collaboration but automatically creates the feeling of psychological failure. It leads either to indifferent passivity or to active hostility. Genuine participation in problem solving removes the causes of these common reactions.

Douglas McGregor [1]

As productivity has increased, gains have been shared with employees through general wage and salary increases, pay incentive systems, and other methods. But *how* to share these gains in a way that will develop an enthusiastic and willing work force is a persistent problem for management. Should all the gains go to employees, or only some proportion? How can we measure the gains in productivity? What approaches and what methods of gain sharing will encourage employees toward still higher productivity? These are among the perplexing questions which continue to face American management and unions, as well as those of other industrial countries. All members of line management and staff specialists, such as the personnel administrator and the industrial engineer, need to be informed on possible approaches in dealing with these continuing problems. This chapter will discuss the uses

[1] Douglas McGregor, "The Scanlon Plan through a Psychologist's Eyes," in Frederick G. Lesieur (ed.), *The Scanlon Plan: A Frontier in Labor-Management Cooperation,* p. 92, John Wiley & Sons, Inc., New York, and the M.I.T. Press, Cambridge, Mass., 1958.

and limitations of pay incentive systems and then consider alternative ways of sharing productivity gains.

DEVELOPING EMPLOYEE INTEREST IN HIGHER PRODUCTIVITY

Employee interest in higher productivity does not develop without some stimulation by management, either directly or through the creation of an atmosphere in which employees want to contribute their best efforts to the job. We have suggested earlier that most employees want to get satisfaction out of their work, but when they distrust management, they do less than they are capable of doing (or even restrict their output). Too often in the past, employees (and their unions) have felt that higher productivity benefited someone else other than themselves, and they have not been convinced that there is any direct relationship between higher productivity, lower costs, and increased sales on the one hand, and more job security and higher wage or salary incomes on the other hand. In many instances, employees seemed to get more satisfaction out of "putting one over" on management by withholding full effort than out of doing their best work in an atmosphere of management interest and approval.

When these attitudes and practices exist in any organization, they are difficult to change. Much of what we have discussed about managerial philosophies and personnel policies in the earlier chapters is relevant to this problem. We have also seen how job changes, resulting primarily from technological change, are resisted by employees under certain conditions and accepted under others—especially when management is able to communicate the need for the change and considers its human impact. Formal programs and industrial engineering techniques accomplish little without a management philosophy that welcomes and rewards employee ideas and efforts toward higher productivity and is

willing to share economic gains as well as job satisfactions with all employees who contribute to achievement of the common objectives of the organization. Unfortunately, some managements often lack these points of view.

When we talk about "productivity gains," we need to consider first what is meant by "labor productivity." The term is widely used, but the problems of measurement are less understood.

PRODUCTIVITY MEASUREMENTS AND THEIR SIGNIFICANCE

The most commonly used measurement of labor productivity is "output per man-hour" worked by production workers in manufacturing. This is computed by the U.S. Bureau of Labor Statistics for all manufacturing and also for certain industries.[2] This measure of "labor productivity" does not measure the efficiency of labor in the sense of increased effort alone, and indeed no overall measure of this is possible. What it does measure is the increase in output resulting from *all* factors that contribute to reducing labor input per unit of ouput—better and more efficient machinery, better work flow, reduced waste, improved processes, more skilled workers, *and* increased efficiency and effort by workers of the same skill. The latter may be relatively less important, because historically the largest increases in output per production man-hour have occurred because more and better machinery, i.e., capital, was introduced by management in the capital-labor mix. The production worker today, in other words, is working with vastly improved tools and

[2] For a fuller discussion of these points along with some examples, see Leon Greenberg, *Productivity and Technological Trends in the Private Economy, 1947-62,* statement presented to the Subcommittee on Employment and Manpower of the U.S. Senate Committee on Labor and Public Welfare, Sept. 26, 1963, U.S. Department of Labor, 1963; *Trends in Output per Man-hour in the Private Economy, 1909-1958,* U.S. Department of Labor, Bureau of Labor Statistics Bulletin 1249, 1960; and *Indexes of Output per Man-hour for the Private Economy, 1947-1965,* U.S. Department of Labor, October, 1966.

equipment, compared with the production worker in the same industry 25 or 50 years ago, and the output per worker is, therefore, correspondingly greater. His "real wages" (money wages adjusted by the Consumer Price Index) have increased as a consequence of higher labor productivity resulting from a number of factors, including his own skill improvement through prior education and training on the job.

One serious limitation of the productivity index related to output per production-worker man-hour in manufacturing is that the proportion of nonproduction employees, such as white-collar workers, research and development staffs, etc., has been increasing. The proportion of production workers to total output has been declining, and the productivity index therefore shows an upward bias. Furthermore, manufacturing is only part of the total economy, and "tertiary" industries such as services, trade, government, etc., are becoming relatively more important. The U.S. Bureau of Labor Statistics, therefore, has introduced estimates of productivity which measure real product per employee man-hour paid for in the private domestic economy. None of these is particularly useful to labor and management in a particular wage negotiation or to management in deciding whether to offer a wage or salary increase. This is equally true of the more widely known "output per man-hour" productivity index, even though both unions and managements often cite this index as justification for their positions on wage increases. Instead, these measurements are useful guideposts for the long-run trends of wages and salaries in the private nonfarm economy.

Furthermore, when productivity measurements are available for a particular industry, there are good reasons for *not* precisely adjusting wage and salary changes *in that industry* to changes in the industry's labor productivity index. If this were done for each industry, wages and salaries would be increased when an industry's productivity was rising, and not increased when an industry's productivity was unchanged or falling. The distortion of the wage and salary structure that would result from such year-to-year adjustments is obvious. Economic analysis suggests that a noninflationary wage and salary policy requires increases in line with long-run changes in productivity for the economy as a whole, so that greater-than-average productivity increases in a particular industry will result in price reductions (or quality improvements at the same price) to offset the necessary price increases in other industries where productivity increases lag behind the national average and where wage and salary increases must therefore be reflected in higher costs and prices.[3]

A familiar example is the cost of haircuts; these have risen substantially in recent years because barbers' wages have increased in line with other wage increases, even though their "productivity" has not risen as compared with the productivity of manufacturing workers. In competitive manufacturing industries, product prices have fallen or product quality has risen. If price competition were more widespread throughout the economy, the gains from higher productivity would be shared among employees, consumers, and investors (who gain through higher dividends or enhanced common-stock values if some earnings are reinvested in the business).

In practice, long-run productivity gains seem to have been shared more with employees and investors than with consumers. Falling product and service prices have not been nearly as conspicuous over the past 25 years as have rising real wages and increased stock values. Furthermore, it is also true that wages and salaries are higher in those industries which have experienced the greatest increases in labor productivity, such as

[3] See Alvin H. Hansen, *Economic Policy and Full Employment,* McGraw-Hill Book Company, New York, 1947, pp. 241-243. This is the principle behind the Wage-Price Guideposts developed by the President's Council of Economic Advisors in 1962.

steel, automobiles, flat glass, etc. Thus, managements and unions have tended to negotiate agreements that share some of the increased productivity gains in the industry with the employees of that industry.[4] As we have seen in Chapter 20, "ability to pay" (which may reflect increased labor productivity as we have defined it) is always a factor in wage negotiations and even in unilateral wage determinations by management in the absence of unions. If higher-productivity industries are also expanding industries and need to attract more labor, then economists would agree that higher wages and salaries are necessary for optimum allocation of labor. But this allocation function is not always involved in wage decisions.

Within a plant or industry, some jobs are affected more by technological changes than others. In other words, labor productivity on these jobs increases faster than the average for the plant or industry as a whole. Some managements and unions agree to increase in wages or salaries on these jobs as a means of getting employee acceptance of the job changes. Perhaps unions tend to push for these more than management would like. If pushed very far, distortion of the wage and salary structure is inevitable.

A more rational method of sharing the gains from higher productivity on specific jobs affected by technological change is to generalize them throughout the work force in across-the-board wage and salary increases. As we have stressed above, these general changes should be related over the long run to the long-run growth of labor productivity in the economy as a whole, not in the particular industry.

[4] One study of the relationship between productivity and wage determination observed: "Our analysis of the wage determination process leads us to conclude that increases in productivity are most likely to result in higher wages by reducing the firm's resistance to wage pressures generated elsewhere. The probability of some increase in the general wage level via this avenue of impact is quite high." William G. Bowen, *The Wage-Price Issue: A Theoretical Analysis*, Princeton University Press, Princeton, N.J., 1960, p. 227.

The General Motors–United Automobile Workers Agreement

One important company, the General Motors Corporation, and one of the largest unions, the United Automobile Workers, signed a notable agreement in 1948 which included a method of sharing the gains from higher productivity in line with principles that we have discussed in the preceding section. This agreement contained two innovations: a cost-of-living escalator clause to protect real wages (mentioned in Chapter 20) and an "annual improvement factor" to increase real wages by a certain amount each year. At first this amount was 3 cents an hour, later increased to 4 cents in 1950, 5 cents in 1953, 2.5 percent of base pay (with a minimum of 6 cents) in the 1955 agreement (continued in the 1958 and 1961 agreements), and 2.8 percent in 1964. The 3-year agreement of 1967 changed the basis of the "improvement factor" from a flat percentage to a general wage increase of 9 to 18 cents, depending on the employee's base rate, effective November 25, 1968, and a similar increase November 24, 1969. This is in addition to the general wage increase effective October 16, 1967, and averages about 3 percent. The same principle was retained in the 1970 agreement. This amount was about equal in percentage terms to the long-term increase in national private nonfarm productivity, although the productivity increase in General Motors was probably greater than the national average.

The GM–UAW agreement contained the following significant clause, which has been incorporated in subsequent revisions of the agreement:

The annual improvement factor provided herein recognizes that a continuing improvement in the standard of living of employees depends upon technological progress, better tools, methods, process and equipment, and a cooperative attitude on the part of all parties in such progress. It further recognizes the principle that to produce more with the same amount of human effort is a sound economic and social objective.

The statements of the corporation and the union when this clause was first agreed upon are interesting. The corporation observed: "Both parties continue to subscribe to the principle that to make the annual improvement factor feasible, technological progress must be encouraged." The union said: "The 4 cents annual improvement factor guarantees the GM workers a share in the fruits of the nation's technological progress. Thus, the GM workers register a major advance in their struggle for progress with the community and not at the expense of the community."

This agreement was hailed by Charles E. Wilson, then president of General Motors, as "a very significant step ahead in labor-management relations [and] . . . full recognition that productivity is the key to progress." Some critics doubted the wisdom of such long-term agreements with deferred wage increases which a firm must pay regardless of its financial condition at a later time. But the General Motors Corporation did free itself of annual bargaining over wages, avoided strikes over these issues, and also gained the uncontested right to schedule production and establish production standards, which some other companies have forfeited in practice by creeping concessions to union pressure.

Partly as a consequence of union opposition, but also because of the nature of the production-line system, wage incentives are not found in the auto industry, and the "improvement factor" may be regarded as something of a company-wide substitute. However, wage-incentive systems are found in other industries and deserve some discussion as an alternative way of sharing increases in productivity with workers.

THE PROPER ROLE OF WAGE INCENTIVES

Wage incentives were first developed by industrial engineers. Prior to the "scientific-manage-ment" movement, led by Frederick W. Taylor, one of the first industrial engineers, the usual method of payment had been by the hour or by the day. Taylor and his followers believed that the worker would produce more if he were given an incentive to do so. Accordingly, a worker's pay should be increased in some proportion to increased output resulting from his own extra efforts. These ideas brought about wider adoption of piecework and other more intricate wage-incentive systems, as well as work measurement or timestudy, work simplification, and other industrial engineering techniques. Industrial engineering techniques for methods improvement are more widely used than are wage incentives as such; less than one-third of manufacturing jobs in the United States are paid on an incentive basis.[5] One of the reasons for this low percentage is that many jobs are not well adapted to wage incentives, another is that some unions oppose this method of wage payment, and still another is that some managements have turned to other methods of encouraging productivity increases.

Industrial engineers and others in the fore-front of the scientific-management movement have made notable *technical* contributions to incentive systems of payment. Unfortunately, however, *the human aspects of these systems have too often been neglected.* It is probably no exaggeration to say that the human problems involved in getting employee and union acceptance of new production standards and new wage-incentive rates or systems are both more important and more difficult to solve than the technical problems of developing and establishing (on paper) these standards, rates, and systems. Too often, engineers and management

[5] *Monthly Labor Review,* U.S. Department of Labor, 1960, p. 461, table 1, reprint no. 2341. This percentage has not changed much since the earlier survey in 1945 to 1946. Piecework is more widely used in European countries. For example, the proportion of hours worked on piecework was 58 percent in Sweden in 1949 and 70 percent in Hungary in the same year. *Payment by Results,* International Labour Office. Studies and Reports, no. 27, Geneva, 1951, p. 55.

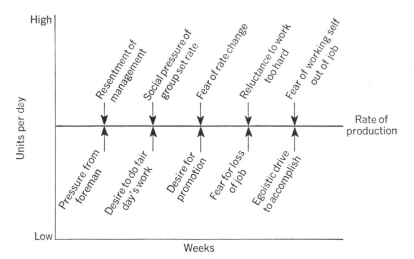

Figure 21-1 Forces affecting individual productivity and pay incentive plans. [*Source: Mason Haire,* Psychology in Management, *2d ed., McGraw-Hill Book Company, New York, 1964. Haire notes (p. 167): "One of the very important effects of this view of the level of production is that it at once becomes clear that it can be raised either by increasing the forces below the line or by reducing the forces above the line."*]

consultants have swept managers off their feet by extravagant promises of productivity gains and cost reductions under elaborate wage-incentive systems. As one writer has said, "It is the worst sort of oversimplification to assume, however, that the mere establishment of an incentive plan can motivate workers to higher output, reduce unit costs, and result in both higher employee earnings and greater company profits.[6]

It should also be repeated here that wage incentives are not the *only* effective incentives. Nonfinancial incentives—especially those which relate to the higher-level needs considered in Chapter 6—may be even more important as motivators for higher productivity. This is more likely to be true when wage and salary relationships are equitable and fairly administered, as we have seen in the preceding chapter. Some of the forces affecting productivity and wage-incentive plans are shown in Figure 21-1.

While the proportion of hours worked on wage incentives has not changed radically in the United States, many employers are having second thoughts about their usefulness in industries characterized by rapid technological change, automation of processes, and even under conditions of "creeping technology" which make it difficult to change incentive rates or to get employee acceptance of changes which may affect their earnings adversely.

These factors have accounted in part for the "demoralization" of some wage-incentive plans, especially under union pressure. Incentive plans become demoralized when there are "(1) substantial inequities in earnings and effort; . . . (2) a growing average incentive yield or bonus; . . . (3) a declining average level of effort; . . . (4) a high proportion of 'offstandard' payment and the . . ."[7] failure to administer an incentive plan after it is established.

[6] Robert E. Sibson, *Wages and Salaries: A Handbook for Line Managers,* rev. ed., American Management Association, New York, 1967, p. 150.

[7] Sumner H. Slichter, James J. Healy, and E. Robert Livernash, *The Impact of Collective Bargaining on Management,* The Brookings Institution, Washington, D.C., 1960, p. 497.

While automation has not widely affected industries in which piecework is common, such as clothing, shoes, and others with more stable technology, automation does change the nature of work by removing it from the direct control of employees.[8] In some cases, percentage of machine utilization may be the basis for incentive pay, but in others there is a movement back to either "measured daywork" related to several levels of production or straight daywork. In fewer cases, automated production may develop work teams which can be put on group incentives.

These changes and developments are important for management to consider carefully before it assumes that wage-incentive systems will always result in increased output and lower costs.[9] Under some conditions, wage incentives can bring these improvements, but they are not a panacea for poor management.

WHEN SHOULD WAGE INCENTIVES BE USED?

Methods of wage and salary payment fall into two basic groups: (1) payment on the basis of time—by the hour, day, week, month, or year—and (2) payment on the basis of output—by the piece or by time spent in completing a piece or a "unit." The relative advantages of each of the two basic methods of payment may be summarized in terms of the circumstances or situations under which each is to be preferred.[10]

1 *Payment on a time basis is more satisfactory when:*
   • Units of output are not distinguishable and measurable.
   • Employees have little control over the quantity of output or there is no clear-cut relation between effort and output, as on some machine-paced jobs.
   • Work delays are frequent and beyond employees' control.
   • Quality of work is especially important.
   • Supervision is good, and supervisors know what constitutes "a fair day's work."
   • Competitive conditions and cost control do not require precise advance knowledge of labor costs per unit of output.
2 *Payment on the basis of output is more satisfactory when:*
   • Units of output are measurable.
   • A clear relation exists between employee effort and quantity of output.
   • The job is standardized, the flow of work is regular, and breakdowns are few or, if many, consistent.
   • Quality considerations are less important than quantity of output or at least are uniform and measurable.
   • Supervision is unsatisfactory, or supervisors cannot devote enough attention to individual performance.
   • Competitive conditions and cost control make it imperative that labor costs per unit be definite and fixed in advance, as in the shoe and garment industries.

---

[8] "Broadly speaking, automation tends to transfer control over the rate of production from the worker to the machine. Hence it tends to undermine the basic rationale of incentive payment." Charles C. Killingsworth, "Industrial Relations and Automation," *Annals of the American Academy of Political and Social Science,* vol. 340, p. 77, March, 1962. James R. Bright puts it even more strongly; he asserts that in automated plants, "Piecework does not seem to be appropriate; incentive systems seem pointless." *Automation and Management,* Harvard Business School, Division of Research, Boston, 1958, p. 208.

[9] For further discussion of points to be considered, see Richard E. Crandall, "Deemphasized Wage Incentives," *Harvard Business Review,* vol. 40, no. 2, pp. 113–116, March-April, 1962; and Garth L. Mangum, "Are Wage Incentives Becoming Obsolete?," *Industrial Relations,* vol. 2, no. 1, pp. 73–96, 1962 (reprinted in Paul Pigors, Charles A. Myers, and F. T. Malm, *Management of Human Resources: Readings in Personnel Administration,* 3d ed., McGraw-Hill Book Company, New York, 1973, selection 40).

[10] For a fuller discussion of these differences, see Sumner H. Slichter, *Union Policies and Industrial Management,* The Brookings Institution, Washington, D.C., 1941, chap. 10. A subsequent study in 1960 concluded: "The advantages and disadvantages of piecework to workers, employers, and unions remain substantially as discussed in *Union Policies and Industrial Management.*" Slichter, Healy, and Livernash, *op. cit.,* p. 523.

Measured daywork combines some of both basic types of wage payment.[11] Production standards are still established, but they may be applied as "low task," "average task," or "high task" or other similar terms. Employees are paid on a time basis. The foreman or supervisor thus has the responsibility for seeing that employees give a fair day's work by meeting the average or attainable standard. A higher time rate of pay is given for achieving the "high task" or "ultimate" standard. Under measured daywork, production standards are also useful to management in establishing cost controls, quite apart from any incentive aspect. Furthermore, some firms claim that measured daywork cuts down employee resistance to changes in methods and equipment, because earnings are not directly affected by these changes.

Clearly, then, payment on the basis of output (wage incentive) is not best under all circumstances. Even where basic conditions seem to favor it, a wage-incentive system needs to be carefully considered before it is introduced. *It is not a panacea for poor morale and low output.*

EMPLOYEE AND UNION ATTITUDES ON WAGE INCENTIVES

When management concludes that some form of wage incentive is desirable, industrial engineers are usually called in to advise and assist in the installation of a plan. The technical aspects of the installation receive considerable attention, and if a system appears to be sound technically, some managements assume that employees should accept it without protest. They forget, however, that a system that depends upon human effort requires for its success more than a knowledge of mathematics and industrial engineering. It is necessary not only that such a system *be* fair but that employees *believe* it to be fair. They have an almost uncanny ability for

devising ways to "beat the system" once they have made up their minds that it is not in their best interest to cooperate. This may take the form of restricting output below what management expects under the new system, to protect the weaker members of the group against discipline or layoff, or in some cases to hold out for a "looser" rate. Unions often help to reinforce these beliefs and practices and challenge managerial authority.

Technical specialists are often unwilling to accept as facts to be reckoned with the attitudes and sentiments of employees toward timestudy and wage incentives. Yet, since the success of these methods depends upon employee acceptance, the personnel administrator should help the technical men and supervisors to discover workers' attitudes in a specific situation and to take them into account in the installation. The person-centered approach is useful in this field, as in all other situations where people are at work. Union representatives should be consulted in advance for worker reactions before grievances develop.

Employee and union attitudes toward timestudy and wage incentives differ from firm to firm and from industry to industry, but some of the fairly prevalent beliefs held by workers and union representatives may be outlined in general terms:[12]

1 A belief that many wage-incentive plans are so complicated that even the experts cannot explain them. As one worker said, "Nobody ever told us how those standards were figured or how we figure our pay. Sometimes we get different

---

[11] For fuller discussion, see Slichter, Healy, and Livernash, *op. cit.,* chap. 18, "Measured Daywork," pp. 530-557.

[12] For examples of worker and union reactions to wage-incentive systems and the industrial engineering techniques used by some managements to establish production standards, see Orvis Collins, Melville Dalton, and Donald Roy, "Restriction of Output and Social Cleavage in Industry," *Applied Anthropology,* vol. 5, no. 3, pp. 1-14, Summer, 1946 (reprinted in Pigors, Myers, and Malm, *op. cit.,* selection 41). For a fuller discussion, see William F. Whyte, *Money and Motivation: An Analysis of Incentives in Industry,* Harper & Row, Publishers, Incorporated, New York, 1955.

pay for the same work, so I don't think they [the engineers] know what it's all about either."

2 A conviction that standards are set unfairly, by using fast workers, juggling allowances, underrating "effort," and selecting the shorter times to be used in computing the standard.

3 The fear of a rate cut and "speed-up" if good earnings are made after a rate is established. Sometimes this belief is held even though workers can cite no actual instance when it has occurred; they have just "heard about" it. Yet the statement, "They'll cut your rate," is a powerful deterrent to increased output and a justification in workers' eyes for restriction of output by pegging it at some fixed figure. The "rate buster" who ignores the sentiments of the group and goes "all out" to increase his output is often hated and ostracized by the group.[13]

4 Unfavorable experiences with wide variations in incentive earnings caused by management's failure to maintain a steady flow of materials, equipment in good condition, and other job conditions on which the computation of the incentive rate was based. This leads to inequities between the earnings on different incentive jobs and is a frequent source of grievances.[14]

5 The difficulties of understanding and policing all changes in rates that are necessary in a firm or industry where methods and processes are constantly changing. The administrative burden on union stewards and officers is sometimes so great that they come to oppose wage incentives entirely, unless they have confidence in the fairness of the company's management and procedures.

When such attitudes exist, management gains nothing by ignoring them or brushing them aside

as "illogical" or "unreasonable." The problem for management is: What can be done to reduce or eliminate these "unfavorable" attitudes?

REQUIREMENTS OF A GOOD WAGE-INCENTIVE SYSTEM

From the record of experience in installing and administering wage-incentive systems, it is possible to list some of the requirements for success. The ability of management to meet many of these requirements will depend upon the background of the company's personnel and labor relations. If management has been fair and reasonable in the past, future problems are easier to solve, as in the case of job changes (Chapter 19), communication and participation are important elements of a successful introduction.

1 Discussion of the need for a wage-incentive system with the supervisors and employees who will be affected and an explanation of the proposed system *before* installation begins. In unionized firms, this means consultation with union representatives and then, in cooperation with these representatives, further explanation with individual employees on the job.

2 A wage-incentive system must be simple and understandable to the employees. Complexity is one of the basic drawbacks in many of the wage-incentive systems that have logical appeal to some engineers. If the employee cannot understand how his pay is figured, the incentive is largely wasted.[15]

---

[13] For specific examples, see Collins, Dalton, and Roy, *loc. cit.* These psychological implications of "economic" incentive systems of payment are brought out by Mason Haire, *Psychology in Management,* 2d ed., McGraw-Hill Book Company, New York, 1964, chap. 6, especially pp. 155-158, 171-174.

[14] See E. Robert Livernash, "Wage Administration and Production Standards," in Arthur Kornhauser, Robert Dubin, and Arthur M. Ross (eds.), *Industrial Conflict,* McGraw-Hill Book Company, New York, 1954 (reprinted in Pigors, Myers, and Malm, *op. cit.,* selection 39).

[15] Some types of wage-incentive plans meet this requirement; others do not. For detailed descriptions of the various types, see J. K. Louden and J. Wayne Deegen, *Wage Incentives,* John Wiley & Sons, Inc., New York, 1959; Charles W. Lytle, *Wage Incentive Methods, Their Selection, Installation, and Operation,* rev. ed., The Ronald Press Company, New York, 1942; *Payment by Results,* International Labour Office, Geneva, 1951; and William B. Wolf, *Wage Incentives as a Managerial Tool,* Columbia University Press, New York, 1957. A good review of the research on wage incentives is found in Edward E. Lawler III, *Pay and Organizational Effectiveness: A Psychological View,* McGraw-Hill Book Company, New York, 1971, chap. 7.

3 The job or jobs must be standardized as much as possible, to determine the best and most efficient method of doing the job with the existing or new equipment. This may involve motion study and work simplification *before* a standard and rate are set on the job. If the job is timed and a rate set before the prior steps are taken, short cuts are soon discovered, the rate becomes known among workers as a "loose" rate, and earnings either rise out of line with other jobs or the operators "take it easy" and peg production to avoid detection.[16]

4 The standard of output (the "task"), on which incentive earnings are based, must be determined by competent timestudy methods, by the use of standard data based on predetermined time values, or from records of past performance, if there have been no significant changes in job methods on a job that has already been standardized. Timestudy is the most widely used procedure, but it involves a number of judgments or "guesstimates," and the validity of its results depends as much on these as on the actual stopwatch readings.[17]

[16] For an interesting example of the use of "kitties" earned on easier jobs to even out earnings on tight jobs, see Chris Argyris, "Organizational Effectiveness under Stress," *Harvard Business Review,* vol. 38, no. 5, pp. 137-146, May-June, 1960.

[17] Some of the limitations of timestudy methods have led to the use of "work-sampling" techniques within recent years. See Ralph M. Barnes, *Work Sampling,* 2d ed., John Wiley & Sons, Inc., New York, 1957. The variation in timestudy results that can occur is illustrated by the example of a simultaneous timestudy made by 11 men. One set a standard 11 percent above the average for the group and another set a standard 12 percent below the average—a spread of 23 percent. After a series of training conferences, in which emphasis was put on training in effort rating, the variation was reduced to 9 percent. Ralph M. Barnes, "Is the Rate of Output Right?," in *Incentives for Management and Workers,* American Management Association, Production Series, no. 161, New York, 1945, p. 15. For an excellent discussion of the limitations of theory and practice in timestudy, especially from the union viewpoint, see William Gomberg (formerly director, Management Engineering Department, International Ladies Garment Workers Union), *A Trade Union Analysis of Time Study,* 2d ed., Prentice-Hall, Inc., Englewood Cliffs, N.J., 1955; and Bertram Gottlieb, *The Art of Time Study: An Exercise of Personal Judgment,* Center for Labor and Management, University of Iowa, Iowa City, Iowa, 1966. For other treatments of time- and

5 An hourly (or "base" or "standard") rate should be established for each job on incentive pay, preferably by job evaluation. This rate should be guaranteed on an hourly or daily basis, or there should be some sort of payment for "waiting time" caused by delays beyond the control of the operator. When the method of payment on the job is changed from a time to an output basis, the time rate is usually the guaranteed rate. It is expected that operators will earn, on an average, 20 to 30 percent more than the guaranteed rate, depending upon the type of work. Piece rates or bonus rates are set with this objective in mind.

6 Earnings above standard or "task," as set by timestudy or records of past performance, should be in direct proportion to the increase in output above standard. Variable relationships at different levels of output are confusing and therefore undesirable. Paying the worker 100 percent of what he produces above the standard ("100 percent sharing") is also generally preferable.

7 There should be a clear system for inspecting, counting, and recording the output of each individual or group, and results should be posted daily, if possible, so that employees know just what they have produced. This will enable them to compute or estimate their earnings, thus increasing the incentive effect.

8 After standards and rates have been established, they should be guaranteed against changes, *except* when there are substantial changes in methods, materials, or equipment. Thus, higher-than-average earnings, due to the superior skill or ingenuity of certain employees, should never be the occasion for an increase in the standard and a reduction in the rate. But if changes introduced by management are responsible for increased earnings, the standard and

motion-study techniques, see Ralph M. Barnes, *Motion and Time Study,* 5th ed., John Wiley & Sons, Inc., New York, 1963; Benjamin W. Niebel, *Motion and Time Study,* 4th ed., Richard D. Irwin, Inc., Homewood, Ill., 1967; Gerald Nadler, *Motion and Time Study,* McGraw-Hill Book Company, New York, 1955; and Marvin E. Mundel, *Motion and Time Study: Principles and Practice,* 4th ed., Prentice-Hall, Inc., Englewood Cliffs, N.J., 1970.

rate *must* be revised to prevent inequities from creeping into the system. They should be revised, however, only to the extent that definite changes in equipment, methods, or materials have been made. Fairness in this respect is essential to success with wage-incentive administration; otherwise employees have reason to suspect management's good faith.

9 There should be careful follow-up to see that production standards are maintained or exceeded or, if they are not, to determine the reasons. Failure to meet standards and reach expected earnings may not be the fault of the employees. Management may be to blame because of improper training, poor equipment, or unequal flow of materials; these possibilities should be investigated first. *The deterioration of wage incentives, as standards are loosened and inequities develop, is the number 1 hazard to their continued effectiveness.*

10 Employees should be encouraged to go to their supervisor and to use the grievance procedure promptly when they think that conditions under the new standard and rate are not right.

11 The incentive plan should cover all employees whose jobs can be adapted to the incentive method of payment. Otherwise, dissatisfaction will result among those employees who have no opportunity to participate in the higher earnings possible under an incentive plan.

There may also be complaints among indirect workers, such as maintenance and service employees, who are paid hourly rates and yet have to work harder because of the increased output under the incentive system of production workers. This is hardly conducive to good teamwork. In some cases, difficulties arising under such incomplete coverage have led to group and plant-wide incentive systems. Furthermore, except for outside salesmen, it is difficult to put white-collar and professional employees on incentives, although incentives have been established separately when favorable conditions are present.[18]

GROUP AND PLANT-WIDE INCENTIVES

Individual incentives are still the most widely used type of pay incentive plan, but when it is difficult to measure individual performance, group and sometimes plant-wide incentive plans may be more appropriate. This may be particularly true in automating plants where machine operators have little or no control over their rate of production. Automation emphasizes the continuous nature of the production process rather than a highly specialized (and measurable) functional operation. Furthermore, as an alternative to individual incentives, group piecework or group bonuses for output above an established standard have the following advantages:

- Individual members of the group do not bear the whole loss if they happen to get a job with a "tight" rate or a job that requires more care than the average because of special technical difficulties.
- Charges of "favoritism" in the assignment of "fat" and "lean" jobs are therefore less likely to occur.
- The members of the group have an incentive for training new members and for helping each other, since individual earnings depend upon the total output of the group, apportioned according to hourly or base rates. The tendency of fast workers under individual incentives to withhold job secrets or short cuts from others is thus averted.

In any incentive system, whether it be individual, group, or plant-wide, management must face the fundamental question: *Will the incentive plan actually stimulate greater production and employee earnings, so that both employer and employee gain; or will it be the occasion for misunderstandings, friction, decreased production, and*

---

[18] J. A. Williams, "A Master Plan for Office Incentives," *Administrative Management*, vol. 26, no. 4, pp. 28–32, April, 1965. General Foods has established office incentive pay when at least four employees do interchangeable work, the rate of production is largely under the control of the employee, there is a continuous supply of work, and the work procedure is governed by definite rules. Work measurement is

spreading into offices, particularly on high-volume, repetitive office work. For a discussion of incentive systems for compensating outside salesmen, see Thomas H. Patten, "Trends in Pay Practices for Salesmen," *Personnel*, vol. 45, no. 1, pp. 54–63, January–February, 1968. Patten noted that salary plus commission or bonus (or both) had largely replaced straight-commission or straight-salary plans.

lower morale? The basic job conditions that exist, the background of personnel relations, and the manner in which the incentive system is introduced and administered will be important factors determining the answer to this question.

ANNUAL-WAGE AND GUARANTEED-EMPLOYMENT PLANS

Another method of paying wages and salaries involves guarantees over a period of time. These are not incentive plans in the narrow definition of the term, but they are based on the assumption that employees may work harder if they are secure in the knowledge that rates will not be cut or that they will not be laid off intermittently. There is a long but limited experience with genuine annual-wage and guaranteed-employment plans. The three most widely publicized plans in the past (Procter & Gamble Company, Nunn-Bush Shoe Company, and the George A. Hormel Company) grew out of the efforts of enlightened managements to provide greater regularity of employment and income for their employees.[19] Experience with these plans suggests that they can be successfully introduced in a particular firm when (1) sales or production are not subject to violent seasonal or cyclical fluctuations, or when stabilization efforts (as outlined at the end of Chapter 17) are feasible; (2) the guarantee is limited to employees with a specified minimum length of service with the firm and with a certain number of hours or weeks of employment per year; and (3) the background of labor-management relations has been good and the plan can be jointly developed.

A number of American unions, led by the Auto Workers and the Steelworkers, made the "guaranteed annual wage" one of their major collective-bargaining demands. While the proposals were designed to put pressure on management to stabilize employment, the 1955 negoti-

ated settlements with the major automobile firms were subsequently called "supplementary unemployment-benefit plans." The Ford agreement, which set the pattern for the others, provided that the company make a 5-cent-an-hour contribution (for each hour worked by hourly rated employees) to a trust fund, out of which supplementary payments would be made after June 1, 1956, to laid-off employees who had at least one year's seniority. The supplement was intended to give laid-off workers 65 percent of their weekly straight-time earnings after taxes for the first 4 weeks of unemployment following a 1-week waiting period, and 60 percent for the next 22 weeks. Thus, the 1955 agreement in essence provided a 60 to 65 percent "guarantee" for half a year. Subsequent liberalization, continued up to the 1967 agreement, which guaranteed up to 95 percent of after-tax pay, minus $7.50 for work-related expenses (lunches, travel, etc.), on a sliding scale per year. Those with 7 years' seniority and over were guaranteed 52 weeks' pay.

While there are many difficulties in the development and implementation of a workable guaranteed-employment or annual-wage plan, the basic drive for job security which is behind the union interest will not be stopped by protestations that "It just won't work in our company." Management needs to study carefully the feasibility of providing more regular employment or income to wage earners and to try to formalize this in some type of commitment to employees who meet specified standards of eligibility. Labor is almost the only factor of production for which management does not make an advance commitment covering a future period of time.

SALARIES INSTEAD OF WAGES

Another development is the payment of salaries to all employees, including production workers formerly on hourly rates. A number of companies have placed all employees on a salaried basis. For example, the Gillette Safety Razor Company did this in 1955, International Business Machines Corporation in 1958, Cannon Electric

[19] For a discussion of these and other plans, see A. D. H. Kaplan, *The Guarantee of Annual Wages,* The Brookings Institution, Washington, D.C., 1947; and *The Guaranteed Annual Wage,* Bureau of National Affairs, Inc., Operations Manual, Washington, D.C., 1955.

Company for two plants in 1959,[20] and Texas Instruments on January 1, 1968, covering 25,000 former hourly employees. The motives were to provide greater income security for employees (since they would not lose pay because of illness, accident, etc.), to eliminate the differences in methods of payment of employees as technological change reduced the number of blue-collar workers, and possibly to avoid unionization.

Under the salaried plans, absenteeism has actually been reduced, and closer identification of employees with the company is reported. Undoubtedly, the pressure for a salaried status for blue-collar workers will grow, as automation and other changes in our labor force reduce the distinctions which have persisted in the past. There should be positive gains in providing greater income security for employees, however, rather than the negative goal of keeping unions out.

Individual, group, and plant-wide incentive systems, more than guaranteed employment plans or payment of salaries, represent a form of productivity sharing. But there are additional specific ways in which firms and unions have shared increases in productivity. These are illustrated by a number of examples which are discussed in the following sections.

PRODUCTIVITY-SHARING PLANS

The 1959 Kaiser Steel-United Steelworkers agreement provided for a committee which was given "the responsibility of studying wages, the cost of living, company progress, and all other

matters that have a bearing on the welfare of employees and the economic life of the company." This committee, composed of three public representatives (two of them professors of labor economics), three management representatives, and three union representatives, recommended after 2 years of study a "long-range sharing plan." This was subsequently adopted by the company and the union and installed on March 1, 1963.[21]

The heart of the plan was a method of "reasonable sharing of productivity and labor cost savings" coupled with stability of employment or income to assure "progress for the Company, the employees, and the public interest." The first of the Committee's "underlying facts and assumptions" is especially worth quoting:

> Progress is achieved by an industrial corporation and its employees as the result of many factors including, but not limited to, capital investment, advances in technology, public investment in community services and facilities, a skilled, intelligent and alert work force, competent and skilled management, mature labor relations, and free collective bargaining.

As a basis for sharing gains in increased productivity, the plan noted that in the case of labor performance, material and supply usage, yield improvement, and utilization of technological improvements, product costs are directly affected by the cooperation and performance of the employees, as well as by management. There is a clear-cut opportunity for improvement in these areas. The gains achieved, are, furthermore, measurable.

These gains were computed monthly, by a rather complicated formula based on a ratio of employment costs to production value of 32.5

---

[20] See Paul G. Kaponya, "Salaries for *All* Workers," *Harvard Business Review,* vol. 40, no. 3, pp. 49–57, May–June, 1962. When he wrote this article, Mr. Kaponya was corporate director of industrial relations for Cannon Electric Company. The payment of weekly salaries has been spreading, according to a National Industrial Conference Board survey of a sample of manufacturing companies; 7 percent paid weekly salaries to all employees, and in firms with 500 or more employees, 19 percent did so. Both unionized and nonunion firms were represented in the sample, but a higher percentage of the nonunion firms paid weekly salaries. Absenteeism was reported as the same as before, or lower. "Salaries for Blue Collar Workers," *Conference Board Record,* vol. 2, no. 11, pp. 15–25, November, 1965.

[21] The full text of the recommendations and the proposed plan are found in *The Long Range Sharing Plan,* Kaiser Steel Corporation, Fontana Operations, and the United Steelworkers of America, Locals 2869 and 3677, Fontana, Calif., December, 1962, revised May, 1965. The plan did not spread to the rest of the steel industry, with the exception of one small firm, the Alan Wood Steel Company.

percent, with certain deductions from the reserve to pay for wages and fringe benefits negotiated by the union, for replacement capital costs, and to even out fluctuations over 12 months. Adjustments were also made to those employees still on wage incentives. A computer was used to make the calculations preceding the monthly distribution. Job or income guarantees were also provided for employees displaced from present jobs as a consequence of technological change; no employee is laid off for this reason, and he receives a "displacement differential" if he is assigned to a lower-rated job.

The initial results and worker response under the plan were good. During the first year (1963) cash bonuses to nearly 6,000 workers amounted to 50 cents an hour; but they dropped to 24 cents in the second year, 18 in the third, and then moved up to 33 cents an hour because of adjustments made in the plan for 1966. Because wage and benefit increases negotiated in the steel industry generally are taken from the reserve, there is less to pay out in bonuses. Employee dissatisfaction with the size of the payout continued, so that in the January, 1968 negotiations, the tripartite committee recommended a further change by eliminating reserve for wage and benefit increases, which are now to be deducted as labor costs. This is intended to increase bonuses somewhat. The plan's advantages to the company have been summarized as follows:

> It has eliminated the plague of wildcat strikes that used to bedevil Kaiser; it has made the employees hospitable to the introduction of new processes; it has encouraged them to cut down on the waste of costly materials; and it has relieved the company and its customers of the necessity for the huge inventory pileups that are a regular accompaniment of the triennial contract negotiations in the steel industry. [22]

[22] A. H. Raskin, "Profit Sharing in the Paycheck: Cure for the Wage-Price Spiral?" *Saturday Review,* Feb. 10, 1968, p. 23. For a more detailed earlier account, see *The Kaiser-Steel Union Sharing Plan,* Studies in Personnel Policy no. 187, National Industrial Conference Board, Inc., New York, 1963.

(Kaiser automatically matches industry agreements.)

One difficulty with plans of this type, however, is that dissatisfaction may develop with the amount of the sharing. When the Kaiser Plan came up for ratification (as it does every 4 years) in February, 1972, the workers voted it down by a small margin, and a strike resulted. The recession in the steel industry, which affected the size of bonuses under the plan, and the fact that some 42 percent of the workers never joined the plan, electing to remain on individual incentives, were cited as reasons for the strike. It was settled in about a month on the basis of guaranteed minimum bonuses to those in the sharing plan and the elimination of "negative" costs savings being carried forward and offset against positive gains, as in the past.

Productivity Bargaining in Great Britain

The Kaiser Plan—like the Scanlon Plan to be discussed later—rewards cost savings (a form of productivity increase) *as they are achieved in the future,* compared to a base period. A different approach to sharing the gains from increased productivity has developed in Great Britain, as a part of an "incomes" (wage-price) policy designed to avoid inflation and reduce consequent deficits in the balance of payments. This is known as "productivity bargaining," and it involves explicit agreements on the reduction of wasteful manning practices in return for a specific offsetting wage increase.

Perhaps the earliest and most notable productivity agreement was reached at the Fawley Refinery of Esso, near Southampton. Here the union agreed to reduce the number of helpers or "mates" with skilled craftsmen, permitted some crossing of craft lines, and reduced systematic overtime in return for a substantial negotiated wage increase. [23] Other similar agreements were

[23] For a full account, see Allan Flanders, *The Fawley Productivity Agreements: A Case Study of Management and Collective Bargaining,* Faber & Faber, Ltd., London, 1964.

subsequently reached in other British firms, including another American subsidiary, Mobil Oil. When the British government instituted a wage-price freeze in 1966–1967, the only wage increases permitted were with "productivity agreements." Thus encouraged, the practice has spread. It is certainly an innovation in British industrial relations and has brought benefits to both labor and management. But there are difficulties: (1) past inefficiencies are rewarded, (2) some unions refuse to be bound by such agreements so far as wage demands are concerned, (3) the agreements tend to be "one-shot" settlements rather than involving further sharing or productivity gains currently, (4) management has the problem of implementing the gains paid for in advance, and strong union leadership is also needed, and (5) the problem of extending production worker agreements to white-collar employees (who may not be able to show commensurate productivity increases) continues. However, as a way of offsetting a wage increase with some gain in productivity by eliminating wasteful work practices, the approach has merit.[24]

PRODUCTIVITY SHARING: THE SCANLON PLAN

An approach to productivity sharing that has become widely known in this country and abroad grew out of some of the work of Joseph N. Scanlon in the early 1940s when he was president of the local steelworkers union in a small Ohio Steel firm. He proposed joint labor-management committees to solicit employee suggestions on how efficiency could be increased, production costs reduced, and waste eliminated. Benefits were to be shared through steady employment, higher wages, better working conditions.

Scanlon later extended his ideas in other firms as director of research and engineering for the national Steelworkers Union, and in 1947 he joined the staff of the Industrial Relations Section at MIT, where he and his associates helped other companies and their unions or nonunionized employees to introduce what came to be known as the "Scanlon Plan." By 1971, the Scanlon Plan had worked successfully in some 70 firms in nearly as many different industries, ranging in size from over 8,000 employees to about 100. The experience with these plans in a variety of firms, under different competitive conditions, has clarified the conditions under which this type of cooperative plan can be successful in increasing productivity and sharing its gains.[25] Most of them have involved unions, but successful plans have been introduced in nonunion companies.

---

[24] For further evaluation of British incomes policy by American students, see Robert B. McKersie, "The British Board for Prices and Incomes," *Industrial Relations*, vol. 6, no. 3, pp. 267–284, May, 1967; and Lloyd Ulman, "Under Severe Restraint: British Incomes Policy," *Industrial Relations*, vol. 6, no. 3, pp. 213–266, May, 1967. For a British evaluation, see Bryan L. Davies, "Incomes Policy; The British Experience," *Labor Law Journal*, vol. 18, no. 7, pp. 427–439, July, 1967. A brief summary of British experience with white-collar employees is found in Gerard Tavernier, "Productivity Bargaining for White Collar Workers," *Personnel Magazine*, vol. 33, no. 327, pp. 26–29, October, 1967. For a later review, see B. Towers and T. G. Whittingham, *The New Bargainers: A Symposium on Productivity Bargaining*, Department of Adult Education, University of Nottingham, England, 1970.

[25] For the most complete account of this experience, see Frederick G. Lesieur (ed.), *The Scanlon Plan: A Frontier in Labor-Management Cooperation*, The M.I.T. Press, Cambridge, Mass., and John Wiley & Sons, Inc., New York, 1958. (Lesieur was president of the local union at Lapointe Machine Tool Company, Hudson, Mass., where the Scanlon Plan had one of its outstanding successes; later he joined Scanlon at MIT and after Scanlon's death carried on the work with the Scanlon Plan there until he established his own consulting firm in 1965.) In addition to articles by Lesieur and others, the book contains three detailed accounts of Scanlon Plan cases; Russell W. Davenport, "Enterprise for Everyman: A Case History of How the Scanlon Plan, as Applied by Union and Management at Lapointe Machine Tool, Has Raised Productivity, Profits, and Pay," *Fortune*, pp. 55–59ff., January, 1950; Joseph N. Scanlon, *Adamson and His Profit-sharing Plan*, American Management Association, Production Series, no. 172, 1947; and George P.

Elements of a Successful Scanlon Plan

The mechanics of the Scanlon Plan are important, but too much emphasis can be put on seeking a "formula." Both the management and the union that embark upon a plan of this sort must be prepared to change their traditional attitudes toward each other. This comes slowly, for at first management may be interested only in a procedure for getting more suggestions from the work force, while the union may see "cooperation" as a way of preserving jobs or getting a voice in matters from which they are usually excluded.

As experience under a plan continues, however, a new spirit develops. This has been described as *genuine participation,* since union representatives on the joint committees now feel free to make suggestions, to criticize, and to ask questions about problems that formerly were considered to be "none of their business." These problems are seen as *joint* problems for the workers, the union, and the management, affecting the welfare of all of them. Workers see a clearer relation between their job and the total product. Management, reluctant at first to reveal "confidential" information and sensitive to criticism, gradually comes to see the value in sharing all types of information with union representatives on joint committees and the benefit from suggestions that reveal managerial weaknesses.

Nevertheless, the fact that attitudes are all-important does not mean that a methodical procedure is unimportant. Experience with successful cooperation plans seems to indicate that the following steps are usually necessary.

1 Find a ratio of labor cost to total sales value of production, or some other measure, which can be used as the basis for computing the savings over normal labor costs under the plan. "Labor costs" means the total cost of wages and salaries of all employees covered by the plan.

2 Provide for sharing the savings (the productivity bonus) each month with *all* the employees in the firm, according to their base rate and earnings. In at least one plan, even the president and owner are included; in others only top-management personnel and salesmen on commission are excluded. Sharing by employees ranges from 100 percent in some plans to 60-40 in cases where the financial position of the firm has been shaky and the agreed-upon ratio favors the workers. A 75-25 sharing is most frequent.

3 Include in the memorandum of agreement a provision for changing the ratio or formula for sharing the gains when a change occurs as a result of an increase or decrease in prices or the wage level, or when a major technological change is introduced by management. The gains to be shared are those resulting from lower costs and higher output under the plan itself. In practice, only major changes result in ratio changes.

4 Hold back some portion of each month's productivity bonus, to build a reserve for paying out some bonus in the months when none is earned because of unforeseen conditions, such as a sales slump.

5 Establish departmental production committees of management and union representatives to gather and act upon suggestions for reducing costs and increasing output in the respective departments. Suggestions of wider scope go to a "screening committee" with top-management and local union representatives.[26] Grievances

---

Shultz, "Worker Participation on Production Problems," *Personnel,* vol. 28, no. 3, pp. 201-211, November, 1951 (reprinted in Pigors, Myers, and Malm, *op. cit.,* selection 36). A more recent account of the Scanlon Plan is Fred G. Lesieur and Elbridge S. Puckett, "The Scanlon Plan Has Proved Itself," *Harvard Business Review,* vol. 47, no. 5, pp. 109-118, September-October, 1969. Three case studies are discussed: Atwood Vacuum Machine Company, Parker Pen Company, and Pfaudler Company, all of which have had success with the Plan for many years.

[26] The screening committee at the Lapointe Machine Tool Company accepted about 2,321 of the 2,927 suggestions received (or nearly 80 percent) during the first 12 years the plan was in operation, before a change in management led to discontinuance of the Plan for a period. The great majority of these were "production" rather than "intangible" suggestions. At a smaller Scanlon Plan company (150 employees), 95 percent of 1,750 suggestions submitted in the first 6.5 years were accepted. The contrast with the usual suggestion-box-system experience is striking.

and other matters involving the collective bargaining relationship are kept out of these committee meetings by agreement, the regular collective bargaining machinery being used for these problems.

6 Discuss all problems facing the business at these joint committee meetings—costs, bids, orders, sales prospects, production bottlenecks or difficulties, customer rejections, quality problems, and materials shortages. In one case it was even discussed whether too many new management officials were being added to the payroll! These problems are important because they are recognized as joint problems, and nothing is held back.

7 Distribute minutes of the meetings to everyone in the plant, and discuss key points in the meetings with workers and management people not on the committees. Information is shared as widely as possible, to avoid misunderstanding and charges that union committee members have "sold out." Improved two-way communication on a wider range of problems is one of the benefits of a cooperation plan.

8 Arrange for transfers to equally good jobs if action under the plan results in displacement of workers.

These steps perhaps suggest a formality that actually does not exist in most cooperation plans. Informality, with more emphasis on changed attitudes rather than on procedures, is characteristic of successful labor-management cooperation plans, such as the Scanlon Plan.

Results under the Scanlon Plan

When a plan is developed in good faith, the gains to workers, the local union, and management are striking. For example, in a machine-tool firm, during the first 12 years the monthly productivity bonus payment *averaged* 16 percent. Included in this period were some months when business was so poor that no bonus was earned. Membership in the local union is now 100 percent of the work force, including office workers and engi-neers; local union officers, with the encouragement of regional union representatives, have developed an unusual level of knowledge and understanding of plant problems. Both union officers and workers get satisfaction out of tackling real production problems, "getting their teeth into them," and seeing their ideas accepted and put into effect. The motives which ordinarily exist in informal groups for restricting output are removed when information and gains are shared.

The productivity gains reported for 10 firms that initiated the Scanlon Plan impressively illustrate the vast untapped potential that exists for improving efficiency. [27] The firms are fairly representative in that they operated in various environments and under widely divergent circumstances. The unweighted 2-year average annual increased efficiency (above the base period) for the 10 firms was 23.1 percent, with a minimum improvement of 10.3 percent and a maximum improvement of 39.2 percent reported.

Finally, management and owners have benefited from lower costs, better quality, and less need for supervision. Management's job under a plan of this sort is not an easier one, but it is a different one. Management officials must "keep on their toes" to plan work ahead and arrange for an adequate flow of orders and materials to the workplace. The planning function of management is increased. Directing the work force and giving orders are less important, since real teamwork and self-discipline have developed.

Success is usually not due to harder work from any group of employees. More savings result from suggestions to eliminate waste, to reduce the number of operations required, or to coordinate the work of groups of employees. For example, in a book-publishing plant, a pressroom worker found that some ink companies would process waste ink and return it in usable form at a cost of 10 to 15 cents a pound, as

---

[27] For a detailed analysis, see Elbridge S. Puckett, "Productivity Achievements—A Measure of Success," in Lesieur, *op. cit.,* chap. 10, pp. 109–117.

compared with 50 to 95 cents for new ink. His suggestion in a committee meeting resulted in a considerable saving. A bindery worker who was a member of a production committee suggested stacking work in a different manner in order to save floor space in an outside warehouse. This space was worth 50 cents a square foot. The pressroom and composing-room production committees met and agreed to print certain jobs from type, thus eliminating the need to make costly printing plates. In another firm that did machine-shop and sheet-metal operations on a job-shop basis, each mechanic agreed to pool his own jigs and fixtures, formerly jealously guarded, in order to share his ideas with fellow mechanics and to reduce the time necessary to complete orders.

Critics may say that an efficient management would have made these changes without the benefit of employee suggestions through a joint labor-management committee. But the fact is that the actual level of efficiency in many firms is below the optimum level; this is partly because employees are neither motivated to produce as a part of a work group nor convinced that higher output will be to their benefit as well as the company's. The essential contribution through the Scanlon Plan is to change *both* employee and management perceptions of what each can do to further their mutual interest.[28]

This approach involves "genuine participation in problem solving," as Douglas McGregor's observation at the beginning of this chapter clearly indicates. A personnel concept of management characterized by Theory Y (or System 4 in Likert's terms) is essential for the ultimate success of the participative effort, as we have noted before. The management system of several Scanlon Plan companies studied by Likert confirms this conclusion.[29]

Some Problems in This Type of Productivity Sharing

We do not wish to suggest that these plans are a panacea for all the ills of personnel and labor relations. No *plan* can be an answer to such problems. Success or failure in personnel administration depends much more on the attitudes and approaches used than in the techniques adopted. Even under the Scanlon Plan, problems continue to arise. Managements and unions should know what these are.

For example, the initial effect of production committees that release the ideas of workers is to bypass the foremen, except those who are committee members. But since in most plans foremen share in the bonus, cooperation on production ideas between workers and foremen may be expected to develop gradually, especially if top management encourages this.

Joint committees are theoretically advisory, but in practice they often make decisions on production problems. This may seem to threaten management's "right to manage" although the issue has not actually arisen in any of the existing plans. Management is often criticized in committee meetings, and management officials have to be able to "stand the gaff." If they survive the initial ordeal, they may find the experience stimulating.

Changes in the "ratio," resulting from changes in prices, wage levels, or the purchase of new machinery, may result in misunderstandings. So far, however, few serious problems have arisen because the committee system with information sharing seems to develop an understanding of the need for changes of all sorts.

The attitudes of local union officials are likely

[28] For a 10-point summary of benefits to management and labor under the Scanlon Plan, based on a survey of experience, see Slichter, Healy, and Livernash, *op. cit.*, pp. 864–868. Some problems are discussed in the following pages, 868–877.

[29] Rensis Likert, *The Human Organization: Its Management and Value*, McGraw-Hill Book Company, New York, 1967, pp. 40–43.

to change. Grievances seem to have declined under cooperation plans. Local union officers and members become much more interested in ways of increasing their productivity bonus and solving plant problems. There is a greater (though not complete) identity of interest between management and labor. Those who think that unions should remain militant, and even class-conscious, are disturbed at this development. The mature relationships that result from recognition by both management and the union of their mutual dependence do not, however, necessarily weaken the ties of the local union with the national. The local union continues to identify its interests with fellow unionists in other plants organized by the national, especially when it comes to collective bargaining matters. Since the Scanlon Plan is separate from the collective bargaining agreement, the national union still must formulate policies and provide services which are essential even for a stronger local union. Managements which look to the Scanlon Plan as a means to weaken the hold of the national union in order to gain an advantage in collective bargaining may find that this attempt backfires.

There have been failures under the Scanlon Plan, in the sense that companies (and some unions) which adopted the plan have subsequently discontinued it.[30] In some, management was not really ready for this new kind of relationship or resented the amount of bonus employees were able to earn by removing what may have been previous output restrictions under a demoralized individual wage-incentive system. Often the Scanlon Plan is introduced when such a

system has deteriorated. In one case, the management of a firm changed and threw out the plan in a fairly autocratic way. In others, there was mutual dissatisfaction when bonuses did not continue, or when there were too many changes in product mix to stabilize a "ratio" for computing the bonus. But there have been many more successes than failures, because of the benefits pointed out earlier.

Who Gains through This Approach?

The experience of Scanlon Plan companies emphasizes the underutilization of human resources that exists in most firms. The productivity achievements of these firms have allowed increased earnings to be shared by the company (including the stockholders) and the employees. In addition, the employees and management have created an entirely new atmosphere, the benefits of which are difficult to evaluate in terms of greater job satisfaction, healthier attitudes, and more mature relationships. The continued existence of free collective bargaining may depend upon the ability of labor and management to recognize their mutuality of interests and responsibility to society in general. To the extent that a labor-management cooperation plan furthers efficiency, sensibly shares the gains of productivity, and reduces the chance of economic warfare, it benefits everyone.

Management has usually been reluctant to enter into union-management cooperation, and the initiative has more often come from the union side. More plans have been started in firms losing money or facing severe competition than in companies that were making a good profit.[31] Have the latter firms nothing to gain from sharing production and cost information with their

[30] For a published account of one failure, in which neither Scanlon nor his associates were involved, see Thomas Q. Gilson and Myron J. Lefcowitz, "A Plant-wide Productivity Bonus in a Small Factory: Study of an Unsuccessful Case," *Industrial and Labor Relations Review,* vol. 10, no. 2, pp. 284-296, 1957. Another was reported by Harold E. Dryer, *The Scanlon Plan: An Analysis and a Case Study,* unpublished doctoral dissertation, Massachusetts Institute of Technology, Department of Economics and Social Science, Cambridge, Mass., 1952.

[31] For an analysis of the characteristics of 19 companies, 21 plants, and 18 local unions employing the Scanlon Plan, see George P. Shultz, "Variations in Environment and the Scanlon Plan," in Lesieur, *op. cit.,* chap. 9, pp. 100-108.

employees? Do they benefit by encouraging employee and union participation in the discussion and solution of these problems? Is the suggestion-box system an adequate alternative to production committees and cost-savings sharing? These are questions that every manager and personnel administrator needs to ask himself, in the light of his own experience and the experience of other firms in stimulating and utilizing the latent ideas and energies of employees on job-related production problems.

Productivity sharing of the Scanlon Plan type, however, is less widely adopted than two other methods which claim to share gains but are not so directly related to the kind of participation which distinguishes the Scanlon Plan. These are profit sharing (including employee stock purchases) and employee-suggestion plans.

Profit Sharing and Employee Stock Ownership

Profit sharing is considered by a number of employers as a better way to share some of the gains in productivity within a firm. More employee cooperation, increased effort, and loyalty to organizational objectives should increase a firm's profits, and employees will as a consequence be able to receive benefits *beyond* those that would be available in the absence of profit sharing. In many cases, however, this incentive aspect of profit sharing appears to be secondary, and so the question arises: Why select this method in preference to others, including increased salaries and wages?

Employee profit sharing is often regarded by employers as a supplementary compensation program. Although plans differ widely in specific details, there are basically three types: profits are shared (1) in cash, (2) in deferred payments, or (3) in a combination of cash and deferred payments. Under the cash plan, payments are usually at specified intervals. Under the deferred-

payment plan, the money is placed in a trust fund to be disbursed usually when the employee is disabled, laid off, or retired. In the last instance, a combination of both, the employee's share is divided (in a prescribed ratio), a part of it is paid in cash, and the remainder is placed in his account in a trust fund. Deferred profit-sharing plans have been growing relative to the other types, primarily for retirement funds.

Profit sharing had its beginnings in the middle of the nineteenth century in France. In the intervening years, it has gone through stages of rapid growth and some decline, especially in the United States. In this country, it is estimated that the U.S. Treasury had approved 48,600 qualified deferred and combination (cash) profit-sharing plans by the end of 1965 and that there were 50,000 to 60,000 straight cash plans.[32] Some are in very large firms such as Eastman Kodak and Sears, Roebuck; but the vast majority of cash plans are in very small firms. The growth of profit sharing within the past 30 years is attributable to government excess-profit taxes and wage and salary controls during the Second World War, to deferred-payment plans, which now enjoy certain tax advantages, to the general growth of pension plans in private business, and to generally good profit levels in many recent years.

Beyond these reasons, it is difficult to generalize about employer motivations in establishing profit-sharing plans. The most frequently mentioned motives in a survey of 298 firms with profit sharing are (1) to instill a sense of partnership; (2) to offer a group incentive; and (3) to provide employee security. Profit sharing, however, appears to be a doubtful means of achieving greater efficiency. In a survey of 199 companies with profit-sharing plans, 62 percent believe

---

[32] Bert L. Metzger, *Profit Sharing in Perspective,* 2d ed., Profit Sharing Research Foundation, Evanston, Ill., 1966, p. 17. See also Bert L. Metzger and Jerome A. Colletti, *Does Profit Sharing Pay?* Profit Sharing Research Foundation, Evanston, Ill., 1971.

these plans affected increased efficiency to some extent, while 22 percent said that they had almost no effect on efficiency.[33] Nevertheless, some strong advocates of profit sharing have pointed out that if workers have a stake in the earnings of the enterprise of which they are a part, they will redouble their productive efforts, avoid wastes that raise costs, and do everything they can to boost earnings. In some instances, these results seem to have occurred under profit sharing.[34] The experience with profit sharing in other companies, however, has sometimes been unfavorable, and many earlier plans have been dropped.[35] One widely publicized plan, the American Motors Company's "Progress Sharing" plan developed by agreement with the United Auto Workers Union in 1961, was discontinued in the 1968 agreement after 2 years with no profits to share.

The major reason that the incentive value of profit sharing is questioned is that many employees apparently tend to regard periodic payments as "so much gravy." Workers in one large firm with a profit-sharing plan stated to an interviewer that the annual distribution had no effect on their effort or output during the year, largely because they could not see any direct relation between their individual work and company profits. Furthermore, when profits declined as

general business conditions became worse, they resented the drop in profit-sharing bonuses to which they had become accustomed.

Some firms have experimented with sharing profits in the form of issuing stock to employees and have encouraged employees to purchase common stock in the company under various arrangements which also involve some cost to the company.[36] As in the case of profit sharing on a cash basis, some employee stock-ownership plans have subsequently been dropped. When stock prices fall drastically, employees lose faith in this form of extra incentive compensation and in the management that sponsored it. In short, there has been only limited success with the attempt to make employees "entrepreneur-minded" through profit sharing or employee stock ownership. Apparently other approaches are needed to identify the workers' long-run interests with those of the specific firm.

As pointed out in one research report,[37] "profit sharing must be considered essentially a form of incentive, or it descends to the level of any fringe benefit." It is precisely because profit sharing may lose its incentive qualities that it becomes merely another means of sharing the existing pie. Unions resent this type of remuneration if it tends to disguise low wages and benefits or to discourage unionization or employee loyalty to an existing union. Further, strongly paternalistic managements may see in profit sharing a way of doing something for their employees, thus losing the opportunity for genu-

[33] *Sharing Profits with Employees,* National Industrial Conference Board, Inc., Studies in Personnel Policy, no. 162, New York, 1958, p. 9.

[34] John J. Jehring, *The Utilization of a Total Systems Incentive: A Case Study of a Cash Profit-sharing Program at Merrill Manufacturing Corp.,* University of Wisconsin, School of Commerce, Center for the Study of Productivity Motivation, Madison, Wis., 1966.

[35] Bryce M. Stewart and Walter J. Couper, *Profit Sharing and Stock Ownership for Wage Earners and Executives,* Industrial Relations Counselors, Inc., Industrial Relations Monograph 10, New York, 1945, p. 49. For more recent evaluations, see Douglass V. Brown, "An Appraisal of Profit Sharing," *Management Record,* vol. 24, no. 12, pp. 27-28, 1962; and Charles Schotta, Jr., "The Distribution of Profit Sharing Plans: An Analysis," *Southern Economic Journal,* vol. 30, no. 1, pp. 49-59, July, 1963.

[36] For details, without any evaluation of their effectiveness, see Mitchell Meyer and Harland Fox, *Employee Stock Purchase Plans,* Personnel Policy Study no. 206, National Industrial Conference Board, Inc., New York, 1967. Approximately 21 percent of the companies with securities listed on the New York Stock Exchange had such plans, 36 percent of stock insurance firms, and 25 percent of large commercial banks.

[37] Harold E. Kubly, *Profit Sharing at Baker Manufacturing Company,* Evansville, Wis., 1899-1958, University of Wisconsin, Madison, Wis., 1958, p. 77.

ine participation in improving efficiency and sharing the gains from higher productivity.[38]

EMPLOYEE-SUGGESTION SYSTEMS

The history and development of suggestion systems have in many respects clearly paralleled those of profit sharing. Suggestion systems were first instituted in the 1880s and grew rapidly during the Second World War. Now formal systems are found in a large number of firms and governmental and nonprofit organizations. Management objectives in installing a suggestion system vary widely from "primarily tangible," e.g., cost reduction, to "leading to administrative techniques," e.g., incentives for employee thinking.[39] Whatever the intangible benefits may be, suggestion systems as a means to share productivity gains with employees have some severe limitations. Experience with these systems has varied, and some firms have introduced suggestion boxes only to discontinue them later when the quantity and quality of suggestions fell off. Often the difficulty is that many of the suggestions are "intangible," they deal with better lighting, safety measures, etc., and less frequently with specific ways of reducing costs and increasing production.

Some suggestion systems, however, are better planned and more successfully operated. It is not unusual to find the percentage of accepted sug-

gestions between 25 and 35 percent and about one out of every three employees submitting suggestions. Suggestion systems that have achieved this degree of success usually have met the following specifications:[40]

• Top management wholeheartedly supports the suggestion system, assigns responsibility for it to a management official (usually in the personnel department), and encourages supervisors to stimulate employee ideas.[41]

• Employees are clearly informed about the kinds of suggestions wanted and even the specific problems on which management seeks help. Rules under which the system operates are also clearly explained to employees.

• All suggestions are promptly acknowledged, and if they are subsequently rejected, an explanation is given for each rejection.

• Awards for acceptable suggestions are monetary and on the liberal side, usually more than 20 percent of the first year's net savings.

• Full publicity is given to award winners.

Unfortunately, however, many suggestion sys-

---

[38] A study of a production-sharing plan (said to be similar to the Scanlon Plan discussed earlier in this chapter) and a profit-sharing plan showed that the latter had higher payouts but largely because the former plan was not administered correctly. John J. Jehring, "A Contrast between Two Approaches to Total Systems Incentives," *California Management Review,* vol. 10, no. 2, pp. 7–14, Winter, 1967.

[39] *Objectives of a Suggestion System,* National Association of Suggestion Systems, Chicago, 1958. This survey also reports: "Although quite a number of responding companies said, one way or another, that their objective was to 'provide a medium for rewarding employees for ideas,' nearly everyone backed off when asked why they chose this as an objective!" (p. 29).

[40] The National Association of Suggestion Systems, Chicago, founded in 1942, reports that nearly 7.5 million employees are eligible to participate in formal suggestion plans. For further details, its survey of suggestion-system operations in 243 companies is reported in the *National Association of Suggestion Systems Annual Statistical Report for the Year 1965,* National Association of Suggestion Systems, Chicago, 1963. The Association publishes the *NAAS Journal* (formerly *Suggestion System Quarterly*), with accounts of experience in various firms. See also Herbert R. Northrup, *Suggestion Systems,* National Industrial Conference Board, Inc., Studies in Personnel Policy, no. 135, New York, 1953.

[41] For a discussion of the advantages of line-management administration, see William S. Wilcox, "What Are Suggestion Systems For?," *Personnel,* vol. 30, no. 5, pp. 382–385, March, 1954. See also Cecil T. Young, "Suggestion Systems: Boon or Bane?," *Personnel Journal,* vol. 42, no. 3, pp. 127–134, March, 1963; Joseph A. Montana, "Managing an Effective Suggestion System," *Administrative Management,* vol. 27, no. 10, pp. 38ff., October, 1966. (A 6-year analysis of one company's experience showed cumulative estimated annual savings of $601,739); and Andrew E. Smith, "Harnessing the Power of Ideas," *Personnel Journal,* vol. 47, no. 11, pp. 770–775, November, 1968 (on the General Motors experience).

tems fail to meet all of these specifications. Examples of inept handling of suggestion awards and rejections are not difficult to find. For instance, one employee made a suggestion and received a form letter stating that his suggestion was being considered. Later he was notified by another form letter that it was rejected as being "impractical." About 6 months after that, he saw the change he had suggested being put into effect. He wrote a letter asking what had been done with his suggestion but received no reply. This experience thoroughly discouraged him, and he refused to make any more suggestions. He thought that the foreman or some "higher-up" had modified his suggestion and taken credit for it. This may not have been the case, but the important fact is that he *thought* so, and nothing was done to explain the situation. Possibly, as in another case, the conditions had changed, and the suggestion then became practical to adopt. In any event, the suggestor was entitled to an explanation.

As in other parts of a personnel program, the climate in which the suggestion system operates is all-important. If management is not sincere in welcoming employee ideas, however critical these may appear to be of existing methods or procedures, the system will be of little value.

SUMMARY

A continuing challenge for management is how to share the gains from higher productivity in ways that will stimulate the interest of employees in improving their own performance on the job and the productivity of the organization as a whole. To measure productivity is a difficult task. Many problems are involved in trying to relate wage and salary changes to a meaningful productivity index, preferably for the economy as a whole. The "annual improvement factor" in the General Motors–United Auto Workers Union agreement is an example of one such attempt.

Systems of wage incentives represent another method of rewarding increases in individual, group, or plant-wide productivity. These systems have too often been considered the special province of industrial engineers. However, in the past, many engineers have neglected the problems that arise in connection with these plans and subsequent changes in incentive pay. Managers and their personnel administrators cannot avoid the responsibility for careful consideration of the conditions under which incentive methods are appropriate and the circumstances under which they should be avoided. Undoubtedly, industries confronted with rapid technological change and automation are not so well suited to incentive systems as those with a more stable technology and production process.

Dissatisfaction with incentive systems which have deteriorated and other factors have led some firms to turn to different methods of sharing productivity gains. One of these is the Kaiser Steel–Steelworkers Union "long-range sharing" plan; another is through "productivity bargaining" as in Great Britain during the period of wage-price control. The Scanlon Plan of sharing labor-cost savings and encouraging employee productivity suggestions through joint production and screening committees is spreading, though slowly. It is a genuine participation plan.

More widespread, but possibly less effective in eliciting employee participation in productivity improvement, are the profit-sharing movement (including employee stock-purchase plans), and employee-suggestion systems. Genuine employee interest and participation in increasing productivity are probably not achievable through any specific plan, technique, or system. If any of the systems reviewed above is successful, it may well be the consequence of changed attitudes of employees and managers toward the common goal of a productive enterprise or organization. This is certainly one of the principal conclusions in the studies of successful Scanlon Plans.

SELECTED REFERENCES

Barnes, Ralph M.: *Motion and Time Study,* 5th ed., John Wiley & Sons, Inc., New York, 1963.

Brown, Douglass V.: "An Appraisal of Profit Sharing," *Management Record,* vol. 24, no. 12, pp. 27-28, 1962.

Collins, Orvis, Melville Dalton, and Donald Roy: "Restriction of Output and Social Cleavage in Industry," *Applied Anthropology,* vol. 5, no. 3, pp. 1-14, Summer, 1946 (reprinted in Paul Pigors, Charles A. Myers, and F. T. Malm, *Management of Human Resources: Readings in Personnel Administration,* 3d ed., McGraw-Hill Book Company, New York, 1973, selection 41).

Crandall, Richard E.: "De-emphasized Wage Incentives," *Harvard Business Review,* vol. 40, no. 2, pp. 113-116, March–April, 1962.

Forms of Wage and Salary Payment for High Productivity, Organisation for Economic Cooperation and Development, Paris, 1970.

Gomberg, William: *A Trade Union Analysis of Time Study,* 2d ed., Prentice-Hall, Inc., Englewood Cliffs, N.J., 1955.

Haire, Mason: *Psychology in Management,* 2d ed., McGraw-Hill Book Company, New York, 1964, chap. 6, "Productivity and Wage Payment Plans," pp. 147-180.

Lesieur, Frederick G. (ed.): *The Scanlon Plan: A Frontier in Labor-Management Cooperation,* The M.I.T. Press, Cambridge, Mass., 1958.

——— and Elbridge S. Puckett: "The Scanlon Plan Has Proved Itself," *Harvard Business Review,* vol. 47, no. 5, pp. 109-118, September–October, 1969.

Livernash, E. Robert: "Wage Administration and Production Standards," in Arthur Kornhauser, Robert Dubin, and Arthur M. Ross (eds.), *Industrial Conflict,* McGraw-Hill Book Company, New York, 1954 (reprinted in Pigors, Myers, and Malm, *op. cit.,* selection 39).

McKersie, Robert B.: "Changing Methods of Wage Payment," chap. 7 in John T. Dunlop and Neil W. Chamberlain (eds.), *Frontiers of Collective Bargaining,* Harper & Row, Publishers, Incorporated, New York, 1967.

———: "Wage Payment Methods of the Future," *British Journal of Industrial Relations,* vol. 1, pp. 191-212, 1963.

Mangum, Garth L.: "Are Wage Incentives Becoming Obsolete?," *Industrial Relations,* vol. 2, no. 1, pp. 73-96, 1962 (reprinted in Pigors, Myers, and Malm, *op. cit.,* selection 40).

Marriott, R.: *Incentive Payment Systems,* Staples Press Limited, London, 1957.

Metzger, Bert L., and Jerome A. Colletti: *Does Profit Sharing Pay? A Comparative Study of the Financial Performance of Retailers with and without Profit Sharing Programs,* Profit Sharing Research Foundation, Evanston, Ill., 1971.

Northrup, Herbert R.: *Suggestion Systems,* National Industrial Conference Board, Inc., Studies in Personnel Policy, no. 135, New York, 1953.

Payment by Results: International Labour Office, Studies and Reports, no. 27, Geneva, 1951.

Shultz, George P.: "Worker Participation on Production Problems: A Discussion of Experience with the Scanlon Plan," *Personnel,* vol. 28, no. 3, pp. 201-211, November, 1951 (reprinted in Pigors, Myers, and Malm, *op. cit.,* selection 36).

Sibson, Robert E.: *Wages and Salaries: A Handbook for Line Management,* rev. ed., American Management Association, New York, 1967, chaps. 6 and 7.

Slichter, Sumner H., James J. Healy, and E. Robert Livernash: *The Impact of Collective Bargaining on Management,* The Brookings Institution, Washington, D.C., 1960, chaps. 17, 18, and 28.

Whyte, William F.: *Money and Motivation: An Analysis of Incentives in Industry,* Harper & Row, Publishers, Incorporated, New York, 1955.

Young, Cecil T.: "Suggestion Systems: Boon or Bane?," *Personnel Journal,* vol. 42, no. 3, pp. 127-134, March, 1963.

Chapter 22

Programs for Employee Health and Safety: An Ecological Approach

Reappraisal and the possible reorganization of the company safety and health function will need to be a comprehensive effort, taking into account the impact of federal legislation on a range of management decisions, the effect of extensive union interest and pressure, and the constantly changing requirements imposed by new technologies and medical and scientific advances. In the light of recent developments affecting the field of occupational health and safety, the routine—and sometimes piecemeal—approach of the past is no longer adequate.

Leo Teplow[1]

In the interrelated fields of employee safety and health, much has been learned and done during the twentieth century. But no one who is conversant with the facts can afford to be satisfied with the stage of understanding and accomplishment currently reached. A brief review of the historical background as well as of recent legislation, and of relevant modern knowledge (including findings in behavioral psychology, industrial hygiene, technology, and modern ways of managing) should facilitate "reappraisal and possible reorganization." Moreover, studying relationships between significant facts and trends should enable everyone concerned with employee safety and health to get beyond the piecemeal approach and achieve a unified view of what remains to be done.

[1] Leo Teplow, "Occupational Health and Safety: The Need for Reappraisal," *Industrial Medicine,* vol. 40, no. 4, July, 1971, p. 24.

BRIEF HISTORICAL BACKGROUND[2]

Changes in management thinking with regard to safety and health of employees have paralleled developmental phases in personnel relations as a whole. In general, the trend has been from paternalism (with indifference to workers as individuals) through a scientific management and engineering approach (with some recognition of costs entailed by excessive waste of human resources and alienation of public opinion) up to modern concepts of business leadership (with participative management).

Common-law Concepts

Until the 1900s, the attitude of most employers reflected common-law concepts such as the master-servant doctrine. Employees were regarded as common labor, mere hands and feet. Such notions fitted well with the assumption that the best way to handle "the worker" was by centralized direction and firm control. During the beginning of the industrial period, as in earlier times, the well-being of employees depended almost entirely upon the humanity of their employers. But by and large, production-centered employers pursued their goals without regard to "incidental" social costs. These had to be borne by employees themselves and by members of the local community.

The situation of factory workers who suffered from chronic ill health (induced by occupational hazards), or from disabling accidents incurred at work, was often tragic. Most employers accepted no responsibility voluntarily to compensate their employees for illness and accidents resulting from hazardous work methods and deplorable working conditions. Court procedures could occasionally wrest from an employer some financial compensation. However, resorting to the law for redress was such a difficult and prolonged undertaking that relatively few employees even attempted it. For one thing, it was difficult to produce witnesses who were willing to risk their own employment by testifying against their employer in behalf of a fellow employee.

Moreover, the principles of common law favored the employer. For example, according to the assumption-of-risk doctrine, an employer was held not liable if he could show that a disabled employee, having been duly informed of the hazards associated with a given job, had voluntarily accepted them.

Two other concepts that favored the employer were (1) contributory negligence (regardless of negligence on the part of the employer, a complainant could not win a damage suit if it could be proved that he himself had been careless in any degree); and (2) the fellow-servant doctrine (evidence that an injury had resulted from negligence by a fellow worker).

Confronted with such legalistic arguments, an employee who had suffered an occupationally induced illness or accident found it almost impossible to prove that his employer's negligence had occasioned his disability.

Finally, the heavy expenses entailed by litigation, which had to be carried while no wages were coming in (and, naturally, no insurance payments), were often such as to cause the unfortunate worker and his family to become destitute.

Early Legislative Reforms

Gradually, an aroused public opinion brought legislative reforms. A series of corrective liability laws, first aimed at counteracting an employer's common-law defenses, finally led to the formulation of an entirely new principle.

Liability without Fault

The old concept of *individual fault* (by an employee) was abandoned in favor of a new con-

[2] For an extensive, scholarly presentation of antecedents, see Herman Miles Somers and Anne Ramsay Somers, *Workmen's Compensation: Prevention, Insurance, and Rehabilitation of Occupational Disability,* John Wiley & Sons, Inc., New York, 1954, especially chaps. 6 and 7, pp. 197-267.

cept: *liability without fault* (on the part of the employer). According to this new principle, risk of industrial accidents, for example, was viewed as an inevitable hazard of industrial employment. Therefore, all expenses associated with accidents became a legitimate production cost for the employer.

State Laws for Workmen's Compensation

The first of these laws came into effect in 1911 (Wisconsin). It held an employer financially liable for all disabling accidents arising out of, and in the course of, employment. Gradually, compensation laws (finally passed in every state) came to be interpreted as also covering occupationally induced chronic illness and injuries suffered in the place of work (even during off hours).[3]

A Giant Step toward Safety and Health

In view of these developments, many employers began to realize that safety is good business. A group of safety-minded professionals took the lead in developing programs for industrial and public safety. For example, the inauguration of The First Cooperative Safety Congress and the organization of the National Safety Council stimulated interest in developing improved conditions for the health and safety of employees.

However, early engineering efforts to make production machinery "foolproof" through the application of mechanical control devices continued to reflect the paternalistic attitude that characterized managerial practices in general. At first, safety was imposed by strict enforcement of safety regulations. Relatively little effort

was made to educate employees or to enlist their participation in safety management.

Gradually, however, a more enlightened "employee-centered" approach began to prevail.[4] An analysis of 75,000 cases demonstrated that most industrial accidents (88 percent) were caused primarily by the *unsafe acts of persons*. It follows that many accidents can be prevented by helping employees to become safety-minded. Accident prevention is thus a joint responsibility requiring the cooperation of management, employees, and the union.

Recent Legislation

The variety of risks to employee health and safety has been growing apace since the beginning of the industrial era. But until the late 1960s most businessmen and industrialists considered that responsibility for programs of employee safety and health could properly be left to staff experts. However, a series of mine disasters focussed national attention on the terrible dangers of mining, including the occupational disease of "black lung." The federal Bureau of Mines (originally established in 1910) had no authority to make inspections or power to enforce established mine safety regulations. Each major disaster resulted in public clamor to strengthen the rule-making and enforcement power of this agency. The Federal Coal Mine Safety Act of 1952 gave the Bureau authority to close a mine on finding that conditions existed that might lead to a major disaster. After the disastrous mine accident near Mannington, West Virginia, an outraged public succeeded in forcing passage of the Federal Coal Mine Health and Safety Act, which became law in 1969.

The Occupational Safety and Health Act of 1971

Another landmark piece of federal legislation in our own day has been the Occupational Safety

---

[3] The costs of such compensation for employees who had suffered partial or complete disability, occupationally induced illness, or death have usually been met by insurance placed with a private carrier. (Such costs have averaged out at 1 percent of a company's payroll. However, a good safety record may lead to a reduction in the cost of insurance premiums.) To reduce such expenses still further, some large corporations have been self-insured. This arrangement conforms to state law if it can be shown that the employer has adequate resources.

[4] H. W. Heinrich, *Industrial Accident Prevention: A Scientific Approach,* 4th ed., McGraw-Hill Book Company, New York, 1959, especially chap. 2, "Basic Philosophy of Accident Prevention," pp. 13–65.

and Health Act (OSHA). This law became effective in April, 1971, and applies to more than 4 million establishments engaged in interstate commerce, employing over 57 million workers. Its general objective is to improve the total environment of workers in the United States and their health and safety on the job.

OSHA was passed only after a 3-year struggle over who should set standards and who should enforce them. Organized labor and liberal Democrats contended that both functions should be carried out by the Secretary of Labor. Representatives of employers and of the Administration argued that there should be two separate presidentially appointed boards. The final bill stipulates that the Secretary of Labor should set federal standards for occupational safety and health. These cover a broad array of hazards including obsolete and dangerous machinery, toxic chemical agents, unprotected radiation devices, and general plant conditions. OSHA is administered by the Assistant Secretary of Labor.

A key feature of OSHA is a general duty clause obligating employers to furnish a place of employment free from hazards likely to cause death or serious physical harm to employees.

In addition to administrative control by the Department of Labor, other significant victories for organized labor were that:

- A union representative is given the right to accompany a federal inspector during his tour of the plant, and
- Individual employees may appeal directly to the Secretary of Labor if they feel that their working conditions are unhealthy or unsafe. [Such appeals began to come in soon after the law was signed (December 29, 1970), even before it went into effect at the end of April, 1971.]

A major victory for employers was that the Secretary of Labor has not been given the power to order an establishment closed even if a federal inspector should find that existing conditions constitute an "imminent danger" to the safety and health of employees. However, citations are issued to concerns deemed to be in violation of OSHA (though employers may appeal such a ruling through the courts). Moreover, new features of the act provide for civil penalties of up to a $10,000 fine and 6 months in jail for "repeated and willful violations." Finally, the government may invoke criminal penalties for willful violations that result in death.

At the outset, emphasis has been on voluntary compliance with safety and health regulations. This feature was a practical necessity because it was anticipated that at first there would be only 200 specially trained federal inspectors. However, if a sufficient number of states take advantage of grants-in-aid, it is expected that eventually some 2,000 federal inspectors will be in the field. (The government allocates 90 percent of available federal funds to help smaller companies plan their own safety programs and 50 percent for administrative costs.)

Growing Concern with the Total Environment

During the 1960s, there was a quickening of interest concerning health and safety in the work environment. Not only employees and union leaders but the general public also became aware of the contaminants breathed by employees while at work (as well as by residents in many large cities).[5]

New developments in technology have been a major cause of air pollution, both on and off the job. Therefore, it is reassuring to know that more and better technology has been instrumental in

---

[5] In this connection it is of interest to note that as early as the seventeenth century, Bernardo Ramazzini, an eminent Italian physician, "conceived the guiding principle that disease must not be looked upon in terms of organs or processes, but rather as complex interactions between the host, the agent, and the environment. Of all the environmental factors to which man is exposed, none is more intimate than the air he breathes. This did not escape the acute mind of Ramazzini, and many of the chapters of his *De Morbis Artificum [Diseases of Tradesmen]* unequivocally bring forward, much ahead of his time, the recognition that volatile and solid wastes that pollute the air can be responsible for pulmonary disease." C. George Tedeschi, M.D., "Bernardino Ramazzini (1633–1714): *De Morbis Artificum,*" *Human Pathology,* vol. 12, no. 2, June, 1970, p. 316.

decreasing environmental contamination in such cities as Pittsburgh and London (England). It is now widely recognized that an understanding of ecological principles can foster health and safety wherever people care enough to expend the necessary brainpower, time, and money. With specific reference to pollution, one employer has pointed out that "fully adequate solutions will call for advance on two fronts: (1) better systems and (2) better habits. . . . No matter how clever our technologists, a cleaner world will also call for something extra from each of us."[6]

Multidisciplinary Cooperation and Systems Thinking

However, to achieve needed advances, this "something extra" from individuals must be supplemented by effective cooperation and coordination between representatives of government, education, science, law, medicine, engineering, and the general public as well as between executives, union leaders, and employees at all organizational levels. Fortunately, a growing and widespread interest in ecology has added a new dimension to understanding needed standards for health and safety. And systems thinking offers a fruitful approach for coping with the whole network of interrelated factors that need to be taken into account if employees—and other people all over the world—are to work and live in an environment that is reasonably healthy and safe.

NEW KNOWLEDGE

Behavioral Psychology and Industrial Hygiene

One field of knowledge, of which managers in earlier times did not have the benefit, consists of findings by behavioral psychologists. For example,

ple, many old-time employers never even entertained the idea that each employee (male or female) is a whole person, living his (or her) life throughout the 24 hours of every day. Nor did they take into account that each individual is, to some extent, unique—so that it doesn't make sense to treat them, and try to communicate with them, as though they were all alike.[7]

Managers who recognize that each employee is a unique individual, and a whole person, know that it is unrealistic to regard "personal" problems of an employee as though such matters were of no concern to management because they could have no effect on the enterprise as a whole. Instead, it is increasingly taken into account that no employee can continue to put forth his best efforts if much of his physical, nervous, or mental energy is dissipated in battling with adverse conditions in any part of his life.

Thus, findings in connection with motivation at work are confirmed by research in occupational health and safety. Taken together, they conclusively show that ill health (mental or physical) and severe stress (such as may be occasioned by family difficulties, pressures generated by organizational conflicts and arduous work assignments, or by fear for one's safety at work) adversely affect not only what an employee *will* do, but even what he *can* do. Executives and managers familiar with such modern research, and who accept these findings as realistic, are in a position to practice the emerging style of managing that implements the broad requirements of the Occupational Safety and Health Act.

[7] In this connection it is significant that physiological research in the field of occupational health and safety has reinforced two of Maslow's conclusions (stated in Chap. 6). Physiologically, as well as psychologically, it is now recognized that (1) each individual is a distinctive biological personality, responding in his own way to environmental factors, and (2) that concentration on target tissues (for example, the liver and kidney in tetrachloride poisoning) is not enough. "The body reacts as a unified whole to all external environmental stimuli. . . ." See May R. Mayers, M.D., *Occupational Health: Hazards of the Work Environment,* The Williams & Wilkins Company, Baltimore, 1969, p. xii.

[6] Raymond H. Mulford, "Environmental Quality—A Challenge to Business," *Michigan Business Review,* vol. 23, no. 4, July, 1971, pp. 7-11, 17.

An Emerging Style of Managing

Employers who practice participative management make it possible for every organizational member to work *with* others toward shared objectives. And such cooperation has often led employees at all organizational levels voluntarily to give that "something extra" which can be even more effective than law enforcement or centralized managerial control. Experienced managers, supervisors, and inspectors know that no degree of externally imposed control can ever wholly close the gap between legal (or management) objectives and the facts of daily performance. The clause in OSHA providing that any employee may appeal directly to the Secretary of Labor is a legislative effort to close that gap. But obviously whenever such action is taken, it is certain to have serious repercussions on personnel and labor relations. Bypassing is deplored by every organization-minded individual. A preferable solution, wherever it can be achieved, is intelligent and informed cooperation *within* each enterprise (including those not engaged in interstate commerce where federal legislation does not apply) toward the mutually beneficial objectives of maximum health and safety.[8]

PRINCIPLES AND POLICY DECISIONS

Principles of Leadership and Mutual Responsibility

Participative management is based on the following principles of leadership: (1) When management strengthens those upon whom it depends for results, it strengthens the organization as a whole; (2) effective and harmonious work-

ing relationships can be established and maintained only when everyone involved is willing and able to do his full share and feels his responsibility for the whole.

The value of leadership, with mutual responsibility for shared objectives (rather than authoritarian management, imposed by inflexible orders and externally enforced rules) is now widely recognized in regard to the technical side of work and standards on the job. All efficient managers expect to set up adequate working conditions, to devise efficient work procedures, and to supply high-grade equipment. In return they expect employees to meet reasonable quantity and quality standards of production and to maintain a responsible attitude toward their work and equipment. The same principle of mutual responsibility is equally valid, and is being increasingly applied, to human factors in the work situation[9]—including those that contribute to employee health and safety.

Having established principles that can usefully undergird all organizational activity, the next step in planning programs for employee safety and health may well be to make policy decisions. These will need to take account not only of technical and medical knowledge in general but also of special circumstances in each enterprise, such as financial resources, available financial and human resources for staffing, working conditions, production processes, materials used, current type of management, and the character of the personnel program as a whole. The following matters for policy decisions will serve to make this general statement specific.

Policy Decisions: Scope and Depth of Programs

The general trend today is toward greater emphasis on preventive medicine and on accident

---

[8] See in this connection stimulating articles by Roderick A. Forsgren, "A Model of Supportive Work Conditions through Safety Management," *Personnel Journal,* vol. 48, no. 5, pp. 351–358, May, 1969; "Developing Employee Psychological Advantage through Safety Management," *Environmental Control & Safety Management,* vol. 14, no. 6, pp. 26–30, December, 1970; "Developing Group Building, Maintenance, and Task Roles through Safety Programs," *Journal of the American Society of Safety Engineers,* vol. 16, no. 5, pp. 16–20, May, 1971.

[9] The Occupational Safety and Health Act does not invoke penalties for heedless violations by employees of safety and health regulations. Nevertheless, it is clear that this law imposes on employees the duty to comply voluntarily with safety and health regulations.

prevention, rather than on postaccident care. *Prevention:* Employers who are interested in building maximum prevention into their health and safety programs are in a position to benefit by the constantly increasing body of knowledge in the field of industrial hygiene. Understanding of the physiological relationship between man and his work environment (the relatively new science of ergonomics)[10] has been growing at an exponential rate. Industrial hygienists, who specialize in this field, have contributed greatly to preventive protection for employees subjected to occupational health hazards such as exposure to toxic chemicals, radioactive materials, and excessive noise.

In relation to employee safety, engineers constantly carry on, with growing expertise, such preventive work as (1) testing new machinery to make sure that it can be used without undue risk, (2) developing new protective equipment to guard against unavoidable risks—both new and old, and (3) cooperating with supervisors, operators, and union representatives to help employees develop safe working habits and a safety-oriented state of mind.

In such a positive program, physical examinations can play an important part both in the preemployment phase and periodically for employees exposed to unusual health hazards. At best, all employees should have the benefit of an annual physical checkup. Such examinations ensure timely diagnosis of ill health such as heart trouble, diabetes, etc. In each firm the policy question is: Will it be a good investment in organizational health to follow up the preemployment physical examination with one or both of the others? (See also later section in this chapter.)

Remedial Care[11]

Regardless of how much is done as prevention, there will always be some need for remedial care.

Over and above requirements as formulated in current state laws of workmen's compensation (and as may further be required by future legislation), every policy-minded employer will want to decide for himself[12] what obligation—if any—the enterprise has to offer help when prolonged remedial care and rehabilitation are needed by disabled or emotionally disturbed employees. Examples of special needs for such care are serious mental ill health and the related disabilities of alcoholism and drug addiction.

Mental Ill Health, Alcoholism, and Drug Addiction If the health department includes a full-time, first-class psychiatrist, or perhaps more than one, an employer may wish to consider offering psychiatric help toward the rehabilitation of regular employees with serious mental health problems. Among the employees who need such help may be persons such as the "half man" (already mentioned in Chapter 11). Trice[13] offers the following suggestions for policy thinking with reference to setting up a rehabilitation program for alcoholics. To be effective, emphasis in such a program must be on the total person in his total work environment and on the interdependent stages of the rehabilitation process: (1) personnel policy, (2) available therapy, (3) early identification knowledge, (4) willingness of supervisors to use a policy and a program, (5) acceptance of treatment by the alcoholic employee, and (6) long-term operation of the program.

In its policy statement, top management should define alcoholism among its employees as a health problem, requiring therapy. The policy statement should then affirm the intention to of-

---

[10] See Etienne Grandjean, *Fitting the Task to the Man: An Ergonomic Approach,* Taylor & Francis, Ltd., London, 1969, especially the section on "The Working Environment," pp. 136–158.

[11] We do not mention first aid, here, as a matter for policy decision, because almost all employers provide this emergency service—some of them for reasons of economy and others partly with an eye to public relations.

[12] Of course, if such help is specified in the labor agreement, as for instance in the UAW contract with General Motors Corporation with reference to mental health, this is no longer a unilateral policy question.

[13] Harrison M. Trice, *Alcoholism in Industry: Modern Procedures,* The Christopher D. Smithers Foundation, Inc., New York, 1968, pp. 12–13.

fer assistance in securing (or providing) therapy. To provide such assistance, management would rely on inside treatment sources (medical personnel and counselors, if available). To secure outside therapy, management would refer the patient to such sources as clinics and hospitals, local affiliates of The National Council on Alcoholism, and Alcoholics Anonymous.

Help for employees who drink to excess can be most effective in the early stages. Unfortunately, fellow workers, union shop stewards, and even supervisors have often succeeded in covering up for employees who begin to turn in recurrent poor work performance and manifest such physical symptoms as periodic hangover, hand tremors, bleary eyes, and sporadic stomach upsets. Before an effective medical program can be set up for such persons, therefore, cooperation from fellow employees is needed.

Employees who are addicted to drugs present their employers with similar questions for policy decision. However, if their addiction was known at the time of their hiring (perhaps because they were veterans of the Indochina war), an employer may feel that he is obligated to offer help toward their rehabilitation.

On the other hand, with both alcoholics and drug-addicted employees, an employer may well feel that the principle of mutual responsibility should be decisive as to how long such assistance should be given. Unless an afflicted employee cooperates fully toward his own rehabilitation, should an employer feel obligated to continue offering help indefinitely?[14]

Special Provisions for Special Categories of Employees

Other matters for policy decision in regard to a company health program concern disadvan-taged employees, long-service personnel, and women.

When the personnel program as a whole is flexible, it should not be necessary to explain—to employees or union representatives—that special provisions to meet special needs do not necessarily represent inequities.

Disadvantaged Employees   Should any part of the company health program be expanded or prolonged to meet special needs of employees recruited from poverty areas? Their health may be substandard at the time of their first employment. Does this create for the employer an obligation to offer them extra medical care? In answering this question, it should be taken into account that physical and psychological health are inseparable. Members from any nonwhite group, especially if they have not previously consorted regularly with whites, are likely to be subjected to severe psychological tension at first. Can an employer (perhaps through a member of the medical department) appropriately offer help to such employees? If so, how much help, and for how long?

Shaw[15] predicted that the "evolution of personnel management [will include] a dramatic new role for industrial medicine in closing the gap between the performance and the potential of individuals . . . ." The policy question is whether a given management considers that closing this gap, with medical care, is any part of its business.

Long-service Employees   A matter for policy decision that arises in many organizations is what to do about long-service employees who can no longer safely carry on their customary duties. For example, a job may require working on a ladder, on scaffolding, or at a high altitude. Many older persons begin to suffer from spells of dizziness. For them such work is unsafe.

[14] Harrison M. Trice and Paul M. Roman, *Spirits and Demons at Work: Alcohol and Other Drugs on the Job,* ILR Paperback no. 11, New York State School of Industrial and Labor Relations, Cornell University, Ithaca, N.Y., January, 1972.

[15] Edward A. Shaw, "Speculations about Man and His Work—A.D. 2000," *Personnel Journal,* vol. 46, no. 7, pp. 419-426, July-August, 1967.

If company policy is to help older employees adjust to incipient infirmities, the chances are good that the handicaps of advancing age will be communicated to supervisors in time to prevent an injury. But this informal opening for protecting employee safety is not enough.

One preventive practice may be semiannual physical examinations for all employees of sixty and over. In this way new handicaps can probably be detected in time to make changes in job assignments or arrange for early retirement.

However, the physical risks associated with advancing age are only part of total health and safety. Uneasiness, or downright unhappiness, at the prospect of retirement often affects employees in the preretirement years. During this period of psychological stress, preretirement interviews (as a matter of company policy) can be useful. Long-service employees can discuss with their supervisors (or with some member of the personnel department) the various options that are open to them. For example, for a given employee:

- Will early retirement be the answer? or,
- Does some physical handicap require modification of current work requirements or change in work assignment before recommending total retirement? or,
- Is gradual retirement advisable, either with increasingly long leaves of absence (without pay but with social security benefits) or as part-time work? Gradual retirement can be mutually beneficial. The organization can benefit by a senior employee's experience while a replacement is being trained. The employee has an opportunity to develop interests and capabilities other than those associated with his former work.

Female Employees Many enterprises are located in states whose laws are inconsistent with federal law (as stated in the Civil Rights Act) with regard to female employees.[16] When this is the case, it is a matter of company policy to decide such questions as whether women should be given maternity leave (without loss of pay or seniority) and possibly brief periods of time off—occasionally—to care for their children if the latter are seriously ill.

Employee Education Still another matter for policy decision is whether, and to what extent, it seems like a good investment in organizational health and safety for management to provide—or sponsor—a special educational program. In such a program information can be supplied as to sensible living habits; nutrition; day-care centers (in the community or provided by the company); company recreational facilities; local agencies (or voluntary groups) that offer help for persons suffering from mental ill health, alcoholism, or drug addiction; and perhaps also current developments and research in regard to industrial safety.

Another possibility in regard to employee education—for example, in safety—is to offer a continuing program in which there can be active participation by staff experts (including engineers, methods men, and personnel from the safety department), operating and maintenance personnel, representatives of management (from various organizational levels), and of the union (if there is one). In our opinion, the case method is an excellent medium for such an educational program. Much can be accomplished, as members from different parts of the organization, at different organizational levels, with different functions and responsibilities, discuss and analyze situations in which safety was a factor. Every member of such a study group can learn more than he knew before not only about safety needs but also about the viewpoints and specific difficulties of employees in other parts of the organization. In this way, education ties in with prevention, facilitates interpersonal communication, and fosters coordination.

Communication and Coordination Needs for improved interpersonal communication and

---

[16] The subject of women workers was treated at some length in Chap. 4. Therefore we touch on it here only in brief, as an illustration.

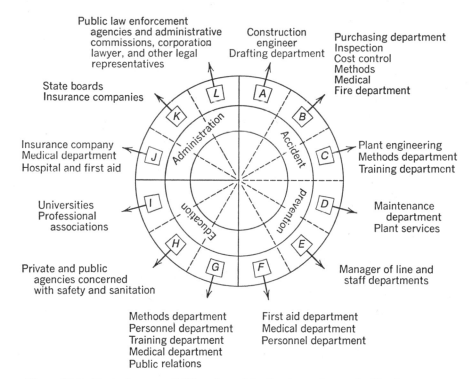

Figure 22-1 Typical responsibilities of a safety director and opportunities for cooperation with line and staff officials. (*A*) Checking plant layout and equipment to ensure conformance with federal and state standards as well as with recognized safety practices and company policies. (*B*) Supervising the purchase, testing, installation, and checkup of protective equipment and fire-fighting apparatus. (*C*) Planning and establishing other measures of safety control, such as specific precautions based on surveys to determine special risks. (*D*) Supervising plant housekeeping and conducting plant inspections. (*E*) Seeing that adequate safety inspections are made and reported. (*F*) Analyzing accidents; correlating and studying accident and injury reports. (*G*) Planning and administering safety education. (*H*) Keeping up to date on such matters as standard codes for safety and health. (*I*) Conducting research projects in matters concerned with safety and health. (*J*) Helping to formulate, establish, and maintain accident procedure. (*K*) Serving as liaison officer with private and government agents and investigators in connection with accidents, injuries, and physical disabilities. (*L*) Corresponding with all interested parties in injury cases and maintaining proper files.

coordination exist in every organization. Effectiveness in these activities is essential for success in a program designed to protect the health and safety of employees. The policy question thus becomes: How much time (and therefore money) is to be invested in furthering such organization-wide objectives? An employer may decide to set up interdepartmental committees that meet regularly. Members of these committees

can serve as "link pins" to carry ideas back to their own work groups, and to stimulate employee motivation for health and safety. The aim of such widespread communication and coordination would be to develop attitudes, conditions, and practices that are conducive to health and safety at all times and in all places where employees are at work—or at leisure—in the work environment. At best, communication and cooperation for employee safety and health should extend even beyond the limits of a given enterprise. Figure 22-1 presents this idea graphically.

When knowledge and experience (both scientific and practical) are drawn from all organizational levels, it should be possible to meet increasingly higher standards for employee safety and health.

Standards Few enterprises can be adequately staffed, in either health or safety departments, to do all the research—in relation to standards—made possible by the growth of interdisciplinary knowledge and necessary by the pace of technological advances.[17] A question for policy decision may therefore be to what extent company health and safety specialists will be expected to develop new and attainable standards within the organization. (Naturally, experts in industrial hygiene, safety, and health should keep abreast of legislation and outside research that apply to their own enterprise.)

Effective communication and coordination can play a significant part in enabling personnel in safety and health to contribute both in planning, and for performance at high standards. For example, is it regular procedure in the company for the medical director to participate in planning with regard to such matters as late shift assignments and schedules for shift rotation? If so, he may be able to offer valuable advice—in relation to preventive measures—by presenting current research findings as to the different effects on various individuals of assignments that

interfere with normal life rhythms of working and sleeping.[18] Similarly, in considering a shorter workweek (with consequently longer workdays) managers need to take into account possible effects of such changes on the health of individual employees and therefore also in the closely related field of employee safety.

Research This activity is implicit in setting, applying, and supervising standards. Moreover, fruitful research depends upon, and can result in, communication and coordination as well as in prevention and continuing education. Thus a matter for top management consideration is whether specialists in employee health and safety are measuring up to the full scope of their responsibilities unless they are constantly thinking about such questions as these: What new needs in this work environment call for new procedures, new attitudes, and altered work habits? What innovative ideas, developed by scientific researchers (nationally and internationally)[19] and by safety and health personnel in other work situations, could be used or adapted to make our own place of work even more healthy and/or safe than it has been heretofore? How might our employees cooperate with outside specialists to develop new ideas for industrial health and safety?

If management is interested in the fruits of such research, it should decide in consultation with specialists (1) what kind of research in employee safety and health is most urgently needed now, (2) whether this needed research can most effectively be done (or is currently being done) by a government agency or private organization,

---

[17] For example, a special report issued by the U.S. Surgeon General in 1966 and entitled "Protecting the Health of 80 Million Americans" states, "It has been estimated that every 20 minutes a new, and potentially toxic, chemical is being introduced into industry. New processes and new sources of energy present occupational health problems of unprecedented complexity." For a revealing analysis of the complex, often synergistic, interactions of numerous physical, chemical, and psychological agents, see chap. 2, "The Chemical Jungle," pp. 7–18, in Ray Davidson, *Peril on the Job: A Study of Hazards in the Chemical Industries,* Public Affairs Press, Washington, D.C., 1970.

[18] See for example, W. P. Colquhoun, M. J. F. Blake, and R. S. Edwards, "Experimental Studies of Shift Work," in *Ergonomics,* vols. 11, 12, and 13; especially W. P. Colquhoun, "Circadian Rhythms, Mental Efficiency and Shift Work," *Ergonomics,* vol. 13, no. 5, pp. 558–560, May, 1970.

[19] See in this connection, Marcel Robert and Luigi Parmeggiani, "Fifty Years of International Collaboration in Occupational Safety and Health," *International Labour Review,* vol. 99, no. 1, pp. 85–136, Geneva, January, 1969.

and (3) whether a joint union-management research project can be used to supplement research by outside specialists. Joint union-management research projects are feasible when union and management representatives are interested and a good working relationship exists between them.[20] A significant byproduct of joint research projects—in employee safety and health, especially if they can be set up as continuing programs—may be increasing mutual respect and a better understanding of what needs to be accomplished.

As a unified point of view, decisions on the foregoing matters may be summed up in two major policy questions: Do we, in this enterprise, want to do anything more than is required of us by legislative enactments? If so, how much more, and in what parts of our program for employee safety and/or health?

DELEGATING RESPONSIBILITY FOR SAFETY AND HEALTH PROGRAMS

Responsibility for employee safety and health should certainly rest with top management, whose thinking characteristically centers on principles and policies. But of course, if responsibility stops at the policy level, it can be of no benefit to employees. The responsibility for implementing top-management policy decisions and long-range plans must be delegated to representatives of staff and line.

The first step in meeting such delegated responsibility is taken when a safety director and a medical director draw up and submit to top management detailed plans and procedures to protect employee safety and health as well as plans for coordinating and reporting. These plans should then be explicitly endorsed, in writing, by the chief executive. This practice ensures due respect from all management representatives who are expected to apply and supervise the various programs. Acceptance and effective action from management representatives, all down the line, can be expected when they understand top management's policy thinking and if they were selected and developed as junior partners in a total effort to manage by shared objectives.

Another requirement for maximum efficiency in implementing policy thinking, with regard to employee safety and health, is that specialists in charge of these programs—the safety and health directors, and possibly also an expert in industrial hygiene—have the status and qualifications commensurate with their weighty responsibilities.

Staffing and Status of Directors   In many large concerns, management has become convinced that there is need for specialists in all three of the above-mentioned areas, each of whom gives full time to his responsibilities and is supported by a staff of competent subordinates.

To indicate the importance of these functions in the eyes of top management, it has often been considered advisable for these specialists to be members of the chief executive's general staff. However, the practical necessity of meeting the requirements of a manageable span of control has often led to other organizational arrangements. For example, these functions are usually considered as subordinated activities of the personnel department.

A special reason why a safety director should also report directly to the head of plant operations is that, unlike other staff personnel, he may—on occasion—have to exercise direct line authority. For example if, during an inspection

---

[20] For example, President A. F. Grospiron, Chemical & Atomic Workers International Union, AFL-CIO, initiated a series of regional meetings in which men and women from the plants could describe their problems and discuss them with scientists, notably Glenn Paulson, Department of Environmental Biomedicine (The Rockefeller University, New York). These discussions were followed up by plant visits and in-depth interviews with several hundred union members. The final report (Davidson, *op. cit.*), while critical of management systems as they affect the health and safety of workers, does not aim criticism at individual managers.

tour, he sees some unsafe practice or condition that entails risk of imminent serious injury, he is empowered to suspend operations immediately. However, if he is wise in administrative matters, he will use this delegated authority sparingly. When time and circumstances permit, a safety director should always work *with* supervisors first so that, as often as possible, his reports to top management can show that any needed corrective measures have already been undertaken by any supervisor who had a safety problem.

Specific Duties of the Medical and Safety Director The duties of these department heads, and priorities among the specific duties, vary according to the nature of the enterprise, specific working conditions, the work environment, and the sophistication of top management.

Detailed consideration of specific duties in both health and safety, along with staffing requirements and facilities in each department, would be out of place in this text. Moreover these matters are amply covered in a growing body of technical literature.[21] However, one major duty of the safety director is worth describing here in some detail, because it illustrates a special application of situational thinking.

Analyzing Accidents[22]—for Purposes of Prevention and General Education

The primary aims of an up-to-date safety director in analyzing accidents are prevention and education. The analytical method used is similar to that which a medical director (and a personnel administrator) need to apply. It includes getting

a range of facts (by correlating different kinds of information, by interviewing, and by studying trends as shown in a cumulative record); noting relationships between key facts and between recurring features of specific situations with the purpose of revealing remediable causes and applying a person-centered approach to special cases. *An important part of the safety director's job is to interpret and communicate top management's policy for safety in such a way as to lift everyone to the level of policy thinking.* For this purpose, he studies the total work environment to see what he can learn and teach that is of general validity. If prevention and education are emphasized as company policy, a safety director naturally tries to increase in himself, and to spread among others, an *understanding of underlying causes of accidents and of what needs to be done to make safe behavior habitual.*

In working toward prevention and education, he can properly begin by asking himself and other employees: *What is an accident?* This apparently simple question has often proved as educational as it is difficult to answer. The difficulty is inherent in the widespread assumption that an accident is something which necessarily costs blood, money, or both. People recognize an accident when it results in material damage, spoilage, or bodily injury. However, they often fail to identify the essential characteristics of the accident itself.

Such preoccupation with *consequences* instead of concentrating on the intrinsic nature *of what happens* was vividly demonstrated in the experience of a safety engineer who conducted numerous accident-prevention conferences. Over a period of years, he obtained a striking uniformity of answers from workers and lower supervisors when he asked the following questions:

• Suppose that a man is trying to put a screw into a window frame and the screwdriver slips. Is that an accident? To this question the immediate answer was almost invariably "no."

[21] See, for example, American Medical Association, Council on Occupational Health, "A Management Guide for Occupational Health Programs," *Archives of Environmental Health,* vol. 9, pp. 408-413, September, 1964; and "Guide to the Development of Company Medical Policies," *ibid.,* vol. 11, pp. 729-733, November, 1965.

[22] In Chap. 11, accident analysis was considered as an indicator of employee morale. Therefore, the analytical techniques described there are different from those presented in the following pages.

- Suppose that the screwdriver slips out of the slot of the screw and smashes the windowpane without hurting the worker. Is that an accident? The answer to this question came more slowly and showed a slight increase in affirmatives.
- Suppose that a man hurts his wrist as a screwdriver goes through the windowpane. Is that an accident? The answer to this question was a prompt and unanimous "yes."

Concentration on results diverts attention from analysis of causes and is often expressed in a fatalistic attitude toward accidents as "acts of God," unpredictable and unavoidable features of industrial life. This attitude was clearly indicated in the following "definitions" of accidents made by lower-level supervisors during conferences on accident prevention: An accident is "something that sneaks up on you," "an unexpected event," or "something that goes wrong and can't be helped."

A safety director is committed to a more far-reaching and realistic analysis and to the view that *what was unforeseen is not necessarily unforeseeable.* He therefore tries to define an accident in such a way as to bring out its typical characteristics. For this purpose, it is useful to develop a definition that centers attention on *the process by which accidents become increasingly probable and, if the process is not halted, or reversed, finally happen.*

The Accident Process

Recognition of continuity in human experience indicates that an accident is not an isolated or arbitrary occurrence. Instead it is a stage in a process by which some condition or mode of behavior leads to an unplanned result. This conception of the accident *as an unplanned incident* emphasizes the importance of planned behavior. Each accident is an integral part of a sequence of happenings which at some stage was probably foreseeable and subject to control. When proper and timely adjustments are made, many unplanned incidents can be prevented.

The accident process can, therefore, be thought of as *a sequence of actions or occurrences during which, for lack of some needed adjustment* (in attitude, in behavior, in mechanical operation, or in environmental conditions), *there is increasing likelihood of an unplanned incident.*

Thus, the only sound aspect of the customary preoccupation with results is the fact that the consequence is part of the process. But, for accident prevention and safety education, the center of interest in an accident sequence should be on what happens *before,* rather than on what happens *during or after* the stage when the unplanned[23] incident occurs.

The Accident Context Accidents should be studied not only as part of a larger segment of time but also as one feature in a situation that includes more than one person and his immediate environment. The larger context contains not only the potential victim and the tangible object or circumstance to which he is not safely adjusted but also all the people, feelings, ideas, and surroundings that make up his environment and experience. An accident may be occasioned by worry about something quite remote from the place where the accident occurs and from the activity engaged in when the accident happens. For example, a truck driver may be so worried about a personal problem that he fails to heed a red light. Whether or not his truck collides with another vehicle, he has driven unsafely. But his state of mind was what "drove him" into unsafe behavior. Or again, *accident-proneness* may be increased by the tension and preoccupation that are set up in one person when he sees another involved in an accident.

[23] H. W. Heinrich, *loc. cit.,* p. 26ff., reviewed over 5,000 cases of potential injury accidents. He estimated that, on the average, in a unit of 330 accidents of the same kind and *involving the same person,* 300 result in no injury, 29 in minor injuries, and 1 in a major lost-time injury. This 300-29-1 ratio spells opportunity, provided that employees who had a "narrow escape" or a "lucky break" use this timely warning signal for self-education or are willing to reveal this information for subsequent analysis.

Differentiating Causes For the purpose of accident analysis, the safety director may usefully differentiate between mechanical and human causes (sometimes termed "accident sources" and "accident causes"). In this way, he can focus attention first on environmental and mechanical sources of accidents, for which management is primarily responsible. One of his major objectives should be to demonstrate how industrial accidents can be reduced if mechanical design is more directly related to the psychological and physiological characteristics of the employees. In cooperating with designers, the safety engineer should study mechanical equipment and arrangements (before they are used, if possible) in relation to the people who are going to use them and the conditions under which they will be used.

Over and above the "human element" in general, individual differences among employees concern the safety engineer. He needs to study the states of body and mind that make different people at various times more safe or less safe in the same environmental circumstances. Even when an accident is *occasioned* by a mechanical risk, there may still be need to explore events and behavior that preceded the accident. If a worker was inattentive or failed to observe rules or to follow instructions, why did this happen? Were the rules and instructions clearly stated? Was there any follow-up to find out whether they were understood? Had the worker failed in the same way before? If safety equipment was not used, why not?

Using a Person-centered Approach Exploration of the circumstances surrounding accidents indicates that psychological factors often deserve attention. In such a case, a person-centered approach is needed to determine whether the condition can be alleviated or remedied. Fears arising out of job insecurity, anger aroused during labor disputes, tension growing out of assignment to an uncongenial work group or due

to the pace of work, boredom because a job seems monotonous—all these accident-causing attitudes should be studied by supervisors. To what extent, and by what means, can they be eliminated or modified?[24]

By analyzing risks associated with certain kinds of work and production processes, supervisors and the safety director can progressively improve their understanding of accident causes. They can then submit to higher management recommendations for more effective procedures to prevent accidents.[25]

Accident Reporting

A safety director's responsibility for accident reporting includes (1) getting full and informal reports from as many as possible of the employees who become involved in *any* stage of the accident process and (2) seeing to it that written reports of accidents are accurate and adequate—though brief—and recorded in a form such that causes may be discerned.

Getting Reports The possibility of getting full reports depends on winning voluntary cooperation from employees who grasp the idea of an accident process and feel ready to work with management representatives toward the objective of accident prevention. Unless employees become interested in what happens *before* an injury accident and unless they feel secure from being penalized *after* they report accidents, management representatives cannot expect to learn much except from what they themselves can see.

Reluctance of employees and supervisors to report minor accidents is a natural response in an organizational environment where management policies (or directives) stress assigning indi-

[24] See Earle S. Hannaford, *Supervisors Guide to Human Relations,* National Safety Council, Chicago, 1967.
[25] This approach is emphasized by M. A. Gimbel, one of the coauthors of the 3d ed. of Roland P. Blake, *Industrial Safety,* Prentice-Hall, Englewood Cliffs, N.J., 1963, chaps. 8–16.

vidual blame and meting out penalties, rather than discovering and correcting all that seems to be accountable (in the company situation as a whole) for faulty behavior and undesirable attitudes. Giving awards for good safety records seems to work better than penalizing people who have, or cause, accidents serious enough to attract the attention of someone in authority (though, of course, repeated, willful disregard of safety rules cannot be overlooked). *But what is all-important is to enlist every employee in noticing and reporting the slight, or embryonic, accidents which customarily receive no attention from anyone.*

The possibility of winning a high degree of such participation and the danger of impulsively imposing penalties are illustrated in the following example.

A Case Example: The Pink Slips

In a large public utility corporation, management had appealed to the workers to provide information about the slight errors and unexpected results in daily work routine that are not usually regarded as accidents at all. The employees responded enthusiastically and submitted brief notations of many such accidents. This opened to the safety engineer a valuable source of first-hand material that would otherwise have been untapped. The data provided clues for a causal analysis that enabled management to answer such vital questions as: Have our supervisors proper training, and do they evince a responsible attitude toward accident prevention? Are all our employees adequately instructed and given the tools and working conditions that promote safety? Do employees exercise reasonable caution in regard to their own safety and to the safety of others?

As management took appropriate steps to get and apply such information the frequency and severity of accidents progressively declined. Several departments established a no-accident rec-

ord. Unfortunately, an operating vice-president, with a mistaken conception of efficiency, threw a monkey wrench into the works. His analysis of the "pink slips," which had been contributed by employees over a considerable period of time, revealed that some of the men were "accident-prone" individuals. To safeguard company interest, therefore, the executive decided that it was more efficient to eliminate these "offenders." When this decision was put into effect by discharging a number of workers, word was passed along the grapevine, and employee cooperation ceased almost overnight. "No more pink slips!"

Recording Accident Data A necessary follow-up procedure (after getting informal reports), and a vital preliminary to effective accident prevention, is developing a system which ensures that written reports of injury accidents will be sufficiently reliable and informative.[26]

Taking Account of Indirect Costs In the field of safety, cost accounting should include emphasis on indirect costs insofar as these can be estimated by tracing the chain of consequences that follow accidents. Indirect costs of injury accidents include such items as time lost to productive work (by injured employee, supervisor, and other employees who gather round to help the injured person or merely stand and gawk), time spent by first-aid or medical department, continuing cost of overhead during lost-time period, and cost of subsequent injuries occurring during an accident cycle. All these expenses, and many more, raise the indirect cost of accidents to a figure that averages four or more times the amount entailed in such direct costs as the wage loss to the injured employee, medical expenses, and overhead cost of insurance and/or compensation. By tabulating and reporting these hidden

[26] For a detailed report on a coding system recommended by the American Standards Association, see Alphonse Chapanis, *Research Techniques in Human Engineering,* The Johns Hopkins Press, Baltimore, 1959, p. 84.

losses, and thus showing himself to be more cost-minded than line management itself, a safety director may be able to win agreement to the idea that unsafe conditions and practices are an extravagance that the organization cannot afford.

Committees for Employee Safety and Health

In a large organization, much of the day-to-day work in eliminating avoidable risks and protecting employee health can most effectively be done through employee participation on committees.

Interdepartmental Committees The directors of the relevant departments should be at least *ex officio* members. In unionized companies it is desirable also to have a high-level union official as a member. If the chief executive (perhaps the plant manager) occasionally chairs such a committee, this is one of the best ways to communicate his continuing concern with employee safety and health, to stimulate managerial interest in ways of advancing these aims, and to ensure that suggestions for improving safety and health programs are communicated up the line where long-range plans and policy decisions are made and kept up to date.

In a medium-sized firm, all these objectives may be met by having one cross-functional committee in each of the related fields of health and safety. In a small organization, there are advantages in having a single committee whose responsibilities span both safety and health. Whether such interdepartmental committees are separate or combined, a useful cross-fertilization of ideas is likely to result. And the outreach of such organization-wide thinking may be increased by rotating the membership.

One special need for an interdepartmental committee is to develop and implement procedures for employees approaching retirement. At best, a policy statement has clarified top management's desire to do its part in matching individual and organizational needs throughout an employee's career in the company, including the preretirement stage (as mentioned in the section on special provisions for long-service employees).

A retirement review committee can appropriately implement that overall policy decision. For example, if, in a given organization, retirement is mandatory (for men at sixty-five and for women at sixty-two), committee members can encourage employees who have reached the ages of fifty-seven and sixty to begin planning for their approaching retirement. (In general, however, women have less need for such timing, partly because their organizational roles have been less absorbing than those of men and partly because family responsibilities help to fill their time satisfactorily after retirement.)

However, many men do not wish to retire at 65 and, depending on the labor market and the existence of a flexible retirement policy, it may not be necessary for them to retire. In fact, it may be beneficial both for them and for the organization to have them remain at work. In such cases, and depending on findings of physical examinations, the retirement committee may recommend that an employee be allowed to continue with his regular work (or with a modified work assignment).

If the employee's immediate line supervisor accepts the committee's recommendation, the length of continued employment should be a matter of company policy. Perhaps the age of seventy has been set as the limit. If so, the review committee should keep informed as to the physical condition of each employee over the age of sixty-five. It should also be made clear that the decision as to continued employment will be reviewed annually—or oftener if there is evidence of inability to meet job requirements safely and without undue physical or mental strain.

Intradepartmental Committees The chief function of an intradepartmental committee, whether for safety or health, is to evoke interest at the level where most accidents happen—namely, the operating level.

Membership on these committees should include first-level supervisors, shop stewards, and a few rank-and-file employees who are elected (or appointed) for this specific assignment. Whether or not the safety and medical directors and the industrial hygienist attend these meetings, each should see to it that (1) relevant material—either as new research findings or a projected change in company procedure—is supplied to each committee chairman; (2) he is kept posted as to the agenda of every such committee meeting, as well as of decisions reached or recommendations made; (3) he is up to date as to action taken for the purpose of implementing those decisions (and of the effectiveness of such action); and (4) prompt steps are taken to communicate these decisions and actions up the line to the highest level (for example, to the plant manager).

In this connection, as in others, it is necessary to reckon on the fact that no organization operates in a vacuum. Federal or state legislation and new risks imposed by the environment must be taken into account. For example, organizations whose activities entail the use of radioactive materials are not the only ones whose employees are—and increasingly will be—exposed to new and serious risks. Even in peacetime, radioactive wastes threaten an increasing number of people and endanger the ecosphere.

EMPLOYEE SAFETY AND HEALTH PROGRAMS

Integral Parts of a Total Personnel Policy System

Even more important than committee work to ensure the success of programs to protect employee health and safety is the extent to which these specialized activities are forwarded by other parts of the total personnel program. If any one of these specialists is appointed in a com-

pany that lacks a system of positive and employee-oriented policies, he is likely to have a hard row to hoe before he can even start getting results. But when he undertakes his duties in a firm where an employee-centered point of view has been accepted and is practiced at all organizational levels, he will find that much of the spadework for his own job has already been done. This general statement can be illustrated by glancing at the following activities and practices that make up a standard personnel program:

• *Selection of applicants* can contribute to both organizational health and safety (see Chapter 15 for details). Adequate testing, thorough preemployment physical examination, and skillful employment interviewing can serve to screen out the unfit and to give some assurance that those who are accepted are physically, mentally, and emotionally suited to fill current vacancies. (If exceptions are made, for example in *recruiting* from among the hard-core unemployed, the safety director and the company doctor should be prepared to undertake special educational and follow-up programs with these temporarily disadvantaged employees.)

• *Proper placement* (see Chapter 15) contributes greatly to health and safety, especially when idiosyncrasies such as accident-proneness or emotional instability are taken into account.

• *Orientation and follow-up.* The importance for safety and health of adequate orientation during induction has not been generally recognized. Everyone knows that new employees need to be carefully inducted in technical matters. Equally important, however, is the fact that new employees have to make social accommodations (establishing mutually satisfactory relationships with fellow employees, members of supervision, and staff experts). Another need for orientation may arise when women are first employed on tasks previously performed by men only.

• *Reorientation* is often a great aid to individual stability (e.g., when an employee has been recalled after a considerable interval and thus needs to learn his way around again in a company situation and work environment that have changed, to some extent, while he was on layoff or on extended leave of absence).

Reorientation, in a different sense, is likely to be even more acutely needed by a person who has never before had regular employment or perhaps has never worked with persons whose behavior and outlook on life seem alien to him because of differences in cultural background.

• The value of a thorough *training* program (Chapter 16) that incorporates safety precautions for both workers and supervisors cannot be overestimated for employee safety and health.

• *Promotion and transfer* (Chapter 17) may call for reorientation and special follow-up to assure that the "new" employee will adapt his attitude and behavior so that he will be safe in a work environment that is new to him and will not in any way endanger those who work with him.

• *Constructive discipline* (considered in Chapter 18) has obvious implications for mental health. The example of the "pink slips" indicates how much an effective program for accident prevention depends on a positive policy for discipline, a policy that needs to be consistently implemented in managerial decisions and supervisory actions.

• Realistic thinking and care for employee health and safety are never more necessary than during the difficult conditions associated with the need to impose layoffs (either for lack of work or as a disciplinary measure), downgrading, demotion, or discharge (Chapter 18).

• When planning *changes in work assignments and work schedules* (Chapter 19) the safety and health of individual employees need to be taken into account. For example, a new work assignment may entail risks for some individuals or for long-service employees, although it would not be hazardous for other individuals or for younger persons. Moreover, as noted earlier in this chapter, planning for changes in work schedules—where late shifts or longer workdays are in question—should include consideration of physiological and psychological factors that affect different individuals in different ways.

• Enlightened policies and practices to ease

the difficulties associated with *retirement* can contribute greatly to the safety and health of older employees. All such critical decisions should be carefully prepared for, demonstrably fair, and carried out with due notice and clear explanations. When this is done, there is less resentment among those directly and indirectly affected and thus less risk of the emotional instability and worry that can undermine health and be a contributory cause of accidents.

• *Wage and salary policies and administration* (Chapters 20 and 21) also affect employee health and morale. For example, a monetary incentive system may tempt employees to ignore safety regulations that necessarily interfere with an accelerated pace of work. Unless safety-minded supervisors are alert, such reckless violations may result in accidents.

SUMMARY

A quick glance at historical developments indicated how much has been done in the twentieth century to protect the health and safety of employees. But despite gains in prevention, technological advances have continued to bring new risks. In the late sixties and early seventies, public opinion made it possible to pass landmark legislation—such as The Occupational Safety and Health Act. Such new laws have set standards higher than ever before. Fortunately, meeting these standards has been possible for employers because new knowledge (developed by multidisciplinary cooperation, new sciences such as ergonomics, and the relatively new technique of systems thinking) has produced a situation in which a new way of managing has emerged.

Participative management—based on principles of leadership and mutual responsibility—makes it possible to enlist employees in all parts of the enterprise, at all organizational levels, and in all phases of the employment process in a joint endeavor to protect safety and health in the total work environment.

Top-management responsibility for these related objectives begins at the level of principles. Policy decisions then determine the scope and depth of safety and health programs. In each enterprise, distinct but related policy decisions add up to a unified approach. This approach can be summed up as two major policy questions: Shall we, in this organization, do anything more than is legally required of us? If so, how much more, and in which part(s) of the two interrelated programs?

Responsibility for implementing policy decisions regarding employee safety and health is appropriately delegated to professionals (a medical director, a safety director, and an industrial hygienist). Each of these specialists should have a status and staff commensurate with the scope and depth of his delegated responsibilities.

However, no such specialist can do all that he might do, in prevention and education, unless he works with and through committees. Ideally, in a large concern, these committees should be both interdepartmental and intradepartmental.

For optimum success in company programs to protect the safety and health of employees, it is essential that these objectives be taken into account in all parts of the total personnel program. Only when the well-being of employees—as individuals—is considered at every step in the employment process (from selection to retirement) and also in regard to such specialized activities as discipline, changes in work assignments and work schedules, monetary incentive, and preretirement planning can management reasonably expect to enlist employees (and representatives of the union, if there is one), in the aim of making the work environment as safe and healthy as it can possibly be.

In working toward this important objective, laboratory research, clinical observations, and continuing experimentation are greatly needed. As will be indicated in the final chapter, these activities are also needed in relation to all the other major aims that have been emphasized in preceding chapters.

SELECTED REFERENCES

Burns, W., and D. W. Robinson: *Hearing and Noise in Industry,* Department of Health and Social Security, Her Majesty's Stationery Office, London, 1970.

Davidson, Ray: *Peril on the Job: A Study of Hazards in the Chemical Industries,* Public Affairs Press, Washington, D.C., 1970.

Gordon, Jerome B., Allan Akman, and Michael L. Brooks: *Industrial Safety Statistics—A Re-examination,* Praeger Publishers, New York, 1971. (A critical report prepared for the U.S. Department of Labor.)

Heinrich, H. W.: *Industrial Accident Prevention: A Scientific Approach,* 4th ed., McGraw-Hill Book Company, New York, 1959.

Marcel, Robert, and Luigi Parmeggiani: "Fifty Years of International Collaboration in Occupational Safety and Health," *International Labour Review,* vol. 99, no. 1, pp. 85-136, Geneva, January, 1969.

Mayers, May R., M.D.: *Occupational Health: Hazards of the Work Environment,* The Williams & Wilkins Company, Baltimore, 1969.

McLean, Alan, M.D. (ed.): *To Work Is Human: Mental Health and the Business Community,* The Macmillan Company, New York, 1967.

Miller, Theron F.: *A Practical Safety and Security Program for Small and Medium Size Plants,* A Dartnell Successful Management Methods Report, 1971.

Peterson, Dan: *Techniques of Safety Management,* McGraw-Hill Book Company, New York, 1971.

Public Personnel Association: *Survey of Medical Examination Practice,* Chicago, 1970.

Pyle, Howard: "Promotion of Occupational Safety and Health in Small Undertakings," *Industrial Medicine,* vol. 39, no. 1, pp. 42-51, January, 1970.

Rush, Harold M. F., and James K. Brown: "The Drug Problem in Business," *Conference Board Record,* vol. 8, no. 3, March, 1971, New York.

Somers, Herman Miles, and Anne Ramsay Somers: *Workmen's Compensation: Prevention, Insurance, and Rehabilitation of Occupational Disability,* John Wiley & Sons, Inc., New York, 1954.

Section F

Summary

Chapter 23

What Future for Personnel Administration?

Throughout this text, we have emphasized policy considerations, and managerial skills other than policy making, that seem to us to have enduring relevance. However, we have also noted developments, during the 25 years since our first edition, that—in our opinion—have affected the roles of managers and personnel administrators alike during this same period. And certainly the pace of change is accelerating as we approach the end of the twentieth century. External conditions that present both difficulties and opportunities to managers and personnel administrators in the 1970s are markedly different from those of the 1940s. And further changes are in the offing. In the years ahead, managers will have to cope with new problems and with new dimensions to old problems. The question is: Will the average personnel executive be equipped to help management deal with these problems, or will he be supplanted by the new specialists who are already getting increasing attention from top man-

agement—experts in information technology (principally the computer), in organization planning, and in manpower planning and forecasting, among others?

One answer to this question was suggested by a 1967 research report for the American Management Association:

> In organization design, manpower planning and development, and electronic data processing, line executives are already bypassing personnel departments. Meanwhile, personnel executives are not actively adopting objectives in these areas, nor are they trying to gain greater acceptance of personnel's role in these areas from members of top management. Moreover, chief executives and operating executives do not seem surprised that the personnel departments are being bypassed.[1]

[1] Dalton E. McFarland, *Company Officers Assess the Personnel Function,* AMA Research Study 79, American Management Association, Inc., New York, 1967, p. 22.

How well do the great majority of personnel administrators measure up to the new challenges? Perhaps not well enough. There are, of course, notable exceptions, particularly among large corporations, many of which are multinational. Personnel administration in these firms, as well as in a growing number of others, has the support of top management and assists all levels of management in their efforts to develop the human resources of the organization. This generalization about effective personnel administration applies to nonprofit and governmental organizations as well as to profit-making ones.

Some Important Changes in the 1970s

If personnel administrators in other firms and organizations are to become effective in helping other managers, they need first to understand some of the external and internal changes which affect their environment. In addition to the changes mentioned in the beginning of this chapter, the following would seem to be of central importance during the decade of the 1970s in the United States. Many of these points have already been made in earlier chapters. We recapitulate them here for greater emphasis.

1 *Changes in the composition of the labor force.* [2] The big bulge in the age group 16-24, which increased 57 percent during the 1960s over the 1950s, will move into the more mature 25-34 group during the 1970s, while the younger age group increases only 16 percent in this decade. The 35-44 group will grow by 12 percent, but the 45-64 age group, from which top managers are likely to be drawn, will increase less than 4 percent.

Occupationally, the technical and professional group, which represented less than 12 percent of total employment in 1960, will grow to 16.3 percent by 1980—the fastest-growing occupational group in the United States labor force. Finally,

the labor force will be better educated by 1980, with an estimated 42 percent finishing secondary school and 17 percent completing 4 years or more of higher education, as compared with 39 percent and 13 percent, respectively, in 1960.

2 *The pressure for "equal opportunity" for minorities—blacks, Mexican-Americans, especially those with labor-market disadvantages—and for women.* The Civil Rights Act of 1964 marked a watershed in the United States, with subsequent federal manpower policies emphasizing the hiring of the disadvantaged. The higher teen-age unemployment rates, especially for nonwhites, are a continuing problem—and challenge—to managerial hiring policies. So are the aspirations of capable women, who are underrepresented in technical, professional, and managerial positions. Managers and personnel administrators will need to give greater attention to this in the next decade. [3]

3 *New lifestyles of people in or entering the labor force.* Hair and dress styles, preferences for certain types of work considered socially useful, and shorter hours or longer weekends (the 4-day week) are becoming more widespread in the 1970s, as is the tendency for some persons to drop out of regular work ("The System"). These changes present new problems for managers. More often than not, those who elect the different lifestyles are younger employees now entering the labor force.

4 *Rapid spread of computer-based information and retrieval systems.* In 1955 in the United States there were only 100 computers in operation; by 1970 the figure was 60,000—with many more on order, and these were of a much more advanced type than the original 100. The projection for 1975 is 80,000. Computers are used increasingly by management and in many other fields. [4] Computer-based personnel systems have been adopted more slowly, but during the 1970s they are likely to have a substantial impact on person-

---

[2] Data are taken from the *Manpower Report to the President,* U.S. Department of Labor, Washington, D.C., April, 1971. Similar data are in the 1972 report.

[3] Charles D. Orth III and Frederic Jacobs, "Women in Management: Pattern for Change," *Harvard Business Review,* vol. 49, no. 7, pp. 139–147, July–August, 1971.

[4] Charles A. Myers, *Computers in Knowledge-based Fields,* The M.I.T. Press, Cambridge, Mass., and London, 1970.

nel record keeping, analysis, skills inventories, and many other personnel functions. The introduction of computer-based systems in offices, including personnel offices, requires attention to the human as well as the technical problems of change.[5]

5 *The economic environment of the 1970s is facing managers, including personnel administrators, with the dilemma of full employment versus rising wages and prices.* No advanced industrial country has really solved this dilemma. A policy of fiscal and monetary stringency to damp down inflation is likely to cost many jobs, as in the United States during the 2 years preceding President Nixon's 3-month wage-price freeze in 1971. The wage and price controls which followed the end of the freeze in November, 1971, affected what employees and managers could be paid.

Some of these external environmental developments are reflected in internal organizational changes, among which are (1) changing organizational structures, such as project groups, matrix structures combining several functional or product groups, profit centers, and the like. These may be less bureaucratic and less hierarchical, reflecting the technology and tasks involved as well as different ways of managing.[6] (2) Greater opportunity for creativity by managers as computer-based systems change managerial tasks and the nature of managerial work by eliminating operations which are routine and structured. Managers should then have more time for the unstructured parts of their jobs, including the responsibility for conserving and developing human resources. There are many opportunities for enterprising personnel administrators to assist operating managers in their changed roles.

Some New Directions for Personnel Administrators

The preceding list of changes in the external environment during the 1970s, together with the shorter review of significant internal organizational developments, suggests new directions for managers and personnel administrators during this decade. Some of these have already been indicated; the following additional directions seem to us important:

1 *Assistance in manpower planning and forecasting,* with particular emphasis on requirements for managerial and technical manpower in the near future. In large organizations, this assignment requires the utilization of computer-based skill banks. From these, information can be retrieved about individuals who possess the combination of skills, education, job experience, and occupational and geographical preferences to fill specific vacancies within the organization. In this way, the final managerial selection process will be made more efficient, not replaced. These skill banks, periodically updated with new information, can also be used in manpower projection models which help top management estimate probable future high-talent manpower requirements in view of forecasts about product or service expansion, replacements for attrition, technical and organizational changes, the condition of the external labor market, etc. As noted (in Chapter 3), manpower planning is an integral part of long-range planning for sales and finance.

2 *Consideration of personnel policies as part of a total system,* rather than as separate policies aimed at specific problems or needs. As Professor Mason Haire has pointed out,[7] policies on

[5] For research on this question, see Enid Mumford and Olive Banks, *The Computer and the Clerk,* Routledge and Kegan Paul, Ltd., London, 1967, and Rosemary Stewart, *How Computers Affect Management,* Macmillan, London, 1971.

[6] The studies by Joan Woodward in Great Britain and Paul R. Lawrence and Jay W. Lorsch in the United States are of particular interest here, as is the book by Warren G. Bennis and Philip E. Slater, *The Temporary Society,* Harper & Row, Publishers, Incorporated, New York, 1964.

[7] Mason Haire, "Managing Management Manpower," *Business Horizons,* vol. 10, no. 4, pp. 23–28 (also reprinted in Paul Pigors, Charles A. Myers, and F. T. Malm, *Management of Human Resources: Readings in Personnel Administration,* 3d ed., McGraw-Hill Book Company, New York, 1973, selection 10).

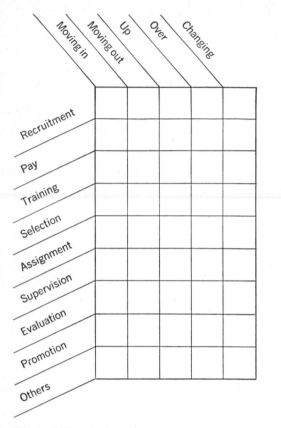

Figure 23-1 Matrix for a personnel policy system. (*Source: Mason Haire, "Managing Management Manpower,"* The McKinsey Quarterly, *vol. 4, no. 4, Spring, 1968, p. 17.*)

recruitment, pay, selection, assignment, supervision, performance evaluation, and promotion all have varied impacts on the flow of manpower into, through, and out of the organization. His suggested matrix (Figure 23-1) includes the activities listed above on the vertical axis; and on the horizontal axis, "moving in," "moving out," "moving up," "moving over," and "changing" are shown as objectives and/or results of the interrelated policies. Some policy decisions have more influence on some of the objectives or results than others, but usually each has *some* impact in a systems sense. The effectiveness of policies in regard to each objective will depend on

more continuing study and research within each organization. It cannot be achieved by taking policies "on faith."

Related to this systems approach is the field of "organization development" (sometimes also called "planned change"), with which personnel administrators should become progressively familiar. This approach, developed by social psychologists working primarily in industrial organizations, is concerned with the *change process* when a need for some change within the organization is seen as necessary. Strategy planning with top management, educational programs to improve managerial competence and skills, further consulting and training efforts, and organizational evaluation are part of the OD approach. Unfortunately, this activity could bypass personnel administrators who are preoccupied with day-to-day chores in their own department.

The spread of computer-based systems, mentioned earlier, to assist managers and personnel administrators in making systems-minded personnel decisions, is unlikely to reduce the need for "situational thinking" (policy-centered *and* person-centered). This approach will continue to be needed in selecting employees, helping them to develop, and stimulating their motivation by humanizing the work environment through job enrichment and job enlargement as well as in improving relations with the community from which the organization draws new employees and public support for its activities. Situational thinking can be especially useful in making the most of the changing nature of the work force.

3 *Development of personnel policies which recognize the changing nature of the work force and new lifestyles.* Executives and personnel managers are already finding that the younger and better-educated managers and professionals reject authoritarian and paternalistic ways of managing. To retain those who can contribute to organizational goals, it will be necessary to practice skills of communication that managers have not traditionally taken much trouble about. The first of these is *listening*—not only to what is said, but also to what speaks in people who do not express their deepest values in words. A second skill is *interpreting* the meaning of what is said—

and what is valued—insofar as this meaning relates to inner motivation.

Having recognized what is important to highly motivated young managers today, executives may find it worthwhile to undertake some restructuring of their organization to make managerial jobs challenging right from the start and to offer all candidates for promotion the opportunity to participate in planning their own careers. Nowadays, young people are unwilling to be moved around within an organization as though they were checkers on a checkerboard. Studies in some of the operating companies of the American Telephone and Telegraph Company have indicated the importance of first-job challenge for retention of capable managers. More recent research also emphasizes their interest in planning their own careers. Many traditional personnel policies and rules, often developed for the blue-collar labor group, are unacceptable to the new breed of employee.

In the young managerial group, which is part of what has been called the "accelerated generation" in the United States, there is impatience with being kept waiting in the wings. "They want to get out there on center stage. They want to be heard." The "organization man" type of younger manager who flourished in the 1950s and 1960s belongs to a vanishing breed. Nowadays such individuals are much less frequently seen: "Today's junior managers, by contrast, reflect the passionate concerns of youth in the 1970's—for individuality, openness, humanism, concern and change—and they are determined to be heard. If they find no response, their deep anger at what they view as imperfections in society and business could infect their colleagues and subordinates, resulting in a sort of industrial mutiny."[8]

A former top executive, now a business school dean, summed up the outlook of the new generation of managers in these words: "The young executive will insist on being a party in the decision-making process. This is part of the new life style. It is the kind of change organizations in the future must make in order to operate in the new

environment, in this new participatory democracy."[9]

The likelihood is that these younger managers will also be less willing to devote themselves exclusively to the company at the expense of neglecting their private lives and lifestyles. Family life may be regarded as separate from company life and not subordinated to company demands. The relative shortage of competent managers because of the smaller absolute size of the age group forty-five to sixty-four will reinforce this assertion of independence by younger managers. The central value of these younger "co-worldly executives" has been described by one who said: "When life is at an end, it is not how well you measure up to others, but how well you stand with yourself."[10]

Changes in lifestyle will also require other adjustments in personnel policies. Acceptance of individual preferences in clothing, hairstyles, etc., is one example; the qualities the individual brings to the job will be more important. Some flexibility in work schedules may be necessary, especially as leisure-time activities grow and lead to the demand for longer vacations or holidays; the 4-day workweek, part-time work for those desiring it, and possibly even the 3-month "sabbaticals" which the Steelworkers Union negotiated for those of its members with 15 years or more of service on the job. The pressure for early retirement will grow as both managers and workers look forward either to a second career or complete retirement, with full pension, and to leisure-time hobbies and other activities.

During a worker's lifetime, furthermore, there may be periodic adjustments, at his own option, in his "package" of fringe benefits. Such adjustments will be made possible by the capacity of

---

[8] Judson Gooding, "The Accelerated Generation Moves into Management," *Fortune,* March, 1971, pp. 101-104ff.

[9] *Ibid.,* p. 115. The statement was by Arjay Miller, former president of The Ford Motor Company and subsequently dean of the Graduate School of Business at Stanford University.

[10] Quoted by Eugene E. Jennings, "The Co-Worldly Executive," *Management of Personnel Quarterly,* vol. 10, no. 2, pp. 4–8, Summer, 1971. This was the comment of one of 34 young managers interviewed by Jennings, who called them "early arrivals" because, as men in their early thirties, they were making $30,000 a year or more and were an extremely mobile group.

the computer quickly to determine different combinations of equal-cost benefits. For example, as a study in the General Electric Company showed, younger workers with families may prefer extensive medical and hospital insurance coverage under private plans to extra benefits at distant retirement; while workers of fifty years and over prefer retirement benefits. Subject to minimum benefit requirements for all employees, an individual should be free to make his own choices as his own needs and those of his family change.

Skilful *listening* will be needed by managers to determine precisely what any individual employee wants and needs at each stage in his family life and working career. Also, skill in communicating and counseling will be needed to ensure that periodic adjustments in the fringe benefit package are *understood* by each employee. Mass communication is inadequate for this purpose. General information should, of course, be presented in writing, supplemented with individual annual statements to each employee on the status of all his benefits. "One important decision that managers of pension programs must make is how and when information should be disseminated."[11]

Selective communication should be adapted to meet the different interests and expectations of various age groups. Individual interviews—each carried out as a genuine interchange of views—are needed to ensure understanding.

4 *Increasing attention to management development, with emphasis on self-development through management by shared objectives.* This point grows out of much of what was said in the preceding section, particularly about the aspirations of "the accelerated generation." Many of the latter are still in their mid-twenties. But some will move into the larger 35–44 age group during this decade. Because of the relative *shortage* of managers in the 45–64 age group (as noted earlier in this chapter), the continued success of most large organizations will depend on developing many managers in the large prime age group for future top-management responsibilities.

As suggested in Chapter 7, an important phase of managerial development can consist in enriching the job of first-level supervisors to the extent that they can function as first-level managers. This change offers ambitious young persons opportunities to show whether their capabilities and breadth of vision are such that, over the years, they can grow into higher-level managers—possibly even into top executives.

Traditional management-appraisal systems with checklists of various desired managerial traits, filled out by superiors about their subordinate managers (much as a teacher grades students), will be even less effective with the new managers than it was with older ones. The spread of managerial styles which encourage the establishment of objectives by the manager in consultation with his immediate superior enables both to evaluate progress toward the achievement of these objectives. Thus it is likely to be more effective with those younger managers who want more responsibility in their jobs and for their organizational careers. This joint planning is made possible through an approach which we have called "management by shared objectives" (in Chapter 1, and elsewhere throughout this book).

5 *Greater attention to the human problems of adjustment to change.* Needs for adjustment will arise not only from the use of computers and other forms of automation but also from realignment of managerial functions as a consequence of acquisitions, mergers, reorganization, and new top-management personnel. Some organizations do need shaking up. In these cases change is essential for the future of the organization. How these changes are made, explained, and interpreted by each individual in the communication process may spell the difference between successful and disastrous change. Effective personnel administrators will be listened to in planning these changes; ineffective ones will be bypassed as outside consultants, skilled in the change process, are brought in.

6 *New forms of compensation which relate pay more effectively to performance.* Piece rate and other incentive wage-payment systems have been declining relatively, particularly when the

[11] Ronald G. West, "Interest in Pensions," *Personnel*, vol. 47, no. 5, pp. 54–58, p. 56, September–October, 1970.

relation between pay and worker output is weakened by technical change and automation. In these cases, measured daywork systems with more effective supervision may be expected to grow in an effort to relate levels of pay to levels of performance. In executive compensation, various devices will also be sought to do this more effectively. There may also be a spread in forms of profit-sharing at lower organizational levels. Put in another way, methods of sharing the gains from higher productivity will assume even greater significance as there is greater acceptance of the principle that pay increases should be related to productivity for the economy as a whole. Translating this idea to payment on the job will result in increasing emphasis on improved performance and the acceptance of new methods, materials, and equipment to increase overall productivity.

7 *The growing importance of occupational health and safety programs within organizations, under the pressure of the Occupational Health and Safety Act of 1970.* Managers will have to become more safety-conscious in view of the large number of workers injured on the job each year. Even more significant, perhaps, occupational medicine will become a more important function either within the personnel department or as a medical department closely coordinated with the personnel department. The medical profession, in the words of one of its members, has not "until fairly recently, officially and effectively pursued the promotion of optimum health among the working population in the environment of their employment." [12] Advances in protecting the health and safety of employees can be expected as medical directors, safety directors, and industrial hygienists—working effectively within the total personnel program—make full use of research in ergonomics and in the behavioral sciences.

8 *Less attention relatively to blue-collar personnel policies except when there is strong union representation.* By this, we mean not that blue-collar

[12] Richard A. Sutter, "A Prediction: Occupational Medicine in the 70's," *Industrial Medicine and Surgery,* vol. 40, no. 6, p. 15, September, 1971.

employees should be ignored but rather that they have too often been the center of the personnel manager's attention, especially when they are unionized. In the future, technical, professional, and managerial personnel—the high-talent and highly motivated people in any organization—will require more attention from the personnel department than they have had in many organizations. Moreover, the blue-collar group is likely to be a shrinking percentage of the work force. Occupational trends in the United States indicate this result. Further mechanization and automation will continue to eliminate many blue-collar jobs, at least for new entrants.

Nevertheless, the problems of collective bargaining, which in the United States have involved primarily the blue-collar work force in the private sector, will demand the best talent in the personnel or industrial relations staff to assist in building constructive plant-level labor-management relations. The extent to which harmonious relations can be developed in each plant will have some impact on wider collective bargaining units. Americans have watched with interest British experience with productivity bargaining. The continued slow spread of the Scanlon Plan idea in a number of plants in the United States is a similar development. But most plant-level relationships involve the periodic negotiation of a fixed-term collective bargaining agreement. During its term, such a labor agreement is enforced less by legal measures than by the willingness of management and the union to submit unresolved grievances and differences over interpretation or application of the agreement to private voluntary arbitration—which is accepted as final and binding.

In a number of states, a similar process, known as "fact-finding," has developed in the public sector as a means of resolving disputes over the terms of new contracts. Examples are found in disputes between schoolteachers and local school boards, between municipalities and municipal workers, and to a certain extent between state governments and state employee organizations. As a consequence of recent state laws in the United States, the spread of public sector collective bargaining at the state and local levels has been rapid. In the private sector, white-collar bargaining is less frequent in manufacturing than in retail trade, for example. But it is largely absent in banks and insurance companies. Whether unionism will spread further will probably depend on the extent to which managers in these organizations can maintain high employee satisfaction with work and conditions of employment. (We have discussed this and other considerations in Chapter 8.)

9 *Changes in the staff role of the personnel administrator, more in certain types of organizations than in others.* Some blurring of staff-line distinctions has already occurred in a number of organizations as line managers have come to depend upon the expertise of the personnel specialist. And, in certain organizational patterns such as project management, matrix management, and other temporary task force groups, the personnel manager is part of a team in which there is no line or operating management in the traditional sense. These organizational arrangements are likely to be found in aerospace, research and development organizations, and other new kinds of ventures.

But we believe that in some of these, as well as in the larger number of other organizations, the effective personnel administrator will continue to be needed as a policy adviser at the corporate or top-management level. Through his own staff, he will continue to function as an adviser and provider of vital services to managers at other organizational levels. As one personnel vice-president with whom we discussed these ideas put it: "The chief executive is the chief personnel officer in our company, and his leadership reflects his own philosophy of management—a willingness to listen to diverse points of view, including my own, before he makes a policy decision." This vice-president sees his role as an educator of line managers rather than as a policeman seeking to get rigid observance of personnel policies established by top management with his advice. He wants to be seen by his line colleagues not as a threat but as a source of help in fulfilling their responsibilities. To the extent that he exercises a "control" function, it is through persuasion, not through orders, even though he may be seen by some as the president's "agent." (In short, we reiterate the essential point of view of Chapter 2.)

10 *More broadly educated personnel administrators will meet the additional responsibilities outlined in preceding paragraphs.* An understanding of significant research in the behavioral sciences will be essential, with additional training in economics and in industrial relations (defined as including labor law and public policy). Familiarity with the literature of personnel administration, especially with research which attempts to evaluate personnel policies, will be part of this necessary educational background. Personnel administrators will have to understand organization planning, manpower planning and forecasting, and computer applications in the personnel function generally. There will also be greater reliance on personnel research.

The intangible qualities needed in the effective personnel manager of the future will not differ greatly from those needed in the past. They are partly the personality traits suggested earlier and partly the wisdom derived from experience. The latter often includes some nonpersonnel experience in other managerial functions, especially if the personnel officer is to be effective as a member of the top-management group.

CONCLUSIONS

A frequent complaint by some personnel people is that they lack the organizational stature to which they are entitled by their education and experience. They say that if only top management would give them more support, they could be more effective in meeting their staff responsibilities. A few may even pine for "authority" to enforce, on recalcitrant line managers, compliance with personnel policies.

However, the major points outlined in this chapter suggest that personnel administrators *will be* or *will become* effective in their organizations to the extent that they *earn* the respect of top executives and lower-level managers by ability to help them in developing the human resources needed to achieve organizational objectives. In profit-making enterprises, this means contributing to "the profit, growth, and resource development of the company through professional application" of specialized personnel policies and techniques adapted to the requirements of the particular firm.[13] In governmental and other nonprofit organizations, the same contribution to specified organizational objectives should be the central goal of personnel management.

The effective personnel manager also needs to relate his contribution to the important changes in the external environment mentioned throughout this book—especially in Chapter 4 and at the beginning of this chapter—as well as to significant internal organizational changes which have implications for personnel administration.

During 1971, a leading financial corporation in New York City advertised in *The New York Times* for a personnel manager described as a "personnel generalist." The advertisement specified at least 5 to 10 years experience "in industrial relations, employment, compensation, man-

power planning, training, policy, development, and organizational analysis." The company sought a "top 2% er! There is no place in our group for the usual personnel mediocrity!"[14]

Is there a place in any organization for "the usual personnel mediocrity"? Only when personnel administration operates at that level would there be relevance in Peter Drucker's often quoted comment that personnel management is "partly a file clerk's job, partly a housekeeping job, partly a social worker's job, and partly 'fire-fighting' to head off union trouble or settle it."[15] Naturally, when personnel work is ineffectual, top management is likely to seek help from other staff specialists to solve the really important problems associated with the development and management of human resources.

Our own conviction is that personnel administration *is* an effective function in a growing number of organizations. With close attention to the changing nature of the work force, introduced by a new breed of employees, and the imagination to envisage new ways of helping employees to develop their productive capabilities—while also satisfying high-level human needs—personnel administration in the future can become even more valuable than it has been in the past. These are the personnel responsibilities of all levels of management, not just those in the personnel staff.

---

[13] David Knox Rowe, *Industrial Relations Management for Profit and Growth,* American Management Association, Inc., New York, 1971, p. 28. An earlier review of the top corporate personnel direction in 171 manufacturing companies concluded: "He is an executive who is profit-minded, who is knowledgeable about his company and the industry of which he is a part, and who backs away from the old 'do-gooder' image that, rightly or wrongly, has been attached to personnel administration." Aileen L. Kyte, "The Personnel Man—in Transition?", *Business Management Record* (National Industrial Conference Board), p. 10, December, 1963 (no volume or number listed).

[14] *The New York Times,* Sunday, June 13, 1971.
[15] Peter F. Drucker, *The Practice of Management,* 1954, pp. 275-276.

Part 2

Case Illustrations

One great advantage of the case method is that it is not primarily focused on what the student knows. In human relations it is primarily concerned with creating an atmosphere and a set of relations in which the students can rethink their experience so as to derive more effective meanings from it and begin to make more precise discriminations in their relations with others.

Harriet O. Ronken[1]

INTRODUCTION

Cases and Case Method: Notes from Experience

As suggested in Chapter 9, case analysis can be carried on, with other people, as a systematic way of learning from experience. To supplement what was said in that chapter concerning the rationale and application of situational thinking

we add here a few notes from our own experience about difficulties frequently encountered by case students, and we offer suggestions for surmounting these obstacles.

Case Reports Should Be True to Life

Studying cases cannot help anyone learn how to deal effectively with life itself unless the case reports faithfully picture actual situations. Not all published cases meet this specification. To the extent that items have been added, omitted, or altered to "improve on" facts, a case report be-

---

[1] Harriet O. Ronken, "What One Student Learned," in Kenneth R. Andrews (ed.), *The Case Method of Teaching Human Relations and Administration,* Harvard University Press, Cambridge, Mass., 1953, p. 65.

comes untrue to life. An entirely fictitious case is worthless, for practical purposes (although analyzing it may be an enjoyable academic pastime). Even a partly fictionalized case may be misleading as a guide to situational diagnosis and decision making in real life.

All the case material in this book is drawn from actual situations and is as accurate and unbiased as we could make it. To conform to the unwritten code of a case writer, names of persons, organizations, and some places have been disguised, but whenever the nationality of a participant is a significant feature of the case, the disguised name indicates that same nationality.

However, students of human relations should recognize that absolute objectivity is unattainable by human beings. Facts in themselves are different from facts-as-perceived, and an individual viewpoint is inevitably reflected in the way a case writer selects and arranges factual material. Yet these human limitations need not be all to the bad, for students. While reading any case report, a student may profitably ask himself: Where and how does the case writer's attitude show up? What changes in the written report might eliminate the effect of that bias?

Prepared Problem Cases Are Relatively Unhelpful

Often, case analysis has been carried on as a purely academic exercise. Problem-solving techniques can be taught in connection with case reports which present an oversimplified picture of what once was a real situation. In our opinion, however, the prepared problem case does too much for students and asks too little of them. All that is expected is that the student find solutions to already formulated problems. That method does not prepare a student for the kind of analytical thinking required by real life. One student who had graduated with honors from a course taught by that method but failed disastrously on his first job made a classic statement of his difficulty, "If only someone would give me a *problem,* I *know* I could solve it. But all I can see here is

a *mess.*" He evidently had not learned how to ask productive questions about real-life situations. Practical people know that in coping with difficulties, the hardest part of the whole job often is to see what is the most urgent need. Every supervisor and manager needs to develop in himself the capabilities to recognize "Here is the place to set to work, now. And this is a practical way to start."

Other difficulties encountered by case students are rooted partly in cases and partly in students.

Students Must Be Able to Connect with a Case

Obviously a student cannot begin to learn from a case until after he has connected with it. Making that connection has often proved difficult. It requires efforts from students, writers, and teachers.

To get full value from any case report, a student must start by trying to put aside preconceptions, prejudices, and personal experiences which could obscure or distort his view of factual material in the case before him. Next, he must make the effort required to explore the whole territory mapped by the case report. What are the facts and relationships which give this particular case its own individual character? A third prerequisite is willingness and ability to reach out toward each case with imagination and empathy. Can a student surmount barriers of space and time to the point where he gets the feel of a case situation and can imagine that he is a participant—or at least an interested onlooker—during current events?

However, even a willing and imaginative student cannot connect with a case that is beyond his reach. The historical or cultural setting of the case may be so remote, the situation so complex, or technical features so far removed from his own experience that he cannot understand what is going on.

We have tried to make sure that all the case material in this book is well within the reach of students in this hemisphere. For students in distant parts of the world, we must depend on teachers to supply explanations as needed and to select, omit, or add cases.

Not all users of this text agree with us about our cases. Some teachers find some cases out of date and suggest that we change actual dates and make such alterations of factual material as would be needed to bring every case up to date. **Having c**onsidered that suggestion, we decided to stick to our principles and not tamper with the facts of any case. To change dates or to fix up other items of historical fact would spoil the integrity of the case report. Moreover, we cannot agree that merely because a case dates back to 1937, for instance, it is necessarily outdated. Some of the old-time cases have been retained primarily because of their historical interest. Studying them may help students appreciate the significance of current trends away from ideas and practices that characterized an earlier day. Other "old" cases have reappeared in successive editions because readers have agreed that the cases offer classic examples of issues that are as vital today and as urgent to think about tomorrow as they were when they were first discussed many years ago.

Some users of this text have objected to the questions for analysis, which, in their view, interrupt the flow of case reports. Those questions were put there for two reasons: (1) subdividing a long and complex case makes it possible for a student to work on it in manageable units; (2) to stimulate interim case analysis at significant turning points, we have inserted questions. (Where lengthy dialogue is part of a case report, numbered lines make it easy to locate passages to which questions refer.) Interim questions certainly do break the continuity of the case report, but analyzing a case is quite different from reading a story. In our opinion, having the plot interrupted is a small price to pay for a stimulus to ask one's self at critical stages in a case: Where have we got to, now? What might have been done differently by insiders at some earlier stage, so that a given difficulty would not have arisen?

What might an outsider learn by analyzing the situation as it is at this point *before* reading about what happened later?

The specific content of some questions has also been criticized. We would like to make it clear that our questions are offered merely as aids, as samples, and as starters. Any that seem likely to be unhelpful to members of a given group should be discarded. Other questions may be reworded to match specific needs and interests of different study groups. Most important, our questions are no substitutes for lines of inquiry initiated by students themselves. Unless new questions are formulated by members of each study group, it cannot be said that they have really connected with the case in the sense of getting close enough to see its relevance to their own experience and interests.

A different kind of assistance, for students who are trying to get into a case which is even relatively remote from their firsthand experience, is offered by the short introductions. These indicate a few of the major issues that we see in the cases and relate case material to the subject matter of the chapters. Any student who takes the trouble to go back and forth between cases and chapters gives himself a doubly good chance of making the most of both parts of this text.

Other Difficulties, Mainly Associated with Attitudes

Another feature of orthodox case method is homework. This standard requirement is perceived as particularly objectionable by experienced men—in business or industry. Many of them feel no need to prepare for case discussion. Moreover, unlike a college student, they are usually expected to do a full day's work in addition to academic study. Even college students have frequently tended to skimp homework requirements, perhaps partly because many of them have little idea of how to prepare themselves adequately for productive case discussion. Yet teachers who use case method know that it is impractical for members of a study group to start analyzing a case until after they have got a good grip on the facts. Unable to convince students on this point (or perhaps unwilling to embark on a lengthy discussion of a work assignment which they are in a position to impose as a course requirement), many teachers have continued to assign lengthy cases to students who scarcely read them. Of course, some conscientious students do read assigned cases. They even take notes and jot down questions to take up in class discussion. But too often these serious students constitute a small minority. When the great majority come relatively (or entirely) unprepared, possibilities for "group discussion" are necessarily limited. And among those who have done little or no advance work, a few try to make up, by boldness or bluff, what they lack in preparation and intellectual caliber.

That kind of irresponsible behavior can constitute the most serious difficulty for students in the field of human relations. When shallow thinking, socially unperceptive behavior, or destructive criticism is given free rein, members of a study group move away from the goals which they frequently recommend for those people in cases whose behavior they are discussing. When the atmosphere and relationships in a study group are poles apart from what is needed for productive interaction between people, then talking and doing are too unrelated to be educational. Little can be gained by talking about cases in human relations unless the situation in which the talking is done matches—or at least reaches toward—standards set up for participants in "those case situations out there."

It has been well said that to live actively is to keep asking questions of life. For students of human relations, another requirement is productive interaction with others. Case analysis, at its best, can help anyone to make progress in learning how to live both actively and productively with others. It can stimulate curiosity and the capacity to ask productive questions. To the extent that case analysis proves rewarding, it can also strengthen the will to maintain an experimental attitude toward firsthand experience.

THE INCIDENT PROCESS:[2] A VARIANT OF TRADITIONAL CASE METHOD

This unorthodox way of practicing case method has now been in use for more than 20 years. The senior author first began experimenting with it, in seminars and courses on personnel administration, at the Massachusetts Institute of Technology in 1950. Since 1952, the Incident Process has been widely adopted, and variously adapted in the United States and overseas by training directors in industry, business, and hospital administration. In the United States it has also been used in government agencies and all three branches of the armed services.[3]

[2] For a detailed description of the Incident Process and how it works, together with complete case studies and discussion plans, see Paul Pigors and Faith Pigors, *The Incident Process: Case Studies in Management Development, Series I: Practical Supervisory Problems,* The Bureau of National Affairs, Inc., Washington, D.C., 1955, *Series II: Government Cases—Federal, State & Local,* The Bureau of National Affairs, Inc., Washington, D.C., 1958, and *Series III: White Collar Cases,* The Bureau of National Affairs, Inc., Washington, D.C., 1965. See also Pigors and Pigors, *Case Method in Human Relations: The Incident Process,* McGraw-Hill Book Company, New York, 1961. Persons interested in human relations in hospitals may read Paul Pigors, Faith Pigors, and Marita Tribou, *Professional Nursing Practice: Cases and Issues,* McGraw-Hill Book Company, New York, 1967. Training directors may wish to refer to Robert L. Craig and Lester R. Bittel (eds.), *Training and Development Handbook,* sponsored by the American Society for Training and Development, McGraw-Hill Book Company, New York, 1967.

[3] Reports on practical experience with the Incident Process have been given in the following articles: D. L. Marshall, "The Incident Process of Supervisory Training: Case Study of Experience in a Small Plant," *Personnel,* vol. 31, no. 2, pp. 134–139, September, 1954; J. L. Centner, "The Incident Process," *Advanced Management,* vol. 21, no. 12, pp. 15–20, December, 1956; S. I. Stone, "The Incident Process," *Journal of the American Society of Training Directors,* vol. 13, no. 3, pp. 17–26, March, 1959; S. H. Schoen and W. L. French, "Experience with the Incident Process in Management Training," *Personnel,* vol. 36, no. 4, pp. 54–61, July–August, 1959. "Incident Process," *Pulp & Paper,* Feb. 20, 1961, pp. 45–47; and Marita Tribou, "The Search before Research," *Nursing Outlook,* vol. 14, no. 10, pp. 51–53, October, 1966.

As a way of learning from experience, the Incident Process has four distinct but related features. Many persons have seen and used only one of them, the five-phase cycle of situational diagnosis and decision making. Yet for purposes of management development, and to acquire skills in human relations, there are three other important aspects:

1 Opportunities to experiment (in the fact-finding phase) with a comprehensive system for situational diagnosis (described in Chapter 9).
2 Use of group-dynamics techniques to establish and cultivate an atmosphere that favors learning with and from other people.
3 Opportunities for job rotation, in a range of roles and relationships which offer experiences in practicing and benefiting by skills of leadership.

The Incident Process as a Five-phase Cycle of Case Analysis

To analyze a case is to embark on a search for meaning at various levels of abstraction. Each successive step in the Incident Process is characterized by a special question or questions. Each of these is a distinct yet integral part of the whole analytical process, and each needs to be answered before taking the next step.

Phase 1: Starting with a Written Incident For each member, group work on a case begins at the start of a conference (or class period) by reading his own copy of a briefly sketched climactic point in the case for the day. Here is a sample.

An Incident: The Nervous Welder[4]

Foreman McCrorie instructed Bell (a welder) to hook the cables of an overhead crane to a rack of

[4] This incident is based on information furnished in the proceedings of an actual arbitration. See *Labor Arbitration Reports: Dispute Settlements,* The Bureau of National Affairs, Inc., Washington, D.C., vol. 21, pp. 410–413, 1954. The report has been reprinted with permission from The Bureau of National Affairs, Inc., as Case 14, "Discharge for 'Proper Cause'?" The *Labor Arbitration Reports* are an excellent and continuing source of current case material for discussion by the Incident Process.

finished work. Bell hesitated to undertake this assignment, fearing that the job was unsafe.

McCrorie called in the shop superintendent and the personnel director. After some inconclusive discussion, in the presence of Harris (welder and shop steward), Bell turned to Harris and said, in effect, "I think this is dangerous. What do you think? Should I pick up the lift?"

Harris sympathized with Bell's fear, adding, "If you feel it is unsafe or too dangerous, you don't have to do it."

At that point, McCrorie discharged Harris, who promptly filed a grievance.

To stimulate responsible and realistic thinking, each written Incident is followed by a suggestion that students imagine themselves in the collective role of a specific insider in the case situation. In that role, and using their best judgment, how might they decide to handle the Incident? And, having coped with the immediate difficulty, what further action, if any, might they take toward long-term goals in the case as a whole? For example, here is a specific suggestion used to help students connect with the case involving the nervous welder: "Try to imagine yourself in the position of the shop superintendent. You have been called to the scene of action at the time of the Incident. The foreman has just discharged Harris in your presence. What might you decide to do about this, both now and later?"

Another kind of decision would be called for from a person who entered the case at a later stage and in a different role. For instance: "The case has been referred to you, as impartial arbitrator, after failure of the parties to settle the dispute themselves. Your job is to hear and to evaluate the evidence, to render an award and to attach your discussion (reasoning)."

There are several advantages in beginning one's case analysis by reading a briefly sketched incident. For one thing, it eliminates the need for advance homework. Second, a reasonably well-written incident arouses curiosity. It stirs people to read not only for surface information but also for underlying implications. When students first begin to connect with a case by searching for the meanings and implications of words in a written Incident, a characteristic question which each reader puts to himself is: *What leads can I find here which, if followed up, might provide the information needed to make the short-term action decision called for by this incident?*

That same question is one which every supervisor and manager might profitably ask himself in connection with incidents he encounters in his daily work. Thus another advantage of starting case analysis by reading a written account (of what once was a real incident) is that it approximates a requirement imposed by a managerial or administrative role.[5]

Phase 2: Getting and Organizing Factual Information on the Case as a Whole By asking fact-finding questions (some of which have been formulated during the 2 or 3 minutes in which the written incident was being studied) members of a case discussion group in effect interview "the man with the facts," the person who is presenting the case and leading discussion on it. In a conference room, of course, this step can be taken more rapidly than in everyday life. Usually, alert and systematic questioning can bring out all essential (and available) information within 20 to 30 min-

utes. When written material is needed to supplement oral answers, it is distributed in response to questions which specifically seek that information.

The general questions which characterize the fact-finding phase may be summed up as follows: What does this incident amount to, at the level of facts? How did it build up? What is the larger context (the total situation) within which it occurred? What leads for constructive action begin to emerge as we assemble verified (or reasonably reliable) information concerning the interactive variables (technical features, space-time dimensions, and aspects of the human element) in this case situation?

When a mass of information has been brought out, it needs to be reduced to manageable proportions. This can be done in a summary[6] which highlights key facts, omits peripheral items, and states the nub of the case objectively. An effective summary answers the question: What does this case boil down to as factual material needed to make a reliable diagnosis and to develop a practical decision for coping with this incident?

Phase 3: Looking for What Is Immediately at Stake, and Formulating an Issue for Prompt, Decisive Action The questions that typify case analysis at this stage are:

1 What is at stake here and now (at the time of the incident), not only for individuals immediately concerned but also for the organization as a whole?

2 Can these constituent elements of the case situation be boiled down (temporarily) to a sin-

---

[5] The Incident Process can also be used by a student of history who seeks "lessons in experience," as suggested in the *Cox Commission Report: Crisis at Columbia,* Random House, Inc., a Vintage Special, New York, 1968, p. 186. The report offers a series of critical incidents which could profitably serve as starting points for situational analysis and decision making. This possibility is suggested by the following comments (taken from the report, pp. 63, 189, 71, and 197): "Neither the issues nor forms of protest exemplified in the April 1968 uprising at Columbia were born full-grown. In 1965, there occurred the first of a series of demonstrations altogether different from traditional political activities at Columbia. . . . The long series of turbulent demonstrations beginning in 1965 . . . an accelerating cycle of violence . . . tolerated by most of the University community, leaves a tragic sense of the inevitability of the final escalation. . . . The sequence of steps was not inevitable but each was the readily predictable consequence of those that went before."

[6] The skill of summarizing is one which comes natural to some persons. Others seem to have great difficulty in separating factual information from their own opinions and in making a statement which is both comprehensive and concise. However, there seems to be general agreement that when someone can effectively sum up items of information which have come in helter-skelter during a fast-paced question-and-answer period, the group as a whole is in a better position than it otherwise could be to take the next step toward decision.

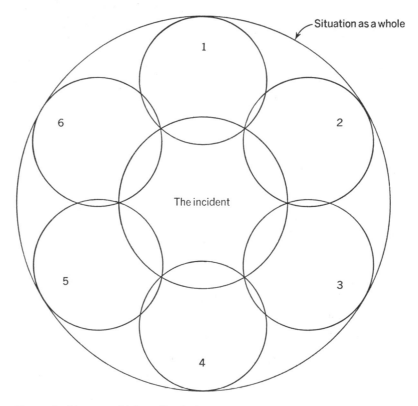

Figure 1 Diagram of interactive factors.

gle, objectively worded question (to which a short-term action decision—in Phase 4—will be an appropriate answer)?

Looking at Interactive Factors in the Case Situation To clarify what is immediately at stake (in coping with the incident), key factors in the case may be diagramed. If a concise and well-organized summary has just been made, the factual material is already at hand. However, further condensation is needed and a diagram emphasizes significant interrelationships between key factors.

Key to Diagram[7] The numbers in the diagram refer to these key features in the situation as a whole:

[7] The words in this key can't have much meaning for a person who does not know the facts of the case. However, in conjunction with the diagram, the key may serve to show what we are talking about.

1 *Safety:* with special reference to responsibilities of a foreman, a shop steward, and a member of the Union Safety Committee; Bell's fears; and objective basis, (if any) for such fears.

2 *Management prerogatives:* especially the right to direct and discipline members of the work force (as specified in the Labor Agreement).

3 *The foreman:* scope of his authority and responsibilities, with special reference to order-giving, appropriate conduct by his subordinates, and a statutory relationship with the shop steward.

4 *The shop steward:* duties and responsibilities entailed by his triple role as a union representative, a member of the Union Safety Committee, and a company employee; facts about the timing of his action in the sequence of events during the incident; his previous record.

5 *Mr. Bell ("The Nervous Welder"):* his duties

as a company employee when given an order to perform work in a way that he considered unsafe; his rights, in regard to safety and to consulting a member of the Safety Committee; his fears (and objective basis—if any—for them).

6 *The change in work routine:* with special reference to use of the new method (introduced on another shift); and previous explanations (if any) to employees on this shift.

Visualizing such a network of situational factors is a tested means to avoid oversimplifying the question for immediate decision. However, if this particular case is used to illustrate thinking appropriate to an impartial arbitrator, the issue is inevitably simpler than if the situation had been taken at an earlier stage (for example, when the plant superintendent appeared upon the scene). For an arbitrator, the issue would naturally be formulated somewhat as follows: In view of the facts as found, and under the existing labor agreement, was shop steward Harris discharged for just cause? At an earlier stage, when the action decision was up to the plant superintendent, the immediate issue might have been formulated as: In view of the circumstances, what action—toward the foreman, the shop steward, and Mr. Bell—would be both practical and organizationally sound?

Members of a case study group soon come to understand that the issue for an administrative decision is necessarily more complex than an issue for arbitration. An ad hoc arbitrator enters the case situation only temporarily to resolve a dispute. But anyone with managerial responsibilities should try to make sure that his formulation of a short-term action decision does not obscure (or unduly restrict) opportunities for long-term action.

Formulating issues is quite different from looking for facts. Case analysis may be said to begin at the point where factual material is organized, in a summary. However, analytical thinking gets into high gear only when we begin

to ask: What do these facts mean—for action? In trying to answer this question comprehensively and objectively, it can be advantageous to work as a member of a group. The first suggestions as to what the issue "is" are often overly narrow or perhaps slanted. If so, such formulations may be questioned, and more thoughtful suggestions may be offered (perhaps by group members who are less quick to express the first idea that occurs to them).

When a discussion group has agreed on a statement of what needs to be decided to resolve the immediate question posed by an Incident, they are ready to take the next step.

Phase 4: Making and Testing Independent Decisions and Group Opinions To provide scope both for independent thinking and for small-group work, this step in the Incident Process is subdivided into four suboperations.

a *Committing to writing an independent, reasoned decision.*[8] At this point each group member, working by himself, gives his own answer to the following questions: *In the collective role assigned to all of us, how would I cope with this incident, assuming that I used my best judgment? If asked to explain how I reached this decision, what would I say?* The signed papers[9] on which these decisive questions are answered are turned in to the discussion leader or to an observer-reporter. They are used to help people sort themselves into opinion groups. Thus small work groups are set

[8] Long experience in leading discussion by the Incident Process has supplied convincing evidence that, valuable though this first suboperation is, omitting it is almost a necessity if the study period is limited to 2 hours and there is to be adequate time for role playing (when desirable) and for Phase 5. If written papers are not available to indicate individual opinions, the discussion leader may jot down a range of options on the blackboard. Study-group members can then indicate their choices by a show of hands. If some members do not like any of the options, they may be invited to state their own decisions (without, however, indicating their reasoning until later).

[9] Subsequently returned to each group member, these papers provide him with part of the record which he needs for appraising his own performance.

up. Each consists of like-minded members—of persons who agree as to how the incident should be handled (though within each subgroup there are always some differences in reasoning).

b *Conferring in opinion groups.* The assignment now is to crystallize group thinking. Doing so in each subgroup, with the guidance of a group chairman, answers the question: *What is the strongest "case" that we can put together to support our decision?*

During this suboperation, the advantages of group dynamics as small group work become apparent. Like-minded members usually find it easy and rewarding to listen to one another. Moreover, in such a group, a strong incentive for effective teamwork often helps someone voluntarily to accept the reasoning of a teammate. Perhaps he now sees it as more compelling, in some respect, than a reason of his own.

The specific form of preparation during this suboperation differs according to whether subgroup thinking is to be presented by a spokesman or a role player.

c *Presenting subgroup opinions.* The third suboperation consists in communicating and testing subgroup opinions. When this is done by spokesmen, each of these elected representatives can serve his constituents by presenting a line of reasoning clearly, concisely, and persuasively.[10]

When subgroup opinions have been expressed by spokesmen, the following question has been answered: *Within the reconstituted discussion group as a whole, what is the range of difference (not only in decisions, but also in reasoning) with regard to how the incident might best be handled?*

When subgroup opinions are presented in role playing, other questions are answered: *Can one role player effectively present a decision that matches the needs of the case? Can he do so in a way that is appropriate to his assigned organizational role and in a manner that would be acceptable to another reasonable person, also cast in a*

specific role? The second role player answers a key question by responding, in a way that seems in character, to his interpretation of what the first role player said.

d *Hearing about what actually happened.* After individual opinions have been presented and compared, a fourth suboperation in short-run decision making is considering the test of history. *What actually was decided and done at the time of the incident? And what happened in the immediate sequel?* The discussion leader may present this information now. Or he may decide to postpone it until after case students have made their own decisions as to the needs for long-term action in the case situation as a whole. Since 1971, the Pigors team[11] has reached the conclusion that it is preferable to offer case analysts the opportunity to test their own insight and foresight with regard to long-term goals in the case under discussion before giving them the last bits of historical information.

Phase 5: What Can Be Learned by Reflecting on Major Issues and Long-term Goals? Characteristic general questions for this culminating phase of case analysis are: *After the immediate incident had been coped with, what more needed to be thought about, and done, by insiders in that case situation? Which of the long-term goals that are obviously worth working for in that case are of special interest to members of a study group because the same goals are equally important in their everyday work situations?* To naturally reflective minds, opportunities for such broad-gauged thinking have a strong appeal. But apparently many training directors who have used the Incident Process have shared the experience of the Pigors team that after short-term decisions have been discussed, most members of a study group feel a sense of letdown. In 1969, we devised an approach that totally eliminates this difficulty.

[10] If presentations by spokesmen are extended into a brief debate, both speakers and listeners can gather material on such questions as these: Is debating an effective technique by which to promote an interchange of ideas? In what important respects does it differ from the experience of conferring with like-minded members in a small work group?

[11] Since the inception of the Pigors Incident Process, the senior author has worked with his wife in demonstrating this method of analyzing and discussing case situations and subsequently evaluating the results obtained.

This device is used after suggesting (as has always been standard practice) that group members now promote themselves to the collective role of an executive. They may have begun working on the incident in the role of a first-level supervisor or member of middle management. But to get the broadest possible perspective on the case, they should now review it from the organizational level of someone in a position to make major decisions: about corporate structure; ways of managing; policies, procedures, and practices for communication; procedures for promotion, transfer, etc.

In earlier descriptions of the Incident Process (including those published by the Bureau of National Affairs), we listed a number of questions on major issues and suggested using these—or others—as starters for reflective analysis. However, such general questions usually proved to be slow starters—or even stoppers (to use I. A. Richards's term). A return to small-group work has proved to be effective in getting active participation from almost every member of a study group. The procedure is to present the group with three specific assignments:

1 What shortcomings (or flaws in the case situation) seem to have been accountable for difficulties that showed up in the Incident? (These are factors *to work on.*)

2 What factors (personalities, organizational relationships, previous managerial actions, etc.) can be identified as actual, or potential, forces that would tend to favor productive interaction in such a situation? (These are resources *to work with.*)

3 What kinds of long-term action might alleviate current difficulties and/or tend to prevent the recurrence of such an incident? (This kind of planning concerns goals *to work toward.*)

These assignments can best be met in small "buzz groups." (A group of three members is ideal. Then there is no need for anyone to move from his seat. And the person in the middle automatically becomes chairman of his subgroup.) If there are six subgroups, the three questions can be assigned alternately, with two buzz groups each considering the same question (but obviously not the subgroups sitting next to one another).

It is refreshing to see the zest with which each buzz group tackles its assignment. And it is interesting and educational to see the similarities and differences in answers reported (after 15 to 20 minutes) by spokesmen whose buzz groups considered the same question. A further point of interest is to note the dovetailing of answers to questions 1 and 3. Moreover, it is usually evident that if the answers to question 2 had been applied in the case situation at an earlier stage, the Incident would probably never have developed.

The discussion leader can be of service to the group by jotting down on the blackboard (or on tear sheets), as reports are made, key words to identify each answer. This makes it easy to see differences and correlations.

If the historical information on the sequel to the incident is now offered, there is the further opportunity—by comparing what was actually decided and done in the case situation itself, with opinions developed by members of the study group—to ask: Is there any such thing as the "one best way" to handle a difficulty in which human interrelationships play a significant part? What are some of the reasons why solutions that look attractive, because they are technically efficient or inexpensive in money, may prove ineffectual and costly in the long run?

Other Group Dynamics Techniques and Job Rotation

This is not the place to go into details concerning all the techniques of group dynamics which can profitably be experimented with during group analysis of a case, but two that were referred to in earlier chapters may be mentioned here. *Projective listening* (described in Chapter 5) can be used to test and develop the attentiveness, objectivity, and insight of members in a case discussion group. One strategic time to test the level of listening comes in Phase 4, when spokesmen for subgroups have finished presenting the various opinions. The spokesmen whose statements were farthest apart may be invited to exchange roles. Has each listened so attentively and objectively that he can now clearly and acceptably present the subgroup opinion that is farthest from his own?

Maier's risk technique (mentioned in Chapter 9) has tested value as a device to stimulate capacity to think clearly and reasonably about alternatives for decision. This technique can usefully be applied in Phase 4—either within subgroups (while members are developing their composite opinion) or after reports from spokesmen (or presentations by role players). Whenever it is used, it is an excellent device for clarifying the relative seriousness and probability of risks associated with each of the various opinions offered.

A unique feature of the Incident Process, job rotation in specific role assignments, applies principles of group dynamics while also offering a range of opportunities to practice managerial skills.

During a series of meetings, all members of a case study group can expect to take turns in various minor leadership roles, e.g., serving as summarizer of factual information and as a spokesman, or role player, who speaks for others as well as for himself.

As soon as group members get the hang of the analytical method (the five-phase cycle), there is also an opportunity to volunteer for one or both of the most responsible roles: (1) serving as discussion leader or (2) as participant observer-reporter, on one case. Persons in these roles work together with mutually supportive functions.[12] Those of the discussion leader can be summarized as follows:

1 Preparing a case, as part of a five-step plan for discussion. This entails:
   a Selecting from firsthand experience (or from documentary material) a situation which seems likely to be interesting and profitable for group members to analyze.
   b Selecting a point of climax and writing it up as an incident (well designed to trigger off fact-finding questions).
   c Making his own analysis of the situation which he has selected as a case.
   d Working out a plan which invites thoroughgoing, objective group discussion and analysis.
2 Leading the group in analysis of that case.
3 During group work on the case, a leader can modify his plan effectively to use behavior which, although unexpected, seems to offer a productive lead for learning.
4 Reviewing his plan and evaluating his leadership, with the aim of learning more about leading.

In each of those responsibilities, the "task leader's"[13] partner, a participant observer-reporter, may work with him. The role responsibilities of this second (and primarily "social") leader include these:

1 Studying or actually collaborating on the case selected, the incident, and the plan for group analysis made by the discussion leader.
2 Making an independent analysis of the case (so that he will not be distracted by trying to

---

[12] Since 1968, we have been impressed by the advantages of having two participant observer-reporters work with each discussion leader. Especially when a series of meetings is not long enough to permit every member to take one of the two leading roles, the increased opportunity to participate in this way can be extremely valuable. The meeting at which a group member is primarily responsible for observing group performance is usually the only time when that person concentrates on the tasks of observing and appraising the actions and contributions of his associates in the study group. Every supervisor and manager needs to develop his full capacity in both these skills. Moreover, a practical point that has appealed to many case students is that having two people share this role halves the work that needs to be done in preparing a written report.

[13] For a discussion of these roles see Robert F. Bales, "In Conference," *Harvard Business Review,* vol. 32, no. 2, pp. 44–50, March–April, 1954.

form his own opinion of it when he is expected to be taking careful notes on developments in the case of the study group itself).

3 Keeping track of who says what, when, in which roles, and with what observable consequences during group discussion of the case.

4 Writing a report, to be delivered to the group, which contains a selection of findings on facts of group performance, some appraisal, and some recommendations for raising the level of group performance.

If invited to do so by his partner, the observer may also offer certain minor services *during group work on the case* (e.g., drawing attention to someone who is waiting to ask a question or suggesting that someone's question may not have been fully answered by the leader), *and afterward,* as the two partners, each from his own angle, jointly appraise the whole sequence of activity which began by selecting a given case for group discussion.

Job rotation among major and minor roles offers opportunities for management development that are more extensive and varied than is possible when all members of a case study group always work on cases merely in an undifferentiated role as discussants. For instance, a person who is preparing to lead a case discussion tends to pay close attention to leadership skills (and shortcomings) demonstrated by other persons. A second step in a process of learning is taken when the fruits of attentive performance appraisal are applied in trying to measure up to responsibilities in that same leading role. Similarly, a participant observer-reporter is in a relatively strong position to make realistic recommendations for improving group performance. A favoring factor is that his responsibility for doing so comes *after* previous experience in case analysis as a discussant and *before* returning to the place where his recommendations (if adopted) would affect his own behavior. Moreover, comments may be particularly effective when communicated by a participant observer. He can speak as one of "us." Consequently, his negative criticisms (if any) and his recommenda-

tions are likely to be more acceptable than if they came from an outsider.

WHAT ABOUT THE TEACHER?

For purposes of management development, a significant advantage of the Incident Process is that the course director can demonstrate managerial responsibilities in the role of a coach. As members of a study group begin to take on the responsibilities of preparing and presenting cases, the teacher can move into the role of one who is "on tap, not on top." Like any other manager, however, he retains executive and administrative responsibilities even after having delegated certain leadership functions.

His primary responsibility, which cannot be delegated, is to stimulate and guide learning. Two ways to meet that obligation are encouraging outstanding group members to volunteer as subleaders and offering them as much coaching as they feel they need (while they are writing cases, preparing discussion plans, and drafting reports on group performance). However, less ambitious members of the group may also benefit from coaching, an effective kind being to hold periodic stock-taking meetings for the whole group. At such times, reports from participant observers can be reviewed for group appraisal of group performance. In this way members of a case study group can apply to their own situation diagnostic and decision-making techniques which they have previously been using only in analyzing cases "out there," situations relatively remote in time and space from the place where they are thinking and talking together.

A course director needs good judgment to know when the time is ripe to embark on this advanced stage in group work. Two developments favor productive interaction in performance appraisal and group coaching by members of a case study group: (1) familiarity with a comprehensive and realistic method of situational diagnosis and (2) ability to maintain the relatively objective attitude which befits a case student.

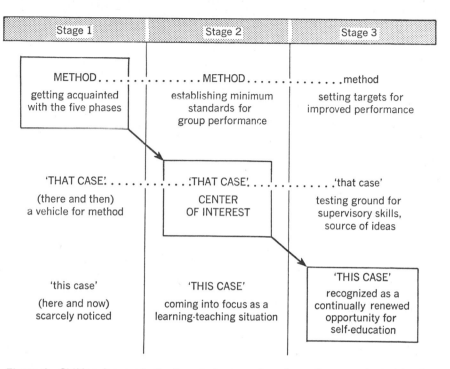

Figure 2 Shifting focus of attention during a series of meetings conducted by the Incident Process of case discussion.

The progressive shift of attention which can be hoped for (and needs to be worked for) may be diagramed as shown in Figure 2. When management representatives reach the third stage (in Figure 2 the place where they apply case method to learn from current experience), they are well on their way toward becoming case-minded. From then on, they have started to use a tested method to ensure that joint evaluation of past achievement can lead to effective planning, which, in turn, can result in progressively improved performance. In this process of self-education with others, case-minded persons readily recognize (and learn from) the idea that many of the mistakes made by people in "those cases out there" are the very mistakes that we ourselves make in "this case right here" (the situation where case students are trying to learn by thinking and talking together).

CASE STUDY IS A DO-IT-YOURSELF ASSIGNMENT

The cases which follow and the Incident Process can help us to understand real-life problems like those faced by managers, supervisors, and personnel administrators every day. By thinking responsibly, and responsively, about these cases, anyone can develop his capacity to understand how a wide range of real-life difficulties can arise and what might be done to prevent or to remedy them. Both the student and the person who already holds a responsible position in some organization can move ahead from the point he has already reached by making full use of his powers to think objectively, to be socially perceptive, to use good judgment, and to take account not only of significant facts but also of significant relationships between facts.

The Old-line Foreman

INTRODUCTION

A first-level supervisor has leadership responsibilities toward employees in the company organization who report to him and also as a management representative in dealings with the union. However, without adequate and continuing orientation he cannot be expected effectively to represent higher management in carrying out administrative procedures, interpreting personnel policies, and working cooperatively with union representatives to handle employee grievances.

An unusually acute need for orientation arises when, as in the following case, a first-level supervisor (1) is an aggressive, independent individual, who (2) was taken over from another, nonunionized organization, and (3) now finds himself in a report relationship which is quite different from that in which he functioned when he first came to the company.

The following case report illustrates several kinds of difficulties that may be expected to develop when a foreman of the old school has been permitted to go his own way, virtually disregarding policies and procedures (for personnel and labor relations) which are accepted for the organization as a whole.

CASE BACKGROUND

Until 1932, Plant 10 of the National Manufacturing Company had purchased from a nonunionized outside supplier all aluminum die castings for its home appliances. In that year, however, the production of food mixers and vacuum cleaners increased to such an extent that management decided to manufacture these parts in its own plant. As it happened, the outside supplier was ready to retire from business at about that time. He therefore proposed that the National Manufacturing Company should take

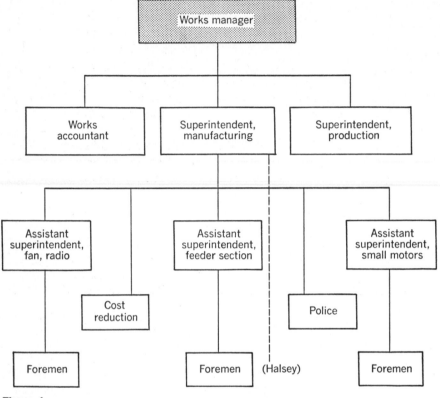

Figure 1

over his foreman, Mr. Halsey, and several of his skilled operators. This seemed convenient for the management of Plant 10, which had no supervisor or operators specially trained for a die-casting department.

The organization of the new department was as shown in Figure 1.

Mr. Morse, superintendent of manufacturing, was put in charge. Since he had no practical experience with die casting, he delegated to the foreman, Mr. Halsey, full authority to set up his own organization. This meant that Mr. Halsey was empowered to hire his own people, buy his own machinery, and in every way assume full charge of the new department in order to set it up on a going production basis. Whenever he felt

in need of advice, he was to report directly to the superintendent.

Mr. Halsey proved to be a die caster of unquestioned ability and a man of independent character. The latter attribute would immediately have created problems in a department more closely allied to the main organization than his own. As it was, the practical convenience to higher management representatives of having a man in the new department who could "go it alone" blinded them to certain human problems that were bound to develop from his methods and attitudes. Mr. Halsey showed no great respect for such of the company rules as interfered with his convenience. For example, he smoked when and where he chose and left the plant whenever he wished. There was evidence that he was somewhat fond of alcohol, which influenced his behavior but not his competence. His previous experience in handling foundry workers, who are on the whole a "rough bunch," had developed his tendency to use coarse language and harsh methods. In the similar setting of the die-casting department, his firm hand and technical ability enabled him to get results. Therefore, he was never reprimanded, and apparently he received no instruction in company policies toward the union.

In the spring of 1934, local management changed hands, and the plant was reorganized. The position of superintendent in charge of manufacturing was abolished, giving place to five divisional superintendents, one for each line of product. Under the divisional superintendents, there were general foremen. The foundry and die-casting departments, as well as the carpentry and pattern shop, were placed under one of these general foremen, Mr. Hermiston, who reported to Mr. Rankeillor, superintendent of the feeder division. Mr. Halsey was now one of the five foremen who reported to Mr. Hermiston. The resulting official organization was as displayed in Figure 2.

Mr. Hermiston was of Scottish ancestry, thirty-five years of age, deeply religious, and an ardent prohibitionist. His previous work history was of a clerical nature; he had been a cost clerk for the foundry before he was promoted to general foreman.

Mr. Halsey ignored his new supervisor and went about his business as before. Mr. Hermiston naturally objected to this behavior but decided not to make an issue of it, hoping that Mr. Halsey could gradually be brought to cooperate. No one interviewed Mr. Halsey about the new organization, of which he was apprised only by

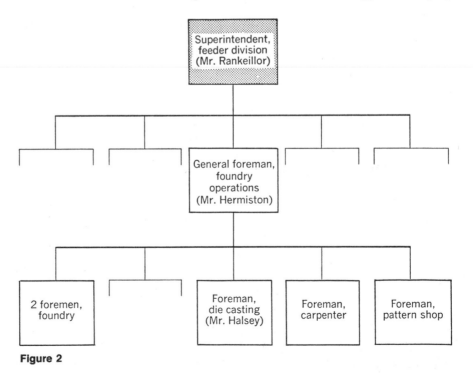

Figure 2

a routine intraplant letter. In spite of Mr. Hermiston's efforts to overlook Mr. Halsey's independent behavior, the situation came to a head on Apr. 15, 1937, when the business agent of the local union presented a written complaint to Mr. Avery, the personnel director, stating that foreman Halsey had refused to recognize the shop steward in his department.

A   THE MEETING

On Apr. 16, 1937, a meeting was held in Mr. Avery's office, the following men being present:

Union:
Mr. Cameron, president of the union
Mr. Oviedo, business agent
Mr. Walker, die-casting cleaner and shop steward

Management:
Mr. Rankeillor, division superintendent
Mr. Hermiston, general foreman, foundry operations
Mr. Halsey, foreman, die-casting department
Mr. Avery, director of personnel relations

Avery: Gentlemen, I have called you together this morning for the purpose of discussing a complaint. *(To the business agent)* Would you like to open the meeting, Mr. Oviedo, or do you wish me to?   5

Cameron: I think you should read the complaint, Mr. Avery.

Avery: All right. *(Reads)*

Complaint Report
Name: John F. Walker   Department: F-10   10
Address: 654 South St.   Badge: No. 20
City:———   Home phone: 6-5357
Complaint:
  The above-named individual has been elected by his department employees as a shop   15 steward. On Apr. 7, 1937, he went to Mr. Halsey, the foreman, to ask him about increasing the ventilating equipment in the department, claiming that there was not enough ventilation for the machine operators. He wanted to   20

know if something couldn't be done about it. The foreman, Mr. Halsey, would not accept Mr. Walker as a representative of the union and, using abusive language, told him to go about his business. We ask that a meeting be   25 called in your office with Mr. Halsey and Mr. Walker in order to clear up this situation.
    (Signed)   Oviedo, *Business Agent*

Avery: Mr. Halsey, inasmuch as this complaint is against you, have you anything to   30 say?

Halsey: Plenty. This guy, Walker, here, doesn't realize that the gang is kidding him. They haven't got anything to kick about. All this stuff he is bringing up is old stuff.   35 We've gone over it before with the other representative. That representative was sick of the job and gave it up, so the gang decided to elect this squirt because nobody else wanted the job. This fellow doesn't   40 know anything about the department. He's only been there 3 months. He's only a kid and doesn't know what it's all about. I haven't got time to rehash this all over again. [1]   45

Oviedo: It's *our* job to decide whether Mr. Walker is qualified to represent his people or not. They have elected him, and that's all there's to it. The reason that we called this meeting is to find out why you won't recog-   50 nize him as a representative and deal with him as other foremen in the plant deal with their representatives.

Halsey: Well, he might be a representative to you, but as far as I'm concerned he   55 don't represent . . . *[indecent language].* He's not qualified to talk about anything that happens in my department, and I haven't got time to waste on him. He brings up all this stuff and nonsense just so he can be a   60 big shot.

[1] With due allowance for Mr. Halsey's informal style, the facts of the situation were as stated here. Some of the older foundrymen had indulged a rather crude sense of humor by getting Walker to complain to Halsey about a matter that they knew was no longer a live issue.

Avery: I wonder, Mr. Halsey, whether you are acquainted with the setup in our whole plant. You know that each department has a shop steward. These employee 65 representatives are privileged to take up complaints with our foremen. It seems to me that you would have used better judgment if you had recognized Mr. Walker as the elected representative and discussed the 70 problem with him. All you would have to do is to sit down with him for a few minutes and discuss any complaints he may bring to your attention. Furthermore, you could have advised him that you had gone over 75 these matters with the former shop steward and that they had been closed to the satisfaction of all concerned. You should have told Mr. Walker that we were not installing new ventilating equipment in the die-cast- 80 ing department because it is shortly to be moved into a new building where the latest and best equipment is to be installed. If you had told Mr. Walker those things, I am sure we should not be here today. 85

Walker: I didn't know anything about what the other shop steward had brought up and would have been satisfied if Mr. Halsey had at least talked to me decently.

Halsey: Don't give me any of that stuff. 90 Don't tell me that you don't know nothing about what the other representative has done. You're not kidding me, Walker, you've been out there long enough to know that the ventilating problem was brought up 95 before.

Cameron: Mr. Avery, I don't believe we are getting anywhere. I think that you or Mr. Rankeillor should tell this fellow what he's got to do. 100

Avery: Well, what d'you say, Mr. Halsey? Do you think we can work this all right in the future? Mr. Walker is the chosen representative of his fellow employees. Let's see if we can't pull together from now on. What 105 d'you say?

Halsey: All right.

Avery: Let's give Mr. Halsey and Mr. Walker a chance to get together on this. If they can't reach a decision, we shall meet 110 again. *(To Mr. Walker)* Do you now understand the ventilating situation, Mr. Walker?

Walker: Yes, I do.

Avery: If anything else comes up, will you take care of it with Mr. Walker, Mr. Hal- 115 sey?

Halsey: Yes, I will.

QUESTIONS ON SECTION A

1 *On higher management's responsibilities toward a first-level supervisor*

  a At the stage of developments when the meeting took place, what responsibilities toward Mr. Halsey had already been omitted or scanted by members of higher management? Ideally, which management representatives should have met these responsibilities? When? And how?

  b For purposes of supervisory development (as reorientation) evaluate Mr. Avery's remarks as quoted in lines 62-85. In your answer take account of the timing, content, manner, and tone of communication from Mr. Avery and cite evidence (drawn from Mr. Halsey's comments) that this meeting did (or did not) provide him with an educational experience.

  c In view of opportunities and requirements in that situation, how appropriate do you find Mr. Avery's concluding remarks (quoted in lines 108-112, and 114-116)? Outline the reasons for your opinion.

  d Imagine that you are in Mr. Avery's position, immediately after the meeting. You now begin to wonder whether all that needed to be done has actually been accomplished. What further action, if any, might you initiate? With whom might you talk? With what specific aim(s)?

  e Suppose you had been in Rankeillor's position before, during, and immediately after the meeting; what action might you have taken in regard to difficulties occasioned by Halsey's behavior?

2 *On communication*

  a Cite remarks by Mr. Halsey during the meeting that reveal an attitude which he evidently perceived as suited to his organizational role.

b How might one reconcile the apparent contradiction between two statements made by Mr. Halsey, and quoted in lines 40-43 and 91-96?

c Why do you (or do you not) feel that (in lines 46-48) Oviedo adequately answered Halsey's challenge (given in lines 40-44) of Walker's competence?

d Given the barriers to communication and to a harmonious relationship that existed between Halsey and Hermiston, do you think it might have been possible for them effectively to coordinate their activities? Why or why not? If you think it could have been done, how might you, in Hermiston's position, have tried to do your share in moving toward this objective?

e What indication of Avery's attitude and assumptions is given by the fact that he apparently made no effort to get either Hermiston or Rankeillor to take any active part in the meeting?

3 *On responsibilities of union officers*

a To what extent do you feel that officers of a union are meeting their organizational responsibilities by making this kind of difficulty the subject of an official grievance? In what other way might they have attempted to deal with it (at least as a first step)?

b What indications were given at the meeting that any union officer had not been thorough in carrying out obligations to Walker in his capacity as newly elected representative? Whose responsibility is it to take corrective action? How?

B MR. HERMISTON'S LETTER

Despite his promise, Mr. Halsey continued to go his own way as before and failed to cooperate either with the union or with his immediate superior. On June 29, 1937, Mr. Hermiston wrote the following letter to the divisional superintendent:

Plant Correspondence   June 29, 1937
Mr. J. H. Rankeillor, Supt.
Feeder Section

At your request, I am outlining below the several reasons why Mr. Halsey cannot be considered a proper person to hold a supervisory position with our company, and particularly in a department under your jurisdiction and mine. I believe that, if he be permitted to continue as foreman of the die-casting department, the morale of the workers will be undermined, resulting in labor trouble more serious than we have yet experienced in that section.

We have received numerous complaints of Mr. Halsey's foul and abusive language to his help, and on one occasion it was the subject of a conference between management representatives and the local union representatives. We cannot hope to get the full cooperation of the employees if their immediate superior approaches them in the manner that Mr. Halsey has used so often.

Much of the unrest in the department can be traced to Mr. Halsey's own indifference to shop rules and regulations relative to smoking in restricted areas at hours when smoking is prohibited. Many of the workers hold him in disrespect because of his uncontrolled desire for liquor, which has undoubtedly been the cause for much of his absence from work. Complaints have reached me from men unwilling to cooperate with him while he is apparently under the influence of liquor during working hours.

As has been already made evident to you, he is decidedly insubordinate.

The past 12-month record of Mr. Halsey's attendance is as follows:

Date	Number of working hours	Hours lost, not includ- ing vacations	Percent
July, 1936	184	16.00	8.70
August	168	0.20	0.12
September	168	0.00	0.00
October	176	0.00	0.00
November	152	16.00	10.56
December	176	45.42	25.80
January, 1937	160	8.00	5.00
February	152	14.23	9.36
March	184	66.92	36.37
April	176	7.07	4.02
May	160	2.13	1.33
June	176	63.00	35.80
Total	2,032	238.97	11.76

None of the above lost time was with permission. Much of it was perhaps due to sickness, but none of the time was voluntarily reported as such. So long as I have had supervision over him, he has never consulted me about leaving the works at irregular hours, but comes and goes as he pleases.

It would not be difficult to replace Mr. Halsey as foreman. For about a year and a half Mr. Fenn, an experienced die caster, has been employed in the department. His duties have been to maintain the dies and make the machine repairs that occur almost daily. He has had an opportunity to take full charge of the department when Mr. Halsey has been absent and he has always done a very good job. In my opinion this man is fully qualified to replace Mr. Halsey as foreman.

(Signed) A. Hermiston
Foundry Operations

QUESTIONS ON SECTION B

1 *On communication and leadership by Mr. Hermiston*
  a Comment on Mr. Hermiston's letter to his immediate superior:
  (1) What information does it contain which would justify terminating foreman Halsey?
  (2) Aside from facts cited, to what extent do the wording and tone (used to describe Halsey's behavior) match requirements for an official statement of performance appraisal? (Cite specific words and phrases.)
  b What inferences can be made as to the way in which Hermiston had been meeting his leadership responsibilities toward Halsey? (In your answer, comment on the date of Hermiston's letter, and note other indications as to what action he had taken toward Halsey before, and since, the April meeting.)
2 *On communication and leadership by Rankeillor*
  a Outline the responsibilities of a division superintendent in such a situation. (In your answer, consider Rankeillor's official relationship with Hermiston, Halsey, Avery, and union officers.)
  b What inference(s) can be made from Hermiston's letter as to action taken by Mr. Rankeillor (in regard to difficulties occasioned by Mr. Halsey's behavior) up to this time?
  c Suppose you had been in Rankeillor's position. What might you have attempted to do (when Halsey first came to the company and afterwards) to prevent or reduce difficulties associated with Halsey's behavior?
  (1) Would you (or would you not) have considered telling Avery that you and Hermiston would handle the matter yourselves? Why?

  (2) If you had decided upon that course of action, what duties would you have delegated to Hermiston, and what part in the plan would you have reserved for yourself? Why?
  d Suppose that Mr. Rankeillor (instead of forwarding Hermiston's letter to Avery) calls Hermiston in to discuss the problem. What do you think he should say and do? Who should talk with Halsey, and what should he say? (This question can be answered by role-playing.)

C SUBSEQUENT DEVELOPMENTS

Hermiston's letter was forwarded to Mr. Avery, director of personnel relations, who on July 2, 1937, arranged a meeting in his office between Mr. Rankeillor and Mr. Halsey.

Avery: Mr. Halsey, we have called you in this morning to discuss something that is quite unusual in my experience and concerns yourself and your future. I have received complaints from your immediate superior, Mr. Hermiston, with regard to your attitude toward your employees, your supervisor, and company rules in general. It seems that you do not consider your department a part of this plant but feel that you can come and go whenever you please, break company rules whenever you want, and indulge in abusive language. What is your side of the story?

Halsey: Well, this is the first time in my experience here that I have been told about it.

Avery: But Mr. Halsey, you must recall the complaint entered in April by the employee representative in your department. It was brought out at that time that you *did* use abusive language. As a matter of fact, you used such language in my presence.

Halsey: Oh, well, you know why. They had just elected that new representative and the kid didn't know what he was talking about. He was just trying to make a big shot out of himself by presenting a lot of damn fool demands. And I wasn't going to take the time to bother with him. I've got something else to do besides fooling around with petty complaints.

Avery: Still, Mr. Halsey, you must realize that you can't handle employees in the same manner that you did 10 years ago and that you have been the subject of several complaints by the union. But at the present time I'm not so much interested in this as I am in your general attitude to the whole situation. You disregard all instructions and come and go whenever you please. Last year, for instance, you had more than 200 hours out of this plant, not counting vacations. None of this time did you ask for, or consider it necessary to tell people about. Furthermore, you have a reputation for drinking, which is not desirable, and I think you have been using poor judgment in going out on drinking parties with your own people. I understand that at one of these parties recently you were engaged in a fist fight. As a rule we are not concerned with what our employees do on the outside or after working hours, but we must be concerned with such activities as tend to affect the internal organization. You show an indifference toward shop rules and regulations relative to smoking in your department. How in the world do you expect your employees to live up to these rules if you don't?

Halsey: Don't worry. They know who is the boss.

Avery: That's another thing. Why do *you* refuse to cooperate with *your* immediate superior?

Halsey: Well, I had an understanding several years ago with Mr. Morse [former superintendent of manufacturing]. When I was hired I was told to set up this department and get it going. I was to have full authority and do as I pleased so long as I got out production. I know the die-casting game from A to Z, and nobody else around here knows it as well. And let me tell you, Mr. Avery, I have worked night and day to get a setup that runs smoothly. When this department first started in the fall of 1932, I spent many a day from 6 o'clock in the morning to 11 or 12 at night. I have been foreman for 20 years, and this is the first time that I've been on the carpet for such complaints.

Rankeillor: Nevertheless, Mr. Halsey, these complaints are based on facts, and we cannot tolerate them. I feel that it is for the best that I have Mr. Hermiston in charge of foundry operations, and none of my other foremen have refused to cooperate with him. On the contrary, Mr. Hill [foundry foreman] has worked very well under Mr. Hermiston.

Halsey: Well, I have no objections to Mr. Hermiston. I've always known him to be a good fellow. But he doesn't know anything about my work. I've never reported to more than one boss, and I don't intend to begin now.

Avery: Who do you feel is your boss, Mr. Halsey?

Halsey: Mr. Rankeillor, here, is my boss.

Avery: Why don't you say that Mr. Abbott, the works manager, is your boss? That would be just as reasonable. Suppose Mr. Kendricks, my employment manager, took that attitude because of his 20 years' experience as employment manager. Suppose he felt that I was not his proper supervisor and just took it upon himself to consider the works manager as his immediate chief. How long do you think my department would last? We've got to have organization, Mr. Halsey, particularly in such a large plant as ours. Our organization may not be the best in your way of thinking. However, here it is *(exhibits company organization chart).* Just look at this chart here, Mr. Halsey. You can see for yourself how impossible it would be for Mr. Rankeillor to contact everybody in his division.

Halsey: When I have to go to my boss, I want somebody who's got authority to decide something.

Rankeillor: Well, Mr. Hermiston has that authority.

Halsey: Oh, yeah!

Avery: Mr. Halsey, I believe we have talked long enough on this subject and I wish I could get you to see our point. There is no question in anyone's mind as to your ability in the occupation which you supervise. However, we may have to sacrifice that ability to gain the cooperation we feel is necessary for the good of the organization as a whole. Unless you are willing to recognize Mr. Hermiston as your immediate supervisor, we shall have to dispense with your services.

Halsey: Well, I don't have to work here. And if I do, I could let Mr. Hermiston take all the worries, even though he doesn't know a damn thing about die casting.

Rankeillor: Well, I don't want you to stay under such conditions. Surely, I would be in the same position, wouldn't I? I don't know anything about die casting. Neither do I know all the details of the work of my other foremen. That is their job and I'm not concerned about any foreman so long as he does his job. And if you want to stay, I would like you to fall in line the same way.

Avery: I think that's the answer, Mr. Halsey. We value your work and would like to keep you in the company. But if you cannot fall in line, I'll have to ask you to resign.

Halsey: Well, all right. I tell you what I'll do. I'll see if I can work with Mr. Hermiston and if I can't, you won't see me here again. I'll pack up and check out.

Avery: That's fine. I'm glad it came out this way, and I know it will work out for the best, Mr. Halsey, if you will only try.

On Aug. 19, the gatekeeper submitted to the industrial relations department the following complaint: [2]

Complaint Record
Employee Complaint or Request
Date: Aug. 19, 1937
Presented by: Guard Lansing

At 7:00 A.M. Mr. Halsey, foreman of the die-casting department, left the works complaining he was sick. The guard at the main gate asked him to go to

[2] In discussing this case by the Incident Process, this complaint could be used as the precipitating incident.

the first-aid station, as is customary when an employee leaves the works sick. This Mr. Halsey refused to do, saying it was not necessary for him.

No action was taken on this complaint. Within the week foreman Halsey left on his vacation and did not return. Subsequently it was learned that he had secured another position as foreman of a die-casting establishment.

QUESTIONS ON THE CASE AS A WHOLE

1 *On communication as a managerial responsibility*
Analyze this case from the viewpoint of interpersonal communication (drawing on material in Chapter 5, including Figure 5-3). For instance,
  a During the meeting (reported in Section A) what effects of activity by any "inner circuit" can you detect? Can you put into words some of the unspoken messages that may have been traveling along the inner circuit of anyone at that meeting?
  b Putting yourself, successively, in the positions of Halsey and Hermiston, give your interpretation of messages—communicated in words and in action—by the one to the other.
  c Identify communication difficulties in each section of the case, and comment briefly on these questions:
    (1) What seems to have been going wrong?
    (2) What, if anything, might have been done to overcome or reduce each difficulty?
2 *On management development*
In view of ideas presented in Chapter 3, what needs for development by which management representatives do you see in this case? If you had official responsibility for management development in this company, what (if anything) might you attempt to do about shortcomings you notice?
3 *On a foreman's competence*
To what extent (and for what reasons) do you think that Halsey's attitude and customary behavior would disqualify him from meeting the responsibilities in the following roles:
  a A production foreman in an independent, non-unionized foundry during the 1930s and 1940s.
  b A first-level supervisor (or first-level manager) in one section of a large, unionized manufacturing organization today.

Who Owns the Improved Tool?[1]

INTRODUCTION

Like many actual situations, this case is far from simple. Analyzing it can be an exercise in practical judgment as to *what difficulties* called for attention by *which management representatives* and *what decisions* for action might usefully have been made at *critical stages* in the sequence of developments as reported.

The specific nature of the diagnosis and decision made by members of a given study group will depend not only on the stage of situational developments at which analysis is undertaken but also on the perspective from which the case is viewed. For instance, is this situation of interest chiefly because it illustrates attitudes of production workers whose aims are sharply at variance with management objectives for the organization as a whole? Or is the case to be analyzed primarily as one which highlights difficulties experienced and occasioned by a foreman who evidently felt and acted like "the man in the middle"? If so, might it be instructive to consider what differences (in events and behavior) could be expected if the role and caliber of that foreman had enabled him to function as a first-level *manager*? (See Chapter 7 for a detailed consideration of that role.) Again, does it seem that major difficulties called for improved administrative procedures? Or might it be most instructive to explore the case from the technical viewpoint? Finally, might it be worth while to analyze the case from all these angles, taking a view which integrates concern for:

1 *Human needs, attitudes, and morale* (a person-centered approach).

[1] Paul Pigors and Faith Pigors, *Case Studies in Industrial Relations,* Addison-Wesley Publishing Company, Inc., Reading, Mass., 1944, ser. II, no. 7 (out of print). With the permission of Addison-Wesley Publishing Company, Inc., we include a revision of "Work-group Ownership of an Improved Tool" as material for this case.

2 *Technical aspects and requirements* (including various kinds and degrees of technical know-how and responsibility for quality and quantity of output).

3 *Administrative procedures, personnel policies, and company-wide aims* (an organization-centered approach).

See Chapter 9 for a description of a diagnostic method incorporating all these different views.

CASE BACKGROUND

The Whirlwind Aircraft Corporation was a leader in its field and especially noted for its development of the modern supercharger. Work in connection with the latter mechanism called for special skill and ability. Every detail of the supercharger had to be perfect to satisfy the exacting requirements of the aircraft industry.

In 1941 (before Pearl Harbor), Lathe Department 15-D was turning out three types of impellers, each contoured to within 0.002 inch and machined to a mirrorlike finish. The impellers were made from an aluminum alloy and finished on a cam-back lathe.

The work was carried on in four shifts, two men on each. The personnel in the finishing section were as follows:

1 *First Shift*—7 A.M. to 3 P.M.; Sunday and Monday off.
  a Jean Latour, master mechanic, French Canadian, forty-five years of age. Latour had set up the job and trained the men who worked with him on the first shift.
  b Pierre DuFresne, master mechanic, French Canadian, thirty-six years of age.
  Both these men had trained the workers needed for the other shifts.
2 *Second Shift*—3 P.M. to 11 P.M.; Friday and Saturday off.
  a Albert Durand, master mechanic, French Canadian, thirty-two years of age; trained by Latour and using his lathe.

  b Robert Bénet, master mechanic, French Canadian, thirty-one years of age; trained by DuFresne and using his lathe.
3 *Third Shift*—11 P.M. to 7 A.M.; Tuesday and Wednesday off.
  a Philippe Doret, master mechanic, French Canadian, thirty-one years of age; trained by Latour and using his lathe.
  b Henry Barbet, master mechanic, French Canadian, thirty years of age; trained by DuFresne and using his lathe.
4 *Stagger Shift*—Monday, 7 A.M. to 3 P.M.; Tuesday, 11 P.M. to 7 A.M.; Wednesday, 11 P.M. to 7 A.M.; Thursday off; Friday, 3 P.M. to 11 P.M.; Saturday, 3 P.M. to 11 P.M.; Sunday off.
  a George McNair, master mechanic, Scotch, thirty-two years of age; trained by Latour and using his lathe.
  b William Reader, master mechanic, English, thirty years of age; trained by DuFresne and using his lathe.

Owing to various factors (such as the small number of workers involved, the preponderance of one nationality, and the fact that Latour and DuFresne had trained the other workers) these eight men considered themselves as members of one work group. Such a feeling of solidarity is unusual among workers on different shifts, despite the fact that they use the same machines.

The men received a base rate of $1.03 an hour and worked on incentive. Each man usually turned out 22 units a shift, thus earning an average of $1.19 an hour. Management supplied Rex 95 high-speed toolbits, which workers ground to suit themselves. Two tools were used: one square bit with a slight radius for recess cutting, the other bit with a 45-degree angle for chamfering and smooth finish. When used, the two tools were set close together, the worker adjusting the lathe from one operation to the other. The difficulty with this setup was that, during the rotation of the lathe, the aluminum waste would melt and fuse between the two toolbits. Periodically the lathe had to be stopped so that the toolbits could be freed from the welded aluminum and reground.

A THE TOOL PROBLEM

At the request of the foreman of Lathe Department 15-D, the methods department had been working on his tool problem. Up to the time of this case, no solution had been found. To make a firsthand study of the difficulty, the methods department had recently assigned one of their staff, Mr. MacBride, to investigate the problem in the lathe department itself. Mr. MacBride's working hours covered parts of both the first and second shifts. MacBride was a young man, twenty-six years of age, and a newcomer to the methods department. For 3 months before this assignment, he had held the post of "suggestion man," a position which enabled newcomers to the methods department to familiarize themselves with the organization of the plant. His job consisted in collecting, from boxes in departments throughout the plant, suggestions submitted by employees and making a preliminary evaluation of these ideas. The current assignment of studying the tool situation in Lathe Department 15-D, with a view to cutting costs, was his first special task. He devoted himself to this problem with great zeal but did not succeed in winning the confidence of the workers. In pursuance of their usual philosophy: "Keep your mouth shut if you see anyone with a suit on," they volunteered no information and took the stand that, since the methods man had been given this assignment, it was up to him to carry it out.

While MacBride was working on this problem, Pierre DuFresne hit upon a solution. One day he successfully contrived a tool which combined the two bits into one. This eliminated the space between the two toolbits which in the past had caught the molten aluminum waste and allowed it to become welded to the cutting edges. The new toolbit had two advantages: it eliminated the frequent machine stoppage for cleaning and regrinding the old-type tools, and it enabled the operator to run the lathe at a higher speed. These advantages made it possible for the operator to increase his efficiency by 50 percent.

DuFresne tried to make copies of the new tool but was unable to do so. Apparently the new development had been a "lucky accident" during grinding which he could not duplicate. After several unsuccessful attempts, he took the new tool to his former teacher, Jean Latour. The latter succeeded in making a drawing and turning out duplicate toolbits on a small grinding wheel in the shop. At first the two men decided to keep the new tool to themselves. Later, however, they shared the improvement with their fellow workers on the second shift. Similarly it was passed on to the other shifts. But all these men kept the new development a closely guarded secret as far as "outsiders" were concerned. At the end of the shift, each locked the improved toolbit securely in his toolchest.

Both DuFresne, the originator of the new tool, and Latour, its draftsman and designer, decided not to submit the idea as a suggestion but to keep it as the property of their group. Why was this decision made? The answer lies partly in the suggestion system and partly in the attitude of Latour and DuFresne toward other features of company work life and toward their group.

According to an informational bulletin issued by the company, the purpose of the suggestion system was to "provide an orderly method of submitting and considering ideas and recommendations of employees to management; to provide a means for recognizing and rewarding individual ingenuity; and to promote cooperation." Awards for accepted suggestions were made in the following manner: "After checking the savings and expense involved in an adopted suggestion [the suggestion committee] determined the amount of the award to be paid, based upon the savings predicted for a year's use of the suggestion. . . . It is the intention of the committee . . . to be liberal in the awards, which are expected to adequately compensate for the interest shown in presenting suggestions." In pursuance of this policy, it was customary to grant the suggestor an award equivalent to the savings of an entire month.

As a monetary return, both DuFresne and Latour considered an award based on one month's savings inadequate. They also argued that such awards were really taken out of the workers' pockets. Their reasoning was as follows. All awards for adopted suggestions were paid out of undistributed profits. Since the company also had a profit-sharing plan, the money was taken from a fund that would be given to the workers anyway, which merely meant robbing Peter to pay Paul. In any case, the payment was not likely to be large and probably would be less than they could accumulate if increased incentive payments could be maintained for a long time without discovery. Thus they felt there was little to be said in favor of submitting the new tool as a suggestion.

Latour and DuFresne also felt that there were definite hazards to the group if their secret were disclosed. They feared that once the tool became company property, its efficiency might lead to layoff of some members in their group, or at least make work less tolerable by leading to an increased quota at a lower price per unit. They also feared that there might be a change in scheduled work assignments. For instance, the lathe department worked on three different types of impellers. One type was a routine job and, aside from the difficulty caused by the old-type tool, presented no problem. For certain technical reasons, the other two types were more difficult to make. Even Latour, an exceptionally skilled craftsman, had sometimes found it hard to make the expected quota before the new tool was developed. Unless the work load was carefully balanced by scheduling easier and more difficult types, some of the operators were unable to make standard time.

The decision to keep the tool for their own group was in keeping with Latour's work philosophy. He had a strong feeling of loyalty to his own group and had demonstrated this in the past by offering for their use several improvements of his own. For example, he made available to all workers in his group a set of special gauge blocks which were used in aligning work on lathes. To protect himself in case mistakes were traced to these gauges, he wrote on them: "Personnel [sic] Property—Do not use. Jean Latour."

Through informal agreement with their fellow workers, Latour and DuFresne "pegged production" at an efficiency rate that in their opinion would not arouse management's suspicion or lead to a restudy of the job, with possible cutting of the rate. This enabled them to make sure of earning an extra 10 percent incentive pay. The other 40 percent in additional efficiency was used as follows. The operators established a reputation for a high degree of accuracy and finish. They set a record for no spoilage, and they were able to apply the time gained on the easier type of impeller to work on the other types which required greater care and more expert workmanship.

QUESTIONS ON SECTION A

1 *On situational analysis*
So far, management representatives have formulated the nub of the difficulty in this case as "a tool problem." What other technical and nontechnical features of the situation can you identify as having contributed to the problem that requires attention?

2 *On staff line relationships*
When a representative of line management has asked for help from the methods department, what obligations (if any) does he have toward the methods engineer who is sent in response to his request? Specifically, if you had been in the foreman's position, what might you have done, immediately after MacBride's arrival, and later, to ensure that his technical ability could make a maximum contribution?

3 *On line responsibility for production*

If a foreman realizes that some of his subordinates are pegging production, what might he try to do about it?

4 *On formal and informal relationships*

a Evaluate the potential advantages and risks, in such a situation, of having a foreman try to work *with* the leader of an informally organized work group. For example:

(1) Do you think that even attempting to do so would be hopeless? Why?

(2) If you think that the effort might succeed, do you think that the price of success would necessarily include a weakening of the foreman's authority? Why, or why not?

b If (in the position of the foreman in this case) you would make that attempt, whom would you talk with first, and what might you say? (This interview might well be role played.)

5 *On line responsibility for personnel administration*

a With reference to ideas presented in various chapters of this text (especially Chapter 2) indicate what responsibilities toward personnel might, in your opinion, have been better met up to this point in the case.

b Considering the tactical move indicated in question 4 as one possibility, what action might you take at this point in the case if you were in the foreman's position? (Indicate your reasons.)

B THE FOREMAN'S DECISION, MACBRIDE'S APPEAL, DuFRESNE'S RUSE

The foreman of the lathe department learned about the new tool soon after it was put into use but decided to let the men handle the situation in their own way. He reasoned that at little expense he was able to get out production of high quality. There was no defective work, and the men were contented.

Mr. MacBride was left in a very unsatisfactory position. He had not succeeded in working out a solution of his own. Like the foreman, he got wind of the fact that the men had devised a new tool. He urged them to submit a drawing of it through the suggestion system, but this advice

was not taken, and the men made it plain that they did not care to discuss with him the reasons for this position.

Having no success in his direct contact with the workers, Mr. MacBride appealed to the foreman, asking him to secure a copy of the new tool. The foreman replied that the men would certainly decline to give him a copy and would resent as an injustice any effort on his part to force them to submit a drawing. Instead he suggested that MacBride should persuade DuFresne to show him the tool. This MacBride attempted to do, but his efforts to ingratiate himself with DuFresne were unsuccessful. When he persisted, DuFresne decided to throw him off the track. He left in his lathe a toolbit which was an unsuccessful copy of the original discovery. At shift change, MacBride was delighted to find what he supposed to be the improved tool. He hastily copied it and submitted a drawing to the tool department. A tool that was made up according to these specifications naturally failed to do the job. When the workers heard of this failure through the grapevine, they were delighted. DuFresne did not hesitate to crow over MacBride, pointing out that his underhanded methods had met with their just reward.

The foreman, however, continued to ignore the friction between DuFresne and MacBride. At this point, MacBride complained to the foreman that DuFresne was openly boasting of his trick and ridiculing him before other workers. The foreman then recognized that he must talk to DuFresne. But the latter insisted that his ruse had been justified as a means of self-protection.

QUESTIONS ON SECTION B

1 *On supervisory responsibility*

a Comment on the foreman's decision and reasoning when he first learned about the improved tool. Even if you do not agree that his decision was justified, to which of his reasons (if any) would you give some weight? As indicated in paragraph 1 of Section B, to what important organization goals does it seem that the foreman gave little or no weight?

b As far as the foreman was concerned, do you feel that either MacBride's appeal or DuFresne's ruse significantly increased the responsibility for supervisory action? Why, or why not? Does one development seem more important than the other as constituting an obligation for supervisory action? If so, which, and why?

2 *On meeting responsibilities in a staff role*
Comment on MacBride's actions up to this point. What else might he have done, or done differently?

C THE SITUATION COMES TO A HEAD, BUT "IT'S TOO LATE NOW"

After having been rebuffed by DuFresne, the foreman at last recognized that he had on his hands something more difficult and perplexing than "a tool problem." But now he did not know which way to turn. He still wished to keep the goodwill of his men. Yet now that the conflict between MacBride and DuFresne had been brought into the open, he could no longer ignore it. To do so would be to expose himself to the charge that he was openly abetting production workers in obstructing the work of a methods man. MacBride would surely make some report of it to his superior in the methods department. Thus the division superintendent would certainly hear of it. At that point, the foreman could expect to hear from the superintendent, who would undoubtedly be critical of his (the foreman's) behavior on several counts. For example, the superintendent would be displeased at not having been informed about the important technical improvement[2] developed by Latour and DuFresne. And what about this fracas with MacBride? The superintendent would want to

know why the foreman had not acted promptly and effectively when MacBride first came into the finishing section.

Awkward questions could, and certainly would, now be raised as to constructive courses of action that should have been taken earlier. But, as the foreman put it, "It's too late now. The best thing I can do is to tell my superintendent the whole story before anyone else gets to him."

QUESTIONS ON THE CASE AS A WHOLE

1 *On management development*[3]
  a What needs for development, on the part of which management representatives, have been illustrated in this case?
  b To what extent, and in what ways, might a formal program for supervisory development be helpful in meeting these needs?
  c In addition to formal programs, what other ways of teaching, carried out by whom, might have been educational?

2 *On motivation and productivity*[4]
  a With specific reference to this case, identify and compare:
    (1) incentives to productivity offered by management.
    (2) inner motivation, as another factor determining output.
  b To what extent, and in what respects, do features of this case seem to illustrate general ideas about motivation which characterize the theories of Maslow, Gellerman, and/or Herzberg? In your answer refer to
    (1) Maslow's hierarchy of needs.
    (2) Gellerman's "self-concept."
    (3) Herzberg's distinction between job content and job context.
  c Do you find any of these ideas helpful in interpreting behavior by employees in the finishing section? If so, how?

---

[2] It should be kept in mind that during 1941 the aircraft industry was expanding. The demand for impellers had increased to such an extent that, in this company, an entire new plant unit was devoted to this product.

[3] In answering this question, consider ideas presented in Chaps. 3 and 7.
[4] In answering this question, take account of ideas in Chap. 6.

3 *On teamwork, team spirit, and cooperative relationships*

a Identify evidences of teamwork and of team spirit (referring to definitions given in Chapter 6) within the eight-man work group in the finishing section.

b Would you say that the foreman's attitude toward production workers showed team spirit? Why, or why not?

c Do you feel that DuFresne's refusal of the foreman's request (described in Section C) proves that he could never have been persuaded to use his influence to promote cooperative relationships between his group and management representatives? Why, or why not?

4 *On taking a systems-minded approach*

a What evidence did you find in this case that employees at various organizational levels did (or did not) take a systems-minded approach?

b In such a situation, what practical steps might be taken to help employees, e.g., a foreman or production operators, harmonize personal goals with organizational objectives?

c Given the same technical circumstances and organizational arrangements as in this case, e.g., the same tool problem in an aircraft company with staff departments available to serve line management, what might a first-level manager have done from the beginning if he had taken a systems-minded approach and tried to encourage other participants to do likewise?

Dissatisfactions of an Expatriate Engineer

INTRODUCTION

This case illustrates, among other things, the need to meet managerial responsibilities that are broader than those imposed by technical requirements of the work situation. For example:

1 In overseas operations, cultural differences between organizational members call for special efforts to achieve mutual understanding.

2 In any organization, the whole life of each employee, including his family life, is a factor which affects his behavior at work and in work relationships.

3 The attitudes of an employee's family members may significantly affect his behavior at work and in work relationships.

4 Therefore subjective forces in an employee and in members of his family may be as significant in a work situation as technical qualifications.

A   CASE BACKGROUND

Engineer Laborde's Initial Contacts with Fabricas Durán

Shortly before obtaining his degree in electrical engineering at a Belgian university, Georges Laborde decided that he could most rapidly advance his career by emigrating to some "underdeveloped" country. Mexico looked promising because of its rapid, though still relatively new, industrial growth. After corresponding with the Belgian Embassy in Mexico City, he selected Fabricas Durán as an enterprise in which he thought his ability could lead to a brilliant future.

Fabricas Durán was a subsidiary of a Belgian corporation, Usines Belges. Located in Monterrey, the Mexican branch had been established in 1960 to manufacture transformers and other station equipment. In 1966, when Engineer Laborde was first employed there, its annual sales volume amounted to 25 million pesos (approximately 2 million dollars), and it had 240 employees. According to information obtained by Laborde, the company was likely to expand rapidly.

After an exchange of letters between Laborde and Señor Vasquez, the general manager[1] of Fabricas Durán, it was arranged that Laborde should be interviewed and given psychological tests at Usines Belges. In November, 1964, he was hired in Belgium with the understanding that after completing his training there he would emigrate to Mexico and be employed by Fabricas Durán.[2]

Points in his favor were judged to be his engineering degree at a first-class European university, where academic standards were higher than in Mexico, his intellectual caliber, his scientific competence, his evident ambition, and the fact that French was his native language. (This circumstance was considered extremely useful for purposes of communication between Usines Belges and its Mexican subsidiary.)

Orientation and Training in Belgium

In the interviews at Usines Belges and during his period of training there, Laborde received no specific information regarding his future prospects at Fabricas Durán with respect to (1) his initial placement, (2) his starting salary, or (3) the ladder of promotion for an engineer.

During the 14 months of Laborde's traineeship, two circumstances apparently contributed to unrealistic impressions that were building up

[1] In Mexico, the general manager functions, in effect, as company president, the latter title usually being honorary.
[2] Advantages (to Fabricas Durán) of this arrangement were that (1) Laborde could study the latest technical methods and equipment (some of which were not then in use in Mexico), (2) salaries were lower in Belgium than in Mexico, and (3) because he would not be employed by Fabricas Durán until he reached Mexico, he would pay his own travel and moving expenses.

in his mind. For one thing, he was rotated among several departments. The purpose was to permit him to familiarize himself with important phases of plant operations, but Laborde took it to mean that he was a management trainee. Second, as a convenience to the company and to expedite Laborde's progress in learning Spanish he was given the unofficial assignment of answering letters from technicians in the Mexican subsidiary. At that time, the manufacture of high-tension equipment was new in Fabricas Durán, and few of their technicians had engineering degrees. It therefore happened that the nature of the questions asked in these letters, combined with Laborde's stereotype of Mexico as a "backward country," made him jump to the conclusion that technicians in Mexico were uneducated and poorly trained. For these reasons, it seemed to Laborde a near certainty that he would (1) begin his career at Fabricas Durán as a management representative "in charge of high-tension production," (2) receive a high salary from the start (owing to his superior technical competence), and (3) be rapidly promoted.

Laborde's Marriage

During the summer of 1965, while still in training at Usines Belges, Laborde (now twenty-four years old) married a Belgian girl (nineteen years of age). No company representative had any contact with her until after the Labordes arrived in Monterrey, Mexico.

QUESTIONS ON SECTION A

1 *On orientation*
   a Identify advantages and disadvantages, for a company and for an employee, of minimal advance orientation.
   b If any disadvantages seem to you serious, what would you recommend doing in a situation such as this one to eliminate or reduce them; and who should act?

B EMPLOYMENT AT FABRICAS DURAN

Orientation in Mexico

Immediately after arriving in Monterrey in January, 1966, Laborde was interviewed by Señor Vasquez, the general manager. At that time he learned that his initial placement would be in the high-tension products department but in a subordinate position, reporting to Señor Perez, the production manager (an extremely capable man, who had made his way up through the ranks without benefit of a college education).

During his orientation interview, Laborde also learned that his starting salary would be 4,000 pesos a month (about $340). Because Laborde had a wife and practically no savings on which to draw to set up housekeeping, the general manager offered him a family supplement of 2,000 pesos a month. Laborde accepted this arrangement. (It later became evident that he never regarded this additional sum as part of his salary.) Nothing was said about when he might expect a salary increase. Nor was any mention made as to possibilities of promotion.

Help with Living Arrangements

Within the next few days, the company treasurer (who at that time undertook certain responsibilities that would normally be met by a member of the personnel department) helped the Labordes in their search for a suitable place to live. Mme Laborde was far from satisfied with the apartment which was finally selected, but she reluctantly agreed that it was the best they could afford.

Initial Placement

When Laborde reported to Señor Perez, the production manager, he received no further orientation. Señor Perez took it for granted that all the necessary information had already been communicated by the general manager.

During the period when Laborde was working under Señor Perez, he developed a number of dissatisfactions. Among them were:

1 Being subordinate to a man without an engineering degree, a mere "Mr."
2 Not being addressed or listed on the payroll by his professional title.[3]
3 Having to punch a time clock (at that period, everyone in the company did so, including the general manager).
4 Having the same working hours as production operators. (This schedule was arranged for everyone who worked closely with shop employees. It meant starting an hour earlier than office employees and having only half an hour for lunch, instead of the 2 hours enjoyed by management representatives.)

All these matters Laborde discussed with Señor Ingeniero Schneider, who also was a professional engineer. Although Mexican by birth, Schneider sympathized with Laborde's feelings, perhaps because of his European background.

At various times, Laborde also complained directly to Señor Perez, who, despite his fiery Spanish temperament, never lost his temper with Laborde. He recognized that the young foreigner was a brilliant and well-educated engineer who might become a real asset to the company—when he settled down. Señor Perez hoped that this accommodation would come about naturally and thought that in the meantime, the less said the better. He therefore declined to become involved in any arguments with the sensitive young man. Instead, he tried to keep their relationship strictly job-centered.

Promotion

After 3 months, Laborde was made head of the product design section. In this position, he reported to Señor Ingeniero Rodriguez, manager

[3] In Mexico it is customary to use professional titles for compatriots. But this is not always done with foreigners.

of the engineering department. Señor Rodriguez had an engineering degree from the University of Mexico.

After Laborde's promotion he was always addressed by his professional title, but none of his other dissatisfactions was ameliorated. Indeed, his feelings about his salary were aggravated by the fact that he received no increase at the time of his promotion although Schneider (head of quality control) received a salary of 5,000 pesos a month. In Laborde's opinion, Schneider was less able than he and had a degree that was inferior to his own—because it had been granted at a Mexican rather than a European university. He did not take into account the fact that Schneider had 5 years of service with the company, and he had not been informed that at Fabricas Durán salary increases were made only once a year. Laborde was surprised, and more affronted than before, to discover that even after being promoted to the position of section head, he was still expected to punch a time clock and still expected to work the same hours as production employees. (Apparently he did not take into account that this was company practice in regard to everyone who worked closely with production employees.)

An Open Communication System

Señor Rodriguez, head of engineering, encouraged Laborde to communicate directly with Señor Perez, head of the production department, in regard to all matters connected with design changes. This arrangement was in line with company practice, according to which everyone was free to talk directly with anyone else in connection with his work.

These contacts with Señor Perez gave rise to occasional friction. Laborde was extremely touchy. He seemed to regard any criticism of his designs as a personal affront, and apparently he could not (or would not) give weight to the practical reasons which made Señor Perez request

some minor change in a new design (to meet the demands of economy, for example, or to avoid the need for the new tools or machinery which would have been required if the design were put into production unchanged).

Señor Rodriguez was vaguely aware that the relationship between Laborde and Perez was not entirely harmonious. However, Perez never made anything of it, and Rodriguez, being a scientist by nature as well as by profession, preferred to spend his time and energy on scientific problems, rather than in "getting involved in personal matters." Therefore, although in theory all problems were to be resolved at the departmental level, Señor Rodriguez took no official notice of the difficulties which his subordinate created for Perez.

Mme. Laborde's Attitude and Social Relationships

Shortly after the Labordes' arrival in Monterrey, several company wives (including Señora Perez, the young Mexican wife of the production manager) called on Mme. Laborde. They felt somewhat rebuffed when she made it plain that she greatly disliked having to live in Mexico, had no intention of learning Spanish, preferred doing her own housework to employing a "dirty" native servant, and continued to send to Belgium for certain items of food and clothing (because she considered Mexican products to be inferior).

QUESTIONS ON SECTION B

1 *On employee dissatisfactions*
   a Which of Laborde's dissatisfactions, if any, seem to you reasonable? On what grounds?
   b If you had been in the position of Señor Perez, the immediate superior of a new employee from overseas, might you have talked with him about any or all of his dissatisfactions? Why, or why not?

2 *On interdepartmental relationships*
   a In Señor Rodriguez' position, why would you (or would you not) feel obligated to intervene if you

became aware that one of your subordinates was creating minor difficulties for the head of another department?

b If you feel that intervention was needed, what would be your plans for action?

C AN INCIDENT: THE REJECTED GIFT

When Señor Perez returned to his office on a Wednesday, in May, 1966, he was surprised to find on his desk a small package. It was daintily wrapped and attached to it was a card addressed in his wife's handwriting to Señora Laborde. He called his secretary and asked in an irritated tone, "What's this?"

The secretary answered nervously, "I don't know, Señor. Señor Laborde brought it yesterday. When he found you were away, he just said, 'Please give this to Señor Perez.'"

Perez "got the message." Feeling that this was the last straw, he went immediately to the general manager's office and poured out the whole story, ending, "If it was *his* wife insulting *my* wife, I wouldn't bother you with it. I wouldn't even give it a second thought, myself. But this is another example of Laborde's impossible attitude. He is negative about everything—can't take the slightest criticism. I know he's a brilliant young man. But I really wonder whether he is the man for us.—Or perhaps I just haven't handled him right.—What do you think?"

QUESTIONS ON SECTION C

1 *Managerial responsibilities for decision making*
If you were in the position of the general manager and had just listened to this report from Señor Perez, how might you handle this incident?

2 *Managerial responsibilities in regard to interviewing*
If your plan for action includes interviewing any organizational member(s):
  a Whom would you talk with? Why?
  b What would be your principal objectives during the interview(s)?
  c What type of interview (directed or nondirected) would seem to you most promising? Why?
  d What interviewing skills might be needed?

3 *Managerial responsibilities for learning from experience*
Afterward, looking back on what may have been accountable for this state of affairs, what changes, if any, might you initiate in any company practice(s)?

The Girl and the Computer

INTRODUCTION

This case illustrates, among other things, interactive difficulties associated with (1) inadequate communication and ineffective coordination between representatives of staff and line, in connection with an important technical project; (2) the individual goals of a highly motivated office clerk; and (3) unskillful interviewing, with no serious effort by a supervisor either to understand the motivation of a clerk who was temporarily reassigned or to explain, in terms which could make sense to her, management objectives toward which she might take pride in contributing.

A THE SPECIAL PROJECT UNIT IS SET UP

In a large insurance company, during early 1963, Section 2 of Division X was swamped with extra work. Even by scheduling all the overtime allowed by the budget, the section head was unable to keep the work from piling up. This overload was occasioned by a new ruling from the Internal Revenue Service to the effect that any concern paying interest or dividends amounting to $10 or more a year must report the amount of each such individual payment to the IRS.

The January dividend notices went out in early February, with a "stuffer" explaining about the tax ruling and asking policyholders whether they would like to have their dividends used to purchase additional insurance, instead of receiving them as annual interest. Returns indicated that the great majority of policyholders wanted to make this change.

Mr. Baker, the division manager, requested higher management (at the department level) to do something as soon as possible to reduce the heavy workload involved in changing the option on so many policies.

In response to this request, Mr. March (assistant to the department head, and a director of the company) whose specialty was conversion to machine operations, was assigned to look into the matter. On his recommendation, it was decided that the data could profitably be processed by UNIVAC, an electronic computer.

To prepare for this electronic processing, a special project unit was set up—across the hall from Division X. Mr. March himself took charge, assisted by staff experts and one female supervisor. He hoped to complete the conversion project in about a year.

Mr. March asked Mr. Baker to send "three good, dependable girls" from his division. (He made no more specific requisition.) In the special project unit, there were ten clerks in all (seven from the other division affected by the new IRS ruling). These clerks received technical supervision in the temporary unit, but general supervision was retained in the divisions from which they had been borrowed and to which they would return.

One of the girls selected to go to the special project unit from Division X was Miss Elizabeth ("Betty") Brown. At that time she was not quite nineteen years old. She had been hired 10 months before, immediately after being graduated from high school (where her scholastic record had been good). When she applied for work, all employment and medical tests were favorable, except for the remark: "Close figure work—limitation." That note took account of the fact that Betty had near-point vision (for which she wore contact lenses). When Betty first started in Division X (as a clerk, job grade 2), her supervisor noticed that apparently she could not see clearly unless her eyes were within about 8 inches of her work. When he called Personnel and Medical, he was assured that Betty's near-point vision should not be regarded "as a handicap for general office work."

Four months later at Betty's first formal appraisal, her supervisor (Mr. Walker) rated her performance as "good" in all respects. Four months after that, she was shifted into Section 2,

as a trainee for a position at the job grade 3 level. She was selected for that promotional opportunity because she had shown herself to be intelligent, adaptable, accurate, and reliable. (The training period for the job grade 3 position was usually about a year.)

She was selected as one of the three clerks to go from Division X to the special project unit for the same reasons. Also, when the conversion project was set up, Betty had been in Section 2 long enough to become familiar with the kind of policies from which data were to be taken for processing by UNIVAC. Yet, since she was a trainee, her leaving would not disrupt the section as much as the loss of a regular clerk.

The three girls who were being lent by Division X were told by their supervisor, Mr. Walker, about their temporary reassignment (on the day after Mr. March called Mr. Baker) a few minutes before they were to undertake their new duties. The interview was brief and nothing was said about what they would be expected to do in the special project unit. (The supervisor had no information about that himself.) The news of this reassignment came as a surprise to the girls. Word of the special project unit had traveled along the grapevine, also that it was to be operated by "staff," but it had not occurred to any of these girls that they might be asked to work there. Two of them took the news calmly, one of them saying, "After all, it's only going across the hall. Our pay will stay the same. And we can still have lunch with our friends."

Betty, however, seemed greatly distressed. She said to Mr. Walker, "Why can't I stay here? I've just started to learn, and now I'm leaving. When can I come back?" The supervisor was unable to answer her second question, for he did not know how long the conversion project was expected to take. He did tell Betty that the matter was all settled and that his temporary reassignment would not interfere with her anticipated upgrading.

The three girls then went across the hall to the special project unit, where one of the staff experts spent about an hour telling the 10 clerks about the work that was to be done in the unit. (It was the first week of operations there.) Betty said later, "It was pretty technical. We didn't understand all of it and he didn't say how long we would be there, but I had a feeling it would be a long time." The girls were then assigned desks, and the supervisor gave them their work.

During the first coffee break, Betty hurried back across the hall and appealed to her supervisor in Division X. Bursting into tears, she begged that she be allowed to return and continue her training, "I just can't stand all that pressure and confusion. Everything is hectic over there. Papers and forms are all over the place—on desks, chairs, everywhere. And we don't know just what we're supposed to do." Mr. Walker urged her to calm down and be patient. He explained that a certain amount of confusion is inevitable, at first, when a unit is being organized for urgently needed work. Things would soon settle down and she would get used to working there. He also pointed out that, with such a high-priority project, there might be considerable overtime, and that the experience she could gain there would be valuable when she returned to Division X. This counseling appeared to reassure Betty. She dried her eyes and said she would try to stick it out.

QUESTIONS ON SECTION A

Comment on the effectiveness of communication, so far, between management representatives, and between management and employees. For example:

1 *A requisition from staff*
   a Under the circumstances, does it seem that a request for "three good, dependable girls" was a sufficiently precise requisition for clerks who were to work in the special project unit? What kind of information might have been provided to help a supervisor in making his selection?
   b How might one account for the fact that a staff expert did not make a more detailed statement about job requirements for these clerks?

2 *Interviewing*
   a What about the timing of the interview in which the girls were notified of their temporary reassignment? (Would you consider it advisable or inadvisable to give them advance notice? Why?)
   b If you had been in Mr. Walker's position as Betty's supervisor, how do you think you would have responded to her initial reluctance to interrupt her training?
   c If you had been in Mr. Walker's position when Betty begged to be allowed to return to Division X, what might you have said to her? (This question might well be answered by role playing.)

3 *Supervisory responsibility*
   Mr. Walker retained general responsibility for supervising the clerks lent by Division X to the special project unit.
   a Do you think he had any obligation to find out, in advance, what their work would be? Why or why not? If you think he had any such responsibility, outline steps that you think he could have taken to meet it (remembering that he had only a few hours between the requisition and the time when the girls were to start their temporary reassignment).
   b Do you think that Betty's second appeal to Mr. Walker did (or did not) put him under any special obligation to check on her performance and state of mind within the next couple of days? Why?
   c Evaluate the practice of retaining general supervision for employees who are reassigned to work in another location.

B   BETTY IS BOUNCED BACK

Three days later, Mr. Baker (manager of Division X) received a telephone call from Mr. March (director of the special project unit). Mr. March angrily demanded that Betty be replaced—immediately. "That girl is *impossible*. She's too slow. And she can't do *anything* right."

Mr. Baker was very much surprised and greatly upset. As he saw it, Mr. March was practically accusing him of sending an incompetent clerk for a top-priority project. Who can afford to make an impression like that on top-level staff? And the thing did not make sense. How could it happen that such an intelligent, reliable girl should suddenly begin making so many mistakes? Mr. Baker had a strong hunch that Betty's poor performance during the last few days was intentional—a form of direct action designed to bring about the result which had now occurred. Quivering with indignation, he called in Mr. Walker, who was equally surprised when he heard about the call from Mr. March. After they had decided on Betty's replacement, Mr. Baker told Mr. Walker that if he found any evidence that Betty's poor performance had been deliberate, she was to be set back to the lower-rated job that she had been doing before she started her recent training. The two men agreed; "We can't let an employee force our hand like that. We might as well pack up and go home."

QUESTIONS ON SECTION B

1 *Opportunities for a manager*
If you had been in Mr. Baker's position after receiving the angry telephone call from Mr. March, what action do you think you would have taken? Be specific and give reasons.

2 *Employee motivation and performance*
What reasons can you think of, besides the one which occurred to Mr. Baker, which might account for Betty's poor performance in the special project unit?

3 *Downgrading as discipline*
If it turned out that Betty had deliberately been making mistakes during her assignment to the top-priority project, what disciplinary step—if any—would seem to you appropriate?
a Why would you (or would you not) advocate downgrading as a disciplinary measure (1) in Betty's case? (2) in general?
b What other alternatives are there?

C   MORE INTERVIEWS AND A HAPPY ENDING

Next morning, Mr. Walker took Betty's replacement to the special project unit and brought Betty back. He and Mr. Baker had a talk with her. It then appeared that Betty didn't know why she had been replaced. When Mr. Baker referred to her being so slow and making so many mistakes, Betty said, with evident sincerity, "No one said anything to me about making mistakes. But I know I was slow. My trouble began from the time I had to work with the data sheets. The lines ran together [columns on the coding sheets were ¼ inch wide] and everything seemed to swim in front of my eyes. Trying to make sure I didn't make mistakes slowed me up. When I told the supervisor about my trouble, she said, 'I'll see what I can do.' The next thing that happened was that Mr. Walker came over with Mary-Anne and brought me back."

Mr. Baker then said, "It seems that we haven't got all the facts. *(To Betty)* You'd better go back to the work you were doing [in training for the higher-rated job]. We'll contact you later."

After Betty had left, Mr. Baker then called Mr. March, who conceded that he was not fully informed about the facts of Betty's case and agreed to make inquiries. Mr. March called back later to say that Betty's story was substantially correct. She *had not* made mistakes, but she *had* been slow. Apparently Mr. March had misunderstood what the technical supervisor had said about Betty, and it seemed that the supervisor, aware of Mr. March's urgent wish to "get the project off the ground fast" had decided that Betty was "impossible."

The same morning that "Betty bounced back," Mr. Walker talked with her again. He expressed regret for the misunderstandings which had resulted in disagreeable experiences for her and told her that she was to continue her training.

Three months later, Betty won her upgrading to the higher-rated job. At that time, she expressed determination to earn her next upgrading the following year. Mr. Baker and Mr. Walker found themselves in agreement that she would probably realize her ambition. As Mr. Baker put it, "She's a plugger. I feel she is good because she is trying hard to make good in spite of her handicap. She does good work. And she's dependable."

QUESTIONS ON THE CASE AS A WHOLE

1 *Personnel administration for line managers*
Try to imagine that you are in Mr. Walker's position, looking back over this case and aware of a line manager's responsibility for personnel administration. What might you wish that you, or Mr. Baker, had said or done differently at any stage in the case? What might you plan to do in the near future, because of anything that happened in this case? (In your answer, consider ideas presented in Chapters 1 and 7.)

2 *Learning from experience*
If you were in Mr. March's position (as director of the special project unit) what do you think you might have learned from your experience in this case?

3 *Situational thinking as diagnosis*
a What are some of the difficulties that might be attributed, at least in part, to *space-time conditions* in this situation? For example:
(1) If the special project could have been carried out in the immediate area where Mr. Walker did his work every day, what actions and consequences might have been different?
(2) Which of the difficulties that occurred in this case may have been associated with being in a hurry?

4 *Employee resistance to change*
What light does this case throw on the general statement that employees tend to resist change? For example:
a What are some of the changes that Betty apparently welcomed and looked forward to?
b Why do you (or do you not) consider that Betty's expressed reluctance to leave Division X was reasonable?
c If you think her reluctance made sense (from her point of view), do you regard it as sufficiently important, organizationally, to justify selecting another clerk instead of Betty in the first place? Why or why not?

Managing Highly Motivated Secretaries

INTRODUCTION

This case illustrates the interactive effects of such situational variables as organization structure, a way of managing, interpersonal communication, individual goals at the secretarial level, and employee discipline.

Key people in the case:

Mr. Ryan, director of the field agency department, Universal Insurance Company
John Lord, division manager
Philip James, agency supervisor
Miss Page, personnel assistant
Marilyn Wiener (secretary to the supervisor of Agency C)
Hope Tetzeli (secretary to Phil James, supervisor of Agency D)

A   THE SEARCH FOR A COORDINATOR

At the Universal Insurance Company, in November, 1970, managers in the field agency department (with 90 to 100 employees) decided to create the position of coordinator (job grade 6) in the field agency department. The coordinator's function would be to ensure that the work load among secretaries was more evenly divided than it had been. Up to that time, some secretaries had been consistently overworked while others frequently had much less work than they could do.

Obviously the qualifications for such a position would include intelligence, reliability, knowledge of the work, and insight into motivational and personality differences among agency personnel, as well as ability to establish and maintain good working relationships with secretaries and supervisors. Promotion from within was company policy, and job posting was a regular procedure.

To understand the importance of effective coordination among secretaries, and the difficulties to be expected in achieving it, the reader needs a minimum of information about functions of the field agency department as well as responsibilities of agency supervisors and their secretaries.

B ORGANIZATIONAL INFORMATION

The overall function of the field agency department (in the home office) was to provide continuous contact with district managers in the field. Each of the 10 to 12 agency supervisors served a marketing group in a specific geographical area. Major objectives of all agency supervisors were to help district managers increase the number of policyholders and to prevent policy lapses. For both purposes it was necessary to keep company representatives in the field fully informed as to all current developments in the insurance business and any changes in home office procedures.

Meeting these liaison responsibilities required prompt and reliable response to all correspondence and telephone inquiries. To help supervisors in this part of their job, each was assigned a personal secretary. However, the amount of activity, and therefore of correspondence, differed considerably among the various geographical areas covered by the agency supervisors. And this fact accounted for the unequal work load that had to be carried by the personal secretaries.

These secretaries had no understudies (though their work was supplemented by clerical employees in *information and service centers* who, supervised by unit heads, could be drawn upon as needed). As is customary, the personal secretaries enjoyed a special status. In this division, the vacation of each was timed to coincide with that of her boss (though normally the secretary's vacation was shorter). And she left for lunch at the same time as he did. (During her absence from the office, telephone calls were answered by any qualified clerical employee who happened to be in the office at the time.)

C TWO OUTSTANDING SECRETARIES

In 1971, two secretaries in the division were outstanding: Marilyn Wiener and Hope Tetzeli.

Marilyn started working for Universal in 1967, as a part-time clerk, during her last 2 years in high school. Immediately after her graduation (at eighteen, in June, 1969), she began full-time employment as a secretary (job grade 4) in Agency C of the field agency division. Her work was consistently outstanding, and she had received both of the annual merit increases that were open to employees at her level. In addition to her technical proficiency and reliability (she had never been tardy and rarely absent) she was well liked because of her pleasant way with people. And, despite her quiet manner, her supervisor and associates were aware that she was ambitious. Some of her friends, but not her supervisor, also knew that by June, 1971, Marilyn had reached the conclusion that secretaries in the field agency department had little chance for promotion.[1] She was, therefore, tentatively planning to leave Universal during the next few months and to continue her education. In this way she hoped to qualify herself for a better position, if not at Universal, then in some other company.

Hope Tetzeli was another outstanding secretary in the field agency division at that time. She was secretary to Phil James (supervisor of Agency D). Hope's parents were Cuban, but she had been born in the United States. She first came to Universal in June, 1970, immediately after graduating from high school (at eighteen years of age). She prided herself on having been an honor student throughout her high school career, having graduated in the top 10 percent in her class of 550 students.

Her employment interviewer described her as "neat and well dressed, petite, vivacious, with a markedly Latin temperament, deeply committed to equal rights for women, and with a keen sense of social justice." In her first performance appraisal, her supervisor (Phil James) rated the quality and quantity of her work as outstanding and commended her willingness to assume extra

---

[1] Usually the only way a secretary got ahead—except by a promotional transfer—was when her immediate supervisor was promoted. However, in the field agency department, even the director was only in his early forties.

responsibilities when necessary. Like Marilyn, Hope had never been tardy and very rarely absent.

However, Hope's office conduct had occasionally been such as to elicit from John Lord (division manager) the comment "Hope is a self-elected moralist. She has an opinion on everything that happens, inside the department and out, and no hesitation about expressing her opinion however unfavorable it may be." In fact, Mr. Lord had gradually become convinced that Hope's outspokenness tended to create unrest in the office. That opinion had been formed on the basis of Hope's behavior in the following incidents.

D SOME OF HOPE'S BEHAVIOR OFF THE JOB, IN THE OFFICE

1 A Misunderstanding

Hope's "keen sense of social justice," as well as her outspokenness, first came to John Lord's attention in January, 1971, as a result of a misunderstanding that had occurred 6 months earlier. In July, 1970, Lord was orienting a group of relatively new girls—including Hope. He told them that after 6 months they would receive an automatic salary increase. However, at the end of the 6 months several of the girls, including Hope, did not receive the increase. Thereupon, Hope appeared in John Lord's office (with three other girls whom she had apparently egged on to join her in making a protest). Serving as spokesman for the group, she demanded to know why they had not been given the promised increase. The division manager expressed regret for the misunderstanding, explaining that he must have forgotten to mention that the automatic increase applied only to low-level entry jobs (grades 1 through 3). He added that after this first automatic increase, pay raises were considered annually for all employees. The other girls appeared to be satisfied with this explanation. But not long afterwards news reached Mr. Lord (through the grapevine) that Hope was harping on the "unjust treatment" that some of them had received in

regard to the promised salary increase. When developing this theme in conversation with her friends, she reportedly cited the incident as proof that Mr. Lord "doesn't know what he's talking about when it comes to company policies."

When John Lord heard about these comments from Hope, he requested Phil James (her supervisor) to counsel her, explaining that her remarks were inappropriate in view of his apology and explanation—which should have ended the matter. James was reluctant to criticize the office conduct of an upstanding girl with whose technical performance he was more than satisfied. It seemed to him that her social shortcomings had nothing to do with her job performance. Therefore, his "counseling" of Hope consisted merely in saying: "You can't be a spokesman for all the girls. Just keep on doing the excellent job you have been doing, and you're sure to get ahead."

2 Hope "Consoles" (?) or "Humiliates" (?) a Co-worker

A week later, another incident occurred which was reported differently by Hope and the other girl immediately involved. After an encounter in the ladies room, one of the girls returned to the office in tears, complaining that Hope had humiliated her by talking in public about a "very personal matter." When asked about this incident, Hope replied that she had merely tried to console the girl (who was pregnant though unmarried), "and other girls gathered around while I was talking."

When Mr. Lord heard about this encounter he sent for Hope and reproved her for "disturbing other employees and creating unrest in the office." According to Hope, he told her that in the future she should mind her own business and ended by saying, "If you keep on like this, I shan't be able to recommend you for promotion."

3 A Progress Review and Hope's Response

Shortly after this reprimand, Hope had her first progress review with the field agency department

personnel assistant, Miss Page.[2] During this
interview, Hope was full of complaints—ranging
from the caliber of the company's medical clinic
to the "injustice" she had suffered with regard to
the "promised" salary increase. Miss Page suggested that Hope discuss her dissatisfactions
with the division manager. But Hope refused.
She said there would be no point in doing so
because Mr. Lord was obviously prejudiced
against her. To substantiate this statement, Hope
asserted that ever since the difficulty about the
pay raise, Mr. Lord had "consistently picked on"
her. She went on to say that Mr. Lord's prejudice
extended to some of the other girls also; that he
had a few favorites; and that, owing to his "ignorance of company policy, he was a very ineffective manager." Miss Page then suggested that
Hope should speak with the department manager, Mr. O'Hara. Hope dismissed that suggestion
also, saying that "everyone" knew Mr. O'Hara
took no interest in personnel matters.[3] She insisted instead on having a confidential interview
with Mr. Ryan (department director). Miss Page,
knowing that Mr. Ryan was a firm believer in the
"open-door policy," acceded to Hope's request.
The interview took place shortly thereafter.

4   Interview with the Director

During Hope's talk with the director, she apparently expressed the same critical views and
strongly negative opinions about Mr. Lord as in
the interview with Miss Page, though she stated
that the supervisors were "fine."

Shortly after this interview, Mr. Lord's record
as a manager was discreetly investigated. The
results completely exonerated him (including the

---

[2] At Universal, a departmental personnel assistant was
responsible for scheduling and conducting progress reviews
and for reporting her findings to the manager. But she was
not expected to initiate any other action with personnel or to
make suggestions to representatives of line management.

[3] This opinion of Hope's was probably based on the fact
that the department manager's responsibilities related entirely to company representatives in the field, though this information had never been relayed to nonsupervisory employees.

charges of favoritism and inadequate information as to company policies).

5   An Effort to Transfer

During the early spring of 1971, Hope became
convinced that she would never get ahead in the
field agency department. She therefore kept
track of posted job opportunities in other departments. In May she found one that appealed to
her because it would entail a promotion. She
therefore told Mr. James that she would like to
apply for it. James, extremely anxious to keep his
competent secretary, tried to dissuade her. Hope
then went to Mr. Lord, who acceded to her request. [Such a request and permission were standard operating procedure (S.O.P.) at Universal,
a prepared form being signed by the management representative receiving the request.]

During the interview in the other department,
Hope was told (according to her own later statement): "Don't get your hopes up, because this
job requires a mature person." When the transfer
failed to materialize, Hope jumped to the conclusion that Mr. Lord had stood in her way, because
of his prejudice against her. Moreover, she was
deeply offended by the implication that she was
regarded as an immature person. On several
later occasions, when criticizing behavior by
other employees, she ended in a dramatic tone,
"do you call *that* mature?" To cite one example:
She told her friends that in the elevator one day
she overheard an elderly man say to an associate: "There sure are lots of good-looking broads
in this company." She added that although she
regarded such a remark as evidence of extreme
immaturity, she had made no official complaint
because the man had a large family and could ill
afford to lose his job.

6   A Verbal Attack

On June 16, Hope had an encounter with Marilyn which brought about immediate and serious
consequences. That afternoon (a Thursday), just
before the end of the working day, Marilyn had
been told that she was to be promoted to the

position of coordinator as of the following Monday. She expressed delight at the prospect. The word spread like wildfire. Immediately after work, Hope waylaid Marilyn in the hallway. According to another girl who witnessed the encounter, Hope accused Marilyn of being unscrupulous in accepting the promotion since, by her own admission, she intended to leave Universal and "go back to school." Hope added that such behavior on Marilyn's part was not only exceedingly immature, under the circumstances, but also selfish, typical of her race, and "unfair to us three girls who want to make a career at Universal." According to another report that reached Miss Page, Hope's remarks were even more bitter. "She accused Marilyn of taking the bread out of other people's mouths, told her she was greedy and ruthless and also that it is typical of your race to think only of yourselves."

After being the victim of this tirade, Marilyn burst into tears and rushed home.

News of the incident reached Mr. Lord the next morning, by telephone. Marilyn's mother called him to say that Marilyn would not be returning to Universal. She blamed Hope for this development. Mrs. Wiener was so angry that she almost hung up at that point. But when Mr. Lord urged her to tell him what had happened, she said that Hope had done "a complete job of character assassination" on Marilyn who was "emotionally destroyed" and might require medical attention. She ended by saying that if this proved to be necessary, she would "hold the company morally and financially responsible."

E QUESTION FOR IMMEDIATE DECISION BY THE DIVISION MANAGER

If you were in Mr. Lord's position at this stage of the case, what might you do? With what objectives?

QUESTIONS ON THE CASE AS A WHOLE

1 *Harmonizing corporate objectives and personal goals*
It has often been said that understanding and managerial action are needed to help personnel reconcile their individual aims with corporate goals. What information in this case report illustrates needs and opportunities *(a)* for which management representatives to achieve such understanding, and take action, *(b)* with which participants in the case situation?

2 *Interpersonal communication*
  a Comment on the open-door policy as a means to develop greater freedom of communication up the line. (In your answer, include advantages and disadvantages of that policy, as illustrated in this case.)
  b What is the difference between "orienting" and "inducting" new employees?
  c In your opinion, can it properly be said that one of these activities is solely a staff responsibility while the other is entirely an obligation of line management? (Give reasons for your opinion.) Also, in your answer consider the following related questions:
    (1) Can employee orientation be completed, once and for all, during an employment interview? Why, or why not?
    (2) If you think that it cannot, cite some circumstances that call for further orientation, and suggest which representatives of management are to be responsible for this.
    (3) If you had been in Phil James's position when requested to counsel Hope, what might you have said to her? (This question can best be answered by role playing.)

3 *Staff-line coordination*
  a What advantages and possible disadvantages do you see in having a personnel assistant assigned to a large department (as in the case under consideration)?
  b To what extent do you approve the responsibilities and limitations of Miss Page's position (as described in this case report)? Why?

4 *Employees' behavior off the job and on their own time*
  a It has often been said that employees' behavior off the job and on their own time is of no concern to management. What light on that general proposition is thrown by Hope's behavior in this case?
  b How would you state a company policy for employee behavior off the job?

Conflict of Interest?[1]

INTRODUCTION

Like most cases in this book, this one highlights the importance of managerial activity to implement employment policies and practices. Of interest here are hiring, placement, follow-up, evaluation, and termination.

However, unlike most of our other cases, this one also points up questions of public relations and public interest—at the community level. (In this respect it has something in common with "The Good-neighbor Policy.")

The setting of this case is unusual in that events and behavior described concern employees of a local newspaper and of a local orchestra. However, for the perceptive student, this setting will not obscure the idea that general principles needed to stimulate and guide employee motivation and to develop employee capabilities are the same as they would have been if the setting had been a factory or an office.

BACKGROUND INFORMATION

In connection with a disputed discharge, the following are pertinent provisions of the labor agreement (between a newspaper called *The Buffalo Courier Express* hereinafter referred to as *The Courier* and Buffalo Newspaper Guild, Local 26).

Article XII, Security
1 Dismissal shall be made only for:
  a Individual just and sufficient cause.
  b Economy to remedy the stability of the newspaper. . . .
6 There shall be a trial period of three months for all employes. Beginners or new employes shall be supplied with monthly reports on their progress

[1] The following case is based on material taken from *Labor Arbitration Reports: Dispute Settlements* (The Bureau of National Affairs, Inc.), Washington, D.C., vol. 48, pp. 77-83, 1967.

and competency if they request them. Beginners or new employes, after completing their trial periods shall have the same security and length of service benefits under this contract enjoyed by all other employes. For beginners or new employes who have passed their trial periods, the benefits depending upon length of service shall be computed from the date of the beginning of their employment with the Publisher.

7 Such employes, if discharged prior to the expiration of the trial period shall not have the right of appeal to the Standing Committee or Board of Arbitration provided in Article XI, if such discharge be solely for inability to perform the duties of the position.

Minimum wage rates pertaining to this case were established by the labor agreement as follows:

Reporters (a full-time position): $86.90 for beginners, $92.40 after six months, and progressively higher thereafter through the fifth year of employment.

Part-time Music Critic: $98.40.

A   MRS. SINCLAIR'S[2] EMPLOYMENT

Hiring

In January, 1965, Mrs. Sinclair (twenty-one years of age) applied for a position with *The Courier,* whose part-time music critic had resigned during the previous month. On the application form, under "position desired," she wrote, "music critic, second choice, reporter." Among her qualifications she listed having majored in music and having obtained a B.A. in music from the University of Buffalo in 1964. During an employment interview with Mr. King (*The Courier's* executive editor) she mentioned that her husband was a first violinist with the Buffalo Philharmonic Orchestra.

---

[2] As reported in *ibid.,* this name is given as "X." We have substituted the fictitious name Sinclair.

On the evening of that same day, she attended a concert by the Philharmonic. Her sample review of that concert was approved by Mr. King, who thereupon hired her.

Placement

Mrs. Sinclair was placed in the job classification of reporter, with the understanding that her duties would consist primarily in covering all musical events, principally the concerts of the Philharmonic, and writing a weekly music column. In this way she would fill the void left by the resignation of the former part-time music critic.

It was made clear to her, however, that she was being hired for a full-time position, that her classification was to be that of reporter covering music assignments, and that the paper would be free, as need arose and her time permitted, to assign her to other work in the reporter classification.

Mrs. Sinclair entered upon her duties, devoting virtually all her time to the activities formerly carried out by the part-time music critic. Her work met with "general approbation." No negative criticisms were made to her at any time before she received notice of her termination. Nor were any evaluation reports made available to her.

Mr. Rosen's Visit

Toward the end of February, Mr. King, executive manager of *The Courier,* received a visit from Mr. Rosen, business manager of the Buffalo Philharmonic Orchestra. Mr. Rosen expressed concern over the fact that *The Courier's* music critic was the wife of a musician whom Mr. Rosen described as being an active member of a dissident group within the orchestra. Rosen stated that in oral interchanges with Lukas Foss (the orchestra's conductor) Mrs. Sinclair's husband had cautioned Foss to bear in mind that his wife was the music critic for *The Courier.* Rosen also mentioned that Foss had been greatly disturbed by what he regarded as an inadequate reference to the conductor's performance as a soloist in a concert covered by one of Mrs. Sinclair's reviews. Rosen added that Foss felt that even when a review by Mrs. Sinclair contained something favorable to the orchestra, it was always qualified by subtle negative comments. Rosen wound up by stating, as his own opinion, that so long as Mrs. Sinclair remained as *The Courier*'s music critic, she had the power to injure Foss by what she wrote. He requested King to assign her to other work.

According to Rosen, his remarks were coldly received by King, who appeared to resent the idea that any question of internal management on his paper should be decided to meet the request of an outsider.

Rosen's visit, his complaint about Mrs. Sinclair, and the request that she be reassigned were not mentioned to Mrs. Sinclair or to any union official until after the case had been submitted to arbitration.

Mrs. Sinclair Gets a By-line

After Rosen's visit and until she was discharged (in mid-April), Mrs. Sinclair continued to cover the Philharmonic concerts, and her reviews were published regularly. Moreover, in March an interview with Foss appeared under her by-line in a Sunday edition of *The Courier*.[3]

Mrs. Sinclair Receives Notice of Her Termination

On March 31, one of the city editors wrote Mrs. Sinclair the following note: "Now that you are nearing the end of your period of probation as an employee of the editorial department, I must in-

[3] It should be noted that it is most unusual for a probationary employee to be granted a by-line. However, on this occasion, Mr. King agreed that the caliber of Mrs. Sinclair's article was such that this mark of distinction should be granted. During arbitration hearings it was also brought out that, at various times, Mrs. Sinclair's work had earned commendations from all four of the city editors.

form you that your services will no longer be required after Sunday, April 4th."

On receiving this note, Mrs. Sinclair immediately went to see the city editor. The latter referred her to Mr. King, who told her that she could no longer be permitted to write music reviews. Thereupon she asked to be assigned to other reportorial work. Mr. King refused, giving as his reason that, since she was almost at the end of her probationary period, the union would not consent to extending this "trial period," even if management were willing to test her ability to perform other assignments.

On April 5, Mrs. Sinclair received the following note from Mr. King: "You are hereby informed that your services are terminated as of the end of your scheduled work, April 19, 1965. The reason for your dismissal is that you are not able to perform the duties of your position."

B   GRIEVANCE PROCEEDINGS

Immediately upon being discharged, Mrs. Sinclair filed an official grievance. During grievance proceedings, the union asked to see the evaluation reports of Mrs. Sinclair's performance. But the business manager, and subsequently the general manager, declined to produce them. Throughout these proceedings, management took the position that its evaluation of a probationer's ability to perform job duties was not subject to the grievance procedure. The general manager also stated that Mrs. Sinclair had given signs of immaturity which disqualified her for her position.

C   ARBITRATION

The parties were unable to settle the dispute between themselves, and the case was submitted to arbitration. During the arbitration hearing, management's reason for discharging Mrs. Sinclair was stated as being different from that given during grievance proceedings. Management now conceded that "outside influences had been brought to bear. . . . [After Rosen's visit[4]] the paper had evaluated the proper weight to be given to the relationship between a musician and the music critic, and had then terminated Mrs. Sinclair's services."

Management's Position

1 Normal contractual provisions, with regard to the employment of a probationary employee, clearly indicate management's right to exercise judgment more freely than in the case of a regular employee, with established tenure.

2 An employer's judgment concerning the ability of a probationer is not subject to review in grievance proceedings or arbitration.

3 In the case of Mrs. Sinclair, management has decided, in good faith, that the interplay of relationships between Mrs. Sinclair, her husband, and Lukas Foss

. . . rendered her unable to perform the duties of the position for which she was hired. Ability to do the job embraces not only educational background, training, judgment, and writing skills, but other criteria as well. In evaluating Mrs. Sinclair's ability to perform the duties of her position, management was entitled to weigh her exposure to the almost inevitable, albeit subtle, bias that marriage to a member of the dissident group [in the Philharmonic Orchestra] could give rise to.

[Management] may also properly consider the relationship between [Mr. and Mrs. Sinclair] because of its possible effect in prejudicing the standing of the newspaper with its readers (some of whom have protested the assignment of the music critic's job to Mrs. Sinclair).

[Moreover, retaining Mrs. Sinclair as music critic] would disrupt good relations with an important and outstanding community organization [the Philharmonic Orchestra].

[4] Inferentially, this visit was not the only occasion on which a representative of the Philharmonic had tried to influence Mr. King.

The Union's Position

1 Mrs. Sinclair is fully competent to perform the duties of her position.

2 The actual reason for her discharge was unrelated to her competence.

3 Except for an evaluation of competence, a probationer may be discharged only for just cause.

4 Management's reason for discharging Mrs. Sinclair does not constitute just cause.

5 Management's lack of candor, in concealing from the union (during grievance proceedings) its real reason for discharging Mrs. Sinclair is evidence of bad faith.

QUESTIONS ON THE CASE AS A WHOLE

1 *On impartial decision making, in the role of an arbitrator*
Imagine that you are the arbitrator who, under the contract, has been called in to resolve this dispute. In view of established facts, and of relevant provisions in the existing labor agreement between the parties, what is your award, and your reasoning, on the issue: Was Mrs. Sinclair discharged for "just cause"?

2 *On placement*
a What information given in this case report suggests a possible answer to the question of why Mrs. Sinclair was hired as a reporter but assigned to do the work of a music critic?
b Why do you consider that this placement was (or was not) legitimate?

3 *On performance evaluation*
In your opinion, why was management justified (or not):
a In failing to give Mrs. Sinclair any progress reports during her employment?
b In declining to produce any such reports during grievance meetings and arbitration proceedings?

4 *On community relationships*
a In your opinion, is the management of an orchestra entitled to demand that the music critic on a local newspaper should be in a position to write unbiased reviews of its performances and its musicians? Why or why not?

b Do you think a local newspaper is entitled to take seriously the displeasure (possibly even a veiled threat) expressed by an important local organization, such as the Philharmonic Orchestra?

c Do you think it could (or could not) be expected that a music critic would write impartial reviews of performances by an orchestra when married to a member of a dissident group within that orchestra? (In your answer, consider any factual evidence given in this case and in other situations that you know about.)

5 *On contractual provisions regarding the status of a probationer*

  a Comment on clauses 6 and 7 of Article XII (for text, see background material at the beginning of this case report).

  b If you, as a management representative, were negotiating such a clause, what changes—if any— would you try to make in the provisions as written? Why?

6 *On terminating an employee*

  a What significant differences do you find between the notes written by the city editor and by Mr. King?

  b Why do you think Mr. King wrote as he did?

  c To what extent, and why, do you feel that Mr. King was justified in refusing Mrs. Sinclair's request that she be tried out on reporting assignments other than music criticism?

The Good-neighbor Policy

INTRODUCTION

The major issues highlighted by the following brief case report include:

1 A corporate image.
2 The policy of being a "good neighbor" in the local community.
3 Procedures and practices designed to implement such a policy.
4 Difficulties deriving from the circumstance that each employee is a whole man (with his own religion, racial background, and inner motivation).
5 Psychological independence of professional employees, whose capabilities give them an unusual degree of economic security.
6 Appropriate action by an employee in a staff role, at a high organizational level.
7 The question of time off with pay for holidays. (Is it discriminatory not to give time off with pay for holy days of non-Christian religions?)

8 Interviewing—opportunities and skills.
9 Decision making, for a management representative in a staff role.

To add immediacy to the following case report, we have written it as though the incident (sketched at the end) had occurred "just now." In this time frame, the management decision called for by the incident therefore needs to be made immediately.

CASE BACKGROUND

The Universal Insurance Company (one of the largest employers in the metropolitan area) has a fine record as a contributor to the United Fund. This is the only charitable drive for which employees are solicited at Universal. Over the years, management's good-neighbor policy has been reflected in a consistently high level of giving from employees. Top management's interest is indicated by the fact that the total of employee gifts to the United Fund is matched, each year, by a contribution from the company itself.

A "suggested guide to giving" (worked out at United Fund headquarters) is distributed throughout every department at Universal. This guide indicates, for employees in each salary bracket, what a suitable weekly contribution would be. (This contribution is set at about 1 percent of earnings, the amount being regarded as far less important, in the long run, than the habit of regular giving.) Lump-sum contributions (in cash, if desired) are acceptable. However, to facilitate weekly giving, a payroll deduction plan was established at Universal, some years ago. Pledges to the United Fund are solicited on punch cards, which are sent to the personnel department (where they are kept on file for purposes of wage and salary administration).

According to a company policy (unwritten), no pressure is to be exerted on any employee to contribute to this charitable fund. In keeping with this policy, no solicitor for the United Fund Drive has line authority over those he solicits. Nevertheless, it is no secret that top management would be glad to see every department meet the goal of 100 percent participation by employees (an aim which is emphasized for all solicitors at United Fund headquarters in the city). For the past 2 years, each department that has achieved this goal has been awarded a wall plaque.

Implementation of the good-neighbor policy at Universal has been so successful that for some years the company has been accorded the honor of serving as a pacesetter for the local business community. Members of the board feel convinced that the corporate image is greatly enhanced by this evidence of outstanding concern for local charities. Other evidences of the good-neighbor policy are participation by employees in the Red Cross Blood Program and in not trying to avoid serving when called for jury duty.

For both these activities, employees receive time off with pay.

THE EDP DEPARTMENT AND THE UNITED FUND

The EDP department (set up 8 years ago) has had a consistently high record of employee participation in the annual United Fund Drive. For each of the past 2 years, the wall plaque (for 100 percent participation) has testified to the success of solicitation in this department. At the time of the "Z-pledge" incident (sketched below) every one of the 450 employees in the department except David Aaron, a junior programmer, has already contributed.

David Aaron

Dave (twenty-two years old and unmarried) has been a junior programmer in this department for about a year and a half, since receiving his B.S. from an outstanding technical institute. (He has been working nights, toward his master's degree.) In the opinion of his seniors, Dave is "extremely bright—a natural programmer." When he has achieved his M.S. and had a few years of practical experience, he can expect to become a programmer, with an excellent salary (and, naturally, also the expectation of finding suitable employment in any organization large enough to operate a computer).

Among his associates, Dave has the reputation of being somewhat of a lone wolf, rather uncommunicative, and fond of his own opinion. However, he does not go around with a chip on his shoulder. Phil Tedeschi, a programmer who has instructed Dave and who is a solicitor in the EDP department this year for the United Fund, said of him, "Dave has well-defined opinions and strong feelings about matters that affect him. And he's not afraid to speak out. In those respects, he's like most of us in this department.

But Dave isn't disagreeable. When he's made his point, he doesn't kick up a fuss."

Although not much of a mixer, Dave has always seemed glad to contribute (periodically) to the Sunshine Fund[1] in the EDP department.

As far as Phil Tedeschi knows, there has never been friction between Dave and other employees in the department. However, when Dave (a member of the Reform Jewish faith) recently took a day off for Rosh Hashanah,[2] he expressed annoyance when told that he would not receive any pay for that day.

Dave already earns a good salary. He lives with his parents in the city where Universal is located. The parents are well off. Since Dave came to Universal, there has never been any indication that he has felt pinched for money. It should be noted, however, that as a member of the Hebrew community, he is undoubtedly solicited for a number of specifically Jewish philanthropies (by their own choice not included in the United Fund) and also for the Jewish hospital.

INCIDENT: THE Z[3] PLEDGE

Phil: Hi, Dave. Have you filled out your pledge card yet?

Dave (firmly, but not in a belligerent tone): No, I haven't. And I don't plan to make a contribution. Here, you can have my card back.

[1] This fund, always small, is used in every department to recognize such events as weddings, the birth of a first child, and long-service anniversaries.

[2] The first two days of Rosh Hashanah are the only ones on which Reform Jews are not permitted to work. "This" year, the second day fell on a Sunday. "Last" year Rosh Hashanah came during Dave's vacation. (During the United Fund drive last year, Dave made a cash contribution of $5.) At Universal, employees receive time off with pay for all recognized holidays (including the Christian holidays, Christmas and Easter). For any holiday designated by his religion, an employee may use vacation days or take time off without pay.

[3] To those who work with computers, "Z" is the customary way of writing "zero."

When Phil looked at the card, he found Z written in the place reserved for the amount pledged. Later that day he submitted Dave's name to Mr. Williamson.[4]

Mr. Williamson asked Dave to drop into his office, and when he did, the following conversation took place:

Mr. Williamson: Hello, Dave. I understand you told Phil you don't plan to contribute to the United Fund this year? May I ask why not?

Dave: Well, as a matter of fact, I have two reasons. For one thing I don't like the idea of being pressured into giving. I prefer to make up my own mind about which charities I'll contribute to. And for another thing, I feel I've already made an extra contribution to this department. Recently, when one of our religious holidays fell on a weekday, I was docked a day's pay for not coming to work.

QUESTIONS ON THE CASE AS A WHOLE

1 *On a management decision*

Imagine that you are in Mr. Williamson's position at the time of the incident. You are aware of company policies (both for 100 percent participation and for "no pressure"). Dave Aaron is now in your office. He has just finished speaking. What would you say to him? Why? (The ensuing dialogue may effectively be role played.)

2 *On a corporate image*

In your opinion, what are the most important factors that determine a corporate image? Which of them are illustrated in this case?

3 *On a "good-neighbor policy"*

For a business organization, especially an insurance company, what advantages might be anticipated

[4] EDP solicitors have been told that if they come up against any holdout they are to report the name(s) to Mr. Williamson, the department coordinator. Mr. Williamson is staff assistant to one of the 10 vice-presidents, who is a division director in the EDP Department. Mr. Williamson scarcely knows Dave by sight. However, he is aware that Dave is regarded as an extremely promising employee.

from establishing the reputation of being a good neighbor in the local community?

4 *On company solicitation for charities*

   a As you see it, what are the chief advantages, disadvantages, and risks associated with soliciting employees on behalf of charitable causes? (In your answer, consider the company, the community, and personnel relations.)

   b Do you think it would be possible to solicit employees, with any expectation of achieving 100 percent participation, without exercising any kind or degree of pressure? (Give reasons for your opinion.)

5 *On company policy with regard to non-Christian holidays*

   a To what extent do you think the company policy at Universal was fair—perhaps even generous—to employees not of the Christian faith? In your answer consider the following statements (made by members of a study group who analyzed this case):

     (1) "It is discriminatory to permit employees who happen to be Christians to have time off with pay for Christian holidays but to deny that same privilege to employees of other faiths."

     (2) "The policy of giving time off with pay for all religious holidays could get pretty expensive, now that the work force of many companies is becoming increasingly internationalized. As a matter of fact, if non-Christians insist on getting time off with pay for all their religious holidays (and refuse to use vacation days or unused sick leave for this purpose) they might find it difficult to get employment outside their own countries."

6 *On a staff role*

If you had been in Mr. Williamson's position why might you (or might you not) have alerted Dave's immediate supervisor to Dave's dissatisfaction at having been docked a day's pay?

7 *On interviewing*

   a In your opinion, would Mr. Williamson's interview with Dave be more likely to succeed if directed or nondirected? Why?

   b Aside from the immediate question of whether or not Dave should (or should not) be expected to contribute to the United Fund, what aims might a person in Mr. Williamson's position have attempted to achieve in the interview?

8 *On motivation*

What illustrations of general ideas about motivation, e.g., as outlined in Chapter 6, do you find in this case? For instance:

   a Does the case throw any light on the question of whether or not a management representative can motivate an employee in a subordinate position? (Document your opinion.)

   b From the little you know about Dave Aaron's personality (and professional status) do you think he would or would not be likely to respond favorably to management pressure? Why?

   c Judging from Dave's statement at the end of the incident, how justifiable do you find his reluctance to contribute to the United Fund?

INTRODUCTION

When a manager, supervisor, or personnel administrator is diagnosing a situation in which a personal problem is part of the difficulty, he should make sure that his decision (or recommendation) for treatment takes account (1) not merely of one symptom but also (2) of the whole condition indicated by a syndrome (a cluster of related manifestations) and (3) accords with positive principles relating to organizational health. In an organization, this last point necessitates considering administrative procedures and personnel policies established for the system as a whole. To overlook the significant differences between a personal problem and a personnel problem, as was done in this case, is to risk aggravating and expanding a small-scale difficulty.

This case also illustrates opportunities and mutual obligations for effective coordination between representatives of a management and a union.

Key people in the case:

Miss Deborah Larkin, inspector, 48 years of age
Mr. Oviedo, business agent of the union
Mr. Avery, director of personnel relations
Mr. Dunstable, interviewer, women's employment

On July 8, 1937, the business agent, Mr. Oviedo, called Mr. Avery on the telephone and asked for an interview, saying that he was bringing with him an employee who deserved special consideration because of her long service. A meeting was arranged.

A THE MEETING

Oviedo: Mr. Avery, I thought this was a   1
worthy case to bring to your attention, and
I wish you would listen to her complaint.
(To Miss Larkin) Will you tell Mr. Avery
your story?   5

495

Larkin: Well, I worked in A-29 as a tester for 15 years, and I was always on the first shift. When I heard that motors were going to Cleveland,[1] I was worried and asked whether I might be transferred. I asked my foreman, and he said he would see what he could do. It wasn't going to be easy, because A-29 was shutting down within 2 weeks, and we were all going to be laid off soon. A little later, the foreman told me to go over to the employment department. There they told me I had to take a second-shift job. I didn't know what else I could do, so I took it. Now I've been working for the last 3 weeks on the second shift in the refrigerator department. I don't like the second shift, and I don't believe I'm getting proper treatment, because I've been here 15 years, and I think I ought to have some pick of my job. I live alone with my sister at home, and she works in a restaurant down the street. She works in the afternoon and late at night. This makes it hard for us to keep our house clean, and I like to work on the first shift because I can be home while she is away.

Avery: Let me call Mr. Dunstable [interviewer, women's employment] and see what he has to say. *(Telephones Mr. Dunstable, who comes in)* Do you recall Miss Larkin, Mr. Dunstable?

Dunstable: Yes, certainly. *(To Miss Larkin)* How do you do?

Larkin: How do you do?

Avery: What information have you got on Miss Larkin's case?

Dunstable: About 3 weeks ago, Mr. Hobbes [foreman, Department A-29] came to my office with a layoff list to tell me that a number of girls with long service were going to be laid off. He asked if I couldn't place them in the plant before the actual layoff. I told him I would do my best. An hour later, Miss Larkin came in to ask what I was going to do for her. She said I had to do something because she had such long service. I told her I would do all I could but that it would take a little time for me to look around and see what kind of work we could put her on. She said she wouldn't consider any other job than a test or inspection job, that she knew of plenty of places where I could put her, and that there were plenty of girls in other departments with less service whom I could lay off in order to give her the preference she deserved. I told her I would look into the situation and let her know. Three different times that day she came to see me, asking what I had done. Each time I let her know that, so far, I hadn't had a chance to do anything but would attend to her case as soon as I could. I told her she needn't worry, we would keep her on where she was until a job had been found. We did keep her on in the department for more than a week. I finally made a place for her as inspector on the second shift by laying off a junior who had been with us only a short time. She took that job, but every day since that time she has been in to see me about a transfer to the first shift. It is difficult to find her a job at the same rate of pay on the first shift, because she's not so speedy as the other girls. I've offered her several other jobs on the first shift, as bench worker or assembler, but she won't take them because they are production jobs.

Larkin: There are plenty of other girls on that shift who have less service than I, and I don't see why you can't transfer one of them and put me in her place.

[1] Management had decided to transfer its small-motors division to Plant 11. This project displaced 1,058 workers. Eighteen of these elected to follow their jobs to the new plant. The others decided not to change their residence. Of this number, 292 employees had 10 years or more of service, 534 employees had less than 10 years but more than 3 years of service, and 214 employees had less than 3 years of service.

Avery: We are doing all we can for you, Miss Larkin. After all, you haven't lost a single day's work in this transfer, and we made sure that your new job was at the same rate of pay. This shows that we are 90 giving every consideration to your service record that we can. Furthermore, we are going to find a place on the first shift for you. Only you must realize that for several reasons this is not so easy. In the first place, 95 you definitely limit the possibilities by specifying the type of work you want. Secondly, you cannot expect that the foreman should jeopardize production by releasing highly efficient girls who have learned to work to- 100 gether in his department.

Larkin: Well, anyway, Mr. Dunstable didn't tell me of any other jobs on the first shift.

Dunstable: I am sorry you take that atti- 105 tude, Miss Larkin. But if you will recall, I showed you three jobs on the first shift. One of them was a bench worker; the others were assembly jobs.

Oviedo: Miss Larkin, I think this is all 110 beside the point. I am certainly convinced that management is trying to place you. And please, don't let us waste our time. I have plenty of other cases where people have not been so fortunate as you have 115 been. They are losing time and money by this transfer and would gladly take any job. Mr. Avery has told you that he will continue to try to place you on the first shift, and I certainly don't want him to fire anybody to 120 do this.

Larkin: Well, please do everything you can, Mr. Avery, and do it quickly, will you? I want very much to get on the first shift.

Avery: I'll do everything I can, Miss Lar- 125 kin. I suppose you wouldn't be interested in taking a job as charwoman on the first shift? We can make a place for you in the office building.

Larkin: Certainly not. I couldn't consider 130 that.

Avery: Well, give us a few weeks to turn around in. Come in to see me Monday, July 26. Will that be all right?

Larkin: Oh, yes, indeed. 135

QUESTIONS ON SECTION A

1 *On staff activity to resolve a personnel difficulty*

a Assuming that Dunstable's statement (lines 41–80) was accurate, comment on his handling of the case at that stage.

b Evaluate what Avery said and did during the meeting. For example:

(1) Why do you approve (or disapprove) of his method and timing in checking facts?

(2) What evidence do you find in Avery's statements (see especially lines 125–129 and 132–134) that he accepted Miss Larkin's formulation of the issue for management action?

(3) Which of Avery's statements indicate that he was assuming responsibility for handling Miss Larkin's request?

(4) To what extent, and in what words, did Avery commit himself to granting her request?

c If you had been in Avery's organizational role, how might you have attempted to help Miss Larkin take a more organization-centered view, or at least state it, as your own view? (A conversation between Larkin and Avery can be an effective way to explore opportunities and difficulties associated with such an attempt.)

d In view of Avery's organizational role, what further action should he have taken, after the meeting, with what specific aim(s)?

e Why do you feel that the kind of decision required by Miss Larkin's request should, or should not, be made by a personnel administrator?

2 *On responsibilities of a union official: for situational diagnosis and action*

a Comparing Oviedo's statements (quoted in lines 1–4 and 110–121):

(1) What inferences can be made as to his general attitude and previous activity in this case?

(2) To what do you attribute the change on Oviedo's part, from an apparently person-centered to a more organization-centered view?

b In view of information brought out at the meeting, do you think that union officials had been well advised in supporting Miss Larkin by making her complaint the subject of an official grievance? Why, or why not?

c If you doubt the advisability of that action, from the viewpoint of policy, can you identify any other angle(s) of view from which such action may seem desirable to union officers?

B THE EMPLOYMENT INTERVIEWER'S REPORT

July 21, 1937
Deborah Larkin

Industrial Relations
Mr. J. Avery, Supervisor

On the case of Deborah Larkin which you 1 asked for a report on, I have talked today with Mr. Masters [foreman, Department L-50] concerning her case and have the following explanation to offer as to why it is impossible at the 5 present time to transfer her onto the first shift.

She is on a job especially suited for her, as it is a simple meter-reading occupation on the stators in Department L-50. Mr. Masters does not feel he could transfer her to any other type 10 of work, and on the particular job on which she is working the two girls on the first shift both have more than 5 years' service on that same occupation. In Mr. Masters' estimation, both girls on the first shift are more valuable 15 to him, and he could not legitimately transfer one of them to the second shift without endangering production.

Mr. Masters has gone over this with Miss Larkin and has absolutely guaranteed that, at 20 the first opening on any occupation for which she might be suitable, he will place her immediately.

Under these circumstances, I cannot see how we can be of any assistance to her at this 25 particular time unless we can place her on a bench job on some easy occupation.

H. N. Dunstable
Employment Department

C INTERVIEW WITH MISS LARKIN

July 22, 1937.   Miss Larkin in Avery's office

Avery: Miss Larkin, we must come to 1 some definite understanding on your case. You have had more consideration than any other employee, and yet you continue to make trouble. 5

Larkin (fumbling for her handkerchief): Oh, Mr. Avery, you're not angry with me, are you?

Avery: Well, I'm not exactly pleased. You agreed to give us time to turn around in to 10 find you a job on the first shift. But, instead of living up to this agreement, you make matters worse by appealing to everybody in sight to do something about your situation.

Larkin (in tears): I don't know what you 15 mean, Mr. Avery.

Avery: I mean just this—your case has bobbed up in this office every single day since we came to our agreement, July 8. You have talked to four people since you've 20 been up here—Cameron [president of the union], Oviedo, and two shop stewards. If there is something that is not clear to you, why don't you come to us?

Larkin: I didn't want to bother you. 25

Avery: Why bother them? Besides, by talking to them you bother both them and me. Naturally, they have to take some action, and the only way they can do that is to come to this office. And it isn't as if we are 30 neglecting your case entirely. We gave you all possible consideration, because we appreciate that you have 15 years of service. We even fired a boy to make a place for you.

Larkin: Fired? 35

Avery: Yes, we fired a junior to give you your present job. And your foreman has absolutely agreed to place you as soon as he can find a job for which you are suited. Why don't you give him a chance? 40

Larkin: I do.

Avery: I beg your pardon. You're not

helping us a bit by misrepresenting your case to the shop stewards.

Larkin: Oh, I didn't do that. 45

Avery: Well, you certainly had Dunstable on the spot by telling one of the shop stewards that he was not taking any interest in your case. What do you expect the shop steward to do when you tell stories like that? 50 He naturally comes right to this office to find out why nothing has been done. More than that, you told Mr. Cameron that we didn't even want to give you the charwoman job on the first shift. Now you know 55 that this isn't true. You can have the charwoman's job right now. I didn't stress the charwoman's job, because I knew you wouldn't like it. Cleaning toilets is different from what you have been doing before. 60

Larkin: Oh, I wouldn't mind cleaning the toilets for office people, so long as it isn't in the shop.

Avery: All right. I am ready to transfer a woman from the office building in order to 65 give you the job.

Larkin: Oh, no, I have no right to ask that.

Avery: Well, you have 15 years of service. You have a right to get preference. 70

Larkin: Well, I don't know. I'll wait till Monday.

Avery: I think that's the best thing. If you will only wait a little while, I am sure we can find a place for you. Mr. Masters has prom- 75 ised. . . .

Larkin (evidently anxious to be gone): Yes, he was very nice to me, and I'm sure. . . .

Avery: Well, give him a chance. Your best 80 bet is in the refrigeration department, because the work there is steadier than anywhere else.

QUESTIONS ON SECTION C

1 *On communication: in words, tone, manner, and expressive behavior*
  a What indications do you find of a considerable

change in Avery's attitude from that expressed during "the meeting"? (In your answer consider both verbal and nonverbal behavior.)

  b What evidence do you find that Miss Larkin immediately "got the message" and reacted strongly to it by changing the tone of her remarks?

  c By comparing events before and at the time of (1) "the meeting" and (2) "the interview," identify verifiable facts which would:
    (1) account for the change in Avery's attitude (at the start of the interview)
    (2) permit a different kind of interchange during the two encounters.

  d In this interview, what communication skills were called for from Avery?

  e To what extent, in what lines of the dialogue, do you feel that Avery met his responsibilities as (1) an interviewer and (2) the head of a staff department?

  f Comment on the appropriateness of Mr. Avery's approach, during this interview, as that of a management representative who might be trying to clarify an organization-centered view: on the scale of company-wide purposes, policies, and procedures. (In your analysis include specific comments on each of Avery's remarks.)

  g In your opinion, what might have been accomplished (and should have been attempted) during this interview that was not achieved (or even attempted)?

2 *On employee motivation and understanding*
  a Comment on communication from Miss Larkin during this interview. For example, by analyzing her words and other behavior, what change do you find in her initial attitude as to what was at stake, in the situation? (Note especially lines 7-8, 15-16, 25, 71-72, and 78-79.)

  b To what extent do you feel that anything said by Avery helped Miss Larkin to extend the scope with which she viewed the situation? On what behavior, verbal or nonverbal, do you base your opinion?

QUESTIONS ON THE CASE AS A WHOLE

1 *On line responsibility for personnel administration*
  a In such a case, what advantages (and/or disadvantages) do you see in having members of line management retain responsibility for making,

and communicating, the needed decision (with regard to possibilities of transfer)? Be specific.

  b If Avery had remained in the traditional role of a staff man, how might he have explained that decision to persons attending "the meeting"? (Role playing can be an effective way to answer.)

2 *On possibilities for management-union cooperation*

  a If Avery had clearly stated his opinion that the decision on Miss Larkin's request was one for her immediate supervisor to make, do you think that a person in Oviedo's role (as a union business agent) might have been able to accept it? On what grounds do you base your opinion? (For general ideas on this matter, see Chapters 8 and 13.)

  b If Miss Larkin's complaint had been processed by representatives of the union and of line management as an official grievance, what part might usefully have been played by any members of the personnel department? Specifically, at what stages in the grievance procedure might they have made what kinds of contribution? (In your answer consider ideas presented in Chapters 7, 8, and 13.)

3 *On a theory of employee motivation*

In analyzing what Miss Larkin said and did, at various stages in this case, in what respects (if any) do you find Herzberg's theory of motivation relevant and enlightening? (For details of that theory, see Chapter 6.)

  a In answering this question, consider Herzberg's ideas about "factors of job context," and "hygiene factors," such as administrative procedures, company policies, and conditions of work.

    (1) Which of the "hygiene factors," if any, seem to have been significant determinants of Miss Larkin's behavior?

    (2) Which seem to have operated as "dissatisfiers," in the special connotation which Herzberg gives to that word?

  b With reference to Herzberg's theory of the duality of man's nature, how would you characterize Miss Larkin's basic orientation at the time of this case? (Document your opinion.)

  c To what extent do you think it might be possible to stimulate an employee with Miss Larkin's orientation (and in her age bracket) to reorient herself so that she would respond positively to such "motivators" as achievement, recognition, work itself, and possibilities for psychological growth? (Indicate your reasoning.)

The "Outside" Inspectors

INTRODUCTION

In this case, a minor change in work assignments turned the situation "inside out" for three inspectors. They had no objections to this change, but another inspector, for reasons of his own, protested management's action.

When reading the case report, questions to bear in mind include the following: What are the uses and limitations of job descriptions as a means to ensure that job duties are understood? What are the chief advantages and risks of joint policy statements by a union and a management? When careful job descriptions have been made out, key terms defined, and policies for using job descriptions agreed on, how can a misunderstanding develop that is serious enough to require arbitration?

In this case, a question that developed into an arbitrable issue was: In what sense are these men

"outside" inspectors? To answer that question yourself, you need to be briefed on facts of the case.

CASE BACKGROUND

During 1949 the Lockheed Aircraft Corporation in Burbank, California, embarked on a job evaluation program. To prevent avoidable misunderstandings, it was arranged that staff experts in the wage and salary department should prepare a glossary of key terms used in job descriptions (see Appendix A, p. 506). In November, 1949, the glossary was issued jointly by the Lockheed management and Lodge 727 of the International Association of Machinists. It was given to supervisors and union officials at the same time, along with a set of recently prepared job descriptions and a joint statement of policy (see Appendix B, pp. 507–508). The stated purpose of the glossary was to provide official definitions of key words in the new job descriptions. The intent of the joint policy statement was to clarify the principles that governed preparation of job descriptions and were to govern their application.

Two Job Descriptions

Two of the descriptions issued at that time were entitled, "Inspector: Outside Production" and "Inspector: Receiving Precision." They were as follows:

Inspector: Outside Production

Occupational Summary. This occupation requires the inspection of aircraft parts, assemblies, tooling and material on outside vendors' and subcontractors' premises.

Work Performed. Performs the functions mentioned below under limited or indirect supervision at vendors' or subcontractors' plants, working in one or more assigned fields. . . .

Determines inspection procedures to be followed at various outside vendors' or subcontractors' plants in order to secure specified quality, giving due consideration to such factors as cost and production time.

Consults with vendors and subcontractors regarding the interpretation of specifications, blueprints, etc.; rejections, possibility of rework, salvage or other disposition; and other problems requiring liaison between outside plant and Lockheed personnel.

May assist vendor with production problems as required, by demonstrating proper methods of production to assure conformance to Lockheed specification.

Rejects faulty parts.

. . . Determines suitability of vendors' equipment and manufacturing practices to meet Lockheed inspection and engineering requirements.

Knowledge and Ability Required. Knowledge of all types of outside vendor and subcontractor inspections on casting, forging, tools, all types of parts and assemblies; ability to use precision measuring and layout instruments, to understand outside shop inspection, practice and procedure, to interpret complex blueprints, to use shop trigonometry.

Inspector: Receiving Precision

Occupational Summary. Inspect all types of complex machined parts and precision assemblies received from vendors, for workmanship, dimensional accuracy, interchangeability and compliance with applicable blueprints and specifications.

Work Performed. Make first-article, percentage, or 100% inspection of machined parts and precision assemblies *received from vendors* for workmanship, dimensional accuracy . . . *[same as above].*

Determine method of inspection, source and application of reference data and type of precision instruments and/or surface plate set-ups necessary to make said inspection.

. . . Improvise or adapt inspection, measuring instruments as required.

Stamp or otherwise approve acceptable parts and assemblies and reject unacceptable items. Prepare documentation as required.

Knowledge and Ability Required. Apply a complete knowledge of Receiving Inspection practice and procedure, A.N., vendor's and company specifications relative to the inspection of machined parts and precision assemblies described herein. Apply a knowledge of precision assemblies, welding, and processing techniques, and the machineability of metals.

To read and interpret complex detail assembly blueprints. To use shop mathematics including trigonometry. To make any type of precision instrument surface plate set-up as required.

To manually pull, push or lift over 25 lbs.

A EARLY DEVELOPMENTS

At the time of this case (1949 and 1950) the hourly rate for the job of "inspector; outside production" was $1.90 an hour. The hourly rate for the job of "inspector: receiving precision" was $1.80 an hour.

However, the official titles for these jobs were not used in the plant. Instead, incumbents were referred to simply as "outside inspectors" and "inside inspectors." The chief inspector saw no reason to correct this technically inaccurate usage. In fact, he too, adopted the simplified titles.

In late 1949, Lockheed was experiencing a period of work contraction. As part of an economy drive, it was arranged that "inside inspectors" should periodically perform routine inspections at plants of nearby suppliers (within a radius of 5 miles from the Lockheed plant at Burbank). The saving made by this arrangement consisted in not having to uncrate and recrate parts on the Lockheed receiving dock before and after inspection. Instead, parts approved by Lockheed inspectors could be sent directly from the suppliers' plants to the Lockheed shipping rooms. The following procedure was set up. When "inside inspectors" were to perform routine inspection on the premises of a nearby supplier, they would first clock in as usual at the Lockheed plant. They would then proceed to the premises of the nearby supplier, where they would perform their regular inspection duties. At the end of their working day, they would then clock out at Lockheed.

At the time of this case, three men who were affected by this occasional change in the location of a work assignment were Mr. O'Brien, Mr. Keenan, and Mr. Sharp. All of them were officially classified as "inspector: receiving precision." When there was inspection to be done at the Menasco plant, 3 miles from Burbank, these three men took turns doing it. Time cards for a typical month showed that this work outside Lockheed amounted to about 6 hours a week for each of the three men.

Neither O'Brien, Keenan, Sharp, nor the union on their behalf, made any complaint about this part-time assignment to do inspection outside Lockheed premises. Nor did anyone ask, in 1949, for reclassification of that work to the higher paid job of "inspector: outside production."

On Jan. 16, 1950, Harry W. Meyer (inspector: outside production) was laid off owing to lack of work. At that time he had been with Lockheed for 6 years. Mr. Meyer did not protest his layoff.

On Feb. 1, 1950, Mr. Meyer was recalled to work in accordance with the following contract provision: "Article IV. Section 3—Layoffs—A-(6). An employee with five (5) years' or more but less than eight (8) years' seniority scheduled for layoff, will be considered for placement in a lower rated classification for which he is qualified." At that time, he was assigned as "inspector: receiving precision." Mr. Meyer accepted without protest the change in status and consequent reduction in hourly rate.

QUESTIONS ON SECTION A

1 *Job titles and job descriptions*
  a Comment on the titles of the two jobs about which a dispute arose in this case. What change(s), if any, would you suggest in either the titles or the descriptions? Why?
  b If you had been chief inspector at Lockheed, why do you think you would (or would not) have made any effort to change the informal practice of referring to men on two kinds of inspection jobs as "outside" and "inside" inspectors? If you had tried to insist on use of the official titles, do you think you would have been successful? (Give reasons for your opinion.)
  c What words in the two descriptions indicate why one job was classified as higher than the other, and therefore paid at a slightly higher rate?
  d Compare these two job descriptions with specifications outlined in Chapter 14. If any differences seem to you important, which would you modify—the description or the text—in what respects, and for what reasons?
  e To what extent do you think the wording of these job descriptions meets specifications given in the joint policy statement (see Appendix B to this case)? Cite specific wording in all three documents to support your opinion.
2 *Definitions and shared understandings*
  a To what extent, and why, do you think that a glossary of key terms used in job descriptions could (or could not) be useful in preventing misunderstandings about job requirements and job classification?
    (1) What more might be done, in addition to issuing a written glossary, to ensure that

everyone concerned has approximately the same understanding of key terms?

(2) What are some of the factors that tend to interfere with shared understanding of job requirements?

(3) Which of these factors cannot be removed by issuing official definitions of terminology?

b Judging by the excerpts given in Appendix A to this case, how useful do those definitions seem to have been? (Support your opinion with quotations.)

c If you were in a position to do so, would you (or would you not) recommend inviting union officers to submit

(1) a list of terms which they think need to be officially defined or

(2) a draft of definitions which they would think belong in such a glossary?

3 *A joint policy statement*

a Using this case as one example, what advantage(s), if any, can you see in having management and a local union issue a joint statement of policy about principles governing the preparation and application of job descriptions?

b Do you consider that a dispute over altered work requirements and the need for reclassification, such as developed in this case, does (or does not) prove that it is a waste of time to agree upon and issue such joint statements of principle? Why?

c When management has participated in preparing and issuing such a joint statement, does that eliminate the need to formulate and issue a management policy on the same subject? (What are your reasons?)

d (This question might well be answered in writing.) What words in the joint statement of policy seem to fit the character of a policy, i.e., a flexible guide for decision making? What sections, if any, of that statement seem more characteristic of a contract clause, a procedure, or a rule? Why?

B A COMPLAINT THAT WENT TO ARBITRATION

However, on Feb. 15, 1950, Mr. Meyer submitted a complaint to the chief inspector. He claimed that employees O'Brien, Keenan, and Sharp, who—like himself—were classified as "inspector: receiving precision" were spending part of their time doing the work of "inspector: outside production." He contended that these three men should be reclassified whenever they did this work and be paid at the higher rate.

The chief inspector rejected this complaint as having no merit. He also pointed out that no complaint had been received from any of the three men for whom Mr. Meyer claimed to speak, and that Mr. Meyer was not an official representative of the union.

Mr. Meyer then filed a grievance through the union, to the effect that (1) O'Brien, Keenan, and Sharp were doing some work as "outside inspectors"; (2) these part-time assignments should be combined into one job; (3) this job should be reclassified as the work of "inspector: outside production"; and (4) on the basis of occupational seniority, he (Meyer) was entitled to this work.

This grievance was processed by the union through the regular grievance procedure. When the parties were unable to settle the dispute at any of the preceding stages of the grievance procedure, the matter was taken to arbitration.

By mutual agreement between the parties, the issue submitted for final and binding arbitration was formulated as follows:

"On the basis of certain duties performed by employees G. B. O'Brien, G. H. Keenan, and L. S. Sharp, is Harry W. Meyer entitled to the classification of "inspector: outside production," with an increase in his rate of pay to $1.90 an hour?"

C POSITIONS OF THE PARTIES

The Union's Position

At the arbitration hearing, the union contended that:

1 The job description for "inspector: outside production" is the only description that mentions the location of work. It specifies "Inspection of aircraft on outside vendors' premises."

2 Employees O'Brien, Keenan, and Sharp have been performing the work of "inspectors: outside production" on landing gear at Menasco Manufacturing Company, but their classification has not been changed from "inspector: receiving precision."

3 Whenever these men inspect landing gear outside the Lockheed plant, they should be upgraded to "inspector: outside production" and paid at the higher rate.

4 Finally, by reason of Mr. Meyer's occupational seniority and of his known ability to do the work required of an "inspector: outside production," he is entitled to job preference.

The Company's Position

Management argued that:

1 According to the provisions in the joint statement of policy for the application of job descriptions (see Appendix B), issued by management and the union on Nov. 9, 1949, "the job description is written to define and illustrate the job standard to be established and as such shall be interpreted and applied in its entirety as a composite picture of the job requirements."

2 The work performed by Mr. O'Brien, Mr. Keenan, and Mr. Sharp at the Menasco plant does not conform to requirements stated in the "Work Performed" section of the job description for "inspector: outside production."

3 Moreover, employees in the classification of "inspector: outside production" do *all* their inspection work outside Lockheed. Thus they are not subject to the kind and amount of supervision given to in-plant workers. They do not check in and out at Lockheed. Often, they even get their initial work assignments over the telephone, when they call in asking where to report for work.

4 Employees O'Brien, Keenan, and Sharp have been doing *the same work* on the Menasco premises that they do at Lockheed. The only difference is in the location of work, a difference which is an inadequate basis for reclassification.

5 The issue is whether a Lockheed inspection, on the premises of an outside vendor, must be performed by an employee classified as an "inspector: outside production."

[Management argued that] in this case, that question must be answered in the negative, because (1) the actual duties performed by these employees are fully covered by the job description for "inspection: receiving precision," and (2) their work does not incorporate essential elements of "inspection: outside production"—elements such as "consultation with, and assistance to, personnel of vendors."

QUESTIONS ON THE CASE AS A WHOLE

1 *On arbitration*
  a How would you formulate the issue that needed to be arbitrated in this case? (In your answer, take account of the issue as agreed upon by the parties, the issue as implied by the union's position, and the issue as explicitly stated in the company's position.)
  b If you were asked to arbitrate the issue as agreed upon by the parties, what would your decision be, and with what reasons would you support it? (If this question is answered in writing, students should outline their reasoning as an arbitrator is expected to do.)
2 *On union policy and action*[1]
  a What was unusual about the manner in which Mr. Meyer's complaint was first presented?
  b How might one explain the difference in wording between Mr. Meyer's initial complaint and the official grievance presented by the union on his behalf?
  c Why might union officers be reluctant to press a grievance which had first been submitted independently by an employee, and had already been rejected by his supervisor?
  d What possible advantages, and disadvantages, for a union can you see:
    (1) In refusing to handle such a complaint?
    (2) In undertaking to press it as an official grievance?

[1] In answering this set of questions, refer to ideas in Chap. 8.

e If you were a union president, to what extent do you think your attitude about taking official action in such a case would be influenced by your opinion about whether or not a favorable ruling could be expected if the case went to arbitration?

3 *On employee motivation*

a What inferences might be made about Mr. Meyer's motives in making his complaint, and about why he first presented it in the form and manner that he did? For example:

(1) Does it seem likely that the 10-cent pay differential would have been his chief motive? Why, or why not?

(2) What other reasons might he have had for feeling dissatisfied with his job classification at the time he made his complaint?

b What motives might have accounted for the fact that Messrs. O'Brien, Keenan, and Sharp made no complaint when their work assignment was modified to include some inspection outside the Lockheed plant?

4 *On job titles*

a Now that you know about Mr. Meyer's complaint and subsequent developments, do you feel any differently about job titles than you did when you answered questions asked on the topic *before* you knew what happened in 1950? If so, in what respects has your opinion altered, and why?

b If you now think that the official titles should have been changed (though you did not think so before) what change(s) would you recommend in either title? Aside from events in this case, what technical reasons might be cited to indicate a need for making one change in both titles? (If a hint is needed, the last paragraph of the company position may be read.)

5 *On handling changes in job assignments*[2]

a With the benefit of hindsight, what action(s) would you say should have been taken, by whom, when an "incidental" change was made in the work of "inspection: receiving precision"? Why?

b What are some of the advantages of *not* offering any explanations until after employees make complaints?

6 *On shared objectives*

a What facts of the case indicate a sharing of objectives by union and management?

[2] Refer to Chap. 19.

b In your opinion, what action by any management representative, at any stage in this case, might have improved the possibilities of working with employees toward mutually desired goals?

c Looking at this situation *after* the arbitrator's award was rendered, i.e., starting at the end of this case report, how might a personnel-minded plant manager plan to help other employees (including union officers) to accept existing facts and to work together more effectively than before toward any long-term organizational goal? (Be specific. This question might be answered by role playing a conference between the plant manager and the personnel administrator.)

APPENDIX A

A Glossary of Terms and Phrases as Used in the Lockheed Aircraft Corporation

The following are a few excerpts from Technical and Office Job Descriptions.

In preparation of the job descriptions the following terms and words are given definition and meaning to clearly indicate the common and consistent interpretation to be placed on them by all persons using the descriptions.

The meaning of words and phrases not included in this glossary shall be as defined by Webster's Collegiate Dictionary.

As Required: Means performance of work operations if and when such are necessary, as long as they are within the level of difficulty described.

Determine: To choose, judge, or decide; to select pertinent data or information from documents, records, etc.

Knowledge: To know and understand the principles, operations and procedures required of a specific job or function and the ability to apply such knowledge to the performance of the specified job.

Liaison: The act of investigating problems, coordinating activities and contacting personnel with a view to arriving at mutually acceptable agreements, changes, etc.

May: When used as the first word of a sentence or phrase, means that the function is performed by *some* of the personnel holding the classification or, that the function is occasionally performed, but is not a requisite for the classification.

APPENDIX B

Joint Statement of Policy for Application of Job Descriptions

The following basic principles governed the preparation of these descriptions; these same principles are to govern their use.

1 The title selected for an occupation and/or classification is that which most clearly indicates the general nature and character of the work performed, and yet serves to set the occupation and/or classification apart from others described.

2 The *Occupational Summary* developed for each occupation is a brief description of the occupation as a whole, the purpose of which is to set it forth in separation from other occupations.

3 The job description describes typical and normal requirements. These requirements are characteristic of the job and illustrate a level of difficulty of work and are not intended to list or describe all work operations, or tasks done within the classification. These requirements may not fit all specific individual work assignments, as the description when written was stated so as to be broad enough to include all variations of work in the occupation and/or classification as it existed throughout the company.

4 The work operations, duties, and other distinguishing characteristics described in a job description are those which are performed under guidance or instruction which is considered usual and normal for the work described.

5 The descriptions were prepared on the basis:

a That as a part of promotional procedure a worker occasionally performs some of the work of higher-rated jobs under close guidance and instruction in order to qualify for advancement.

b That a worker performs the work of lower-rated jobs when required.

c That the normal duties of any worker may include assistance to other workers on work operations, and

d That normal job relationships between workers include giving guidance and instruction to each other, as long as such guidance and instruction is not extended to conflict with the duties of a Leadman.

6 The job description is written to define and illustrate the job standard to be established and as such shall be interpreted and applied in its entirety as a composite picture of the job requirements. This means that the *Occupational Summary, Work Performed* (*Typical Materials, Tools and Equipment Used*—when applicable), and *Knowledge and Ability Required,* all must be considered in arriving at the proper classification.

In order to secure or hold the classification, the employee must be assigned regularly and consistently to that work which distinguishes the occupation and classification from other occupations and classifications.

An employee's classification shall be determined in the light of the highest requirements for knowledge, ability, and skill necessary to perform his regular assigned duties. In making this determination, duties that are performed infrequently or rarely shall not be considered or made the basis of granting the higher classification. This would not be applicable, however, to intermittent duties of a higher level to which the employee is specifically assigned in an area where the prevailing day-to-day routine may fall in lower-level requirements. If the employee on such an assignment is expected to possess and apply the knowledge, skill, and ability necessary for performance of the higher-level work, he is entitled to the higher classification even though the majority of his work time may be spent on the lower-level work. In such a case the employee is assigned to bring to the job the higher skills which he is expected to use as requirements demand.

To cite examples:

a An employee in a jig where Structures Assemblers are working, is assigned the responsibility and is retained in the group for the specific purpose of working off difficult M.C.N.'s and difficult reworks. His other daily activities are no different from those of the remaining employees on the assembly. The employee has had only three difficult rework jobs in three weeks and four difficult M.C.N.'s in the last month. This employee is properly classified as a Structure Assembler—General, due to his assigned responsibility of performing, as requirements demanded, difficult structures work on the assembly.

b At a production rate of one ship every two weeks, assume that the ship's hydraulic system requires two days for checkout. Assignment to this work would require classification as a Hydraulic and Plumbing Checkout Mechanic.

7 The job descriptions herein referred to are of a composite nature and thereby do not require an individual employee to perform all of the work therein mentioned, except where the job description indicates otherwise.

8 The job descriptions are not intended for, and should not be confused with operation sheets, work instructions, or work assignment sheets, etc.

9 The job descriptions are to be interpreted in the light of the purpose for which they were written and not for the purpose of accomplishing mass upgradings or downgradings of employees. The classifications assigned in the initial application of these descriptions shall be taken as generally indicative of the proper future application of such descriptions. This statement, however, is not intended to approve any miscalculation, nor is it intended to bar correct classification of any work or any employee, or to bar grievances alleging improper classification.

The Rejected Applicant for Employment (new engineer)

INTRODUCTION

This brief case report offers opportunity for analytical thinking about:

1 Recruitment and selection procedures for professional and technical personnel.
2 The relative value of interviews and scientific tests.
3 Effective coordination between representatives of line and staff.
4 The pros and cons of reversing a management decision that may have been made on inadequate evidence.

CASE BACKGROUND

In the fall of 1959, the Zenith Electric Company in upstate New York carried on an extensive advertisement campaign to recruit design and development engineers for its new atomic power division. One of these advertisements was as follows:

Creative Men
An excellent opportunity awaits specially qualified engineers with a minimum of 5 years' experience in the analysis and system design of high-energy electromechanical equipment.

We need men with initiative, inventiveness, and a liking for new and challenging problems.

Applicants must be capable of project leadership and active participation on our development team now, when our organization is on the threshold of an unprecedented expansion program.

Please send résumé and salary requirements to:
Zenith Electric Company
Department 100

Mr. Raphael Niosi, currently employed in Long Island, was attracted by this advertisement. He was looking for an opportunity to develop himself professionally and also desired to make his home in upstate New York, where his parents lived. A position with the Zenith Electric Company would satisfy both requirements. Mr. Niosi promptly sent in his application for employment. His résumé set forth the following background information:

Born: June 25, 1925, in Syracuse, N.Y.
Married; 3 children.
B.S. in Mechanical Engineering, Syracuse University, 1947.
Attended Graduate School of Carnegie Tech, 1947–1948. Took courses in electrical engineering and industrial management.
Attended the General Electric Training Program in Commercial Power, Transmission and Maintenance, 1948–1950.
Worked 8 years for Con Edison in New York.
General job activities involved design of mechanical and electromechanical equipment in the Main Power Plant and Subject Stations. Acted as troubleshooter and supervisor of maintenance. Has considerable knowledge and interest in atomic power as applied to public utilities.
Extracurricular activities include:
Captain of Syracuse University football team.
Part-time on New York newspaper writing a sports column.

As a result of his application for employment, an interview was arranged at the company's office. The interview was conducted by Mr. Featherston, employment manager of the atomic power division; Mr. Brigham, department head of development engineering; and Mr. Beckman, project supervisor. Mr. Featherston directed the employment interview, although both Mr. Brigham and Mr. Beckman asked questions with reference to Mr. Niosi's professional experience.

At the conclusion of the interview, the three company representatives met to discuss their impressions. All three agreed that Mr. Niosi's background and experience entitled him to serious consideration. However, Mr. Brigham and Mr. Beckman were put off by Mr. Niosi's physical appearance. His heavy build and fleshy jowls, combined with drooping eyelids, gave them the impression that his temperament was lethargic to the point where he might have difficulty in keeping awake. They were both of the opinion that Mr. Niosi's application for employment should be rejected.

Accordingly, Mr. Featherston wrote to Mr. Niosi:

Dear Mr. Niosi:
Since you were here yesterday, I have discussed your qualifications with Mr. Brigham and Mr. Beckman. We feel that there has been such a great divergence between your experience during the last 5 or 6 years and the requirements of our openings that to ask you to make such a change would be too great a gamble for both you and us. We appreciate your interest in our organization and are very sorry that we are not able to offer you a position at this time. If in the future an opening should occur in Maintenance' or Electrical Equipment, we shall give your application serious consideration.

On receiving this letter, Mr. Niosi was bitterly disappointed. At first he felt inclined to accept the decision passively. However, after further thought, he wrote the following letter:

583 Summit Avenue
Somerset, New York
Oct. 22, 1959

Mr. George S. Featherston
Employment Manager
Zenith Electric Company
Dear Mr. Featherston:
I read your letter concerning the results of our interview with disappointment. I am well aware of my apparent lack of experience in machine design; also, I can appreciate your reluctance in "taking a chance," due to that lack of experience.
In my conversation with Mr. Brigham and Mr. Beckman, I tried to emphasize to them that my duties require an intimate knowledge of mechanisms and electrical circuits, both as a means of determining the location of trouble in our equipment, and in instructing our electrical maintenance crews on procedures for performing their duties. Further, I have on many occasions revised existing control circuits to meet special needs in the field. I know that I must have failed to get this across to them because at one point in our conversation Mr.

Beckman voiced the mistaken impression that I was a substation operator. I am convinced that this misunderstanding occurred because I have a natural tendency to use expressions that are generally understood in the power utility field although they could be easily misunderstood by anyone not involved in that field.

When Mr. Beckman asked me whether or not I was a substation operator, I knew that I had failed to enlighten him concerning my duties here. At that point in our conversation he was questioning me on whether I could read electrical layout prints and whether I had an understanding of schematic diagrams. As a means of convincing him of my proficiency in this field, I suggested that he bring in a suitable control layout print, from which I would, in his presence, make an acceptable schematic diagram. This unfortunately was not done.

In fairness to myself, I must say that yours is the only company to which I have gone in seeking a change of employment. The type of work that you offer is what I want, and I have known your company all my life. This, coupled with your geographic location, provides the conditions under which my family and I can secure our greatest happiness.

Since the burden of proof regarding my abilities in design and development rests with me, I ask that you give me a chance to prove what I can do. I know that it may be generally unethical to ask you to reconsider your decision, but I do not feel that it is improper under the following conditions:

Provide me with a problem, or part of a problem, with which you are faced currently or which you have already solved. Supply the necessary specifications and generally explain the functional operation of the device in question. Let me develop a solution for this problem. If the problem is electrical control, I will provide you with detail work drawings and schematic diagrams and a general explanation of its operation. If the problem is mechanical, I will provide such drawings as you may suggest together with an explanation of operation. If you wish, make it a combination of the two.

I would prefer to work on the problem in my spare time here at home where my textbooks are available. You may set a time limit for the accomplishment of the project. If, however, you wish to keep my progress under observation I could work out the problem there, on weekends, in your presence or that of Mr. Brigham.

I can think of no other way to prove my ability. I am both willing and anxious to make the change which you have described as too great a gamble for me and hope that you will give me the opportunity to prove that yours will not be the gamble you believe it to be.

I have already stated that I would be willing to start at a reasonable reduction in salary. Because I do wish to join you, I would consider $800 a month as reasonable to start. This in anticipation of proper adjustments as my value to you increased.

Respectfully yours,

(Signed)   Raphael Niosi

The employment manager was favorably impressed with Mr. Niosi's determination and discussed the letter with the interested parties. It was finally decided to give Mr. Niosi an opportunity to prove himself, and one of the development engineers set up the following problem.

It is desired to move a finished perfect steel spur gear along a conveyor and allow the gear to be transferred from the conveyor to a sorting device. The gear should then be automatically identified in discrete sizes and placed in a bin according to its diametrical pitch, pitch diameter, face width, and pressure angle.

Assignment:

The design of some workable solution to the problem should be roughly sketched along with a suitable description. If it is of value to state the reasons for the choice of some design factor for the sake of clarity and better understanding, this is desirable.

Specify any type of conveyor necessary for carrying the gear to the transfer point. It may be necessary to make some assumptions during the solution of the problem. This is permissible as long as they are stated as such.

The overall device can encompass any variety or combination of factors such as mechanical, hydraulic, or electrical components.

If any additions to the manufacturing process of the gear are desired which would aid in operation of the conveyor-sorter and not interfere with normal operation of the gear, they should be specified and assumed as being applied to the gear before it reaches the conveyor.

However, before this problem was sent to Mr. Niosi, the latter thought up a problem of his own, solved it, and submitted the solution to the company for evaluation. Three experienced development engineers reviewed the problem submitted by Mr. Niosi. Their conclusion was that his solution was very thorough and well developed.

QUESTIONS ON THE CASE AS A WHOLE[1]

1 *On recruitment*
  a What are the chief advantages and disadvantages of advertising as a way to recruit engineers?
  b What other methods are likely to yield better results? Why?
2 *On selection*
  a To what extent does an applicant's physical appearance offer a valid criterion for selection when

[1] In answering these questions refer to Chap. 15.

the position in question is that of a development engineer? (Indicate your reasoning.)
  b What criteria would you use for selecting a development engineer?
  c In your opinion, what are the relative advantages of interviews and scientific tests for selecting professional personnel?
  d In your opinion, how reliable a substitute for scientific tests was the homemade sample of problem-solving ability offered by Mr. Niosi? (Give your reasons.)
3 *On a management decision*
Suppose you had been in Mr. Featherston's position and had just received the development engineers' report on the problem and its solution, submitted by Mr. Niosi.
  a Would you invite Mr. Niosi to return for another interview? Why, or why not?
  b Might you, instead of making that decision independently, confer again with Mr. Brigham and Mr. Beckman? (If you were considering that step, what potential advantages and risks might you envisage?)
  c If (in Mr. Featherston's position) you wished to recommend reversing the decision against Mr. Niosi, how might you present your opinion to Brigham and Beckman? (This question may well be answered by role playing.)

Will More Money Be a Motivator?

INTRODUCTION

This case illustrates, among other things, some typically interactive effects of ways of managing, supervisory responsibilities, management development, career development, communication, and inner motivation.

Key people in the case:

Mike Walker, senior project engineer, operations

Lee Hartwell, supervising engineer, performance

Henry Hall, lead engineer, Subgroup B, analytical studies

Bill Brown, engineer, Subgroup B, analytical studies

A PROPULSION DEPARTMENT EXPANDS, A NEW LEAD ENGINEER IS PROMOTED

In 1964, the propulsion department of Aerodynamics (a large aircraft company on the West Coast) was considerably expanded. At that time,

Mike Walker (senior project engineer, operations) then forty-five years of age, selected Lee Hartwell for the position of supervising engineer, performance. (Two other supervising engineers were in charge of operations and controls respectively. But those subgroups do not come into this case.) Hartwell (forty-one years old at that time) was put in charge of three subgroups, of which Subgroup B—whose function was making analytical studies—was the unit in which the following case situation developed.

Walker had a high opinion of Hartwell's competence as an engineer. But during the period in which Hartwell had already functioned as supervisor, Walker had sometimes felt that Hartwell needed a bit of coaching (which he—Walker—could supply) about the human relations responsibilities of his job.

In April, 1968, John Rouge, lead engineer in charge of Subgroup B, requested a lateral transfer[1] to another department. He reportedly felt

[1] In Aerodynamics at that time, promotional transfers could not be requested, and no salary increase was permitted before the end of the first year in the new position.

that his chances for rapid advancement would be better there than in propulsion. From the organizational viewpoint, a major argument in favor of this transfer was the expectation that in the other department lead engineer Rouge could make an outstanding contribution to company goals. Before leaving propulsion, he was asked for his recommendation as to his successor as lead engineer in Subgroup B. However, he replied that he had no recommendation and would prefer to leave the matter entirely to Hartwell.

Hartwell felt that the only choice was between Henry Hall and Bill Brown. (Promotion from within was company policy.) Both Hall and Brown were technically competent. The other three engineers in Subgroup B had seniority of less than 1½ years, and none of them had as yet demonstrated outstanding ability.

Henry Hall (thirty-two years old, and with a B.S. in mechanical engineering)[2] had been with the company for 2 years and in the propulsion department for 14 months. For 8 years before coming to Aerodynamics, Hall had been doing similar work in another aircraft company. In Subgroup B he had shown himself to be a dedicated and effective worker; consistently enthusiastic not only about work assigned to him but also about departmental goals. He had received merit increases at the end of each 6-month period of his employment in the company. Moreover, in the opinion of Hartwell (supervising engineer) Hall was "a natural leader who could rapidly develop into a real driver." Hall was a big man (6 feet tall and weighing 200 pounds). He also seemed to have an unusually large store of physical energy. Hartwell felt sure that, as lead engineer, Hall could stimulate the other engineers in Subgroup B to get out production of maximum quality and quantity.

Bill Brown, the other man under consideration for promotion to the position of lead engineer, was thirty-seven years old (also with a B.S. in mechanical engineering). He had been with the company for 15 years and in the propulsion department for 2 years. He had shown himself to be a steady and competent worker, and his salary was the highest in Subgroup B (only one step below the top level for his job classification). He had shown unusual ability in problem solving. However, in Hartwell's opinion, Brown would not function as effectively as Hall in the position of lead engineer. Physically, he was a small man (5½ feet tall, and slender). His temperament appeared to be quiet, and his manner was mild—in Hartwell's opinion, too mild to command respect from the other engineers. He totally lacked Hall's charisma.

When Hartwell had made up his mind that Hall, rather than Brown, should get the promotion, he went to Walker with his recommendation. The latter immediately asked, "How do you think Bill Brown will take this?" Hartwell replied, "Well, it's true Bill has been with the company a long time. But he has never shown any real leadership ability. Technically he could handle the job, I'm sure. But I don't think he would inspire the men beneath him to move the way John Rouge (the former lead engineer) had them going. With a bit of seasoning, Henry [Hall] could do just fine."

Walker, though with some mental reservations, then approved Hartwell's recommendation.

Hartwell communicated the decision by issuing a memo to all five engineers in Subgroup B. He did not discuss the matter with Brown, or give him any advance notice.

When Brown received this written communication, he immediately went to Hartwell, ex-

---

[2] In Subgroup B, all engineers were required to have at least a B.S. in mechanical engineering or aerodynamics. This amount of academic background was necessary because each of them worked—with relatively little supervision—as an expert in a specific area such as vibration, sound, aerodynamics, and model testing. The lead engineer gave out the assignments, usually requiring individual reports on tests made on aircraft installations or on research in wind tunnels. These tests were set up and directed by the engineers and carried out by technicians assigned to them from a technicians' pool.

pressed strong dissatisfaction at having been passed over, and insisted on taking his complaint directly to Walker. Hartwell, though greatly surprised and somewhat put out to find that Brown was not willing to accept the decision without going higher up, arranged for the interview with Walker.

During the talk with Walker, Brown made it plain that he had counted on getting the promotion, because of both his excellent work and his long service with the company. Also, to meet Hartwell's objection that he (Brown) lacked leadership ability, he stated that during the Korean War he had risen to the rank of major in the army. (Later, Walker learned that Brown had been with the Supply Services at the time.) Walker was surprised to learn about Brown's military rank and assured him that his whole record would be reviewed, for possible future promotion. However, Walker made it clear that the choice of Hall as lead engineer was final. And he told Brown that he would be expected to cooperate with Hall to the limit of his ability.

B   BROWN REQUESTS A TRANSFER

The next day Brown submitted to Hartwell a written request to transfer out of the propulsion department and into the R&D department.

Hartwell was again surprised at such an aggressive reaction from a man whom he had previously thought of as "a mouse." However, he checked with the R&D department, with supervisors in other operating departments, and with the personnel department. But he found no promising openings for a man of Bill Brown's "particular capabilities and preferences." (Hartwell did learn of a vacancy for the position of field engineer. But he did not mention this to Brown because the latter had previously indicated that as a family man he would not be interested in a job that required much traveling.) Hartwell reported his findings to Brown (with the previously noted exception), adding that the

personnel department would be on the lookout for suitable opportunities. Brown accepted Hartwell's report with a brief word of thanks, but with no comment.

C   BROWN'S MORALE SEEMS TO SUFFER

After this second disappointment, Brown seemed somewhat less enthusiastic about his job than before. He continued to perform his assignments satisfactorily, but a shade less quickly. Also, his manner became increasingly withdrawn. And his attitude toward Hall, although not openly hostile, was decidedly cool. As Hall himself put it, "All the other men work *with me,* but Brown just works *under* me." Evidences of these intangible changes were given by the fact that Bill never joined the group that usually gathered around Hall during coffee breaks and that he volunteered no suggestions during the team problem-solving sessions that were one of Hall's innovations.

D   BROWN IS NOT RECOMMENDED FOR A MERIT INCREASE

Two months later, when recommendations for merit increases were being considered in the propulsion department, Hartwell[3] decided that Bill should be passed over—chiefly on the basis of a lack of cooperation (a factor that was regarded as extremely important at Aerodynamics). When Hartwell had filled out the rating form, he discussed it with Walker. He then took it to Brown, who signed it (according to standard proce-

---

[3] Normally, each employee was rated by his immediate supervisor, who then discussed with his own immediate superior the employee's strong and weak points. But in this instance, it was decided that Hartwell should rate Brown. Both he and Hall thought that, under the circumstances, Brown might not accept Hall's opinion as objective. The rating sheet for engineers which had recently been revised, consisted of 6 factors: judgment; initiative; follow-up [on assignments given to technicians]; quantity of work; accuracy; and cooperation.

dure)—to indicate that he had seen it—and forwarded it to the personnel department for purposes of salary administration.

When Bill Brown did not receive the merit
increase (which was also withheld from two
other engineers in Subgroup B), he made no
complaint. (Indeed, he had never indicated that
he felt pinched for money.) But it seemed to
Henry Hall that Bill became even more withdrawn than before and the pace of his work ever
so slightly more deliberate—though the quality
remained high.

E   DECISIONS MUST BE MADE

In December, 1968, Walker learned that Bill
Brown's name was not to be included on the list
when recommendations for merit increases were
forwarded to the personnel department the following week. Hartwell had told him that
Brown's latest performance appraisal (made out
by Hall and reviewed by Hartwell) did not warrant any increase at this time. However, Walker
was uneasily aware that, in all probability, neither Hartwell nor Hall had given any thought to
the possible effect on Bill Brown's morale of
being passed over for the second consecutive increase. Moreover, Walker felt sure that it would
not occur to either of these men to make any
effort to soften the possible blow to Brown's
pride, nor to reassure him as to management's
continuing confidence in his capabilities. Another difficult feature in the situation, as Walker
saw it, was that Bill Brown would almost certainly find it difficult to accept Hall's judgment as the
basis for an adverse decision as to his performance, still less to discuss the matter with him in
a friendly way.

Walker therefore decided to have a talk with
Hartwell—partly because this seemed a good
opportunity to provide some coaching for a supervisor who had not previously shown much
perceptiveness as to the human relations aspects
of his job. In thinking about the contemplated
talk with Hartwell, Walker wondered whether
the latter would take the position that, since a
merit increase is strictly a matter of money, the
recent across-the-board cost-of-living increase
granted by the company would take care of the
matter. Would Hartwell also argue that, at Aerodynamics, merit increases were supposed to be
based strictly on performance appraisal, and
that Brown's attitude and performance had certainly not improved during the 6 months since he
had been denied the previous increase?

On the other hand, might it be useful for Hartwell to consider the possibility that the company
could not afford to deny the upcoming increase
to a man of Brown's proved capabilities? Would
being passed over again (when others in his unit
would receive increases) further demoralize
Brown—possibly to the point where he might
leave the company? Was this perhaps one of
those special cases in which flexibility would be
more productive for the long run than adhering
inflexibly to S.O.P.? (Exceptions had occasionally been made before.)

In visualizing the interview with Hartwell,
Walker felt that he should also consider whether
it would be advisable to put any pressure on
Hartwell to change his mind (especially since
Hall already knew that Hartwell agreed with his
appraisal of Bill's performance).

Questions for Prompt Decision by Walker

What it boiled down to, then, with regard to
Brown, was: Should Brown be recommended for
the upcoming merit increase? If so, on what
grounds? Whatever the decision on that point,
who should communicate it to Brown, when,
and how (orally or in writing)? If the decision not
to recommend Brown for the increase remained
unchanged, could any other way be found to
help him reverse his evidently increasing trend
toward demoralization, to change his attitude
toward Hall, and to stimulate his inner motivation so that he would want to put forth his best

efforts—in partnership with his colleagues—to advance company goals?

If you were in Walker's position, how might you answer those questions?

QUESTIONS ON THE CASE AS A WHOLE

(Notice that all topics listed below represent interactive factors in the case situation. For this reason, many of the questions dovetail or even overlap. For example, inner motivation and ways of managing and of communicating are implicit in every aspect of the case, even where they are not brought out by specific questions.)

1 *Communicating*
   a Comment on Hartwell's method of communicating (by a memo) the decision to promote Hall, rather than Brown, to the position of lead engineer. (Specify advantages and disadvantages, and for whom.)
   b What possible advantages might there have been in telling Bill Brown (when he requested a transfer) about the vacancy for the position of field engineer?
   c What seems to you significant about Hartwell's reply to Walker's question (see end of Section A) as to how Bill Brown might feel about being passed over for the promotion to lead engineer?
      (1) Did Hartwell actually answer Walker's question? If not, what question did he answer?
      (2) How does Hartwell's reply illustrate the concept of "the inner circuit"? (See Chapter 5, Part 1, of this text.)
2 *Ways of managing*
   a What is meant by the terms "production-centered" and "person-centered" as applied to ways of managing?
   b In your opinion, which style is more likely to increase productivity? Why?
   c From information provided in the foregoing case report, what behaviors illustrate these two ways of managing?
   d What information in the foregoing case report illustrates the practice of making decisions *for* a subordinate, rather than *with* him, on matters

that concern his personal goals? Comment on the advantages and disadvantages—both short- and long-term—of that practice.
   e What underlying assumptions indicate which style of management is associated with that practice?
3 *Supervisory responsibilties*
   a *What* supervisory responsibilities, for persons in *which* organizational roles, are illustrated by *what* information in the foregoing case report?
   b In your opinion, what are the most important supervisory responsibilities? Why?
   c Do these responsibilities need to be met only by employees whose job titles include the term "supervisor"? If not, what other management representatives share these responsibilities? Why?
   d In your opinion, might any supervisory responsibilities have been more effectively met, in this case situation, than they were? By whom? In what ways?
   e What advantages (if any) might there have been in having Hall rate Brown's performance in June (only 2 months after his own promotion), and then follow the company procedure of reviewing that appraisal with his own immediate superior?
4 *Promotion*
   a In your opinion, what are some of the advantages of a company policy for promotion from within?
   b Can you cite any factors in this case situation that illustrate a difficulty—or difficulties—associated with that policy?
   c Comment on Hartwell's stated reasons for thinking that Hall would function more effectively than Brown as lead engineer. To what extent, and why, do you agree with that line of reasoning?
5 *Performance appraisal and merit increases*
   a Evaluate the factors on the merit rating form (see footnote in Section D). To what extent does each lend itself to an objectively verifiable judgment?
   b What changes, if any, would you recommend in such a form?
   c What advantages can you see in not using a merit-rating form at all?

d What are some of the objectives in having a supervisor discuss his appraisal of a subordinate with his own immediate superior?

e What advantages can be expected if opinions are exchanged between an employee and his supervisor as to his strong and weak points (instead of having such an interchange of views confined to managerial representatives at two levels)?

f For what purposes can performance appraisal be used in addition to salary administration?

6 *Transfer*

a What advantages, and/or disadvantages, can you see in the company rule against requesting promotional transfers?

b From your reading about transfers as an index of organizational health, what would you suggest needs to be done in a situation like this case—when a requested transfer cannot promptly be arranged?

7 *Seniority*

a What facts given in this case situation illustrate the pros and cons of company-wide versus departmental seniority?

b When promotion is in question for a professional person (for example, an engineer as in this case) do you consider that seniority (either departmental or company-wide) is an important factor to consider? (Give your reasons.)

8 *Inner motivation*

a Drawing on Chapter 6 (in Part 1 of this text) and on other readings, as well as on your firsthand experience and observation, do you think that a man like Bill Brown

(1) Would be greatly interested in a merit increase on account of its monetary significance?

(2) Might be affected by any other aspects of merit increases? If so, what aspects?

b Judging from the timing and manner of Bill Brown's request for a transfer, what can be inferred as to his motives?

c Do you think that Bill Brown's attitude toward money (insofar as it can be inferred from information provided in the case report) might illustrate Herzberg's theory that money can be a "dissatisfier" and cannot be a "motivator"?

9 *Management development and career development*

a According to information given in the case report, which individuals showed any need for management development? Give your reasons.

b In this case situation, what attempts were made to develop any management representative(s)?

c In your opinion, what more needed to be done—by whom, for and with whom, by what method(s)?

d What are some of the advantages to be anticipated, and possible limitations to be reckoned with, in having employees (1) take management-development courses, and (2) receive coaching on the job?

e What advantages may be gained by having the development program include employees at all levels, instead of being confined to management representatives?

10 *Stereotyped thinking (labeling)*

a What examples, if any, of stereotyped thinking do you find in this case? And what developments in the case situation do you see as results of such thinking?

b If you were a manager and noticed that one of your supervisors showed a tendency toward labeling, how might you try to help him overcome this block to realistic perception?

An Engineer and a Machinist (needs for orientation and explanation)

INTRODUCTION

It has often been said that the outlook which is characteristic of scientific personnel makes it difficult for them to understand rank-and-file employees. This case illustrates among other things:

1 Some unfortunate consequences of unwarranted assumptions made by a young engineer.
2 That the word "explanation" has different meanings for different people.
3 That "showing 'em" without first "telling 'em" what they are about to see can amount to administering a severe shock treatment.

A CASE BACKGROUND

In a machine shop attached to a metallurgical laboratory, a highly skilled and reliable journeyman machinist had been selected by his supervisor to prepare test rods. His job was a vital link in a research process that began with melting various kinds of ore, was continued by preparing alloys in the foundry, and ended with laboratory testing for tensile strength.

The machinist turned rough castings to specifications. This was a highly skilled operation which entailed threading both ends of each specimen to fit the tensile testing machine, holding the central portion of each test rod to an exact diameter, and producing a mirrorlike finish. The machining of each test rod, from the rough cutting to the high-quality finish, took from 2½ to 3 hours. As each test rod was completed, the machinist carefully wrapped it in masking paper to protect the surface from the slightest scratch while it was being handled.

Apparently no one had ever told the machinist why he had been selected for this important work or explained to him how his job fitted into company operations as a whole. But it seems that he wondered, at times, what happened to the rods after he had finished his work and they

519

had been sent to the laboratory, and apparently he was particularly curious as to why so many of them were needed.

One day when the test engineer, a recent college graduate, was walking through the shop, the machinist asked, "Say, what happens to all my rods?" The engineer was about to tell him, when he happened to recall some remarks made during a lecture on training in industry. "Demonstrate whenever possible! *Show,* rather than tell!" So he answered, "Why don't you come and see for yourself?" So it was arranged through the machine-shop foreman that the next time a test run was scheduled, the machinist would be allowed to come to the laboratory.

QUESTIONS ON SECTION A

1 Comment on the lack of explanation to the machinist, either about his selection for an important job assignment, or about the reason for job requirements and the place of his job in company operations as a whole. According to good personnel practice, who should have provided such explanations, when, and with what aims?

2 In your opinion, to what extent would the general advise, "Show, rather than tell!" be applicable in a situation like this one? (Give reasons to support your opinion.)

B A CRITICAL INCIDENT

As recalled by the engineer some time afterward,[1] the circumstances during the test were roughly as follows. In the presence of the machinist, the engineer removed the wrapping from one of the machined rods and screwed the specimen into the tensile testing machine (which could apply a gradually increasing force up to 100,000 pounds). He then pressed a button, and

[1] The following is not an exact reproduction of the account first given by the engineer. A few background facts and some interpretation that he supplied later have been fitted in. Also, most of his technical terminology has been translated into everyday language.

the test began. A pointer on a dial indicated the increasing amount of strain to which the test rod was being subjected. Simultaneously, an automatic recorder drew a graph of the stress-strain relationship. The engineer watched this graph with concentrated attention. He temporarily forgot all about the machinist.

After about 1½ minutes the engineer disconnected the recorder. (He did this in order to prevent the imminent rupture of the specimen from injuring the delicate recording mechanism. Alloys were never supposed to be used except within a wide safety margin, as indicated by test results. Therefore, there was no need to have an exact record of the last phase of the test.) But the pointer on the dial continued to indicate the amount of increasing strain. About 30 seconds later, the specimen snapped with a loud noise.

The engineer completed his procedure by recording (on the stress-strain diagram) the figure for the breaking point. He was delighted with the results of the test. Suddenly, he was reminded of the machinist's presence when the latter indignantly exclaimed, "So, that's what happens to my rods!"

It struck the engineer as extraordinary that anyone should be surprised, apparently even upset, by seeing a test specimen destroyed when "tested to destruction." Why should the machinist seem to react to this planned result as though it were a personal affront? But there was no time now to ask questions. The machinist abruptly turned around and marched out of the laboratory. The next day the engineer heard that the machinist had gone straight back to the shop, packed up his tools, and quit.

From this experience, the young engineer drew the following conclusions: "That machinist was certainly dumb and emotional. All workers are that way. They are incapable of taking an objective view of things, or of appreciating what science is all about. It was too bad I ever invited him to the laboratory. If I hadn't tried to help him understand how important his work was to us, he would never have quit. He was a good machinist. But trying to explain anything scientific to hourly rated workers is just a waste of time—or worse."

QUESTIONS ON SECTION B

1 *On the effect of an "inner circuit"*
What clues to the machinist's interpretation of the "critical incident" are offered by his words and actions at that time? Try to imagine yourself in his position: a craftsman with no understanding of engineering aims and methods. Try to describe the "test to destruction" as the machinist might have told his wife about it when he got home that day.

2 *On learning from experience*
Comment on the conclusions which the young engineer drew from that experience. State to what extent you agree with his statement:

a In general, regarding the limitations of hourly rated workers.

b As specific conclusions warranted by the circumstances and immediate consequences of the "critical incident."

C EXTENDING A FORMER "EXPERIENCE" IN ANOTHER SITUATION

The foregoing case example was cited at a discussion meeting in a seminar on industrial relations. Most of the participants were laboratory engineers. The discussion leader had just been talking about the supervisory responsibility of explaining things to subordinates: "Every contact is a training opportunity." "Management is partly teaching." "Ego involvement on the job is an excellent motivator to secure employee participation in management objectives."

One participant (the young test engineer in the above case situation) spoke up in sharp disagreement. He challenged such slogans as misleading, not to say dangerous, generalizations. He knew, from his own experience, he said, that such concepts are "oversimplifications." Rank-and-file workers just cannot understand scientific procedures and objectives. To illustrate his point, the engineer then cited his experience with the machinist. As the discussion leader watched other seminar members, it seemed to him that the engineer's dramatic account of a firsthand experience had been a clincher for many of his fellow students.

At that point, the discussion leader recognized that he had been unrealistic in assuming that everyone has the same idea of what the word "explanation" means. What could usefully be done, on the spot, to uncover the roots of this multiple misunderstanding?

The discussion leader decided to backtrack. He invited the group to discuss the question: *What constitutes adequate explanation?* To start the ball rolling, he led the talk to the case example that had just been reported with such dramatic effect. He asked the engineer, "In your laboratory, was it necessary to have such perfectly machined test rods?"

Engineer: Of course. Any fool knows that.

Discussion leader: Well, I didn't. And even now I don't know the reason for it. Would you mind explaining it to me?

Engineer (in the patient tone of one who talks to a child): Well, obviously, the slightest surface irregularity would set up a stress-strain center of its own. And if that happened, it would vitiate the whole experiment. *Now,* do you understand?

Discussion leader: Yes, I think so. . . . But did you explain any of that to the machinist?

Engineer (with evident embarrassment): Well . . . no . . . I didn't. (*After a pause, and as though to himself*) I see. . . . I guess I really never explained anything, after all.

QUESTIONS ON THE CASE AS A WHOLE

1 *On discussion leadership*
Try to imagine yourself in the discussion leader's position. How might you have followed the lead offered by the engineer's last remark?

2 *On "explanation"*

How would you define the word "explanation" in operational language?

3 *On remedial and preventive action*

a If you had been in the young engineer's position, immediately after hearing that the machinist had quit, what if anything might you have tried to do (either in relation to that machinist, or to avoid a recurrence of any of the same difficulties for the jobholder who replaced him)?

b In view of all that you now know, how and by whom should the machinist have been told about the importance of his job to the laboratory?

4 *On motivation*

a What light is thrown by this case on differences and common denominators between factors that motivated an engineer and a machinist?

b To what extent does this case, and other situations that you know about, confirm or refute the following hypothesis: professional personnel need to understand why they are expected to meet demands presented to them as job requirements. Therefore, in supervising professionals, a way of managing different from the traditional authoritarian system had to be developed.

Factors in Promotion Policy (selection of a head lift-truck operator)

INTRODUCTION

In unionized plants, it is difficult to settle the question: Shall seniority or ability be the governing factor in making promotions? Even when management does secure a contract clause providing for ability as the primary factor, there remain many problems of day-to-day administration. Some difficulties may be eliminated by careful wording of the policy statement or of the contract clause, but differing interpretations are still possible, as in the case here reported. Can management decide immediately which of several candidates is the most competent for a better job, or should it give the senior man an opportunity to show whether he can perform the new job capably?

Besides the main issue of defining and weighing seniority and ability, the difficulties described in this case also illustrate other points, such as:

1 A need for employee rating and job evaluation.

2 A typical opportunity for preventing dissatisfaction and a need for improved policy thinking about a complaint before it develops into a grievance.

3 The unfortunate results of "horse trading" in a problem involving a policy issue.

4 The inefficiency resulting from poor coordination among line officials and from confusion about the proper role of a staff expert.

CASE BACKGROUND

The company in which this case arose had an agreement with a CIO union which provided that:

> When an employee is promoted to a higher-skilled or higher-paid job in the same department which has a functional relationship, the promotion shall be made upon the basis of seniority, provided the

employee is qualified and competent to fill the position. Competency shall be considered a large factor. When such promotions are made by management on grounds of qualification and competency to perform the work required, without regard to seniority, the union and the employee or employees with higher seniority than the employee promoted shall be entitled upon request to a statement of the reasons for disregarding seniority, and the matter shall be arbitrable.

Other relevant clauses were:

Seniority shall be by job classification, and shall be based upon length of continuous service in each job classification. Periods of layoff shall not interrupt continuous service.

An employee shall lose all seniority rights if he or she *(a)* quits or terminates his or her employment or *(b)* is discharged.

On Apr. 12, 1945, the Wister Corporation purchased two forklift trucks for use in loading and unloading materials and finished goods in its warehouse. This purchase was part of a program to improve material handling in which the company had the advice of a consulting traction engineer. When the trucks arrived, the plan was to use one on the ground level to unload boxes from freight cars onto pallets (wooden platforms into which the fork fitted for lifting) and then to move the pallets full of boxes to the elevator. On an upper floor, another forklift truck would be driven into the elevator to pick up the pallets and move them to a storage area, where they could be piled for later use.

With these lift trucks, the men were able to handle materials more efficiently and quickly than by the former hand-trucking method. Several similar trucks were already in use in the warehouse and in other parts of the plant, and at least 12 men had operated these trucks at one time or another. At this time, there was no problem of labor displacement, because drafting of men for the armed services had made male labor

extremely scarce. There was no opposition on the part of the warehousemen to the new trucks. In fact, they welcomed these mechanical aids that lightened their jobs. Most of the men were anxious to have an opportunity to operate these trucks. The skill required to drive a lift truck was similar to that needed in operating an automobile, since it had a clutch, gear shift, accelerator, brake, and gasoline engine.

A THE NEW JOB AND THE PROMOTION

When the new trucks were received, Samuel Soluka, the foreman of the warehouse, assigned one of his men, John Fortineua, to get them ready for operation. When the consulting engineer arrived to supervise the new system of handling, Fortineau and another warehouse employee, Earl Chadwick, were asked by the foreman to operate the new trucks temporarily. Chadwick was a new employee and had to be shown how to operate this type of truck. Fortineua, however, had operated one of the trucks before and was quick to grasp the ideas of the consulting engineer and the additional instructions that were given.

The engineer was so favorably impressed by Fortineau's intelligence and ability that he requested the plant superintendent, James Allerdice, to assign Fortineau to the special job of head lift-truck operator. This job was created at the request of the consulting engineer. He felt that, in his absence, it was necessary to have someone responsible for seeing that the trucks were properly used. When promoted to this job, Fortineau received a pay raise of 5 cents an hour. He was expected to check on all points of the work, such as piling boxes straight on pallets, the number of pallets on hand, proper sizes of pallets, and care of the two new lift trucks.

At this time, no one except Fortineau and Chadwick was asked to operate the new trucks, and no one except Fortineau was given the opportunity to try out for the new job of head lift-truck operator. However, several other warehouse employees had considerable experience in operating such trucks. The relevant parts of the work histories of the various men were as follows:

---

1 John Fortineau (thirty-nine years old)

First employed in company (Department B)	Mar. 2, 1925
Quit	May 9, 1925
Rehired, Department C	Oct. 19, 1926
Quit	Jan. 15, 1927
Rehired in warehouse	June 29, 1933
Quit	Aug. 19, 1933
Rehired in warehouse	Feb. 21, 1934

(Served as a general warehouse hand, trucking cartons and cases on the main floor for shipping; general all-round man; has been gang leader)

Quit to go into taxi business	Dec. 7, 1940
Rehired in warehouse	Mar. 12, 1942

2 Andrew Conté (thirty-three years old)

First employed in company (Department B)	June 6, 1927
Discharged	June 30, 1927
Rehired in warehouse	July 19, 1933
Quit	Jan. 6, 1934
Rehired in warehouse	Feb. 20, 1934
Laid off temporarily because of slack work	Feb. 1, 1936
Recalled to work	Feb. 13, 1936

(Served as general warehouse hand, and for last 4 years has marked location slips on cartons for shipment)

3 Edward Paradise (forty-two years old)

First employed in company, in warehouse	May 18, 1927

(Served as general warehouse hand, and, after Fortineau quit in 1940, he was made gang leader; worked with and supervised three men in loading and unloading trucks, loading cars, and working on the shipping floor; also has done some labeling; continuous service in the warehouse since date of first employment)

On the seniority list which was prepared by job classifications in accordance with the union agreement, these three men and others appeared as follows:

Edward Paradise (gang leader)	Dec. 7, 1940
William Cassidy (general warehouse man)	Aug. 15, 1944
Andrew Conté (location slip marker)	Feb. 8, 1941
John Fortineau (general warehouse hand)	Mar. 12, 1942
Louis Watkins (general hand in yard)	Apr. 4, 1944
Thomas Coté (general hand in yard)	Mar. 26, 1945
Leo Lamb (machinery mover)	June 25, 1944
Arthur Dumont (machinery mover)	Nov. 9, 1944
Albert Teriault (helper on auto truck)	Sept. 7, 1943
Kenneth Altman (helper on auto truck)	Oct. 27, 1944
Earl Chadwick (general warehouse hand)	Jan. 10, 1945

QUESTIONS ON SECTION A

1 *On administration of a promotion policy*
  a Should the promotion policy apply to this case? Give your reasons.
  b Assuming that the promotion policy as stated in the union agreement is applicable, what would be the proper procedure to follow in selecting a man for the new job?
  c Do you see any difficulties in determining which man has the greatest seniority? If so, what difficulties?
  d On the basis of the information presented up to this point, whom would you have selected, and why?

2 *On the role of a consultant*
  a Comment on the activity of a consulting engineer in selecting an employee for advancement to a better job.
  b What would you have done if you had been the consulting engineer?

3 *On the data necessary for decision making*
  What further information would management need to have before making a sound decision in such a case?

4 *On a foreman's duties and responsibilities*

What implications for the foreman's status as a management representative has the episode described in Section A?

5 *On placement*

Consider the placement of Chadwick as temporary lift-truck operator, and give your reasons for or against the proposition that this was a satisfactory step for management to take.

B THE GRIEVANCE

On May 7, 1945, Mr. Evans, labor relations **1** director of the Wister Company, received the following letter from the business agent of the union:

Dear Mr. Evans: **5**

The following matter was brought up at a meeting held by employees of the warehouse. The major complaint of all the workers is that they cannot see clearly why John Fortineau was given a job with a higher rate when he had **10** very little seniority. There are workers with much more experience and greater seniority than he had, and yet they were not given the opportunity to go on as lift-truck operators. Not only was Fortineau given a lift-truck op- **15** erator's job, but he was also classified as head lift-truck operator.

The union is requesting that a conference be held for this particular matter, because of the fact that the workers are very much dis- **20** turbed by this procedure. May I hear from you at your earliest convenience?

> *Business Agent,* Local No. 215
> Very truly yours,
> (*Signed*)   John B. Coté   **25**

After a brief investigation of the case, Mr. Evans replied on May 11, 1945, as follows:

Dear Mr. Coté:

John Fortineau was appointed head lift-truck operator on the strength of his outstand- **30** ing qualifications and demonstrated competency to perform the work required. The char-

acteristics, aptitudes, and abilities of the available men were given due consideration at the time of this appointment. Fortineau was **35** the unanimous choice of the management and the consulting engineer, Mr. Collins, who has been employed by the company to supervise the installation of the new lift trucks.

Management takes issue with your state- **40** ment: "There are workers with much more experience. . . ." It is management's position that this was a proper appointment substantiated by the facts.

> Very truly yours,   **45**
> (*Signed*)   A. D. Evans

This reply failed to satisfy the union business agent, who took the case to the vice-president of the company. On the advice of the labor relations director, the vice-presi- **50** dent refused to reconsider the decision and agreed with the union to take the case to arbitration. At this point, the company attorney was called in to assist in preparing a brief to support the company's position. He **55** asked for an opportunity to review the case with company officials who were familiar with the facts. A meeting was arranged the next day in the office of the labor relations director, with the following persons present: **60**

D. K. Jackson, company attorney
A. D. Evans, labor relations director
James Allerdice, superintendent
Samuel Soluka, foreman of the warehouse   **65**

The meeting opened with a statement by the company attorney:

Jackson: I asked for this meeting, gentlemen, because, if we are going to win this case at arbitration, we have to be absolutely **70** sure of our facts and of our position. If we are weak, we'd better find it out now rather than have the arbitrator tell us. Now, I have read the material that Mr. Evans gave me about the case, and some further questions 75 have occurred to me. First, as between Fortineau, Conté, and Paradise, did their last jobs have any "functional relationship" to the new job that was created and to which Fortineau was promoted? 80

Evans (to Soluka): I guess you'd better answer these questions, Sam, because you know more about the specific facts of this case than anyone else.

Soluka: Well, the general warehouse 85 work and experience in gang leading that Fortineau had was a help in this new job. Conté's job of marking location slips has no relationship with this new job, though he has a good sense of general warehouse 90 work. Paradise's job as a gang leader and his general warehouse experience was good, the same as Fortineau's.

Jackson (taking notes): All right, now what about the physical strength of these 95 three men, their eyesight, quickness of operation of automobiles, and other specific evidence of qualifications?

Soluka: All three are strong men—they have to be to work in the warehouse. Forti- 100 neau has good eyesight and is an expert at handling automobiles because he had his own taxi for a while. He has a good appearance; he is neat and a quick thinker and talker. He is steady at work. Conté has good 105 eyesight and drives a 1½-ton truck around his farm. His appearance is good; he is fairly neat and a fairly quick thinker and good talker. He is a steady worker, too. Now Paradise is good, too. His eyesight is 110 good. I don't know how he handles automobiles, but he drives his own. He is neat and has a good appearance, maybe is not so quick a thinker, but he is a steady worker.

Jackson: Did these other two fellows who 115 might be considered eligible for the job have any opportunity to demonstrate their qualifications?

Soluka: No, because at the time I didn't know there was to be any new job out of it. 120 As I told Mr. Evans, Fortineau did a fine job right away of handling the fork-lift truck and grasped the ideas of the engineer, Mr. Collins, who was showing him what to do and the way he wanted it done. He 125 showed an intelligence about the work that took the engineer's notice, and the engineer requested of Mr. Allerdice that John Fortineau be appointed to see that this work went along as he, the engineer, had laid it 130 out, during the times that he was not in town.

Allerdice: That's right, Mr. Collins thought that Fortineau would be just the man for this special job and asked me to 135 make him sort of a special assistant to him. So we created a new job and called it head lift-truck operator. I agreed on Fortineau because he has always been a good worker and has shown a real interest in his work 140 and has made many constructive suggestions. His attitude is good too. He's not always complaining about something, but I don't think he gets along very well with the union steward in the warehouse, who is also 145 the president of the union.

Soluka: Yes, about 2 months ago, my assistant foreman, Al Bandeau, asked Fortineau to put up cards showing carload lots and arrange the cases. There were about 150 four cases not placed just right, and he asked another fellow to help him move them. The steward heard him and went over and told this other fellow he need not do anything Fortineau told him, because For- 155 tineau was no boss. He seems to have it in for Fortineau.

Jackson: Well, we are treading on thin ice when we bring up things like this. But you think Fortineau is the best man? 160

Soluka: He was excellent for the job, and his capabilities have been proved. He can converse intelligently with the engineer about the work and all in all is, I think, much better than anyone else in the ware- **165** house that I might have got. We were not making a choice for this job at the time Fortineau was put onto this work, because, as I have said before, I didn't know any new job was in the making. But, if I had, I think **170** that, all things considered—capabilities and personalities—John Fortineau is the best man for the job.

Jackson: Could either Conté or Paradise have handled it? **175**

Soluka: Well, I guess they could have done it. Maybe Conté was entitled to more conscious consideration for the job than he got, because I think well of him. He's younger than Fortineau, though. Recently, **180** Paradise has felt aggrieved because he was not considered, and I'll have to admit he's a pretty good man. But I still think Fortineau is better.

Jackson: Have these other two run lift **185** trucks?

Soluka: Yes, both Paradise and Conté have run the first trucks that we got before these new ones came.

Jackson: Ordinarily, when there is an **190** opening on a better job, how do you go about filling it?

Soluka: We look at seniority and capabilities.

Jackson: Did you consider seniority here? **195**

Soluka: No, because as I told you I didn't know there was going to be a new job at the time.

Jackson: Does the new job involve any supervisory duties? **200**

Soluka: Yes, the man must have in mind the whole operation from the start in the freight car to the end where the boxes are piled up in the warehouse.

Jackson: Well, could we consider it a real **205** supervisory job? Our position would be stronger if we could say that this case came under Paragraph D of the seniority clause of the union agreement. *(Reading)* "Promotions of employees to jobs outside the bar- **210** gaining unit (for example, to assistant foreman) shall be at the sole discretion of management, shall not be restricted in any way by seniority, and shall not be the subject of a grievance, dispute, or arbitration **215** hereunder." What about it?

Evans: I'm afraid we couldn't claim that, could we, Jim?

Allerdice: No, the job is not really a supervisory job. It's paid by the hour, further- **220** more, and has been listed on the department job list as a nonsupervisory job.

Evans: I think our strongest argument is that under the union agreement management has the right to consider competency **225** as a large factor in making promotions. We are not bound to follow seniority alone.

Jackson: Well, that gives me about all the information I need. Frankly, this case isn't as strong as I thought it was at the begin- **230** ning, but I'll see what I can do to work up something for the arbitrator. We have four other cases going to arbitration, and maybe we can win some of them.

QUESTIONS ON SECTION B

1 *On interpretive analysis*
  a On what evidence do you think the union business agent is basing the statement quoted in lines 11–17?
  b What appears to be the union's interpretation of the promotion clause of the agreement?
  c Evaluate Mr. Evans's letter in the light of the information presented in Section A of this case.
2 *On the role of a labor relations director*
  a Comment on Mr. Evans's position in the grievance procedure.

b Should Mr. Evans have taken a more active part in preparing the case for arbitration? If so, what should have been done?

3 *On evidence for decision making*

a What would be the implications of the two possible answers to Mr. Jackson's question (lines 76-80)?

(1) Which answer would support management's contention?

(2) Which answer would support the union's position?

b Evaluate the evidence given by foreman Soluka on the relative qualifications of the three men (lines 85-93 and 99-114). What other information would have been helpful in this case?

(1) Which of the facts stated are relevant to this issue?

(2) Which, if any, justify management's decision?

(3) Which, if any, justify the union's contention?

c Why do you think Mr. Jackson rejected (lines 158-160) the evidence given (lines 133-157) by superintendent Allerdice and foreman Soluka? Do you or do you not agree that this is a valid objection?

d What is the importance of the information that is brought out so late in the discussion (lines 176-184)?

e Would you agree with Mr. Evans that the argument mentioned in lines 224-227 is the "strongest argument" management has in this case? Compare his statement with his earlier letter to the business agent (Section A).

f Do you share Mr. Jackson's feelings about this case (lines 228-230)? Why or why not?

4 *On administration of a promotion policy*

a Should Mr. Conté and Mr. Paradise have been given an opportunity to demonstrate their qualifications for the new job of head lift-truck operator? Why or why not?

b Comment on superintendent Allerdice's reasons (lines 133-146) for favoring Fortineau for the new job.

c In the light of the statements made in lines 187-189, what consideration, if any, should have been given to seniority in this case? What is the seniority of these three men?

5 *On promotion policy*

Do you or do you not think it is wise to include in the union agreement such a provision as that mentioned in lines 209-214? Give reasons.

6 *On top-management action on a grievance*

What would you recommend that top management do at this point?

7 *On the foreman as a management representative*

Comment on the relative prominence given to the foreman

a When the decision to promote Fortineau was made.

b During the subsequent meeting.

(1) What effect is this sort of inconsistency likely to have in the long run on a foreman's prestige and on his loyalty to higher management?

(2) How well does the foreman show up during the meeting? On what evidence do you base your opinion?

(3) If the foreman had made the decision independently, what evidence is there that he might have decided differently, and what advantages did he have that the superintendent lacked?

C THE INFORMAL SETTLEMENT PRIOR TO ARBITRATION

Arbitration of this case and four others was scheduled for July 25, 1945. Prior to the hearing, however, the president of the company arranged to meet with the regional director of the union in an effort to settle some of the cases. He also had a number of other matters he wanted to discuss with the representatives of the national union, and he thought this would be a good opportunity to "trade off" some of the weaker cases for others that were of greater concern to the company.

In preparation for this meeting, he asked the company attorney and the labor relations director to give him a memorandum summarizing briefly the strong and weak points of each case from the company's standpoint. He also requested the attorney, the vice-president, the superintendent, and the labor relations director to be present at the meeting. The union was represented by the regional director, another representative of the national union, and the local union business agent.

At this meeting, the president and the regional director agreed on a settlement of this case as well as on the other four that were in dispute. Three of them were settled in favor of the company, two in favor of the union. None was taken to arbitration. The memorandum of agreement contained the following paragraph:

> In the head lift-truck operator case, it was agreed that Paradise be given a reasonable trial in the position. John Fortineau may be permitted to retain his present rate and is named as an assistant to a supervisor. His rate in this position is to be a "present incumbent" rate. It was agreed that this disposition of the case settles all questions relating to the head lift-truck operator.

Paradise was given a trial period on the new job, and he performed it to the satisfaction of the warehouse foreman. Fortineau's new position was "created" to save him (and management) the embarrassment of his return to a lower-rated job. He continued, however, to be of real assistance to the foreman, relieving him of many minor details.

QUESTIONS ON SECTION C

1 *On labor relations policy*
  a What do you think of the wisdom of the president's proposal to "trade off" some grievance cases against others?
  b Was it wise to invite the superintendent and labor relations director to this meeting? Why, or why not?

2 *On decision making*
In the light of previous information, subsequent developments, and policy requirements, do you think that the agreed-upon settlement was the best possible solution of the case at this stage of developments? What weaknesses did it contain?

QUESTIONS ON THE CASE AS A WHOLE

1 *On promotion policy*
  a Discuss the relative advantages and disadvantages of two types of promotion policies: (1) one in which seniority is reviewed first and the senior employee is given a trial period in which to demonstrate his ability, or (2) one in which management considers ability first and makes its selection without a trial period. Under what conditions would the second type of policy be feasible?
  b Can you suggest any improvements in the promotion policy as stated in this case?
2 *On related procedures*
In a case of this sort, how can "competency to do the job" be established clearly enough to convince the union, the other employees, and, if necessary, an arbitrator that management's selection is right?
3 *On labor relations policy*
As a general practice, would you advise that management discuss a proposed promotion and the reasons for it with a union steward or business agent before the promotion is actually made? Why or why not?
4 *On responsibility for executive action and/or policy thinking*
In view of the promotion policy as stated in the union agreement, how would you have handled this case if you had been
  a The warehouse foreman?
  b The superintendent?
  c The labor relations director?

Discharge for "Proper Cause"? (shop steward Harris)[1]

INTRODUCTION

The following report, of a case that went to arbitration, offers a range of opportunities to practice skills of fact finding (by distinguishing between substantiated and unsubstantiated statements about facts), weighing facts (to determine their relative importance in relation to critical issues), reasoning from facts to relate them to principles which an impartial thinker would regard as decisive, and articulating reasons in such a way that a decision (based on established facts and on principles that are relevant and valid) is presented as a well-organized, considered opinion.

Full value can be derived from this case *only* if the questions following Section C are answered before reading Section D.

A STATEMENTS OF FACT

John Harris was discharged (from the Copco Steel & Engineering Company) on Sept. 16, 1953, for allegedly exercising the prerogative of management by telling another employee not to follow his foreman's instructions. By this appeal he seeks reinstatement with full seniority rights and payment for time lost.

A hearing was held at the office of the American Arbitration Association in Detroit, Mich., on Oct. 30, 1953, at which time the parties presented evidence and argued their respective contentions.

John Harris, welder A on the second shift, had seniority from 1946 and was a union committeeman. On Sept. 16, 1953, Marshall Bell, also a

[1] *Labor Arbitration Reports: Dispute Settlements,* The Bureau of National Affairs, Inc., Washington, D.C., vol. 21, pp. 410-413, 1954. For a complete discussion plan of this case, prepared for use by the Incident Process, see Paul Pigors and Faith Pigors, *The Incident Process: Case Studies in Management Development: Practical Supervisory Problems, Series I,* The Bureau of National Affairs, Inc., Washington, D.C., 1955.

welder, who had been working together with Harris, was instructed by his foreman to hook some racks, which were loaded with so-called "sailboats," onto a truck. The sailboat pieces had been loaded onto the rack by the first-shift operators, and the process of "hooking" required that cables from an overhead crane be fastened to the racks, after which the crane would lift the racks onto a truck. Bell had never performed this particular operation in the past, but he had hooked individual pieces, which had formerly been the practice. The new method of loading the pieces on a rack had been instituted several days before, but this was the first time that it was attempted on the second shift. On receiving the instructions from his foreman, Bell refused to comply, stating that the job was unsafe and dangerous. Bell was afraid that the pieces, which weighed 200 pounds each, 10 to a rack, might fall as the rack was being lifted by the crane. Bell felt that unless the pieces were banded, they might slide off the rack, as a result of the vibration of the crane, which, according to the evidence, had defective wheels. Bell continued his refusal after a discussion with the personnel director and superintendent, in which Bell had asked for some written assurance that his family would be provided for in case of his injury. Such written document was refused, but Bell was assured that he was fully covered by insurance.

The Aggrieved was Bell's committeeman, and Bell asked his opinion about whether he should "pick up the lift." Both the Aggrieved and Bell testified that the Aggrieved replied in effect that "if you feel it is unsafe or too dangerous, you don't have to do it." Harris claims that he was merely asked his opinion, which he freely gave, but left the ultimate decision with Bell. Harris agreed with Bell that the lifting process was dangerous unless the pieces were banded, since otherwise they could slide off the rack.

The personnel director testified that the Aggrieved, in his presence, told Bell he did not have to do the job, and that the Aggrieved's discharge at that time was accordingly justified, since he

thereby improperly exercised a management prerogative. This contention, of course, assumes that Bell would have complied with the foreman's instructions but for the intervention of Harris, who allegedly instructed Bell not to perform the job.

The evidence established that, after Bell's refusal, the foreman prepared and handed to Bell a pass indicating that Bell "refused to carry out instructions." Bell refused to accept this pass, after which further discussion ensued between Bell and representatives of the company. Later, Bell sought advice from another committeeman, Vickery, who informed him that "if the job was unsafe, you don't have to make the lift, but if you don't, the company can send you home." Thereupon Bell, after Harris was discharged, informed his foreman that he would agree to make the lift but that actually he was too nervous to make it. At this point, he was given a gate pass by his foreman for "illness" and he went home.

B CONTENTIONS OF PARTIES

The union contends that the wrong man is on trial, because if Bell refused to make the lift, he should have been disciplined rather than Harris; that the Aggrieved merely exercised his duty as a committeeman in advising Bell at the latter's request; that even if the Aggrieved's opinion was wrong relative to the safety of the job, he should not have been discharged; that while the company has the right to direct the working force, it cannot insist that an employee be required to do an unsafe job; that the Aggrieved's past record did not show a similar offense and therefore his past record is not material to the issue.

The company contends that Bell was a victim of circumstances brought about by the Aggrieved's improper advice; that the Aggrieved as a committeeman should have advised Bell to do the job and if a grievance resulted, the contractual grievance procedure should have been followed; that the Aggrieved, by advising Bell to refuse to do the job, improperly exercised a prerogative reserved to management; that the circumstances of the case together with the Aggrieved's poor record in the past justify the discharge.

C   THE ISSUE

As framed by the submission agreement and the evidence: whether the Aggrieved was discharged for "proper cause" within the meaning of Article XII, Section I, of the collective bargaining agreement between the parties. Important subissues to determine would be:

1 Did the Aggrieved tell Bell not to comply with his foreman's instructions?
2 If so, did the Aggrieved exercise a management prerogative?

QUESTIONS ON SECTIONS A TO C[2]

1 *On a management prerogative*
Why do you (or do you not) subscribe *in principle* to the following ideas:
  a That management has the right to direct the work force by unilateral decisions?
  b That under certain circumstances, a union official has a right to challenge a management representative, who is exercising that prerogative, about the fairness or propriety of his decision?
  c That if committeeman Harris told welder Bell not to obey his foreman, he (Harris) was acting improperly?
2 *On interpretation of facts*
  a As you interpret the facts, did welder Bell refuse to obey his foreman?
  b If you think he did so refuse, do you attribute his refusal to a statement by shop steward Harris that Bell should not "make the lift"? (Give your reasons.)
3 *On safety, as one issue in this case*
  a Why do you consider that an arbitrator would (or would not) need to decide whether—as a matter of verifiable fact—it would have been dangerous

for Bell to carry out the new work assignment as given to him by his foreman?
  b What information given in this case report could be used to throw some light on the question as to whether or not performing the work assignment was unsafe?
4 *On weighing the validity of arguments*
In your opinion, what is the merit of the following arguments, and what is your reasoning:
  a "The wrong man is on trial."
  b Because the record of the Aggrieved did not show a similar offense, that record is immaterial in this case.
  c The Aggrieved acted improperly. He should have advised Bell to do the job as instructed by his foreman and, if he wished, to file a grievance afterward.
  d The circumstances of the case, together with the Aggrieved's poor record, justify his discharge.

D   THE ARBITRATOR'S OPINION AND AWARD

Opinion. Article XII, Section I, of the agreement provides as follows:

"The management of the works and the direction of the working forces, including the right to hire and discharge or suspend for proper cause, and the right to transfer or relieve employees from duty because of lack of work, or for other legitimate reasons, is vested exclusively in the company, provided that this will not be used for the purpose of discrimination against any employee, and does not conflict with any other provisions of this contract."

The above provision qualifies the company's right to discharge or suspend an employee by requiring the discharge or suspension to be for "proper cause." The term "proper cause" is not defined in the agreement and it must, therefore, be given that meaning which is ordinarily accepted for such term, and which is reasonable under the circumstances. In general, it means such "proper cause" as would appeal to reasonable and fair-minded persons as warranting discharge. The "cause," however, should be in connection with the work, and should reflect a disregard of the employer's interests. Thus, any conduct, action, or inaction by an employee which arises out of, or is directly connected with,

---

[2] In answering these questions, consider the ideas presented in Chaps. 8, 18, and 24.

the work, and which is inconsistent with an employee's obligations to his employer either under his contract or hire, or under the provisions of the collective-bargaining agreement, might very well be determined to be "proper cause."

In the present case, can it be said that the Aggrieved's conduct and language was of such a nature as to constitute "proper cause" for his discharge? For the reasons hereinafter given, I find that the answer is in the negative, and, therefore, the discharge will be set aside.

It is undisputed that Art. XII, Sec. I, of the agreement recognizes the exclusive right of management to direct the working forces, and this Arbitrator subscribes to the principle that the company's exercise of its honest discretion and judgment in managing its business should not be lightly disturbed by an Arbitrator, unless there is an abuse of discretion. However, in this case, the real issue is not whether the company abused its discretion by exercising a management prerogative in directing Bell to make the lift, but rather whether the Aggrieved improperly exercised a management prerogative in allegedly informing Bell that he did not have to follow his foreman's instructions. It is true that neither the union nor any individual employee may properly exercise a management function any more than management has the right to exercise the functions and prerogatives of the union. It is my impression that the parties are in agreement on these general principles, but it is the application of such principles to the particular facts of this case which has caused the current dispute.

I am impressed by the fact that Bell, in the original instance, and *prior* to the intervention of the Aggrieved, had refused to follow the foreman's instructions, because he felt that the job was dangerous and unsafe. I am satisfied that Bell had a genuine fear of the job based upon his knowledge of the operation. Whether this fear was well founded, and whether the job was in fact unsafe, need not be determined in this case. The point is that Bell, at least in his own mind, had reasonable grounds for fearing the job. In this context, and after repeated urging by management, Bell then turned to the Aggrieved, his committeeman, for advice and guidance in the matter. The Aggrieved, together with other committeemen, had been previously instructed by the chairman of the union's safety committee

with respect to matters of safety and health. It cannot be denied that Bell was within his rights in speaking to the Aggrieved about the matter.

There is a conflict of testimony with respect to the language used by the Aggrieved in advising Bell. Witnesses for the company testified that the Aggrieved definitely told Bell that he (Bell) "did not have to do the job," thereby exercising a management prerogative. The Aggrieved and Bell testified that the Aggrieved in response to Bell's query stated, in effect, that if Bell "felt that the lift was unsafe or dangerous, he didn't have to do it," thus leaving the choice exclusively with Bell. Harris stated he was merely giving Bell his opinion. A careful analysis of all the evidence compels the conclusion that, whatever the exact language used by the Aggrieved, the import of such language was not to direct or order Bell to refuse to do the job, which the Aggrieved clearly had no authority to do, but rather to advise Bell as to a possible course of conduct. In the last analysis, the decision was Bell's, not the Aggrieved's, and the latter in his capacity as a committeeman was assisting Bell in making his decision, which the Aggrieved had a right to do.

It is urged by the company that the Aggrieved should have advised Bell to comply with the foreman's instructions, and then if there was a complaint, the contractual grievance procedure should have been followed. This contention has considerable merit where there is no element of alleged danger in connection with the job. But the argument loses much force in a case, such as the present one, where, if the employee's contention is correct, performance of the job might result in serious injury, so that the subsequent filing of a grievance would be meaningless.

As previously stated, I do not consider it necessary to determine whether, as a technical matter, the job in question was unsafe. It is sufficient to note that both Bell and the Aggrieved considered the job unsafe, and there is some evidence to support their views. Under such circumstances, I cannot find that the Aggrieved improperly exercised a management prerogative by his advice to Bell, who already had refused to do the job, and who was quite disturbed about the possibility of being required by management to do it. Bell's frame of mind at the time and his genuine fear represented a hazard too compelling to be ignored by the Aggrieved.

If the element of danger had not been involved and the Aggrieved had advised Bell not to perform a job assignment, for which type of case the grievance procedure provides an adequate remedy, an entirely different case would be presented. But here the stubborn fact is that, from the standpoint of Bell and the Aggrieved, there were reasonable grounds for believing the job to be unsafe. Therefore, a committeeman could hardly be expected to take the responsibility of advising an employee to take the risk which might have been involved.

It is my opinion that the Aggrieved felt that he was acting in the best interests of Bell, and, as a committeeman, that was his function. However, I am not persuaded that the Aggrieved, at the same time, intended to exercise a management prerogative in violation of the agreement between the parties.

The company contends that Bell, who has an excellent record, has never before refused to do as he was told. It is, therefore, urged that Bell's refusal must have been due to the Aggrieved's undue influence. The evidence does not completely support this view, for Bell had originally refused to do the job before consulting with the Aggrieved; Bell also consulted with Vickery, another committeeman, after he spoke to the Aggrieved, and Vickery informed Bell that he did not have to make the lift if the job was unsafe; and finally Bell was sent home because of "illness," arising out of his nervous condition.

The Aggrieved's past record with the company was submitted in evidence. Such record established that the Aggrieved's conduct in the past left much to be desired. However, the infractions and "charges" which are involved in the Aggrieved's past record shed no light on the present case, for there is no prior record of a similar charge or prior warnings. An employee's past record is often of major importance in determining the proper penalty, after the guilt of the Aggrieved has been established. But, here, since I find the Aggrieved innocent of the charges, his past record becomes immaterial.

The company is fearful that, if the discharge is set aside, any employee in the future may, with impunity, arbitrarily refuse to do a job merely by claiming that it is unsafe, no matter how unreasonable the claim may be. I cannot share the company's anxiety in that regard, for my conclusions in the case are obviously not to be interpreted as a license to employees to violate management's instructions. It is to be noted that this decision does not involve the propriety of Bell's refusal. It only involves the question of an alleged exercise of a management prerogative by a committeeman. The conclusions are based on the peculiar facts of this case.

Finally, I felt it pertinent to mention the question of burden of proof. The extreme penalty in industry is the discharge, for the employee's job, seniority, and other benefits are at stake. The burden is on the company to prove that the discharge was for "proper cause" within the meaning of the Agreement. Here, such burden of proof must be sustained by the company by a preponderance of the evidence, or such clear and convincing evidence as is sufficient to convince a reasonable mind of the Aggrieved's guilt. Upon a careful review of all the evidence and arguments presented, I find that the company has failed to sustain the burden of proving that the Aggrieved was guilty of the charge.

Award. The discharge of John Harris was without proper cause and it is hereby set aside. He shall be reinstated with full seniority rights and paid compensation for time lost at his regular rate, less any wages earned or unemployment compensation benefits received since the date of his discharge.

QUESTIONS ON SECTION D

1 *On an arbitrator's reasoning*
   a Regardless of whether or not you agree with the arbitrator's award, comment on his reasoning. To what extent do you think he has usefully factored out the main issue, subdividing it into questions whose answers—taken together—would add up to a reasoned decision?
   b If you disagree with some of the arbitrator's reasons, what other conclusions did you reach on those same points, and why?
2 *On case study for supervisory development*
   If you were in charge of a program for supervisory development, what features of this case and which ideas presented in the arbitrator's opinion might you present for discussion by supervisors? Why?

Discharge for "Insubordination" (Irene Mason)

INTRODUCTION

Sound disciplinary action can be taken only within a constructive disciplinary policy. In the case here reported, a clear-cut policy, well formulated and soundly administered, might have prevented the discharge of Irene Mason. Thus, as in so many other instances, constructive discipline would have been of value both to management and to the worker.

Furthermore, the situation is typical in that the central issue was beclouded in the minds of the participants by other aims and preoccupations. For instance, the problem of dealing with the case of "insubordination" was complicated for management by its concern with educating an old-line foreman. Another complicating element in the situation was the presence of a newly organized union.

Thus a case that at first seems to center on the question of discharge for cause can fully be un-derstood as an evolving situation only by considering all the following points:

1 The elements of a constructive disciplinary policy.
2 The kind of disciplinary action to be taken by line officials.
3 Opportunities for union participation in securing good discipline.
4 The importance of an appropriate disciplinary policy and opportunities for supervisory development offered by such a policy.
5 The need of building and maintaining respect for management's authority.
6 The need for policy thinking in personnel and labor relations.

CASE BACKGROUND

The Winston Mill was a small woolen textile factory that had been a family business for more than 50 years. It had never employed more than

150 workers. During the depression of the thirties, financial difficulties resulted in absorption
by a large New England textile firm. The Winston Mill became a branch plant, although in
practice the local manager was given considerable authority in handling day-to-day problems.
There was also an assistant manager who took
care of the office, the accounts, and some of the
purchasing, and a superintendent who scheduled
production, gave instructions to department
heads, and handled disciplinary problems. There
was no personnel administrator and no employment manager. The superintendent handled the
limited personnel functions, and informal relationships continued much as they had in the
past.

There was one important difference, however.
About a year prior to the episode described in
this case, the Textile Workers Union, CIO, won
an election conducted by the National Labor
Relations Board and was certified as the exclusive bargaining agent for all production and
maintenance employees. Contract negotiations
began soon afterward; but, for a number of reasons, final agreement was delayed for more than
9 months. The union had not notified management of the selection of stewards, so that the
formal grievance procedure specified in the contract was not yet operative when the events described below took place.

A   THE DISCHARGE

In April, 1945, Irene Mason had been em-   1
ployed in the mill for about 6 years. At the
time of this case, her job was that of cloth
inspector. She had the responsibility for final checking of the cloth and was frequently   5
in contact with various representatives of
management. Irene had been transferred to
this job 2 years earlier, when another girl
left. Then, according to the mill manager,
"something happened to her." After a series   10
of episodes in which she was reprimanded

by the superintendent and by the assistant
mill manager, she was finally discharged because she told the superintendent, Bill Smolokas, that he "didn't know what he was   15
talking about." According to the records,
the reason for discharge was "insubordination."

The episode leading to this discharge
took place one Saturday morning. Earlier,   20
the superintendent and the foreman had
been given instructions by the mill manager
in regard to pieces of cloth that came
through to the inspection table with too
much "shive," or foreign matter, in the wool 25
nap. He told them to send the pieces back to
the napper (a machine that "naps" the
cloth). Accordingly, Irene had been instructed to put aside such pieces and call the
foreman or the superintendent for instruc-   30
tions. Not all these pieces had to be sent
back, and the judgment of the foreman or
the superintendent was needed.

On this Saturday morning, one such piece
came to Irene at the inspection table. Since 35
the foreman was busy helping to repair a
napper that had broken down, she called
superintendent Smolokas. He looked at the
piece carefully and told her to put it aside to
be sent back to the napper. In what he later 40
described as a "sassy" tone of voice, Irene
said, "You don't know what you're talking
about." The superintendent made no answer to this but laid the piece aside, went to
the front office, and asked the mill manager 45
to come and look at it. He did not tell the
manager what Irene had said but simply
asked him what he would do with the piece.
The manager said that it should go back to
the napper. The superintendent then told   50
him the rest of the episode, but nothing further was done about it that day. The manager later explained that he had wanted to
talk to the foreman about Irene's conduct.
Since the foreman was busy on the broken-   55

down napper, the discussion was postponed until Monday morning.

On Monday morning, the foreman was still busy. It was not until Monday after-noon that the foreman, the superintendent, 60 and the mill manager met to discuss the episode. Both the superintendent and the manager felt that Irene should be asked to apologize for her remark to the superinten-dent and should also be transferred to a 65 different job where she would not be in con-tinual contact (and conflict) with manage-ment. The foreman said very little during the discussion.

On Tuesday morning, however, the fore- 70 man told the superintendent that he did not think Irene would either apologize or accept a transfer. The superintendent wondered whether the foreman had discussed the whole matter with Irene in his car when he 75 took her home the night before, according to their usual share-the-ride arrangement. However, the superintendent said nothing. The mill manager then called Irene into the foreman's office and tried to convince her 80 that she should apologize to the superinten-dent for saying that he did not know what he was talking about. This she refused to do, explaining that she had spoken "as she felt" and that she was still of the same opinion. 85 The mill manager then said that, if she would not apologize, she would have to leave the mill.

The manager sent a notice to the union office, as required by the new contract, stat- 90 ing that Irene had been "suspended" for "insubordination" and that within 7 days the suspension would become a discharge.[1]

At the same time, he called the union office and told one of the assistant business agents 95 the whole story. According to the manager, this business agent said that he thought the right action had been taken under the cir-cumstances.

The next morning, the head business 100 agent of the union called the mill manager for an appointment to discuss the matter. His attitude was quite different from that of the assistant business agent. He was in-censed at Irene's discharge and threatened 105 "to blow the place apart." The manager said nothing in reply to this, except that he would be glad to see him at two o'clock the following afternoon.

QUESTIONS ON SECTION A[2]

1 *On discharge for cause*

  a Was Irene Mason's discharge justified?

    (1) For what cause was she discharged?

    (2) Did her behavior constitute insubordination?

    (3) What is insubordination?

    (4) If superintendent Smolokas had discharged Irene on Saturday morning, could he justifi-ably have alleged insubordination?

    (5) How might superintendent Smolokas have brought the issue to a head on Saturday morning?

  b How much responsibility should the "home of-fice" of a branch plant have in cases of this sort?

  c What official should have the responsibility for discharge in this case?

---

[1] Article VII of the union contract stated: "No employee shall be discharged except for just cause—just cause to mean, among other things, inefficiency, insubordination, or persis-tent or serious infraction of rules relating to the health or safety of other employees, or to rules reasonably promul-gated by management relating to the actual operation of the plant, or engaging in a strike or group stoppage of work of any kind, slowdown, strike, sabotage, picketing or failure to abide by the terms of this agreement or by the award of an arbitrator."

The suspension-discharge procedure was also specified in the contract. "A grievance alleging such suspension as unjust or discriminatory must be mailed to the employer within three (3) regularly scheduled working days of the union's receipt of the employer's written notice of the suspen-sion and of the specific reason or reasons therefor. If the employer specifically directs that such suspension shall not become a discharge, the employee involved shall be given pay for all time lost by reason of the suspension."

[2] In answering these questions, refer to general ideas pre-sented in Chaps. 1, 2, 5, 8, and 18.

d Is it advisable in a situation of this sort to discuss the case with the foreman? Why or why not?

2 *On disciplinary policy*

a Judging by the action described thus far, what can be said of the disciplinary policy here?

b Comment on the fact that superintendent Smolokas said nothing to Irene after her impertinent remark (line 42).

(1) Why do you think he may have acted as he did?

(2) What bad effects are likely to follow such indecisive behavior by a management representative?

(3) Comment on the validity of the manager's reason for postponing discussion of Irene's conduct (lines 55-57).

c What instructions and orders relating to this episode were given to Irene? Did she disobey any of them? If so, which?

d Comment on the timing of top management's first step in disciplining Irene.

3 *On executive responsibility*

If you had been the superintendent, what would you have said when the foreman brought the "message" from Irene (lines 71-73)?

4 *On getting evidence to review a decision*

On the basis of the information thus far presented, what points should be checked further before the meeting with the head business agent of the union?

5 *On labor relations*

How should management interpret and reply to a "threat" such as that expressed by the head business agent of the union?

B EMPLOYEE DISCIPLINE AND SUPERVISORY DEVELOPMENT

The mill manager knew that he had had little experience in handling cases with a union, since the union had been officially recognized for only a few months. Therefore, although he was busy with a number of other matters that he felt were more directly connected with production, he decided to devote some time the morning before the meeting with the union to getting the facts on the case. He sat down with the assistant manager and with the superintendent to review all the difficulties they had experienced with Irene Mason. During the discussion, the manager did not review in any detail the problem that was uppermost in their minds with regard to foreman Williams. But they all recognized that it was an important element in the discharge case. When the superintendent had been hired 3 years before, it was with the understanding that he develop uniformity of practice throughout the plant. Having come from the outside, his presence was at first resented by many foremen, but gradually he won the respect of most of them and had continuing difficulties with only a few. Ed Williams, an old-timer, was one of these, and the superintendent devoted considerable time to working with him in trying to improve the standards and practices of his department. The superintendent's desire to educate Ed Williams was his main reason for handling the case as he had.

The following facts were brought out in the course of the discussion: Soon after Irene was placed on the inspection job, superintendent Smolokas noticed that she was talking and "kidding" with some of the truckers who occasionally came past her work station. In his judgment, both she and the truckers were neglecting their work, so he went to Irene's foreman, Ed Williams, and asked him to check up on this and stop the practice. In carrying out these instructions, Williams went over to Irene and said, "Bill says you should get back to work. You're bothering the boys." At this remark, Irene walked out of the plant "in a huff." When she came back the next day, she was reinstated only after a private talk with the superintendent, who outlined what was expected of her on the job.

The "campaign to educate Ed Williams" had continued. According to superintendent Smolokas, Ed as "lax on details," such as record keeping, and he was "lax on handling the help." He was inclined to be easy-going, except where he formed definite opinions about someone. Apparently he often got these opinions from Irene, whom he drove to and from work in his car. (She was a "friend of the family" and lived near his home.) Although they could not prove it, both the manager and the superintendent believed that the girl influenced the foreman against people whom she did not like. According to statements of present workers, several girls had left the mill "on account of Irene."

At various times, the superintendent had spoken to the foreman about his work, telling him that he must "tighten up" his management of the department. One day, Irene came to the superintendent's office and asked to see him. She opened the conversation with the question, "Why do you pick on Ed all the time?" The superintendent replied that although he would be glad to discuss her work with her at any time, he could not discuss with her any problems that merely concerned the foreman. He said to her, "Go back to your work and mind your own business. Your job is inspecting, not acting as a nursemaid for Ed Williams. If Ed has any complaints he should be man enough to come to me himself and tell me." As Irene left the office, she said something over her shoulder that sounded to the superintendent like "You damn Polack." So he added, "The next time you interfere in anyone's business you will be discharged." She then asked, "What is my job?" The superintendent again outlined her duties and finally said, "I don't want you influencing Ed."

One morning about 6 months later, a temporary worker was sent home by foreman Williams at 9:30 A.M. because there was no more work for her that day. Later the same day, the office girl came back to the foreman's office to get his "OK" on the girl's time card, marked for 2½ hours. The foreman said he thought that the new "reporting-time" provision of the union contract applied in this case. (This clause provided 4 hours' reporting pay or work at the employee's regular rate of pay if there was insufficient work for an employee at the beginning of a day.) He thought that the girl should get 4 hours' pay.

Irene was working near by and was either called over by the foreman or came into the discussion on her own initiative (the facts are not wholly clear). She sided with the foreman and insisted that the girl's card should be marked for 4 hours' pay. This confused the office girl, who had not been told about the reporting-pay provision, so she called over superintendent Smolokas, who happened to be walking past at the moment. She said, "Ed and Irene say we must pay this girl 4 hours' reporting pay." Superintendent Smolokas then told foreman Williams that the reporting-time provision of the union contract was not to go into effect until it had been approved by the Regional War Labor Board; and, since this approval had not yet been received, the provision did not apply at this time. He then told Irene to go back to her work, since the matter did not in any event concern her. She did not go immediately, however, and continued to insist that she was right.

At this point, another official had entered the discussion, Mr. Forbes, the assistant mill manager, who was on his way to check up on another matter, when he saw one of the girls from his office talking with Ed, Irene, and superintendent Smolokas. The superintendent explained the problem to Forbes and asked his opinion. The assistant manager replied that the reporting-time provision was not yet in effect. He then turned to foreman Williams and added, "Ed, you let the office handle things like that. I'll tell my girls when any new provisions apply. Furthermore, you shouldn't 145 have let Irene get into the discussion. It didn't concern her."

At this remark, Irene observed, "It's a free country, and I guess I can say what I think is right if I want to." 150

"Your job is inspecting, not butting into other people's business," replied the assistant mill manager. "You have no right in this discussion. You're not a union representative." 155

He then called the foreman aside and told him that he was "off base" on two points: (1) in his opinion of the applicability of the reporting-time provision and (2) in permitting Irene to leave her work and enter the 160 discussion.

Shortly after the episode involving the temporary worker's time card, Irene joined the union. When the union had first won bargaining rights, Irene had been most out- 165 spoken against it. She said that she could not see any benefit to be derived from it. It seemed that she reflected some of the feelings of foreman Williams, who had previously said, "I don't want the union telling 170 me how to run my department." Now, without any explanation to her fellow workers, Irene signed a membership card in the union. The "grapevine" reported that she had told several people that she was out to 175 "get" superintendent Smolokas.

Another difficulty with Irene, preceding the one leading to her discharge, occurred when she told Ed Williams that the girl on the second shift had not inspected her cloth 180 properly. The foreman then told the second-shift girl (apparently without checking the facts), "Irene says you haven't inspected your cloth right." The second-shift inspector denied this and was much upset. When 185 Williams later asked Irene what she meant, she denied that she had said the girl was

doing poor work. She said that she just meant that the work was not being done as well as she thought it should be done. 190

QUESTIONS ON SECTION B[3]

1 *On supervisory development by higher management*
   a Comment on the methods used by members of higher management to "educate" foreman Williams as to his responsibilities (refer especially to the superintendent's action, lines 33–43).
   b What seem to have been the foreman's principal weaknesses?
   c What might have been done about them, other than what was done?

2 *On line authority*
   a Comment on superintendent Smolokas's handling of the situation when Irene accused him of "picking on" the foreman (lines 75–85). If you had been in his place, what might you have said and done? Why?
   b As an example of line authority, what do you think of the superintendent's order to Irene (lines 81–83) and of his neglect to follow through on it? (Consider it especially with reference to his warning, lines 89–90.)
   c Evaluate the advantages and risks of direct intervention by a top-management official in a situation such as that described in the temporary worker's timecard incident (lines 132–140).

3 *On fact-finding*
   Why is it important to determine whether foreman Williams brought Irene into the discussion or whether she came in on her own initiative (lines 109–110)?

4 *On reviewing a decision*
   a In what respects has the review of these earlier episodes shed additional light on the points you checked in question 1 after Section A?
   b Has any of this information made you change your mind? If so, what information? And what is your present opinion as to the propriety of the discharge?

5 *On executive action in a grievance case*
   Comment on the manager's activity in preparing for his conference with this union business agent. Do

[3] In answering these questions, refer to ideas in Chaps. 2, 3, and 7.

you feel that he took unnecessary trouble? Why, or why not?

6 *On the responsibilities of a foreman*

  a Comment on foreman Williams's remark to Irene (lines 45-46).

  b How might a first-level manager have handled such a situation?

  c If you had been in the foreman's position, after hearing Irene's comment on the second-shift cloth inspector (lines 181-184) how might you have handled the matter? Why?

  d What objections, if any, do you see in a foreman's sharing his car with a worker? If you see any difficulties, how might these have been overcome?

C THE GRIEVANCE MEETING

Two days after Irene's discharge in May, 1945, the representatives of the union and the company met in the mill manager's office. The following were present:

Mr. Wilson, manager of the mill
Mr. Forbes, assistant mill manager
Mr. Smolokas, superintendent
Mr. DuFresne, head business agent of the union
Mr. Leboeuf, assistant business agent

After the usual preliminaries and introductions (some of the men had not met each other before), the head business agent of the union "came to the point."

DuFresne: We came over to straighten things out about Irene Mason. You can't just discharge a person for saying what she thinks. That's free speech. Furthermore, she has been working for you for a good many years; she must be a good worker.

Wilson: She is good when she sticks to her work. The trouble is that she didn't mind her own business. But let's not argue before we have all the facts. We have reviewed the

case, Mr. DuFresne, but we should like to hear your side of the story first.

DuFresne (glancing at a typewritten statement): Well, she told me a lot of things. There was this matter back a couple of years when she was told not to bother the truckers. She tells me *they* were bothering her. Anyhow, Mr. Wilson, you know as well as I do that, if people work next to each other, they will talk. You can't fire them for that.

Then there was the time she was told to go back to work and mind her own business when she gave her opinion about the 4 hours' reporting pay. She says the foreman called her over and that the talk was near her workplace, where she could have heard everything anyway. Now, she was wrong about the reporting pay being in effect, but she was just saying what she thought was right, when the foreman asked her.

And now last Saturday. She expressed her opinion again, and probably she shouldn't have said what she did. But she didn't refuse to do the work, and you can fire a person for insubordination only if he refuses to do the work. If one of my office girls says I'm wrong about something, I don't fire her. This is a democratic country, where everybody has a right to express an opinion. Well, that's all I have. There just aren't sufficient grounds for discharge.

Wilson: Now, we've looked into the case, as I said, and our information doesn't check with yours at a lot of points. There were at least five times in the last 2 or 3 years when we had trouble with Irene. *(He then recounts the four episodes outlined in Section B and the discharge episode described in Section A.)*

DuFresne: Well, if she caused that much trouble, why didn't you discharge her before? Why didn't you fire her when she called Mr. Smolokas that insulting name?

Forbes: Because we were trying to convince her that she was in the wrong and should change her ways. We were short of help, and we wanted to hold onto her. She was a good worker, except for that.

DuFresne: Well, I can't help what she did before. She was discharged—or suspended—on Tuesday for something she did Saturday, and I say what she did Saturday, and refusing to apologize for it, is not reason enough for discharge. If she isn't put back on her job with back pay, I'm going to take the case to arbitration. And I don't think any arbitrator will rule against me in this case.

Wilson: We discharged her Tuesday because it was the last straw. All these other episodes are important as background. We did offer to move her to a different job where she wouldn't cause so much trouble, but she refused.

DuFresne: I'm not interested in another job for her. I want her back in her old job. She came to the union with her grievance, and we're going to do something for her, even if we have to go to arbitration. I told her I thought she had a good case and would go to bat for her, and I'm not going to let her down. What d'you think would happen to the union if I didn't do something about cases like this?

Forbes: Well, Mr. DuFresne, just what will happen here if we put her back, supposing we do? Will that help anything? There is a clash of personalities here that just can't be remedied. We've tried enough times, but it won't work. She'll do the same thing again.

DuFresne: What I want you to do is to give us a chance to show how the union can help you. If you put the girl back, I'll call her in and have a good talk with her. I'll tell her that, even though this is a free country, she shouldn't express opinions that don't involve her, especially if they are insulting to management. I'll tell her that she is expected to do her work.

Smolokas: Well what if she does the same things all over again, as she will? If it is wrong for her to do them then, why isn't it just as wrong for her to do them last Saturday and before? I don't understand the difference.

DuFresne: The difference is this. You have given the union the chance to see what it can do to straighten this girl out. Then if she doesn't come around, we won't go to bat for her again. I'll tell her it will be her last chance.

Forbes: But why should you do that? Isn't that management's job? Do we have to depend on the union to discipline our workers?

DuFresne: You can do whatever you like. But we want a chance to show you that we can be helpful, too. Why, the other mills in this town tell us if they are having trouble with certain people—acting up or loafing too much—and I call the people in if they are union members and ask them what the story is. If they admit what the mill has told me, I tell them that they will have to turn over a new leaf if they expect to get any help from the union. If their stories don't agree, we go right down to the mill and get the thing straightened out before it goes too far. If you had called me about this girl when the trouble first started, maybe all this could have been avoided.

Wilson: Well, you know that we didn't have a union here until last year, and we don't have much experience with one. Why, we don't even know who the shop stewards are in each department. But we were talking this morning about the angle you mentioned. I think in the future when we have trouble with anyone in discipline, Mr. Smolokas should call the union office about it, so

that you know the story before it is neces- **140**
sary to take action.

DuFresne: That would be fine. We want
to help. But what about this case? What are
we going to do—go to arbitration?

Wilson: I don't know yet. Suppose you **145**
give us a chance to talk it over—to discuss
what you have offered to do about her.
Then I'll get in touch with you by tomorrow
morning at the latest.

DuFresne: That's all right with me. I want **150**
to do the right thing, and I think you do,
too. And I'll send you a list of the shop
stewards that have been appointed in each
department.

After the meeting adjourned, there was **155**
further discussion among the three management officials. They agreed that if the case
went to arbitration, the foreman would
probably be called upon to testify, which
might weaken the company's position. This **160**
company had no experience with arbitration and wanted to avoid it on a case that
was not "airtight." On the other hand, the
officials felt that their case was strong
enough so that they might reinstate the girl **165**
on her old job without back pay. The loss of
pay would be something of a penalty for her
actions, they reasoned, and, furthermore,
the "talk" that the union business agent had
agreed to give her would strengthen their **170**
position later if she persisted in her actions.

The assistant manager wondered whether
the union business agent would back down
if management told him that it would not
change its position and would carry the case **175**
to arbitration. The manager and the superintendent, however, felt that this challenge
might be hazardous, since they were convinced the union would carry the case to
arbitration. **180**

The manager then called the union office
and told the union business agent what the
company was prepared to do. The offer was

accepted, and there was no argument over
the denial of back pay. The business agent **185**
assured the manager that he would have a
talk with the girl the next morning.

After reporting this conversation to his
colleagues, the manager suggested that they
call in the foreman the next day and "have **190**
a talk with him." He also said that the superintendent should tell Irene when she
came to work that "bygones would be bygones" but that she was expected to do her
work and "mind her own business." **195**

QUESTIONS ON SECTION C

1 *On defining an issue*
  a Why do you think the statements of the head
  business agent (lines 1-6, 13-41, and 58-67) are
  or are not helpful in clarifying the issue?
  b How well does Mr. Wilson, as a management
  representative, bring out the central issue (lines
  7-12, 42-48, and 68-73)?
  c At what point in the discussion, and by whom, is
  the issue with regard to Irene Mason clearly
  stated? What advantage of this clarification is
  taken by the parties to the dispute?
  d If you had been at this meeting as a personnel
  administrator, what might you have said to clarify this issue at the outset?
2 *On discipline as a management responsibility*
  a In relation to personnel policy, is the union's proposal (lines 91-99 and 115-127) acceptable or
  not? Why?
    (1) Do you see any risks in it? If so, what risks,
    and for whom?
    (2) What other issues (side issues with regard to
    Irene's discharge) were mentioned, by
    whom? (Refer to specific lines in the quoted
    dialogue.) Which of them seems to have been
    an important factor in the case?
  b Comment on Mr. Wilson's statement (lines
  137-141). What possibilities for future difficulties
  in labor relations does this statement contain?
3 *On management and union attitudes toward arbitration*
  a In your opinion, should management have "stuck
  to its guns" and taken the case to arbitration?

b What gains and losses might have been anticipated in plant morale and relations with the union?

c How strong is management's case? Briefly outline management's contentions and list supporting evidence.

d How strong is the union's case? Briefly outline the union's contentions and list supporting evidence.

4 *On management's technique to correct a mistake*
What advantages might there have been if the mill manager had frankly admitted that the discharge was a mistake and reinstated Irene with back pay?

D FOREMAN TRAINING

On the morning following the conference with the union, the foreman was called in by the manager and "put on the carpet." He was told that his actions had placed the mill in an embarrassing position and that he must handle his department differently if he expected to keep his job. His relations with Irene were criticized, and the foreman admitted, "Maybe that's true." According to the manager, he took his reprimand "like a great big kid that had had a spanking." He agreed he was "all wrong" and said that he "would try to do better."

The superintendent had a talk with Irene before she went to work, pointing out that "we will start with a clean slate, but you are expected to do your work and mind your own business."

Irene said nothing. During the first week after her reinstatement, she was surly, but this attitude gradually changed. One day about 2 weeks later she came to the superintendent's office voluntarily to say that she realized that she had been "loafing on the job" and that her actions had hurt the work of the department, bringing criticism on the foreman.

After this confession, Irene "settled down," according to the superintendent, and "she is almost like her old self before all this trouble started." But the difficulties with the foreman continued, and 8 months after the discharge episode, he was replaced by a new foreman. Irene continued to do her work well under the direction of this new supervisor.

Six months later, no further difficulties of this nature had been experienced with the union. Relationships improved, and, in negotiations for subsequent contracts, the attitude of the business agent was friendly and reasonable.

QUESTIONS ON SECTION D

On supervisory development
Comment on the manager's technique in criticizing foreman Williams. In your opinion might any other approach have been more instructive for the foreman? If so, what approach? (Role playing can be an effective way to answer this question.)

Approaches to Introducing Job Changes (Caledonia Woolen Mills)

INTRODUCTION

One of the central problems of management is how to get employee and union cooperation when technological changes are constantly taking place in a dynamic industry. Changes in output standards and work loads or work assignments, dilution of skills, demotion, transfer, and sometimes layoffs are associated with technological changes. These account in large part for the frequent opposition of workers to the introduction of new machines, methods, processes, and work assignments.

In his capacity as a staff adviser to line management, the personnel administrator has an opportunity to urge the adoption of policies and procedures which reduce the resistance of workers and their unions to changes. This case considers different approaches used in the same firm.

CASE BACKGROUND

Early in 1949 the Caledonia Woolen Mills, producers of woolen blankets, employed about 2,000 workers. They were represented by the Textile Workers Union (CIO). As the woolen industry expanded in the South after the Second World War, Caledonia and other Northern mills began to face greater competition. The Caledonia president expected that this would become especially severe after the postwar boom in textile products ended. Several inquiries convinced him that, in comparable Southern mills, work loads or work assignments were 15 to 20 percent higher than in his mill, and he believed that the mill's survival depended upon a combination of more modern machinery and higher work loads for new and existing jobs. He considered it unlikely that the union would agree to a wage reduction, and so in his talks with local union leaders he stated that, unless costs were reduced by the methods he proposed, the firm would not be able to maintain its present rate of operations.

The union officials agreed to consider workload changes proposed by management, in accordance with the clause in the collective agreement. This clause required the company to notify the union of proposed changes and then discuss them over a 2-week period. If no agreement was reached, the change could be put into effect for a 4-week trial period, followed if necessary by arbitration.

A THE TIMESTUDY ENGINEER'S APPROACH

The company president first asked the timestudy engineer to prepare a number of work-load proposals for present jobs which were considered "less than full jobs." In the textile industry, a weaver may tend a certain number of looms, or a doffer may be assigned to remove ("doff") bobbins from a certain number of spinning frames. A "full job" is usually considered to be one which, except for rest and delay periods, requires the full-time attention of the worker during the hours scheduled.

The timestudy engineer, with the help of his assistants, made studies of 15 jobs, using "effort rating" or "leveling" in addition to elapsed times to get a computed time required to do each job. He prepared detailed summaries of the timestudies, each of which showed that workers could handle more machines than they were currently handling. The president had asked the timestudy engineer to present the results of these studies to the union committee. He expected the union to accept these results without much question.

The local union representatives on the committee included a full-time business agent and several departmental stewards. They knew very little about the intricacies of timestudy, and they were "floored" by the detailed figures in each proposal. Several of the stewards in the departments affected by the proposals asserted that "no human being can take care of that many machines." Following is an excerpt of the discussion between the union business agent and the company timestudy engineer.

Business agent: Now on this proposal that doffers take on four more sides [of spinning frames]. How do you figure that time per doff? Here on page 2 you have one figure you got by taking the actual average time to doff a frame, then you have here on page 3 a new figure which you say is the final one. How come?

Timestudy engineer: Well, that second figure is the right one because we estimated by "effort rating" that the worker we studied was working only 70 percent as fast as a normal worker. So we had to compute the rate at which she would normally have worked. Otherwise, timestudy data wouldn't be accurate.

Business agent: That sounds fishy to me. How do we know you got it right? And how do we know you didn't juggle around a lot of other figures?

Timestudy engineer: You'll just have to accept our honesty about this. I could take that as an insult, but I won't. Timestudy methods can't be learned overnight, and it is hard to explain everything to you fellows. Once you understand it, you see that timestudy is a scientific way of measuring how long it takes a normal worker to complete a task. We can argue about some things, but we can't argue about the figures: they're facts. If you can't accept the accuracy of the figures, I don't know how we can ever reach any agreements. Maybe we ought to stick to the contract and just put these proposals into effect for the 4-week trial period. I think you'll see that the work loads we propose are reasonable. And if we can't agree after that, we might as well go to arbitration.

Business agent: We don't have to take your word for everything. We just want to know what is behind these figures, what you base them on, so we know that nothing is **80** being pulled on the workers in this mill.

Timestudy engineer: We certainly aren't trying to put anything over on you. But we ought to be clear on one thing. The basis for timestudy is not a matter for collective bar- **85** gaining, and nothing in the contract requires us to discuss this with the union. If we expect to get anywhere in this, we have to keep the discussion on a factual basis, and here are the facts *(picking up a copy of* **90** *the work-load proposals).* I don't want to be unreasonable, but we ought to try to agree on a sound basis for handling these changes.

Business agent: Well, if that's the position you take, I'll have to get in touch with our **95** national office to see what our next step is. (The meeting is adjourned.)

During this discussion, the president of the company and the mill superintendent were absent from the city on other business. **100** The assistant superintendent and several overseers (foremen) were present, but none of them took part in the discussion. Later it was learned that they had not been consulted in detail on the proposals and knew **105** very little about the timestudies. The timestudy man was the sole company spokesman.

Subsequently, the company put into effect three work-load proposals for the 4- **110** week trial period, as the contract provided. In the meantime, the regional director of the union wrote a letter to the company stating that the union could proceed with work-load discussions only if the company (1) fur- **115** nished answers to a long list of specific questions about each work-load proposal and (2) agreed to certain "principles" to be followed in future proposals. The most important of these was the discontinuance of "ef- **120** fort rating" in making timestudies.

The timestudy engineer objected to the extra work entailed in answering the union's questions, many of which he regarded as irrelevant or "none of the union's business." **125** Most of the union's proposed "principles" he considered unsound, and when he was asked whether he would agree to drop effort rating, he replied, "Only over my dead body." **130**

There were no further meetings, and the timestudy engineer reported to the company president that discussions with the union were stalled because of the business agent's unreasonableness and obstinacy, **135** backed up by the union's regional director. He recommended that the work-load proposals be taken to arbitration, since he saw no other alternative.

The assistant superintendent felt that **140** part of the difficulty was that the company was trying to introduce too many changes in too short a time. "It took a couple of Southern mills 2 or 3 years to make their studies **145** and put in higher work loads," he added. "Well, maybe so," was the comment of the timestudy engineer, "but I don't think we'll have as much trouble later on if jobs get scarce here. The help have to be hungry a **150** while before they take higher work loads."

QUESTIONS ON SECTION A

1 *On management's approach*
   a What do you think of the president's decision in asking the timestudy engineer to represent the company in discussions with the union? Were there any other alternatives?
   b Should the timestudy man have attempted to answer fully the business agent's questions? Are these matters any of the union's business?
   c What do you think of the timestudy engineer's position that "time-study is not a matter for collective bargaining"?
   d Do you think any other approach would have worked better in gaining employee and union acceptance of the proposed changes?

2 *On resistance to change*
  a What features of the timestudy engineer's approach are likely to increase, rather than reduce, resistance to change?
  b To what extent did the business agent's attitude account for this resistance? How do you explain the regional director's position?
  c Might the number of proposed changes have anything to do with resistance encountered?
  d Comment on the final remark made by the timestudy engineer.

3 *On the nature of timestudy*
  a To what extent do you agree with the timestudy engineer's statement that timestudy is scientific and accurate?
  b Does your answer to the preceding question have any bearing on the way in which you would have handled these discussions?

4 *On union-management relations*
  a What possible effects could this episode have on union-management relations?
  b If you were company president, what would be your next step? How would you attempt to get discussions off "dead center"?

B   ECONOMIC CRISIS AND A NEW APPROACH

About mid-summer, 1949, the woolen-blanket industry was gripped by a serious recession, and layoffs were general. High-cost mills were hardest hit, and Caledonia's failure to reduce costs through work-load changes was especially serious. Only a few of the promised new machines had been installed, and definite work loads for these had not yet been established. Faced with declining orders, management decided to discontinue some of the blanket lines that were least profitable or losing money, and 500 workers were laid off.

At the same time, the company president decided to replace the mill superintendent with a new man brought in from another more successful firm. The new superintendent was given a free hand in cost reduction, with particular emphasis on the work-load question. He brought with him a personnel director from the other firm, and together they resolved to try a different approach in work-load discussions with the union. One of their first steps was to replace the former timestudy engineer with a new man who remained strictly in a staff role. Then the personnel director arranged for a conference with the union business agent, to explain how they proposed to proceed on work-load changes.

QUESTIONS ON SECTION B

1 *On management's general approach*
  a What other alternatives, if any, did the president have?
  b Should the new personnel director "take the bull by the horns" and handle the matter himself, as suggested, or should he take a different approach? If so, what?

2 *On resistance to change*
  a What should management do to change the union's previous opposition to timestudy results?
  b To what extent do you think union and employee resistance to changing workloads will be reduced—or increased—by the economic recession which affected the woolen textile industry after the experience in Part A?

3 *On the exactness of timestudy*
  a What should management's position be now on the exactness of timestudy? Should the original position be maintained, or would you suggest more flexibility? Are there dangers in "horse trading" in the application of timestudy?

4 *On union-management relations*
  a How would you suggest management proceed to get better union understanding of the company's competitive problems?
  b What problems, if any, does the union have which management needs to understand better if this impasse is to be resolved?
  c Would better union-management relations help resolve the conflict present in Section A, or should management assume that labor peace has too high a price?

Difficulties Connected with Work Scheduling[1]

INTRODUCTION

In any organization, an important managerial responsibility is to schedule work in a manner such that (1) all necessary tasks will be performed (2) with necessary assignments equitably distributed among available employees. A hospital has special scheduling difficulties because care for patients must be *continuous* and must be performed by specially trained personnel. The hospital in which the following case occurred had the additional difficulty that some patients had serious mental disturbances. It was therefore necessary in the "disturbed ward" that all personnel be temperamentally suited to their tasks

[1] This case, prepared for discussion by the Incident Process (described in the Introduction to Part 2), is published under the title "A Last-minute Request for Time Off," in Paul Pigors and Faith Pigors, *The Incident Process: Case Studies in Management Development, Series III: White Collar Employees,* Bureau of National Affairs, Inc., Washington, D.C., 1965.

and—insofar as possible—be in a suitable frame of mind when on duty.

However, aside from these special requirements, supervisors and administrators in that hospital had to meet managerial responsibilities that also exist in many other kinds of organization. A number of these are listed below. Each is illustrated in this case, and all were mentioned in Part 1. We therefore append chapter numbers for easy reference.

1 *Personnel administration as a line responsibility,* especially for supervisors (Chapters 1, 2, 5, 7, 14, and 19).

2 *Setting up and administering procedures and rules* for scheduling work and shift assignments (Chapter 19).

3 *Communicating to employees* about work assignments and making arrangements for receiving communications from employees about desired changes in assignments (Chapters 5 and 19).

4 *Trying to understand the inner motivation* of an employee who is disregarding established procedures and rules; trying to hear the messages being relayed along that employee's "inner circuit" and thus learning how to respond effectively both to that employee's behavior and to the human needs which occasioned that behavior (Chapters 5 and 6).

5 *Sanctioning informal arrangements* by employees to exchange shift assignments (Chapter 19).

6 *Formulating and administering a policy* and a procedure (in this case also rules) in regard to credit for extra time worked and requests for unscheduled time off. (Chapters 1 and 5 suggest differences among policies, procedures, and rules, indicating why consistency of administration is necessary so that each means of control may reinforce the others.)

7 *Administering rules and interpreting disciplinary policy* (Chapter 18).

8 *Developing and retaining competent employees* (Chapter 3). In this case, a special difficulty was introduced by acute shortage of trained personnel.

9 *Interviewing and counseling* (Chapter 10).

10 *Coordinating the activity of supervisors* with various kinds and degrees of responsibility and authority (Chapter 7).

11 *Diagnosing and preserving organizational health* (Chapters 9 to 13).

In the following case, a point of climax was reached when an employee made a last-minute request for time off. In deciding how, when, and by whom that request should be answered, a seasoned administrator would recognize intuitively that all the responsibilities in the above list are factors in *a situation which needs to be thought about as a whole.*

A   CASE BACKGROUND

At the time of this case, in 1955, Hill Hospital (for psychiatric patients) in Boston had 600 beds. It employed over 900 people in a variety of services and occupations. One job was that of "hos-pital attendant"—a relatively new occupation which had been developed to meet the severe shortage of registered nurses. The hospital's "Personnel Policies and Practices Manual," revised in April, 1953, stated that a hospital attendant was to accept assignments designated by the assistant director of nursing services and the head nurse. Ward assignments included care of difficult patients; transfer of patients and belongings; care of untidy patients; taking patients to departments for special work; taking patients for walks, drives, etc.; bed baths; tub baths; shampoos; and enemas. Other duties included bringing and clearing trays at meals, spoon feeding, cleaning rooms, and running errands within the hospital.

The hospital preferred that attendants be between eighteen and forty years of age, although the minimum hiring age was seventeen. High school graduates were also preferred, and 2 years of high school was the minimum requirement. The usual personal qualifications of good physical health, physical energy, dignity, good manners, etc., were expected.

Duty for attendants was scheduled on an 8-hour shift (day or night) and a 40-hour week, with 2 days or 2 nights off each week. Normal day duty was from 7 A.M. to 7 P.M. with 4 hours off, as designated by the head nurse. Regular relief duty consisted of 8 consecutive hours: 2:30 P.M. to 11 P.M., assigned as often as 1 week out of every 3. Night-duty assignments were from 11 P.M. to 7 A.M., and attendants were expected to have these night assignments 2 months out of every year.

Holiday time consisted of 1 day off for every officially recognized holiday, either on that day or on some other day "to be arranged when convenient to the ward and personnel." Ten holidays were observed: New Year's Day, Washington's Birthday, Patriot's Day (Apr. 19, a holiday in Massachusetts), Memorial Day, Fourth of July, Labor Day, Columbus Day, Veterans Day, Thanksgiving Day, and Christmas Day.

All the above information was given to new employees in writing when they were hired. After reading it, each employee was asked to sign the following "contract": "It is understood that the foregoing statements of working conditions at the Hospital have been read and agreed upon by the undersigned."

The young girl, Jane Ordway, who is the principal figure in this case, was twenty years old. Her home was in northern Vermont near Burlington. For medical reasons, she had left high school in the middle of her senior year in 1953. After recuperating from her illness, she decided to come to Boston. She began employment at

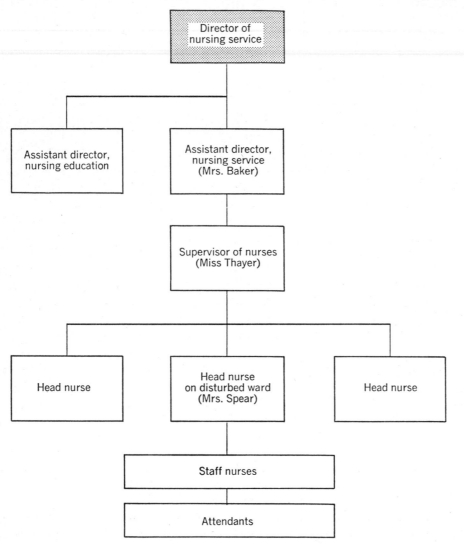

Figure 1

Hill Hospital on Sept. 9, 1954. Miss Ordway expected to finish her high school requirements during the next year while continuing to work as a hospital attendant. After that, she planned to enter training as a student nurse.

In the organizational hierarchy of nursing services at Hill Hospital, the hospital attendant is at the lowest level. The partial organization chart given in Figure 1 indicates supervisory and administrative personnel who had different kinds and degrees of responsibility for Miss Ordway's performance.

Notes on Key People and Their Duties in Regard to Scheduling Work Assignments

1 Mrs. Baker: Registered Nurse, college graduate; age forty-six; 20 years' experience; inclined to be authoritarian, but trying to change her behavior to more democratic leadership. Mrs. Baker was expected to help when difficulties arose in preparing work schedules for the coming week. She was in a position to make temporary transfers if required for ward coverage and, if necessary, to call in part-time employees who had previously worked at Hill Hospital.

2 Miss Thayer: Registered Nurse, college B.S., 1953; in her twenties; 1½ years' experience. Impulsive, relaxed, easygoing but efficient. Saw herself as a "go-between," or buffer, between the assistant directors and nursing service personnel. Miss Thayer was expected to help when "personnel problems" arose in connection with current schedules.

3 Mrs. Spear: Registered Nurse; no college degree but has 15 college credits in adult education; age thirty-five; 9½ years of experience, 7 of these years on convalescent ward, 2½ years on disturbed ward. Easygoing, affable, above average in practical ability, and well suited for service on disturbed ward. Good interpersonal relations with patients and hospital personnel. Mrs. Spear was expected to prepare the weekly schedule for ward coverage, to post this schedule each Thursday, showing assignments for the week be-

ginning on the following Monday, and to handle special requests for time off (in accordance with established policy, procedures, and rules).

A Policy and Procedures; a Practice and Rules

At Hill Hospital, there was a long-standing (though unwritten) policy that when any regular employee requested special time off, the request would be favorably *considered* (though not necessarily granted).

Flexible interpretation of that policy had resulted in a departure from established procedures and the expectation that in any personal or family emergency special requests for time off would be granted.

Established procedures for scheduling and for making time-off requests were these: Special requests for time off were to be entered in the "Time-off Request Book," which was kept in the head nurse's desk in each ward. The deadline for submitting such requests was Thursday of the week preceding the week during which time off was requested. By a gradual slippage of practice, it had become customary for employees to make many requests *orally, after the Thursday deadline,* presenting these requests either to *head nurses* or to the *supervisor of nurses.* Such requests had often been granted.

Another practice which departed from established procedures was that employees had begun to accumulate *"time-off credits"* for extra days worked (beyond the regulation 40-hour week). Such extra work had often been undertaken as a "buddy" arrangement when employees were trying to make last-minute changes in scheduled assignments for holidays.

To regularize that practice and bring it in line with established procedure, a rule about meeting scheduled assignments had been revised about 10 months before the point of climax in the case.

The following revised rule was posted on ward bulletin boards.

Hill Hospital
Official Notice
All Part-time Workers, Nurses and Attendants:
　From this day forward, you will be expected to work on days agreed upon when you began your employment, regardless of holidays or school programs, unless arrangements are made with the head nurses or supervisors by Thursday for the following week.
　The only alternative is for you to secure a satisfactory replacement.

(Signed)　　Eleanor Baker
Assistant Director
Nursing Service

February 1, 1955

Miss Ordway's Schedule for the Week in Which She Requested Extra Time Off

Miss Ordway was on a special relief schedule, from 10 A.M. to 7 P.M. (with 1 hour off for lunch). Her assigned schedule of days on and off was as follows:

Monday, *on*
Tuesday, *off*
Wednesday, *on*
Thursday, *off*
Friday, *on*
Saturday, *on*
Sunday, *on*

A　AN INCIDENT: MISS ORDWAY'S REQUEST

At 9:25 A.M. on Wednesday, Nov. 23, 1955, Miss Ordway came to see Mrs. Spear, head nurse on the disturbed ward. She was scheduled to go on duty at 10 A.M. During the following conversation, Miss Ordway's manner seemed hurried and nervous:

Miss Ordway: Mrs. Spear, I just realized that I have 3 days off coming to me, because I worked for other girls on three holidays since I started. I worked on Labor Day, Columbus Day, and Veterans Day, and now I'd like to have Friday, Saturday, and Sunday of this week off, since I'm off on Thursday which is Thanksgiving Day.

Mrs. Spear: Do you really have 3 days coming to you? I'm surprised at this, because you know we don't like our people to accumulate so many credits for days off. But let me check the records. *(She checks her "Ward Time Sheets" and finds that Miss Ordway is correct in her statement that she has worked three previous holidays.)* You're right, Miss Ordway, you do have 3 days coming to you. But there isn't much that can be done about it this late in the week. I don't believe we could find anyone to cover for you, now. Why do you need these 3 days all of a sudden?

Miss Ordway: I'd like to go home for a visit. I haven't been home since my vacation in June. This long weekend would be just right for me as it takes a day's traveling each way for me to get home. That would leave me 2 days to spend with my family. I *must* go home.

Mrs. Spear: Has something happened at home that requires your presence at this time?

Miss Ordway: Nothing has happened, so far as I know, but. . . .

Mrs. Spear: Well, if nothing is wrong, we can arrange for you to be off next weekend.

Miss Ordway: No, I want to go home this weekend . . . so I'm going.

Further conversation between the head nurse and the attendant merely underlined Miss Ordway's determination to go home regardless of the risk to her position at the hospital. An impasse was reached. Mrs. Spear then suggested that Miss Ordway discuss the matter with Mrs. Baker, the assistant director of nursing service. (Miss Thayer, supervisor of nurses, to whom such a matter would ordinarily have been referred, was not on duty that day.)

Miss Ordway left immediately for Mrs. Baker's office. It was then 9:30 A.M. While Miss

Ordway was on her way to Mrs. Baker's office, Mrs. Spear telephoned Mrs. Baker:

Mrs. Spear (over the telephone): Oh, Mrs. Baker, I've just sent Miss Ordway over to see you. I referred her to you because Miss Thayer is off duty today.

Mrs. Baker: What's the trouble?

Mrs. Spear: It's this. . . . I've been having quite a time with Miss Ordway. She has tomorrow off. But now she is insisting on having Friday, Saturday, and Sunday off, too.

Mrs. Baker: Well, wait a minute. Do we owe her 3 extra days?

Mrs. Spear: Yes, we do. I checked that on the ward time sheets. But I reminded her that it's too late to do anything about it for this weekend. I asked her if there was any reason why she *had* to have these 3 days off all of a sudden.

Mrs. Baker: Was there? Is someone ill in her family?

Mrs. Spear: No. But she hasn't been home since June. You know, coming from Vermont, it takes her a day to get home and another to get back again. So I told her that, if nothing goes wrong, we can arrange for her to get off next weekend. But. . . .

Mrs. Baker: Here she is now. I'll talk to her and call you back. *(to Miss Ordway)* Well, Miss Ordway, what is it?

Miss Ordway (with a rush, and in a tone of urgency): Mrs. Baker, I'm off tomorrow. And I'm on for the weekend. But I have 3 days coming to me. So I want Friday, Saturday, and Sunday off.

Mrs. Baker: But Miss Ordway, you've been assigned to ward duty. And we're counting on you for the holiday weekend.

Miss Ordway: I don't care. I need the time off to be with my family.

Mrs. Baker (more sternly): That's not a very constructive attitude, Miss Ordway. I'm not sure we can give you that time off, and if you persist, you will leave us in a very difficult position. Why don't you come back to see me during your lunch

hour. I'll see what I can do in the meantime but I certainly can't promise anything, and you must realize your obligation to the hospital.

Miss Ordway (belligerently): I do, but I think I'm also entitled to those days off after Thanksgiving, and I want to go home very much. I don't see why I can't go.

Mrs. Baker: Well, I've explained all that, but come back and see me later. Maybe you can find someone to take your place.

Miss Ordway: All right, I'll try, Mrs. Baker. But I think I can catch a night bus to Burlington at midnight tonight and I want to go. *(She leaves the office.)*

Mrs. Baker then looks in the files for Miss Ordway's last performance-evaluation report. She finds the following:

Hill Hospital
Evaluation Report—Attendants
Date: March 1, 1955
Name: Jane Ordway
Quality of work: Excellent
Interest shown in work: Pronounced interest shown
Attitude toward patients: Shows empathy and helpfulness
Ability to follow directions: Quick to grasp details
Alertness: Well demonstrated
Cooperation: Good teamwork
Punctuality: Good—some improvement needed
Reliability: Very dependable
Personal appearance: Neat at all times
Disposition: Pleasant and congenial, relates well with personnel and patients, quiet and well-mannered individual
Strong or weak points observed: Takes work seriously; memory poor at times
Improvements shown: Makes effort to overcome forgetfulness (uses written notes at times). Takes direction well; only occasional self-initiative shown. At times has resented students who are given charge duties and tends to regulate own assignments when graduates are off duty. This has been discussed with her, and she said that she would be more attentive to this problem.

s/s _____　　　　　s/s _____
Attendant　　　　　　　　Head Nurse

QUESTIONS ON SECTION A

1 *On employee motivation*

    a How would you explain Miss Ordway's apparent determination to get the weekend off? (In your answer, consider what she said to Mrs. Spear and Mrs. Baker, and what had been said about her in the "evaluation report," as well as what you infer from other information given about her and her family.)

    b From Miss Ordway's standpoint, why might her request have seemed perfectly justifiable?

2 *On management communication to employees (in words and in actions)*

    a What is communicated to employees about an organizational policy when it is administered as though it were a rule; in this case to grant time off for an emergency?

    b When established procedures and rules have been disregarded to some extent by both personnel and management representatives, what managerial action would you recommend to "tighten up" the procedures and rules? Why?

    c Comment on the revised rule as stated in the bulletin board notice. In what respects, if any, does it seem to you inadequate? How, if at all, would you change any of the wording?

3 *On supervisory responsibilities (at the level of a head nurse)*

    If you were in Mrs. Spear's position:

    a Do you think you would follow up a new employee to make sure that she fully understood her commitments under the contract that she signed when she was hired? Why or why not?

    b Why do you think you would, or would not, have passed Miss Ordway along to Mrs. Baker?

    c In theory, who should settle this kind of question? And how might such a situation be handled to develop supervisory potential?

4 *On interviewing*

    a If you had been either in Mrs. Spear's position or Mrs. Baker's, what might you have said to Miss Ordway in trying to help her take an organizational view of what was at stake? (The answer to that question may be role played, in two parts if time allows, to bring out differences in attitude and opportunity at the time of the two interviews.)

    b What educational opportunities were provided for Miss Ordway by Mrs. Baker's suggestions that (1) Miss Ordway should come back during her lunch hour and (2) in the meantime Miss Ordway should try to find a replacement?

5 *On making an administrative decision*

    In Mrs. Baker's position:

    a How might you formulate the issue for immediate decision? (In your answer consider, in addition to Miss Ordway's request, other aspects of the work situation that will be affected by your decision.)

    b In working toward a decision on that issue, what is your opinion on the following points:

        (1) Should you or Mrs. Spear try to find a replacement for Miss Ordway if she cannot do so herself? Why or why not?

        (2) Why would you, or would you not, be prepared to risk her quitting (or going without permission) if you or Mrs. Spear decided to refuse her request?

        (3) If Miss Ordway takes off without permission but returns on Monday, what disciplinary action, if any, should be taken? By whom? Why?

B   MRS. BAKER'S ANSWER

In the afternoon, when Miss Ordway came back to Mrs. Baker's office, she was told that arrangements had been made to cover her duty time until she returned on Monday.

Mrs. Baker: But I hope you realize, Miss Ordway, that this arrangement has been made only because you are overdue in receiving your holiday time. Please be careful in future and do not allow it to accumulate again.

Miss Ordway: I didn't deliberately allow it to accumulate. It's just that I forgot about it, for the time being.

Mrs. Baker: Your work here has been most satisfactory, and we want you to stay. But you must realize that an ultimatum such as you gave me will not be accepted again. A repetition of such behavior will probably mean termination of your services.

(During the last part of this conversation, Miss Thayer, supervisor of nurses, was present. She had come in to pick up her pay check.)

Miss Thayer (to Mrs. Baker): What's all this about?

(Mrs. Baker told her what had happened.)

Miss Thayer: I left a note on your desk one day last week telling you about three people on the staff who were overdue on holiday time. Miss Ordway's name was on that list. Didn't you read it?

Mrs. Baker: It must have been misplaced, as I don't recall reading it.

Miss Thayer: Miss Ordway, I'm sorry that you didn't get that holiday time sooner. But I guess all's well that ends well. Now that accumulated time has made it possible for you to go home for a few days.

Miss Ordway (apologetically): I'm sorry I made such a fuss over it. But I do want to go home very much to see my folks.

Mrs. Baker: Well, have a good time, Miss Ordway. And remember in future, please give Mrs. Spear more notice when you want a specific day off.

Miss Ordway: Yes, I will. And thank you both.

Miss Thayer: Before you go, are you still serious about entering school next fall?

Miss Ordway: Yes, I am.

Miss Thayer: Well, remember that you will be faced with many more difficult problems about time off as a student. So think about your feelings about this before you apply for admission.

Miss Ordway (turning to go): I will. And thank you again.

QUESTIONS ON SECTION B

1 *Appraising an administrative decision*

  a To what extent do you think Mrs. Baker's decision met the needs of this case because:

   (1) It represented a person-centered view and showed (a) understanding and sympathy for a young employee who might later become a valuable member of the organization, (b) perception of what might help that individual develop her full potential for nursing service?

   (2) It strengthened management authority?

   (3) It reinforced established procedures and rules?

   (4) It was a wise interpretation of management policy (in regard to requests for special time off)?

   (5) It was fair to other employees?

   (6) In all, or most, of these ways it established a desirable precedent for future answers to similar requests?

  b What indication do you find that Mrs. Baker herself was not entirely satisfied with her decision?

2 *On administering a disciplinary policy*

  a What step in a positive process of discipline was taken by Mrs. Baker during this interview?

  b Why do you, or do you not, agree that this disciplinary step was appropriate at that time?

3 *On organizational roles and relationships*

Comment on Miss Thayer's part in the preceding interview. For example:

  a If you had been in Miss Thayer's place, why might you have postponed your questions and comments to Mrs. Baker?

  b If you had been in Mrs. Baker's position, why might you have felt that Miss Thayer's questions and comments, as well as her tone, were unsuitable under the circumstances?

4 *On coordination and communication between management representatives*

Regardless of the suitability of Miss Thayer's remarks, what do they reveal about:

  a Her relationship with Mrs. Baker?

  b The effectiveness of a control procedure (designed to prevent the accumulation of time-off credits)?

5 *On employee motivation*

  a Why do you suppose Miss Ordway's attitude suddenly changed from belligerence to apology?

  b If you were in Miss Ordway's position, do you think that having such a request granted would make you more (or less) careful in future to adhere to established procedures? Why?

  c What information given in this case suggests that

Miss Ordway might have been able to accept, and even to learn from, a denial of her request?

6 *On diagnosing and preserving organizational health*

a Suppose you had been one of the other staff people with accumulated credit for time off, how might you have felt when you heard that an attendant had got the holiday weekend off in response to a request which had been made in disregard of established procedures and rules?

b If you had been in the position of a head nurse or a nursing supervisor, how might you have felt about Mrs. Baker's decision? Specifically:

(1) What guidance would it seem to give for future decisions in matters where personal wishes of employees run counter to requirements imposed by procedures and rules?

(2) What effect would such a decision tend to have on behavior by hospital personnel?

QUESTIONS ON THE CASE AS A WHOLE

1 *On case analysis*

a How would you classify the nub of the difficulty in this case? For example, would you call it:

(1) A scheduling difficulty? Why?

(2) Lax administration? Why?

(3) A "personnel problem"? Why?

b Can you cite specific features of this case which illustrate the theory of situational diagnosis described in Chapter 9?

2 *On generalizing*

Some might say: "I don't work in a hospital and never expect to. So there's no point in my studying this case." Regardless of whether or not you agree with that statement, cite features of this case that might be worth analyzing by supervisors and managers in any organization.

A Dispute over Rates on Three Jobs (Wilshire Shoe Company)

INTRODUCTION

The following case illustrates some of the problems confronting a management when wage rates on specific jobs are in dispute, especially in a unionized situation. Unions frequently apply the pragmatic test in adopting those arguments that best support their current demands. In this case, the union business agent is making an understandable effort to get "equal pay for equal work" in all plants in which the union is the bargaining agency. Confronted by this position, the employer is making an equally understandable objection to paying the same rates in a country town as in an urban labor market. The union business agent, representing only one group of workers, is interested only in their wages and not in the entire wage structure of the plant. But the company president must think in terms of his total labor costs, and he is genuinely concerned about the ultimate effect of piecemeal increases.

BACKGROUND OF THE CASE

In April, 1945, the Wilshire Shoe Company employed about 350 workers in the manufacture of Army shoes. Production of shoes for the armed services was its regular line of business, supplemented in peacetime with work shoes and police shoes. The company was located in a small country town about 35 miles from a larger city in which a number of shoe companies were located. For many years, a shoe workers' union, which was an amalgamation of 14 locals of the various shoe crafts, had represented the shoe workers in the city. In 1942, following a consent election, it won bargaining rights for employees of the Wilshire Shoe Company, and this was one of the few firms outside the city that the union had succeeded in organizing. General wage changes and other matters affecting all employees were negotiated by the top officials of the amalgamated craft union with this company and with a manufacturers' association in X city. But all grievances and requests for changes in job rates affecting a particular craft were handled separately by the business agent of the craft union involved.

The case here reported took place early in 1945, beginning with a meeting between the business agent of the Goodyear operators' local and the president of the company. The business agent had made an appointment to discuss a grievance on wages for the crafts he represented.

A   THE GRIEVANCE MEETING

After the usual preliminaries, the business agent stated his case:

Business agent: A couple of days ago, the   **1**
Goodyear operators asked me to come up and hear their gripe. I talked to them a little while ago, and they tell me they can't earn as much as operators do in X city. I looked   **5**
at their earnings slips, and this seems to be true. So I'm asking an adjustment of the piece rates on welting, rounding, and Goodyear stitching, so that they can earn just what they would in X city, which is about   **10**
$1.27 an hour.

Company president: Well, I'd want to check their actual earnings here first, but you know, we've been all through that question before. This little company just can't   **15**
pay the city rates and stay in business. We aren't competitive with the city companies, and we aren't in that labor market.

Business agent: But you're making the same kind of shoes those companies are   **20**
making for the Army now. We're not talking about dress shoes or police shoes or work shoes; we're talking about Army shoes. I don't see why our members here, who pay the same dues and belong to the   **25**
same union, should get less money than they do in the city for doing exactly the same work on the same type of shoe.

Company president: I repeat, we just can't pay the city rates, and we never have in the   **30**

past. The X city companies have continued to make some dress shoes during the war, and they took this Army business on to help cover their overhead. They don't care too much what rates they have to pay on Army   **35**
shoes, because the business is all gravy to them and is temporary. But it's different with us. We will go on making Army shoes after the war, and our competitors in other parts of the country already pay lower rates   **40**
than we do. How can we keep in business? We've already given a lot of increases during the war. Since December, 1940, they've totaled about 40 percent.

Business agent: Oh, you'll do all right. But   **45**
let's get back to the main point. We should get the city rates here, because our membership pays the same dues in both places and should get the same pay for the same work.

Company president: Have you checked   **50**
how many jobs here pay more than the city rates? I know we have some. Our wage structure isn't what it should be, I'll admit, but I've urged you union people to join me in a real job evaluation or wage-classifica-   **55**
tion program, so that we do the fair thing for everyone, not just for a few people who happen to kick the most. Maybe some of our rates ought to be raised and some ought to be reduced. But we can't keep on making   **60**
a few increases here, and a few more increases there, and expect to stay in business. Do you know that last year [1944] we lost money? Our losses were half as great as our profits the year before, and it was all due to   **65**
increased labor costs.

Business agent: How can that be? We haven't had any general increases in the last year.

Company president: Well, the War Labor   **70**
Board ordered us to give paid vacations, and you remember there were several other cases in the other crafts that resulted in retroactive adjustments. And we've had to transfer skilled operators to less skilled jobs   **75**

at their higher rates to keep a production line going when labor was scarce. We've also had to pay some overtime for the same reason.

Business agent: Well, maybe so, but the **80** companies in the city are making money and you must be too, even though you say you had a net loss this year.

Company president: Our accounts are audited, and I don't know how else to con- **85** vince you that these are the facts. I'm willing to let any impartial person look at them to verify what I say. Furthermore, I think we must pay at least as much as any other shoe firms in small towns in this area out- **90** side of the city. That's a high-rate place, you know.

Business agent: That's because we've raised wages for our people there, and members of the local here should get the same **95** rates as members of the local in the city.

Company president: I'm not willing to concede that, but let me check the actual earnings of our operators here and also what some of the other shoe firms outside of **100** the city pay. I'll get in touch with you in a week or so.

Business agent: All right, but I'd like to get this thing settled pretty soon. The men are dissatisfied. **105**

QUESTIONS ON SECTION A[1]

1 *On wage policy*
 a What factors should influence the determination of this company's general level of wages? Have they been adequately considered in the discussion between the company president and the union business agent?
 b What assumptions are implicit in the union's claim that the same rates should be paid on the three jobs in the city companies and in this company (lines 7-11, 19-28, and 46-49)?

[1] In answering this set of questions, refer to ideas presented in Chaps. 8 and 20.

 c Is it important to make a wage survey of other shoe plants outside the city? Why or why not?
2 *On job evaluation*
 What might be accomplished by the company's suggestion that a job-evaluation program be introduced in the plant (lines 54-56)?
3 *On wage negotiations*
 What do you think of the manner in which the company president presented information on his inability to meet the increases requested (lines 60-66)?
4 *On grievance procedure*
 Is there anything unusual in the way in which this grievance was presented by the union? How do you account for this procedure?

B THE WAGE SURVEY

During the next week, the company president telephoned executives in three other shoe firms, two located in another small town 20 miles away and one larger firm located in a medium-sized city 50 miles away. He asked them what piece rates they were paying welters, rounders, and stitchers in the Goodyear room, and he then tabulated the following information on rates per 24 pairs:

Goodyear operators	Company A	Company B	Company C
Welters	$0.3630	$0.3444	$0.2880
Rounders	0.2178	0.2220	0.1680
Stitchers	0.5929	0.6202	0.5400

Goodyear operators	Average A, B, C	Wilshire	X city
Welters	$0.3318	$0.3333	$0.3600
Rounders	0.2026	0.2361	0.2402
Stitchers	0.5844	0.5139	0.5701

He also asked the paymaster to compute the average straight-time hourly earnings of the operators on each job during the third quarter of 1944. These were reported as follows:

Welters	$1.2952 an hour
Rounders	$1.1394 an hour
Stitchers	$1.1027 an hour

Only one of the firms that the president telephoned could give him quickly the average hourly straight-time earnings figures for these jobs, and this firm reported that, for the current week in 1945, stitchers' earnings averaged $1.23 an hour and rounders' earnings averaged $1.34 an hour. He did not consider that these figures provided a fair comparison, however, for the particular company was one noted for very efficient production and high piece-rate earnings. Further study of his own payroll figures also revealed that the average hourly straight-time earnings of individual operators in the third quarter of 1944 fell between the following ranges:

Welters	$1.2367 to $1.5443
Rounders	$0.9005 to $1.3012
Stitchers	$0.8899 to $1.4284

These figures, he thought, showed that individual operators could earn well above the X city average of $1.27 an hour on these three jobs.

Finally, the president asked the paymaster to check the location of the homes of present employees, to determine whether any came from the city and its suburbs. He received the following report:

Live in town	156
Live in adjacent towns	249
Live within 11 miles of town	322
Live in X city area	None

When the union business agent returned a week and a half later, the company president showed him the figures that he had collected and maintained his original position that he could not pay the city rates. He added that there was no train or bus service between the city and the small town in which the Wilshire Company was located, and consequently they must be considered two separate labor markets. As for other communities, he felt that Wilshire rates and earnings compared favorably, on the whole, and that he could not agree to an isolated increase for one craft. He again urged that the union join him in beginning a job evaluation program or some other procedure to determine proper wage relationships and "what would be fair labor costs for this type of business."

The union business agent put a different interpretation on the figures. He argued that "only the welters were earning their rate" (city rate) and that the piece rates of the rounders and stitchers should be increased to enable them to earn at least $1.27 an hour. He again repeated his argument that union members should be paid the same rates for the same work regardless of where the plants were located.

Unable to reach an agreement in the dispute, the parties agreed to submit it to arbitration.

QUESTIONS ON SECTION B

1 *On wage policies and administration*
   a Could there have been any improvement in the method used in making the wage survey?
   b Is there any significance in the figures showing the location of the homes of Wilshire employees?
   c Suppose that you were the personnel administrator in this company; how would you have suggested to the company president that the case be handled, in terms of both the data needed for reaching a decision and the manner in which the problems of the company should be presented to the union representative?

2 *On differentials in earnings*
   What might explain the wide variation in earnings of individual operators on the same jobs? Do you agree with the company president's conclusions based on these data?

3 *On impartial decision making*
   As an arbitrator, what would have been your decision on:
   a Whether the company should pay the city rates?
   b If not, what rate should be paid on the three operations? Give your reasons.

Fear? Or Featherbedding?

INTRODUCTION

This case report provides specific data to illustrate the following general statement by the administrator of consumer protection and environmental health services for the Department of Health, Education and Welfare: [1]

Occupational health and safety—and a good many other environmental problems—remain the subject of controversy. . . . In one camp are those who maintain that all work involves, to a greater or lesser degree, some element of risk and that . . . the worker should look out for himself, stay alert, be responsible—because most accidents . . . are the result of human failure. Then there are those who would issue hard hats, safety shoes, respirators and what have you to every employed American, and

[1] Charles C. Johnson, Jr., "The Problems Are Growing," in *DANGER: MEN AT WORK,* Proceedings of the 1969 Occupational Safety and Health Conference of the Industrial Union Department, AFL-CIO, pp. 13-19. Quotation, pp. 13-14.

would set and enforce standards for every type of occupation. The aim would be to make the industrial world perfectly "idiot-proof." The course of reason surely lies somewhere in between, but I think these two divergent views could be brought closer together if all could come to share a common view of the fundamental nature of man and of the physical environment in which he works.

A CONTRACTUAL BACKGROUND

A typical provision in labor agreements negotiated by the Oil, Chemical and Atomic Workers International Union was as follows: "WORKING CONDITIONS: The Company shall continue to make reasonable provisions for the safety and health of its employees at the plant and in the event of an accident or near-accident, the Union President shall upon request, receive full information from the Safety Supervisor and Operating Supervisor concerned, such meeting to be arranged by the Personnel & Service Supervisor."

B A SEQUENCE OF EVENTS[2]

At the beginning of the day shift (Monday, January 19, 1970), Joseph Keenan (instrument and electrical foreman) gave the following work order to Tom Osborne, (first class mechanic-electrician): "Clean No. 3 Compressor in the DMT Compressor House."

Osborne protested that he could not accept the assignment because it was unsafe. He gave the following reasons to support his position: (1) This had always been a two-man job, (2) the solvent used for cleaning the motors made him dizzy, and therefore (3) he feared that, working alone in the compressor room, he might slip, fall, and injure himself without help being immediately available.

Foreman Keenan then told Osborne to do that part of the job (90 percent of the task) that did not entail spraying with solvent.

Osborne accepted the restricted assignment without further protest and started to comply with the order.

Later that day, Foreman Keenan checked Osborne's progress. He found that Osborne had done all the work involved in cleaning the compressor unit except spraying with the solvent. The foreman then told Osborne to finish the job.

At this point, Osborne repeated his protest. This time he mentioned only reasons 2 and 3 (listed above).

Foreman Keenan then requested Safety Supervisor Addison to check the job.

Addison came to look at the job and explained to Osborne that, in his opinion, it would be perfectly safe to perform the spray job because (1) management would be supplying a new type of solvent, furthermore, (2) Osborne would be sup-

plied with the following safety devices: a blower and a fresh air safety mask. Addison also emphasized that the risks of slipping and falling were minimal. He added that the mere presence of another employee would not lessen these risks, such as they were. His final argument was that on occasion this work had been done by a mechanic working alone. But there never had been an accident.

However, Osborne was not convinced that even with the new equipment it was safe to perform the spray portion of this work assignment alone. In fact, so far as he was concerned, he felt that the hazards were now greater than ever because:

- The new solvent had not been used before. Therefore its possibly toxic effects were not known.
- The Fresh Air Mask would be a handicap because it would limit his vision during the spray operation.
- Furthermore, having to drag the attached air hoses after him while he worked would hamper him in his efforts to avoid falling when the surface of the steel platform (on which the compressor was located) became even more slippery than before owing to the overspray.
- Osborne reiterated that the cleaning operation was traditionally a two-man job. He conceded that on one occasion (in 1965) the assignment had been completed by one man working alone after his teammate had been called away because of an emergency. However, Osborne pointed out that the mechanic who stayed on the job by himself had been able to arrange to have someone check him at frequent intervals. Thus, if an accident had occurred, immediate help would have been available. His final position was that unless another employee could be assigned to work with him while he completed this job he would be unwilling to take the risk.

The foreman then objected that assigning another employee to work with him would be a

---

[2] The data are taken from a Summary of Labor Arbitration Awards published by the American Arbitration Association, Report no. 147, June 15, 1971, case no. 147-7, Hercules, Inc. (Wilmington, Del.), and OACAW, Local 8-667, 1/22/71, Charles L. Mullen, Jr., public member of a tripartite board of arbitration. Names of participants in the case situation have been disguised.

clear case of featherbedding and an unwarranted addition to the cost of doing the work. He then added that if Osborne continued to persist in his refusal to complete the work assignment his behavior would be considered a clear case of insubordination calling for disciplinary action.

When Osborne persisted in his refusal, Foreman Keenan sent him home for the remainder of the day, pending further action on his case.

Subsequently, Keenan assigned the unfinished task to another mechanic. The latter also refused to accept the "unsafe" assignment and was sent home for the balance of his shift, thus losing 3 hours' pay.

The next day (Tuesday, January 20), Osborne was given a 3-day disciplinary suspension beginning immediately.

Osborne promptly filed a grievance with the Union.

Three days later (Friday, January 23), Osborne was given a written reprimand (which was to remain in his record for 6 months) for refusing to accept a work assignment.

Two months later, on March 25, the Union, in Osborne's behalf, filed the following grievance: "The Union feels that the suspension and reprimand were unwarranted and that the reprimand should be rescinded and all lost time be reimbursed to the aggrieved."

When the parties were unable to resolve this dispute through the regular grievance procedure, the Union demanded arbitration.

C A LABOR RELATIONS QUESTION

Assume that you are in the position of the personnel and service supervisor. In view of the sequence of events (as presented above), give your considered opinion as to whether it would be advisable for the company to settle the matter short of arbitration. State reasons for your opinion.

D GENERAL QUESTIONS

1 *Terminology*
   a What different kinds of consequences are lumped together in the term "near-accident"? (See Section A of case report.)
   b What words might usefully be substituted for "accident" and "near-accident" in such a contract clause?
2 *Administrative communication*
   How might more effective communication, at various stages in the case situation, perhaps have removed Osborne's fears—if he had any—of completing the work assignment as ordered?
3 *Staff-line relationships*
   In your opinion, how appropriately did the safety supervisor function in this case? (Give reasons for your opinion.)
4 *Way of managing*
   a What way of managing is illustrated by Keenan's behavior?
   b If Foreman Keenan had been convinced that Osborne was genuinely afraid to complete the work assignment by himself, how might Osborne's objection have been met without assigning another man to do the job?
5 *Motivation*
   In your opinion, does Osborne's behavior (as described in this case report) indicate (1) "resistance to change," (2) fear for his safety, (3) a wish to go along with the practice of featherbedding, (4) a combination of two or more of these motives, or (5) some other motive?
   (In answering this question, take into account the various statements made by Osborne as reported in Section B.)
6 *Summary question*
   What general ideas about employee safety and health (for example as stated by Johnson, in the case introduction, and as outlined in Chapter 22, Part I of this text) are illustrated in this case?

Name Index

Subject Index

Page numbers followed by *C* indicate case in Part II illustrating the point under discussion. Page numbers followed by *Ex.* indicate case examples in Part I.

573